IN DEFENCE OF CANADA

In Defence of Canada

GROWING UP ALLIED

❖❖❖❖

JAMES EAYRS

UNIVERSITY OF TORONTO PRESS

Toronto Buffalo London

© University of Toronto Press 1980
Toronto   Buffalo   London

Printed in Canada
Reprinted 1985

ISBN 0-8020-2345-2 (cloth)
ISBN 0-8020-6608-9 (paper)

Canadian Cataloguing in Publication Data

Eayrs, James, 1926-
  In defence of Canada

  (Studies in the structure of power : decision-making
  in Canada ; 1, 3, 6, 8 ISSN 0081-8690)

  Includes bibliographies.
  Contents: [1] From the Great War to the great
  depression. – [2] Appeasement and rearmament. –
  [3] Peacemaking and deterrence. – [4] Growing up
  allied.
  1. Canada – Armed forces. 2. Canada – Foreign
  relations. 3. Canada – History, Military. I. Title.
  II. Series.

  FC542.E29   327.71   C72-7513
  F1029.E29

To Muriel and Peter Aylen

STUDIES IN THE STRUCTURE OF POWER:

DECISION-MAKING IN CANADA

EDITOR: JOHN MEISEL

STUDIES IN THE STRUCTURE OF POWER:

DECISION-MAKING IN CANADA

The series 'Studies in the Structure of Power: Decision-Making in Canada' was sponsored by the Social Science Research Council of Canada for the purpose of encouraging and assisting research concerned with the manner and setting in which important decisions are made in fields affecting the general public in Canada. The launching of the series was made possible by a grant from the Canada Council.

The studies of decision-making are not confined to any one of the disciplines comprising the social sciences. The series explores the ways in which social power is exercised in this country and encompasses studies done within a number of different conceptual frameworks.

J.M.

Preface and Acknowledgments

A reviewer of *In Defence of Canada: Peacemaking and Deterrence* (1972) complained that much of importance during the period with which it dealt – 1943 to 1949 – had been omitted from its text. 'How come,' my reviewer asked rhetorically (and colloquially), 'a historian writes a history of Canadian defence thinking in those years without a chapter – rather than a few fleeting mentions of it – on NATO's founding'? Nor is that the end of his complaint: 'As for the 1948-49 Berlin Blockade that loomed then so large in Cold War psychology, it gets one brief allusion.'

These are truly large omissions; but they were not oversights. For in the preface to that volume – third in the series – I'd noted that another was in the works: '... I have started ... on a fourth volume ... which will deal with Canada's experience as a North Atlantic ally and global peacekeeper.' *In Defence of Canada: Growing Up Allied* is my effort to deliver the first part of that two-part undertaking. As it contains a section on the Berlin blockade and three or four chapters on 'NATO's founding,' I hope my reviewer is now mollified. Anyway, that's 'how come.'

Still, the second part of the undertaking remains undelivered. My promise to 'deal with Canada's experience as a global peacekeeper' reiterated an earlier commitment made in the preface to *In Defence of Canada: From the Great War to the Great Depression* (1964): 'All being well, [a] later volume ... will be concerned with para-military skirmishing along the periphery of the Great Powers' spheres of influence.' That business, while begun, is unfinished.

Illustrious is the company of authors who have promised future work whose time has yet to come: Chaucer, Spenser, William Wordsworth (whose completion of *The Recluse* has been awaited since 1814). It is no dishonour to join them. So here goes: a fifth and final volume of *In Defence of Canada* will deal with those topics of 1947-57 which the fourth volume leaves out: our involvement in war and peacemaking in East Asia ('para-military skirmishing' inadequately describes the ordeals in Korea), South-East Asia, and the Middle East.

Research for this volume began as long ago as 1953, the year I was privileged to work as a research assistant on the official biography of W.L. Mackenzie King – whose active role in its events is confined to Chapters 1 and 2 (though his spirit lingered – lingers? – on) – , to be resumed in earnest only in 1972-3 when, as an Izaak Walton Killam Senior Research Fellow, I was able to devote myself to studying the diplomatic documents on which it is largely based. It is a pleasure to acknowledge again my indebtedness to A.E. Blanchette, then Director of the Historical Division, Department of External Affairs; he and his associates, particularly Agnes Ireland, made my regular visits to their cramped quarters above the Ottawa Post Office on Confederation Square as expeditious as could be desired. I am grateful to the Killam Trust and the Canada Council for financial aid to relieve me of teaching duties at the University of Toronto that year and the next; and to Professor J. Stefan Dupré, Chairman of its Department of Political Economy, for doing in good humour the administrative chores that were created by my absence.

I completed the book as the Skelton-Clark Visiting Fellow at Queen's University, Kingston, Ontario, during 1977-8. I appreciate my nomination to that high honour by the Department of Political Studies and its acceptance by the Advisory Board of the Skelton-Clark Memorial Foundation. Professor Ronald L. Watts, Principal and Vice-Chancellor, made me feel fully accepted as a member of the Queen's community, as did his predecessor, former Principal J.A. Corry. To Professor J.A.W. (Jock) Gunn, Head of the Department of Political Studies, and his congenial colleagues there, I offer warmest thanks for their hospitality, good fellowship, intellectual stimulation, and moral support. Irene Hogarth and Jane Hinchey of the Department's office facilitated arrangements for my visit and graciously assisted in many ways (Mrs Hogarth going so far as to let me use her office on occasion, Mrs Hinchey as to help me carry trunks). Ian Hodson and his able staff of the Documents Unit of the Douglas Library attended with unfailing efficiency and courtesy to my inordinate demands upon it.

Two good friends at Queen's took time from hectic schedules to read my manuscript chapter by chapter. Professor C.E.S. (Ned) Franks, tamer of white water and unruly prose, excised infelicities in scores; if any remain, they are all my fault. Of Professor John Meisel I wrote in an earlier preface: 'His ... counsel has been invaluable, not least because he has refused to allow our friendship of over twenty years to stand in the way of the sternest critical comment:' amending 'twenty' to 'thirty-five,' I can repeat that here. To express adequately my appreciation of all that John Meisel did to make my year at Queen's so memorable, 'words fail.'

Meanwhile, back at Toronto, members of the National Office of the Canadian Institute of International Affairs – Marion Magee, general editor, Jane Barrett and Katherine Webb Nelson, librarians, and Heather Wright who so agreeably enlivens the premises – met my frequent requests for information accurately and promptly.

Dr T.A. Hockin kindly made available for my use transcripts of interviews conducted under the auspices of the Oral History Project, York University.

Jean Wilson resolutely shunned the delights of a Galiano Island spring so as to speed the manuscript, enhanced by her editorial skills, on its way. R.I.K. Davidson, social science editor at the University of Toronto Press, has been my mentor and impresario since this series was begun; for navigating its fourth volume safely past the shoals of jettison and cutback I am more than ever grateful to him.

This volume is published with the benefit of grants from the Social Science Federation of Canada, using funds provided by the Social Sciences and Humanities Research Council of Canada, and from the Publications Funds of the University of Toronto Press.

25 April 1979   JE
Toronto

Contents

DOCUMENTS

IN DEFENCE OF CANADA

1

Creating the Coalition

O what are they doing with all that gear,
  What are they doing this morning, this morning?
Only their usual manoeuvres, dear,
  Or perhaps a warning.

W.H. Auden

CHARTER OR TREATY?

The Charter of the United Nations had been approved by the House of Commons, with no dissenting vote, on 19 October 1945. The event was not marked by ceremony, nor by celebration. The mood was sombre. In the mood, prayer and pessimism comingled. Coming months brought much to justify the pessimism, little to reward the prayer.

Canada, like other troubled Middle Powers at San Francisco, had hoped – sometimes against hope – that the Great Powers of the post-war world, Stalin's above all, would display a sense of *noblesse oblige* and be guided by discretion. Instead, in every mode save military, the Soviet Union was behaving not as an ally but as an enemy.

The Soviet embassy at Ottawa had been used for espionage (as Soviet embassies in other capitals doubtless were as well). The Soviet seat at the Council of Foreign Ministers had been used for hostile propaganda and invective. The Soviet permanent membership of the UN Security Council had been used to block the early efforts of other governments to create a semblance of world order by a flurry of vetoes often frivolously cast. The Soviet presence in the UN General Assembly had raised obstruction to the level of a form of art.

It was within the General Assembly that Canada's diplomats encountered the Soviet Union's tactics of disruption at first hand and close quarters, and the experience was chilling. The representative of Canada at the first meetings of the Assembly at London during February 1946 conveyed to his government a dispiriting account of Soviet negotiating manners, which left so much to be desired. 'The tactics of the Soviet delegations were to use the proceedings to the uttermost for purposes of propaganda,' Hume Wrong* reported on 27 February. 'Their arguments often were addressed not so much to the delegates in front of them as to the outside world. ... The result was to strain severely the effective operation of the Charter at its first trial, and to make it apparent that talk of turning the United Nations into an agency of international government, by the delegation to it of a portion of the sovereignty of the members, is in present conditions wholly unrealistic. ... What took place at London,' Wrong concluded,

has shown that the General Assembly and in particular the Security Council can be and are being used as instruments in the war of nerves, especially by the Soviet Government. ... The Security Council was not meant to be an agency for the prosecution of psychological warfare or an arena for gladiatorial contests between national champions. Without a great alteration, therefore, in the attitude towards each other of the great powers ... the first meetings of the Security Council and the Assembly leave open the question whether the establishment of the United Nations has in fact furthered its primary purpose – the maintenance of international peace and security.[1]

What kind of threat did Soviet behaviour pose to peace and security? How gravely was it to be assessed? If its gravity were judged to be great, what should and could be done to counter or contain Soviet power?

Opinions were bound to differ on how such questions, at once so fundamental and so baffling, should be answered. The assessment on high was unique. 'I confess I personally believe that as regards Russia,' the Prime Minister of Canada recorded on 5 March 1946, 'the rest of the world is not in a very different position than other countries in Europe were when Hitler had made up his mind to aim at the conquest of Europe.'[2] Few of Mackenzie King's† senior advisers, then or later, would have accepted that analogy – had they known he made it, which they did not.

The Prime Minister's opinion had been registered by him after he had heard on the radio Winston Churchill's 'iron curtain' address at Fulton, Missouri, which Mackenzie King described in his diary as 'The most courageous speech I have ever listened to,' 'in every way most opportune.' Churchill's speech touched off a flurry of assessments of Soviet intentions around the Western world. Among Canadian officials who set down

---

* See James Eayrs, *In Defence of Canada*, III, *Peacemaking and Deterrence* (Toronto 1972) [hereafter cited as *In Defence of Canada* III], 32-3.
† See *In Defence of Canada* III, 4-7.

some impressions was L.B. Pearson,* then Ambassador at Washington. Pearson's reflections are markedly at variance with his Prime Minister's. 'It may well be that Soviet policy is fundamentally defensive,' Pearson advised the Department of External Affairs on 11 March,

an effort to exploit a fluid post-war situation for all it is worth in the interest of their own domestic security; of squeezing the last ounce of advantage out of their own relatively strong position. The Soviet authorities may feel that they can now take with impunity steps which would provoke a war if made ten years from now when an international pattern has been re-established. They expect to encounter diplomatic resistance and incur resentment; but nothing more, unless they go beyond a line which has not yet been fixed and the boundaries of which they hope themselves to be largely instrumental in determining. Once determined, however, they will, as realists, not seek to go beyond it. The risk would be too great.[3]

Such a code of operations would be most un-Hitlerian: the leader of the Third Reich had been ready, even eager, to risk everything on a gambler's throw. Hume Wrong, Pearson's close colleague and his successor at the Washington Embassy, explicitly rejected the analogy with Nazism. 'Soviet policy is defensive,' Wrong affirmed forthrightly on 28 June 1946. 'While there is a resemblance in technique between the diplomatic practices of the Kremlin and those used by Hitler, it would be most misleading to push the comparison too far. For instance, the Soviet Government completely controls one-seventh of the earth's surface and already possesses, unlike Nazi Germany, a vast field for internal development. The Russian peoples,' Wrong added, 'also do not share the German illusion that they are a master race.'[4]

A third notable assessment – prompted like King's and Pearson's by the Fulton speech – came from the Ambassador at Moscow, who had returned to that capital on 6 March 1946, three years to the day since he had arrived at Kuibyshev to assume the representation of Canadian interests in the Soviet Union during the war. Dana Wilgress[†] reported that the fortnight since his return had witnessed the crisis over Soviet forces in Iran; the recriminations between the Soviet Union and the Western allies over Bulgaria; the protests by the United States and the United Kingdom

---

* See *ibid.*, 33-7.

† See *ibid.*, 40-1. When Wilgress was recalled from the Moscow Embassy to indicate official displeasure at the discourteous and hostile treatment accorded him by his Russian hosts following the revelations of Soviet espionage in Canada, it was decided to appoint him High Commissioner to the United Kingdom. 'He has shown himself in Moscow to be a wise and shrewd observer,' a colleague wrote in recommending Wilgress for that important post, 'and a first-class diplomatic reporter of conditions and attitudes of mind.' Quoted in Donald M. Page (ed.), *Documents on Canadian External Relations, 12, 1946* (Ottawa 1977), 5.

at the removal by the Soviets of industrial equipment from Manchuria; and, to cap it all, the stir in Moscow caused by Churchill's speech. 'I have never known a time,' Wilgress admitted, 'when relations between the major allies were so strained or the prospects of co-operation with the Soviet Union so depressing.' Nevertheless, Wilgress was emphatic in his judgement that the Kremlin was not bent on military aggression.

I am ... convinced that the Soviet Government are anxious to avoid war, that they desire above all else a long period of peace in which to repair their shattered economy and strengthen it still further for a possible future trial of strength and that they are no longer interested in spreading communism for its own sake. But because the Soviet Government is run by a handful of men and is dominated by a strong personality with absolute dictatorial power, without having to pay regard to the will of the people, they cannot refrain from following the dictates of personal ambition which lead them to seek the exploitation of the advantages to be gained from temporary situations.

This interpretation of Soviet policy as opportunist is at variance with that expressed by those who hold that the Soviet Government are working to a definite plan and know just what they want. ... I believe that the day-to-day manifestations of Soviet policy are nothing more than revelations of the intuitions of Generalissimo Stalin and of his beliefs of the extent to which he can go in pushing Soviet interests without incurring undue risks.[5]

While Mackenzie King became ever more deeply pessimistic about the prospects for peace, his advisers remained calm. There was at any rate no panic. Officials agreed with the assessment of the British Foreign Office reaching them at the end of 1946: 'Russia, so far as we can judge, is neither prepared for nor in the mood for war, and Stalin is a sober realist. But the general outlook is one of friction, disputes, recrimination and unrest.'[6]

Such an outlook persisted throughout 1947, a year when the enigma of Soviet intentions received much systematic attention within the Department of External Affairs. L.B. Pearson, on being appointed its Under Secretary, agreed to the suggestion of his second-in-command, Escott Reid, that an assessment of the likelihood of war be prepared for the guidance of the Prime Minister and the Secretary of State for External Affairs. Work on it went forward. The earliest draft was done by C.S.A. Ritchie,* based on the despatches of Dana Wilgress from Moscow.

---

* Charles Ritchie, then head of the First Political Division, had served in what was then the Legation at Washington and in the High Commission at London, later becoming Ambassador to the United States and High Commissioner to the United Kingdom. Perceptions of self and scene, recorded in a diary (in contravention of departmental regulations), are piercingly acute and plainly truthful.

All morning a stream of interesting and informative telegrams and despatches from missions abroad comes pouring across my desk. I am tempted to read them

Ritchie's analysis dealt with prospects for Soviet aggression in the long run and the short. Imminent attack was deemed questionable. 'On such information as is available to the Canadian Government,' Ritchie wrote on 30 November 1946,

it appears most unlikely that the Soviet Union would be in a position to wage another major war in the near future, and for this reason it is highly improbable that the Soviet Government would run the risk of deliberately provoking such a war. As a result of the last war, the Soviet Union has suffered so heavily in terms of a general disorganization of the economy, material destruction and loss of manpower that a breathing space seems clearly indicated as a main objective of Soviet policy...

To this short-term estimate, however, three qualifications were attached. First, the Soviet Union might sooner than expected acquire the capacity to produce atomic weapons on a large scale, and be tempted to employ them. Second, the death of Stalin might usher in a period of political instability such that a contender in the power struggle would resort to war not for the national interest but for personal ambition. Third, the Soviet Union might be led inadvertently into conflict, through, say, the imprudence of a theatre commander (as with the outbreak of war in Manchuria in 1931), or some other breakdown in command and control; this eventuality was considered unlikely.

In the long run, three factors predisposing the Soviet leadership towards war with the West had to be taken into account. One was its ideological heritage. Marxism postulated that 'an ultimate struggle between communism and capitalism is inevitable and that communism will emerge victorious. It is difficult to say,' the memorandum commented, 'how much the present rulers of Russia are affected by this concept but it is certainly not without influence on Soviet policy.' National interest rather than ideology could be expected to be the deciding factor. More germane to the possibility of conflict was the totalitarian nature of Soviet power: 'Between such a state and the Western democracies a fundamental cleavage inevitably exists. ... Moreover, the insecurity which makes it

all and try to understand what is really happening, but if I do that I have not time to draft answers to the most immediate telegrams and despatches crying out for instructions. I must skim through everything with my mind concentrated on immediate practical implications. If I try to be objective and to comprehend all the issues I am lost. I draft telegrams and speeches under pressure, short-term considerations upper-most – "Will the Prime Minister sign this?" – "Are we not too short of personnel to be represented at this or that international meeting?" This is the way policy is made on a hand-to-mouth basis out of an overworked official by a tired politician with only half his mind on the subject.

Diary entry for 7 September 1945. Quoted in Charles Ritchie, *The Siren Years: A Canadian Diplomat Abroad, 1937-1945* (Toronto 1974), 208.

necessary for the Soviet government to rule by such methods, also makes it essential that the people of the Soviet Union should not be exposed to the unsettling effects of contact with the Western democracies or their nationals. The Soviet Government, therefore, not only keep their people in ignorance of our conditions of life, but employ unceasing propaganda to instill into their population fear and suspicion of the intentions of the Western democracies. ... Such methods are obviously dangerous to international peace.'

Second, the Soviet Union, ill disposed to the West by reason of ideology and form of government, was clearly in an expansionist phase. Its conquests and its spheres of influence represented 'formidable acquisitions of power ... and there are no signs that the Soviet Government is willing to set bounds to its appetite for further expansions.'

Third, the Soviet Union could opt for war out of fear of the threat posed to its security by aggressive and provocative moves – or what its leaders perceived as such – on the part of the Western powers. This did not mean that the Western powers should shrink from taking prudent action in their own defence; on the contrary: 'So long as they think the western democracies and in particular the United States are strong and united and so long as firm but fair-minded policies are pursued by those powers in dealing with the Soviet Union, the Soviet Government may be disposed to proceed with caution. ... On the other hand, should they become convinced (perhaps as the result of inaccurate reports from their representatives abroad) that the Western powers have aggressive intentions against the Soviet Union, they might feel impelled to provide in haste for their security by further annexation of territory or infiltration into countries in strategic positions.'

By these arguments the paper was led to its conclusions. '[W]hile the threat of immediate aggression is slight, there is little prospect of co-operation with the Soviet Union.' '[E]xisting international machinery cannot be relied upon as a deterrent to aggression by the Soviet Union.' 'The best likelihood of averting such a catastrophe would be for the Soviet Government to be convinced of the strength and unity of the western democracies and at the same time persuaded that they have nothing to fear from them. It is possible that they might then postpone indefinitely the accomplishment of their ultimate aims and the world might settle into a period of uneasy peace.'[7]

Ritchie's analysis – in hindsight so perceptive – became the basis of the Department of External Affairs' assessment of Soviet intentions. Other papers were produced, and from the results of the exercise Escott Reid compiled the master document of 30 August 1947 – 'a scissors-and-paste job,' by Reid's own admission, but wide-ranging enough 'to help us clear our minds on this fundamental question.'* The Reid paper reflected general agreement among the policy community[†] that while war with the Soviet Union might occur by accident, it was unlikely to happen by design. The Russian people were war-weary. The Soviet economy was war-devastated. The Soviet dictators 'despised ... bourgeois adventurism.' Accordingly, 'the prospect of war during the next tear years appears to be remote.'[8]

Such a view of Soviet intentions did not necessarily lead to the conclusion that other members of the United Nations should keep on trying to make the Charter work as if the Soviet Government were not trying to obstruct at every turn. Nor did it necessarily imply that other countries should turn a blind eye to Soviet provocation around the world. If the Soviet horseman continued his maverick ride to the disadvantage and even danger of the herd, ought not others – in the absence of any sheriff taking on the role of vigilantes – attempt to rein him in?

That one of Franklin Roosevelt's 'Four Horsemen' (five when joined by France) might turn upon the rest was a prospect few analysts had cared to dwell upon before the war had ended – still less upon what the rest in that event should do. One Canadian analyst did not hesitate to speculate upon both problems. Escott Reid, whose restless and fertile mind was preoccupied by the shape of things to come to a degree most diplomats would deem excessive (and which he had himself once deemed excessive),** addressed himself during the winter of 1944-5 to what should be done if a great power were once again to try to dominate the world by force. In that event, Reid wrote, 'the only way to prevent a world war from breaking out will be for the other great powers to form immediately an alliance against that power and to declare that the moment it commits aggression they will wage total war against it....' His memorandum made

---

* 'The United States and the Soviet Union: A Study of the Possibility of War and Some of Its Implications for Canadian Policy.' This document, twenty-three pages long, is carefully analysed by Don Page and Don Munton in 'Canadian Images of the Cold War 1946-7,' *International Journal*, XXXII, 3, Summer 1977, 577-604.

† The term 'policy community' is used throughout to denote the group of persons – politicians, civil servants, and military officers – both at home and abroad which formulates national policy. For profiles of its leading personalities, see *In Defence of Canada* III, 4-74.

** '[It is] with the near future that a statesman in office must be mainly concerned – not with the distant future. ... A minister for foreign affairs must be mainly concerned ... with what his country's policy should be to-day, tomorrow, or during the next twelve months' ('Canada and the Threat of War,' *University of Toronto Quarterly*, VI, January 1937, 242). Reid joined the Canadian foreign service soon after propounding this dictum and spent much of his career defying it.

clear that this drastic step would not be taken under United Nations authority and auspices. 'The alliance ... will not be an alliance growing out of the undertakings of member states under the [Charter]. Its effectiveness will depend not on legal obligations contracted in 1945 but on the will for peace of the peoples of the world when the threat of another world war arises.'[9] (This memorandum was published, anonymously, on the eve of the San Francisco Conference.)[10]

This proposal pre-dated Hiroshima. The United States' monopoly (until 1949) of nuclear weapons could be said to strengthen it. When the atomic bomb was under feverish development in wartime, the few Allied statesmen to know the secret supposed that whichever country won the race to fission would win, for once, the peace. The British minister in charge of the United Kingdom side of the Manhattan Project had told Mackenzie King in 1943 that nuclear weapons (in the latter's words) 'would be a terrific factor in the post-war world as giving an absolute control to whatever country possessed the secret,'[11] while the American Secretary of State assured President Truman in April 1945 that nuclear weapons would put the United States 'in a position to dictate our own terms at the end of the war.'[12] It was not to be. Nuclear weapons might deter a would-be aggressor from attack, but they would not compel a trouble-maker to desist. And would those in a position to use nuclear weapons in a compellent role find the nerve to dare to? Churchill told Mackenzie King in December 1947 that he thought the Russians should be ordered to be reasonable or be annihilated;* but the statesman who a quarter century before had sent troops to Russia to 'strangle the infant Bolshevism in its cradle' was not then in a position to attack Bolshevism in its loutish maturity.

If nuclear threats could not be relied upon to quell Soviet provocations, what else might be done to stop them or protect the West against them? L.B. Pearson added to his analysis of Soviet conduct and intention a pro-

---

* Mackenzie King's diary recounts vividly Churchill's advocacy of preventive war against the Soviet Union.

> He turned to me sharply, his eyes bulging out of his head, and said ... What the Russians should be told at the present conference, if they are unwilling to co-operate, is that the nations that have fought the last war for freedom, have had enough of this war of nerves and intimidation. We do not intend to have this sort of thing continue indefinitely. ... We will meet you in regard to conditions generally. What we will not allow you to do is to destroy Western Europe; to extend your regime further there. If you do not agree to that here and now, within so many days, we will attack Moscow and your other cities and destroy them with atomic bombs from the air.

Quoted in J.W. Pickersgill and D.F. Forster (eds.), *The Mackenzie King Record*, IV, *1947-1948* (Toronto 1970), 112.

posal for action. 'There is, in my mind, only one effective reply to this Russian policy,' Pearson told the Department of External Affairs.

A Big Three Conference should be held where all the cards are placed on the table; where all the issues will be faced and a genuine effort made to resolve them. No such conference has yet been held, and it is long overdue. ... Such a conference might have to remain in session for months, but should be prepared to do so. The Foreign Ministers must be willing to take whatever time and make whatever efforts are required to clear away suspicions and differences and to bring about a definite understanding of each other's desires and designs.

And if this endeavour to dissipate East-West differences by friendly persuasion should fail? 'Then the United States and the United Kingdom should convert the United Nations into a really effective agent to preserve the peace and prevent aggression. This means revising it radically.' And if the Soviet Union were to veto such a proposal, as it would be almost sure to do? Then 'a new organization must be created which, as the guardian of the peace of all nations ... can function without the Russians and, as a last resort, against them.'[13]

Here were ideas which were, to say the least, imperfectly thought through. From Ottawa, Hume Wrong put his finger on one of several weaknesses. 'Perhaps the metaphor about putting the cards on the table is misleading,' Wrong wrote to Pearson on 23 March.

It implies that the issues between the great powers can be clearly defined; and that, by arranging the pack so that each of them gets a hand satisfactory to itself and to the other two, the game would continue in amity in accordance with the book of rules.

The trouble is that in the sort of game that is now being played each of the great powers can, if it wishes, manufacture new cards, add new suits and decide for itself what are trumps. That is what the Russians have been doing with vigour during the past few months, and the others are forced, willingly or not, to disregard the rules or to invent new ones. I cannot conceive a conference really facing the issues honestly at present because the issues are not clearly enough defined and because, like most international problems, really serious issues cannot be solved but only changed in form and urgency. Such a conference would, I think, at the best end merely in the application to the world as a whole of the old Hapsburg motto of "divide et impera." It would create a balance of power which would have less stability than the balances achieved during the 19th century...[14]

Pearson himself soon abandoned his early advocacy of a confrontation with the Soviets. Of a fellow Canadian who had put the case for showdown then and there, Pearson commented: 'I can certainly understand his pessimism at the possibility of developing friendly relationships with the USSR. Nevertheless, that is the only possible approach, ultimately, to peace.'[15]

From Moscow, Dana Wilgress recommended resolving not to truckle to or knuckle under Soviet demands. To the 'irresponsible opportunism' which characterized the post-war policies of the Soviet Union there was, Wilgress considered, 'only one possible rejoinder. Not that policy of touchiness which in the minds of its advocates means treating the Soviet Union as an inferior or a pariah, but a policy of firmness based on a coalescing of American and British policies on a high moral plane. This high moral plane should be intimately associated with the purposes and principles enunciated in the Charter of the United Nations. There should be no more compromising with these principles,' Wilgress added graphically, 'for the sake of brief vodka honeymoons in Moscow.'[16]

A major concern of Canadian policy-makers during 1947 was to avoid any move that would drive the Soviet Union and its client states out of the world organization. 'I feel that the main danger over the next twelve months,' Escott Reid wrote on 29 October 1947, 'is hasty action on the part of the United States which might have the result of the Soviet group of states seceding from the United Nations. I feel,' Reid continued, 'that this further crystallization of the existing political division in the world would be dangerous and unnecessary. It would be dangerous because it would destroy one of the few bridges between the two worlds. It would be unnecessary because the Western world can do everything that it may want to do to organize itself against the Soviet Union, without driving the Soviet Union out of the United Nations.'[17]

Was such a Western organization somehow to be accomplished within the United Nations by some tinkering with its Charter which the Soviet Union could accept? Reform of the Charter was an appealing approach, and some ideas about it were tentatively put forward. 'The greatest danger to the future of the United Nations,' L.B. Pearson declared in a speech at Toronto on 2 September 1947, 'a menace which will kill it if it is not brought under control, is the irresponsible use of the veto power in the Security Council.' What could be done about that?

We can try to do three or four things. We can amend the Charter. Or rather, we can't amend the Charter, because the Big Powers have a veto on amendment, and any amendment has to be passed by all of them. We could agree on certain conventional rules and regulations for the exercise of the use of the veto, and get the Great Powers to accept those rules. This also will be difficult...[18]

Charter reform was also the theme of a speech by the Ambassador at Washington delivered at Tarrytown, New York, on 15 September 1947. 'We must remember that a two-year-old constitution for the international community is a very young constitution,' Hume Wrong told his audience on that occasion. 'It must be changed sooner or later, and the sooner the better.' Wrong conceded, however, that it 'would not be wise to be cocksure about what change should be made'; and he noted that 'use of the veto is a symptom, not a cause, of that profound division of our single world which baffles the statesmen, the diplomats, the publicists, and the ordinary man in the street. Almost any constitution,' Wrong added, 'national or international, can be made to work if there is the will to work it.'[19]

Charter reform, Escott Reid argued convincingly, was the wrong path. The Prime Minister had received a letter from the British authority on international affairs, Sir Alfred Zimmern, in which Zimmern had enclosed the text of a speech he had delivered at Hartford, Connecticut on 4 July, advocating that the United Nations Security Council be replaced by a body of seven representatives elected by an international electoral college, three-quarters of whose members would be chosen by national legislatures. Zimmern had solicited Mackenzie King's opinion of his scheme, and it fell to Reid to draft the Prime Minister's reply. In a covering minute on his draft, Reid had observed: 'This is a pretty unrealistic proposal. The Soviet Union is not likely to agree even to minor revisions of the Charter which relate to the Security Council. ... It is surprising that Zimmern should have suggested seriously this unrealistic constitutional panacea for our ills.' The reply which went to Zimmern over the Prime Minister's signature sums up the policy community's attitude to projects of Charter reform in the autumn of 1947.

The United Nations can be of great help in maintaining a preponderance of power on the side of peace and in upholding moral values. If the Charter could be improved, the United Nations could be an even more effective instrument.

But the possibility of reforms in the Charter of the United Nations is narrowly limited by the obvious unwillingness of the Soviet Union to agree to substantial reforms since no formal changes in the Charter can be made without Soviet consent.

Therefore, if the United Nations is to be kept in existence as a meeting ground between the two worlds and if, at the same time, a more effective system of international security is desired, are we not forced to the conclusion that we shall have to get that security in some other way than by amendment of the Charter?

Perhaps those members of the United Nations who are willing to accept more specific international obligations in return for greater national security will have to consider whether they should not be prepared to agree to a treaty of mutual defence against any aggressor...[20]

In that final paragraph was adumbrated the idea of the North Atlantic Treaty – although not, as will be shown below, for the first time.

The Canadian who earliest placed on record the opinion that the United Nations system could not suffice as a bulwark against Soviet imperialism was a journalist rather than a statesman. Willson Woodside was among the first individuals in the Western world – if not the first – to proclaim in print that the Soviet Union, nominally the ally of the Western democracies, had reverted to its pre-war enmity. Woodside warned in his column in *Saturday Night* magazine that the Soviet Union would seek to expand its rule until Western counter-pressure compelled it to halt. He maintained that the West must organize to pool its strength in order to defend its interests against Soviet imperialism. 'If Russia continues to break solemn agreements,' Woodside wrote on 26 May 1945, '...she will soon provide the impulse for the democratic world to organize itself. Far from leading to another war with Russia which nobody in our country wants ... such a democratic union would muster so overwhelming a proportion of the military, or particularly aerial-naval, strength of the world that it might well ensure peace for a century. ... Such a consolidation of the power of the free world,' Woodside concluded, 'may be the only way of preventing war.'[21] And on 6 October 1945: 'If the coming months prove conclusively that we cannot organize the peace of Europe and the world on the basis of a frank and open co-operation with Russia, we will be faced squarely with the alternative of consolidating the preponderant, but at present dispersed, strength of the free world.'[22]

In this prediction, so soon to be proved correct, the journalist was ahead of the policy-makers.* Their early pronouncements were enigmatic. Official statements pointed out that neither the letter of the Charter nor the spirit of the United Nations stood in the way of member states forming among themselves special associations for purposes consistent with those of the world Organization; but the statements did not specify what such purposes might be. Thus, L.B. Pearson observed in a lecture at Princeton University on 13 May 1946, when still Ambassador at Washington, that 'We do not expect our membership in the UN to prevent our working out special arrangements with powers who wish to co-operate with us and which are consistent with our obligations under the Charter.'[23] A year later, in a speech delivered at the University of Rochester, Pearson was a bit more specific about what such 'special arrangements' might be designed to provide. 'If mutual tolerance between two basically opposed

---

*   And also out of step with most of his fellow countrymen. 'Woodside has said that during 1945 and 1946 he was denounced repeatedly in letters to the *Toronto Star* and *Saturday Night* as a "fascist rat," "the voice of Goebbels," "breeder of World War III," or just an "anti-communist".' Donald Liesemer, 'The Nature of Canada's Crusade for NATO' (unpublished MA dissertation, Bishop's University 1973), 13.

forms of society within the United Nations should prove impossible,'
Pearson stated on 16 June 1947, 'the nations of the west would then have
to decide whether to adjust their pace to that of the slowest member, or to
go ahead to a really effective international order with those states who are
really willing to co-operate.'[24]

On 4 July 1947, L.S. St Laurent* (who had become Secretary of State
for External Affairs the previous September) reiterated Pearson's comment with (as the latter notes) 'greater authority' and, perhaps because of
that authority, lesser precision. St Laurent noted 'a serious danger to the
peace of the world' posed by 'its division, both politically and ideologically, into two great groupings. Somehow, methods which can make possible peaceful co-operation, political and economic, must be found. The
sources of fear and suspicion between them must be removed. ... No government,' he added, 'least of all the Canadian government, can accept the
view that there is any fundamental hostility or division between the common peoples of the several nations.' The government still hoped, its foreign minister told the House of Commons, that the United Nations could
be 'the agency to counteract these divided forces. ... It is because it still
thinks that this can be done that the Canadian government feels that the
growth and strengthening of the United Nations must be a real corner-
stone of Canada's policy in foreign affairs.' St Laurent then stated:
'Within the United Nations there is room, of course, for closer associations not inconsistent at all with the ideals of the world organization,'
adducing the Commonwealth of Nations as a working example of such an
organization.[25] (It is reading too much into that statement to represent it
as does Pearson in his memoirs: 'Mr St Laurent ... told the House of
Commons that there was room in the UN for closer associations for collective security...':[26] St Laurent gave no hint that the 'closer associations' to
which he referred might be invested with a security function, and the
Commonwealth of Nations then as now is conspicuous by its resolute
avoidance of any measures for collective defence.)

On 13 August 1947, the Assistant Under Secretary of State for External
Affairs delivered a statement which went well beyond anything hitherto
said in public in the name of the Canadian government. The occasion was
the annual study conference of the Canadian Institute on Public Affairs
held at Geneva Park on Lake Couchiching, Ontario; the venue of this
statement together with its importance have led students of Canadian
foreign policy to refer to it as 'the Couchiching speech.' The speaker was
well aware of its significance: despite his seniority, he had it cleared before

---

* See *In Defence of Canada* III, 10-15.

delivery: 'The speech was approved by Mr Pearson,' Escott Reid informed Hume Wrong some weeks later, 'and subsequently Mr St Laurent
approved of its being published in the printed proceedings of the Couchiching Conference.'[27]

The key passage of the speech was set in the context of a comprehensive analysis and review of Canada's role in the United Nations. 'It would
have been possible for Canada after San Francisco to have taken the line
that the Charter needs radical amendments,' Escott Reid told his audience at Geneva Park. But that would have risked, and probably brought
about, the secession of the Soviet Union from the United Nations. 'Such
a secession would mean the destruction of the only constitutional structure which now exists which includes both of the two worlds into which
our one world has now so tragically been divided. It seems to me that as
long as that structure remains in existence – faulty and weak as it is –
there is some hope that the two worlds can learn to live together.' It was
important, then, to preserve the United Nations structure.

But that was not to say that nothing could be done. 'A rejection of
proposals for immediate, drastic revision of the Charter does not necessarily mean that those states of the Western world which are willing to
commit themselves to a much closer degree of union than that embodied
in the Charter should not, if they so desire, work out such arrangements. ... The states of the Western world are not debarred by a Soviet
veto or by Soviet membership in the United Nations from the creation of
international federal institutions to deal with international economic and
social questions if they decide that such institutions are required. Nor are
they debarred by the Charter of the United Nations or by Soviet membership in the United Nations from creating new international political
institutions to maintain the peace, if the time should come when it was
generally agreed by them that this was necessary.' Then followed the key
passage:

If the peoples of the Western world want an international security organization
with teeth, even though the Soviet Union is at present unwilling to be a member
of such an organization, they do not need to amend the United Nations Charter in
order to create such an organization; they can create it consistently with the
United Nations Charter. They can create a regional security organization to which
any state willing to accept the obligations of membership could belong. In such an
organization there need be no veto right posessed by any great power. In such an
organization each member state could accept a binding obligation to pool the
whole of its economic and military resources with those of the other members if
any [italics in original] power should be found to have committed aggression
against any one of the members.[28]

Of this passage, Reid wrote of it later: 'This may be the first public state-ment advocating a collective defence organization of the western world '[29] It is almost certainly the first public statement by a government official advocating a collective defence organization of the western world.

Because the Assistant Under Secretary of State for External Affairs was, as Escott Reid wrote afterwards, 'a civil servant putting forward in public ideas not yet adopted by the government,' he used what he described as 'guarded language.'[30] Even so, it was not guarded enough for L.B. Pearson who, when shown the draft by Reid, 'suggested that it would be just as well if this particular passage were omitted from the copies of the speech given to the press at the conference.'[31] If so inconspicuous a *ballon d'essai* was not likely to get shot down at once, it was not likely to get attention, either. Nor did it, hovering aloft for several days getting no attention whatsoever, then drifting out of sight. The Department of Ex-ternal Affairs then decided to publish the speech as delivered, including its key passage, in its series of 'Statements and Speeches.' Thus was the grand design of what would become the North Atlantic Treaty Organiza-tion revealed to the world: quiet diplomacy, indeed.

Escott Reid prepared his speech at the same time as he was preparing his memorandum of 30 August 1947, 'The United States and the Soviet Union: A Study of the Possibility of War and Some of the Implications for Canadian Policy.' Like the speech, the memorandum in similar wording recommended the creation of 'a new "regional" security organization in which there would be no veto and in which each state would undertake to pool all its economic and military forces with those of the other members if any power should be found to have committed aggression against any members.' Unlike the speech, the memorandum employed – for the first time – the term 'alliance.'[32]

The memorandum differed from the speech in two further respects. First, it addressed itself to the question of whether an alliance of western nations might provoke the Soviet Union into pre-emptive war. This possi-bility was dismissed – provided the alliance itself did not act in a pro-vocative manner. 'In order to diminish the possibility of war, the first requirement is that the Western powers maintain an overwhelming bal-ance of force relative to that of the Soviet Union, that they use the threat of this force to hold back further extensions of Soviet power, but that they do not provoke the Soviet Union into any desperate gamble.' And again: 'It is ... essential that the policy of firmness and of containing the Soviet Union should not be pushed too hard and too fast and that we should keep our heads.'[33] The second respect in which the memorandum differed from the speech was that it elicited responses from those members of the policy community – as noted previously, almost a score – among whom it had been circulated. None of the respondents disputed the 'firmness and fairness' approach recommended by the memorandum; only one took exception to its advocacy of a western security alliance, expressing his preference for driving the Soviet Union out of the United Nations altogether and for transforming the latter into a collective security system capable of meeting the Russians on all fronts.[34]

It may thus be concluded that by the fall of 1947 there existed within the policy community of Canada a consensus that the time was approaching when it would be prudent and expedient to create a Western security alliance of some kind to meet the threat of Soviet imperialism and to prevent the outbreak of a war. From that consensus the Prime Minister alone remained aloof. It was up to his cabinet colleagues and officials to try to draw him into it. In that endeavour they were aided by events.

Rumination became policy when the Secretary of State for External Affairs spoke at the United Nations on 18 September 1947. L.S. St Laurent's address to the General Assembly may fairly be described as the most important initiative by Canada in world affairs since her Advisory Officer at the League of Nations had proposed imposing oil sanctions against Italy twelve years earlier. (St Laurent, however, unlike W.A. Riddell, spoke with the authority of his government.)*

St Laurent proposed that, if the security machinery provided for by the United Nations Charter continued in its enforced idleness, member states wishing to enter into a mutual security arrangement of their own should be free to do so. How strongly this proposal should be stated had been debated by two of St Laurent's senior advisers, as one of them – Escott Reid – has since recalled.

When the time came to draft a speech for St Laurent to deliver to the UN General Assembly in the autumn of 1947, I found that Pearson wanted to maintain in St Laurent's speech an ambiguity between whether Canada was proposing a radical revision of the UN Charter, even at the cost of driving the Soviet Union out of the United Nations, or a collective security pact to supplement the UN Charter, whereas I wanted St Laurent to come down unequivocally in favour of a supplementary agreement. Pearson won...[35]

---

* On the 'Riddell incident,' see James Eayrs, *In Defence of Canada*, II, *Appeasement and Rearmament* (Toronto 1965), 16-27; and Robert Bothwell and John English, '"Dirty Work at the Crossroads": New Perspectives on the Riddell Incident,' *Historical Papers 1972*, 263-85.

The address, prepared by Pearson in some haste – 'I ... spent most of the night in my hotel room writing a draft' – contained two key passages. The first suggested a return to the Charter or its revision.

The veto privilege ... if it continues to be abused, may well destroy the United Nations. ... Our peoples cannot be expected to accept indefinitely and without alterations, voting procedures and practices which ... reduce agreement to a lowest common denominator of action that in practice often means inaction. ... [These] procedures and practices ... must be changed. This can be done by the voluntary abandonment of these practices, by agreed conventions or by amendments to the Charter. We hope that no member of the Security Council will flout clearly-expressed world opinion by obstinately preventing change, and thus become responsible for prejudicing, and possibly destroying, the organization which is now man's greatest hope for the future.[37]

The second suggested a supplementary agreement.

Nations, in their search for peace and co-operation, will not, and can not, accept indefinitely an unaltered council which was set up to ensure their security and which, so many feel, has become frozen in futility and divided by dissension. If forced, they may seek greater safety in an association of democratic and peace-loving states willing to accept more specific international obligations in return for a greater measure of national security. Such associations, it has already been pointed out, if consistent with the principles and purposes of the Charter, can be formed within the United Nations. It is to be hoped that such a development will not be necessary. If, however, it is made necessary, it will have to take place. Let us not forget that the provisions of the Charter are a floor *under*, rather than a ceiling *over*, the responsibilities of member states [italics in original].[38]

'[O]nce the Canadian government had agreed six months later to support a supplementary agreement or agreements,' Escott Reid has pointed out, 'it was this [second] part of the speech which was emphasized to the exclusion of the other part.'[39]

Reports of reaction to St Laurent's address differ. Pearson, quoting in his memoirs only the 'supplementary agreement' passage, remarks of it that 'These words gripped the attention of the world assembly. ... At once we were asked by many other delegations, especially by the British and Americans, to elaborate on them. We did. We emphasized that what we had in mind was not a revision of the procedures of the Security Council, with its vetoes, but a more limited collective security arrangement under Article 51 of the Charter, which affirmed the "inherent right of individual or collective self-defence" of the United Nations members against armed attack.'[40] Escott Reid felt that the statement, cautiously worded and coupled with the 'Charter return or revision' approach as its alternative, did not receive the attention it deserved. 'The significance of this statement was not apparently appreciated at the time by the newspapermen who were covering the Assembly,' Reid wrote to Hume Wrong some weeks later. 'I think, however, that I am right in saying that in making this statement Mr St Laurent went further in the direction of [advocating a regional security organization] ... than any other head of delegation.'[41] In so doing, Pearson thought, St Laurent may have caused his Prime Minister to feel 'some uneasiness at the important initiative....'[42]

From the rostrum of the United Nations General Assembly, L.S. St Laurent next took his message to an altogether different but no less significant forum – an audience in Quebec City. 'It was an important occasion,' St Laurent's biographer observes, 'since he had to prepare public opinion in French Canada for a further period of international tension, and forestall a new withdrawal within the frontiers of Quebec, the instinctive reaction of French-speaking Canadians in time of stress.'[43] St Laurent spoke much more bluntly at Quebec City on 7 October than he had done at New York on 18 September. He portrayed the Soviet leadership as ruthless imperialists: 'It is perfectly clear that the Soviet Union wishes to see what it calls Capitalist Regimes destroyed and Communistic Totalitarianism established everywhere.' He quoted the two key passages from his speech to the UN General Assembly, then added:

[I]f theory-crazed totalitarian groups persist in their policies of frustration and futility, we will not, for very much longer, allow them to prevent us from using our obvious advantages to improve the conditions of those who do wish to co-operate with us...

You may be assured this whole problem is being given and will continue to be given the most careful consideration by the government and by those from whom it takes expert advice in that regard. We are not going to jump at hasty conclusions, but we are not going to stand idly by and allow situations to develop to the point where they would be apt to be irremediable.'[44]

St Laurent's biographer comments: 'Not only was this forthright warning the first announcement to the Canadian people that the country would be taking a firmer stand in the cold war, but it was made in the heart of Quebec, from which most resistance to such a policy was bound to come. No other Canadian could make the important statement with such hopes of a favourable reception...'[45]

In mid-October 1947, reports reached Ottawa from the Ambassador at Washington that it was possible that the United States government would within the next year or so be ready to take an initiative of its own in support of a regional defence pact. This information prompted Escott Reid to try his hand at drafting a treaty. Reid's purpose was only to limber up for future negotiations, not to prepare a text to be put forward by the government. It would be premature to bring a proposal of this nature before the present session of the General Assembly,' Reid wrote to Hume Wrong on 7 November. 'I am pretty certain that this is not the kind of matter on which we would want to take any initiative.' But since the United States itself might take an initiative, it would be 'useful if we were to try to clear our own mind a little on some of the problems which are raised.' He sent the result of his labours to Wrong with the probably unnecessary injunction not to take it 'too seriously. It is something which I wrote out at the end of last week,' Reid added, 'when I had to stay home for a few days with a cold.'[46] Later, he described his draft as

based on the Anglo-Polish treaty of mutual assistance of August, 1939, and including provisions from the Rio treaty [the Inter-American Treaty signed in September 1947] and the abortive Geneva Protocol of 1924. It was a treaty open to all members of the UN. In order not to exclude countries whose admittance to the UN had been vetoed by the Soviet Union it was also open to any country whose application for membership in the United Nations had been supported in the General Assembly by a two-thirds majority of the members present and voting. The treaty was to come into force when ratified by three of the five permanent members of the Security Council (meaning the United States, Britain and France), and by a majority of the other members of the UN.[47]

The principal institution required by the treaty would be an assembly of its signatories to be known as a 'Board for Collective Self-Defence,' because, as Reid explained to Hume Wrong, '"collective self-defence" is the phrase used in Article 51 of the Charter.' He added: 'The powers of the Board are set forth in very general terms. ... I think that experience in the United Nations has shown that it is much better to give a general grant of powers than to be too specific...'[48]

Between Escott Reid's draft treaty and the North Atlantic Treaty signed at Washington seventeen months later there was little similarity. (A noteworthy difference was that Reid's was open to signing by all like-minded countries regardless of their location in the world.) Reid's effort was greeted coolly by the policy community. 'My own view would be that we should not ... at the present time take any initiative in regard to the proposal for a Mutual Defence Treaty,' a member of the Department of External Affairs wrote to its Minister after perusing Reid's handiwork. '[W]e should confine ourselves to learning as much as possible about the intentions of the United States and the United Kingdom. If the proposal develops,' the official added, 'I am doubtful if there is any over-riding advantage to be gained from our being amongst those who initiated it.'[49] On which L.B. Pearson noted: 'I agree.' Reid did not. 'I was disappointed when nothing happened in December [1947],' he wrote years later, 'and when I could not get support for Canada taking some kind of initiative.'[50]

The Prime Minister, in Britain to attend the wedding of Princess Elizabeth, was briefed on the international situation at 10 Downing Street on 24 November 1947. (Besides Mackenzie King, Prime Minister Jan Smuts was present at the briefing, along with Prime Minister Clement Attlee, Foreign Secretary Ernest Bevin, other British minsters, and the Commonwealth High Commissioners at London.) Bevin told a tale of turmoil provoked by the Soviet Union everywhere in Europe, confessing – so Mackenzie King recorded – to feeling 'more pessimistic than he had felt at any time in his life.' The Council of Foreign Ministers, soon to resume its meetings in London, was on the verge of final failure. Bevin expressed his fear 'that the Russians would keep up the attitude they had assumed. He felt that the Americans and British and French must make a stand to save Western Europe. The Russians would try to make this impossible. ... [H]e feared there would be conflict...' At this stage, Mackenzie King interrupted the Foreign Secretary.

[W]hat do you mean by conflict? Do you mean conflict within the conference or without? ... Bevin then said: I mean without. ... What he feared was not an open declaration of war, or the intention on the part of Russia to bring on a war immediately, but rather that the Americans with their sense of power might become impatient at Russia's behaviour and that matters would drift unintentionally but quickly into overt acts which would lead to war...

At this clarification, Mackenzie King rejoined: 'I said this was a most serious statement – the most serious statement I had ever heard in the years I had been in Downing Street.'[51]

Following this meeting, the Prime Minister exchanged impressions with the High Commissioner at London, Norman Robertson.* 'We each agreed it was the most serious situation that we could possible have imagined,' Mackenzie King recorded, 'and indeed was altogether beyond anything I had hitherto thought possible. In a word, it came down to this: that within three weeks, there may be another world war. This world war will grow out of the unwillingness of the Russians to make any peace settlement with respect to Germany at this time, and their determination to go on fomenting unrest in all countries...'[52] After talking alone with the British foreign secretary next day, King noted: 'As Bevin went away, I told him I deeply sympathize with the great load he was carrying. Would welcome any opportunity to lighten his burden where I was sure the Cana-

---

* See *In Defence of Canada* III, 29-32.

dian people would understand the situation well enough to cause the influence of our country to be felt.'[53]

On 4 December, having returned to Ottawa, the Prime Minister relayed to his Cabinet what he had learned in London. '[T]old them perhaps more than I should have about inside of situation in Europe as I knew it and believe is about to break. I could see what I said had a very sobering influence among all the Members. They were not surprised about conditions in France, but they seemed stunned at the thought of a possible conflict coming on immediately between Russia and the other nations. ... It is just too terrible to contemplate,' Mackenzie King reflected afterwards, 'but it does look increasingly to me as if the men at the head of affairs in Russia have got it into their minds that they can conquer the world.'[54]

On 15 December, Mackenzie King learned that, as Bevin had feared and predicted, the Council of Foreign Ministers had broken off its meetings in London without arriving at any agreement. 'We have now reached the point that Bevin feared might lead to war,' King noted on that date. 'It is clear that the United Kingdom, the United States and France intend to work together to save Western Europe. ... It is equally clear that Russia intends to hold all her satellite powers together to seek to become the Master of Europe.'[55] What was not yet clear was how Canada, in so stark a situation, might react.

Following the adjournment in disagreement of the Council of Foreign Ministers on 15 December, the British Foreign Secretary spent a soul-searching evening alone with the American Secretary of State. Over dinner at Ernest Bevin's home, Bevin told George C. Marshall that the fruitless meetings of the past few days had convinced him 'that there is no chance that the Soviet Union will deal with the west on any reasonable terms in the foreseeable future. The salvation of the west depends on the formation of some form of union, formal or informal in character, in western Europe backed by the United States and the Dominions – such a mobilization of moral and material force as will inspire confidence and energy within and respect elsewhere.'[56] Two days later, on 17 December, Marshall paid a farewell visit to the Foreign Office during which Bevin elaborated his proposal.

His own idea was that we must devise some western democratic system comprising the Americans, ourselves, France, Italy, etc. and of course the Dominions. This would not be a formal alliance, but an understanding backed by power, money and resolute action. It would be a sort of spiritual federation of the west. He knew that formal constitutions existed in the United States and France. He, however, preferred, especially for this purpose, the British conception of unwritten and informal understandings. If such a powerful consolidation of the west could be achieved it would then be clear to the Soviet Union that having gone so far they could not advance any further. ... The essential task was to create confidence in Western Europe that further communist inroads would be stopped. The issue must be defined and clear...[57]

From this statement (which is a British record), it is evident that Ernest Bevin had in mind some arrangement which would differ from a conventional military alliance. 'I do not think that at that stage he was thinking in military terms only,' Gladwyn Jebb (then Bevin's close adviser) has written since, 'but rather of some sort of friendly association of democratic peoples determined to resist the expansive tendencies of totalitarianism.'[58] Of Bevin's initiative, an American commentator observed: 'It was a simple idea, the kind of idea that comes to a shrewd, hard man who has been organizing [within the trade union movement] for thirty years of his life. ... When things got tough you organized.'[59]

General Marshall was persuaded by what Bevin said to him, and told him so. But he warned the British foreign minister not to count on immediate American support. Congress had just voted enormous sums for the economic reconstruction of Europe, and was in no mood to follow up with troops. Bevin should get on with the job of uniting the Western European countries. That done, the US Administration would see how best to help.

Before flying back to Washington, Marshall told the US delegation of his exchange with Bevin, and the delegation mulled over Bevin's proposal while returning to the United States by sea. One of its members, J.D. Hickerson of the US State Department (who, along with Theodore C. Achilles, customarily dealt with the Embassy at Washington and would be closely involved with Hume Wrong and Escott Reid in the negotiation of the North Atlantic Treaty), became an enthusiastic supporter. Hickerson recruited John Foster Dulles, then acting on behalf of Senator Arthur Vandenberg as the Republican Party's adviser to the delegation. Dulles, in turn, converted Vandenberg. The conversion of the isolationist from Grand Rapids, Michigan, to the creed of internationalism symbolizes the end of that tradition of American indifference to the fate of Europe – 'let it stew in its own juice' – that reached back with few interruptions to George Washington's farewell.

The conversion of the Prime Minister of Canada was to be more arduous than any of these.

By 1947, Mackenzie King had become an isolationist again. '[B]efore he left office,' L.B. Pearson has testified, 'he had reverted to the fears of the thirties about international commitments, though he continued to preach the proper sermons about peace and international co-operation.'* The more grave the world scene appeared to the Prime Minister, the more determined he became to keep Canada clear of it. Asked to indicate in some way support for the 'United Europe' movement, King's immediate instinct was to withhold it. 'I have never been too sure about the extent to which Canada should become involved in the European situation,' was the Prime Minister's guarded reply. 'There is much to be said on both sides.' He would say nothing on either side. 'I very much doubt the wisdom of anyone in Canada at this time entering too actively upon a campaign on behalf of the 'United Europe' movement. I may be quite wrong in this view,' he conceded in a context admitting no possibility that he could have been wrong at all, 'which I hope you will regard as wholly personal and not in any way official.'[60] Less than a fortnight before retirement, Mackenzie King confided to a political associate that 'there was great danger of our getting beyond our depth in some of the international obligations that we were assuming, and that we would be well advised to have the Great Powers – the US and the UK – accept the main responsibility for initiating matters of major and world wide significance. We would get little thanks if they succeeded but would get plenty of blame if they were a failure. Above all, we were running the risk of making Canada the first target for Russian aggression.'[61]

But the old man, worn out by his long run, had all but lost his grip on the helm. He could no longer shape foreign policy to his liking, let alone his whim. His Secretary of State for External Affairs – a portfolio Mackenzie King had held himself until 1946 and was even then reluctant to relinquish – became, with the backing of the senior officials of his Department, the foremost exponent of a new internationalist outlook. 'When Mr St Laurent was the responsible Minister,' L.B. Pearson testifies again, 'he was the framer and strong supporter of our ... policy. ... Mr King felt differently.'[62] Colleagues and officials humoured their Prime Minister, they reasoned with him, they would on occasion stand up to him. 'He did not try to restrain Mr St Laurent in the expression of his views on collective security,' is how Pearson recalls Mackenzie King's role in 1948, 'which, however, he felt were too greatly influenced by the department [of External Affairs], more particularly by myself. While the Prime Minister favoured, in principle, the idea of a North Atlantic coalition, he thought Canada should keep in the background, leaving the promotion

* *Mike: The Memoirs of the Rt Hon. Lester B. Pearson*, II, *1948-1957* (Toronto 1973), 132. 'For this reversion he offered no ... justification ... but sought simply to impose his will ... by the sheer force of his personality and by the authority of his office.' *In Defence of Canada* III, 13.

and development of the idea to the Americans and the British...[63] Asked
in an interview in later years 'To what extent were the earlier overtures,
the earlier speeches ... a matter of government policy, to what extent did
Mr King stand behind what you and Mr Reid and Mr St Laurent were
doing?,' Pearson responded:

He didn't know too much about what was going on. ... He was getting ready for
his own retirement and I have a feeling ... that when we discussed these things
with Mr St Laurent as we did, that if he had held back there would have been
nothing done. ... But Mr St Laurent went along 100%. In fact, he used to encourage us. He was the author of this policy because he was the Minister. I don't know
how much he discussed it with Mr King and I suspect it wasn't discussed in the
Cabinet very much....[64]

The then head of the Prime Minister's office and, by his own account,
Mackenzie King's 'most trusted adviser,' confirms Pearson's impressions. 'This revolutionary change from a policy of no commitments in
peacetime to a guarantee of collective security was announced by Mackenzie King,' J.W. Pickersgill* wrote when retired, 'but I do not believe
he would ever have reached that point without the pressure from St Laurent, backed by Pearson and [the then Minister of National Defence,
Brooke] Claxton.'[65]† Escott Reid recalled that 'St Laurent and Pearson
were constantly apprehensive that Mackenzie King might switch from
suport of the treaty to his prewar isolationism.'[66] And again: 'During the
war he had urged the creation of an effective collective security system
but as soon as the war was over he began to retreat to his pre-war isolationism. We, in the External Affairs Department, never knew which way
he would jump.'[67]

The querulous state of the Prime Minister's mind is indicated by his
dour reception of the message sent to him by the Prime Minister of Britain on 14 January 1948. (A similar message had been sent to Washington
the day before.) It elaborated on what Bevin had said to Marshall at London after the breakdown of the Council of Foreign Ministers. It was a
moving and persuasive plea – J.D. Hickerson of the US Department of
State described it as 'magnificent' – but Mackenzie King fastened unerr-
ingly on only one of its sentences: 'If we are to stem further encroach-

---

*   See *In Defence of Canada* III, 45-7; also James Eayrs, 'Houdini Among the Mandarins,'
    Toronto Star, 25 October 1975. Close as he was to Mackenzie King, Pickersgill felt
    himself to be even closer to L.S. St Laurent and placed a higher value on that rela-
    tionship. 'I doubt if, in Canadian public life, there has ever been a more intimate
    working association between two men than the association I had with Louis St Lau-
    rent from 1948 until his retirement from public life....' J.W. Pickersgill, *My Years with
    Louis St Laurent: A Political Memoir* (Toronto 1975), 327.
†   See *In Defence of Canada* III, 45-7.

ment of Soviet ties, we should organize the ethical and spiritual forces of Western Europe backed by the power and resources of the Commonwealth and the Americas, thus creating a solid foundation for the advance of western civilization in the widest sense.' That he did not like, and said so in no uncertain terms to the British High Commissioner at Ottawa who had delivered the message to him:

I went over the note with Clutterbuck, and pointed out that I was in general sympathy with the point of view expressed, but took decided exception to one paragraph which could be read as implying that through use of the words "the power and resources of the Commonwealth to be devoted to the defence of civilization" might mean military power, finance, resources, etc., but I thought it was quite wrong that any paragraph should be so framed. ... I wished he would tell his Government that I would not accept that paragraph – that it was objectionable to me. As to what referred to a spiritual outlook, etc. I was in full accord but did not like the use of the word Commonwealth as though it was one entity instead of several nations.[68]

The Prime Minister called L.B. Pearson by telephone, told the Under Secretary of State for External Affairs of his objection to the wording in the British message and charged him with preparing a reply to it. Pearson, Escott Reid wrote later, 'was delighted that the British had made this opening move. If the campaign for a security pact was to gather momentum, it was clearly essential that Canada should welcome the British initiative.'[69] Pearson was well aware of Mackenzie King's deep-seated suspicion of anything smacking of imperial centralization and 'Downing Street domination,' and knew how crucial it was to the success of the British initiative that it not be deflected by Mackenzie King's ire at the terminology in which it had been couched. 'He thought the use of the word "Commonwealth" in this connection,' Pearson wrote to L.S. St Laurent in sending him the draft reply for the approval of the Secretary of State for External Affairs, 'to mean the centralization of those powers and resources under a common direction and for a common use, a doctrine which, as you know, is anathema to him. I agree that these words are somewhat unfortunate and might lead to misunderstanding, but any danger from them is, I think, sensibly diminished by joining the Commonwealth with the Americas. If there is no greater centralization suggested for the Commonwealth than for the Americas in this context, then I suppose there is little to worry about.'[70]

St Laurent approved Pearson's draft reply. It remained to secure Mackenzie King's approval. Pearson had accepted an invitation to dine with Escott Reid on the evening of his interview with the Prime Minister. 'Mr Pearson was late in arriving,' his host recalls. 'He looked drawn and tired.

He whispered to me: "I got the reply through. But it was the worst struggle I've ever had".'[71] Reid described Pearson's feat of persuasion as 'his most important accomplishment as Under- Secretary.'[72] That takes in a lot, but it may be true.

The Prime Minister's reply to Attlee's message had asked him to clarify the sentence to which Mackenzie King had taken such strong exception. On 3 February the mollifying reponse arrived: 'Mr Attlee asks me to reassure you on the point of interpretation and to confirm that these words were not intended to imply any military commitment for the countries of the Commonwealth or the Americas.' The episode may well have been in Clement Attlee's mind when writing of Mackenzie King in his memoirs: '[H]e had for the greater part of his career been apprehensive of being dominated by the government of the United Kingdom and had been almost morbidly fearful lest Canada should be drawn into European entanglements without her consent.'*

On 22 January 1948, fortified by positive responses from both Canada and the United States to the messages of 13 and 14 January, Ernest Bevin made his project public in a speech in the British Parliament. Gladwyn Jebb (who had a hand in drafting it) calls it in retrospect 'A very clever speech,' for it did not at this stage actually propose a multilateral treaty, still less a multilateral defence pact. '[Bevin] only hinted, very inferentially, at the military aspect by his reference to the Treaty of Dunkirk. Nor did he positively suggest any wider grouping which might at that stage have disturbed the Senate of the United States.'[73] Bevin could have been a bit more daring, for the US Administration, at least, was disappointed at the proposal's tepidity. 'In the State Department,' Hume Wrong reported, 'they certainly regard the project of a closer union with warm fervour. They are inclined to think, however, that a better start would have been made if Mr Bevin had proposed something broader and more imaginative as the first step than the conclusion with the Benelux coun-

---

* C.R. Attlee, *As It Happened* (New York 1954), 250. L.B. Pearson provides a more shaded interpretation of Mackenzie King's attitude towards the United Kingdom at this time. 'In general,' Pearson wrote to Norman Robertson on 29 January 1948,

> I should say that this anxiety about Commonwealth commitments has been over-shadowed by his anxiety over United Nations and United States commitments. In fact, the latter anxiety has become so strong, and with some reason, that he is beginning to counsel close contact with the United Kingdom, notably at [the United Nations] ... to make sure that we are not pushed too far by the United States. This, I have always been sure, was an inevitable development, but it has not proceeded to a point where the old fears do not occasionally emerge, even against the background of the newer and greater ones.

Quoted in *Mike* II, 42.

tries of treaties on the model of the Anglo-French Treaty of Dunkirk. ... The Treaty of Dunkirk is an alliance against the possibility of German revival as a military menace. This barely touches the central problem of Europe today...[74]

Bevin's speech, in Jebb's description, may have 'had a great echo all over Europe,' but it failed to rouse America. It also failed to deter Russia. Barely a month later occurred the *coup de Prague*.

A week after the brutal and unceremonious ouster of President Beneš, the Department of External Affairs prepared a statement on the communist takeover in Czechoslovakia for delivery by St Laurent in the House of Commons. St Laurent showed it to Mackenzie King, saying he thought it was 'excellent.' The Prime Minister thought otherwise.

I confess I was perfectly horrified if not terrified at the thought of anything of the kind read in the House of Commons at this time. It was a long story of what the press had contained of how the Government had changed. To me, it was a real interference with the domestic affairs of Czechoslovakia in an unpardonable way. Would certainly if cabled to Czechoslovakia create very bitter feeling against Canada at once. ... It was almost equivalent to an open declaration against Russia on the part of Canada. I confess that I get increasingly alarmed at the lack of judgment on the part of External Affairs in these matters and am beginning to mistrust St Laurent's judgment in them. I think he has been carried away by the clerical feeling against Communists which has caused him to lose judgment on how these matters when expressed in Parliament in a certain way, may affect our own international relations.[75]

Despite this emphatic disapproval, Mackenzie King does not seem to have remonstrated with his colleague, and did not alter the text of the statement which St Laurent duly delivered in the House of Commons. 'St Laurent's situation as Minister for External Affairs became increasingly difficult as international tension continued to grow,' writes his biographer, 'and the divergence of views between his advisers and the Prime Minister was accentuated. His own position was usually much closer to Pearson's than to Mackenzie King's, but he recognized that the latter had the final word in determining the government's policy, and he hesitated to differ with a man who had so much more political experience. In his public statements, however, St Laurent continued to warn Canadians of the Communist threat, and to urge firmness and unity in resisting it.'[76]

More than mere 'clerical feeling' motivated the Secretary of State for External Affairs in undertaking what would later be called his 'crusade' for the Atlantic Alliance. The *coup de Prague* had been the turning point. 'Whatever the longer range causes for NATO may have been,' L.B. Pearson observed years later, 'the overthrow of the Beneš government in Czechoslovakia was the immediate reason. ... I think I was more frightened than anybody in Washington because, well, my reaction – with the memory of 1914 and 1939 – was "Here we go again, it's the third time we'll be over in Europe fighting and, by God, we've got to do something about it..."'* But what? To Pearson the response seemed obvious. 'Until the Western world has forces in being rather than merely potential forces,' he wrote on 3 May 1948, 'there is little that the Western world can now do to prevent a Soviet occupation of the whole of Western Europe. The immediate danger now, it seems to me, is that the Soviet leaders may decide to occupy Western Europe before the United States and the other Western countries have been able to build up their forces to a sufficient extent to give them some reasonable chance of holding Western Europe. This danger may last for two years or longer, depending on how long it takes the United States and the other Western countries to build up their forces in Western Europe. They may be able to do it in less than two years,' Pearson added, 'if their publics are not fooled by some new Soviet gesture of conciliation.'[77]

A useful corrective to the mood of fear induced by the *coup de'état* in Prague was provided a few weeks later by the High Commissioner at London. Dana Wilgress possessed as much expertise about the Soviet Union acquired at first hand as any other Western diplomat of his generation.[†]

---

* Oral History Project, Pearson interview. Escott Reid, however, did not think that the Czechoslovak crisis in itself would have been sufficient to generate the momentum for an alliance. 'Another difference between the facts and the public story,' Reid wrote in 1951,

> is that in public the pressure for the initiation of the negotiations is said to have arisen because of the Soviet seizure of Czechoslovakia. Actually, while the seizure of Czechoslovakia led to the Brussels Treaty, I am not certain that it would have led to the launching of negotiations for the North Atlantic Treaty if the seizure of Czechoslovakia had not been followed by threats to Norway, and if this Russian pressure in the North had not been accompanied by threats in the Mediterranean.

'Memorandum for Mr Soward,' 20 June 1951, DEA files, 50030-40.

† 'At the Rome meeting [of the North Atlantic Council, 24-8 November 1951],' Brooke Claxton has recalled,

> one of the matters which came up for discussion was trends in Soviet policy, a paper which had been drawn up by the Council Deputies. Dean Acheson, like most of us, did not think much of this paper and suggested that a group of experts should be gathered together to work out this kind of a paper. "While," he said, "the deputies are an estimable group of people, none of them were really qualified, none of them were Russian, or had ever been to Russia." ... I intervened to say that while I held no brief with the paper, I could not let this unwarranted attack on the Council Deputies go unanswered. ... Our Deputy, Dana Wilgress, probably knew as much about Russia as anyone else. He had spent a considerable time there at the end of the First World War, he had served there in various capacities, both during and after the war, he had been our Ambassador there, he understood Russian well and spoke it fluently and ... he had married a Russian...

Claxton memoirs, 1293-4.

Wilgress's calm assessment could hardly have been more at variance with Mackenzie King's panic images of a world soon to be ablaze. 'I have, as you know, clung to the view that a major war is not likely in the near future,' Wilgress wrote to L.B. Pearson on 25 May 1948,

because (1) it would not suit the Russians to start a war unless they knew for sure that they would win, and (2) it is not possible for the democratic countries to secure the necessary popular support to wage a preventive war.

To predict that there will be no war always involves greater risk than to predict that there will be a war. It is possible that my view may be disproved before you and others in the Department have had time to forget about it, whereas those who predict an early war can always continue to say, "Not yet, but soon." However ... I still think a careful appraisal of the situation leads to the conclusion that the Soviet leaders are not likely to take the great risk involved in provoking a major war now or in the course of the next few years...

Recently, when I have seen the Western European countries getting together for the purpose of forming a defensive alliance against Russia, I have thought it might be possible for Stalin to launch a preventive war on his own – that is, to conquer Western Europe before it has time to unite – but, when I have considered all the other factors, I have come to the conclusion that Stalin is not the kind of man to run such a risk. He would know that this would involve him in war with the United States, and would come to the conclusion that the Soviet Union is not yet ready to take on the United States.

The conclusion I derive from all of this is we are likely to see, for some time to come, a continuation of the "cold war," the purpose of which will be to divide and weaken the Western powers. Every possible advantage will be taken of international developments to provide an opportunity for causing embarrassment to the United States and creating differences between the Western powers themselves. Probes will be made here and there to see that further territory can be acquired without running the risk of a major war, but care will also be taken to prevent the "cold war" from turning into a "hot war"...

Just as during the period of appeasement efforts in North America were directed to white-washing the Bolsheviks, now nothing is spared in attempts to blacken them. ... The danger of overstating the case against the Russians is that it is apt to defeat itself. It builds up the atmosphere in which one bold peace offensive by Molotov can throw confusion into the ranks of the Western countries....[78]

On 11 March 1948, there arrived for the Prime Minister of Canada a communication which its recipient described as more 'serious and solemn' than any of the despatches which had reached him before the Second World War.[79]

The message from Prime Minister Attlee of the United Kingdom was delivered by the British High Commissioner at Ottawa to Mackenzie King's residence shortly before noon. (A similar though not identical communication had been sent by Attlee to President Truman.) Sir Alexander Clutterbuck had just returned to his post following a visit to Britain, and was able to convey to Mackenzie King a sense of the mood of anxiety and alarm which was gripping London and other capitals in Western Europe. It was the belief of the British government, Clutterbuck told King, that only the boldest of counter-strokes could restore the morale and self-confidence of the Western democracies then threatened by a Soviet political offensive of unprecedented effrontery.

These views Attlee's message bore out in full. Events were moving, it contended, far more quickly than had been foreseen. Flushed by their successful extinction of Czechoslovak democracy, the Soviet leaders had turned their attention to Norway.

Norwegian Government have consulted United States and ourselves as to the help that they could expect if attacked. As a first step we think that United States and United Kingdom representatives in Oslo should be instructed to infuse some courage into Norwegian Government, pointing out that Turkey and Persia have successfully resisted Soviet demands and that Norway would be ill-advised to put her foot on the slippery slope by sacrificing her right to conclude pacts with whomsoever she chooses and that if she eventually requires outside support she is more likely to get it by showing resolution than by temporizing. We cannot be sure, however, that encouragement of this kind will alone induce Norwegian Government to hold out. On the other hand, we cannot at this moment afford to risk Norwegian defection which would not only involve the collapse of the whole Scandinavian system but would also prejudice our chances of calling a halt to expansion of Soviet influence over Western Europe and would in fact mean the appearance of Russia on the Atlantic.

In these dire circumstances the British Government considered it essential to form a security alliance – 'a regional Atlantic pact of mutual assistance in which all the countries threatened by a Russian move on the Atlantic could participate. These countries might be, besides the United States and the United Kingdom, Canada, Eire, Iceland, Norway, Denmark, France, Portugal and Spain when it again has a democratic regime.'

Such an Atlantic pact should form, in the opinion of the British government, one of three interlocking security systems. In addition, the United Kingdom, France, and the Benelux countries should be loosely linked with the United States, and a Mediterranean security system, of which Italy would be a member and the intended beneficiary, should be created. Because of Soviet pressure on Norway, the proposed Atlantic pact should take priority. 'In this grave situation,' Attlee's message concluded,

I think it right to put our ideas at once before you and the United States Secretary of State. I am convinced that we should study without delay the establishment of such an Atlantic security system so that we inspire necessary confidence to consolidate the West against Soviet infiltration and at the same time inspire Soviet Government with sufficient respect for the West to remove temptation from them and so ensure a long period of peace. Our idea would be that if the Canadian and United States Governments agree, officials of the three Governments should meet in Washington and very secretly explore the proposal for an Atlantic system. I hope that this will commend itself to you.[80]

Mackenzie King sent first for L.B. Pearson, with whom Clutterbuck, on King's instruction, had left copies of Attlee's message. A meeting was arranged for the Prime Minister, Pearson, L.S. St Laurent and Brooke Claxton at King's office in the East Block that afternoon. '[A]ll agreed,' Mackenzie King recorded, 'that collective security was essential to preservation of safety and preservation of Canada. That no time should be lost in seeking to bring this about.'[81] In the words of St Laurent's biographer: 'In the moment of real crisis, Mackenzie King proved still able to rise to the occasion; he cast aside his preoccupation with politics and his isolationism, and agreed to send an affirmative reply to London.'[82] Pearson did a draft, which the Prime Minister revised at Laurier House that evening. 'Gave him the revision over the 'phone about 8 o'clock. The message went off to Attlee tonight.'[83] It read as follows.

Your High Commissioner has shown me the very important message contained in your telegram of March 10th regarding possible Soviet demands on Norway, and proposing, as a constructive measure against this and other such aggressive moves the early conclusion, under Article 52 of the Charter, of a regional Atlantic Pact of mutual assistance. I am deeply impressed with the gravity of these developments. Certainly everything possible should be done, and that speedily, to avoid a possible repetition of the disastrous experiences of pre-war years when peaceful states allowed themselves to become victims of aggression, one by one. Collective measures seem to me to be essential to establish some sense of security and to preserve the peace. Such collective measures will, of course, require the active leadership of the United Kingdom and of the United States. To permit of the earliest possible consideration by the Canadian Government of the proposal for an Atlantic system, I shall arrange to send one of our officials to Washington just as soon as he is required, to join officials of the United Kingdom and the United States Governments in the exploratory talks suggested.[84]

That message embodied a transformation of Canada's foreign policy. But in one respect its sender had not changed. 'I was careful,' Mackenzie King noted in his diary, 'to make no commitments.'[85]

At the end of the day, the Prime Minister reflected on its historic event. 'I am quite positive that we were right in not delaying an hour in getting off our reply to the British Government; also that if Britain and the United States were drawn into the war with Russia, nothing could keep our country out. If we did not join in at once with the United Kingdom and the United States in seeking to arrange a situation that might help to preserve peace, we would certainly be destroyed in no time.' Gloomily he surveyed the world scene: 'At this moment, there is the almost certainty of war in the present conflict between Arabs and the Jews developing into what might well be the beginning of a world war. There is a conflict between Russia and the Greeks. ... The elections in Italy may upset the Government there and put a Commnist Government in power. France would not last a day were the Russian armies ... to cross her territory. Spain is not to be relied on ... Portugal is a weak power. All other countries pretty much look to the United States and Britain for assistance. ... Then there is war being fomented in Manchuria and again in Korea. This is being done by Russia. The whole world,' Mackenzie King concluded, 'may be in flames before very long.'[86]

The Prime Minister's next task was to begin preparing public opinion for the sudden right-about-face in foreign policy to which his government was not yet formally committed but which he had come to believe, however reluctantly, to be well-nigh inescapable.

A radio address to warn fellow citizens of the peril they now faced was not Mackenzie King's style. He could hardly bring himself to divulge to three fellow politicians, in strictest confidence, that the lights of Europe were going out. '[R]ead to them what was in a statement of the background of the situation in Europe – not tell them more than that. I could not read the other messages but I would like them to know they were very grave. I would some day let them see them. Could not do so now.' With that much John Bracken, leader of the Conservative Party, Solon Low, leader of the Social Credit Party, and M.J. Coldwell, leader of the Co-operative Commonwealth Federation (CCF) Party, had to be content. 'I read the statement to Bracken,' Mackenzie King recorded. 'I gave him to understand this was a talk entirely between ourselves.'[87] A newspaper report of a speech by L.S. St Laurent, in which St Laurent had said that Canadians might have to fight for freedom, drew their Prime Minister's displeasure. 'I become increasingly alarmed,' King wrote in his diary on 13 March, 'at the extent to which both he and Claxton are apt to talk of the international problem.'[88]

When the Cabinet met on 15 March, Mackenzie King divulged to his ministers no more than he had told the opposition party leaders. He said nothing of Attlee's proposal for an Atlantic pact. 'Members listened very attentively,' Mackenzie King recorded, 'and looked in some way deeply concerned.'[89] After the Cabinet meeting, King again briefed the opposition leaders, this time in the presence of his Minister of National Defence. 'We might see fire around the world before very long,' he told them sombrely. 'I did not wish to say these things in public.'[90]

On the morning of 17 March, the Prime Minister spoke to the Liberal Party parliamentary caucus. The meeting had been so arranged as to permit the group to listen afterwards to the speech that the President of the United States was to broadcast at noon, giving the Administration's response to the Brussels Pact signed earlier that day. Mackenzie King confided to the Members his fears that Soviet expansion in Europe would lead to general war unless the Western nations united to stop it. The group then went into the adjacent lounge to hear Truman's radio address – 'an exceptionally fine, manly, courageous, direct speech,' Mackenzie King wrote of it, '...much along the lines that were expected.' The speech contained one statement that had not been expected. The United States would be introducing Universal Military Training – what Canadians called conscription, which so many in French Canada had come to fear and loath.*

The possibility that so soon after the crisis of 1944 conscription might again become an issue in Canadian politics filled Mackenzie King with consternation. His diary entry suggests that he panicked beyond reason: 'I am afraid if conscription becomes an issue in Canada, we will find in some parts, large numbers joining the Communists. They will say if we are to risk our lives fighting Communism, we better save our heads by joining with them.' The utter remoteness of that happening notwithstanding, the Prime Minister believed it to be likely, and was so unnerved as to have gone straightaway to his office to pray 'very earnestly for strength and guidance.' Then he met with ministers.

I said nothing until six or seven were present. I then said: You have heard what President Truman has proposed. We are now faced with a very real situation. All the old questions will come up. The last war will be revived. I shall have to make a statement of some kind when I get into the House this afternoon. I want the advice of the Cabinet; one of the first questions likely to be asked is what we intend to do in the matter of conscription. Claxton said the Chiefs of Staff would not favour that step at this time. They would regard it as a hindrance to our collective effort. ... St Laurent pointed out that the real problem was how we could best make our contribution to the maintenance of world peace. We had always been prepared to take our share of duties. I said I assumed that we would stand

---

* 'Conscription may theoretically be the best, the fairest, and the most expeditious way to raise an army; it may equalize the demands and equalize the suffering far better than the hazards of voluntarism. All this may be so, but not in Canada. Here conscription has divided French-speaking Canadians from their compatriots. Here conscription has created chaos, shattering the political system and fostering mistrust and division in the country. And here conscription has had scant military impact, certainly not enough to provide a *post facto* justification for it. Conscription has simply not worked in Canada, and there seems no reason to believe that it ever will.' J.L. Granatstein and J.M. Hitsman, *Broken Promises: A History of Conscription in Canada* (Toronto 1977), 269.

behind the Western Union – but I imagined there would be no difference of view in the Cabinet as to our being prepared to do our part in helping to support the Western Powers from Europe [ie, the Western European powers]. St Laurent said the question of the methods of implementation was something that we would have to give further thought to. He mentioned the joint defence of the Continent was already something that had been worked out. Our generous attitude had always been to do our full part. We would be ready to do that now in ways that seemed best. Someone said something about a league of free people and we either had to be in it or out of it. I said I was sure there could be no doubt on the part of anyone as to our being in it.

Claxton read the words which he had taken down from the President's address to the effect that the United States was prepared to help the Western Nations of Europe with the same determination as they might show themselves. I asked in order to get consensus of opinion of the Cabinet whether we might not take that definite stand ourselves as the basis of our policy. We could say that we assumed our attitude would be the same. St Laurent used the expression the rest was a matter of implementation [sic]. It need not follow that we would take exactly the same steps [as the United States] or at the same time. We would be governed by the conditions as we had an opportunity to review and study them.

Of St Laurent's interventions in this discussion, his biographer observes: 'There was no doubt in the minds of any of the men listening to him that his comment implied the reintroduction of conscription if necessary to resist the current threat.'

Only after this exchange of views had taken place did the Prime Minister see fit to disclose to his colleagues the exchange of messages between himself and Attlee.

I then said we would be faced with a question of being prepared to join a regional security pact of which the United Kingdom, the United States and ourselves would be the principal persons. I ... said that I had urged one of our officials (Pearson) to go to Washington to meet the British and United States representatives purely for exploratory purposes; would have no power for commitment but I assumed that all parliament would feel that we should join in such a security pact for the Atlantic. There was agreement on the part of all. I brought up the question three or four times. Each time saying I wanted to be sure we were all in agreement. Used the expression one time, there is no dissenting voice. [James] Gardiner [Minister of Agriculture] spoke of not wishing to agree to military service, conscription, at once. Saw no need for it at present. I said certainly there would be no commitment of any kind. What we would want to know would be what would be expected; who the parties would be, etc. That when we got this information, Pearson would return and I would then give the Cabinet the particulars. We could reach a decision. I stated I really intended to wait until I got the result of the explorations before saying anything of the matter. Was so exceedingly secret but in view of the President's statement I thought I should let them know immediately what the situation was so that when Pearson (I did not mention his name) went to Washington, he would go with the knowledge that, on the general principle, we were all agreed.[95]

The time had come to prepare a statement for the House of Commons that afternoon. 'As Pearson and Heeney* were comparatively fresh, I suggested they might start and draft something,' Mackenzie King recorded. He did not think too much of their handiwork: 'Made some modifications. The last paragraph of all I thought was drafted exceedingly poorly so I changed it considerably but it still appeared to be rather involved ... much less clear type of statement than I would have liked to have made.'[96] But there was no time for further improvement. The division bells were summoning Members to their seats. When the House met at three o'clock, the Prime Minister was in his place and rose immediately.

Mr Speaker, Members of Parliament will have already learned with much satisfaction that a treaty of mutual guarantee was signed this morning at Brussels by representatives of the governments of the United Kingdom, France, Belgium, the Netherlands and Luxembourg. This pact represents a partial fulfilment of the idea of a Western European Union put forward by the United Kingdom foreign secretary on January 22 last. This pact is far more than an alliance of the old kind. It is a partial realization of the idea of collective security by an arrangement made under the Charter of the United Nations. As such it is a step towards peace, which may well be followed by other similar steps until there is built up an association of all free states which are willing to accept responsibilities of mutual assistance to prevent aggression and preserve peace....

The Canadian Government has been closely following recent developments in the international sphere. The peoples of all free countries may be assured that Canada will play her full part in every movement to give substance to the conception of an effective system of collective security by the development of regional pacts under the Charter of the United Nations.[97]

None of the opposition party leaders took exception to this statement. John Bracken, for the Conservatives, welcomed Canada's participation in an Atlantic regional defence pact: 'This nation, in association with other nations, must be strong – strong economically and collectively – so strong collectively that no other nation will dare attack us.'[98] M.J. Coldwell, for the CCF, called the Brussels Treaty as 'a step in the right direction,' 'a step for the rehabilitation of western Europe economically, and I am one of those who believe that if western Europe be rehabilitated economically we shall have gone a long, long way towards maintaining peace and defeating the onward march of communism, because communism thrives on poverty, misery and want.'[99] Solon Low, for the Social Credit party,

* A.D.P. Heeney, then Secretary to the Cabinet. See *In Defence of Canada* III, 43-4. Heeney subsequently became Under Secretary of State for External Affairs, Permanent Representative on the North Atlantic Council, and was twice Ambassador at Washington. A colleague has paid tribute to his professional qualities: '[W]ell-briefed, articulate, master of a terse and muscular prose, and always in control...' John W. Holmes, 'Foreword,' Arnold Heeney, *The Things that are Caesar's: The Memoirs of a Canadian Public Servant* (Toronto 1972), x.

confined himself to urging the government to drive communists and crypto-communists from all walks of Canadian life. Mackenzie King was well satisfied by these reactions. He reflected that he had, 'without disclosing anything ahead, more or less prepare[d] the House as I had the Cabinet for a Security Pact and, to all intents and purposes, secure[d] their tacit assent to Canada becoming a party thereto.'[100]

Not exactly a clarion call to arms. Nevertheless, the *Winnipeg Free Press* (which had been among the very few pre-war critics of isolationism and appeasement) judged the Prime Minister's statement to be 'an historical declaration of foreign policy' which all Canadians should welcome.[101] Mackenzie King himself believed that he had crossed the Rubicon. 'This was a day that had its place in History,' he wrote of 17 March 1948 in his diary. 'It really is the line of demarcation between the past and efforts to adjust difficulties with the USSR by conciliation and beginning of settlement by force, should the USSR not back down immediately.'[102]

Yet the historic commitment to the first peacetime alliance in Canada's history had not been made with confidence. Mackenzie King had crossed the Rubicon, but all his doubts crossed with him. 'I found myself perspiring from sheer anxiety.'[103]

The following day the Prime Minister assented, with little reflection, to L.B. Pearson's proposal that Canada should play host to the Atlantic Pact's founding conference when the time came for it to be held. As Mackenzie King thought more about the idea, he liked it less and less, and soon countermanded his previous agreement. 'It would lead,' King wrote, 'to ... discussion in Quebec, throughout Canada generally, of such questions as compulsory military service, focussing in addition on immediate prospects of war, uncertainty of affairs, etc. ... It would be a mistake to make Canada a sort of apex to a movement which would be linking together United States and United Kingdom and other nations in a project that is intended to offset the possibility of immediate war with Russia. ... These things fill me with a sense of trepidation and fear.'[104] He was not alone. A few days later, the Embassy at Paris, reporting certain improvements in the political and economic situation in France, went on to comment that 'All these hopeful symptoms are, however, jeopardized by the fear of war which more and more with every week is becoming an obsession with the peoples of Europe.'[105] The Atlantic Pact, like Thomas Hobbes, was born a twin to fear.

BLOCKADE, AIR AID, CRUSADE

'Lexington and Concord, Sumter, the *Maine*, the *Lusitania*, Pearl Harbor. American history is filled with dramatic episodes which define the nature of wars in the popular mind, and afterward become contested issues among historians. The Berlin blockade of 1948 serves this function for the cold war.' So writes an American historian a quarter of a century later, adding: 'From the beginning, the Berlin blockade acquired mythic qualities. Soviet propaganda charged that the West had no desire to reach agreement. ... Americans called Berlin an ultimate showdown for control of the world, a test of freedom versus slavery. If Communism forces us from Berlin – so ran a thousand speeches and editorials – all of Germany will fall, then Europe, then even our own freedom.'[106] That perception was shared by most Canadian policy-makers reacting to the news of 22 June 1948 that Soviet troops were preventing railway traffic from leaving or entering Berlin if destined for or arriving from the three Western zones of occupation. But it was not shared by the most important of them.

The Prime Minister had been following the mounting pressure on Berlin with acute apprehension. Mackenzie King had recorded Bevin's prediction on 24 November 1947 that '[m]atters might even come to the point where in three weeks' time, Russia might seek to keep within her zone, the part of Berlin which she now controls. This would mean that the British would be cut off from getting into the part of Berlin which they control. This is also true of the Americans.'[107] He had added: 'I am not sure that I have this wholly correct;' and indeed he had not. But he had been forewarned of grave trouble from Berlin. When Bevin asked 'point blank the question as to whether, if the Russians sought to prevent free access between Britain and the British zone in Berlin, Britain could afford to allow them to do so,' King noted: 'I made no reply to this...'[108] The following day Bevin told him that the British government might 'have to order the shooting.'[109] On 15 December, Mackenzie King thus assessed the situation: 'The issue will reach the critical point when ... Russia may seek to prevent them going through the Russian zone. Should she do this, and threaten to enforce her position by threat of arms, war will be inevitable.'[110] On 13 April 1948, the Prime Minister referred to Berlin in a talk to the Liberal Party parliamentary caucus. He reminded his followers that he had warned them on his return from his visit to Britain late in 1947 that

I had told the Cabinet but had not told the public, that I had gathered that when the spring of this year came ... the Russians would begin to try to make it impossible for the Americans and the British to get into their own zones of Berlin. This might occasion some active conflict and ... someone might be killed and in no time a conflagration would start in Berlin itself which would lead to the Russians immediately taking a step that would enable them to sweep across Europe through France and the other countries to the sea. Take possession of the whole of Europe.

I said I did not think members of Caucus took much stock of what I had said at the time. Seemed to think it was fanciful...[111]

During the days following the news of 22 June 1948, the Prime Minister wrote in his diary of his 'deep concern,' his 'great concern,' at what might happen next. 'One can only pray,' he recorded on 25 June, 'that so-called "cold" war may continue cold but ultimately cease and let nothing too precipitate take place as a result of constant goading and irritation by Russians in Berlin.'[112] When word arrived next day from the High Commissioner at London that the British government expected a clash with the Russians over Berlin but not war, King expressed his disagreement in his diary. 'My own feeling is, if men are killed, American and British soldiers, the resentment will be so strong that nothing will avert a situation that might soon become one of affecting the whole of Europe, if not also the whole of the world. Of those around me,' the Prime Minister added petulantly, 'no one seems to give this appalling possibility so much as a thought. They just reason that anything so terrible cannot be.'[113]

These fearful reflections forecast, and to a large degree account for, Canada's policy when the crisis came.

On 28 June 1948, the British Foreign Secretary called the High Commissioners of the Commonwealth to his office. Ernest Bevin told them that his government, with those of France and the United States, were agreed in their determination to resist Soviet pressure to force them out of Berlin. Plans were being made to fly food into the Western sectors, and the occupying powers were ready to respond to the Soviet challenge by feeding two and one-half million people by means of airlift until the blockade was lifted. For this task an enormous number of transport aircraft would be needed. The three Western occupying powers would contribute to the limit of their ability, but they needed and would welcome help. 'At this point' – so Norman Robertson's account of the meeting relates – 'whether by premeditation or not I do not know – he turned to me and said that the United Kingdom and United States would be very grateful for any assistance other countries could give in making additional transport aircraft available for this operation.' Robertson added his recommendation that 'the Foreign Secretary's appeal for assistance ... should be given prompt and serious consideration...'[114]

L.B. Pearson wanted to do more than consider Bevin's appeal for help, he wanted to respond to it with help. 'It seems to me,' Pearson wrote at once to L.S. St Laurent after receiving Robertson's cable,

that the trial of strength which is now going on in Berlin is of crucial importance. I cannot believe that the Russians want to push things to the point of war but I believe they may be prepared to do everything short of war to get the Western allies out of Berlin. Rightly or wrongly the situation has now got to the point where the withdrawal of the Western powers from Berlin, leaving the two million Germans in the lurch, would be a tremendous blow to the prestige of the Western powers, not only in Western Europe but elsewhere.

On the other hand, a successful demonstration of the ability of the Western powers to act together on this matter and to force the Russians to change their tactics might well have a very considerable effect in strengthening the determination of the Western Europeans to resist Soviet pressure...[115]

When the House of Commons met on 30 June, the Prime Minister was immediately asked if the government intended to join with the three Western occupying powers in helping to run and break the blockade. 'I felt how careful I should be in reply,' Mackenzie King recorded, 'so as to avoid a stampede in the country or anything being said that the Russians might take as some evidence of the over-concern on the part of the three other nations occupying Berlin, so I simply said I had no answer to the question at the moment but would wish to confer with my colleagues about it...'[116]

Whatever chance – and it was slight enough – that the Prime Minister might respond affirmatively to the British request for air transport from Canada was reduced to none at all by the leak of Bevin's meeting with the High Commissioners to the London newspapers, and by the manner in which that leak was reported in one of them. The noon edition of the *Evening Standard* for 30 June ran a banner headline: 'EMPIRE ASKED TO BREAK BERLIN SIEGE.' That headline, Pearson sorrowfully cabled Norman Robertson at once, 'has caused great irritation here, for reasons which you will appreciate.'[117]

Indeed it had. Mackenzie King at once lost sight of both the issue and the stakes. It had become for him as if Britain, rather than the Soviet Union, had done the major wrong. The Prime Minister dwelled at length on this aspect of the matter when he met with his Cabinet colleagues later in the day. 'In speaking to the Cabinet, I stressed mostly the feeling of indignation I had that on a matter as grave as this, it should be projected into the press of the world by some persons in Britain who, as I said, I believed would prefer Empire and war, to no war and separate nations of the Commonwealth. ... I said the whole position reminded me of the Chanak incident,' details of which he proceeded to relate.*

The Prime Minister introduced the policy question – whether or not to provide the air transport for which Britain had asked – by outlining 'in a sketchy way what the telegrams [from Norman Robertson] stated, draw-

---

* Quoted in *Record* IV, 191. On the Chanak incident, see James Eayrs, *In Defence of Canada*, I, *From the Great War to the Great Depression* (Toronto 1964), 20-5.

ing attention to the fact that Bevin ... had used the expression that the situation was such that it might mean war. That the British, Americans and French had decided to face that possibility and would not leave Berlin, even if attacked. I described the city [as] in a state of siege by the Russians. Also referred to the presence of troops and tanks in the streets of Berlin, and what might be expected at any moment, if some precipitate action were taken. I said I could not understand the reference Bevin had earlier made, that there might be a clash in Berlin but not war. My own view was that if a clash came, war would be next to inevitable.' Mackenzie King then asked L.S. St Laurent to read the telegrams to the Cabinet, and then, changing his mind, proceeded to read them himself. 'I did this,' King explained in his diary, 'because I have noticed right along that St Laurent seeks to avoid reading out communications and indeed has frequently said to me he did not think that we could get along, telling the Cabinet as a whole this and that. ... I had too in mind the memo which was attached to one of the despatches by Pearson and which advised the Minister that he should take the position that we should send transport and food at once. This, of course, is right along the lines that External Affairs has been taking for some time past, to get into every international situation and as much in the front of it as possible, not realizing what the appalling consequences are.'[118]

After the Prime Minister finished reading the despatches, there was, he recorded, 'a dead silence in the room. Ministers looked anxious. St Laurent, I could see, was deeply concerned.' There being no spoken response, Mackenzie King launched into his digression about Chanak. It reinforced his feeling, he said, that 'we should proceed with great caution.' He then turned to his Minister of National Defence to ask whether a formal request had been received from the British government to supply air transport and whether the Royal Canadian Air Force was in a position to supply it. 'I had expected Claxton, in the light of the advertising he is giving Canada's armed services,'* King recounted in his diary,

[to] immediately say something to the effect that they were ready to supply a certain number of planes with crew, etc., and that we should send word immediately as to what we were prepared to do. Instead of that, to my amazement, he took the very opposite view. He said he thought we should keep out of the situation altogether if we possibly could. He said if we were to send planes over and one of our planes were shot down, it might lead to war or we might be credited

---

*   In the most literal sense: 'I was in effect the head of the recruiting effort,' Claxton wrote of his campaign. 'I felt it necessary to examine and pass on every single advertisement ... and frequently made substantial changes or even redrafted an entire advertisement....' See *In Defence of Canada*, III, 120-2.

with having been responsible for shooting down some other planes. He thought the whole business was much too dangerous. Besides we had not been drawn into any of the councils respecting matters concerned with Berlin and had been left out. He did not think we should be drawn in if it could possibly be avoided. Immediately I heard a note of acquiescence from different parts of the room...

From one corner came a note of something less than acquiescence. L.S. St Laurent was caught between the advice of L.B. Pearson – which was to offer air transport – and the opinion of his Cabinet colleagues which was to stay out of the operation altogether. Mackenzie King's record of St Laurent's intervention suggests that the Secretary of State for External Affairs wanted to follow his Under Secretary's advice.

When speaking of the supply of planes at the request of Britain, I was rather surprised to hear St Laurent say we might have to consider the request. The United States might wish us to supply them and we have to consider that. There again I detected a note which is characteristic of Pearson with his close association with the United States. ... I think the Cabinet saw for the first time that I had been wise in the fight that I had been making right along against getting too quickly and easily and unnecessarily drawn into situations in all parts of the world which we should be extremely careful about assuming. They saw in a moment when faced with decision as to war just how grave that decision was.

...I said I felt it was quite certain that if war broke out, between the three great powers and Russia, Canada would wish to come in instantly. The Cabinet agreed with that. They felt that there could be no two views on that score. They were, however, pretty chary about how far they were prepared to go at this time.[119]

The Prime Minister then asked Brooke Claxton and A.D.P. Heeney to draft the government's reply to Norman Robertson's telegram forwarding the British appeal for transport aircraft and his recommendation that it should be considered (by implication, favourably). 'Claxton had suggested that we should telegraph him to see Bevin at once and tell him that it would be a great embarrassment to us if any request were made for transport planes. That he hoped it would not be put forward. This coming from Claxton,' Mackenzie King commented, 'surprised me beyond words. He has been boasting of what we were ready to do.'[120]

After the Cabinet meeting, the Prime Minister told L.B. Pearson of its decision. 'For the first time,' Mackenzie King noted, 'I have seen Pearson look really frightened. He looked almost terrified. Quite evidently he had at last come to see what the decision was. Quite all right to be in on all these things; when it comes to actually have one's country involved in war, there were limits to what we might be able to do, and [to] the commitments that it was wise to make. I think if anything he was relieved at the Government's attitude which really was quite the opposite of what his memo to St Laurent had proposed earlier in the day as to the policy of External Affairs.'[121] It is more than likely that Pearson's reaction, construed by King as fright, was really acute concern at the government's reaction. Certainly there is no hint of relief in the memorandum Pearson prepared for St Laurent that day.

Supplementing my previous memorandum on Canada's participation in the efforts to supply Berlin with foodstuffs by air, the following points are, I think, important:

1 Mr Bevin has stated to our High Commissioner that the United Kingdom Government did not believe that the Berlin situation would lead to war. He thinks that the Russians will try everything short of war, but that, if the Western powers hold firm, the Russians will back down, and that this will have a tremendous effect on the world because it will be the first time since the war that any country has really stood up successfully to the Russians. Mr Bevin added that, if we can get through this present difficulty successfully, there is a real possibility of ending the age-old feud between France and Germany, with all that this would mean for Western European unity.

2 This Berlin situation is one in which the United Kingdom, the United States and France are pursuing a common policy.

3 If we accept the request to participate, we may be making our contribution to a successful stand against the Russians and, therefore, eventually to a solution of present international difficulties.

4 If we refuse to participate, it would mean that, even in a matter of such importance when the three great Western Powers are acting together, we stand aloof.

5 If we participate by sending aircraft, it might of course develop that an incident would take place which would concern a Canadian aircraft and might become the occasion of war. However, it would only be the occasion and not the cause, and I doubt whether we would be justified in refusing to participate by this risk alone.

6 It may be argued that this was a battle of power politics rising out of the policies of the Western powers towards Western Germany for which we are not responsible and, therefore, they have no right to implicate us in the results. Against this, however, is the fact that we have been kept informed of developments in regard to the formation of the West German state, the issue of the new German currency, etc., and that if we had any doubts as to the wisdom of these measures we could, and should, have expressed them.

7 It is of course true that whether we take action or not in regard to the United Kingdom suggestion we will be involved in any trouble which might result from the present situation in Berlin. It is inconceivable that a war resulting from these difficulties which finds the USSR on one side and the three great Western democracies on the other would not involve Canada. This being the case, it might be argued that we should do what we can to stop the Russians, short of war. The best way of doing this is to show them that they cannot starve Berlin and in this way drive the Western allies out of Berlin. If they are convinced of this, then I think Mr Bevin's optimism will be justified, and an arrangement will be made with the

Russians, possibly along the lines of acceptance of the new Russian currency in the whole of Berlin in return for abandonment by the Russians of the blockade [122]

These are not the reflections of a 'frightened' and 'terrified' man.

If any member of the Cabinet may be singled out as responsible for the Government's decision, it is the Minister of National Defence. Brooke Claxton's intervention in its discussion was crucial, setting the tone for other ministerial responses. On Claxton's Department would have fallen the responsibility for mounting Canada's share of the airlift operation, and he was in a position to veto it on logistical, if not on other, grounds. But he had his other grounds. He set these out in a memorandum to the Secretary of State for External Affairs, with whom he apparently sensed disagreement. 'In connection with the discussion at Cabinet today regarding the enquiry made through the High Commissioner at London as to whether we would assist in meeting the emergency in Berlin,' he wrote to L.S. St Laurent on 30 June,

I thought I would set down here the reasons for the view I took so as to make sure there is no misunderstanding about them.

It seems to me that the course I suggested can be supported on five main grounds.

In the first place, the fact that [if] Canadian military aircraft were used to assist in carrying out the Occupation of Germany[, that] would appear to commit us to support the Occupation with all its consequences, even war, and this although we had no say whatever in determining the policy which set in [sic] this course of events. This might be put more extremely if it should turn out that some action in connection with one of our planes had precipitated hostilities.

The second point is that bringing in Canadian assistance may appear to be provocative. We have no status as one of the occupying powers. Again, the Russians would make a good deal of this should it happen that a Canadian plane was made the actual occasion for an incident which led to war.

The third point is that we have in fact no status in the matter except as the subsidiary or paid help of the United Kingdom or of the United States.

The fourth point relates to the manner in which the enquiry was made by the United Kingdom. It seems to me that no friendly power, certainly not a power having the special relations which Britain has with Canada, should put us in the position where we might feel that we had to take a course of action just because of the fact that an enquiry had been made. In such circumstances the right course for the country which is wishing to make the enquiry would be to ask very privately and very discreetly if we would have any objection to an enquiry being made. Otherwise we might be put in the position where we would feel it necessary to adopt a course because publication of our refusal to do so would assist another nation, in this case the Soviet Union, or prove a source of embarrassment to us.

A fifth point is that it would appear that here our assistance would be of a token character, invited primarily for the purpose of giving the impression of Imperial solidarity. We have not got the same interest in this phase of the matter as have France, Belgium or the Netherlands, both because of their situation and because of their membership in the Western Union as well as because of the fact that they are, I understand, powers which in fact have occupying forces.

Unlike Pearson, who confined his arguments entirely to those in support of offering aircraft, Claxton dealt with the case against his own. 'In favour of our helping in every way possible,' he wrote, 'is the fact that this is a vitally important test of strength which might determine the course of events for months and years ahead. If the Russians succeed it will be a major disaster for us, whereas if they do not succeed it will be a setback of at least some consequence for them. Eventually if there is war, we would take part and go all out to help in bringing victory to our side. It might be argued,' Claxton conceded, 'that we should go all out now, despite the objections I have made, in order to do everything in our power to set back the Russians over this issue.'[123] From this last point it might be inferred that the Minister of National Defence was not so implacably opposed to Canada's participation in the airlift as his Prime Minister had thought him to be. Or perhaps in this communication Claxton was not so much revealing his true motives as attempting to appease St Laurent and bring their differing views together. 'Many of the points made by Mr Claxton are sound,' Escott Reid observed to Pearson after examining them a fortnight later, 'but sound only ... because of the way in which the matter was brought to our attention. They would, in large part, not be relevant if the United Kingdom, the United States and France, as the three Western occupying powers, had made a request of a number of democratic countries including Canada.'[124]

The Cabinet's decision on 30 June required communication to the House of Commons. Its announcement there was complicated – and delayed – by the appearance in Canadian newspapers of stories to the effect that the British government had requested Canada to offer air transport for supplying Berlin with food. This was not Mackenzie King's understanding of the matter. 'My statement [drafted for delivery in the House of Commons] had just indicated that while there had been conversations, there had been no request.' Further drafting ensued and, before the House of Commons adjourned at 6 PM, the Prime Minister delivered the following statement in reply to the question which had been directed to him at the outset of the day's proceedings.

An inquiry has been received through our High Commissioner in London as to what stocks of concentrated dehydrated foodstuffs might be available in Canada to assist in supplying food to Berlin in the present circumstances. A reply has been sent to the effect that there are considerable stocks of such food which would be available for that purpose.

I understand that on Monday last [28 June] Mr Bevin, in informal conversation with the High Commissioners in London, touched upon the question of the adequacy of present air transport facilities for supplying the civilian population in Berlin. No request has, however, been received from the United Kingdom government either for food stocks or air transport.[125]

The statement, Mackenzie King wrote, 'helped I think to quiet matters'[126] – but by some sacrifice of candour. Bevin had not so much 'touched upon' the provision of air transport as he had put the touch on Canada to provide it. Pearson's memorandum of 29 June referred specifically to 'the United Kingdom request for assistance in providing aircraft.' Both Pearson and Norman Robertson had construed Bevin's overture not only as a request but as a request to which the Canadian government ought to return a prompt and affirmative reply. The same verdict applied to the Government Leader's statement in the Senate on 15 June 1938 about the United Kingdom's request for air training may be applied to the Prime Minister's statement in the House of Commons on 30 June 1948 about the United Kingdom's request for air transport: 'On any reasonable reading of the evidence ... a plain mis-statement of what was known to be fact.'[127]

The High Commissioner at London was informed of the Cabinet's reaction by L.B. Pearson who, at the Prime Minister's suggestion, did so by trans-Atlantic telephone rather than by cable. The next day, Pearson followed up by a telegram to Norman Robertson. 'I hope that if any request is to be made in the future for air transport assistance from Canada or other countries for Berlin, it may be possible to let us know in advance. ... I rather feel myself,' Pearson added, 'that the Berlin situation will have resolved itself one way or the other before any assistance of the kind requested could come from overseas countries and that therefore we will not hear of the matter again.'[128] That was wishful thinking.

The government of Australia (whose High Commission at London was thought by the Canadian authorities to have been responsible for having leaked Bevin's appeal on 28 June)* announced that it would send ten Dakota air transport planes, with Royal Australian Air Force crews, to

---

* 'Original leak ... probably came from Australia House ... The Commonwealth Relations Office, who are most genuinely upset and exasperated by the handling of the whole business from beginning to end, will be cabling their regrets....' N.A. Robertson to L.B. Pearson, 1 July 1948 (telegram), DEA files, 11840-40.

participate in the Berlin airlift. 'The Australian offer,' L.B. Pearson predicted, 'will undoubtedly provoke interest and possibly controversy in this country.'[129] That prediction proved correct.

Brooke Claxton had been attempting to defend in public the government's decision not to participate in the airlift, using in his speeches some of the arguments put forward in his explanation to L.S. St Laurent of 30 June. L.B. Pearson was not well disposed to these efforts. 'It is of course true that we have had no part in the German occupation,' Pearson wrote to St Laurent about a press report of one of Claxton's speeches, 'but to state that merely invites the reply that we refused to take part. There is an answer to that reply, but the argument can become pretty unprofitable.'[130] Nor did Pearson think much of Claxton's point 'that we have no desire to take part in a situation that might easily explode into war. That really doesn't seem to me any argument either against or in favour of assisting. Explosion into war would have nothing to do with our assistance. Furthermore, we would inevitably be involved in the consequences of any such explosion, so I think it is conveying the wrong impression to suggest that because we remain aloof from the situation, we may be able to remain aloof from the possible explosion arising out of it.'[131]

Canada's policy, already under attack by opposition and newspaper critics, became still more difficult to defend when it became known in mid-August that while Australia's offer of aircraft had been turned down on the ground that the Dakotas were not needed, its offer of aircrew had been eagerly accepted. Ottawa's predicament was further intensified by the decision of the government of South Africa on 1 September to offer no fewer than fifty transport aircraft, complete with aircrew. The South African offer was, if anything, more embarrassing to the Canadian government than the offer by Australia. 'The fact that a South African Government which is considered to be so unfriendly to the British connection has made this gesture,' Pearson commented, 'naturally points up the problem so far as Canada is concerned.'[132]

The issue of possible Canadian participation was discussed by the Cabinet on 9 September and again on 25 September. At the latter meeting, the Minister of National Defence told ministers that the Royal Canadian Air Force was ready and able to take part: a squadron of ten Dakotas with a complement of ninety aircrew and 219 ground crew could be made available immediately.[133] But the Cabinet once more rejected participation in the airlift. Meanwhile the head of the Canadian Military Mission at Berlin had sent a gloomy report from the scene of the action: '[A]s I see it, the outlook is bleak and it seems to me quite likely that sooner or later in Berlin we shall find ourselves left without much more than a flagpole.'[134]

In mid-October, Norman Robertson, recently returned to Ottawa from the High Commissionership at London, turned his attention to an examination of the difficulties, diplomatic and technical, that stood in the way of a Canadian contribution. (The main obstacle, of course, was political.) 'The major diplomatic difficulty,' Robertson considered, 'is a fear which I find held by responsible people that the Soviet Union might challenge, perhaps by indirect interception, participation in the airlift by planes flying the flag of a country which is not one of the occupying Powers with a legal claim under the terms of the Articles of Surrender and subsequent Inter-Allied Agreements to participate in the occupation of Germany and the Government of Berlin.' That factor, Robertson thought, could have led the United States and the United Kingdom to discourage an offer by The Netherlands to contribute some of its army transport aircraft, and might have been behind the British suggestion to Australia to furnish aircrew but not aircraft. Robertson also examined the option of Canada's relieving Royal Air Force units from other transport and patrol duties, so enabling the RAF to step up its run to Berlin. This proved unpromising as well, partly because the RAF had practically abandoned its other duties to give its all to the airlift, partly because (as Hume Wrong pointed out from Washington) 'the assumption of relay responsibilities on the North Atlantic seems to be open to the strong political objection in Canada that the Government is dodging the issue and adopting an ineffective, indirect and safe modicum of aid.'[135] Robertson came to the conclusion that 'it is not presently practicable to arrange the sort of direct and distinct Canadian contribution to the airlift which on general grounds of policy might have seemed appropriate...'[136]

That seemed to leave the provision of Canadian aircrew and ground-crew as the only practicable form of contributing. The British Secretary of State for Air had taken advantage of a lull in the proceedings at the Commonwealth Prime Ministers' meeting at London to tell Norman Robertson that 'it would be a great help if it were feasible for Canada to provide, say, 10 or 12 four-engine bomber crews.'[137] This proposal was found objectionable on the ground that, as Hume Wrong put it, 'in view of the fact that Australia, New Zealand, and South Africa have already provided air crew, it would ... be hard for the Government to come along at this stage with an offer of air crew which would be represented as belated...'[138] A more formidable objection was stated by L.S. St Laurent. 'He feels that the difficulty about ... the provision of air and ground crew to assist the RAF,' Escott Reid reported to L.B. Pearson, '[is that it] could be interpreted in certain quarters in Canada to mean that Canada is behaving very much as a colony in that the Canadian Government would, in effect, be recruiting forces in Canada for the United Kingdom.'[139] Where there is no will, there is no way.

On 15 November 1948, Mackenzie King resigned as Prime Minister to be replaced by L.S. St Laurent. L.B. Pearson had entered the Cabinet as Secretary of State for External Affairs on 10 September (St Laurent having become Minister of Justice during the brief interim). Pearson's first trip abroad as foreign minister had taken him to Berlin, and that experience reinforced his conviction, held since the onset of the crisis, that Canada should play a direct part in what he described as 'a magnificently impressive operation.' He put the case for Canada's participation to Escott Reid.

I think that we should begin now to reconsider our position ... All concerned at Berlin and Wiesbaden felt that irrespective of the diplomatic difficulties in regard to the participation of RCAF planes (which the Australians, though not the British, were inclined to minimize), there would be no real advantage in an offer of Canadian transport aircraft, partly because two-engined planes are not required as they are too small and partly because our North Stars are not entirely suitable because of the difficulty in maintenance and repair of the Merlin engine. However, great stress was laid by the United States and United Kingdom officers on the immense practical help which could be given by participation of Canadian air crews. The resources of personnel, both British and American, are now being strained to the limit and Canadian help of this kind would be very greatly welcomed. I myself think that we should give serious consideration to an offer of such help...[140]

But the new Prime Minister was no more taken with the idea of helping out with aircrew than the old had been with helping out with aircraft. L.S. St Laurent continued to balk at providing Canadian armed forces personnel to serve in British units – not for reasons of state but for reasons of status.

Meanwhile Canada (on her second try) had been elected to the UN Security Council. In that election a way out of the impasse was detected. As a member of the Security Council, Canada could become involved in negotiating a settlement to put an end to the blockade. If she was at the same time running the blockade, her position as peacemaker might be impaired. So Escott Reid, in a brief of considerable ingenuity, maintained. 'It could be argued that the greatest contribution Canada could make to the dispute, as a member of the Security Council,' Reid wrote on 20 December 1948,

would be to assist in reaching an agreement which would remove the blockade and eliminate the necessity of the aircraft. If Canada's participation in the airlift would lessen Canada's value in the Security Council's efforts to resolve the dispute, then participation in the airlift might be judged to be the less useful of the two functions. This line of reasoning remains valid for as long as any hope remains that the Security Council may bring about a solution before Canada could participate in the airlift...[141]

This argument at least and at last provided the government with an answer to critics persisting in asking what Canada was planning to do to help the Western powers supply Berlin. 'The question of the Berlin airlift is now before the United Nations for consideration,' L.B. Pearson replied to such a question in the House of Commons on 25 February 1949. 'Efforts are being made by the Security Council to arrive at a solution of the problem by way of raising the blockade of Berlin. This would make the airlift unnecessary. ... Pending consideration of this matter by the Council, I would prefer to postpone answering the question...'[142]

Shortly thereafter, the American and Soviet representatives on the Security Council met privately in the delegates' lounge: out of this chance encounter between Philip Jessup and Yakov Malik developed the series of discussions eventually resulting in the lifting of the blockade of Berlin on 11 May 1949. Throughout its duration, not a bag of flour or a box of powdered milk or eggs had arrived in Berlin under Canadian power. (Australia, by contrast, flew 7000 tons of supplies, 7000 passengers, and her airmen logged 6000 hours in flight.[143]) Canada had neither helped to run the blockade nor helped to end it. 'The better part of valour is discretion': never more than during the Berlin blockade could Falstaff more appropriately be cited as the patron saint of Canadian diplomacy.

The period of the Berlin blockade coincides with St. Laurent's 'crusade' on behalf of Canada's becoming a founding member of the North Atlantic alliance. Is his zeal in that mission to be construed as atonement for his government's failure to come to the relief of the beleaguered Berliners? While there is no evidence, it seems reasonable to speculate that it was.

The score or so of speeches delivered in and out of Parliament by St Laurent, L.B. Pearson, Brooke Claxton, and senior government officials throughout 1948 on behalf of coalition and Canada's inclusion was more than routine stumping. The *Ottawa Journal* called it a 'crusade,' a reference that St Laurent was quick to pick up. 'That title of "crusade",' the Secretary of State for External Affairs declared in the House of Commons on 19 June 1948, 'perhaps justly describes the attitude we have adopted.'[144] The crusader's mission is seldom easy, and St Laurent's was no exception. 'It meant for Canada a complete break with the past,' Escott Reid was to comment later. 'Up to then we had resolutely rejected any proposal from any source that we enter into any kind of military treaty, even with Great Britain. Opposition to such proposals was nation-wide but it was especially strong in French Canada. It was, therefore, especially difficult for a French Canadian to lead a crusade for a North Atlantic treaty. Yet Mr St Laurent did.'*

There were three potential sources of opposition: among intellectuals; on the political left; and within French-speaking Canada.

Among intellectuals – their number in the Canada of that era was not great, nor was yet their influence – Donald Creighton, Harold Innis, and Frank Underhill were notable opponents of the government's foreign policy.

Harold Adams Innis, economic historian, philosopher of communications, chairman of the Department of Political Economy at the University of Toronto, had returned from a lecture tour during the summer of 1948 deeply suspicious of the United States for exacerbating, as he believed its government had done, the tensions of the Cold War. 'A visitor from North America to Great Britain and the continent,' Innis wrote of his experience, 'can scarcely fail to sense a feeling of hostility. Much to his surprise he is regarded as coming from an area behind a gold curtain, and to find that he is in a sort of no man's land between iron and gold curtains ... It is clear that European countries feel more directly exposed to American influence and that the threat of "the cumulative advantage of size and technological progress" of the United States is in the impact of uniformity and standardization and its disastrous implications to the artistic culture of Europe and to western civilization.' Holding such a view, Innis could not consistently regard the crusade for an alliance which embraced Western Europe and Canada and was led by the United States as a crusade on behalf of western civilization. Nor did he. 'Whatever hope of continued autonomy Canada may have in the future,' Innis wrote, 'must depend on her success in withstanding American influence and assisting in the development of a third bloc designed to withstand the pressure of the United States and Russia, but there is little evidence that Canada is capable of these herculean efforts and much that she will continue to be justly regarded as an instrument of the United States.'[145] These views, if they reached no further than the audience of undergraduates at the University of Toronto who read the *Commerce Journal*, had a pro-

---

* Escott Reid, 'Memories of Louis St Laurent, 1946-9,' in Norman Penlington (ed.), *On Canada: Essays in Honour of Frank H. Underhill* (Toronto 1971), 80. It would, however, be possible to argue that St Laurent, as a Québecois himself, stood a better chance of converting French Canada than any Anglophone.

found influence upon it,* and put Innis on a collision course with the would-be architects of coalition. 'Pearson seems to be as active as possible,' Innis wrote to a colleague at that time, 'in selling us down the river to the United States.'[146]

Another gadfly to the body of orthodoxy was the historian Frank Underhill. Underhill's reaction to the *coup* in Czechoslovakia was wholly at variance with that of L.S. St Laurent. Whereas St Laurent spoke of 'a frightening case history of Communist totalitarianism in action,' Underhill belittled the strategic significance of what had taken place. 'Let us console ourselves in our present acute state of jitters by reflecting that what has happened is only that Stalin has demonstrated to us that Czechoslovakia is in the Soviet sphere of influence. ... Apart from this, the most significant feature of the events in Czechoslovakia is the place which they occupy in the time-table of the moves and counter-moves that have marked the ever-intensifying crisis of the past year. ... The Czech coup has galvanized the western European governments into energetic action toward military and economic union. But it is clear that military alliances among them, spreading out from the nuclear [in the non-atomic sense] five-power alliance of Britain, France and the Benelux countries, are an ineffective instrument to meet the particular technique of communist aggression with which they are threatened this summer. It is not an invasion by Russian armies that they have to face, but the assault of revolution or civil war manipulated by the communist state-within-the-state.'[147]

To rebut and discredit such critics – it would have been expecting too much to try to convert them – L.B. Pearson and Escott Reid attended the annual study conference of the Canadian Institute of International Affairs† held that year at Vancouver during June, at which they were expected to be in full hue and cry. And so they were. Harold Innis and Donald Creighton rounded on Reid – so the latter recalled years later in an interview – for involving Canada in a movement 'in which we were selling our independence to the United States.'[148] Underhill challenged Pearson to a debate, declaring that Canadians were being 'sold another bill of goods.' He repeated the argument of his *Forum* article: 'The aggression of the Soviet Union is non-military. ... We are facing a religious aggression. ... We need non-military defence.'[149] The officials did their best to counter such views, with only qualified success. Pearson wrote

* As the author, who was among Innis's students at the time, can testify: Innis had already become a cult figure, and we hung on every (often inaudible) word.
† See *In Defence of Canada*, III, 170-1; and Alex I. Inglis, 'The Institute and the Department,' *International Journal*, XXXIII, 1, Winter 1977-8, 88-103.

afterwards that 'the presence of foreign representatives tended to restrain Canadian officials from speaking as frankly as they could.' Marcel
Cadieux, another foreign service officer in attendance, complained of
'the academic tone of the meetings' which, to his regret, had been top-
heavy with theorists to the exclusion of practical men of affairs.[150] Minds
engaged but did not meet. Not for the last time was it shown that the
tension between policy-maker and intellectual can be exploited but seldom dissipated.

Another source of opposition was the political left. Along the farther
shores of leftism, crusading was unnecessary. The Labor Progressive
Party was without representation in Parliament and unlikely to acquire it;
its membership was small and scattered. Crusading would also be futile,
for the party line had been set. In its dogma, St Laurent's crusade was
made out to be 'a propaganda campaign which is designed to make you
believe that war against Russia must be prepared for because Russia is
preparing to attack us. Our great ally, whose losses in the war in lives and
property outweighed the rest of all the Allies combined, is all of a sudden ... declared to be our enemy. The Atlantic War Pact is concocted as
the Western war alliance, for aggression.' There was more in this vein,
much of it singling out the St Laurent government as arch-villains in the
piece.

The record of the Canadian government in this shameful story, which has all but
obliterated in public discussion the grand alliance which defeated the Axis ... is
one of perfidy and deception, base commitments to the war plans of Wall Street
and the surrender of our national independence. At each step the King-St Laurent
government – fully supported by the Tories, the CCF leaders, [Maurice] Duplessis
[premier of Quebec] and the Social Credit Party – has pursued the role of an eager
jackal for the US war beast.

...Without recourse to public opinion, the St Laurent regime, which refused to
commit Canada to collective action against the Hitler Axis*, has already committed this country, in open and secret agreements with the US government, to
full-scale war against Socialist Europe and the New Asia.

...Canada is a vitally strategic area for the warmakers. That is why the Atlantic War
Pact was first raised by St Laurent, flying a kite for Wall Street...[151]

It was the near left, not the far, about which the policy-makers were
concerned. The strategy of the Labor Progressive Party was to divide the
membership, and if possible the leadership, of the Co-operative Com-

---

*   A reference, presumably, to the controversy over when the Western allies should
     open up a 'Second Front' against Germany during the Second World War. As the
     Dieppe raid, of which so many Canadians were casualties, had been in part mounted
     to placate Stalin's demands for a Second Front, the reference is egregious.

monwealth Federation (CCF). Its propaganda was aimed at the CCF rank-and-file: 'As a trade union man, or a CCF member or supporter, you have a special responsibility, because the labor movement must not let the people of Canada down in this critical hour. Labor has had enough of appeasing imperialists and fascists. The labor movement's rank and file must go after those leaders like [M.J.] Coldwell [leader of the national CCF party], [A.R.] Mosher [president of the Canadian Congress of Labour]* and the rest, who once appeased Hitlerism by rejecting labour unity, and who now appease Yankee warmongers because they all together believe in the domination of "the West" over the rest of mankind. ... Labor men and women, wherever you are, should resist these agents of the ruling class in the labour movement and refuse to be led by Mr Coldwell and Co. into the trap of supporting the foreign policy of the government.'[152]

The CCF national leadership, sensing early that the LPP's declaration of support for the party could mean the kiss of death for it in the impending federal election (held on 27 June 1949), did all it could to disassociate itself. In January 1948, M.J. Coldwell issued a statement rejecting the LPP's demand for unity on the left.

In the 1945 elections, Canada's communist party, the LPP, called on the Canadian people to support Mackenzie King and the Liberals. Today the party has switched its line again and is now declaring its support for the CCF. ... Naturally what Canadian Communists decide to do is entirely up to them. But I want to make the position of the CCF crystal clear. ... The CCF will not collaborate with the Labour Progressive Party in any way, direct or indirect...[153]

A year later, the CCF National Council stated the party's position on Canadian membership in an Atlantic alliance.

The Cooperative Commonwealth Federation believes that Canada should support and join such a North Atlantic Security Pact. Efforts must be continued to build the world security system called for in the United Nations Charter. But until such security is assured, a regional pact, in line with the provisions of the Charter, will increase the degree of mutual aid and assistance among the western democracies.[154]

For this statement, in which the word 'defence' is notably absent, the national leadership of the CCF was hard-pressed to secure the unwavering support of its rank-and-file. M.J. Coldwell forced its adoption by threatening to resign from party leadership if it were not adopted.[155] Members of the provincial party in Western Canada were outspokenly critical. J.P.

---

* On 5 March 1948, the Prime Minister recorded that he had received a Canadian Congress of Labour delegation led by Mosher, which brought cordial greetings and a brief praising 'the Government's ... policy of helping Europe...' Quoted in *Record* IV, 253.

O'Brien of the Manitoba CCF described the statement as 'a most amazing collection of half-truths, samples of confused thinking, and naive conceptions,' while Colin Cameron of the British Columbia CCF argued that 'the alliance, which would divide the world into two camps, represented a flagrant betrayal of the United Nations.'[156] In April 1949, two CCF members of the Manitoba legislature repudiated the CCF statement.[157] The CCF's foreign policy platform was further damaged by the LPP's creation of the Canadian Peace Congress and of so-called 'peace councils' across the country, ostensibly for the purpose of obtaining signatories to a petition calling for the unconditional banning of atomic weapons but actually for the purpose of undercutting the CCF's support for the government. The national party warned its members in January 1949 not to sign the petition or associate themselves with the Congress and the councils which it described as fronts for the LPP and international communism.[158] But these public defections on the hustings led to private defections in the polling booths. The federal election of 1949 cut CCF representation in the House of Commons from twenty-eight seats to thirteen – a drastic decline 'which experienced observers, both inside and outside the party, attributed to the strange differences of opinion within the Cooperative Commonwealth Federation about the Atlantic pact.'[159]

The communist attack on the leadership of the CCF for supporting the government's policy towards an Atlantic alliance did not have the effect of eroding public support for that alliance. Votes lost by the CCF in the 1949 election went to Liberals, not to Communists (the LPP failed to gain a seat). But the LPP campaign to draw CCF supporters away from their party's official foreign policy caused spokesmen for the government to emphasize more than they probably would have done otherwise the so-called 'non-military' aspects of the proposed alliance. This emphasis is reflected in the rhetoric of the St Laurent crusade and in the text of the North Atlantic Treaty itself.*

---

*   See Chapter 2. One unidentified official, said to have had 'an important influence on Canadian policy in 1946-49,' remarked at a Canadian Institute of International Affairs Study Conference held in 1967 that 'Article II was a necessity in order to win Canadian public opinion to the unprecedented step of engaging in a permanent peace-time alliance. The Cooperative Commonwealth Federation would not have accepted the NATO treaty without this provision.' Escott Reid, questioned on the point in 1971, did not go quite so far, but readily conceded the political utility of stressing the non-military functions of the alliance: 'If the Cooperative Commonwealth Federation had not existed, Mr St Laurent and Mr Pearson would have argued for an Article II. But they knew that the chances of getting full support from the Cooperative Commonwealth Federation for the North Atlantic Treaty were increased the stronger the provisions in the treaty on economic and social co-operation and on democracy.' Quoted in Liesemer, 'The Nature of Canada's Crusade for NATO', 147.

The third source of opposition to Canadian membership of an Atlantic alliance was within French Canada.

'*Je me souviens*': within the collective memory of *les Québecois* the resentments created by their experience of militarism did not so much smoulder as burn. *La conquête* itself, the political murder of the leader of the Riel rebellion, the trauma of 1917, the near-trauma of 1944, attained the properties of myth. The searing denunciation of the nationalist Henri Bourassa in July 1916 – 'I find that Canada, a nation of America, has another mission to accomplish than to bind herself to the fate of European nations. ... To speak of defending French civilization in Europe while harrying it in North America seems to us an absurd inconsistency'[160] – echoed down three decades. Nothing in Quebec's past justified the complacent assumption that by 1948 the French-speaking majority of that province were ready to support Canada's membership in a military alliance for the defence of Western Europe just because Stalinism had replaced Kaiserism and Hitlerism in the allegation of Anglophones as the menace to freedom.

In view of its history, French Canada's opposition to the proposed alliance and Canada's membership therein was surprisingly muted. Its critics were confined to one or two members of Parliament, a handful of intellectuals, and the editorials of a single newspaper – the small but influential *Le Devoir* of Montreal* (whose founder, fittingly enough, had been Bourassa); in its columns a trio of publicists (Gérard Filion, Paul Sauriol, and André Laurendeau) mounted a sustained assault upon the foreign policy of the St Laurent government and on St Laurent for contriving it. Membership in the alliance, it variously argued, would compromise Canada's democracy, sovereignty, identity, and even safety. Canada should remain neutral. St Laurent was denounced as 'a half-French Canadian showing himself more bellicose and imperialistic than the people of the Montreal *Gazette* and the Toronto *Globe and Mail.*'[161] This fusillade was not ignored by the policy community who thought it well to fire back. 'As you may have noticed, *Le Devoir* is becoming even more violent in its advocacy of neutrality for Canada,' Escott Reid wrote to the new Prime Minister's chief political aide on 6 December 1948. 'For this and for other reasons, it might perhaps be useful if one of the Ministers were to give a

---

* A survey of 13 French-language daily newspapers in Quebec finds *Le Devoir* to have been alone in 1948-9 in opposing Canada's entering the alliance. See J.I. Gow, 'Les Québecois, la guerre et la paix, 1945-60,' *Canadian Journal of Political Science*, III, March 1970, 98. '[N]ous avons trouvé,' the author concludes, 'qu'après 1948 le débat sur la politique étrangère qui a eu lieu au Québec s'est fait en termes de la guerre froide et avec des arguments qui se retrouvaient dans tous les pays de l'Ouest.' *Ibid.*, 121.

speech before Christmas following up the Prime Minister's speech on November 11.'[162]

Such were the crusaders' enemies. What of the crusade itself?

Several leading members of the policy community took part in the campaign to persuade Canadians that membership in a defence pact with Western Europe and the United States would be in the best interest not only of Canada's prospective European allies but of Canada herself.

The Prime Minister – a reluctant participant in this cause – was prevailed upon by his advisers to open the campaign in January 1948. 'So long as Communism remains a menace to the free world,' Mackenzie King declared at Ottawa on 20 January, 'it is vital to the defence of freedom to maintain a preponderance of military strength on the side of freedom, and to ensure that degree of unity among the nations which will ensure that they cannot be defeated and destroyed one by one.'[163] On 24 June, the Minister of National Defence, speaking in the House of Commons on the defence estimates, declared that one of Canada's objectives was 'to work out with other free nations plans for joint defence based on self-help and mutual aid as part of a combined effort to preserve peace and to restrain aggression.' Present defence plans were flexible, Brooke Claxton added, and would require modification 'if, as we hope, Western Union grows into a North Atlantic security understanding.'[164] On 21 September, L.B. Pearson, making his first speech as foreign minister, told an audience that 'the Canadian Government has made it clear that it is not only willing, but anxious, to join the other North Atlantic democracies in establishing a regional collective security pact for the North Atlantic.' Disclosing that negotiations for this purpose had been in progress at Washington – 'it is not ... possible for me to tell you today how these discussions are going' – Pearson added:

The Canadian Government has taken these steps towards the creation of an effective regional security system with, I am sure, the overwhelming support of the people of Canada. The people of Canada have given this support knowing that Canada's participation in such a security system may require that, in an emergency, we share not only our risks but our resources. It would, for instance, be the task of a North Atlantic security system, once it is established, to agree upon a fair allocation of duties among the participating countries, under which each will undertake to do that share of the joint defence and production that it can do most efficiently.

Such a sharing of risks, resources and obligations must, however, be accompanied by, and flow from a share of, the control of policy. If obligations and resources are to be shared, it is obvious that some sort of constitutional machinery must be established under which each participating country will have a fair share in determining the policies of all which affect all. Otherwise, without their consent, the policy of one or two or three may increase the risks and therefore the obligation of all.[165]

In the vanguard of the crusade, made tireless by zeal, was L.S. St Laurent. Not only did he carry the case for the coalition within his own province, he made it across the country, arguing for the alliance in 'almost every speech ... on a 6000 mile barnstorming tour of the West.'[166] Escott Reid has since paid tribute to his boldness.

A cautious man would not have got out in front in an international crusade for the North Atlantic treaty. A cautious man in the private diplomatic negotiations would have thrown his weight on the side of those who wanted a weak treaty, with ample provision for every nation to decide for itself what it should in fact do if one of its allies were attacked. There were plenty of opportunities to do this during the negotiation of the treaty. Instead Mr St Laurent campaigned in private and in public for a strong treaty – in speeches, in cabinet and in instructions to our representatives in the international negotiations. The North Atlantic Treaty is a monument to his foreign policy.[167]

Of scores of speeches, three are especially noteworthy; and of the three, the most remarkable was the earliest – the address delivered by the Secretary of State for External Affairs in the House of Commons on 29 April 1948. Into its text were incorporated many of the ideas and some of the phrases used by St Laurent's officials in their confidential papers on the proposed Atlantic pact. He recalled his speech to the UN General Assembly on 18 September 1947: 'I stated then that it was not necessary to contemplate the break-up of the United Nations or the secession from it of the Soviet group in order to build up a stronger security system within the Organization.' Perhaps, he suggested, the time for action was approaching. 'It may be that the free states, or some of them, will soon find it necessary to consult together on how best to establish such a collective security league.' St Laurent then outlined his conception of such a body.

Its purpose, like that of "Western Union," would not be merely negative; it would create a dynamic counter-attraction to communism – the dynamic counter-attraction of a free, prosperous and progressive society so opposed to the totalitarian and reactionary society of the communist world. The formation of such a defensive group of nations would not be a counsel of despair but a message of hope. It would not mean that we regarded a third world war as inevitable; but that the free democracies had decided that to prevent such a war they would organize so as to confront the forces of communist expansionism with an overwhelming preponderance of moral, economic and military force and with sufficient degree of unity to ensure that this preponderance of force is so used that the free nations cannot be defeated one by one. No measure less than this will do. We must at all costs avoid the fatal repetition of the history of the pre-war years when the Nazi aggressor picked off its victims one by one. Such a process does not end at the Atlantic. I am sure,

he added, 'that it is the desire of the people of Canada that Canada should play its full part in creating and maintaining this overwhelming preponderance of moral, economic and military force and the necessary unity for its effective use.' But, St Laurent warned, Canada should not act in any spirit of philanthropy. 'One thing we must constantly keep in mind as we approach this fateful decision is that the western European democracies are not beggars asking for our charity. They are allies whose assistance we need in order to be able successfully to defend ourselves and our beliefs. Canada and the United States need the assistance of the western European democracies just as much as they need ours. The spread of aggressive communist despotism over western Europe would ultimately almost certainly mean for us war, and war on most unfavourable terms. It is in our national interest to see to it that the flood of communist expansion is held back.' And he concluded:

Our foreign policy today must therefore, I suggest, be based on a recognition of the fact that totalitarian communist aggression endangers the freedom and peace of every democratic country, including Canada. On this basis, and pending the strengthening of the United Nations, we should be willing to associate ourselves with other free states in any appropriate collective security arrangements which may be worked out under Articles 51 or 52 of the Charter.

In the circumstances of the present, the organization of collective defence in this way is the most effective guarantee of peace. The pursuit of this course, steadfastly, unprovocatively, and constructively is our best hope for disproving the gloomy predictions of inevitable war.[168]

This speech, St Laurent's biographer records, 'made banner headlines.' The *Winnipeg Free Press* declared it to be 'perhaps the frankest statement of foreign policy ever made in the Canadian Parliament.'[169] The *Globe and Mail* of Toronto, a newspaper normally unfriendly to the Liberal government of that day, described St Laurent's statement as 'a great parliamentary performance and a major document in Canadian history.'[170] The snipers at *Le Devoir* denounced it as an incitement to war. ('St Laurent,' writes his biographer, 'found himself being criticized in Quebec as too soft on Communism for refusing to ban the Labor Progressive Party, and too belligerent for preparing to resist any attack by the Soviet Union.'[171]) Across the Atlantic, at least one statesman picked up St Laurent's signal: 'The House will have noticed ... a remarkable speech by the Canadian

Minister of External Affairs,' the British foreign secretary observed to his legislature on 13 May. 'Mr St Laurent pointed to the eventual constitution of some world-wide system of regional defence arrangements based essentially on Article 51 of the United Nations Charter. For my part,' Ernest Bevin added, 'I agree that nothing could so successfully reinforce the Charter as a ... system such as he proposes.'[172]

The speech-maker himself was well aware of the boldness of his message. Having delivered what Escott Reid rightly calls 'the first unambiguous public statement of Canada's willingness to enter a North Atlantic military alliance,' St Laurent leaned across his desk to whisper to his adviser: 'I wonder how that will go down.' Reid responded: 'I think it will go down very well in the country.' St Laurent rejoined: 'I wasn't thinking of the country. I was thinking of Laurier House.'[173] (Laurier House was the residence of the Prime Minister.)

A second notable address of the crusade was likewise a parliamentary performance. On 19 June, St Laurent returned to the theme of the need for a coalition. 'We think there would be value in a regional pact whereby these western European democracies, the United Kingdom, the United States and ourselves agreed to stand together,' the Secretary of State for External Affairs told the House of Commons,

to pool for defence purposes our respective potentials and coordinate right away our forces, so that it would appear to any possible aggressor that he would have to be prepared to overcome us all if he attempted any aggression.

We do not think that a pact that did not include those major powers would be sufficiently impressive to require us to be a party to it. We think this Western Union is a good thing, but our adhesion to it without the United States would add very little to it. We are hopeful that it will develop into something which will comprise the United States along with those who are already members, and in that event we think the people of Canada would wish that we also be associated with it, not because we want to assert domination over anyone, but because we realize that if the group in this regional pact became involved in war we would necessarily be involved with them.

That is something that the people of Canada might prefer to avoid, but it is something which they could not avoid even if they wished to. That being so, if there is any value in preparedness, we think the people of Canada would be glad to see us making that preparation in an orderly fashion with others whose way of life is the same as ours and whose security is part of our own security. That,

St Laurent admitted, 'has not proceeded very far.'[174]

The third noteworthy address in St Laurent's crusade was delivered by him on the national radio network four days before becoming Prime

Minister. He had chosen, 'with a fine sureness of touch,' Armistice Day – 11 November 1948 – for the occasion of his final major appeal to the public on behalf of an Atlantic alliance for Canada. He described the proposed commitment as a form of insurance against unimaginable disaster. A prudent citizen would no more resent the premiums to be paid for insuring his country's security than would a prudent householder resent the premiums to be paid for insuring his dwelling-place, even though his home had never been on fire. 'When I ask you to support a North Atlantic treaty,' St Laurent told his fellow countrymen, 'I am simply asking you to pay an insurance premium which will be far, far less costly than the losses we would face if a new conflagration devastated the world.'[175]

The metaphor came naturally to the prudent lawyer from Quebec City who displayed a national characteristic of buying large amounts of life insurance by accumulating no fewer than thirty-three policies with annual premiums of several thousand dollars. But it is likely that St Laurent was aware of its historic significance. A quarter of a century earlier, another statesman from French Canada, speaking at Geneva in 1924, had described the League of Nations as 'an association of Mutual Insurance against fire.' Whereas St Laurent urged Canadians to buy more of such insurance, Raoul Dandurand had thought they should buy less. Since the risks assumed by members were unequal, the premiums paid by each should be adjusted to the degree of danger which for Canadians – living 'in a fire-proof house, far from inflammable materials' – was small. It was only fair – so Dandurand had argued – that Canada should be assessed less dues for peace than those countries closer to where the flames would start.[176] Dandurand had invoked the metaphor of insurance to defend his country's isolationism. St Laurent – probably with Dandurand's invocation in mind – invoked the same metaphor to defend its new-found internationalism.

NORTH ATLANTIC LATITUDES

The public speeches of ministers and officials during their 'crusade' for a trans-Atlantic coalition in which Canada would join do not fully account for their strong support of this proposal. The US Secretary of Defense, visiting Ottawa during April 1948, was struck and even startled by what he described in his diary as 'the curious fact' that his hosts were such fervid advocates of a North Atlantic treaty; no such advocacy then existed at comparable levels in Washington.[177] Why were Canadians so keen so soon?

Early in 1948, discussions had begun to explore the possibility of creating a free trade area between Canada and the United States.* Perhaps to the surprise of the participants, agreement in principle was quickly reached and easily secured. A set of proposals commanding the full support of officials on both sides had been formulated by March 1948. The first of its provisions called for 'Immediate removal of all duties by both countries.' An American representative commented at the time: 'The Canadians consider the proposal, if implemented, to be one of the most momentous decisions in their history.'[178]

The Americans involved were elated, for there seemed to lie within their grasp what one of them termed 'a unique opportunity of promoting the most efficient utilization of the resources of the North American continent and knitting the two countries together – an objective of United States foreign policy since the founding of the Republic.'[179] The Canadian negotiators – two senior officials of the Department of Finance and the Chairman of the Tariff Board – were hardly less elated. The proposal, the Minister of Finance later assured the Prime Minister, 'would be the answer to all our present restrictions. If we could get complete reciprocity' – so Mackenzie King recorded D.C. Abbott having told him – 'he felt we would no longer be dependent on uncertain markets of Europe ... and that this would give what was needed to maintain, as far as could be maintained, the prosperity of this country.'[180]

But when the Prime Minister reflected further on the proposal for 'complete reciprocity' he took fright. Reciprocity had defeated a government of which he had been a member, it could defeat a government of which he was the head. 'The cry would be raised at once that it was commercial union that we were after,' Mackenzie King told L.S. St Laurent, C.D. Howe,[†] and the three officials who had drafted the agreement for Canada – W.C. Clark, J.J. Deutsch, and Hector McKinnon – at a meeting on 22 March. '[T]he Tories would say this is Mr King's toy. He has always wanted annexation with the States. Now he is making his last effort toward that end.'[181] Even if the Prime Minister successfully got the plan past opposition from Parliament and people, it would be at the expense of his rightful niche in history. '[F]or me to be placed in the position of being the spearhead of furthering a commercial union as the last act of my career would be to absolutely destroy the significance of the whole of it.'[182] Reinforced as usual by an 'extraordinary experience which I took to

---

* The initiative had come from the United States and the Prime Minister had authorized his officials to explore it. See Robert Cuff and J.L. Granatstein, 'The Rise and Fall of Canadian-American Free Trade, 1947-8,' *Canadian Historical Review*, LVIII, 4, December 1977, 459-82.

† See *In Defence of Canada* III, 9-10.

be a perfect evidence of guidance from Beyond,'[183] the Prime Minister reached his decision. Salutary for Canada as reciprocity might prove to be, Mackenzie King would not touch it with his walking cane.

But how to explain this sudden reversal to the Americans? How to convey to them Canada's rejection of a proposal which her own officials had helped to draft and which they had greeted with such enthusiasm? How to represent to them that its summary rejection had been on the highest plane of statesmanship when in reality the grand design had been shredded by partisan political considerations?

At the same time as financial officials were attempting to convince the Prime Minister of the value of a free trade agreement, diplomatic officials were meeting at Washington with those of the United States and the United Kingdom to discuss for the first time the project of a North Atlantic security pact.* In this circumstance, Mackenzie King realized at once, was a way to get off the hook of reciprocity. What was the point of pursuing a free trade area for North America if there existed an opportunity to pursue a free trade area for the North Atlantic? He could tell his financial officials to withdraw their initiative, at least for the time being. When the proposal reappeared – if it ever did – Mackenzie King would no longer be prime minister.

A minor difficulty was that the Washington talks on North Atlantic security were being conducted in such extraordinary secrecy that the Canadian participants in the Washington talks on North American reciprocity were unaware – indeed until that moment possessed no 'need to know' – of their existence. That need the Prime Minister now created. 'I said I would have to swear [the] three members of the [Civil] Service present to absolute secrecy,' Mackenzie King recorded on 22 March, 'and to tell them that, at the moment, negotiations were on at Washington for the establishment of an Atlantic Security Pact – negotiations between the United Kingdom, United States and Canada. ... That I felt trade proposals might be made to fit as it were into the larger Atlantic Pact. That if, for example, the Atlantic Security Pact were agreed upon and were brought before Parliament and be passed as it certainly would be, we might immediately follow thereafter with trade agreement as being something which still further helped to further the object of the Pact, namely, the removal of restrictions to trade within the area arranged by the Pact.'[184]

As Mackenzie King expounded this ingenious mode of prevarication on bilateral reciprocity to L.S. St Laurent, C.D. Howe, and the three officials, he grew expansive. 'It might even lead,' he told them, 'to the

---

* See below, Ch. 2, 72-8.

United States coming to move in the way of greater freedom of trade ... I felt that both the United States and the United Kingdom would go very far in the direction of anything that would disclose a closer unity of interest between them. That, later, certain other countries, France, for example, might be brought into a larger, freer trade area, etc. All three – Clark, Deutsch and McKinnon – were strongly taken with the idea.'[185]

Having thus successfully side-tracked the reciprocity proposal in Ottawa, it remained for the Prime Minister to side-track it in Washington. On 1 April 1948, the Ambassador explained the reasons why, as Hume Wrong put it in a 'Top Secret and Personal' letter to J.D. Hickerson of the US Department of State, 'the Canadian Government was not in a position to take immediately a favourable decision on the economic proposals which have been developed...' There were, Wrong stated, two main reasons for postponement. First, it would be overloading the public's capacity to absorb major changes in policy to confront the people of Canada almost simultaneously with the proposal to enter a security alliance and a proposal to enter a free trade area with the United States. Such a double confrontation, Wrong suggested, 'would be of doubtful wisdom from the point of view of obtaining both objectives with a minimum of controversy. It is believed, therefore, that at the moment the energy and attention of the Canadian Government should be concentrated on the problems involved in the security pact and on the necessity of rallying Parliament and the public wholeheartedly around that pact and the policy which it embodies.' The second reason given for the desirability of delay was that the government considered it would be preferable to broaden the proposed free trade area from North America to the North Atlantic, once a North Atlantic treaty had been signed. 'It would be natural for the trade discussions to be related to the pact, since they are concerned with measures for economic defence against aggression. It might also turn out to be desirable later to add the United Kingdom to such discussions. If, in fact, the discussions could be somewhat widened in this way,' Wrong concluded, 'it would remove one of the political obstacles to bilateral arrangements at the present time for free trade between the two countries.'[186] (In the event, nothing further developed from this suggestion: on the contrary, a Canadian proposal that the treaty should pledge its signatories 'to develop the great possibilities of trade between them' was turned down during its negotiation by the United States.)*

The North Atlantic treaty proposal appeared attractive to the policy community at Ottawa for a reason additional to that of helping Canada to

* See below, Ch. 2, 121-8.

deflect ill-timed proposals for reciprocity. A multilateral treaty was seen as well as a device for reducing the pressure of the Pentagon. A United States administration pledged to co-ordinate its defence policies with those of allies in Western Europe as well as those of its ally in North America would be less likely than a United States administration going it alone to lean as heavily upon its northern neighbour. Canada, allied to the United States within the North Atlantic coalition, would have more room in which to breathe and to manoeuvre than would be hers if locked into a stifling bilateral embrace. 'Under such a treaty,' L.B. Pearson pointed out in a memorandum for the Prime Minister setting out the advantages for Canada of a multilateral defence association over some form of United States unilateral guarantee of Western Europe's security, 'the joint planning of the defence of North America would fall into place as part of a larger whole and the difficulties arising in Canada from the fear of invasion of Canadian sovereignty by the United States would be diminished.'[187] (A part of this memorandum is printed below as Document 1.) That was an aspect of the proposed pact which appealed to Mackenzie King. 'I felt sure that the long objective of the Americans was to control this Continent,' the Prime Minister remarked soon afterwards in a discussion with the Ambassador at Washington. 'They would want to get Canada under their aegis. If I was an American,' King added, 'I would have the same view...'[188]

The argument that Canada needed a multilateral defence pact as a kind of fender against intense pressure from the United States was one which officials, naturally enough, used privately or not at all. Only later would hints at it be heard in public statements. '[I]n my view,' L.B. Pearson told the House of Commons some years after the North Atlantic Treaty had been signed,

any idea that the great coalition which we have formed for peace should be replaced by an entrenched continentalism would make no great appeal to Canadians as the best way to prevent war or defeat aggression. Nor would it be likely to provide a solid basis for good United States-Canadian co-operation.

Indeed, the idea of continental self-sufficiency, in the military as in the economic or political fields, makes no appeal, I suggest, either to our sense of reality or to our deepest Canadian instinct. And so NATO, with the United Kingdom, the United States and France in it, is for us an indispensable instrument both for co-operation and defence...[189]

A further argument in favour of Canada's membership in a North Atlantic security pact was that the coalition could be used to constrain the United States from pursuing provocative policies and taking headstrong actions. Not all believed this to be a danger, but some believed strongly that it was. '[W]e should in the next few months take particular care to leave the Russians ground for retreat,' the *chargé d'affaires* at the Embassy in Moscow wrote to L.B. Pearson on 9 April 1948. 'It seems to me of desperate importance that we use our considerable influence in the coming months to prevent the United States from taking heady action without calculating the consequences.'[190] A United States administration pledged to consult with its allies was less likely to take 'heady action' than a United States administration going it alone. The notion of the Atlantic alliance as a coalition of constraint upon its leading member was also not for public display – least of all by Canadians – but privately it counted. '[T]he United States may press the Russians too hard and too fast and not leave them a way out which would save their faces' – so L.B. Pearson put it for the benefit of the Ambassador at Paris whose instruction it was to argue the merits of an alliance to a reluctant Quai d'Orsay. 'To lessen this danger, the Western European powers will have to exert a steady and constructive influence on Washington. The establishment of a North Atlantic Union will give them additional channels through which to exert this moderating influence.'[191]

These several strands of advocacy were neatly gathered by an exceptionally sagacious official of the gifted group which provided post-war Canada with foreign policy guidance. 'I am more than ever impressed by our own good fortune,' Norman Robertson observed to L.B. Pearson on 21 April 1948, from his High Commission at London – a post affording an incomparable overview of North Atlantic latitudes.

Ever since we have been in a position to shape our policy abroad, we have had to wrestle with the antimonies created by our position as a North American country and as a member of the Commonwealth, by our special relationship with the United Kingdom and at the same time, although in less degree, with other countries in Western Europe as well. A situation in which our special relationship with the United Kingdom can be identified with other countries in Western Europe and in which the United States will be providing a firm basis, both economically and probably militarily, for this link across the North Atlantic, seems to me such a providential solution for so many of our problems that I feel we should go to great lengths and even incur considerable risks in order to consolidate our good fortune and ensure our proper place in this new partnership....[192]

From virtually every perspective of Canada's external policy, it thus appeared to those in charge of it that membership in a North Atlantic coalition would be for their country – in more ways, perhaps, than for any of its other members – a beneficial outcome. It now remained for them to obtain a treaty to Canada's advantage.

2

Drafting the Treaty

The negotiation of the treaty went smoothly...

J. W. Pickersgill

[T]he public story of the negotiations for the North
Atlantic Treaty differs in a number of very important
respects from the truth.

Escott Reid

My recollection of the birth of NATO ... is that it was a
conspiracy by the British and Canadians to entrap the
United States Senate into a commitment to defend
Europe and that it was largely engineered by Escott
Reid...

John W. Holmes

WASHINGTON: BEHIND (ALMOST) CLOSED DOORS

'It looks as though you may be required here,' Hume Wrong cabled to
L.B. Pearson from Washington on 13 March 1948. 'You will have to
devise a good cover story. ... Everyone agrees that the completest secrecy
must be observed.'[1]

Before setting out for the 'Security Conversations' held among representatives of the United States, the United Kingdom, and Canada at the
Pentagon between 22 March and 1 April 1948, the Under Secretary of
State for External Affairs spoke with the Prime Minister about his ideas
concerning what he expected to be the two principal issues that would be
discussed at Washington: the countries which might be invited to join a
defence pact; and the commitment by which their governments ought to
be bound.

On the issue of membership, L.B. Pearson considered France to be the
key adherent. Belgium, The Netherlands, and Luxembourg should certainly be included, so enabling the Brussels Treaty to be replaced by 'a
more inclusive Atlantic Pact.' Sweden, Pearson felt, should be invited,

for otherwise it would 'be left dangerously exposed...' So, too, should Italy, and for the same reason. 'An attempt at a complete Russian conquest of Italy by constitutional or extra-constitutional means may take place during the next month. If the USA and the UK consider that exclusion of Italy from the Communist bloc is as important as the exclusion of Norway, then it would seem that a guarantee to Italy is at least as urgent as a guarantee to Norway.'

On the issue of commitment, Pearson displayed at the outset what would remain Canada's unwavering attitude throughout the prolonged negotiations leading to the alliance and thereafter. '[T]he purpose of the pact,' he reminded the Prime Minister,

is to rally the spiritual as well as the military and economic resources of Western Christendom against Soviet totalitarianism. To do this it should not be a merely negative anti-Soviet military alliance but should be the basis for a positive liberal and democratic counter-offensive. The pact may succeed in giving us a long period of peace if it results in creating an overwhelming preponderance of force against the Soviet Union. This force, however, to be overwhelming should not be only military and economic force; it should also include the force that comes from ability to rally to our side all non-Communists in all countries, including our own, who are now apathetic, fearful or doubtful.

The proposed pact should make as clear as possible the methods which the peoples and governments of the Free World intend to follow to make good their faith in human rights and fundamental freedoms, in the worth and dignity of man and in the principles of parliamentary democracy, personal freedom and political liberty. If it can do this it will underline that this pact is something far removed from alliances and arrangements of the old kind.[2]

The two issues – of membership and of commitment – were therefore of a piece. If the pact was to be no more (if no less) than an alliance and arrangement 'of the old kind,' then the democratic credentials of prospective members need not be closely scrutinized. If, however, the pact was to be an inspiration to freedom-loving peoples everywhere, signatory states ought to exhibit a reasonable love of liberty themselves. In a less than perfect world it could not be expected that all the members would be models of perfect freedom; compromise was necessary. But it was seen from the beginning that compromise would not be easy. '[C]onstantly ... keep in mind the necessity of the pact being a basis for what one can call the spiritual mobilization of the liberal democracies,' Escott Reid enjoined L.B. Pearson on the eve of the Washington discussions, 'as well as being a basis for economic and military co-operation against Soviet threats. This involves a nice problem of balancing tangible and intangible considerations.'[3]

The first of six 'Security Conversations' was held on 22 March. Their venue was the 'War Room' of the US Joint Chiefs of Staff, deep in the bowels of the Pentagon. Extraordinary efforts had been made to prevent knowledge that the meetings were taking place from becoming public. Each of the participants contrived a 'cover story' to offer some spurious reason for his presence: thus, L.B. Pearson's excuse for being out of Ottawa was that he was going to New York to assist in atomic energy negotiations there; General Charles Foulkes,* Chief of the General Staff, was allegedly in Washington to pay a courtesy call on the new US Army Chief of Staff; while Hume Wrong, Ambassador at Washington and therefore needing no reason for his presence there, skipped the first two meetings 'because he had, before the talks were agreed to, made engagements in Toronto which he said he could not get out of "without giving an awkward explanation".'[4] Participants were delivered by staff cars to a secret entrance in the basement where they entered the Pentagon through a kitchen door.[5] To preserve the fiction that the Security Conversations had never been held, their end product – an undated memorandum entitled simply 'Final Draft' and referred to in related documents as the 'Pentagon Paper' – was 'cast in the form of a "Working Paper" setting forth tentative proposals which might be put forward by the United States administration.'[6] Many years later, those associated with the 'Security Conversations' treated them as a non-event, an 'unhappening' – some even while they purported to write the history of the negotiations. As in Orwell's Oceana, 'Everything faded into mist. The past was erased, the erasure was forgotten...'†

These measures successfully kept the very existence of the Washington Security Conversations from being known to any Westerners other than

---

* See *In Defence of Canada* III, 61-5.
† George Orwell, *Nineteen Eighty-Four* (London 1954), 63. 'Forgotten' until 1972, when a British participant referred to the 'Security Conversations' in his memoirs, so becoming the first to disclose their existence. 'I have some vivid recollections of this encounter,' Lord Gladwyn wrote,

> which took place in the recesses of the Pentagon, great trouble having been taken to maintain secrecy, in this case with fairly good results, though I believe that the celebrated Joe Alsop must have had some wind of what was taking place since he published only a fortnight after the end of our talks a piece to the effect that the American Administration was considering joining an Atlantic pact!

The Memoirs of Lord Gladwyn (London 1972), 215. While disclosing the existence of the talks, Gladwyn did not disclose their substance: 'Until they are published it would not however be proper for me to disclose any details of what was then said.' *Ibid.*, 215. Pearson's memoirs, published the following year, are more revealing: see *Mike* II, 43-6. The minutes of the six meetings, as recorded by Maj. Gen. Alfred M. Gruenther, are published in *Foreign Relations of the United States 1948*, III, *Western Europe* (Washington, DC 1974), 59-61, 64-7, 69-72; these minutes were used by Escott Reid to reconstruct the first phase of the negotiation in his *Time of Fear and Hope: The Making of the North Atlantic Treaty 1947-1949* (Toronto 1977), *passim*.

the participants themselves and a handful of officials of the three governments concerned. ('At the beginning of July, 1948 ... information about
the discussions had been given to only two officers of the Department of
External Affairs in Ottawa in addition to Pearson and [Escott Reid]...')[7]
But it is possible that more Easterners knew than Westerners. Participating in the Washington Security Conversations, present at each of the six
meetings, was Donald Duart Maclean – a Second Secretary in the British
Embassy at Washington and a spy for the Soviet Union.

The chagrin of Maclean's colleagues when word of his defection to the
Soviet Union reached the West in June 1951 may well be imagined. There
is little doubt in their minds that Maclean reported to the Kremlin on the
'Security Conversations.' 'I should imagine,' Pearson remarks in his
memoirs, that Maclean 'reported immediately to Moscow.'[8] 'However
"secret" the negotiations,' Lord Gladwyn comments wryly, 'there can be
little doubt ... that the Soviet Government had a pretty full record of what
happened from the very moment they took place.'[9] Maclean's labour of
love would have been eased by his assignment, within the British team, to
help draft its minutes and telegrams on the progress of the meetings for
perusal by Bevin at the Foreign Office.[10]

Did Maclean's presence matter? His Soviet connection was not necessarily disadvantageous to the West. It could have been so had he mis-
chievously let slip the tale of the talks to some national reporter or
isolationist senator: 'I have sometimes thought,' writes Robert Cecil
(who, with Maclean, accompanied Jebb on the British side), 'that, at that
juncture, Maclean could have created more confusion in the Western
world by a leak in Washington than by his secret line to the Kremlin,
where news that a common front was being constructed in the West
probably had a salutary effect.'[11] But Maclean, apparently, leaked only to
the Kremlin. It would have been disadvantageous to the West had the
negotiation ended in failure, for then Moscow would have had material
with which to foment discord among Western governments and publics.
As things turned out – so Escott Reid and Cecil have speculated – 'his
presence may well have been advantageous for the West. In his reports to
Moscow, he presumably informed the Soviet Government that no one in
the top-secret discussions evinced any desire to embark on a preventive
strike against the Soviet Union while the United States still had a monopoly of the atomic bomb.'* Reid observes further: 'The Soviet Govern-

---

*   The word 'presumably' in this passage bears a heavy load. An anonymous letter
    delivered to the US Embassy in London shortly after Maclean's defection contains
    what purports to be a deposition made by him to its sender on 24 May 1951, which
    reads in part:

ment would make a great contribution to an understanding of the Cold War if it were to publish Donald Maclean's reports to them on the making of the North Atlantic Treaty'[12] – as would leopards to zoology were they to change their spots.

Discussion at the first of the Security Conversations on 22 March was free-wheeling and informal; there was no break for lunch, and the participants munched sandwiches. British and Canadian representatives sought to ascertain American intentions: it will be recalled that the United Kingdom government, not the United States government, had requested that the talks take place. They were told that United States support 'should be assumed, for purposes of the current conversations'; but not what it was that the Americans would support.

Three varieties of coalition were weighed: an extended Brussels Pact; a new Atlantic Pact and possibly other regional pacts, such as a treaty for Mediterranean states; and 'a world-wide pact of self-defense based on Article 51 of the UN Charter, which might be approached initially on the basis of regional arrangements.' The United States minutes state that Canada and the United Kingdom preferred the creation of a new Atlantic pact to an extension of the existing Brussels Treaty. All three parties

> I am haunted and burdened by what I know of official secrets, especially by the content of high level Anglo-American conversations. ... I hold identical copies of the minutes of all Anglo-American conversations relating to the use of the North Atlantic Treaty for the preparations and launching of assault on the Soviet Union...
>
> I have decided that I can discharge my duty to my country only through prompt disclosure of this material to Stalin, whom I shall beg to release it at once...

Quoted in David Leitch, 'Secrets of the FBI Spy File,' *Sunday Times*, 27 November 1977. Is this document, released under the US Freedom of Information Act, a forgery? If so, the motives of the forger are not readily apparent. Is it authentic? If so, it reveals Maclean's state of mind in 1951 but not necessarily in 1948. If in 1948 Maclean was warning the Kremlin that the West was about to attack the Soviet Union, it is indicative of the caution and conservatism of the Soviet leadership that Stalin did not act pre-emptively as Western governments – Canada's among them – feared he might. It seems probable that Maclean's conviction (if such it was) that the West harboured aggressive designs against the Soviet Union was formed, if not confirmed, by the events touched off following President Truman's press conference on 30 November 1950 (see below, Ch. 4, 248). 'After he had absconded, when I succeeded to the post [Head of the American Department],' a Foreign Office colleague has recorded, 'I found in the filing cabinet reserved for the Head of the Department a numbered copy of the Cabinet paper containing Prime Minister Attlee's account of his hasty visit to President Truman in December 1950, the aim of which was to ensure that General MacArthur should not be permitted to use the atom bomb in the Korean War.' Robert Cecil, 'Legends Spies Tell: A Reappraisal of the Absconding Diplomats,' *Encounter*, L, 4, April 1978, 16.

agreed that in whatever arrangement that might be worked out, it was crucially important to provide for the security of Italy: 'Italy, more even than Norway, is now most directly menaced.'[13]

L.B. Pearson reported to Escott Reid in Ottawa that he had supported the idea of a new Atlantic pact. '...[W]hile great importance and value would naturally be attached to United States accession to the Brussels Pact,' Pearson observed, 'this would not be the case with regard to Canadian accession, for which, in fact, there is neither more nor less reason than for accession by, say, Brazil or Australia. I doubt myself whether we should take any action of this kind merely because the United States of America does.'[14] But this way of looking at it did not commend itself to the Prime Minister and the Secretary of State for External Affairs. 'They feel that the essential thing is for the UK and US to underwrite the security of the signatories of the Brussels Treaty and the Scandinavian countries,' Reid noted after conferring with St Laurent.

They would therefore accept anything which the UK and the US jointly agree is required to defend our common interests. They would be prepared to recommend to Parliament, if need be, accession by Canada to a Pact of which the UK, the US and France were members even if no other Atlantic nations were signatories. They would, however, prefer an Atlantic Pact which would include other Atlantic nations as well as the signatories of the Brussels Treaty.

They do not at the moment wish to preclude from consideration the admission of Italy and perhaps some other states to the Pact now in contemplation...[15]

At the second meeting on 23 March, the field of possible arrangements was narrowed. A world-wide pact of 'free nations' was abandoned as being 'too cumbersome and too long in implementation,' although as an ultimate objective it should not be discarded. A Brussels Pact augmented by the adherence of the United States and possibly Canada was also rejected, on the grounds that retention of the Brussels Treaty in its existing form was desirable for the eventual development of a United States of Europe. The main drawback of an Atlantic Pact appeared to be that it would exclude Italy as lying outside the treaty area; that difficulty could be overcome by calling the pact 'Western' rather than Atlantic. A defence pact in which all parties offered reciprocal guarantees appeared preferable to a unilateral guarantee of security to be offered by the United States 'to free nations menaced by Soviet Communism'. The American participants, Pearson reported, had favoured a United States unilateral guarantee on the grounds that it could be given 'speedily and effectively, and would not require any prior agreement or the negotiation of any political arrangement with the European powers. Its disadvantages, however, and these were considered over-riding, were that it was a purely unilateral act, without any quality of reciprocity, and that, as such, it might be open to attack both in North America and among the European states as too one-sided.'[16] For this reason, the participants agreed that 'the objective ... should from the outset include a pact of mutual defense against aggression to which the US (and Canada) would finally adhere.' The meeting adjourned until the following day, when each delegation would have ready for discussion a paper suggesting how 'A Western Mutual Defense Pact might be developed.'[17]

Hume Wrong, who had not been present at the first two meetings (in order, as noted, not to draw attention to them) offered some comments on reading the minutes of the second.

The immediate steps proposed to deal with the threat of Soviet aggression in Scandinavia and in the Mediterranean seem well designed to meet the situation. But it is perhaps arguable that the ideas which emerged on the method for dealing with the long term situation are not so well fitted to generally accepted ideas on Soviet behaviour.

In the first place, it is agreed that Soviet expansionism will take place wherever it is not stopped. Another usually accepted axiom is that the possibility of isolating aggression anywhere in the world is remote. By this time most people seem to subscribe to the theory that the best place to deal with aggression is where it breaks out. If these two principles are accepted, some simple conclusions seem to flow from them.

First, scattered regional arrangements with gaps in between them might invite the expansion of Soviet power into the holes. This seems to be a danger in the regional approach. To meet the threat of Soviet world wide ambitions, perhaps the Western powers should not run the risk of excluding by implication vulnerable areas. But what is the alternative? Perhaps the West should have the known intention of dealing with Soviet aggression anywhere if it constitutes a threat to the peace. Thus, instead of drawing rings around certain areas which are definitely *verboten*, a looser and more flexible arrangement might be better designed to meet the long term threat...

Alternatively, if tight regional groupings are established, the dangers inherent in them might be obviated by a concurrent announcement that a threat to the peace in the form of Soviet aggression would not be tolerated anywhere in the world...

One of the disadvantages in the inclusive Western Pact idea seems to be that it is ideologically messy, i.e., Spain and Portugal. It seems a pity to sacrifice, if it can be avoided, ideological forces at our disposal. A looser arrangement might be less vulnerable to charges of hypocrisy.[18]

The third meeting, on 24 March, considered the three papers from each delegation and appointed a drafting committee (Theodore Achilles for the United States, Gladwyn Jebb for the United Kingdom, and Pearson for Canada) to reduce these to one. The resulting document proposed the creation of a 'Security Pact for the North Atlantic Area,' of which the United States would be a member 'along with all nations bordering the North Atlantic (including Iceland).' Italy would be invited to join at once if its government desired. 'The way would be left open for accession later by Western Germany, Austria and Spain.' The designation 'North Atlantic' – used for the first time – was employed 'to prevent efforts of Latin America, Australia, etc. to adhere, which would make the arrangement unwieldy, especially as none of these are now directly threatened by Soviet Communism.'[19]

Between the third Security Conversation and the fourth, L.B. Pearson returned to Ottawa to brief the Prime Minister (he had kept in touch with St Laurent by telephone). Pearson's memorandum to Mackenzie King indicated his preference for 'a separate and more broadly based North Atlantic Security Pact' over an extended Brussels Pact, and for reciprocal over unilateral guarantees. As to membership, the Americans had suggested that invitations to take part in a conference to negotiate a security pact should go out from the US President to fourteen countries, including Portugal (whose air base facilities in the Azores were judged to be of paramount strategic importance). While Britain seemed prepared to regard with indulgence the prospective candidacy of its 'oldest ally', Canada, through Pearson, had expressed her doubts. 'I mentioned the disadvantage of the inclusion of Portugal from the ideological point of view, but it was felt that this disadvantage was more than neutralized by the strategic advantage of Portugal's membership.'

There had been contention, too, Pearson reported, over what kind of pledge members should be required to make. The Americans and, with slight reservations, the British considered a traditional military pact sufficient. Against this conception Canada had stood fast. 'I stated more than once,' Pearson informed the Prime Minister, 'that the document should not be exclusively military in character and that there were economic and even spiritual defences against communist attack which should not be overlooked. I felt that the Brussels arrangements had taken these important factors into consideration and that it was even more important that the North Atlantic Pact should do so. Otherwise, it would be considered as merely another old fashioned military alliance.' To make sure that the treaty would not be regarded in that light, Pearson had proposed that a preamble should be written in such a way as to emphasize the more than 'merely military' nature of the alliance. The preamble should provide in clear and moving language 'a firm economic and social basis for defence against aggression, both direct and indirect.' So that this statement of purpose would not be dismissed as so much windy rhetoric, an article within the treaty should recite the signatories' readiness to 'make every effort, individually and co-operatively, to promote the economic well-being of their peoples, and to achieve social justice, thereby creating an overwhelming superiority of moral, material and military force on the side of peace and progress.'[20] (Here, Pearson would comment in his memoirs, 'was the genesis of the famous Article 2 of the treaty, which came to be known as the Canadian article, and which has had a chequered and disappointing life.'[21])

By these ideas, amplified by the Under Secretary of State for External Affairs in discussion with the Prime Minister, Mackenzie King was much attracted. 'The form the scene is now taking,' King wrote in his diary on 26 March after being briefed, 'is a declaration by the President ... in which the United States will offer to support the members of the Brussels Pact and invite other countries to join in mutual security around the Atlantic. Matters so arranged as to keep it in the Northern Atlantic zone. I liked the idea very much. Pearson thinks a conference will be held in about two or three weeks – possibly at Washington.' What Mackenzie King liked most about the idea was that the Americans – apparently – were in the vanguard. 'It seems to me in every way best that the whole matter should become one of United States leadership. It puts increasingly on the United States the obligation of maintaining peace in the Atlantic.'[22] Pearson reported the Prime Minister's reaction to Hume Wrong: 'Mr King expressed himself as greatly pleased with the course that the discussions had taken and the resulting recommendations. He thought that from our point of view they could not be better.'[23] Wrong, too, was satisfied. 'If an agreement along the lines that were discussed becomes a reality,' he wrote to Pearson from Washington when the 'Security Conversations' had been completed, 'it should considerably ease our problems in handling defence relations with the United States. ... I have for a long time been worried,' Wrong confessed,

lest our current defence arrangements with the United States should result in too great a concentration of effort and resources on the static defence of the continent, particularly in the case of Canada but also in some measure in the case of the United States. If the North Atlantic is bridged by a new defensive alliance, the problems of North American defence would become a small part of a larger plan; the purpose of which would be the means of defeating the potential enemy. In such a plan, the offensive aspect would be the primary consideration.

Furthermore, our own political difficulties about permitting US forces to conduct certain operations or maintain certain facilities within Canadian territory ought to be substantially diminished if such activities could be seen as a fraction of a larger scheme...[24]

After conferring with the Prime Minister, L.B. Pearson returned to Washington where the Security Conversations resumed on 29 March. At this fourth meeting, the nature of the pledge was broached for the first time. The United States delegation took the position that 'any treaty article committing the parties to war in the event of aggression should in terms of American realities either be on the model of the Rio pact* ... or should be explicit in indicating that each party would determine "municipally" for itself whether an armed attack had in fact occurred.'[25] This position was confirmed at the fifth meeting on 31 March, at which a further draft of what would become the final paper to emerge from the Tripartite Talks was presented by the American participants. The new draft incorporated 'changes suggested by ... "indirect" soundings concerning the probable attitude of Congressional leaders. ... Effect of the alterations is to:

a. Introduce Rio Treaty language wherever possible.
b. Abandon any attempt to define "indirect aggression" ...
c. Provide that each party determines for itself "whether there has occurred an armed attack within the meaning of the agreement" and the immediate measures it may individually take in fulfilling its treaty obligations until coordinated measures have been agreed upon.[26]

In the final position paper, it was stated that the proposed treaty should contain two provisions dealing with the pledge.

b.. Provision that each Party shall regard any action in the area covered by the agreement, *which it considers an armed attack against any other Party*, as an armed attack against itself...

c. Provision following the lines of Article III, paragraph 2 of the Rio Treaty to the effect that, at the request of the State or States attacked ... *each one of the Parties shall determine the immediate measures which it will individually take* in fulfillment of the obligation contained in the preceding paragraph...[author's italics][27]

The US minutes of the Security Conversations do not record any Canadian intervention on the subject of the pledge. Nonetheless, L.B. Pearson was disturbed by the italicized portions of these provisions. They allowed, in his view, far too much discretion to member governments for the pact to be effective. A pledge so diluted, Pearson told Hume Wrong on 1

---

*   A reference to the Treaty of Rio, or Inter-American Treaty of Reciprocal Assistance, signed on 2 September 1947 by the United States and eighteen other American republics. At the time of the Washington Conversations on an Atlantic pact, the Treaty of Rio had not yet come into force (it did so on 3 December 1948). Article 3 of the Rio Treaty pledged its signatories to 'agree that an armed attack by any States against an American State shall be considered as an attack against all the American States,' and to undertake 'to assist in meeting the attack...'

April, 'will have a very discouraging effect on those who might wish to sign the Agreement and an equally encouraging effect on those who are expected to be deterred from aggression by it. It will be interpreted as reducing to almost nothing the obligatory character of the obligation. I realize,' he added, 'that the determination of whether an armed attack has in fact taken place is the right of the individual signatories, but surely that can be left implicit rather than be made explicit...'* The only consolation for the Canadians was their realization that, as the British foreign secretary had emphasized at the meeting through his representative, that the 'work thus far had gone forward only on the pick and shovel level,' and that no promises were being made or implied. They could attempt to strengthen the commitment formula at later stages of the negotiations, as they did.[†]

The sixth and final meeting on 1 April adjourned in general agreement 'that a treaty should be accomplished and as soon as possible, the optimum possibility being that it might be accomplished prior to the end of the current session of Congress.'[28] It would take a lot longer than that.

The North Atlantic Treaty has for more than three decades been the foundation on which United States foreign policy is built, and that foundation was laid only with great difficulty. A diplomatic tradition to which all alliances were anathema, alliances with Europe especially so, was not lightly set aside. The momentum generated by the Security Conversations at Washington was not sustained. Doubts and reservations slowed the negotiations down. The treaty that some had hoped would emerge within a matter of weeks took more than a year to draft.

---

* L.B. Pearson to Hume Wrong, 1 April 1948 (telegram), DEA files, 283 (s). Some months later, Pearson again expressed his dissatisfaction with the Rio Treaty type of pledge.

> The advantage of the Brussels formula is that the parties promise to fight an all-out war if one of them is attacked. They obviously will have to fight an all-out war so why not say so instead of using the vague term "assist in meeting the attack" which hostile critics could say means the kind of assistance Mexico gave in the last war...

Pearson to T.A. Stone, 10 August 1948 (telegram), quoted in Reid, *Time of Fear and Hope*, 146-7. And yet again:

> "Assist in meeting the attack" is certainly susceptible of the meaning "all aid short of war". ... If this were the nature of the undertaking in the North Atlantic treaty, might it not mean that Canada would be fulfilling its obligation under the treaty in the event of a Soviet attack upon the United States, if its assistance to the United States went no further than United States assistance to Canada in the last war up to Pearl Harbor.

Pearson to Stone, 16 August 1948 (telegram), quoted in *ibid.*, 147.
† See below, 107-14.

Doubts and reservations emanated from two main quarters, both of them in Washington. One was within the US State Department. The other was within the US Senate.

When the American participants in the Security Conversations – Lewis Douglas, J.D. Hickerson, and Theodore Achilles – displayed their handiwork in the form of the 'Final Draft' position paper to their colleagues of the State Department, there was by no means unanimous praise for their achievement. 'There was dissension as to the need for a treaty,' one witness at the scene has since recalled. 'Certain officials opposed it. ... We had constantly to break all rules of procedure to get the Secretary's approval as matters progressed.'[29]

The opponents of the treaty fell into two camps. In one were to be found those who opposed it on the ground 'that it would never pass the Senate.' In the other were far more formidable opponents – those who opposed the idea of an Atlantic security pact even if it were to pass the Senate. Their opposition derived not from expediency but from principle. Of them Escott Reid would write disparagingly: 'Some of these people never really liked, or even understood, the very idea of an alliance. They weren't very anxious to learn the complex and subtle art of how the leader of an alliance conducts its relations with the other members of the alliance. They hankered after unilateral declarations, unilateral decision-making, unilateral actions.'[30] Their views were articulated by two of the most experienced and gifted members of the American foreign policy community, both specialists in Soviet affairs – George F. Kennan and Charles E. Bohlen. Bohlen in his memoirs so forgets his position at the time as to make it appear that he was in favour of the alliance from the outset,* but Kennan in his memoirs offers a forthright statement of the reasons why he opposed what he describes as 'a treaty unprecedented in our history.'

I saw, in the first place, no need for a full-fledged reciprocal military alliance at that state of the game. It seemed to me regrettable that attention should even be drawn in a major way, in the circumstances of the moment, to the relationships of military strength as between Russia and the West. I was well aware that we had demobilized and the Russians had not. This I considered unfortunate but not fatal or even very important. The Russians had no idea of using regular military strength against us. Why then should we direct attention to an area where we were weak and they were strong?...

---

* 'NATO was simply a necessity. The developing situation within the Soviet Union demanded the participation of the United States in the defense of Western Europe. Any other solution would have opened the area to Soviet domination...' Charles E. Bohlen, *Witness to History, 1929-1969* (New York 1973), 267.

Secondly, I had little confidence in the value of written treaties of alliance generally. I had seen too many instances in which they had been forgotten, or disregarded, or found to be irrelevant, or distorted for ulterior purposes when the chips
were down. I had no confidence in the ability of men to define hypothetically, in
any useful way, by means of general and legal phraseology, future situations
which no one could really imagine or envisage. What was needed, it seemed to
me, was a realistic consciousness of where one's interests really lay. Given that,
military policy would flow of its own accord – it needed no legal obligations or
prescriptions...[31]

If such arguments made converts up the chain of command, they
would stop the project for an Atlantic pact in its tracks; for a while it
seemed that they had stalled it. 'I am somewhat worried that the Americans seem to be drifting away from a Pact to a Declaration,' L.B. Pearson
wrote to Hume Wrong on 13 April 1948. 'The latter would, I feel certain,
be much less satisfactory from every point of view.' And a month or so
later: 'I think that Bohlen and those who feel like him are on the wrong
track, and that the idea that all that is required to back Western Europe by
some form of unilateral guarantee and by supplying arms is wrong and
possibly dangerous. It is especially discouraging to hear talk at this stage
about an Atlantic Pact provoking the Soviets.' Perhaps, Pearson mused
disconsolately, the West had missed the bus: 'I have the unhappy feeling
that the big moment has passed when a genuine regional security arrangement could be negotiated on a reciprocal basis ... and that the United
States is now relapsing into policies which are short-sighted and insufficient. ... Certainly the hopes that were inspired by the meetings that we
attended some weeks ago now seem to have been largely dissipated and
there is, I think, real danger of a reliance on old fashioned alliance policies, dictated by purely military considerations. It would be disastrous,'
Pearson concluded, 'if the Article 51 approach so hopefully begun should
now be abandoned.'[32]

The following day, at Pearson's suggestion, the Ambassador at Washington attempted to persuade the US State Department's foremost opponent of the pact that it was a good idea after all. 'I began my talk with
[George] Kennan at lunch today,' Hume Wrong reported to Pearson,

by saying that I was firmly convinced in my own mind that a formal commitment
was necessary fully to achieve the purpose in mind. He said that they were still
debating this in the State Department and left me with the impression that he was
opposed to a formal commitment. He argued that the United States would inevitably be involved from the first in war against the Soviet Union if there was Soviet
aggression anywhere in Western Europe. ... He thought, therefore, that the same
results would be achieved whether or not there was a pact.

I opposed this view on two grounds. I said that many people in the European
countries and also in Canada would not be content with a unilateral assurance of

US policy, which might be changed if there was a change in the Administration. They wished something to build on which would span a presidential term at least. Even if it were true that they were as much assured of US support now as they would be under an alliance, plenty of people would not think that this was the case, and would therefore refrain from running risks which it was in our interest that they should run...

My second point related to the position of Canada. I said that it would be far more difficult for Canada to collaborate in planning defence against Soviet aggression on the basis of a unilateral US assurance than it would be if both countries were parties to an Atlantic agreement. Furthermore, under such an agreement the joint planning of the defence of North America fell into place as part of a larger whole and would diminish difficulties arising from fears of invasion of Canadian sovereignty by the US. It would become easier to advocate a policy of Canadian aloofness if the present state of affairs was maintained. An Atlantic pact would go a long way towards curing our split personality in defence matters by bringing the US, the UK and Canada into regular partnership.

Kennan told Wrong that 'he was much impressed by this latter argument, which had not occurred to him before,' and that 'he would think it over carefully.'[33] Unknown to Canadian officials, Kennan had been even more impressed by the speech of L.S. St Laurent in the House of Commons on 29 April 1948.* 'I think the statements of the Canadian Foreign Minister ... add a new and important element to this problem,' he had written on 24 May to the US Secretary of State and the Under Secretary. 'I think we must be very careful not to place ourselves in the position of being the obstacle to further progress toward the political union of the western democracies...'[34] On 28 May, Wrong reported from Washington that 'Kennan is much more receptive now to the pact idea,' adding that 'Bohlen ... remains to be converted.'[35]

The wooing of the Director of the Policy Planning Staff of the US Department of State reached a peak of intensity early in June 1948, when the policy community invited George Kennan to Ottawa. L.B. Pearson's memorandum to the Prime Minister of 1 June (see Document 1), outlining the reasons why a multilateral security pact was thought to be preferable to an American unilateral guarantee, was distributed to those officials with whom Kennan would be meeting. The confrontation took place after a dinner given for Kennan by the US ambassador, when L.B. Pearson, Brooke Claxton, J.W. Pickersgill, and others

launched at him the reasoning set forth in the memorandum. The main argument ran as follows. Because a treaty would have to be ratified by the [US] Senate it would commit the United States much more firmly. It would embody the element

* See above, 59-61.

of mutual assistance. Why should the United States and Canada come to the assistance of European countries if those countries were not willing to accept similar obligations to us? A unilateral guarantee gave unnecessary prominence to the dependence of the European states and seemed to underline the satellite character of their relationship to the United States. As such, it might unnecessarily offend their pride. Moreover, the United States and Canada needed the assistance of the Western European democracies just as they needed ours. A Russian conquest of Western Europe would mean for us war and war on most unfavourable terms. A unilateral guarantee smelled of charity (in the worst sense of the word); the Western European democracies were not beggars asking for our charity, but were potential allies whose assistance we needed in order to be able to defend ourselves. A pact would be an important demonstration that security arrangements could be worked out under the Charter, in this case under Article 51. Eventually other arrangements could be negotiated for other areas until all free countries might be brought in. Most important of all, a unilateral guarantee would be nothing more than a pledge of military assistance.

Pickersgill added two specifically Canadian arguments. In the last two world wars Canada had gone to war two years before the United States; a treaty commitment by the United States would be more likely than a presidential declaration to lessen the danger that this would happen again. Second, Canada and a number of other North Atlantic countries would find it politically easier to grant defence facilities to a North Atlantic alliance than to the United States.

During the discussion, Kennan retorted that 'he was impatient with the pressure from the United Kingdom and the Western European states' – to which he might have added Canada – to make a formal treaty commitment. Those states did not seem to realize that if the United States gave this guarantee it would be doing something which would be in the interests of Western Europe but not necessarily in the interests of the United States itself, since it could at any time make a deal with the Soviet Union.'[36] This was too much for his hosts. 'We naturally took him up on this,' Escott Reid reported to Hume Wrong, 'and he withdrew from this exposed position. However it did give me a feeling that if you scratch almost any American long enough, you will find an isolationist. They suffer, and you can hardly blame them, from a homesickness for isolation.'[37]

This encounter seems to have had its intended effect. 'It is still uncertain whether the State Department is fully convinced that a treaty commitment is desirable,' was Wrong's final report on the American line-up. 'I think that Lovett is inclined to be sympathetic but not fully satisfied on the treaty proposal. Bohlen still tends to oppose it, while Kennan appears to be converted. [J.D.] Hickerson [then Director of Office of European Affairs, US Department of State] is the staunchest advocate.'[38]

The other main opposition to a security pact in Washington came from within the US Senate. The catastrophe of 1920, when the Senate rejected

the Treaty of Versailles, cast a long shadow. But whereas Canadian officials could try to convert sceptics within the US State Department, they
had little purchase upon Senators, and could only look on, helpless and
hopeful, as pro-pact American officials sought to persuade the Congress
to make their cause its own. The key figure was Senator Arthur Vandenberg, chairman of the Senate Foreign Relations Committee (and thought
to be front-runner as the Republican Party's presidential nominee). Secretary Marshall and Under Secretary Lovett danced attendance upon the
Senator with exceptional solicitude, eventually inveigling him into sponsoring the resolution which bears his name. Vandenberg's statement during hearings of the Foreign Relations Committee was to L.B. Pearson
disappointing in its tepidity; Pearson wrote of its 'inadequacy in so many
respects' and of 'the indifferent reception that this statement has been
given. I feel certain that the Western European states will be discouraged
by these developments...'[39] The passage of the resolution on 11 June 1948
by a vote of sixty to four placed the Senate behind a policy aimed at
'association of the United States ... with such regional and other collective
arrangements as are based on continuous and effective self-help and
mutual aid, and as affect its national security.'[40] This vote is rightly judged
historic, but at the time the resolution's language seemed to sound a
muted, not a clarion, call. Hume Wrong foresaw obstacles ahead. 'Whether
this vote records in fact a momentous change in United States foreign
policy,' Wrong cautioned Ottawa on 16 June, 'will depend on how the
policies approved by the resolution are developed. ... I have doubts
whether the discussion of the resolution in the Senate and the press has
been explicit enough to make people realize that it blesses the participation of the United States in entangling alliances in Europe. As usual,' he
added, 'the pathway from the general to the particular is likely to be steep
and devious.'[41]

Between the arrival of Attlee's telegrams at Washington and Ottawa in
an atmosphere of alarm and panic and the passage of the Vandenberg
Resolution, exactly three months had elapsed. There was not much to
show for them. Among the many questions which years later still perplexed one of the principal Canadian architects of NATO was whether the
chance of a lifetime had been allowed to slip by.

[W]as an opportunity lost in April 1948 to rush the treaty through quickly while
the sense of urgency was so great? Pearson, in his memoirs, outlines the agreement which was reached by the end of March. It contains as he says, "the basic
features of what was to become the North Atlantic Treaty." The United States
negotiators had the complete text of a treaty drawn up at that time. This first draft
of the treaty was made by [Theodore C.] Achilles [then Director of Office of West

European Affairs, US Department of State]; according to him, "The eventual North Atlantic Treaty had the general form, and a good bit of the language, of my first draft..." The United States could have put this initial draft of April 1, 1948 before a conference of the Brussels powers, Canada and themselves in April. Indeed on March 15, 1948, Pearson informed Mackenzie King that, in order to check the communists in Italy, he considered that it might be essential to have the treaty concluded and published a week or more before April 18, the date of the Italian elections. He had been ambassador in Washington only a year and a half before, and, nevertheless, he believed that the Administration would be able to get a North Atlantic treaty ratified by the Senate even though consultation between the Administration and the Senate during the negotiations had been severely limited because of the need for haste.[42]

Could the North Atlantic Treaty signed on 4 April 1949 have been signed a year before? It is one of history's charms that we shall never know.

'DEAR JOE' OR 'FELLOW DEMOCRATS'?

During the lull in diplomatic activity that developed between the adjournment of the Washington Security Conversations on 1 April 1948 and the resumption of intergovernmental discussions on 6 July, a difference of opinion emerged within Canada's policy community over the nature of that security pact which all agreed was needed.

Spurred on by the imminence of the Tripartite talks, which as Escott Reid engagingly admitted had 'aroused my apocalyptic fervour and my passion for drafting international agreements,'[43] the deputy Under Secretary of State for External Affairs had tried his hand at yet another treaty text (his first effort having been in November 1947).* Reid had given a copy of this document, dated 20 March 1948 and entitled 'Provisional and Tentative Draft of a Collective Security Agreement,' to L.B. Pearson before the latter departed for the Washington discussions, together with an explanatory memorandum setting out his views on the kind of treaty he thought the government should strive to bring about.

On three main issues Escott Reid had strongly held opinions.

The first was that of membership. Reid advocated a much wider range of members than that of a regional grouping confined to the North Atlantic area. While he would strike Portugal from the United Kingdom's list of prospective invitees for failing to aspire to democracy, he wanted to invite Italy and even Finland. He also proposed inviting Australia, New Zealand, and South Africa, because their membership 'would help to pre-

---

*   See above, 21.

serve the unity of the Commonwealth and would remove the possibility of criticism of the pact by Commonwealth-minded people in Canada.' And, since it would be invidious to invite from the Commonwealth only those formerly so-called 'White Dominions' while excluding the Commonwealth in Asia, Reid proposed as well inviting India, Pakistan, and Ceylon. 'Their inclusion in the pact would most certainly extend greatly the commitments of all the other signatories since India and Pakistan are exposed and weak states, but their very exposure and weakness is a source of weakness to the United States, the United Kingdom, and ourselves.' But there were limits to Reid's profligacy. 'I would think that the list of invited states should stop here,' he wrote. 'To bring countries in which do not inherit so directly as these states the traditions of Western Europe would be to complicate matters at this stage when the paramount necessity is speed.' Later, 'it might be found to be possible to make those necessary amendments in the pact which would enable it to be signed by all the states of the world now outside the Soviet sphere.'

The second issue on which Reid had a strongly held opinion was the nature of the commitment. 'The important thing here,' he had written to Pearson,

is to get rid of the absurd weakness in Article IV of the Brussels Treaty under which the obligation of the signatories to come to each other's assistance is restricted to their being subjected to "armed attack." The whole game of the Russians is obviously to conquer without armed attack. So far they have been successful in playing that game and it is to be assumed that they will continue to play it. The new treaty will be pretty futile if it is a treaty to guarantee us against the kind of attacks on our independence which might have been made thirty years ago but not the kind of attacks which may be made during the next weeks and months. The treaty must therefore be a treaty of defence against not only armed attacks but also against "attempts by any state to undermine the political or economic independence of another state by intimidation or by subversive processes of political or economic penetration"...

The third issue concerned the scope of the pact. Reid felt most strongly that the treaty for which Canada should strive ought to transcend the merly military aspects of security. 'There is great danger that in the present atmosphere of crises,' he had written in his memorandum for Pearson,

Foreign Offices may be tempted to have recourse to something which would be not much more than an old-fashioned military alliance and that clauses in the pact other than those providing for mutual guarantees would be merely window dressing. Such a pact would not, I am convinced, meet the necessities of the day. We have to establish rapidly an overwhelming preponderance of force and we have to remember that it is not merely military and economic force with which we are concerned but also with what can be described as spiritual force. Or, to put it another way, mere force is not enough. There has to be the determination to use the force if necessary and a determination accompanied by a fervent belief in the society which one is trying not only to defend but to make the basis of an eventually united world. The new treaty must therefore be a living document and create a new living international institution.

The main enemies in Western Europe must now be despair, apathy, doubt and fear. A pact of mutual guarantee will not by itself overcome these enemies, for, if the pact should not preserve peace, the peoples of Western Europe may have to go through for many years the trials of Soviet occupation.

All this, it seems to me, underlines the importance of ... a bold move to raise in the hearts and minds and spirits of all those in the world who love freedom that confidence and faith which will restore their vigour.

It seems to me that a new treaty would give evidence of boldness and vigour if we carried a great deal further some of the provisions of the Brussels Treaty. ... We should set forth much more precisely the goals of economic co-operation. We should in some way make it clear in the treaty that the treaty is based on the principle that there should be equality of sacrifice between the free nations in the struggle for a Free World. This means acceptance of proposals for pooling our economic resources.

It also means that we should go further than the Brussels Treaty in setting up revolutionary new political instruments for the alliance. That is why I feel that we should have not only a Board for Collective Self-Defence but a parliament, a president (Spaak?), a chancellor (yourself?), and a chief of staff (Eisenhower?) This would give the impression that we mean business when we talk about forming a new society of the free nations...[44]

On 3 June 1948, Escott Reid sent a copy of this memorandum, together with a copy of the draft treaty on which it commented, to Hume Wrong in Washington, saying that he would be 'very interested in your comments...'

Much of what Reid had written concerning the need for the treaty to be more than an old-fashioned military alliance commended itself to L.S. St Laurent and L.B. Pearson, and had already figured – if not so floridly – in their public statements. But it was one thing to use these views as aids to rhetoric, quite another to use them as guides in negotiation. Hume Wrong, as Ambassador at Washington, would have the job, if a security pact were to emerge, of negotiating its terms. Familiar as he was with the mood of scepticism in Washington about entering into any sort of military alliance however traditional, Wrong was certain that Reid's views stood no chance of acceptance, and wrote to tell him so. 'I am far from sure that I would like to see a collective defence agreement in which "all the free States of the world" would be partners,' was Wrong's opening comment.

My own conception of possibilities is more modest and, I believe, more practical. It envisages perhaps four or five agreements covering different areas, with the connecting link between them the participation of the United States in all except the inter-American treaty. If the fear of war were to diminish greatly, a general superstructure might be erected. In the present state of affairs I would prefer to limit the participating countries in each case, because the larger the alliance, the more unmanageable and ineffective it tends to become. Coalitions are hard enough to control in wartime, but they are a great deal more difficult to manage in time of peace...

If we do get a North Atlantic defence agreement, it is going to be simpler than the sort of treaty proposed. ... I see no prospect that the United States would in the next year or so sign a treaty that goes as far as the Brussels Treaty. If that is the expectation in Ottawa, I think that steps should be taken to disabuse those who hold it. Certainly it is essential that we should be ready to approach the establishment of a real North Atlantic community by stages and not expect to get there at a rush. I believe that the central thing to concentrate on now is to secure a military undertaking ... with some simple general article which would cover economic collaboration and set up some sort of consultative organ or organs. If the other parties to the negotiation insist on something more they will wreck the whole project. ... The most that we should aim at is a modest elaboration of the Pentagon suggestions embodied in a treaty of not more than ten articles.[45]

Thus two senior officials of the foreign policy community came to hold conflicting views as to what kind of treaty was desirable. Hume Wrong had the opportunity to shape the outcome by his participation in the negotiations. Escott Reid had the opportunity to influence events by his proximity to the decision-makers at Ottawa. Both would exploit these vantage points during the months ahead. Meanwhile, Reid went directly to Pearson to press his position on the government. 'I would myself disagree with Wrong's view ... that we should not aim at a more elaborate treaty than that outlined in the Pentagon document,' he wrote to Pearson on 26 June,

and I would not wish to pass Wrong's message to the PM and the Minister without considering whether we should not at the same time pass on an alternative recommendation.

... [Wrong] develops somewhat his argument that we should not set the sights too high in the discussions with the United States and he goes on to say that, if the other parties to the negotiation insist on something more than a simple document, "they may wreck the project."

It seems to me that Wrong has made too big a jump in this paragraph. There is a profound difference between setting one's sights high and taking the line that if you can't get what you want you won't take half a loaf. I shouldn't think that any one of the participants in the Washington talks would break the negotiations because the United States would not go as far as they want them to go. That doesn't mean that we should not press the United States to go as far as we think they ought, in their interest as well as ours, to go...[46]

And a few days later, Reid attempted to persuade Pearson that his own views were more in line with stated government policy than Wrong's: 'Mr Wrong ... is far from sure that he would like to see a collective defence agreement in which "all the free states of the world would be partners." ... [T]his is a matter on which Mr St Laurent has taken a clear and consistent position. ... We should not, I think,' Reid added,

assume too easily that the United States administration and Senate cannot be persuaded to accept something more than the minimum set forth by Mr Wrong. I think Mr St Laurent is convinced that something more than that minimum is required by the existing international situation and that his view on this is shared in the United Kingdom, France and Benelux. Moreover, it is not only in Western Europe that something more imaginative than the Brussels Pact might create greater enthusiasm and public support. Sometimes it is politically easier to put through a big imaginative scheme than to get agreement on a half-way measure, particularly if the half-way measure is written ... in the language used by tired civil servants...[47]

Such were the opening shots in what Reid would later call a 'duel' between the two senior officials – one in Ottawa, the other in Washington – which lasted throughout the drafting of the North Atlantic treaty and impeded the attainment of Canada's objectives.

With the adoption by the US Senate on 11 June 1948 of the Vandenberg Resolution, the way was open for the expansion of the intergovernmental talks from three participants to six. Joined by representatives of France, Belgium, and The Netherlands, United States, British, and Canadian delegates participated in a series of meetings at Washington from 6 July to 10 September. Their discussions were officially described as 'Exploratory Conversations on Security Problems of Common Interest.' Because of the greater number of participants – and of the participation of the French whose capacity for keeping secrets was justifiably in question – it was decided not to attempt to prevent the very existence of the meetings from becoming public knowledge, as had been done during the tripartite Security Conversations, but to do everything possible to prevent leaks. At the first meeting, the head of the American delegation, Robert A. Lovett, 'emphasized the need for absolute security. A leak, particularly during the political campaign in the United States, might throw the whole enterprise into jeopardy. Political heat in this country will increase up to election day, and scars will be left afterwards. Any leaks as to the subjects of discussion in these meetings, therefore, might cast a cloud over the whole plan.'[48]

Among those present to receive this stern injunction, a participant to the end of August – one imagines him, inwardly amused, nodding his head in agreement – was Donald Maclean.

At the second meeting, the representatives agreed to adopt in the interests of security the procedure known as 'Metric', which precluded the transmission of documents except through a diplomatic bag in the custody of a special courier who would deliver it to the registry of the British Foreign Office for distribution from that point. Metric also forbade the participants from engaging in telegraphic and telephonic communication with their governments on the subject matter under discussion. This latter procedure, which would have been wholly unrealistic in a process of negotiation as distinct from exploration, was simply ignored by those agreeing to abide by it. 'The rules which were adopted to ensure secrecy were not adhered to strictly by the Canadian and United States governments,' Escott Reid has testified,

and presumably not by other governments. Governments had agreed in July not to refer to the discussions in telegrams or over the telephone. Yet there was a voluminous exchange of telegrams between the Canadian embassy in Washington and the Department of External Affairs in Ottawa about the discussions; and Pearson and Wrong had many talks about them over the telephone. We assumed that our cyphers were unbreakable and that only the United States was likely to intercept our telephone calls and we were accustomed to take this into account when speaking over the telephone. Moreover, if we didn't break the rules, we in Ottawa would not be able, when discussions in Washington were proceeding at a fast pace, to give effective guidance and instructions to our representatives. In order to give guidance and instructions in time we had to receive reports by teletype and reply by teletype. Perhaps in July and the first half of August of 1948, when the discussions in Washington were leisurely, the British, French, Belgians and Dutch did not refer to the discussions in telegrams or over the telephone. By the end of August, however, they were probably all using telegrams to give instructions to their delegations.[49]

In the light of these systematic violations, the layman may pardonably wonder why the conferees bothered going 'Metric' to begin with.

Between 6 July and 9 July 1948, five meetings of the 'Exploratory Talks on Security' were held. The participants for Canada were L.B. Pearson, Hume Wrong, and Thomas A. Stone, Minister in the Embassy at Washington. 'The talks here are going very well along lines which should be satisfactory to us,' Pearson reported after the third meeting on 7 July. 'The Americans have apparently decided that the basis for any security arrangements should be broad and have emphasized that neither a military alliance of the old sort nor a unilateral guarantee is sufficient to achieve the purpose desired. Mr Lovett keeps refering to a "North Atlan-

tic system" and to the fact that arrangements agreed on should be positive
and not merely negative; that co-operation should be wider than merely
military and should be closely related to the principles and purposes of the
United Nations.'[50] Pearson comments in his memoirs: 'Bob Lovett was
talking "Canadian".'[51]

According to the minutes of these discussions, the most important
Canadian intervention occurred at the fifth and final meeting of the
series on 9 July 1948, when Pearson stated 'that the Canadian government could not make any contribution to the collective security of the
area by any unilateral guarantee of western union security.' Following
Lovett's interjection that the United States government had no intention
of offering such a unilateral guarantee, Pearson continued

by saying that what he had in mind was the creation of a new system. He thought
that even if there had been no Brussels Pact the Canadian Government would still
be interested in an Atlantic security system. The members of such an Atlantic
system would be associating themselves with the security of each and all. As he
saw it there were already two groups of states who were willing, in the hope
thereby of obtaining greater security, to take on obligations greater than those
involved by membership of the United Nations. The Brussels countries were one
group; the United States and Canada were the other. There was a third group of
states concerned with the Atlantic which, though not members of these other two
groups, should somehow be associated with them. Some of these states were as of
much importance to the national security of the western hemisphere as were certain countries of the Brussels Pact. There were certain principles concerning the
nature of such an association upon which agreement should be sought before an
attempt was made to work out details. Firstly, there should be as close a connection as possible with the United Nations, not only under Article 51 of the Charter,
but also under Article 56, which concerned co-operation for economic, cultural
and spiritual purposes. ... Mr Pearson wished any new pact to involve positive
co-operation in fields other than purely military. Secondly, while the obligations
undertaken by a party to the new arrangement would be conditioned by certain
constitutional arrangements, that did not prevent the creation of something far
reaching.

The Rio Pact stated that an attack on any signatory was to be considered as an
attack upon all the signatories. This was the kind of obligation which should eventually be considered in connection with an Atlantic Security Arrangement. Such
an obligation did not mean that each party to the pact was obliged automatically to
go to war if one of the others was attacked. The obligation called for "assistance"
which did not necessarily involve a declaration of war. Moreover, each country
would be able to decide for itself whether an attack, the occasion for "assistance,"
had occurred...

The actual machinery for implementing a pact would probably have to be worked
out later. But as regards the idea of a pact, the Canadian government were already
on record in favour of participation in some sort of North Atlantic collective assis-

tance or mutual assistance arrangement. They were also on record as saying that their participation would not be effective unless the United States also participated.[52]

Following this fifth meeting, the participants agreed to set up a 'Working Group' to be charged with the task of preparing papers on '(1) the general security needs of western civilization, (2) the geographical limits implicit in any regional security arrangement and (3) the differing, individual needs of each of the countries concerned.'[53] This Working Group held fifteen meetings between 12 July and 9 September 1948, during which the Canadian participants were Thomas Stone and R.L. Rogers, third secretary in the Embassy at Washington. (Contrary to Pearson's recollection in his memoirs, Hume Wrong did not participate in these meetings.)

The level of representation within the Working Group was low, the summer was hot, the pace was sluggish. The Americans insisted that the intergovernmental talks were being held at the request of the Brussels powers and that it was therefore up to the Brussels powers to make proposals; this the Brussels powers were disinclined to do. 'Because the United States took this line,' Escott Reid explains, 'it refused to submit the ... Pentagon paper as a basis for discussion in the talks in the summer of 1948. The fact that no paper was put before the participants in these talks resulted in diffuse discussions, confusion – and a slow rate of progress which was probably what the United States wanted. At one time Stone ... even suggested to Ottawa that he might submit a revision of the Pentagon paper as his own product.'[54]

Backsliding set in. 'The Americans, perhaps expecting a [Thomas E.] Dewey victory in their upcoming elections, again became worried about the attitude of the Senate towards any broadly based Atlantic treaty and began to talk about a security pact which would have three parties, the United States, Canada and the United States of Western Europe. This might be an ideal arrangement,' Pearson concedes in his memoirs, 'but we thought it completely unrealistic, as was the hope that a security commitment by North America could be used to force the unity of Western Europe.'[55]

The Canadians while dismayed at the delay within the American camp could at least understand the reasons for it. But the backsliding – or foot-dragging – by the Western Europeans seemed to them wholly misguided. 'I think it is most unfortunate,' L.S. St Laurent wrote to Hume Wrong on 27 July,

that the Benelux countries and the United Kingdom and France are not pushing ahead with the Working Party. I suppose the delay has been due to ... the general feeling that there is no need to hurry this work because the immediate problem is one of getting arms to the European countries rather than tying up the United States to any Atlantic security arrangements. I suppose the European countries feel, in fact, that such a tie-up has already taken place because of the presence of United States troops in Europe and the fact that the United States would be involved from the beginning in any Soviet attack on Europe. This point of view is, I think, profoundly wrong and short-sighted. I feel myself that it would be folly for the European states concerned not to push ahead with the North Atlantic security pact because of their worry about immediate military assistance. Their main hope, it seems to me, lies in the development of a genuine regional mutual assistance system in which the United States will play a leading part. Circumstances favour such a development in the United States now, but it may be different two or three years from now...[56]

To convey this sense of concern to Western European governments, the policy community selected the Ambassador at The Hague, in all probability because Canada's prestige among the Dutch remained high as a consequence of her armed forces having liberated The Netherlands barely three years earlier. Pierre Dupuy* was accordingly supplied with an unusually full statement of the reasons for Ottawa's displeasure at the tepid response of the Western European governments to what L.B. Pearson, in his lengthy despatch to Dupuy, described as a unique opportunity for them to gain security.

It would be surprising to me if representatives of France and Belgium, in the light of the history of the last forty years, expressed less interest in a long term security policy than in measures to meet the short run emergency. Surely they must realize that there is now an opportunity to work out formal treaty arrangements by which the United States will accept its full share of responsibility for the security of the Western European and North Atlantic democratic community, and that it is vitally important to take full advantage of this opportunity. If discussions to this end interfered with arrangements for meeting the present emergency or increased the danger of Soviet aggression, I could understand the hesitation of the French and Belgians. But, as I see it, this is not the case. The Americans have made it clear that they will do what they can to help immediately, provided the Brussels countries are themselves doing everything possible, individually, and, even more important, collectively to strengthen their own defences. Naturally, with American troops in Europe they are bound to take this attitude because they know that, along with the Western European countries, they will at once be at war if and when the Russians commit an act of aggression. But to build long range policy on this situation; to assume that all that is required is a flow of arms to the European countries from the USA and to assume that first priority should be given to the consolidation of the Western Union Group with United States military support displays, so it seems to me, a serious misunderstanding of the present position. What is required, I think, is for the Brussels Powers to push ahead with a regional

---

*   See *In Defence of Canada* III, 38.

security pact under the United Nations, which would include the United States and Canada. The European powers have everything to gain and nothing to lose by this, as it would not interfere with an immediate assistance to Europe which the USA is willing to give. There is no possibility of any formal unilateral backing of the Brussels countries by North America, and it is folly for the French and Belgians, misled possibly by the fact that Germany is now garrisoned in part by US troops, to think so...

Reiterating Canada's position that the government would not be willing to offer any form of unilateral guarantee as an alternative to an Atlantic security pact, Pearson described the mood in Washington which, he emphasized, propitious as it then was for internationalist initiatives, was likely to be transitory.

For the first time in United States history, developments in domestic policy and the consciousness of a great menace to her security (the two are, of course, tightly related) have made it possible for Washington not to follow but to take the lead in working out collective security arrangements – not merely for an emergency but as part of long term policy. These arrangements will cover countries which have suffered grievously in the past because such arrangements did not exist until after war had begun. I should have thought that a change of this kind in US policy would have been greeted in Paris and in Brussels with great relief and enthusiasm and that they would have pressed ahead with all speed to reduce to a treaty commitment a policy which would have saved them in 1914 and 1939 and which may be more difficult to implement in 1952 than in 1948. Any holding back or reservations now by European countries would be disastrous. If the USSR attacked Western Europe during the next, say twelve months, nothing that the USA would be able to do during this period – under any emergency arrangements – could prevent Soviet forces over-running continental Europe. But if the USSR were tempted to commit an aggression three or four or five years from now, the certainty that an attack on any one European state would be an attack on the USA as a signatory to an Atlantic pact, might prevent the aggression taking place. Furthermore, the other signatories to that pact during those years would secure more material help from North America for their own defence than they could do in any other way. I suggest, in fact, that only within the framework of such a security arrangement can the maximum military assistance which may be required in the years ahead be granted.

That is why I feel certain that the European countries concerned have everything to gain and nothing to lose by concluding such a pact at the earliest possible moment. It is depressing that some of them seem unable to see this...[57]

It may be assumed that the Ambassador at The Hague passed this pep talk from the sidelines along to his Western European colleagues – with what effect remains unknown.

By the third week in August, the Working Group at Washington had met a dozen times with scant result. On 20 August, the US Under Secretary of State arranged a special meeting at his home to seek a way out of the impasse. L.B. Pearson, with T.A. Stone, attended for Canada. The Belgian ambassador, at whose request the meeting had been convened, led off by saying that 'he feared that we might not be coming to grips with the basic question. ... By this' – so Robert Lovett's notes of the discussion record – 'he meant quite bluntly whether ... a North Atlantic Pact of some sort was necessary or whether some defensive arrangements could be made with Western Europe without having a North Atlantic Pact. He, therefore, would like to ask me and Pearson, in that order, to give our frank personal answer to this question.' Lovett responded by saying that he thought a North Atlantic pact was necessary and that no alternative defensive arrangements were possible. Pearson, according to Lovett, replied as follows.

Pearson said ... that he could summarize [the Canadian position] ... best by making four short statements: (1) Canada was not interested in joining the Brussels Pact, as it would make no sense for them to have an obligation 2500 miles away with all the areas in between being insecure. (2) They were not in a position to contribute to the rearming of Western Europe simply for the purpose of building up Western Europe no matter how desirable that would be for the over-all view of their security. (3) They would not be interested in any pact which did not cover the North Atlantic approaches. (4) They were definitely interested in such a pact and felt it had a direct bearing on their security.

He said that he understood the United States position fully and perhaps better than did his colleagues, and recognized the tremendous advance in thinking which the Vandenberg Resolution represented. He also was aware of the Congressional difficulties in the way of making arms to Europe on a loan or grant basis in view of the very heavy charge on the American budget for ERP [European Recovery Programme] and its own rearmament program. It was his opinion that it would be far easier, if not essential, for this country to have an association with some sort of a regional pact which met its national defense need than it would be to deal with the rearmament of Europe as a project which, while obviously improving the security of this continent, did so in a remote rather than a direct fashion.[58]

This exchange clarified the issue to the satisfaction of the Belgian and The Netherlands' representatives present, but not to that of the French ambassador who, as Lovett noted tartly, 'obviously had a prepared speech which he had to get off his chest and ... occupied about an hour in doing so.'[59]

From this meeting, and from other diplomatic activity, it became evident that the slowest ship in the North Atlantic convoy was flying the *tricolore*. 'The French,' Pearson writes in his memoirs, '...became more negative as the summer went on ... I wired Georges Vanier,* our Ambas-

---

*   See *In Defence of Canada* III, 38-40.

sador in Paris: "There is, I think, a real danger of the whole project being wrecked." So I told him to talk some sense into his French friends who, of all people, should be the most enthusiastic about an Atlantic security system."[60] Among the points Pearson suggested to Vanier that he might make were the following.

The French, particularly from their experience in the last war, must be worried by the possibility that if war should break out they will have little or no say in the making of the larger political and strategic decisions by the Western allies. The conclusion of a North Atlantic Treaty would make it possible to set up formal international bodies, not only for making plans for preventing war, but also for making plans for the waging of war. The establishment in peace time of these bodies would help ensure that in the event of war France and other Western European countries had a say in the making of the larger political and strategic decisions.

I know it is easier for someone reared in the British constitutional tradition to accept imprecision in a matter of this kind than it is for a Frenchman. However, I hope the French will realize that a North Atlantic treaty, even if it is not as precise as they would like it to be, will create a new living international institution which will have within itself possibilities of growth and of adaptation to changing conditions. The North Atlantic community is a real commonwealth of nations which share the same democratic and cultural institutions. If a movement towards its political and economic unification can be started this year, none of us can forecast the extent of the unity which may exist five, ten, or fifteen years from now.[61]

By 9 September, the Working Group had finally produced a document which 'represents ... an agreed statement on the nature of the problems discussed and the steps which might be practicable to meet them.'[62] The document, subsequently referred to as 'the Washington Paper,' contained as its penultimate paragraph the following statement.

The Canadian representatives emphasized the importance which they attached to provisions, in any treaty which might be concluded, for the encouragement of cooperation in fields other than security. Such cooperation would contribute directly to security. In other words, they felt that the purpose of a treaty should be not merely negative and that it should create the dynamic counterattraction of a free, prosperous and progressive society as opposed to the society of the Communist world. The treaty should provide a basis for the organization of an overwhelming preponderance of moral, economic and military force and a sufficient degree of unity to assure that this preponderance of force may be so used as to guarantee that the free nations will not be defeated one by one.[63]

At the seventh and final meeting of the Exploratory Talks on Security held the next day, Hume Wrong stated that when 'commending consideration of the project to the Canadian Government,' he intended

to express his firm conviction that if a pact along the lines of that currently under discussion had existed in the later 1930s, there would have been no war in 1939, and that a similar pact probably would have prevented the outbreak of war that began in 1914. Consideration of what horrors the world might have avoided, he believed, sharply underlined the enormous significance of what this present group was attempting to achieve. If a pact of this nature would have deterred Hitler, he continued, it would certainly be likely to have a strongly deterrent effect on the leaders of Russia; Hitler was a fanatic with a mission, but the Marxists were under no such dictates of urgency, since their very ideology required them to refrain at a given time from taking any action which might prejudice the eventual overthrow of capitalism. He therefore hoped that the governments represented at this table would eagerly pursue the project outlined in the paper, despite the other manifold preoccupations which required immediate attention. Some of these preoccupations, in fact, would be more easily dealt with once the framework of a North Atlantic system had been created. Mr Wrong believed that one of the greatest advantages which the creation of such a system would bring would be the attainment of certainty, and particularly of continuing certainty about the long-term position of the United States as a partner in a North Atlantic security system; in his judgment this alone far outweighed whatever new risks might conceivably arise from the conclusion of the pact.[64]

This statement had not been delivered on the spur of the moment. 'I had had it in mind for some time,' Hume Wrong told L.B. Pearson, 'to speak with a good deal of emphasis on this ... in the hope that my colleagues in referring the matter to their governments would not confine themselves to an analysis of the document and the means whereby it was produced, but would also seek to put the proposals in a broader setting. I think that I was at least partially successful,' Wrong added, 'since the Belgian, French and British ambassadors are including my statement in their telegraphic reports to their governments.' (The Belgian ambassador also requested that Wrong's statement be included in the minutes of the meeting, which was done.) 'Mr Hickerson also greeted it enthusiastically,' Wrong reported, 'and said that he agreed with every word. Mr Bonnet, to whom it was really addressed, was not so responsive.'[65]

Early in October 1948, the Cabinet Defence Committee considered the Washington Paper, and authorized L.B. Pearson to recommend to the Cabinet that the government inform the other parties to the Exploratory Talks on Security that Canada was ready 'to enter into a Treaty ... along the general lines of the document of September 9, 1948.'[66] Pearson's memorandum embodying this recommendation – his first ministerial representation to Cabinet – was submitted on 4 October. It contained the following paragraph.

The project for a North Atlantic Treaty, as set forth in the document of September 9, would appear to meet the objectives of Canadian policy as set forth during 1948 by the Canadian Government. By the membership of the United Kingdom, the United States, France and Benelux, it would provide the basis for the organization of an overwhelming preponderance of force – military, economic and moral – over the Soviet Union and a sufficient degree of unity to ensure that this preponderance of force may be so used as to guarantee that the free nations will not be defeated one by one. It is based on the concept that the Western European countries are our allies whose assistance we need to defend ourselves. It carries out the principle of a pooling of risks, of resources, and of combined control over policy. It establishes a constitutional basis for a devolution of power in peace and war from the Grand Alliance to its organs and agents, as compared with the arrogation of power by the Big Two or the Big Three in the last war...

The paragraph concluded with the words used in Pearson's message to Vanier on 13 August to point out that the proposed alliance would be a 'real commonwealth of nations' with a capacity for growth and adaptation such that no one could foresee the degree of unity it might in time attain.[67]

In the interests of secrecy, the Cabinet had not been kept informed of the intergovernmental discussion which had been in progress since March 1948. Its members may well have been startled by the content of the document which came unexpectedly before them. 'My memorandum was given a close examination by my colleagues and a vigorous discussion took place,' L.B. Pearson recalls cryptically, 'since it represented a highly important change in Canadian foreign policy. Agreement was given and our decision was then conveyed to the other governments.'*

The next step after the decision to negotiate a North Atlantic treaty for Canada to sign was to prepare instructions for Canada's negotiator. In charge of the preparation of instructions would be Escott Reid; in charge of the negotiating would be Hume Wrong. The exercise renewed the conflict between the two officials at a more acrimonious level.

---

* *Mike* II, 54. It is regrettable that the Prime Minister was not present at this meeting to provide in his diary a fuller version of this 'vigorous discussion' than Pearson's reticent account. Mackenzie King had gone to London, where illness prevented his attending the Prime Ministers' Conference there. On 30 October – a fortnight before the old man's long reign came to its end in resignation – Pearson visited King at his hotel. The Prime Minister's final counsel on national security policy embodies the convictions of a lifetime.

> I spoke to him about Claxton's ... continuous references to Russia and our preparations for war against Russia. Said I thought he should use general terms of our wishing to do our part with other nations in being prepared against aggression from whatever source it might come etc. Claxton was really helping to focus Russia's enmity on Canada. I feel there is great danger of this in the way some other policies are being handled. I do not like Canada attempting to assume position and take on responsibilities greater than those which belong to the US and the UK, not to speak of other nations...

Quoted in *Record* IV, 426.

As soon as the Cabinet agreed that Canada should negotiate on the basis of the Washington Paper of 9 September, Escott Reid began preparing a set of draft instructions, 'drawn up in such a way as to make it possible to circulate it to the other governments participating in the Washington talks.' Reid's first effort was dated 7 October 1948; his second, dated 26 October, was revised in the light of Wrong's comments on the first; his third, dated 6 November, was revised in the light of Pearson's comments on the second. The third edition had grown into a memorandum of thirty-six paragraphs, and the end was not in sight. Reid's draft drew hostile responses from Norman Robertson at London and from Hume Wrong at Washington. 'In general I think your paper is written in larger language than is appropriate or required,' Robertson cabled tartly on 9 November. 'I see no need for rhetoric in a secret working paper for circulation to governments which, when they meet together, will have already agreed on the main objectives. ... Specifically, I would cut out all the three-decker phrases ... most of the double-barrelled ones, and any remaining echoes from the Anglican prayer book' – a reference to the assertion in Reid's third draft that 'the North Atlantic Pact must be ... the outward and visible signs of a new inward and spiritual unity and purpose in the Western world.' Reid had wanted to dispense with diplomatic jargon. 'Because the Treaty should be a human and compelling document, calculated to strike the imagination of the peoples of the Free World, it is important that every effort be made to write it in simple, every-day language understandable by the ordinary man. This means that ancient forms and terms should be avoided.'[68] Robertson would have none of this. 'I fear you still have your phobia about lawyers' jargon,' he responded tartly. 'It is hackneyed, but it often helps precise statement; I see no need to work in sub-crusades for basic English and simplified spelling with the principal object of getting the countries around the North Atlantic to combine their strength for their security.' The paragraphs on 'The Treaty as a Basis for an Ideological Counter-Offensive,' arguing that the 'North Atlantic Treaty should provide a basis ... for what might be called a "spiritual mobilization" of the liberal democracies ... to counter the demoralizing and insidious propaganda weapons of Soviet diplomacy,' Robertson declared he did not like at all. 'I do not ... think that they belong in a document of this kind. ... I think the argument of these three paragraphs could be safely left to Walter Lippmann and Dorothy Thompson rather than spelled out in a communication from the Canadian Government to the other Governments taking part in the discussions.'[69]

Hume Wrong was if anything more critical than Robertson of Reid's third draft: he acknowledged that his comments were 'severe.' He considered that it would be 'a mistake to commit the Canadian Government to support most of the positions taken. ... Put the ideology of the treaty in the preamble where it belongs ... and let the rest be put in as direct language as we can find, without frills or use of phrases such as North Atlantic Community, North Atlantic Assembly, or free world in capitals. Some of your phraseology,' Wrong added, 'seems designed to establish a semi-commitment to set up a super-state. Nothing would more surely bring about the rejection of the whole project. ... These suggestions,' Wrong commented on the paragraphs in Reid's draft proposing North Atlantic institutions, '...have no chance of acceptance and ... might endanger United States ratification of the treaty if they were accepted. I should omit them altogether. They are not really comments on the Washington proposals of September 9th. Diplomatic papers should err on the side of understatement, particularly at this stage of an important and tricky negotiation. ... I repeat, we are making an alliance not a federation...' Like Robertson, Wrong took exception to the parts of Reid's draft designed to make the treaty into an instrument of counter-propaganda. 'Cut them out, as they are material for a speech, not a contribution to a negotiation.'[70]

Bloodied but unbowed, Reid returned to his drafting board. Another version emerged, and then still another. Reid sent the latter to L.S. St Laurent on 15 November – the day St Laurent became Prime Minister. 'I enclose for your consideration and if you agree, for submission to the Cabinet, a draft dated November 14 of a statement of Canadian views. ... This is the fifth draft...'[71]

Reid had gone over the head of the Ambassador at Washington, but he could not go behind his back. Hume Wrong had seen the draft of 14 November, and he did not like it any better than its predecessors. 'I note that it keeps growing longer instead of shorter,' Wrong commented in evident irritation, 'and I think it should be cut down sharply.' He had no use for the economic and cultural agencies which Reid's draft instructions urged should be created; these would only 'create confusion and get in the way of effective work by existing amenities.' Nor did he see any need for Reid's 'deliberative body,' a North Atlantic parliament. 'Surely the Council ought to deliberate as well as decide. We have too many international agencies already.' There followed this appeal.

I am most anxious at this stage that we should stick to the central purpose in these negotiations, which is, put bluntly, the creation of a military alliance encircling the North Atlantic. The numerous omissions I suggest are designed to avoid confusion of the issue and to facilitate rapid negotiation. If we pushed hard for all the proposals in your draft, we would secure no support at all in many cases, and the

greater the support we get for some of them the more protracted would the negotiation be. If we put forward a project like your draft treaty and it was seriously
considered, the negotiation would last at least until midsummer.[72]

The two officials were now close to showdown. Escott Reid at once
took his case to his Minister. 'I received yesterday from Wrong a somewhat disturbing teletype,' he cabled to L.B. Pearson (who was then in
Paris), 'in which he took the line that we ought to "stick to the central
purpose" in the forthcoming discussions, which is "the creation of a military alliance encircling the North Atlantic" and, for this reason, he made
a number of suggestions, among which were the deletion of references, in
the draft statement of preliminary Canadian views, to economic and social
co-operation and so on.' Reid told Pearson that he had prepared a reply to
Wrong's message. 'I will not, repeat, not, send [it] off until I hear from
you...'[73]

Reid heard first not from Pearson but from A.D.P. Heeney, who was
soon to become Under Secretary of State for External Affairs (a position
then held by Reid in an acting capacity only) and so Reid's immediate
superior at the East Block.* Heeney's letter, possibly written at Pearson's
behest, was intended both to mollify Reid and to head him off. 'An able
document,' was his tactful if patronizing opening comment on the set of
draft instructions. 'It is, however, my perhaps unreasonable opinion that
it is too complete at this stage and that it would be preferable to leave out
much of the detail at least until the Washington discussions have got
under way again.' As Secretary to the Cabinet, Heeney stressed the
importance of not making ministers feel that they were being pushed or
rushed.

There is absolutely no chance of the Cabinet deciding next week, even tentatively,
upon more than the most important general principles of the kind of treaty they
would be prepared to recommend to Parliament. The Cabinet have already gone
some distance in accepting for further discussion the Washington document of
September 9th. I think they should not be asked to go much further until we have
some idea of what the other governments are likely to do.

It is felt, I know, that it would be helpful tactically if Wrong could be given, before
the talks resume, the kind of detailed guidance which would enable him to circulate early in the talks a Canadian draft. I simply do not believe that authority for
this can be obtained, and I am not sure that it should.

---

* This transition contained seeds of discord, but none seem to have sprouted. 'I was
   very much an innocent in diplomacy and had a great deal to learn,' Heeney engagingly
   confessed later. 'I don't suppose that many have had a more concentrated or more
   sympathetic crash course in diplomacy than I received those first few months at the
   hands of Escott Reid...' Arnold Heeney, *The Things that are Caesar's: The Memoirs of a
   Canadian Public Servant* (Toronto 1972), 97.

It may turn out that we shall be substantial contributors to the North Atlantic pool because of our position and resources, but we should not take too leading a part in the negotiations until we have got more definite indication of what our treaty obligations are to be in men, money and materials. There is, in my view, real danger that we may be open to the charge of speaking loudly but carrying a pretty small twig...

Heeney granted that his comments were 'almost wholly negative. Not that I am unenthusiastic about the "crusade" – quite the contrary. But I am far from being convinced that the Canadian people have as yet by any means such a clear and specific opinion upon the objectives of the treaty as is indicated in paragraph 10 of the draft memorandum of November 15th to the Prime Minister.'[74] (In that paragraph, Reid had proposed that Canada should press for the inclusion in the treaty of provisions for creating not only a consultative council but also a North Atlantic Council of Defence Ministers, a North Atlantic Chiefs of Staff Committee, a North Atlantic Commanders-in-Chief Committee, and a North Atlantic Military Supply Board. All these institutions, if under other names, would in time appear; but in 1948 their time had not yet come.)

Escott Reid now had arrayed against his set of draft instructions the three most influential officials of the Department of External Affairs – Hume Wrong, Norman Robertson, and Arnold Heeney. But policy was for the Minister to decide. On 21 November, Reid was gratified to receive from Pearson a message of support. 'I think that on the whole this is an impressive document,' Pearson stated of the set of draft instructions, 'and the sooner it gets to Washington the better.'[75] Reid's gratification may have been cut short by a further message from Pearson the following day: 'In view of the likelihood that Washington talks may not begin for another fortnight, I think Atlantic treaty papers should not be circulated to the Cabinet at its meeting on Wednesday. You will appreciate that in the rush of Assembly business I have not had time to think over the issues involved as thoroughly as I should have liked to do. I am, therefore, glad of the opportunity of this delay to give these questions the fuller and more detailed consideration they deserve and which now seems possible.'[76] Under the circumstances, Reid deemed it prudent not to send the cable to Hume Wrong that he had composed two days before. That message had said in part:

I had hoped that I had made it clear ... that what I had been trying to do is not to make proposals for the kind of treaty which I want, but to make proposals for the kind of treaty which the Canadian Government wants. My own view as to the kind of treaty which I would like to see drawn up as soon as possible is set forth in my draft treaty of a year ago.

My reading of the statements made publicly by the Canadian Government leads me inevitably to the conclusion that the Canadian Government would not be satisfied with the mere creation ... of "a military alliance"...

It would seem to me, therefore, that unless you would desire, at this late date, to ask me to put before the Prime Minister a message from you setting forth your reasons why you think his policy is mistaken, and ask him to reconsider the basis of his policy, there is no alternative but for us to use our best efforts in discussions in Washington and through normal diplomatic channels to secure the kind of treaty which Mr St Laurent has declared that he wants.

...Unless this is done, an important section of Canadian opinion may feel that the Canadian Government has failed in what Mr St Laurent has called its "crusade"...[77]

It was well for the morale and harmony of the policy community that this message was never sent. Its prospective recipient realized soon enough that his criticism of Reid's set of draft instructions had been intemperate, and offered its author a guarded apology: 'I regret that my message to you of November 19th was so abruptly worded. It was dictated in a great hurry just before leaving to catch a train...' All the same, Hume Wrong did not retract its substance. 'The purpose of the negotiation,' Wrong yet again reminded Reid, 'is to tie up the United States with the defence of Western Europe, and no one but ourselves will be much impressed by Canadian electoral considerations. ... Your aim seems to be wholly to merge the Western Union movement in a North Atlantic Union, and this will not go down here.'[78]

During the next week, Reid's draft was gone over by both L.B. Pearson and Brooke Claxton, and revised in the light of their comments. 'The Commentary, as revised, is now reduced to eight pages,' Reid informed Pearson after a sixth and final go at it. 'Wrong ... said that he considered it to be "very respectable," which is high praise from him.'[79] The document was considered by the Cabinet on 1 December, and approved in its entirety except for the paragraph on Portugal's membership. That paragraph had read:

10 All the contracting states should be able to subscribe to the principles of democracy, personal freedom and political liberty. There will be difficulty in reconciling these principles with Portuguese membership in the Organization. Only the most important strategic considerations can therefore justify Portugal's inclusion.[80]

The Cabinet decided to delete this paragraph from the commentary. If the question of Portugal's admission were to come up during the negotiations, the Canadian representative was to state that his government did not wish to oppose it on purely ideological grounds. The draft thus amended was in its final form. It was called, simply, 'Commentary on the Washington Paper of September 9, 1948,' and dated 6 December 1948. (Its text is printed below as Document 2.) The paper was circulated to the other delegations at Washington on 14 December.

No sooner had Hume Wrong got down to the business at hand of the intergovernmental discussions which had resumed on 10 December than the 'feud' between himself and Escott Reid flared up once more. Reid had hit upon the idea of supplying Wrong with supplementary instructions. For Wrong, 'supplying' meant 'saddling,' and that he did not want. 'I doubt whether much in the way of supplementary instructions is really needed,' he cabled to Reid on 11 December, 'and I hope that I shall not receive a very lengthy and detailed document which would limit my capacity in seeking to compromise conflicting views of the other participants. ... I do not wish to have a long debate by teletype on what should go into the instructions while simultaneously engaged in the actual negotiations...'[81] Reid remained adamant and once more appealed to the Minister. 'I think there would be some merit in sending supplementary instructions,' he wrote to Pearson. 'First, it would be useful for the record. Secondly, it would make our position clear on certain points which will arise...'[82] In the event, no supplementary instructions were sent and no debate on them ensued; instead, a letter drafted by Reid, to be signed by Pearson, was prepared for Wrong's 'information and guidance during the forthcoming discussions.' Reid wrote later: 'Pearson did not sign it and I believed at the time that he had not given it to Wrong.' However, Reid subsequently discovered that when Pearson saw Wrong in New York on 29 December 1948, 'he gave him this letter unsigned and "for information".'[83] Such a document, presented in such a way, fell considerably short of the status of 'supplementary instructions'; Wrong had won that round.*

'We agreed on most aspects of Canadian foreign policy, but disagreed fundamentally on the North Atlantic Treaty.'[84] So Escott Reid would state later of his troubled relationship with his colleague. Three reasons for their disagreement may be discerned.

---

* Pearson, as well as Wrong, seems to have been put off by Reid's tenacity. In a first draft of his memoirs, he used the words 'almost feverish' to describe Reid's efforts 'to bring into being the perfect North Atlantic Treaty'; in the published memoirs those words are deleted but the words 'single-minded intensity' are not. See *Mike* II, 59; Reid, *Time of Fear and Hope*, 276 (note for 228). '[O]ne can well imagine,' writes Lord Gladwyn, 'that hard-worked and competent politician, busy presiding over the General Assembly of the United Nations, being confronted by an admirably argued, if perhaps rather long, disquisition on the exact significance of a word in Article 2 demanding an immediate reply.' Lord Gladwyn, review of *Time of Fear and Hope*, *International Journal*, XXXIII, 1, Winter 1977-8, 261.

One is surely temperament. Wrong and Reid were too much alike to work in harmony – each self-confident, sure of his judgement, tenacious in debate, proud of his career. In Reid's case these traits were fortified by those of zeal and perfectionism with which, as he came later to admit, he was overly endowed and to which he ascribed his inability to win Wrong over to his views. 'I would have suffered fewer disappointments and frustrations and accomplished more if I had played my cards better,' Reid confesses in his study of the making of the North Atlantic Treaty. 'I should not have disclosed that my ambitions for the North Atlantic alliance were so far-reaching. This aroused opposition. ... I would have been more effective if I had not given the impression that my intensity was almost feverish.'[85]

Their disagreement was as well the product of perspective. Reid looked out from headquarters, Wrong from in the field. Reid was more attuned than Wrong (or believed himself to be) to the play of politics in Canada; Wrong was preoccupied with the play of politics in Washington, and tended to exaggerate (or so Reid believed) the forces there opposed to a North Atlantic treaty – let alone to a North Atlantic Community. Reid later speculated that Wrong's dual role as Ambassador at Washington and negotiator of the North Atlantic treaty was harmful for the attainment of Canadian objectives.*

More important in accounting for the differences of opinion between Hume Wrong and Escott Reid than their respective temperaments and perspectives is that they desired of the negotiations differing results.

Hume Wrong wanted the negotiations to produce a treaty which would deter armed attack on Western Europe by 'the creation of a military alli-

---

*   Reid wrote to Pearson on 30 August 1972:

> Could you somewhere discuss a thesis of mine that ambassadors in a capital, and especially ambassadors in the capital of an important power, should never be used in multilateral negotiations on an issue which is important to the country to which they are accredited, and where the views of the government to which they are accredited are likely to be at variance on important points with the views of their own government. Ambassadors to the US, for example, are peculiarly subject to pressure by the US: they have other fish to fry than the multilateral negotiations; they don't want to damage their good relations with the President or the State Department by being tough in the multilateral negotiations...

Quoted in Reid, 'Canada and the Creation of the North Atlantic Alliance, 1948-1949,' in Michael G. Fry (ed.), *Freedom and Change: Essays in Honour of Lester B. Pearson* (Toronto 1975), 130. 'When I said this to Pearson,' Reid explained, 'I was ... thinking of Wrong's decision not to press our maximum demands ... I am confident he did not [use] the often blunt language of the telegrams from Ottawa.' *Ibid.*, 130-1, 131n. Pearson picked up Reid's suggestion and wrote in his memoirs: 'Hume Wrong's job as our Ambassador in Washington was considerably complicated by his having to pursue a Canadian line in these multilateral negotiations which was often at variance with that of the United States.' *Mike* II, 54.

ance encircling the North Atlantic.' What was needed was the deterrent of a force in being, and Wrong toiled 'forcefully and elegantly' (it is Reid's own gracious tribute) to draft a treaty that would make decision-makers in Moscow think twice before attacking. If such a treaty required a preamble at all, two words (as The Netherlands' ambassador had wittily suggested) would suffice: 'Dear Joe.'

Escott Reid wanted the negotiations to produce a treaty which would render ineffective Soviet efforts at subversion and disruption by bringing about 'a "spiritual mobilization" of the liberal democracies.' The alliance would be military, but should be more than merely military. The treaty should be aimed as much at Western publics as at Stalin. Its articles should be so designed as to capture the imagination and steel the resolve of scores of millions of people, so drafted as to dispel their fears and raise their hopes. If two words must suffice for a preamble to such a treaty, they would be 'Fellow democrats.'

These two differing objectives were by no means incompatible: a treaty might be and indeed was contrived which aimed at both. But the treaty would emphasize one more than the other, and the 'Dear Joe' conception prevailed in the end.

While the North Atlantic Treaty bears the imprint of both Wrong's labours and Reid's, the latter believed his to have been largely unavailing. 'My chief disappointment about the results of the negotiations on the treaty,' Reid would write in later years,

was that the non-military provisions of the treaty were weaker than what I had hoped for and what I believed were needed. I wanted comprehensive provisions on economic, social and cultural co-operation and the promotion of democracy within the member states. I did not want Portugal and Italy in the alliance or to have the pledge in the treaty cover Algeria. I wanted a North Atlantic Parliament. I wanted the members of the alliance to agree to refer to the International Court of Justice all disputes between them over existing legal rights. I wanted the treaty to make clear that the military organs of the alliance, in peace and war, were responsible to the North Atlantic Council. I wanted the treaty to be couched in the form of a constitution for the North Atlantic community ... and to be written in language capable of inspiring the citizens of the member states. ... I wanted the treaty to be a long first step in the direction of a close union of the North Atlantic countries.

This was a lot to ask for – in the event, too much. 'The treaty included provisions on economic and social co-operation and on the promotion of democracy,' Reid reflected in retirement, 'though these provisions were not as far-reaching as I wanted them to be. The language of the treaty went some way to meet my wishes. For the rest, my efforts were abortive either because of opposition within the Canadian group which was directly concerned with the negotiations' – an obvious reference to his sparring partner in Washington* – 'or because of lack of support or opposition from the other countries participating in the negotiations.'[86] The reader of Reid's account of the making of the North Atlantic Treaty is left in no doubt that its author considered the first of these two sources of opposition to have been the more obstructive.

THE 'CANADIAN ARTICLE' AND ITS ENEMIES

On 13 December 1948, at the second meeting of the Exploratory Talks on Security that had resumed in Washington on 10 December (it is recorded as the ninth meeting, following the eighth held on 10 September), Hume Wrong presented a 'general outline of the views of the Canadian Government.' Wrong's statement (as recorded in US minutes) touched on three main problems that would preoccupy the government throughout the remainder of the negotiations over the next four months: the problem of the pledge; the problem of membership (and the associated issue of the treaty area); above all, the problem of 'general welfare.'

The issue of the pledge had from Canada's standpoint turned out badly during the Tripartite Talks of the preceding March. Wrong accordingly led off by stating that 'The Canadian Government would like to see the commitments clause in the treaty made as definite as possible, which probably meant as close as possible to the formula used in the Brussels Treaty. This was desirable both in order to achieve as exact a definition as possible of the nature of the obligation and in order to prevent the Soviet countries from belittling the importance of the undertaking in the Pact.' Wrong also stated that 'there should, if possible, be no guarantee without reciprocity.'

As to membership, Wrong continued, 'the Canadian Government ... would like the original members of the North Atlantic Pact to include Norway, Denmark, Sweden, Iceland and Ireland,' in addition to the seven governments present at the meeting, 'and wished every effort to be made to persuade these countries to join as full members. Italy ... raised special problems requiring further discussion; the Canadian Government had no pat solution for Italy.'

---

*   'I was ... an opponent of Escott Reid and seem to have had an ally in Hume Wrong...' Gladwyn, *op. cit.*, 255. 'Wrong was not much in sympathy with Reid's views ... or with the intensity of his expression thereof...' *Mike* II, 57.

The Ambassador then turned to what by this time his colleagues may have regarded as Canada's hobby-horse (it was not, as has been shown, his own).

The Canadian Government continued to attach a good deal of importance to including in the treaty some general provision which would encourage economic and social collaboration between the members. ... The Canadian Government did not wish to advocate the establishment of new agencies in this field between the North Atlantic countries, but they did believe that the Treaty should be something more than a defense treaty or a defensive military alliance. The idea of the treaty was based on a community of principles and ideas, and the Canadian Government wished this to be recognized in the body of the treaty rather than only by a phrase in the preamble. The proposal made in the third article of the annex of the Washington paper would meet the Canadian views.* Mr Wrong said that recent experience had shown that if the resources of different countries in war are .to be pooled, it is necessary to have close collaboration between the economic systems of the countries concerned. From the point of view of defense alone, therefore, he thought the treaty should encourage, in explicit terms, economic collaboration.[87]

How did these three negotiating positions fare during the fifteen weeks to follow before a North Atlantic treaty was signed?

The United States met in two respects the demands of the European and Canadian participants in the Exploratory Talks concerning the pledge. No longer would the Americans insist that the commitment article explicitly state the right of each signatory to determine for itself if an armed attack had occurred. And they agreed that the pledge should include a reference to the provision of military assistance. Both these desiderata appeared in Article 5, paragraph 1, of the Draft Treaty which a so-called International Working Group presented to the Ambassadors on Christmas Eve.

1 The Parties agree that an armed attack against one or more of them occurring within the area defined below shall be considered an attack against them all: and consequently that, if such armed attack occurs, each of them, in exercise of the right of individual or collective self-defense recognized by Article 51 of the Charter of the United Nations, will assist the party or parties so attacked by taking

---

* The Annex to the Washington Paper of 9 September 1948 was in the form of an 'Outline of Provisions Which Might Be Suitable for Inclusion in a North Atlantic Security Pact.' The third of such provisions was as follows:

3 Provision for the encouragement of efforts between any or all of the parties to promote the general welfare through collaboration in the economic, social and cultural fields.

Foreign Relations of the United States, 1948, III, *Western Europe* (Washington, DC 1974), 246.

forthwith such military or other action, individually and in concert with the other Parties, *as may be necessary to restore and assure the security of the North Atlantic area* [author's italics].[88]

The italicized clause represents the price which the United States delegation had charged the other participants for agreeing to their two demands for strengthening the pledge. The change had been made to suit the US Joint Chiefs of Staff, who had stressed, in the words of General A.M. Gruenther, the 'necessity for being entirely clear that no commitment to aid a state, victim of attack, should require that aid should be delivered locally.'[89] Hume Wrong explained the change to Ottawa. 'If, for example, Sweden became a party and was invaded by Russia, the agreement must not state or imply a commitment to send forces to Sweden. The commitment would be to defeat Russia according to the best strategic concept that could be devised. The offensive against Russia, however, should be undertaken anywhere and in any way that seemed best to the high command.'[90] That made sense to the Canadians – even if the representative of a small and exposed West European country might glumly reflect that it postponed the day of its eventual liberation. Escott Reid would later describe the insistence on the point by the US Joint Chiefs of Staff as 'scrupulous, perhaps excessively so.'[91]

From the Canadian standpoint, the wording of the pledge was satisfactory. It soon enough was placed in jeopardy. On 20 January 1949, the United States acquired a new Secretary of State. Dean Acheson took over from Robert Lovett, who had been Acting Secretary, the chairmanship of the Ambassadors' Committee. Acheson's first move in that capacity was to sound out US senatorial opinion on the Draft Treaty of 24 December. He discussed the Draft Treaty with Senator Tom Connally, the new Chairman of the Foreign Relations Committee, and Senator Arthur Vandenberg, now reduced to its ranking Republican member, on 3 and 5 February 1949. Among the articles to which the senators took strong exception was that dealing with the pledge.

On 8 February, at the twelfth meeting of the Exploratory Talks in Washington, the US Secretary of State explained to the six ambassadors the reasons for the senators' displeasure. 'The Senators thought that the language used gave an impression of crescendo and haste which perhaps overstated the problem,' Dean Acheson delicately put it. 'It implied that the United States was rushing into some kind of automatic commitment. The Senators wanted the Pact to avoid overstatement or rhetoric. There would be preliminary talks, there would be plans, but the ultimate action would depend upon the decision of each member country and would have to be in accordance with international and moral obligations. ... [I]t was a question of finding more neutral language than that contained in the present draft.'[92]

Here loomed a major setback to the attainment of a major Canadian objective. Hume Wrong did not let it pass unchallenged. He stated that his government had become impatient at the delay in producing a treaty. 'The negotiations had aroused considerable public interest' – so the US minutes of the meeting records Wrong's intervention – 'and there was the danger that those opposed would gain adherents. Opposition was already beginning to increase to some degree in Canada.'* Wrong then turned to the proposed alteration of the pledge. 'The Canadian Government was in favor of the present wording of Article 5 and would be sorry to see any change which might give rise to the idea that it had been watered down. In particular, he felt it desirable to retain, if possible, a reference to military action. If the negotiations had just been starting, it might have been possible to avoid such a reference. But such a change of wording after so much had appeared in the press about the present wording would cause difficulties and might be of considerable advantage to Soviet propaganda.'[93] Wrong's own briefer account of his statement is as follows. 'When it came to my turn to speak,' he cabled Pearson on 9 February,

I said that while everybody agreed that the State Department must carry the Senate along with it the rest of us were under pressure from our own governments to get something done and were hearing of the rise of opposition to the Treaty in some quarters. I said that the Canadian Government liked the language of Article 5 and wanted to keep the reference to military action. I did not think the language could be watered down very much because the public already knows too much about the language of this Article for us to let it appear that we have weakened the obligation...[94]

In a further cable to Ottawa next day, Hume Wrong expressed his opinion that 'the violence of the reaction of the two senators to the language of the draft pledge might have been caused in part by their dislike of Acheson's incisive style when he discussed the pledge with them.'[95] Commenting on this interpretation years later, Escott Reid believed it to

---

* Apart from the strident campaign against Canada's entering a security pact being mounted by the Labor Progressive (Communist) Party, and the shrill vendetta conducted in the columns of *Le Devoir*, there was in fact little significant public opposition to the project. See above, 52-8. Wrong was doubtless aware of this, and invoked a fictive opposition as a negotiating ploy. 'The year-long discussions on the North Atlantic treaty threw light on the methods governments use in efforts to strengthen their hands in intergovernmental discussions. There is the tough guy waiting in the back room; and this "person" can be the Senate, Cabinet, Parliament, etcetera.' Escott Reid, *Time of Fear and Hope*, 58. Or public opinion.

have been correct. 'Acheson was not at that time arrogant of heart and mind but he was sometimes arrogant of expression and it was an arrogance of expression that irritated the ambassadors when he discussed the pledge with them on February 8,' Reid writes in his account of the making of the North Atlantic Treaty.

The draft of the pledge on which Acheson was commenting had been agreed to unanimously on December 24 for submission to the governments. This agreement had come after long debate. The Ambassador of Canada had been working on the pledge for almost 11 months of intergovernmental discussions. ... Every word in the draft had been weighed on delicate balances by the ambassadors and their governments. Acheson was the new boy at the negotiating table; this was his first appearance there. ... Yet he spoke to the ambassadors not as a neophyte but as a teacher lecturing not very intelligent students.[96]

Acheson was not part of the solution, he was part of the problem.

On 14 February, 'the crisis over the pledge was greatly exacerbated by a storm which suddenly burst out on the floor of the Senate.'[97] An isolationist senator goaded Connally into an extemporaneous outburst which was probably ill considered and certainly intemperate. Connally declared that he was against 'giving carte blanche assurances...,' that he did not believe that the United States should 'blindfold ourselves and make a commitment now to enter every war that may occur in the next 10 years, and send our boys and resources to Europe to fight,' that the American people 'cannot ... be Sir Galahads, and every time we hear a gun fired plunge into war and take sides without knowing what we are doing, and without knowing the issues involved. ... [T]here are many people, and we have found them in government and elsewhere, who would favour automatically going to war, which would mean letting European nations declare war and letting us fight.'[98] After this outburst – whether as a result of it or by previous arrangement is not clear – Connally and Vandenberg went to the US State Department for an audience with Dean Acheson. The US minutes of that meeting record that 'Connally even questioned the advisability of a statement in Article 5 that an attack on one would be considered an attack on all. He preferred that this should read "an attack on one would be regarded as a threat to the peace of all".' Vandenberg, while not going so far as Connally on that point, went even further on others: he 'was most insistent ... that it should be made plain that the determination of the type of action should be a matter for individual determination and also that the word "military" should be omitted.'[99]

Should the Senators prevail, Canada's position on the pledge would be, quite simply, shredded. 'If the type of reservation is written into the treaty which Senator Connally's remarks would imply,' Hume Wrong reported of the US Senate exchange, which had made that chamber resonate to the kind of rhetoric which had not been heard there since 1940, 'it will, of course, seriously reduce the effectiveness of the treaty as a deterrent to aggression and will also assist Soviet propaganda in belittling the value of the pledge...'[100] And again: 'The worst feature of the debate ... was the denial by Connally and others that the signature of the treaty would create a moral obligation to go to war...'[101]

Neither the Ambassador nor the Government could have known of Connally's clarification of his remarks to Acheson, but the outburst in the Senate made headlines. The policy community at Ottawa was so disquieted that, for the first time, it canvassed the possibility that no treaty at all would be preferable to the only kind that Connally seemed to be prepared to countenance. This canvassing took place at the request of Hume Wrong who, on 16 February, asked for a restatement of Canada's views on the pledge which would leave him 'wide discretion in employing the statement.' Escott Reid drafted it, L.B. Pearson revised it, the Prime Minister approved it. 'If there is no satisfactory pledge in the Treaty,' the long despatch began,

and if that Treaty is interpreted by the Senate merely as a mechanism for getting the European states out of difficulties which really don't concern the USA directly, then its value is greatly reduced and we might have to re-examine our whole position. It might be that in the light of such re-examination we will be compelled to decide that the Canadian national interest involved in this kind of treaty interpreted in this way by US opinion is not sufficiently direct and immediate to warrant the government recommending to Parliament our adherence to it.

We would do this, of course, with the greatest regret, but we might, in the circumstances, conclude that it is better to have no treaty at all than to have a treaty which is so weak and ambiguous as to be meaningless and therefore mischievous, especially since the conclusion of such a treaty might render less likely the conclusion of a really effective arrangement in the future.

The over-riding purpose of the proposed treaty is to preserve peace. In our view, the only way to preserve peace today is to make clear to the Russians beyond shadow of doubt that, if they attack any one of the North Atlantic countries, all the other North Atlantic countries will immediately take action to defeat the aggressor. Two things are essential if we are to get people in this country behind a treaty. It must represent a sufficient concentration of force to prevent aggression, and it must give some reasonable assurance that this force can be quickly and effectively mobilized when required.

The treaty must make clear to the exposed countries in Western Europe that they are protected against Russian attack by the Russian knowledge that Russia will be defeated in the end if it attacks Western Europe, even though it may win the initial victories. Such a feeling of confidence in Western Europe would enable the work of economic reconstruction to proceed. This concept is so far removed from that put forward by Senator Connally that there doesn't seem to be much possibility of reconciling the two.

These purposes of the treaty are not going to be fulfilled by an undertaking which is so watered down that it does not create even a moral obligation to take effective action, but is put forward as a charitable donation from the United States. This is reducing the proposed North Atlantic Treaty to the level of a Kellogg-Briand peace pact.

It seems to us that the opponents both in Canada and in the United States of an "automatic commitment" to take action, subject, of course, to constitutional processes, are still thinking in the pre-war terms of the North American nations being producers and not consumers of security. They are not, in our opinion, thinking in realistic terms; for surely it is only realism to recognize that the Western European countries are allies whose assistance we in North America may well need in order to defend ourselves and our freedom. Today these Western European countries are more exposed to direct Russian attack than is North America. However, in ten years' time it may be that the first shock of an aggressive attack will be against the industrial centres of North America which are the arsenal of the whole Western world.

Is it not in the long-run interests of Canada and the United States to bind Western Europe to us in a close security arrangement so that if that attack should come the Western European nations will be in honour-bound to come to our assistance with all the forces at their disposal? A vague understanding in the treaty would presumably make it possible for the United Kingdom, France, Belgium and the Netherlands to remain neutral if the Soviet Union should attack the United States...[102]

This message reveals how deep was Ottawa's concern at the turn of events. It contains the Canadian government's ultimate threat: either the treaty would contain a pledge along the lines of the wording that had been agreed to by the Ambassadors on 24 December 1948, or the Canadian Government might decide not to sign a treaty at all. Its ambassador had authority to make the threat if he deemed fit.

In the event, the threat proved unnecessary. On 18 February, Secretary Acheson appeared before the US Senate Foreign Relations Committee and secured its tentative agreement to the 24 December draft of the pledge, with one major concession to the senators: a signatory would be obliged to take 'such action as it deems necessary, including the use of armed force,' rather than – as prescribed in the 24 December formula – 'such military or other action ... as may be necessary.' On 21 February, Hume Wrong reported to Ottawa that 'the changes in the situation here made it unnecessary for me to use a number of your arguments' – including, presumably, the threat that Canada might pick up her marbles and go home. On 25 February, at the thirteenth meeting of the Exploratory Talks, Wrong told his fellow ambassadors that while 'the Canadian

Government favoured the original language [of Article 5], or perhaps something even stronger ... in view of the problems that had been faced by the United States negotiators, he felt gratified that they had been able to restore a situation which looked seriously endangered only a week or ten days before.'[103]

Recollecting this episode in the tranquillity of retirement, the surviving Canadian participants recorded their satisfaction at the outcome. Escott Reid pronounced it 'a partial victory,' noting that the Canadian and West European governments could 'congratulate themselves that the pledge in the North Atlantic treaty was, on balance, stronger than the pledge in the Rio Treaty.'[104] L.B. Pearson likewise expressed this view. 'The key article dealing with the obligation for mutual assistance in case of aggression was satisfactory,' Pearson states in his memoirs. '[I]ndeed it went further than some Congressional leaders would accept. One or two changes, not of great substance, were made to remove that difficulty. The inclusion of the words "as it seems necessary" instead of "as may be necessary" in reference to action taken to assist the victim of aggression, made clear that it was the responsibility of the individual state to make that decision, as, indeed, it was to decide whether an aggression had in fact taken place. We could understand Congressional preoccupation with this point.'[105] (That understanding came more easily after two decades.) In an interview in 1970, Pearson talked of his feeling at the time.

I certainly felt on the basis of past experience that Article 5 should be a precise engagement to take part in a war, not mainly to declare war but to take part in it. I knew perfectly well, as a parliamentarian, that we couldn't constitutionally send troops out of the country without parliamentary approval but so far as the executive was concerned, I felt we had obligated ourselves to participate in war. I don't think the British felt that and I'm sure the article would appear to the Americans in a different way. What they were worried about was not initiating action against an aggressor but that somebody in the alliance, like Denmark or Norway, or a minor move against Berlin, might engage the US obligations under the Pact and they would find themselves in a major war...[106]

Article 5 of the North Atlantic Treaty was sufficiently oracular to permit politicians defending the pact against detractors to stress whichever element they chose – that of automatic response or that of discretion. Oddly enough, in the light of the history of its negotiation, American defenders chose to emphasize the automatic aspect, Canadian defenders to emphasize the discretionary. The American foreign minister, closely questioned by newspaper reporters as to whether the United States would be committed under the North Atlantic Treaty to go to war on behalf of a European ally, replied with some spirit: 'Decent people ... carried out their contracts. ... We have an international legal commitment here to do certain things. It was true nobody could force us to do it, but we would do what we contracted to do.'[107] The Canadian forerign minister was more cautious. 'Under this treaty, then,' L.B. Pearson told the House of Commons on 28 March 1948,

each North Atlantic nation declares that it will in future consider an armed attack against any one of its allies as an armed attack against its own territory. That does not mean that Canada would be automatically at war if one of our allies were attacked. ... I have heard no one suggest that the full weight of the North Atlantic alliance will be brought into play over some minor event of little importance. In whatever action is necessary, however, we agree to play our proper part in co-operation with the others to restore peace. This action on our part may be small or it may be great; it may be brief or it may be of long duration. We shall have to decide upon it in terms of the situation which makes it necessary and the end to be achieved.

To be properly understood, I suggest that the commitment under this article would be compared with others which Canada has been prepared to take. ... When we entered into war with Germany and Japan, the Canadian people accepted a commitment far more general, far more exacting, than those imposed by the terms of this treaty. The Charter of the United Nations also imposes on us an extensive commitment. ... So far as this Government is concerned, Mr Speaker, in view of a national emergency so grave as to call into force our commitments under this pact, it would immediately desire to consult parliament.[108]

Such a national emergency has not so far arisen, and the pledge of the North Atlantic Treaty's signatories has yet to be put to its test.

Who should be invited to become members of the security pact? By December 1948, it had become Canada's policy to exclude Italy and Portugal from the list of prospective invitees – although not to the extent of mounting a drive to keep them out.

The policy on Portugal is quickly and best told in Pearson's words. 'We ... worried about the inclusion of Portugal in a coalition of free democracies,' is how he put it in his memoirs, 'but accepted, reluctantly, the view of the Americans and British that strategic considerations must override ideological.'[109] An even more succinct explanation was offered by Pearson at the time. Escott Reid had written, in a memorandum of 26 October 1948: 'To invite Portugal to become an original member of the Alliance would seriously weaken its effectiveness as a basis for mobilizing an effective spiritual counterforce against Soviet aggression.' In the margin of Reid's memorandum, Pearson wrote: 'Surely we cannot insist on the exclusion of Portugal against US opposition.'[110] And that would settle that.

'... worn out by his long run ...' (25)
W.L. Mackenzie King
(Prime Minister)

'In the vanguard of the crusade ...' (59)
Louis S. St Laurent
(Secretary of State for External Affairs, Prime Minister)

'... North Atlantic seer ...' (187)
L.B. Pearson
(Under Secretary of State for External Affairs,
Secretary of State for External Affairs)

TOP '... deals with paper, and what quantities ... there are!' (123)
Brooke Claxton
(Minister of National Defence)

'Such were the crusaders' enemies.' (58)
Demonstration for a 'Peace Pact,' Toronto, c. 1948-9

'... occupational bias ... of wary frugality ...' (286)
Douglas Abbott
(Minister of Finance)

'... each ... tenacious in debate, proud of his career.' (104)

Escott Reid
(Assistant Under Secretary of State for External Affairs,
Acting Under Secretary of State for External Affairs,
Deputy Under Secretary of State for External Affairs)

Hume Wrong
(Ambassador to the United States)

OPPOSITE

TOP '... [W]ell-briefed, ... always in control ...' (37)
A.D.P. Heeney
(Secretary to the Cabinet, Under Secretary of State for External Affairs,
Permanent Representative, North Atlantic Council,
Ambassador to the United States)

'... King's "most trusted adviser" ...' (26)
J.W. Pickersgill
(Head of the Prime Minister's Office, Secretary to the Cabinet,
Clerk of the Privy Council)

TOP '... exceptionally sagacious ...' (67)
N.A. Robertson
(High Commissioner in the United Kingdom,
Clerk of the Privy Council,
Secretary to the Cabinet)

'... nothing if not wily.' (135)
Lt-Gen. Charles Foulkes
(Chief of the General Staff,
Chairman, Chiefs of Staff Committee)

The policy on Italy was less easily fixed. The Canadian government, in responding to the Washington Paper of 9 September 1948, had declared its opposition to Italy's membership. 'It would be difficult to support an invitation to Italy,' its commentary of 6 December had observed, '...since Italy not only does not fall within the North Atlantic region, but she could contribute little to the common pool of resources.' As an alternative to membership, the Canadian government had proposed some sort of special arrangement for Italy, perhaps one in which Italy would grant base facilities in exchange for a military guarantee.[111] The reasons for Canada's misgivings about Italian membership are more complex than those stated in the commentary of 6 December. They were subsequently elaborated by Escott Reid.

The main argument advanced against the inclusion of Italy was that Italy was not a North Atlantic country and if it became a member, it would be difficult to keep Greece and Turkey out; their admission would weaken the alliance by making it less homogeneous; commitments under the treaty would become extended and diffuse; and it would be more difficult to use the alliance as a chrysalis for a North Atlantic community. ... [T]he Canadian [government] also believed that the admission of Italy would weaken public support for the treaty...*

In addition, the Canadian government opposed Italy's membership lest that make it easier for France to press its case for the inclusion of her Mediterranean possessions in North Africa.

The Canadian position was explained by Hume Wrong at the tenth meeting of the Exploratory Talks on 22 December 1948. 'Canada did not think Italy should be a full partner in the North Atlantic Pact, but if that country should nevertheless become one, there would be a good case for including the Mediterranean coast of North Africa.' He hoped, however, that the European commitments could be limited to countries bordering on the North Atlantic.' Later in the discussion, Wrong returned to the issue of Italian membership, saying that while agreeing with the Americans and British that, whatever happened, Italy must not be left without protection, 'Canada had doubts about the advisability of including Italy as a full partner on geographical and political grounds.'[112] Wrong reported to Ottawa that he had 'taken the line that Italy should not be a party to the Treaty and that French North Africa should not be specified as part of the North Atlantic area. I have, however, expressed our attitude in terms which would permit our agreement to the inclusion of both Italy and

---

* Escott Reid, *Time of Fear and Hope*, 200. For this assessment of diminished public support for a treaty which included Italy, no explanation was proffered. Perhaps the government assumed that many Canadians would not welcome as an ally a country which had been so recently an enemy and – for Canadian soldiers – a theatre of war.

North Africa if it becomes evident that this is the only solution for which general acceptance can be secured. I propose,' he added, 'to resist strongly any suggestion that the North Atlantic group should give special assurances to Greece or Turkey, since I think that if we were to do more than promise to consult, if danger comes from that quarter, we should find that the obligations of the Pact would tend to become world-wide.'[113]

On 12 January 1949, the Ambassador of Italy called at the US State Department to request, formally, that his country be invited to participate in the alliance. This request complicated Canada's position. '[T]he complete exclusion of Italy from participation in the Pact would ... be much more difficult now than before,' Hume Wrong cabled from Washington on 15 January. 'If we continue to oppose the inclusion of Italy it would be well if we could offer some other alternative suggestion...'[114] On 17 January, L.B. Pearson replied: 'I still hope that it may be possible to refrain from accepting the Italian request for full membership and that Italy may be covered either by a declaration on under the special arrangements provision. ... You should not, however, oppose too strongly the admission of Italy.'[115] It was not necessary to sustain the opposition much longer. On 19 January it became known that the United States had switched from wanting to extend a military guarantee to a willingness to allow Italy to enter the alliance as a full member. Other European governments then indicated that they would not continue to oppose Italy's full membership if the United States strongly supported it. Canada duly fell into line. On 26 January, the Italian ambassador at Ottawa was informed by the government that Canada was dropping her opposition to Italy's inclusion in the pact.[116] On 25 February, at the thirteenth meeting of the Exploratory Talks, Hume Wrong conveyed this decision to the Ambassadors.

Mr Wrong said that the Canadian Government's original view was that the definition of North Atlantic countries should be severe. Initially the Canadian Government had desired to limit the parties to the countries bordering on the North Atlantic, or almost so, in order to cover the inclusion of Sweden, and not to penetrate into the Mediterranean. This was not because of a desire to leave Italy exposed, but because it was difficult to know where to draw the line. As the discussions proceeded, however, the force of the arguments against leaving Italy out became even more apparent. From the strategical point of view, if the question were asked whether this agreement would, in practice, come into operation if there were an all-out attack by the Soviet Union on Italy, his impression was that all of the governments would probably have to answer affirmatively. Although strategically Italy could add little to the arrangement, on balance, provided there was a genuine meeting of minds on the subject, the Canadian Government would be prepared to support the admission of Italy. This was a decision which had, in a sense, been reached reluctantly, and it involved a delicate weighing of the arguments on both sides...[117]

Article 6 of the North Atlantic Treaty, defining the treaty area, includes within it 'the Algerian departments of France...' These five words, Escott Reid comments, 'are a monument to a prolonged and bitter disagreement in the intergovernmental discussions.'[118] Canada was in the thick of the argument.

The government of France, on joining the negotiations, had proposed that the area in which an armed attack would bring the pledge into play should include Algeria as a part of France, and in addition all of the North African littoral north of 30° North – the Mediterranean coast of Egypt, the Suez Canal, the whole of Tunisia, and the north of Libya and Morocco. When this extreme proposal – doubtless made as a bargaining tactic to secure the inclusion of Algeria – was unveiled by the French ambassador at the tenth meeting of the 'Exploratory Talks' on 22 December, Hume Wrong responded, in understated language, that his government, he was sure, would be surprised to learn 'that a considerable stretch of North Africa facing the Mediterranean' might be included in the treaty area.[119] After reporting to Ottawa on 4 January 1949 that he had taken the line that 'French North Africa should not be specified as a part of the North Atlantic area' without, however, indicating fundamental opposition, Wrong was telephoned by L.B. Pearson to take a 'stiffer attitude.' This emphasis was the Prime Minister's. L.S. St Laurent, 'whose conservative appearance,' according to his biographer, 'belied his progressive views,'[120] did not take kindly to the notion that the Atlantic alliance, on whose behalf he had conducted so energetic a crusade, should serve to protect and so to perpetuate colonial territory of any kind. 'Mr Pearson and I discussed the North Atlantic treaty ... with the Prime Minister yesterday,' Hume Wrong informed Escott Reid on 8 January. 'The Prime Minister said that he had read the draft with great care. There were three points which struck him as being important for the public acceptance of the treaty in Canada.' The first of St Laurent's requirements, Wrong reported, was that 'the areas specifically covered should not include any colonial territory. This applied to Algeria as well as to the rest of French North Africa.'[121]

St Laurent's insistence on the exclusion of Algeria put Canada on a collision course with France which, Wrong reported, was ' "adamant" in insisting on the inclusion of Algeria...' At Wrong's suggestion, the Ambassador at Paris was instructed to try to persuade the French foreign minister to change his representative's instructions. General Vanier's meeting with Robert Schuman on 12 January was futile. 'It would be quite impossible for any French government to accept the idea of excluding Algeria which was part of metropolitan France,' Vanier reported Schuman as having told him, 'on political grounds because no French government could possibly propose this to Parliament, but also on purely strategic grounds because the general defence of France could not be envisaged without the inclusion of Algeria as a base for defensive action as well as for purposes of retreat. ... Algeria,' Schuman declared, 'bore the same relation to France as Alaska to the United States. It would be even difficult for the government to accept the exclusion of Tunisia and Morocco, but that of Algeria quite impossible.'[122] This authoritative statement of the French position was not known to the Canadians who attended Working Party meetings at Washington on 11 and 12 January, and in reporting to Ottawa they referred to the 'rather rash statements about the complete unacceptability to the French of a pact which did not include at least the three departments of Algeria,' rather as if to indicate their belief that the French representative was moving beyond the letter of his instructions from Paris. But this was not the case.[123]

On 12 January, in response to the representations of other governments (which included the United States' and the United Kingdom's as well as Canada's), the French abandoned their North African proposal and announced that they would be content with a pact that covered Algeria. On 14 January, at the eleventh meeting of the Exploratory Talks, Hume Wrong's reaction (according to the US minutes) was low-keyed: '[T]he matter had caused concern on the part of the Canadian Government which was reluctant to see the area extended to include part of North Africa. He reserved his position, but was glad to note that the proposal was now concerned only with Algeria.'[124] Wrong's own account is more specific: 'I said that we were still of the view that it would be unwise for domestic political reasons in Canada to include Algeria. We quite appreciated the constitutional situation, but its inclusion, nevertheless, could not fail to raise in the public mind the whole question of colonial overseas territories.'[125] That Wrong's account more faithfully than the US minutes records the gist of his remarks is evident from the retort they provoked from M. Bonnet, which is anything but low-keyed: 'France did not see how a Pact could include part of the Arctic regions and the northern part of Canada without including the three departments of Algeria which were a part of France.'[126]

The other West European governments, and the British, having by then dropped any objection to the inclusion of Algeria within the treaty area, Canada and the United States stood alone in opposing it. On 15 January Hume Wrong reported that 'the French are not prepared to budge on this matter, even to the point of sacrificing the treaty...'[127] Independently, and at about the same time, the Canadian and United

States governments reached the conclusion that a treaty without Algeria would mean an alliance without France, and the decision that France would have to be appeased. The two governments exchanged this intelligence on 24 January, but the United States left France in ignorance of the decision until 1 March 1949. The Prime Minister summed up the reason for Canada's attitude: '"Algeria was not a matter of great importance to the main purposes of the Treaty, but France was essential".'[128]

Canada's most difficult struggle in the drafting of the North Atlantic Treaty was over what became Article 2.

At the ninth meeting of the Exploratory Talks on 13 December 1948, Hume Wrong had told his fellow ambassadors that his government wanted to have in the treaty an article pledging the signatories to promote economic and social collaboration among them. The article came to be referred to in the negotiations as the 'general welfare' article. It devolved upon Wrong to advocate its inclusion in the body of the treaty against deep-seated United States opposition to it – and despite his own antipathy towards it,* of which its opponents may or may not have been aware.

Canadian advocacy during the negotiations had produced agreement on a version in the Draft Treaty that the negotiators decided on 24 December to recommend to their governments.

Article 2 (General Welfare)

The Parties will encourage cooperative efforts between any or all of them to promote the general welfare through collaboration in the cultural, economic and social fields. Such efforts shall, to the greatest possible extent, be undertaken through and assist the work of existing international organizations.[129]

This formulation, which represented a compromise between the Canadian view that a 'General Welfare' article was essential and the British view that it was redundant, was not acceptable to Escott Reid. (Reid's early draft of such an article, submitted to L.B. Pearson on 18 March 1948 before the latter embarked for the Tripartite Talks that month, had proposed not just one article on the subject but four.[130] '[A]s soon as I saw it, I urged Pearson that we should not give up the struggle for a more strongly worded provision and I suggested amendments to him. Pearson agreed that the article "should go further if possible but [he thought that it was] not likely to be possible." Wrong agreed with Pearson that there

---

* '[T]he two Canadian spokesmen at Washington, Wrong and [T.A.] Stone, were never convinced that the non-military aspects of the North Atlantic alliance were essential.' Escott Reid, *Time of Fear and Hope*, 167. Wrong was never 'personally convinced that the non-military aspects of the proposed alliance were essential...' *Mike* II, 47.

was not much chance of making the article stronger but said that he would see what he could do, possibly by including some such words as, "The parties agree to make every effort in common to eliminate conflict in their economic policies and to develop the possibilities of trade between them." This was based on a proposal I had made to Pearson. Wrong reported on January 5, however, that "we shall not be able to secure agreement on strengthening [the article's] language." I did not accept Wrong's judgment..."[131]

Prospects for a General Welfare article of any kind took a sharp turn for the worse on 20 January 1949, when Dean Acheson became Secretary of State and chairman of the Exploratory Talks. Acheson's attitude towards the concept embodied by Article 2 was undisguisedly hostile. 'Dean Acheson didn't like it a damn,' one of his fellow negotiators has since recalled.[132] Consequently, when Acheson consulted with the two key Senators on 3 and 5 February, to find that Vandenberg and Connally were as implacably opposed to the draft of Article 2 as they were to the draft of Article 5, their complaints were sympathetically received. These Acheson has described in his memoirs.

The early drafts, the senators thought, went too far on ... three issues. The first was the Canadian proposal of Article 2, which got us into cultural, economic, and social cooperation. The senators were strongly opposed. We had all just been through a harrowing experience. On February 2 I had been before the Senate Committee doing my best to support agreements that came out of the Bogota Conference attended by General Marshall. The Senate would have none of them. The agreements announced sweeping alleged human rights to education, the good life, welfare, and so on ... [that] posed serious constitutional implications. ... Our senators saw Article 2 threatening our treaty with the same danger for no important benefits. I agreed...[133]

On 7 February, Escott Reid persuaded L.B. Pearson to instruct Hume Wrong to try not merely to preserve the draft Article 2 but to strengthen it. 'What had happened,' Reid explains, 'was that St Laurent and Pearson, with a general election impending, had become increasingly apprehensive that if the article were not strengthened the necessary degree of public support for the treaty in Canada would not be forthcoming.' Accordingly, Pearson agreed to telling Wrong for the first time 'to explain to his colleagues in the negotiations in Washington the practical domestic political considerations which lay behind the insistence by the Canadian government that Article 2 be strengthened: the existing draft of Article 2 could scarcely be much weaker; the Parliament and people of Canada would expect the government to secure something much stronger; failure might result in the government facing "a definite weakening of support for the treaty in the House [of Commons] and in the country".'[134] Wrong was instructed to attempt to have inserted in the draft Article 2, after its first sentence, the following two sentences.

The parties agree to make every effort in common to eliminate conflict in their economic policies and to develop to the full the great possibilities of trade between them. The parties also undertake to make every effort in common to promote the attainment of a higher standard of living by their people and greater economic and social justice, and to bring about a better understanding of the principles which form the basis of their common civilization.[135]

Hume Wrong responded to these instructions by warning Pearson that they stood scant chance of being implemented successfully. 'We are now the only party to the negotiation that really favours the inclusion of anything in the treaty about social and economic collaboration outside a general reference in the preamble,' Wrong pointed out. Moreover, he continued, 'I have learned privately that the Secretary of State does not like the present Article 2 on the ground that it means next to nothing' – a view Wrong himself shared – 'and that Senators Vandenberg and Connally may wish it to be deleted because it seems they want the Treaty to be a straight defence agreement.' Wrong promised to do his best to strengthen the wording as he had been instructed, but doubted that he would prevail.

I think that the most that we may be able to do is to retain the existing language. ... In any case there would be difficulties about your suggestion for a phrase requiring the parties "to eliminate conflict in their economic policies" because of the issues of free enterprise vs. socialism that might be considered to be involved. The use twice in your addition of the words "in common" might also be taken to require the establishment of special agencies in the North Atlantic area, against which there is very strong opposition...[137]

The next day, on February 8 at the twelfth meeting of the Exploratory Talks, Hume Wrong tried to persuade his fellow ambassadors to accept the new wording his government had proposed for Article 2. The US minutes thus record his effort.

Mr Wrong said that he had just received instructions from the Canadian Government urging the strengthening of Article 2. For political reasons, the Canadian Government was anxious to emphasize the fact that the Treaty was not merely a military alliance. Article 2 was the only non-military article in the Treaty and, as at present drafted, it was weak. The Canadian Government therefore suggested an additional sentence for insertion after the first sentence of the article on the following lines...

There appear in the minutes, with the word 'great' eliminated from the Ottawa drafting of 'great possibilities,' the two sentences with which he had been furnished (not just the single 'additional sentence' referred to).

Following this intervention, the US Secretary of State responded. He too faced political difficulties. 'Mr Acheson said that the Senators were worried about Article 2 as at present worded,' the US minutes record.

It detracted from the main purpose of the treaty and got involved in social and economic questions which might raise internal political problems. What, for instance, was the meaning in the Article of the words "the general welfare"? Did this refer to the whole world?

Mr Wrong said that he did not want to go into details at this time, but wanted to point out that it would cause great political difficulty in Canada if there were no article in the Treaty of a non-military nature. There was need for something which reflected the ideological unity of the North Atlantic Powers.

Mr Acheson suggested that this might be done in the Preamble.

To have kept composed at that suggestion, Hume Wrong may well have drawn on all his years of experience: one imagines his eyes rolling ever so slightly upwards at the recollection of his advice to Escott Reid only weeks before: 'Put the ideology of the treaty in the preamble where it belongs...' The chickens now coming home to roost had not been hatched by him. Nevertheless, like the professional he was, Hume Wrong soldiered on in a cause he believed to be not only hopeless but unwise.

Mr Wrong said that it had always been understood that there would be some wording in this sense in the Preamble, as well as in Article 2. The Canadians had originally suggested much stronger language for Article 2. They wanted now to find words which would be more explicit. The Government would be able to win more support for the Pact in Canada if it was not purely military in character. This point would carry considerable weight with several political groups. He hoped that the political necessities in Canada would be borne in mind in any further discussions between Mr Acheson and the Senators.[138]

Wrong's own account to L.B. Pearson of this exchange is as follows.

On Article 2 I informed Mr Acheson that I had received instructions from you to secure stronger wording. I read part of your message ... to the meeting. In reply to Mr Acheson's objection that the Senators were fed up with treaties for the general welfare I said that I wanted him to tell them about your political difficulties in Canada. I pointed out that it would be difficult to secure support in Quebec for a purely military pact and that some Article along the lines of Article 2 was important to get the support of that province and of other political elements...

I brought up our views on Article 2 toward the end of the meeting (which degenerated into a straggling discussion of various points) so that Acheson would know of the great importance which we attach to an improved article on economic collaboration before he had another meeting with the Senators. There was next to no discussion of our suggestions. I think we can at least maintain the present article, subject to finding some alternative to the phrase "to promote the general welfare,'' which seems to rouse in senatorial minds a vision of endless hand-outs to the other parties. I am sure we shall not get acceptance of your addition, but it seemed good tactics to propose it in order to emphasize our point of view...[139]

Pearson was still not satisfied. 'I continue to object to the thesis that the Treaty should be merely a military alliance designed for the immediate emergency,' he cabled to Wrong the following day. 'It must, I think, if it is to be acceptable in Canada, go much deeper. You should therefore continue to press for a strengthening of Article 2 and should you meet with no success, for the maintenance of the Article as it now stands as the *minimum* requirement.'[140]

Escott Reid considers that Hume Wrong made two errors during the negotiation of Article 2 which contributed to the failure of Canada's efforts to strengthen its wording: 'The first was on February 8 when he indicated that Canada would be prepared to compromise.'[141] Presumably the alleged 'compromise' consists in Wrong's having told the meeting, according to the US minutes, 'That the Canadians had originally suggested much stronger language for Article 2. They wanted now to find words which would be more explicit.' Reid evidently believes that Canada's objective would have stood a greater chance of attainment had Wrong not indicated in this way that the government had retreated from an earlier version. He explains the lapse as deriving partly from Wrong's 'consistent overestimation of the strength of the opposition to a strong Article 2,' and partly to 'his own lack of enthusiasm for a strong Article 2. Even the most conscientious and able negotiator,' Reid adds by way of extenuation, 'and Wrong was extremely conscientious and able, is apt to see more difficulties in the way of a proposal that he is not keen on than he is of one that he is enthusiastic about.'[142]

Be all that as it may, Hume Wrong did offer a compromise formula on 9 February – but not before clearing it with Ottawa. If he could not, as he expected he would not, obtain acceptance of the two-sentence addition, Wrong proposed to Pearson, he should be allowed to put forward a draft article which, while going further than that of 24 December, would fall short of the two-sentence proposed addition by omitting the stipulation to 'eliminate conflict in ... economic policies.'

It now became Ottawa's strategy to muster political support for a strengthened Article 2 – whether by the two-sentence addition or, that failing, Wrong's proposed compromise. To that end, the High Commissioner at London was instructed on 9 February to secure the backing of the British Government and, on 17 February, the ambassadors at Paris, Brussels, and The Hague were similarly instructed to enlist in Canada's cause the governments to which they were accredited. (Escott Reid considers the delay – for which he assumes responsibility – in rounding up West European support to have been an error; had this support been obtained earlier, the Americans could have been told that all parties except themselves now favoured the Canadian amendment.)[143] The support requested was duly forthcoming – the French promising it '*au fond*,' the British only because Canada had asked for it, not because they liked the idea.*

The set-piece of this strategy was the meeting between the Prime Minister and the US President in Washington on 11 February – their first as heads of government. L.S. St Laurent told President Truman of Canada's commitment to a strongly-worded article on economic and social collaboration. 'When the Prime Minister mentioned the great Canadian interest in a satisfactory article to the President and Acheson,' Wrong reported of their discussion, 'they listened sympathetically, and I think we should have no difficulty with the Administration in securing at least the maintenance of the current draft.'[144] L.B. Pearson states that Truman 'seemed to understand and sympathize, if not with the Canadian Atlanticist viewpoint, at least with the realities of Canadian domestic politics.'[145] But St Laurent's biographer doubts whether the meeting made much impact: 'The Canadian visitor ... argu[ed] that the North Atlantic Treaty, almost ready for final approval, should not only be a military alliance, but should also provide for closer economic and social co-operation between member countries. Truman was clearly not as interested in that possibility...'[146]

The Ambassadors met again in Washington on 19 February, although not in a formal convening of the Exploratory Talks. After the meeting, Hume Wrong discussed Article 2 with Dean Acheson, Charles Bohlen, and John D. Hickerson. Acheson 'described the almost universal reluctance of the members of the Senate [Foreign Relations] Committee to include any Article of this nature in the Treaty itself,' Wrong reported to Ottawa.

This was based on a growing resistance to general commitments in economic, social and cultural matters, in part derived from the language of the Bogota Treaty, in part for their distaste for some of the activities of the [UN] Economic and Social Council and UNESCO, and in part from a desire to keep the Treaty strictly limited to the organization of defence...

I repeated, I think, all the arguments which we have adduced in favour of a respectable Article of this nature, stressing the position consistently adopted by

---

* 'I pressed London to help us,' L.B. Pearson has recorded, 'but the best I could get, for all Norman Robertson's ingenuity in putting our case, was an assurance of support for some "economic clause," not because they wished it but ... to meet our wishes.' *Mike* II, 57.

the Canadian Government, the expectations aroused with the public, and the evidence of the political desirability of making the Treaty more than a defence pact.

...I gave them my compromise text. ... There will ... be very great difficulty over the phrase included in it "to develop to the full the possibilities of trade between them." ... Acheson said he would have another try with the Senators and would inform them more fully than he had done of the importance attached to the Article by the Canadian Government...[147]

By showing the US State Department officials the fall-back position of Wrong's 'compromise text,' the Ambassador had disclosed to them that the government did have a position to fall back upon and that it was not determined, therefore, to regard the two-sentence addition as non-negotiable. This Escott Reid considers to have been the second of Wrong's two errors in handling the negotiation. 'Once he had retreated to a fall-back position it was difficult, if not impossible, for him to press vigorously for our maximum demands when he later learned that we had the full support of all five Brussels treaty powers for those demands. ... The reason Wrong gave for not pressing our maximum demands on February 19 was that this would increase Acheson's difficulties with the senators. Wrong's task was to get the strongest possible language for Article 2 in order to diminish the difficulties of St Laurent and Pearson in getting support for the treaty in the House of Commons ... and in the country. Whether this increased Acheson's difficulties in getting support for the treaty in the Senate of the United States was relevant only if the additional burden on Acheson would result in his not attempting the task of persuading the senators. Acheson could scarcely have refused to undertake the task if all the other participants in the negotiations had asked him to.'[148]

On receiving Wrong's report of his discussions with the US State Department on 19 February – discussions in which he allowed that he had tipped his hand to them – he was immediately instructed by Pearson to put forward the maximum demand (ie, the two-sentence addition) at the next Ambassadors' meeting. 'If you get substantial support ... from all the representatives other than the United States, Acheson could report this back to the Senate Committee and in the light of the reaction from the Senate Committee we can decide whether to press for these two sentences or to be content with your compromise.'[149] But crossing these instructions was what Escott Reid describes as 'a very pessimistic' message from Wrong: 'If strong objection continues to be taken to the inclusion of anything on the lines of Article 2, do you think it would be possible for us to get by with Article 3 and suitable language in the preamble? That may be the most that we can secure.'[150]

This assessment from the Ambassador that there might be no Article 2 of any kind, coming as it did after his assurances that the 24 December draft article, at least, was secure, doubtless alarmed St Laurent and Pearson. In the absence of any written message in the files, it may be assumed that Wrong received their response by telephone. In the light of what Wrong then told J.D. Hickerson of the US State Department, both in writing and in person, their response must have been insistent. 'If the Canadian government were to agree to sign the treaty without a pledge of this nature,' Wrong's memorandum for Hickerson stated,

it would be essential to explain to the public that the pledge was dropped at the insistence of the government of the United States. The Canadian government has received assurances of support from the French and Netherlands governments for the inclusion of an article stronger than the present draft of Article 2 as well as a general promise of support from the British government. It is understood that the Belgian government is also favourable. It would be very difficult to explain satisfactorily why the United States government was unwilling to accept a general article of this nature in view of the many more specific engagements to which the United States is a party, including a number of inter-American treaties now in effect and the Lend-Lease and OEEC agreements.[151]

What Wrong said to Hickerson in person was more drastic. 'I told Hickerson that unless we could get an article on these lines in the Treaty the Canadian Government would have to review its position on the whole project.'[152] On this statement, Escott Reid comments: 'This diplomatic formula was the equivalent in ordinary language of a threat not to sign the treaty, and it would be interpreted by Hickerson as such. One must assume that Pearson not only gave firm instructions to Wrong to say this but that the language was Pearson's and that on a matter of this importance Pearson would have secured St Laurent's concurrence.'[153]

At any rate, the threat worked. Hickerson, aghast that the treaty might fall apart over the wording of what Dean Acheson regarded as its least essential article, at once got to work on a new draft of Article 2. He and Theodore Achilles of the US State Department, and Wrong and Thomas Stone of the Embassy at Washington, met at Hickerson's house on 23 February – a Saturday – and worked out a new draft of Article 2 that satisfied them all. It would still have to satisfy Acheson. The next day Wrong and Hickerson went to Acheson's home, where he lay ill with influenza. 'Hume on one side and I on the other,' Hickerson would later describe the scene at his bedside, 'beat the poor sick man over the head.'[154] Acheson's resistance was low; he gave in. Of what the US Secretary of State had thus approved, Wrong cabled to Ottawa: 'I think that this is as strong a text as we can secure because of the cantankerous attitude adopted by the Foreign Relations Committee towards any article at all. Indeed, I doubt that they will take this as it stands.'[155] But they did.

On 25 February, at the thirteenth meeting of the 'Exploratory Talks,' the West European ambassadors made good their governments' promises of support to Canada for the kind of article she so urgently desired. Then Hume Wrong spoke of the new draft now before them. 'The language of the present draft Article did not go as far as the Canadian Government would wish,' the US minutes record him saying. 'They would like more specific language. If this was as far as the United States could go he would do his best to persuade the Canadian Government to accept this wording. Possibly the Canadian Government would make some suggestion for the amendment of the Article.' Acheson responded by saying 'that he would not like to try to expand the wording of this draft. He had been surprised at [the] success in getting the draft past the Senators. The President also had been helpful after his conversations with St Laurent. He thought the Senators had been co-operative and reasonable. For domestic reasons the Senators were wary of ideas concerning welfare and cultural development. If the present draft could be accepted by the Canadian Government it would make the task of the United States administration much easier.' After more sparring between the US Secretary of State and the Ambassador, the Belgian representative asked if the text before them 'gave satisfaction, at least personally, to Mr Wrong.' Wrong, giving the two-sentence addition a hearing for the last time,

replied that at the end of the second sentence of the present text he would like to add "to encourage economic collaboration between any or all of them with a view to determining the great possibilities of trade between them." He would also like to add another sentence which would refer to the attainment of higher standards of living and greater economic and social justice as general objectives. He understood that these proposals would cause great difficulty with the Senators. He considered them reasonable proposals coming within the general purpose of the Treaty and that was why he could not, at the moment, say whether the present text would satisfy the Canadian Government. Mr Acheson demurred at the suggestion to include any such wording.[156]

After the meeting, Wrong reported on the proceedings to Ottawa. 'I argued this morning for a stronger Article on the lines of our own proposal, making reference directly to the development of trade, higher standards of living and greater economic and social justice,' he cabled to Pearson. 'Mr Acheson and Mr [Ernest A.] Gross [US State Department legal adviser] were both firmly of the view that they could not secure Senatorial approval for these additions, and urged me to seek to persuade the Canadian Government to accept the present language. They were sur-

prised that the Senate had not opposed this, and are most anxious not to
have to go to them again with a new text.'[157]

At last the Ambassador was able to persuade his government that it had
gone as far as it should go: field and headquarters finally saw eye-to-eye.
The Prime Minister and his foreign minister decided to end the quest for
a more perfect wording. 'I feel that this article is perhaps as strong as we
can secure,' L.B. Pearson told Hume Wrong on 27 February, 'and it is
therefore acceptable as it stands.'[158] Wrong must have been greatly relieved to hear so. He communicated the good news to his fellow Ambassadors at their fifteenth meeting on 4 March. It was because his Minister
had recognized 'that it would cause great difficulty to the United States
Government if they had to try and secure the acceptance of an Article
more in accordance with the original Canadian proposal,' he told them,
that the Canadian government 'did not wish to press for any further
changes.'[159] The draft, with slight amendments, passed into the North
Atlantic Treaty.

The Parties will contribute toward the further development of peaceful and
friendly international relations by strengthening their free institutions, by bringing
about a better understanding of the principles upon which these institutions are
founded, and by promoting conditions of stability and well-being. They will seek
to eliminate conflict in their international economic policies and will encourage
economic collaboration between any or all of them.

Such is the text of Article 2 which, as one of the United States architects of the Treaty would later remark, 'is the Canadian Article of the
Treaty and was called that during the negotiations. If it had not been for
Canada, Article 2 would not have been in the Treaty.'[160] In the event it
would not make much difference, either in or out. But that is another
story.*

---

*   See below, Ch. 3, 175-89.

3

Organizing the Alliance

Away with ... the idle supposition that it is the harness
and not the horses that draw the chariot along.

George Canning

PLANNERS AND PLANS

Drafting of the North Atlantic Treaty, except in very minor matters, had
been completed by 7 March 1949. '[T]here was now an agreed text,' the
US Secretary of State declared at the sixteenth meeting of the Exploratory
Talks on Security in Washington on that date, 'which should be sent to
the various governments for comment and approval.'[1] The government
of Canada, without comment, approved the agreed text on 10 March. The
following week brought approval from all twelve prospective signatories.
The text was made public on 18 March and ten days later was debated in
the House of Commons. 'When the vote was taken,' L.B. Pearson recorded in his memoirs, 'only two were against.* Thus I had the backing of

---

* The two, both from Quebec, were Josephe Irenée Hamel and Maxime Raymond.
Hamel offered no reason for his dissent, Raymond several reasons:

> Based as it is upon a series of contradictions, that treaty affords no guarantee that the
> intentions of many of the signatories are sincere; on the contrary, it inspires mistrust
> and under such circumstances it cannot be deemed a contribution to an equitable and
> enduring peace. Rearmament is resorted to for the defence against a prospective en-
> emy to whom weapons are supplied; an alliance is arranged against Russia with coun-
> tries already pledged with her by a treaty involving alliance, co-operation and mutual
> aid, which precludes them from concluding any alliance or participating in any coali-
> tion directed against her; it is desired to fight communism while Spain, an enemy of
> communism, is excluded from the pact; it is the aim to ensure the security of Canada
> in America, but there is a refusal to associate through a security pact with countries
> of America; an anti-aggression alliance is made with a country like Holland which, at
> the same time, launches the most brutal aggression against the Indonesians.

an almost unanimous Parliament when Hume Wrong and I signed the treaty for Canada.'[2]

The signing ceremony, held in Washington on 4 April 1949, was enlivened by a US Marine band. 'At the precise moment that Acheson, our Secretary of State, signed the first commitment of this sort ever made by the United States,' one of the American officials present has recalled, 'they struck up "It Ain't Necessarily So".'[3] As its other number from *Porgy and Bess* the band played 'I Got Plenty of Nothin'.' Dean Acheson considered the repertoire to have added, however fortuitously, 'a note of unexpected realism.'[4] L.B. Pearson rather stuffily describes the selection as 'regrettable.'[5] It provided, in any case, an overture which was to prove peculiarly appropriate.

The Parliament of Canada was the first among the North Atlantic legislatures to ratify the Treaty, on 29 April 1949; the government of Canada was the first among the North Atlantic cabinets to deposit its instrument of ratification, on 3 May 1949. With the completion of the process by 24 August 1949, a treaty was now on file. An organization had yet to be created.

About organizing the alliance, the Treaty was mostly silent. 'The Parties hereby establish a council' – so they had recited in Article 9 – 'on which each of them shall be represented, to consider matters concerning the implementation of this Treaty.' To this they had added: 'The council shall set up such subsidiary bodies as may be necessary; in particular it shall establish immediately a defence committee which shall recommend measures for the implementation of Articles 3 and 5.' That was what there was to go by.

The Treaty's silence on alliance institutions had intended to be golden, and it probably was so – though the point has been debated both at the

Offered as a peace program, it is an armaments race which may lead any day to an undescribable [*sic*] catastrophe. And Canada is bound for twenty years to come, having given up, through her signature, her right to remain neutral.

I am not an isolationist, nor am I opposed to an alliance aimed at ensuring, in international life, the triumph of justice and charity principles; but I am not ready to give a free hand to any government, whatever it be, to plunge us, without consulting parliament, into armed conflicts, in order to serve, in the four corners of the world, the interests of powers actuated by a spirit of domination rather than a spirit of justice.

Canada, *H.C. Debates*, 1949, III, 2687. The irrepressible Jean-François Pouliot, a remorseless critic of senior military officers, refrained from voting: 'The brass hats are out of the war, but they are preaching war; they are war-mongers. ... That is why I am very cautious about this treaty.' *Ibid.*, 2103. The vote on the Treaty was carried 149 to 2.

time and since. 'With public opinion in the United States moving as fast as it has been for the last eight years,' Escott Reid had written in a memorandum for the Prime Minister on 15 November 1948, 'we should not reject the possibility that large and influential sections of the United States public might welcome enthusiastically the inclusion in the North Atlantic treaty of a provision setting up a North Atlantic assembly, and that instead of criticizing their government for going too far they might criticize it for agreeing to a treaty [that did not go far enough]...'[6] And in 1975 an American commentator wrote: '[W]hen the NATO treaty was drafted in 1949 no one had the foresight to give it a "parliamentary coiffure".'[7] But it was not a lack of foresight, rather a sense of prudence, that caused Canada,· and others, to hold back. To attempt to insert into the treaty articles creating an Atlantic assembly or other institutions would – so L.B. Pearson considered at the time – 'provoke unnecessary controversy and discussion though some development of this sort may ultimately be desirable.'[8]

The approach, then, had by design been organic. The drafters of the Treaty did not wish to bind themselves and their successors by a host of do's and don'ts. The allies should proceed by trial, and if necessary by error, adjusting to new realities, responding to new needs. 'The flexibility which the Treaty gained from not being detailed has been one of NATO's strengths': such is the judgement of the historian of the Alliance's Staff/ Secretariat, and he adds: '[T]he Organization has been able to deal pragmatically with the varied administrative needs which have arisen.'[9] Each member government thus had the opportunity to draw on the blank pages of a constitution largely unwritten those organization charts deemed most congenial to its purposes; some member governments would seize that opportunity.

Canada's policy community was not likely to fret over the reticence of the Treaty in matters of North Atlantic organization. Working within a political system of which the written constitution, amended down the years, gave but imperfect guidance to how public affairs were actually conducted, led by experience of Commonwealth relations to a distrust of exercises in definition, willingly accepting the traditional foreign office aversion to planning for the future,* officials of the government – Escott Reid signally excepted – were not conditioned to crusade for a North

---

* 'Canadian foreign service officers, like so many others in the largely British tradition of professional diplomacy to which they belong, have tended in matters of foreign policy to be wary of large intents and grand designs.' Daniel Madar and Denis Stairs, 'Alone on Killer's Row: The Policy Analysis Group and the Department of External Affairs,' *International Journal*, XXXII, 4, Autumn 1977, 728.

Atlantic Treaty organization in the same way as they had crusaded for a North Atlantic treaty. 'I think that the Secretariat ... will be unimportant,' the Ambassador at Washington predicted early in the life of the Alliance. As for needed personnel, he thought 'an archivist and a few clerks' would do.[10]

One important sector of the policy community did not share the pervasive scepticism towards planning. This was the military establishment. Taking over as Minister for National Defence in 1946, Brooke Claxton discovered his senior officers to be up to their epaulettes in plans. 'The planning began during the war,' Claxton later recorded,

and went much further than has ever been divulged. From 1945 until they were absorbed in the NATO framework, Military Co-operation Committees of the United States and Canada worked at Washington and Ottawa on every problem of defence planning. This was tied in with similar co-operation with Britain. ... The plans included what would have to be done to meet the shock of an immediate world war. There was even a "Black Plan" on what should be done if Europe and Britain were over-run...

The great danger of planning activities of this kind is that the planners, generally very bright officers of the rank of colonels, majors or captains, live and work without regard for the facts of national life. Unless they are very closely supervised, they are apt to draw up plans that are utterly unrealistic and impossible of fulfilment. Military planning on this scale sought ideal solutions; military programming invariably has to be aimed much lower...

It was in 1947 that General Foulkes and I found the planners were getting out of hand...*

General Charles Foulkes was at the time of the creation of the North Atlantic alliance the most senior officer in the armed forces. Four years earlier, on 5 May 1945, he had accepted from Colonel-General Johannes Blaskovitz the surrender of the German armies in The Netherlands and north-west Germany. The advent so soon after that crowning moment of what, despite Canadian disclaimers, was first and foremost a military alli-

---

*   Brooke Claxton memoirs (no page reference), Claxton papers. Compare the observation of a veteran of the US State Department's Policy Planning Staff (later Council):

    The military planning process, in so far as it relates to the ponderables of real or hypothetical campaigns, turns out tidy and complete results. ... It is easy for the unwary to jump to a fallacious conclusion that if all human affairs were laid out with the precision of military plans, then all problems could be brought to as complete solution as can the problem of force in the conduct of a victorious military campaign.

    Charles Burton Marshall, *The Exercise of Sovereignty: Papers on Foreign Policy* (Baltimore 1965), 51.

ance must have come as manna from the skies, a tonic reprieve from the *longueurs* of the profession of arms when arms are silent. Foulkes eagerly immersed himself in the managerial affairs of the new coalition. 'He deals with paper,' the Minister of National Defence wrote admiringly of his Chief of the General Staff, 'and what quantities of it there are!' Colleagues in the Department of External Affairs were less admiring. 'Like you, I am rather worried lest the CGS gets way ahead of himself,' the Under Secretary in that Department wrote to his Minister on receiving yet another memorandum from Foulkes on organizing the Alliance, 'to say nothing of the rest of us.'[11]

It sometimes helps to be first in. Foulkes, if not first, was early in the field of organizing the alliance, and held much of his ground. 'It is interesting to note,' he wrote with pardonable pride in later years, 'that the organization of the military aspects of NATO suggested in our proposal of 7 March 1949, is very similar to the present organization.'[12] 'Our proposal' had been Foulkes' proposal. 'Never negotiate on the other fellow's draft': the other fellows – Generals Bradley and Gruenther for the United States, Generals Hollis and Templar for the United Kingdom – negotiated on Foulkes' draft. Largely because of the enterprise of Canada's Chief of the General Staff, her government was more successful in giving SHAPE – Supreme Headquarters, Allied Powers in Europe – its shape than in obtaining a treaty exactly to its liking. 'Even at that early date,' Foulkes would recall of his 1949 paper, 'we had been recommending the necessity of a Supreme Allied Commander ... which ... was not obtained until two or three years afterwards.'[13]

On the civilian side of the policy community, there was less enthusiasm. What interest existed in the problems of alliance organization stemmed primarily from a perennial (and justifiable) concern lest Canada find herself excluded from the councils of the new coalition. Apprehension at the prospects of such exclusion arose early in 1949 as the result of rumours reaching Ottawa that the United States and the United Kingdom intended to retain the Combined Chiefs of Staff (that postwar hold-over from their wartime partnership) for strategic planning and the direction of operations. Were this to come about, prospective North Atlantic institutions would be subordinate to an Anglo-American military directorate. 'If the United States and the United Kingdom are successful in this,' Escott Reid objected in a telegram to Hume Wrong in Washington,

and if hostilities should break out, we would find ourselves in almost exactly the same position as we were in during the last war when we were not consulted on questions of policy and when decisions were taken by individuals and bodies who had received no authority from us...

It is ... of very great political importance to us that Canada should be a full member of a Chiefs of Staff Committee along with the United States as a full member. How can we or the United States be full members of a Western Union Chiefs of Staff Committee? This smacks of the old "Allied and Associated Powers," which is an out-of-date concept.

Reid suggested to Wrong that he try 'to get some clarification from the United States and the United Kingdom representatives as to what they are driving at.' If it turned out that they meant what they said, Reid concluded, 'there seems a danger that we will be omitted from the strategic planning under the North Atlantic Treaty.'[14]

The recipient of this suggestion did not find it at all constructive. Hume Wrong's patience (never his strong point) at what he regarded as Reid's overly intrusive interventions in the exacting negotiations then under way in Washington had been by this time sorely tried.* 'I think that you need not worry about this,' Wrong remonstrated. 'The Working Group has only discussed in a very general way the military organization which might be built up under the Treaty...' The important thing was to go for the Treaty, not to complicate the negotiations by anticipating alliance problems of the future.

I am strongly of the view that it would be unwise for us to introduce a detailed discussion of this problem ... I would much rather have the Treaty in existence than run the risk of prejudicing its acceptance or prompting the introduction of unwelcome amendments by raising now matters which cannot in fact be settled until the Treaty is in effect. ... My belief is that we shall get a better solution in the Council to be established under the Treaty, so long as we are assured, as we are now assured, that the military agencies must be established by the Council.[15]

With that, Escott Reid had to be content. But the problem of Canada's being adequately represented on alliance bodies which could decide the disposition and fate of her armed forces remained. The memorandum by General Charles Foulkes of 7 March 1949 – 'North Atlantic Pact: Military Organization' – was the earliest effort to solve it.

A North Atlantic pact – so Foulkes' paper argued – would not only cover a vast treaty area, it would bring together 'a large number of sovereign countries with divergent outlooks, strong nationalist pride and varying military and logistical capabilities.' This circumstance suggested two competing methods of organizing the alliance. One was to centralize command. The other was to devolve control. Foulkes' memorandum ingeniously found room for both centralization and devolution.

---

* See above, Ch. 2, 98-106.

Centralization was to be accomplished by the appointment of a supreme commander – 'this officer,' so Foulkes stipulated, 'to be an American.' The supreme commander would 'be primarily concerned with the building up and employment of the Strategic Reserve...' – that is, the formation of troops and weaponry which in conventional military doctrine is to be withheld from the theatres of fighting until the settling dust of battle reveals how it might be most gainfully deployed. The issue of deploying the strategic reserve had been productive of what Foulkes described to his United States counterpart as 'quite divergent opinions.' He explained the problem to General Alfred Gruenther.

Western Union visualizes that they will require reinforcing from this continent while, as you are aware, our joint planning does not visualize any reinforcement of Western Europe. It is quite obvious that if, and when, the Scandinavians start to plan their defence scheme they will similarly expect reinforcing from outside. Both these areas will most likely want hard and fast commitments of the number and type of divisions et cetera which will be put at their disposal. Some of the rest of us may feel that any troops which would be available should not be committed to Western Europe but somewhere else, like the Middle East. It has occurred to me that the only way to shelve these divergent views would be for a frank statement that the strategic reserve would be put at the disposal of the Supreme Commander and that while plans should be made for every contingency, including the reinforcement of the various groups, those decisions will have to be left to the Supreme Commander. In this way we could, therefore, shelve this whole problem of reinforcing the various regions and get over this serious difficulty in the concept of how the next war should be fought...[16]

The Supreme Commander was to have at his disposal not only a strategic reserve but also a Strategic Reserve Group, to include representatives from those countries 'which can provide uncommitted reserves of personnel and material;' this Group would do the planning for the strategic reserve under the guidance of the Supreme Commander. Only three countries were qualified for membership on the Strategic Command Group: the United States, the United Kingdom – and Canada. Foulkes was nothing if not wily.

Canada might gain admission to decision-making in two further North Atlantic forums. One was the Council of Ministers, which had been bestowed upon the pact's members by Article 9 of their Treaty; on that Council, each of them would be equally represented – most appropriately, Foulkes considered, by its minister of defence (most appropriately, Pearson considered, by its foreign minister). The other forum for Canada could be the regional group – a device affording Foulkes' ingenuity full play.

The regional group, Foulkes proposed, should be composed of countries possessing 'a common vital interest which, if threatened, would call for *immediate military action* [Foulkes' italics] by all the countries in that group.' The armed forces of member countries not so threatened would then be available to the Supreme Commander, along with the strategic reserve, for disposition as he saw fit. Each group was to be made responsible for planning the region's defences, and no other. Each group was to have a defence committee advised by the group's chiefs of staff committee, the chairman of which would advise the Supreme Commander. Foulkes discerned three such regional groups which he deemed feasible to form immediately. These were a North American group, composed of the United States, Canada, and (for the defence of Greenland only) Denmark; a Scandinavian group, composed of Norway, Denmark, Iceland, the United Kingdom, and the United States; and a Western European group, composed of 'those countries which form the land mass of Western Europe, together with the USA.' The omission of Canada from the Western Europe group so shocked General Hollis of the British Army that he told the Canadian officer who had brought Foulkes' memorandum to him for comment that he thought 'it must be a typographical error.'[17] It was anything but.

Foulkes' advocacy of the regional group as a basic instrument of alliance planning stemmed from at least three considerations. One was his conviction that (as he put it to General Gruenther) 'useful military planning can only be done by small groups who have a vital interest in the particulars of that planning...' Another was the need to stop leaks. 'I realize that one of the over-riding problems connected with planning is SECURITY,' he had written in his memorandum. 'It is for this reason that I suggest all planning connected with the Strategic Reserve is retained within a special group, which for several years can only comprise Canada, US and UK. Group planning will also assist overall security by dividing plans into comparatively watertight compartments.'* And to Gruenther: 'I know you are as well aware as I am of the difficult security problems which will arise if too many nationals have access to the planning such as that which is being done lately. It has occurred to me that if in some way or other we can isolate the various nations into groups where their own vital interests are paramount they, perhaps, can be kept away from the other planning, at least in the early stages.'[18]

---

* At this observation General Hollis had noted: 'Won't be accepted by Fr.' Prophetically so: it was in response to the rejection of a French demand for a Franco-Anglo-American NATO directorate that General de Gaulle took France out of NATO (without repudiating the North Atlantic Treaty) and ordered NATO out of France, in 1958.

The third reason for Foulkes' advocacy of regional grouping within the alliance had nothing to do with its effectiveness in planning or its prevention of leaks. The device could ensure that Canada would not be made to bear too great a share of the load. This consideration was not for the eyes of allied generals, and Foulkes put it only to his Minister. 'From the papers of the Western Union Finance and Economic Committee,' he informed Brooke Claxton in mid-March,

it appears that they are attempting to work out a formula for the allocation of defence costs on the basis of equitable contributions in accordance with the proportion of the national budget spent on defence. I am a bit alarmed that the Western Union Powers may attempt to have this formula adopted by the Atlantic Pact, and I can see considerable trouble ahead for us if this is the case. The organization which I suggest in the attached paper [the 7 March memorandum] would prevent any such thing and would keep the Western European Powers in their own bailiwick, attending to their own defence matters and not meddling too deeply in our affairs.

'I am quite certain,' Foulkes added, 'if this Atlantic Pact is to work that it must be organized on the basis of Groups of Nations with similar interests and problems...'[19]

Foulkes described his memorandum as 'a purely private paper,' but by mid-March it formed the basis of discussions between its author and senior military officers in the United States and the United Kingdom. What had originated as a purely private paper could be taken for 'the Canadian proposal': already the memorandum had elicited what Foulkes described as 'some favourable comments from the Americans,'[20] and the Vice Chief of the Imperial General Staff had pronounced it to be 'of extreme value,' 'the first time that any other Commonwealth country had produced concrete proposals on a subject of such importance on defence matters...'[21] Foulkes had evidently got things moving. In the Department of External Affairs there was some concern at this, perhaps due as much to departmental rivalry as to the feeling that Foulkes was beyond both his field and his depth. Was it time to rein him in?

On March 25, the two sides got together – Claxton and Foulkes for National Defence, Norman Robertson and A.D.P. Heeney for External Affairs – for what Heeney described as 'a brief chat about defence organization of the Atlantic Pact.' He reported that 'nothing definite was decided. Foulkes explained his idea in greater detail and will, I assume, continue his exchange of views with Gruenther and Hollis. Mr Claxton took no exception to this.'[22] But Claxton while a member of the government of Canada was not the government of Canada. Whether the government would adopt Foulkes' ideas (or some of them) as its own proposals was for the Cabinet to decide; and in such matters the Cabinet (not invariably but usually) consented to what the Secretary of State for External Affairs advised.

L.B. Pearson was briefed on the issue by Heeney on the eve of setting forth for Washington to sign the North Atlantic Treaty for Canada. Heeney strongly urged against pushing Foulkes' memorandum at the Americans and the British, and tried instead to have it consigned to limbo. 'It would clearly be inappropriate and unwise for us to take a leading part in putting forward proposals for the form that defence organization might take under the Atlantic Treaty,' Heeney advised his Minister. 'It could indeed prove very embarrassing if we were to insist on any given scheme for our own representation and then find that we seriously disagreed with the criteria proposed by other countries for apportioning the burden in men, money or supplies.'[23] Mackenzie King (who had lured Heeney into public service) would have very much approved of his protégé's advice on this occasion.

There was in any event no sense of urgency. The Americans (so General Foulkes had reported after visiting the Pentagon) had not yet been able to make up their minds. 'It will clearly be some months before any new organization can be agreed on,' A.D.P. Heeney had written on 1 April. A working group was to be established in Washington to prepare proposals for organization under the Council, including proposals for defence organization. But the North Atlantic Treaty Working Party was not to get to working until its first meeting on 22 August (a delay caused not by the lassitude of diplomats during the heat of a Washington summer but by the desire of the Americans, British, and French to reach agreements in principle before allowing the Working Party to get down to details).

On 18 May, the Cabinet approved guidelines for the Canadian representatives to follow during the course of the Working Party's discussions. These allowed them to assent to locating the North Atlantic Council and its subsidiary organs in different places, but not to agree to a geographic separation of the military and supply organizations; both should be situated together, preferably at Washington. They were to lend their support to the principle that defence planning be done on a regional basis. They were to approve of the formation of a small committee, or steering committee, to plan the co-ordination of regional arrangements and oversee the deployment of the strategic reserve; it should be composed of the Chiefs of Staff of certain North Atlantic countries – the United States, the

United Kingdom, France if it wished, Canada if invited.[24] Foulkes'
'purely private paper' now stood some chance of becoming public policy.

Of these agreements in principle, the most contentious had been the
issue of Canadian membership on the proposed steering committee: the
decision to accept if invited but not to press for invitation had been a
compromise. Those in favour of Canada's membership argued that it
'would ensure that Canada had an equal voice with the United Kingdom,
the United States and France in the determination of all questions of
North Atlantic defence policy. It would avoid the position where Canada
would be presented with more or less final plans which at that stage would
be difficult and possibly embarrassing to argue against.' There was the
additional argument that 'as Canada, like the United States, will have on
the outbreak of war uncommitted forces, it would be desirable for Canada
to be a member of the Group which would be responsible for recommending the allocation of the forces to the various theatres.' And finally:
'Canada, as a supplier nation, should have a full voice in the making of
war plans, which will call for the production and allocation of various
types of equipment and supplies.' The argument against seeking membership was much like Heeney's objection to Canada's taking initiatives on
issues of alliance defence organization.

If Canada accepts membership on such a high level body, it may be expected that
she will be called upon to make a contribution commensurate with such membership. The Minister of Finance has argued against Canada accepting an invitation
to participate in the Western Union Finance and Economic Committee on the
grounds that such participation would lead to demands of a financial and economic character on Canada which we are not prepared to meet. If this is indicative
of the attitude the Government is likely to take toward economic and financial
commitments under the Atlantic Treaty, then membership on a "Steering Committee" might well prove embarrassing to the Government.[25]

It turned out that Canada was not to be invited, after all. The United
States authorities, particularly the Joint Chiefs of Staff, felt that too
many cooks would spoil the broth. It was an argument Canadians had
heard before, too often at their expense. Second thinking set in at
once.

A new set of guidelines to be followed by the Canadian representative
in the North Atlantic Working Party submitted for Cabinet approval on 9
August had at the head of the list the following:

In the event that Canada is not a member of the Steering Committee, representation should be made at the outset of the discussions in the Working Group that
Canadian representatives participate fully in any discussions in the Steering Com-

mittee concerning the use of employment of Canadian resources in areas outside
those of the regional defence organizations of which Canada might be a member.*

It became the task of the Ambassador in Washington, and of George
Ignatieff, the Canadian representative in the Working Party, to obtain the
most explicit recognition of this requirement by other member governments, principally the United States. 'You should emphasize the importance we attach to its acceptance in theory and practice. In putting it
forward you should do so in general terms which would be applicable to
any signatory, although in practice its application would be particular to
Canada which would be the only non-member of the Steering Group having resources likely to be required outside its own regional grouping.'[26] A
telegram to Hume Wrong next day on the same subject betrays mounting
concern in Ottawa.

We continue to regard it of great importance that ... "in any case where the Steering Group planned the use of forces or facilities of any signatory outside the
regional grouping of which that signatory were a member, that signatory should
have a right to participate, as a member, in the deliberations of the Steering
Group." It is true that the functions of the Steering Group are in theory advisory
in character and that decisions could not be taken by that Group on the use of
Canadian forces or resources without the consent of the Canadian Government.
However, we consider it extremely important that our representatives should participate from the initial stages in any planning involving the use of Canadian resources or military manpower. We must avoid the contingency of having plans
presented to us for approval in the framing of which we had no voice and the
rejection of which might prove politically embarrassing...[27]

Next week brought perturbing news. The Canadians were having heavy
going with their requirement. The American member of the Working
Party had spoken to Ignatieff, Hume Wrong reported from Washington,

in order to ask that we should not continue to press too hard for a "watertight"
formula on the question of participation of non-members in the Standing Group,†
as he said that Canada could be quite assured of having its interests fully protected
as far as the Standing Group was concerned because of our special relations with
the United States and the United Kingdom. He suggested that it was to our interest as much as to that of the United States and the United Kingdom that the
Standing Group should be enabled to operate effectively. ... The United States
Chiefs of Staff ... were somewhat perturbed at the idea that non-members should
have too frequent an access to the Standing Group...[28]

---

*   Minutes of Chiefs of Staff Committee, 9 August 1949, Department of External
    Affairs files (50030-40). Much the same formula had been sought, with success, by
    the Canadian delegation at San Francisco in 1945, to assure access to the United
    Nations Security Council.
†   'Steering Committee' or 'Steering Group' was at Canada's suggestion replaced by
    'Standing Group' – 'steering' being thought too authoritarian.

This bad news sent Ottawa's top people into parlay: Heeney met with both Pearson and Claxton and on their instructions replied that 'the formula for participation by non-members in the working of the Standing Group should be regarded as a minimum Canadian requirement. The Canadian Government would not be willing to accept the concept of a Standing Group on which Canada was not represented without such a formula.'[29] Pearson wrote to Heeney: 'I am somewhat disturbed by the [American] attitude. ... We must stand firm on this, no matter what the United States Chiefs of Staff may think...'[30]

The Canadians stood firm, and had their way. The Working Party agreed to a formula much like that proposed by the Canadian government.

It is understood that before the Standing Group make any recommendations on any plans or course of action involving the use of forces, facilities or resources of a party not represented on the Standing Group, going beyond or differing from arrangements previously agreed by the party concerned, that party shall have the right to participate in the work of formulating such recommendations.[31]

This outcome – 'largely the results of our efforts in the meetings' – was described by the Under Secretary of State for External Affairs as 'reasonably satisfactory.' The formula, A.D.P. Heeney assured Brooke Claxton, 'should enable Canadians to participate adequately in North Atlantic planning so as to advance and protect our interests.' But the advancement and protection of those interests, so far from being automatically assured, would 'require the will to make [the formula] work on the part of the US and UK authorities, as well as intelligent and continuing attention on the part of our representation in Washington.'[32]

L.B. Pearson's satisfaction was marred by what he took to be an erroneous interpretation of Canada's position in the press. On 3 September, the *Ottawa Citizen* reported that the Canadian government would likely be excluded from 'the important defence standing committee,' and described the reaction of 'authorities here' as one of 'disappointment.'[33] This report, Pearson told his Under Secretary, 'quite disturbed' him, all the more so because he had taken the precaution of calling in the reporter beforehand precisely in order to head off the misconception which his story contained. During the interview, Pearson told A.D.P. Heeney, he had emphasized to the writer that 'there was no disappointment, and that our sole aim was to make sure that Canadian interests were protected by Canadian representatives whenever they were discussed by the Standing Committee. One way to ensure this would be by membership on that Committee; the other way by participation in its work whenever anything of direct importance to Canada was under consideration. ... Either of the above procedures would be quite satisfactory to us.' Pearson pinned the blame for what had happened on officers and officials in the Department of National Defence. 'They are apparently talking to and misleading the press...' He had telephoned the offending reporter after his story appeared, 'expressing my irritation ... I told him that any of the soldiers or others in National Defence were misleading him if they took this line, and that they did not know what they were talking about if they attempted to represent it as government policy. I pointed out to him that no doubt some of them would be disappointed if Canada were not represented on this inner group, but that their disappointment was personal and not governmental.' Pearson thought such misrepresentation should be nipped in the bud. 'I think that it would be a good idea,' he told Heeney, 'to have a word with [Brooke] Claxton about this, or even better, to send him a memorandum on these lines, a copy of which could go to the Prime Minister.'[34] Pearson, like Mackenzie King, could not abide talkative soldiers – and inquisitive reporters.

Relations between the Standing Group and the rest of the member countries' representatives remained, from the latter's standpoint, unsatisfactory for many years. In 1951, Brooke Claxton put in 'a good deal of work behind the scenes trying to get the Standing Group to appreciate the meaning of the word "consultation." I must have had a dozen talks during these two or three days with people like [General] Bradley,' Claxton wrote,

and in the end they seemed to realize for the first time that consultation in drawing up a plan meant something more than their drawing up a plan and handing it to us for comments which, when received, were attached to the plan, which then remained unchanged. In the case of the Standing Group countries, every figure put down for them was naturally cleared with their own Chiefs of Staff and governments in advance of it being put down. Consequently, they found no difficulty in agreeing with it enthusiastically. For the other countries they put down figures without consultation of any kind. When we questioned these, the Standing Group had some rancour at all the other countries which did not leap to their feet with their hand upstretched to say "Me too, teacher"...[35]

Lack of adequate consultation by the Standing Group remained in the memory of both L.B. Pearson and Brooke Claxton years later. 'On the general question of our worries about not being consulted and the danger of an inner directorate,' Pearson would testify,

we did talk a lot about that. However we didn't feel more strongly about it than some of the smaller European members, not a bit. Some people find it hard to believe, but it is true that Norway and Belgium and the Dutch had always been telling us, "Well, why don't you talk to the Americans and British, you can talk to them in a way that we can't. You know them so well." So we did more of the grousing than they did. This used to annoy the Americans, but we had a very legitimate concern with these developments...[36]

Claxton confirms Pearson's testimony that the Canadian representative on the Military Committee – the Chairman of the Chiefs of Staff Committee or his representative – became something of a mediator between the Military Committee and the Standing Group, and that the Canadians became a spokesman for other aggrieved members. 'At almost every meeting of the Defence Ministers several of the lesser powers would discuss privately with members of the Canadian team some high-handed action of the Standing Group. Almost invariably the Netherlands and Norwegian ministers would see us, Mike Pearson, General Foulkes, or myself, on the eve of such a conference and they would urge us to be their spokesman in taking some stand or asserting some point of view *vis-à-vis* the Standing Group Powers, particularly the United States.'[37]

Just as the Standing Group dominated the Military Committee, so the United States dominated the Standing Group. 'Propinquity in Washington,' Claxton recalled, 'combined with the vastness of the interests, contributions and resources of the United States, gave the Pentagon a position of dominance over the Standing Group. Why, the Standing Group even had its offices and staff housed in the Pentagon! All things considered, it is surprising that the partnership worked as well as it did.'[38]

The Standing Group's practice, noted above by Claxton, of putting down figures for other countries' force commitments without consulting them about these, on occasion created difficulty for Canada. When that happened, it was Claxton's job to try to undo what the Standing Committee had done. A particularly vexing episode occurred at the meeting of the Defence Committee at Washington in October 1950. Before the meeting were a series of papers – an appreciation of the Soviet threat, an estimate of the military forces needed to meet that threat, and a proposal as to how the responsibility for raising those forces should be allocated among NATO members. 'These documents had been considered at various levels by the Standing Group powers and this consideration was still going on to the very eve of the meeting,' Claxton recalled.

None of the smaller powers had been able to get so much as a sight of the papers before they were presented to the meeting of the Military Committee, consisting of the Chiefs of Staff ... two days before our ministerial meeting. Immediately on getting the papers, General Foulkes saw that the Standing Group had made an error of some significance to us in that they had counted twice over one of the ships for which we would be responsible. This would increase by one the number of ships for which, if the paper was passed, we would be committed, a ship, be it noted, which did not exist. There was another similar error under which we would appear to be agreeing to provide a military formation well in advance of the time when it was physically possible to have it transported to the scene of action. More important than these errors which were really errors of editing was a sentence which, in effect, declared that it should be the aim of all nations to have at least two years of military service. This was, of course, not aimed at us. There would be no possible use in our having two years of military service and no one had ever suggested or even considered it. It was, however, aimed at the European countries and had, in fact, been inserted at the express suggestion of the representatives of two or three of the nations who wanted such a provision as a stick with which to get their reluctant parliaments into line. We would not be bound by and would not act on any such recommendation. But the fact that it was there might in the future prove embarrassing to us. However, if it was taken out, it would materially weaken the prospects for increasing the military strength of the countries of Europe which were then woefully weak. We were in a tough spot...

How to extricate Canada from it? Claxton lined up appointments with the defence ministers of the three Standing Group countries, Foulkes sought out his American counterpart General Omar Bradley and the personnel who had drafted the documents. Time was short: the Defence Committee was to meet at 10:30 that morning. It was, Claxton remembered, 'the day I ate three breakfasts.' A formula was contrived wherein the reference to two years of military training, with its dread connotation of conscription, was deleted in favour of a reference to two years of reserve training. 'This was not entirely satisfactory,' Claxton observes in his written record of the incident, 'because all of us knew that we would not have a reserve of the type described.' However, better to fib about reserves – in the interest of the security of Western Europe – than to to fib about conscription. 'I thought it best to let it go. Actually the matter was never mentioned again...'[39]

The errors about 'Force Tabulations' in the papers prepared by the Standing Group were of less consequence to Canada, but Claxton was unwilling to let them go as well. 'The officers of the Standing Group responsible for the paper admitted they had made a mistake,' Claxton recalled.

However, the members of the Standing Group were most anxious to avoid, if possible, all discussion of force tabulations as some of the countries had agreed to some of the figures put down only with the greatest reluctance and any discussion would throw the whole comprehensive plan wide open. It was urged upon me that the force tabulations were put down for "planning purposes only." I was all too familiar with this expression from my experiences with Canada-United States defence co-operation, and I would not let it pass. Everyone agreed that the figures were put down in error: why not be grown-up and correct the error? I said that any figures we agreed to let stand would later be used by others as indications of commitments and if we made a commitment we kept it. I was simply not authcr-ized by my government to make such a commitment and I would not ask the government to accept figures put down by mistake. All of the others knew that the figures were, in fact, wrong, and they should be changed...

In the event, they were: '[T]he matter was dealt with by the subsequent circulation of a revised allocation with the right figures for us.'

Was Claxton being too much the stickler in making such a fuss? His own delegation thought so for, as he records, 'they unanimously took a view contrary to mine. They said that everyone knew our position, which I would make clear at the time of the meeting and, as it would appear cn the record, no one would ever dream of raising it again or we could igno-e anything that was said. I still refused to change.' His advisers, Claxtcn considered, had missed the point. 'The fact that we took the stand we did,' he wrote afterwards,

was useful quite apart from its being necessary in our own interest. It showed the Standing Group and the other agencies of NATO that they must discuss with the nations concerned figures affecting them. This I pointed out at the conclusion of the meeting and it resulted in assurances being given that this would be done in the future. I may say that either General Foulkes or myself or some other Cana-dian had to point this out at virtually every meeting or every organ of NATO until it gradually came to be accepted...[40]

In pressing [this point], we were, of course, completely right. Unless the "Big Three" accepted our point of view and acted on it, the alliance might not long survive. ... What we were driving at was that the over-all direction of the alliance must be carried on by the alliance as a whole, an alliance in which we were all equal partners though not of equal strength. All nations agreed with us in this, but the "Big Three" frequently reverted to type and, despite repeated assurance to the contrary, acted without the participation of the rest.[41]

The Standing Group's task in peacetime was to plan the overall defence of North Atlantic Treaty countries. But what was to be its scope? Were the planners to take the world for their potential operations? Or were they to plan only within the treaty area as defined by Article 6?

These questions would divide the Alliance down the years. But as early as its first year, a major and potentially damaging division was caused by them.

Of all NATO members, France was from the outset the most forceful and unyielding advocate of the necessity of planning on a global scale. Soviet power was deployed, French policy-makers argued, according to world-wide perspectives; only a global strategy, therefore, could effec-tively contain and contend with Soviet power. There was logic in this argument, but there was also self-interest. France faced politico-military threats from the proxies of Soviet power far outside the treaty area – most menacingly in South-East Asia. How was it possible fairly to assess the French contribution to the common defence of the North Atlantic countries without taking into account French resistance to communist imperialism in areas remote from them?

The British, and to a lesser extent the Americans, did not at first accept France's position in favour of a world-wide strategy. They contended that planning, at least during the Alliance's early years, should be restricted to the regions of the North Atlantic. These, they argued, afforded scope enough. North Atlantic planners might in time develop a global reach, but for the present it should not exceed their regional grasp. Realism dictated a less ambitious mandate. Behind this stated argument lay an unmentionable one. The United Kingdom and the United States had, in conjunction with Canada, engaged in global strategic planning since the Second World War had ended; visible products of these exercises existed in the form of planning papers. The three governments concerned did not wish to divulge these, for security reasons, to the government of France.

On the issue as to whether NATO should plan regionally or globally, the Canadian position was described, in a Chiefs of Staff memorandum of 30 June 1949, as 'somewhat involved.' The memorandum attempted to explain:

When the Canadian Government agreed that if Canada were invited to sit on the top level planning body, the invitation would be accepted, it was felt by certain officials that the discussion concerning this subject had included the problem of overall strategy as being part of the North Atlantic responsibilities. Other officials are of the opinion that all the Ministers were not clear that our acceptance of a position on the top level North Atlantic Defence planning body would involve us in global strategic planning...[42]

This unusually murky passage of bureaucratic prose suggests that the Canadian position on global planning was not so much involved as confused.

There was no confusion, however, in the minds of the Chiefs of Staff. They were globalists like the French. 'The primary objective of the North Atlantic Defence Organization' – so the Chiefs put forward for the Cabinet's consideration – 'must be the development of a global strategy which will bring about, quickly and effectively, the destruction of the Russian war machine and at the same time will provide for the territorial defence, as far as is practicable, of all countries of the North Atlantic community.'[43]

By August 1949 the rift between the two sides had widened. Canada made an attempt to bridge it. The Ambassador at Washington was instructed to tell the American authorities how Ottawa thought this might be done. 'You should say that it is the conclusion of the Canadian chiefs and senior officials concerned,' Hume Wrong was told on 2 August,

that the general interest would best be served by limiting the reference of the Senior Military Committee to general terms and by avoiding any attempt at this time to define the Committee's role with any greater precision than does the Treaty itself. Thus the instruction to the Defence Committee from the Council of North Atlantic Foreign Ministers might merely be to "recommend measures for the implementation of Articles 3 and 5."

'I think if we can keep to general terms of this kind,' A.D.P. Heeney concluded, 'we might be able to avoid an open and possibly irreconcilable conflict particularly with the French whose strong views are well known.'[44]

A few days later A.D.P. Heeney again turned to the scope-of-planning problem. Heeney described the issue as 'fundamental.' He lamented that he had seen 'no indication to date that a reconciliation has been achieved.' He repeated his instruction to Hume Wrong to place Canada's suggestion for compromise before the American government, this time formally. 'If such terms of reference (which admittedly avoid the issue) are accepted by the United Kingdom, the United States and France,' Heeney recapitulated,

the possibility of an early impasse in the establishment of the organization might be averted. We would hope that the conflict between the notions of regional and global planning could in practice be reconciled within the organization as experience dictated. ... I do not see how it would be possible to avoid some discussion of the wider issues in the North Atlantic Organization...*

Meanwhile, General Foulkes had been conferring in Washington with the senior US Army officers, among them General Omar Bradley. Possibly to Foulkes' surprise, Bradley agreed with the Canadian approach. 'Bradley's view,' Foulkes reported to Ottawa,

was that he thought the Pact in its early stages should be mainly concerned in the organization of the regions; in other words, the settling of the territorial defence of the regional groups. He felt that the ultimate aim must be that of a deterrent and an organization to plan, fight and win the next war. He agreed, however, that it would not be advisable to try and spell out now the scope of the Atlantic Pact. He felt that this was a matter that could well be decided by the Council after the Pact was set up.[45]

* A.D.P. Heeney to H.H. Wrong, 19 August 1949 (telegram), DEA files, 50030-40. In the event, it not only was possible, it happened: see below, 156-63.

    As the result of these efforts, the report of the North Atlantic Working
Party submitted to the North Atlantic Council at its first meeting on 17
September 1949 proposed that the Council create a Military Committee to
'recommend measures for the implementation of Articles 3 and 5.' The
issue had been avoided. It would not disappear.
    Any lingering antipathy in Ottawa towards the concept of global plan-
ning by NATO was banished by the outbreak of war in Korea on 25 June
1950. 'It is obvious that war in the Pacific, particularly if it should spread,
will affect the probability of attaining the objectives of North Atlantic
planning,' a member of the policy community commented three weeks
after hostilities began.

The North Atlantic Treaty Organization cannot go on indefinitely without taking
stock of the changes which the Korean War is bringing about and of the possible
results of more extended trouble in the Pacific. The whole balance between the
defence needs of the North Atlantic Treaty area and of the Pacific area, respectively, will require to be reconsidered. This is as much a political problem as a
strategic one. If a disproportionate involvement is undertaken in the Pacific area,
this may undermine not only the security but the morale of Western European
nations...

Note was made of an item on the agenda of the forthcoming first meeting
of the Council Deputies – 'Round-up on World Situation' – which, the
official felt, 'would permit consideration of some of the implications of
the Korean affair upon the problems facing the North Atlantic Treaty. It
is doubtful,' he concluded,

whether some major political issues, as, for example, United States policy on
Formosa or the admission of Communist China to the United Nations could
profitably be discussed in this forum. On the other hand, the bearing of the Pacific
War on North Atlantic plans is an obvious general topic for discussion...[46]

The Under Secretary agreed. 'A discussion of Korea among the North
Atlantic Deputies at this time would, it seems to us, be almost unavoidable,' A.D.P. Heeney responded, 'if the North Atlantic countries are to
take the meetings of the Deputies as seriously as the Council obviously
intended...'[47]
    If NATO members were now enjoined to discuss issues around the
world – even if only as these were thought to bear on problems of the
North Atlantic area – ought not NATO members be permitted to plan globally as well? The French government, with armed forces engaged in
South-East Asia and North Africa, proposed that the Standing Group be
entrusted with the task of developing a global strategy for the Alliance.
Ottawa now favoured global planning, but was reluctant to have it done by

the Standing Group. 'I think there is little likelihood of the French persuading the rest of us that the Standing Group should be the agency for global planning and strategy,' the Secretary of State for External Affairs told the Permanent Representative at Paris on 3 October 1952. 'Nevertheless, I think it is almost as important now as it was in wartime that there should be planning on a wider-than-NATO basis.'[48]

That 'planning on a wider-than-NATO basis' was imperative if the Alliance was to make its decisions in a reasonably rational manner was soon borne in upon A.D.P. Heeney after arriving in Paris to take up his new duties as Permanent Representative on the North Atlantic Council. 'In organizing resistance against a Communist aggression, the Free World has to make a difficult decision in regard to the allocation of its resources, e.g., what proportion of these resources should be assigned to the various theatres: the Far East, the Middle East, the Atlantic area,' Heeney pointed out in one of his first despatches.

At present, however, there is no single agency to make this decision. NATO is not in a position to provide the forum for discussion of global strategy and take decisions on the overall allocation of Allied resources between the Atlantic and other areas.

The present procedure seems to be to set up progressively regional organizations ... without formal links between each other, liaison being provided by those countries like the United States and the United Kingdom which are members of all or many of these various bodies. This arrangement leaves it implicitly to these countries to make the basic decisions as to priority between the various areas. The smaller countries, in times of crisis, unless they themselves are directly threatened, may not follow, claiming that they have not been adequately consulted. In a period of cold war, the regional groups are likely to be weakened by disagreement over the priority which is assigned to them by the members who have interests in other areas...

Planning on a world basis is nevertheless required...

What then should be done? It was not Canada's business, Heeney conceded, to tell the Big Three how to co-ordinate their respective global plans. 'It is, however, in our interests that NATO plans should be integrated with those which are related to the world-wide scope of the threat. We would therefore be justified,' Heeney concluded, 'in urging in the interests of NATO that its members should be informed of and should have some opportunity to comment on, global plans which might envisage the allocation of particular responsibility to the NATO area.'[49] L.B. Pearson agreed, but not without reservation. 'I still think, however, there must be difficulties about using any NATO agencies for the purpose – certainly some of the smaller European member countries would be worried about any such development. But global planning in some way is obviously necessary.'[50]

As the policy community at Ottawa tried to grope its way to some resolution of these 'difficulties,' it occurred to some of its members that it might be helpful to develop a distinction between 'strategy' and 'planning.' The Standing Group could be encouraged 'to take into account overall global strategy in formulating NATO strategy,' but not to undertake global planning, since the latter 'might imply extension of our commitments beyond the NATO area. ... We can see the political problem clearly,' the Under Secretary of State for External Affairs argued in a memorandum for the Defence Liaison I division of his Department,

if we endeavour to relate it to our own position. It is true that increased defence efforts by the NATO powers in such areas as South-East Asia or the Middle East might lead to calls being made on Canada for greater efforts in the defence of the NATO area, but it would be much more difficult to get the Canadian people to respond to this effort if it is put in global terms than if it is put in the simple terms of the defence requirements of the NATO area. That is, we can make our people see that the defence of the NATO area is vital to Canadian defence, whereas they cannot be made so readily to respond to an appeal which relates the interests of Canadian defence to such areas as the Middle East or South-East Asia.

In any event, Dana Wilgress concluded, 'I think this whole question is very academic because for reasons connected with atomic energy legislation the United States is not yet ready to discuss either global strategy or global planning with other powers.'*

But the question was not 'very academic.' Canada's NATO commitment and a fellow NATO member's global commitment were in practice interrelated. The interrelationship indeed came close to creating a crisis within the government – and did create a *contretemps*.

On 30 June 1952, the French Embassy in Ottawa informed the Department of External Affairs that its government wished to divert a quantity of military equipment which Canada had given to French forces for the defence of Western Europe under Mutual Aid. The equipment included seventy-two tractor-drawn anti-tank guns, seventeen anti-aircraft guns, 14,000 rounds of ammunition for these weapons, rangefinders, and telescopic sights. The French government wished to send it to the theatre of war in Indochina.

Officials consulted the Defence Appropriation Act, 1950, which authorized transfer of military equipment to Western European allies, and discerned there no legal impediment to the desired transfer. The Act

---

* USSEA, memorandum for Defence Liaison Division I, 5 March 1953, DEA files, 50107-40. See below, Ch. 4, 236-38.

prescribed a sole qualification – that weapons transferred be used by their recipient to 'help assure the preservation of peace.' L.B. Pearson, whose opinion as Minister was then solicited, took the view that 'the preservation of peace' was the mission of the French Army in Indochina, and that the French Government should be informed that Canada accordingly would have no objection to the weapons being transferred from France to Indochina.

'I was clearly not a born politician': the admission is Pearson's own, and while uttered as jesting self-deprecation it was on this occasion justified. The highly developed – indeed, overdeveloped – antennae for detecting distant political trouble possessed by the Minister of National Defence* produced in Brooke Claxton an altogether different reaction. 'I must say this gives me a good deal of concern,' Claxton wrote to the Under Secretary of State for External Affairs, 'and I think it should be brought before the Cabinet.'[51]

The Minister of National Defence was not the only member of the Government to feel apprehensive about the prospect that Canada's Mutual Aid for the defence of Western Europe would be diverted for service in what could – and would – be called a 'colonial' war. The Prime Minister was even more concerned. Louis St Laurent learned of the proposal on 24 July. He at once

expressed grave doubt as to whether such a diversion would be within the scope of the present law and left no doubt that, in his opinion, it was beyond the scope of government policy at the present time. He pointed out that Canada had been among those countries which had insisted that the scope of the Atlantic Treaty area should not include North Africa but be confined to Metropolitan France. He added that we had taken the view consistently that our mutual aid was to strengthen the North Atlantic forces in Europe and that we had been very careful to indicate at all times that we accepted no responsibility for the defence of British colonies or dependencies and that he felt that the public would not understand anything which might be construed as accepting responsibilities in relation to the French Empire which we would not accept in relation to the British Empire.[†]

* 'He approached a problem apprehensively, as if it were an ambuscade from which would leap some monstrous complication to overwhelm the Liberal Government and Liberal Party.' *In Defence of Canada* III, 27.

† J.W. Pickersgill to C.M. Drury, 24 July 1952, DEA files, 50030-L-5-40. St Laurent's attitude stemmed less from his desire to keep Canada's commitments to Britain and France in balance than from his distaste for the colonial policies of each: 'A pox on both your Empires' fairly renders a feeling so agitated by the Suez crisis as to prompt his outburst in the House of Commons on 26 November 1956. 'With the sense of relief of a man unburdening himself of a grievance of long standing, the Prime Minister threw back his shoulders defiantly, reddened, and retorted: "...the members of smaller nations are human beings just as are other people; because the era when the supermen of Europe could govern the whole world is coming pretty close to an end".' Dale C. Thomson, *Louis St Laurent: Canadian* (Toronto 1967), 485-6. Pickersgill later described these words as 'fatal.' J.W. Pickersgill, *My Years with Louis St Laurent: A Political Memoir* (Toronto 1975), 313.

St Laurent remained unmoved by the argument, put to him by J.W.
Pickersgill, that the proposed transfer was 'a mere substitution of material
to avoid shipping one lot of supplies to France to replace another lot
which would be taken from France to Indochina, and that, in that sense, it
might be regarded in fact if not in form as a strengthening of the North
Atlantic forces in Europe.' That to him was sophistry. The form was the
fact. The most that the Prime Minister would concede – and it was a concession wrung from him reluctantly – was that Canada would *sell* the
equipment to France if, and only if, the Standing Group were to state that
the diversion was in the best interests of the Alliance.[52]

From the Ambassador at Paris, meanwhile, had come advice strongly in
support of Canada's giving outright and forthright aid to the French military effort in Vietnam. 'I see no reason why the proposed diversion of
mutual aid should not take place,' General Georges Vanier cabled from
his embassy. 'I believe the best way to help Europe now is to help France
in Indochina where the French are putting up a valiant and costly fight
against Communism. ... The immediate Communist threat is to Asia not
Europe. If Indochina goes, other countries will follow.'[53] There was nothing in this analysis to contradict anything that L.B. Pearson, speaking for
the government, had been telling the people of Canada. Yet St Laurent
recoiled from it. His views on France's war in South-East Asia were closer
to what Roosevelt's had been. ('The case of Indochina is perfectly clear.
France has milked it for one hundred years. The people of Indochina are
entitled to something better than that.')[54] Defence equipment reaching
France from Canada was to be used in the defence of Western Europe,
not in a colonial war.

The policy community was now aroused and agitated. This sort of com-
motion was not its standard operating procedure. The Prime Minister
seemed to some to be idiosyncratic. The Chairman of the Chiefs of Staff
Committee let it be known that had France not committed what had
turned out to be its tactical error of seeking permission for the diversion,
but had simply shipped the equipment on the quiet, no one would have
been any the wiser and the matter would not have come up. The military
adviser to the delegation at NATO headquarters insisted that Europe's defence would not suffer as a result of the diversion: the twenty-five-
pounder guns which the French wanted for the Indochina battlefield were
not in use in France's European forces. That let a cat out of the bag: 'If
metropolitan French forces do not use 25 pdr. guns,' the Defence Liaison
Division of the Department of External Affairs inquired pointedly, 'why
did the French Government put bids for such guns when offered by Canada to NATO countries through the Standing Group?' The counsellor at

the French Embassy, confronted by this evidence of possible bad faith and double-dealing, replied evenly that the Standing Group knew very well that the French Army did not use such weapons and must have therefore assumed all along that they were destined for the Indochina theatre.[55]

By all of this the Prime Minister remained unimpressed and unmoved. To agree to allow the shipment to proceed overseas, St Laurent noted, 'would involve our assumption of some responsibility for the colonial or dependency burden of the metropolitan members of NATO, and that is something which we decided originally we would not do. I see no sufficient reason to change our stand.'[56]

St Laurent was stubborn, but there were limits. He was by now holding out against the advice of everyone to seek a compromise. He told his advisers that 'if his colleagues in the Cabinet were convinced that action ought to be taken ... he was prepared to have himself over-ruled. He wanted it to be known, however, that he was quite unconvinced that it was desirable to take any such action.'[57]

That attitude made it unlikely that his colleagues could change his mind. Nor did they. On 26 August, St Laurent told the Cabinet Defence Committee that he did not want the Mutual Aid equipment to go to Indochina. The French Government was duly informed that the Mutual Aid equipment should remain in Europe. If the French Government decided to send it to Indochina, that was their responsibility. 'The ultimate destination of this equipment is a matter for the French to clear with the Standing Group. ... We, for our part, have no further concern with the matter.'[58]

It was not exactly a noble way out of the impasse, but at least it was a way out.

HARNESS AND HORSES

Between the first session of the North Atlantic Council, on 17 and 18 September 1949 at Washington, and its second, from 15 to 18 May 1950 at London, the Alliance had acquired a rudimentary organization – in fact, if not yet in name. An organization chart (see overleaf) tells something about the institutions it depicts, but little of their power structure and less of ambience. How did these appear to Canadian officials taking part in them?

Of the North Atlantic Council, expectations had been modest. 'Made up, as it will be, of representatives of States of all sizes between that of

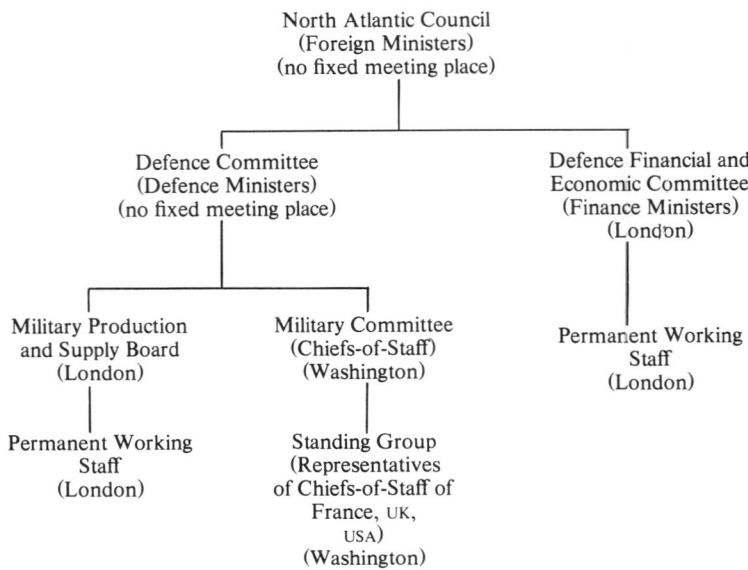

Iceland and that of the United States,' Hume Wrong commented some weeks before it first met, 'it is not likely to become a body which meets frequently or requires lengthy sessions. It will in practice, I think, register decisions for formal submissions to the parties which have already been agreed upon in the subordinate treaty agencies or in diplomatic negotiations. ... There will be reluctance in Washington,' Wrong predicted, 'and I think in some of the other capitals, to [allow] the development of the Council into a substantial body of machinery with Standing Committees and Special Committees busy drawing up reports.'[58] However reluctantly, they would watch that happen.

The date proposed by the US State Department for the first meeting of the North Atlantic Council was for L.B. Pearson both inconvenient and inappropriate – inconvenient because Parliament was to meet at about the same time, inappropriate because the date was shortly before that of the convening of the UN General Assembly, and Pearson feared that this timing 'would certainly be seized on for propaganda purposes,' allowing critics of the alliance to accuse its members of attempting to downgrade the importance of the world organization.[59] The meeting took place on 17 September as the Americans had wanted it to and moreover decided that 'for general convenience the ordinary annual session should normally be held at about the same time and in the same general geographic area as the annual session of the General Assembly.'[60] Friends of the Soviet Union pounced eagerly upon this practice, as Pearson had foreseen they would. 'Underlining the fact that the Atlantic Pact organization is in direct opposition to the UN,' the *Daily Worker* of London told its readers on 4 May 1951, 'it was announced yesterday that the annual meetings of the full North Atlantic Council will be held at the same time and the same place as the UN Assembly.'

The first meeting of the Council was timed by a Canadian official at fifty-three minutes; it went, he thought, 'very smoothly.' The US Secretary of State presided. There were no public speeches, and a text prepared for such an occasion went undelivered. Its author, Escott Reid, was told by a colleague that his draft 'might be very useful for a statement in Parliament which will presumably have to be made'; to which Reid responded dryly: 'Thanks for the consolation. You might put this on the proper file so that the oratory can be resurrected when needed.'[61] The episode led Hume Wrong to express doubt about 'the value of preparing in Ottawa draft speeches for use at the Council. I think both the form and the content of statements such as this cannot be determined in this instance much, if at all, ahead of the opening session. ... My general impression is that Mr Pearson will in fact need to play by ear at the Council meeting.'[62]

As the date of the Council's second session approached, senior officials reflected on how its meetings might best be conducted. 'The North Atlantic Council, like the constitutional organs of any national community, suffers from defects,' Escott Reid ruminated in a memorandum to his Minister.

Its members are of unequal calibre. The states which they represent vary greatly in size and in importance and, at least so far as Portugal is concerned, differ in certain fundamental characteristics. However, it is the only general organ which the North Atlantic Community possesses and, if we are to make progress towards our goal of a more united and stronger North Atlantic Community, there seems to be no alternative but to make the fullest possible use of this organ, imperfect as it is.

It is therefore all to the good that it has been decided that the Council, at its next meeting, should discuss some of the fundamental questions of foreign policy which affect all the members of the North Atlantic Community.

The Council in its first discussion of these fundamental questions will have to feel its way much as the meeting of Commonwealth Foreign Ministers at Colombo felt its way, and my guess is that the discussion in London will be somewhat similar to the discussions at Colombo both in their general characteristics and in the value to be derived from them. Each member of the Alliance will have the opportunity to learn more at first hand of the general approach of the other members to common problems, and each member, after the meeting has taken place, will be in a better position to make its own decisions in the light of a greater understanding of the aims and policies of the other members. This could be the beginning of a process ... of a pooling not only of risks and resources but also of control over policy...

There will obviously be certain important subjects which, for one good reason or another, it would not be wise to discuss formally at a certain meeting of the North Atlantic Council. This does not, however, mean that a subject should be kept off the agenda merely because discussion of it would embarrass one of the members of the Council. If the Council is to discuss important questions of foreign policy, the discussions are bound at times to embarrass one or more members of the Council. That, indeed, may be the main purpose of the discussion...

From our experience at the Colombo Conference, I suggest that the Working Party in Washington discuss not only the agenda of the meeting in London but also the physical arrangements for the meeting. The smaller the conference table, the fewer the people who are in the room, the more informal the atmosphere, the more likely it is that the discussions will be useful. I would suggest, for example, that the table at which the Foreign Ministers meet should be no larger than to seat comfortably fourteen people – the twelve foreign ministers and two secretaries or interpreters, and that each Foreign Minister be restricted to having three advisers in the room and that there be no other people in the room...[63]

If Reid stressed the importance of format and ambience, A.D.P. Heeney was concerned with the agenda. 'In general terms,' he wrote for Pearson's benefit,

it is clear that there is a good deal of interest among the North Atlantic countries in using the next meeting as a time for stocktaking, both as regards the progress that has been made during the first year in implementing the Treaty and as regards the relations of the North Atlantic Community with the Soviet Union...

We propose to have a frank exchange of views on political developments of common concern in much the same way as we did at the meeting of Commonwealth foreign ministers in Colombo. There will be no commitments or any attempt to formulate common policies on outstanding issues, but simply, by an exchange of views, to try to achieve closer coordination of our foreign policies...[64]

Looking at the Council's agenda as it had evolved towards the end of April 1950, Pearson pronounced it 'quite satisfactory. On its face it should give an opportunity for realistic examination of the progress to date and for constructive discussion with regard to future policy.' He was, however, worried lest the talk be rushed and superficial. 'I am inclined to think that the time allotted is much too short. ... Part of this time will probably be given up to a public session and to the preparation of a press release. At best this leaves little more than two days for serious discussion.' He hoped that the participants would undertake to remain in session as long as required for them to do justice to the subject-matter.

'Meetings at the ministerial level have hitherto been largely *pro forma*,' Pearson complained to Hume Wrong in Washington.

There is the more need for adequate consideration by the Council of all topics on the agenda. It is, of course, difficult to say how the forthcoming meetings will develop or to predict what functions in the organization the Council will ulti-mately perform, but if NATO is to become a really effective instrument for peace and for promoting the community interests of the North Atlantic area, I should think that the Council must take seriously its responsibility as a supreme governing authority of the organization...[65]

The second session of the North Atlantic Council fulfilled Pearson's hopes for it. The ministers talked for four days, rather than three, and he considered the time well spent. 'The Council meeting has gone off ex-tremely well,' Pearson reported from London. 'Really important things have happened this week...'[66] And at the next session, held in New York in mid-September in an atmosphere of emergency brought on by the war in Korea, Pearson was struck by 'the remarkably high level of discussion '[67]

From this pinnacle of excellence there could only be a fall. 'It is pretty plain that the Americans want to keep discussion to a minimum,' an offi-cial of the Department of External Affairs noted on the eve of the North Atlantic Council session at Brussels in December 1950.[68] So it proved: Dean Acheson's performance was perfunctory and Pearson (then in New York negotiating with the Chinese communists on behalf of the United Nations) did not miss much. A ministerial meeting of the Council held two years later was described by one of the Canadians present as 'singu-larly unproductive,' and he speculated that issues were being deliberately avoided 'in order to escape responsibility.'[69] The approach of the annual ministerial meeting in 1953 found Pearson apprehensive: he feared that 'the forthcoming Council meeting will provide very thin fare.' He was dismayed to learn that the session was being scheduled for 17-19 Decem-ber. Such a date, he complained, 'would advertise to the world that...we expected to accomplish little; that the meeting would not be much more than a formality – sandwiched in between a [French] Presidential election and Christmas.'[70] Pearson plumped for an earlier date, but in vain. An American journalist on the scene concluded that the North Atlantic Council was at a nadir. 'Nobody – and that includes Eden, Mike Pearson, [Halvard] Lange or any of the other so-called bright boys – contribute anything. Everybody is just glad to get the meeting over and done with.'[71]

'Everybody' did not include L.B. Pearson. So far from wanting to get the meeting over and done with, Pearson urged that the participants take their time and lamented the fact that they did not. 'Too often meetings on this [ministerial] level last only a day or so,' he complained in a public lecture at Princeton University early in 1955, with a substantial part of the time taken either by set speeches, or by consideration of a draft communiqué. The Ministerial participants are often as much the victims of a deadline as any cub reporter, and the requirement of exact precision in the language recording a decision becomes secondary to the necessity of being at the airport in two hours so that an appointment can be kept next day at home, thousands of miles away. As a result – and this has happened more than once in the last few years – misunderstandings have been created which could have been avoided if there had been more time for careful and painstaking discussion between all the participants...[72]

The Secretary of State for External Affairs, believing as he did that the North Atlantic Council was a potentially valuable instrument of coalition diplomacy, expressed his gratification about those of its sessions he considered to have been productive, just as he voiced his criticism of those he considered to have been futile. L.B. Pearson quoted with approval an assessment of the May 1955 session by his Belgian colleague Paul-Henri Spaak: 'Our discussions were ... becoming more and more like Cabinet discussions in a Commonwealth of Atlantic powers.'[73] And of the meeting of the North Atlantic Council convened at Paris on the eve of the Big Four summit conference at Geneva in July 1955 (to allow other alliance members to receive and comment on the views of the three NATO governments which, with the Soviet Union, would be represented at the summit by their respective heads), Pearson told the House of Commons that it had been 'the process of consultation at its best. ... [T]he three foreign ministers who were going to Geneva told those representing the other 12 member states quite frankly and quite fully their hopes and fears about Geneva, their plans and their policies, and gave us an opportunity to express our views. ... In that sense it was valuable...'[74]

The North Atlantic Council Ministerial Meeting scheduled for December 1955 appeared to L.B. Pearson to be particularly crucial, convened as it would be in the aftermath of the Geneva summit. Pearson instructed the Ambassador at Washington to so inform the US State Department. This was done. 'I said it seemed to you, particularly after Geneva, that it was important that there should be no undue sense of rush about the December meeting,' A.D.P. Heeney* reported to his Minister. 'That is to

---

* Heeney had replaced Hume Wrong as Ambassador at Washington in July 1953. 'My contacts with the East Block,' he recalled later of this posting,

> and with the Ottawa hierarchy, were all that I could have asked. Pearson seemed to trust me. In addition to communication by teletype, he used to telephone me frequently, and from time to time we met. ... I felt that we were on a frank and confident basis in our dealings.

A.D.P. Heeney, *The Things that are Caesar's: The Memoirs of a Canadian Public Servant* (Toronto 1972), 126.

say, that there should be an opportunity for deliberation; the Alliance was at a perhaps critical stage and this was an opportunity to tighten it up. For this purpose time should be given for real consultation, not only in the formal meetings, but behind the scenes as well...'[75] These representations were without the desired result. Pearson was once more dismayed when he saw the agenda proposed for the meeting. It hardly reflected, he wrote, 'the seriousness of some of the problems which we shall have to consider. ... I am more than ever convinced that ministerial meetings should be the place where substantive discussions are held and not merely the occasions for giving formal approval to decisions already reached.'[76] Aggravated by the seemingly cavalier attitude of the NATO summiteers, he told the Permanent Representative on the North Atlantic Council of his distress 'at the way the United States ministers on the one hand and Mr Macmillan on the other seem to have combined forces to reduce to a bare minimum the time available for the next NATO ministerial meeting. ... We are seriously concerned here at the inability of the US and UK Ministers to see their way clear in attending a full meeting as originally scheduled. The decision of Mr Macmillan not to be in Paris on ... the 17th is quite disconcerting. I am afraid,' Pearson added, 'that this can only be interpreted by some of our NATO partners – and I am thinking mostly of our German colleagues – as a lack of interest in political consultations at the Ministerial level between NATO partners.'[77] The meeting, when it took place, was short but, for Pearson at least, sweet – 'the best informal exchange of views that has ever taken place.' The delegation reported from Paris that a discussion of general political problems 'had lasted for three hours, and was characterized by frankness, which augurs well for the future of political consultation within NATO.'[78]

In March 1956, L.B. Pearson became one of three 'Wise Men' assigned by the North Atlantic Council to investigate, among other matters, the role of the NATO ministerial meeting as a venue for improved political consultation. Here was his chance to try to breathe new life into the meeting scheduled for May of that year. There was much to discuss. Beyond the hardy perennials of NATO agendas – Soviet intentions, battle-worthinesses, Atlantic community – loomed prospective new items. Two NATO members – Britain and Greece – were at odds over Cyprus. France was distracted by a war in Algeria which was dividing and demoralizing the metropole. Iceland wanted its American guardians to leave. Was it not unrealistic to ignore such developments which were depleting resources urgently required to meet the threat of the common enemy?

The question might be thought to be rhetorical; but it was far from that. If debate over these issues led to a clearing of the air, obviously well and good. But there could be a different outcome. 'Naturally our main aim should be to consolidate the Alliance,' L.B. Pearson pointed out to the Permanent Representative on the North Atlantic Council in mid-March 1956, 'and there would be no point in discussing these problems in the Council if the end result were to widen the gap between the members most immediately concerned.'[79] If these intra-Alliance disputes were to be usefully discussed, Pearson considered, there should be prior consent from the disputants.

Still perplexed as to whether candour in the Council would help or hinder alliance solidarity, the Secretary of State for External Affairs sought guidance from NATO's Secretary General. In a 'personal and confidential' message to Lord Ismay, L.B. Pearson outlined the dilemma. On the one hand, alliance solidarity was threatened by the crises over Cyprus and Algeria, and it obviously behooved its members to do all they could to lower the tension. On the other hand, 'both situations have an important bearing on the political and military effectiveness of the Alliance and many member Governments must be wondering whether those directly concerned would consider that consultation with their political friends would be a help rather than a hindrance in working out solutions. ... I hate to add to your burdens,' Pearson thoughtfully added, 'but I would be very grateful indeed if, in the meantime, you could give me, through Wilgress, the benefit of your thoughts...' In a later message to Dana Wilgress, Pearson explained what had led him to make this overture.

My personal message to Ismay was prompted by my concern about what the next Ministerial Meeting will do to cope with the critical developments in the Mediterranean which obviously pose most serious and immediate problems for the solidarity and efficiency of the Alliance. What I would hope for in the comparatively short time before this meeting are joint efforts by the Council and Member Governments to see if some solutions could be found to these problems. What I should hope to avoid is the Ministerial Meeting merely providing ..."an excellent opportunity to wash our dirty linen but '*en famille*'." Likewise in the present circumstances it would be frustrating and perhaps even positively harmful if the Ministers merely met to have a general discussion of the international situation and various long term problems of the kind we have had in the past and make no useful impact at all on the current situation facing the Alliance.[80]

NATO's Secretary General received Pearson's message as he was about to take a holiday. 'For the time being my brain has stopped functioning,' Lord Ismay engagingly admitted, and asked if he might respond when refreshed by his vacation. This he did, unhelpfully. 'To be quite honest, I could not think of any reply that would be either constructive or helpful,' the old soldier wrote bluntly. 'And I am still in that quandary...'[81]

In the absence of guidance from Ismay, the Permanent Representative ventured the opinion that whether discussion of sensitive issues within the North Atlantic Council would prove helpful or otherwise would depend on the issue itself. To debate Cyprus, for example, would be worse than useless: 'The result would be three outspoken speeches by the countries concerned which could not help to solve but might aggravate the situation...' Algeria was different. '[B]y asking the Permanent Council to issue a communiqué on the recent withdrawal of French troops from Germany for Algeria,' Dana Wilgress pointed out, 'the French Government can no longer claim that this is a purely domestic matter. I believe, therefore, that the Algerian question should be discussed at the next ministerial meeting. ... [T]he emphasis should be on encouraging the French Government in their efforts to reach a liberal solution...'[82]

Ten days before the session opened, policy makers were still divided as to whether discussion of such issues would help or harm the Alliance. 'I do not see that a discussion can be avoided...,' the Under Secretary of State for External Affairs argued in a memorandum for his Minister on 25 April 1956. '[I]ndeed, if political consultation is to serve any useful purpose between the allies, I do not think that a discussion should be avoided. ... I for my part think it would be a mistake if we were simply to gloss over a decisive problem in the Council.' But, Jules Léger added, 'I do not think that just "washing NATO's dirty linen" even in private will of itself help to find solutions to these difficult problems ...'[83]

The meeting to which Ottawa had given so much consideration when held proved disappointing. 'Despite the fact that the Canadian Government, ... as on other occasions, had urged that at least three or four days should be allotted to discussions,' L.B. Pearson wrote afterwards, 'the Chairman ... in opening the meeting indicated that the discussions would have to be concluded within two days. As a result not only were the most interesting discussions which developed necessarily superficial but also there was little or no opportunity for the Foreign Ministers to consult one another in private...'[84]

The most urgent session of the North Atlantic Council since its discussion of West German rearmament in September 1950 took place at Paris during December 1956. 'This meeting of the Council was a difficult, as well as a very important one,' L.B. Pearson reported to his Prime Minister on 18 December, 'in the sense that it reflected some of the differences – and irritations – that can been created over the Suez intervention by the United Kingdom and France. It also presented an opportunity for easing those differences.' The talk was frank – and therefore tough. 'The British ... were sensitive and defensive,' Pearson told L.S. St Laurent. 'They were not able to resist the temptation to try to justify their Suez actions at every opportunity. They were also inclined to exaggerate casual critical observations by the Americans – even if they were merely made as social gossip – into proof of either hostility or lack of understanding or both.' The stage had been set for a show of righteous indignation by the US Secretary of State, but John Foster Dulles did not play his moralizer's role to the hilt.

Dulles' speeches often take the form, even when they do not possess the substance, of moral lectures and this was the more noticeable at this session because of the somewhat suspicious atmosphere which existed. The British and French, smarting under the failure of their enterprise, were in no mood to receive sermons gracefully. Their sensitiveness and Dulles' natural insensitiveness made for one or two awkward moments in the discussion.

On the other hand, it is only fair to add that some of Dulles' observations were very friendly and constructive. ... He adopted a "more in sorrow than in anger" attitude...

Summing up the mood of the meeting and its results, Pearson told St Laurent that the discussion had made plain that in the United States view, 'the United Kingdom and France were still "on probation" though likely soon to be respectable again, while that of the British and French was "unrevised and unrepentant" ... I would say that this Council session confirmed that the breach between Washington and London and Paris is a serious one. It also, however, began the process of repairing the damage. The communiqué was better for this purpose than we could have expected earlier in the week, and the session ended on a friendly and co-operative note...'[85]

After the psychodramatics of the post-Suez session, the next meeting of the North Atlantic Council in May 1957 – the last that L.B. Pearson would attend as foreign minister – was bound to be an anticlimax. 'There was little opportunity ... for private conversations,' Pearson reported to Ottawa in what had become by then his perennial lament, 'and official entertainment took up all the time.'[86]

The following year, in the course of a series of lectures at the Fletcher School of Law and Diplomacy, Tufts University, Pearson offered his reflections on the work of the North Atlantic Council from his long experience of it. As in the earlier lectures at Princeton in 1955, Pearson favoured giving the Council 'greater power and authority than it now possesses. It is true,' he continued,

that there were periodic meetings of this council when ministers, the policy makers, are present. But these meetings are short, formal at times to the point of being almost perfunctory, and often more concerned with private conversations, and with the council communiqué to follow, than with the hammering out of a collective policy. I do not wish to deprecate them. It is good and it is valuable for ministers of the governments of a coalition to meet in this way and develop the practices, and even more the habits, of consultation. It would be even more useful if Council members with ministerial authority could meet continuously and thereby lift the NATO Council from the diplomatic to the political level.

A North Atlantic Council that functioned in this manner would not be just a substitute for its members' ways of dealing diplomatically with one another; rather, it would 'make diplomacy in its formal sense entirely unnecessary by working out common policies in the fields of action covered by NATO, in the same way that policies are worked out by and become binding on all the members of a Cabinet.' Pearson then put forward this proposal.

I believe that the time has now come, both in order to facilitate the formation of an effective and united foreign policy, and for the development of Atlantic unity generally, to convert the NATO Council – or as many of its members as are willing to accept the obligations for united action involved – into a kind of political general staff, with greater power and authority than it now has...[87]

Here was a bold suggestion – as such, offered more easily by an opposition party leader (which the lecturer had by then become) than by a foreign minister who before presenting his ideas in public submits them to the scrutiny and approval of professional advisers from which they seldom emerge intact and sometimes not at all.

'Really important things have happened this week...': so L.B. Pearson had reported from the second session of the North Atlantic Council in May 1950. Among those really important things had been its decision to create a Council of Deputies to serve as the ministers' permanent *alter ego* during the long stretches between ministerial meetings.

This new institution had been carefully examined in Ottawa, not without mixed feelings. 'It is all too easy to devise new machinery,' Pearson reflected. But he admitted that 'the need for additional central machinery to function in the intervals between Council sessions seems to us to be becoming increasingly evident. We have been thinking,' Pearson informed the Ambassador at Washington,

along the lines of a Permanent Commission or group of deputies to Foreign Ministers. ... I think it only sensible to have a clearer idea as to what jobs would be given the Permanent Commission before trying to draw up a detailed constitution for it...

It is now suggested ... that the Commission should coordinate "the essential military, financial and economic factors into an effective defence programme and
consider the equitable division of the financial burden and of production tasks."
This all adds up to a pretty tall order even for a group of "top level civil service
representatives." ... In practice, the deputies of the foreign ministers meeting in
the Commission would inevitably have to refer back any question of policy to
their governments for decision. It would be illusory to suppose that they could
wield any greater or different powers than these...[88]

Pearson also consulted his Prime Minister. 'It becomes clear that one of
the most important steps to be discussed by North Atlantic Council,' he
cabled to L.S. St Laurent on 9 May 1950, a week before it met, 'will be
establishment of continuing or permanent body of some kind to meet
between sessions of Council.' He observed that 'deputies to Foreign
Ministers will obviously have considerable difficulty in imposing on
Finance Ministers and Defence Ministers their ideas about an integrated
programme, especially in countries where principle of cabinet unity is not
strong.'[89]

A Council of Deputies was duly created, the North Atlantic Council
declaring at its May 1950 meeting that 'the time had come for the creation
of a permanent civilian body which would be responsible for carrying out
the policies of the NATO governments in the intervals between meetings
of the North Atlantic Council.' The Deputies were based at London. In
July 1951, a little more than a year after coming into existence, they
acquired a secretariat – having first acquired a budget.

Canada showed her respect for the new institution by appointing as her
Council Deputy the then High Commissioner at London, Dana Wilgress,
whom the American Deputy, elected chairman of the Council, told Pearson he considered to be 'one of the more effective colleagues.'[90]

In February 1952, the North Atlantic Council Ministerial Meeting at
Lisbon decided to replace the Council Deputies by a Council of Permanent Representatives, one for each member country, who were to be 'sufficiently close to their governments and entrusted with adequate authority
to enable the Council to discharge their collective tasks and to reach
prompt decisions.' Each Permanent Representative was head of his country's mission to the North Atlantic Treaty Organization. NATO missions,
like national delegations to the United Nations, would be maintained at
the Organization's headquarters; NATO's would be located at the Palais de
Chaillot in Paris.

Canada again displayed her regard for the importance of this new post
by appointing as her first Permanent Representative on the North Atlantic Council the then Under Secretary of State for External Affairs, A.D.P.

Heeney. Heeney, ablest of diplomats, had able helpers. 'I was particularly fortunate in my Canadian colleagues in the Permanent Delegation,' Heeney wrote in his memoirs, 'of whom Wynne Plumptre and Marcel Cadieux headed respectively the economic and political sections.' Morale among the Permanent Representatives at first ran very high.

Generally speaking the atmosphere in the Council and within the delegations in those early days was one of optimism, mutual respect and mutual confidence. The permanent representatives felt they had been given an important task by their governments and the manner in which the organization had been launched in Paris gave ground for the belief that the alliance would be backed up materially from the various capitals. Our behaviour those first few months reflected this conviction and the assumption around the table that each country would discharge in good faith its commitments to the alliance to the best of its ability. There was thus a spirit of unity in the council and a freshness...[91]

That freshness soon turned stale. The Permanent Representatives were made scapegoats for the persistent discrepancy between alliance professions and member country performances.* The blame lay elsewhere. 'Each government in the alliance insisted on determining by its own domestic processes the nature and extent of the forces it would commit and the funds it would obligate,' Arnold Heeney wrote of his NATO 'interlude.' 'Their representatives in NATO had no authority to make decisions on their own. The council, in fact, was a continuing conference of delegates subject to instruction and little more.'[92] Even L.B. Pearson partook of the general discouragement. 'Much of our optimism and most of our brave talk,' Pearson wrote to Heeney in July 1952, 'about the value of the new and permanent council ... seem to have disappeared.'

The North Atlantic Council had created a Defence Committee at its first meeting on 17 September 1949 – thereby complying with the instruction of Article 9 of the Treaty that such a committee be established 'immediately.' The Defence Committee, composed of the defence ministers of each of the member governments, first met on 15 October 1949. The meeting was held in the Pentagon, the newly incumbent US Secretary of Defense, Louis Johnson, presiding. Johnson's chairmanship struck the Minister of National Defence, Brooke Claxton, as 'rather like that of the benevolently inclined president of a minor fraternal order,' and the atmosphere as 'strangely informal for an event which was making history.' There were no speeches: 'We got down to business.' That business was to establish, as the North Atlantic Council had directed, the Military

---

* See below, Ch. 4, 223-4.

Committee and Standing Group. In this way the Defence Committee got off, as Claxton recalled, 'to an early start on the path to frank, friendly and full co-operation. All of us were anxious to do everything possible to break down formality, not to make speeches unnecessarily, to stop talking "for the record" and still less "for the folks back home"; to preserve reasonable security while giving as much information out as we could in order to arouse wider understanding and more general support for our great undertaking.'[94]

The second meeting of the Defence Committee took place at Paris on 1 December 1949 where, in the words of the first NATO Secretary General some years later, it 'agreed on a strategic concept for the "integrated defence of the North Atlantic area," and on the methods by which a programme of production and of deliveries of military weapons and equipment should be devised'[95] – a singularly cryptic description of a torrid debate over a document of extraordinary importance and sensitivity.* An American participant considered that 'the general atmosphere was one of harmony with a general impression of greater solidarity among the Defense Ministers than in their first meeting on October 5.'[96] This was not Brooke Claxton's impression. The US Secretary of Defense, still in the chair, pushed the meetings through with what Claxton thought to be 'almost indecent haste,' remaining in Paris for no more than thirty hours. 'Johnson's steamrolling created some resentment,' Claxton noted at the time, adding, however, that 'several of those present expressed their pleasure that he was applying himself with such drive to the task of getting the organization going.'[97] Harmony is in the ear of the hearer.

The third Defence Committee session took place at The Hague on 1 April 1950. By then there were signs of stress. 'Before the meeting,' Claxton recollected, 'friends in The Netherlands, French and Belgian delegations told me of their trouble with the Americans which they were not even willing to discuss with Louis Johnson.' Politicians and officials in the three countries bitterly resented what Claxton called 'the bull-headed and inconsiderate way in which the Americans were telling [them] to change their plans.' In The Netherlands, a political crisis was brewing as a result of the Standing Group's proposal that the Dutch – 'a sea-faring people,' as Claxton noted, 'and proud of their naval tradition' – should not proceed with plans to construct a major new naval base and two new cruisers and five destroyers, but alternatively should build up army and air forces instead. It was not so much the substance of the proposed change that

---

*   The document, 'Strategic Concept for the Defense of the North Atlantic Area,' is printed in *Foreign Relations of the United States*, 1949, IV, *Western Europe* (Washington, DC 1975), 353-6. See below, Ch. 4, 237-8.

rankled, Claxton noted, as 'the way in which it was made. My friend, the Minister of Defence ... had told me of this with anger and almost despair ... Belgians and French complained of similarly heavy-handed treatment by the Americans...' On the other hand, he reflected,

That the Americans had cause for concern was plain. How could the Administration or Defense Department justify giving aid to countries and put large forces in Europe unless the Europeans were moving promptly to help themselves? Not one of the three countries was taking its military commitments very seriously at the time. The Americans felt that the Alliance must "get on with it"; if NATO was to progress at all they must play their part.

Claxton accordingly took it upon himself to try to acquaint the US Secretary of Defense with the depth and sincerity of the Europeans' resentment at being, as they felt it, pushed around and leaned upon. Johnson's response was unhelpful. 'He was surprised, upset, and, in his naive ignorance of the way other nations felt, more hurt than anything else,' Claxton recollected. 'How could these others be so ungrateful for what the US and himself were doing?'[98]

All in all, the Hague sessions had not gone well. 'Unfortunately the atmosphere of these meetings is such that any discussion at them is almost impossible,' Claxton wrote after their adjournment. 'The work done is limited to expressing approval of documents put forward by subsidiary committees.' He conceded that

by these means very considerable progress has been made without having to face any awkward questions. I think, however, the time is coming when the Defence Committee should face up to a number of problems, which it should deal with itself during the course of a single meeting. So far there are plans and programmes and paper. These have produced a stronger faith, but we are coming to the time when faith must be shown by works and that is going to be a rather difficult proposition.[99]

The contretemps at the second and third sessions of the Defence Committee were as nothing compared with those of the fourth. These took place in Washington, DC, beginning on 28 October 1950. The previous month had witnessed the great debate over German rearmament within the North Atlantic Council.* The debate continued in the Defence Committee. Papers prepared for the meeting by the Standing Group included a resolution recommending, in general terms, participation of Western German armed forces in European defence. The Military Committee approved. When the resolution came before the Defence Committee, Brooke Claxton recalled, the French Minister, Jules Moch,

* See below, Ch. 6, 327-8.

at once opened up in a statement charged with emotion on the French position regarding Germany. ... This ... led [Emmanuel] Shinwell [United Kingdom Minister of Defence] to make a sharp reply ignoring the background of France's attitude towards Germany. ... Seated next to Shinwell was the Minister of Defence of Denmark. ... Either Shinwell or Moch said something which irritated him. ... His speech poured oil on the flaming fire. Altogether it was the worst scene I remember in NATO. Shinwell spoke insistently and with extreme acerbity. Then I got into [it] alternately speaking French and English, trying to explain to the French the British position, and to the British the French position. ... My efforts, I am glad to say ... helped us to get through the meeting without blows...[100]

The Defence Committee met for what proved to be its fifth and last session at Brussels on 18 December 1950. The Committee was done in by what L.B. Pearson described as a 'radical' proposal for reorganizing the North Atlantic Council. This proposal originated in Ottawa as early as May 1950, a year before its acceptance. The idea was to have the Council absorb the functions of the committees of defence and finance ministers. 'If this were to happen,' Pearson observed, 'Council might well be attended by more than one Minister and representation of each State from day to day during Council meetings would depend on subjects discussed.'[101] He floated the proposal at a meeting of the North Atlantic Council on 18 September – 'Suggested ... having but one council at ministerial level, at which appropriate ministers could appear as required'[102] – and on 17 November a memorandum elaborating the proposal and setting forth the reasons of the government for putting it forward was presented by the Council Deputy to his colleagues.

Under the present structure, with three separate Committees of Ministers, the problem of coordination is difficult, if not impossible, to resolve simply through the Council Deputies. The NATO hierarchy of Foreign, Defence and Finance Ministers does not correspond accurately to any precise division of responsibilities in the Government of member countries. Further, if the present Ministerial structure of NATO is not modified, the increasing importance of production and supply problems may well lead logically to proposals for the establishment of a fourth body at the Ministerial level, to correspond with those on defence and finance.

The prospect of four separate Committees of Ministers, each composed of colleagues of equal status in their own governments although three of the Committees are formally subordinate to the fourth, emphasizes the necessity for combining all activities of the NATO under one Supreme Council which would represent governments. At such a Council, Governments might, according to their own domestic requirements and the nature of the agenda, be represented by one or more Ministers. (Representation by Prime Ministers should not be excluded. For example, if the Council were to meet in Ottawa the Canadian Prime Minister might represent the Government of Canada.)

We recognize that such a solution would increase the number of persons attending Meetings of the Council. Nevertheless, the advantages to be gained by introducing into the highest body of the NATO where policy is formulated, Ministers
directly responsible in their own Governments for defence, finance and supply
seem to us sufficient to outweigh the disadvantages of numbers...

Such a reorganization of the Council would confirm and enhance the prestige and
importance of the Council Deputies which would then emerge quite clearly as the
active continuing authority of the NATO. The Deputies would no longer be merely
the Deputies of the Foreign Ministers as they are now at least in form. They
would also represent their other Ministers concerned with North Atlantic matters;
in fact, between Council Sessions, they would represent Governments and be in a
position to speak for the NATO...

The general argument for drastic simplification of the NATO machinery at this
time needs no further emphasis. As the scope and scale of activity increase and we
pass from the planning stage to execution, the decisions to be taken at the top
level will emerge as being primarily political – that is, questions which can be dealt
with only by Governments and not by experts. For these reasons, we believe that
the time has come to concentrate on one Council of Governments the full authority of the Organization.[103]

The Canadian proposal did not find favour immediately in Washington,
where it was opposed by the Department of Defense. 'After looking into
the matter,' US Defense Secretary George C. Marshall wrote to the US
Secretary of State, 'I have concluded that we should not agree to a major
reorganization of the Treaty structure at this time.' The existing committees of the Organization, Marshall argued, had been preoccupied with
planning and had not yet been in roles where their capacity for practical
action could be fairly tested. 'If there is fault in coping with NATO responsibilities I think it is not primarily because of the type of organization.'
The United States Council Deputy should be instructed to take 'a sympathetic interest in the Canadian proposal' but not to the point of backing its
implementation.[104]

Canada's plan was put to the Council Deputies on 12 December 1950,
where it received support from the French, British, and Netherlands representatives. In view of this developing consensus, the United States
Council Deputy, as chairman, adjourned the discussion for three days,
during which he sought to persuade the Canadians to hold back. On 14
December he reported to Washington that he had been successful: 'Canadians are being thoroughly co-operative in not pushing for action at this
time,' Charles M. Spofford told the US Secretary of State, 'and have
agreed that Council should merely endorse proposal's objectives and recommend further study.'[105] Further study duly undertaken, the proposal

was approved by the Council Deputies and adopted by the North Atlantic Council Ministerial Meeting at Paris in May 1951.

The North Atlantic Treaty Organization had by then come to need a North Atlantic Treaty organizer – a chief executive officer on its civilian side who could act as administrator, expeditor, public relations officer, coach and, if need be, mediator.

Two conceptions of this office emerged as its necessity became apparent. One inclined to the notion of a figurehead, the other to the notion of a father figure. Backing the former were the British: 'Under the British proposals the Secretary-General would be a weaker figure, who would have to share with the Council's standing committees control over the staff of the non-military agencies. In the main, he would be a co-ordinator and supervisor of civilian activities – literally a secretary-general.' Backing the latter were the Americans who (consistently with Franklin Roosevelt's vision of a chief executive officer for the United Nations so exalted as to deserve the title of World Moderator) preferred to emphasize the potentials inherent in the office not of secretarial skill but of generalship.[106]

These competing conceptions of the office of a secretary general for NATO had come before the Department of External Affairs by the end of 1951. Discussion there centred on the merits of appointing 'a civilian Eisenhower.'

In the Under Secretary's view, the Director General would have to be an American. The suitable man would, of course, overshadow the Chairman of the Deputies and would amongst other duties be responsible for making reports and keeping in touch with national governments. He would, of course, have to be independent of the national representative of his own country.

The Under Secretary stated that he had little faith in the appointment of a superman as a panacea for the Organization's procedural difficulties. He could, indeed, help avoid tangles ... and have contacts with the Governments, but it seemed to be another reflection of the American practice of appointing a man of reputation to an impossible job, keeping him there until his reputation is destroyed and then replacing him.

In Mr Heeney's opinion it was imperative that a Director General should be formally subject to the Deputies – otherwise, if they were superceded, the Deputies would waste away. In practice, the personal prestige and influence of the Director General would, much more than his formal terms of reference, control the sphere of his influence...[107]

The terms of reference for the office of Secretary-General approved by the North Atlantic Council meeting at Lisbon in February 1952 were deliberately enigmatic. They neither elevated nor unduly constrained whatever individual might be appointed to the post. He would, as A.D.P. Heeney had forecast, be free to make of it what his gifts of leadership and judgement might permit. 'A Secretary General should be appointed by, and be responsible to, the Council,' the resolution adopted at Lisbon prescribed. 'He should not be a member of any national delegation. He should be responsible for organizing the work of the Council and directing the work of the International Staff/Secretariat. He should initiate and prepare matters for Council action and ensure that appropriate steps are taken to follow up Council decisions. He should have direct access to all NATO agencies and to governments.'[108] Figurehead or father figure: it could go either way.

The office of Secretary General thus created, what paragon should occupy it? Unlike the post of Supreme Commander, which had been tailored to specifications suitable for General Eisenhower, member governments had developed no consensus about who should be appointed. The names of the foreign ministers of The Netherlands and Belgium, Dirk U. Stikker and Paul-Henri Spaak, had been mentioned in previous months. (That of the foreign minister of the United States had not been mentioned: Heeney's conviction that the Secretary General 'would have to be an American' was not shared by others, even though Dean Acheson would have been available for the position after November 1952.) But the name of the foreign minister of Canada was mentioned most of all.

L.B. Pearson was highly qualified to become NATO's chief executive official. Five years earlier he had been out front in the running for an even senior secretary-generalship, that of the United Nations.* 'He had been an enthusiastic supporter of NATO, and an advocate of an "Atlantic Community" concept embracing economic, social and cultural ends as well as military ones. He was also the 1952 Chairman of the NATO Council.'[109] It was in all probability this last qualification which put Pearson so prominently in the running, for at the meeting at Lisbon at which the selection was made he had, as Council Chairman, been maintaining a high profile. His colleague, Brooke Claxton, who was with him at that time, believed that, while Pearson could not have had the job for the

---

*   '...Pearson was strongly pushed by the British and supported by the Americans in their first choice,' Hume Wrong had reported to Ottawa from London on 30 January 1946. 'The Russians, however, were unyielding in their insistence that the Secretary General should not come from the "Anglo-Saxon Bloc"...I think ... Pearson is well out of it. I doubt that the best man on earth would have much chance of enhancing his reputation during the initial years.' Quoted in Donald M. Page (ed.), *Documents on Canadian External Relations*, 12, *1946* (Ottawa, 1977), 627-8.

asking, he was nonetheless a strong contender for it. 'Mike Pearson had been presiding at the Council with his customary skill,' Claxton recalled later.

People naturally thought of Pearson himself. He was already president of the Assembly of the United Nations. He had had twenty-five years extensive experience in the diplomatic business, probably more than anyone present. He was one of the real parents of NATO. He was popular and able. Canada had done its full share in NATO and had earned the respect of everyone. It looked as if Mike would get the call...

[H]e told me of the possibility ... and asked me what I thought. He was rather disposed to take it out of hand if the offer was firm. Certainly it was a wonderful appointment, a great opportunity to be of major service and one could assume that the position would lack nothing in the way of amenities.* I asked him if he had discussed this with the Prime Minister. He said he had not – up to now it had not got that far – and I said no doubt he must feel he would have to do this before definitely committing himself. He said he supposed he would. I think he had hoped that I would simply confirm his own inclination which was to take the post then and there if it was offered to him...

[A]n international appointment at this altitude [is not] ... something to be decided ... on the sole basis of the qualifications of a particular man for a particular job. ... In the game of international chess, the position of Director General [sic] was a major piece only to be given up or exchanged for some equivalent consideration. As the United States had the top command position through Eisenhower, the feeling of the British and French was that the top civilian position should go to one of them. At this time the Deputies were located in London. The French were very anxious to have the location of the Deputies, that is of the Permanent Council, changed to Paris. Therefore, there was bargaining. ... The French agreed that the British could get the [Secretary Generalship] ... if the British would agree to the headquarters moving from London to Paris. So it turned out.[110]

L.B. Pearson's version of the affair is different from Claxton's. A letter Pearson wrote to the Prime Minister at the end of 1952 about the possibility that he might again be considered as UN Secretary General refers to the dissimilarity between the two prospective nominations: 'As I see it,' Pearson wrote to L.S. St Laurent on 29 December, 'the situation is not the same as that which arose over the NATO Secretary Generalship where there was no possibility of deadlock over candidates, and where the Organization had such a close and direct relationship to us that the position

---

* This assumption proved ill founded, at least for a time. For several months after arriving in Paris, Lord Ismay experienced difficulty obtaining suitable accommodation, saying 'he was stateless, because he was serving 14 different governments; and homeless, because he hadn't been able to find a flat.' Quoted in Robert S. Jordan, *The NATO International Staff/Secretariat, 1952-1957: A Study in International Administration* (London, New York, Toronto 1967), 84.

of a Canadian as Secretary General might be misunderstood in our country and complicate Canadian policy to NATO.'[111] Here Pearson suggests that even had the NATO job been offered to him, he would have turned it down on the grounds that accepting it could impair – for some unspecified reason – Canada's membership in the alliance. In his memoirs, however, Pearson states that loyalty to his Prime Minister led him not to seek the position that could very well have been his. 'The British felt that the first Secretary General should be British, as the first Supreme Allied Commander Europe had been American,' was his later recollection.

They said that they would be glad to support me – I was at least "Commonwealth British." I had also been approached by other delegations, including the American, to accept the post. It was a most attractive prospect and, personally, I would have been happy to become Secretary General. I felt, however, that to resign as Canada's Secretary of State for External Affairs would have been a poor way of showing my appreciation for all that Prime Minister St Laurent had done for me and for the confidence that he had shown in me. So I indicated that I was not available for NATO.[112]

A reviewer of Pearson's memoirs finds this passage lacking in candour.* So it is – if Claxton's version is correct.

With the creation of the Secretary Generalship, the appointment of Lord Ismay as the chief executive office of the Alliance and Vice-Chairman of the North Atlantic Council, and the nomination of Permanent Representatives to take the place of Council Deputies, NATO's political machinery was substantially in place. (See overleaf for what it looked like on a chart.)

As early as March 1949, General Charles Foulkes, then Chief of the General Staff, had proposed that the Atlantic alliance should have at its disposal a supreme commander. Little had been heard of this suggestion during the first few months of alliance activity. War in Korea drove home the need for a NATO force in Western Europe and a NATO military officer to lead it. The North Atlantic Council recommended the creation of the force and the appointment of a force commander in September 1950. Disagreement over how, if at all, West Germans would participate delayed prompt action on both recommendations. At the Council meeting in December 1950, agreement in principle was given to the proposition 'that German participation would strengthen the defence of Europe with-

---

* The passage is cited as an example of Pearson's 'reluctance to discuss anything remotely resembling his ambitions. (Could it be that he never confronted these things himself?) What we get instead is the curious rhetoric of the successful ex-athlete.' Morris Wolfe, 'At Arm's Length from Mike,' *Saturday Night* (Toronto), November 1973, 49.

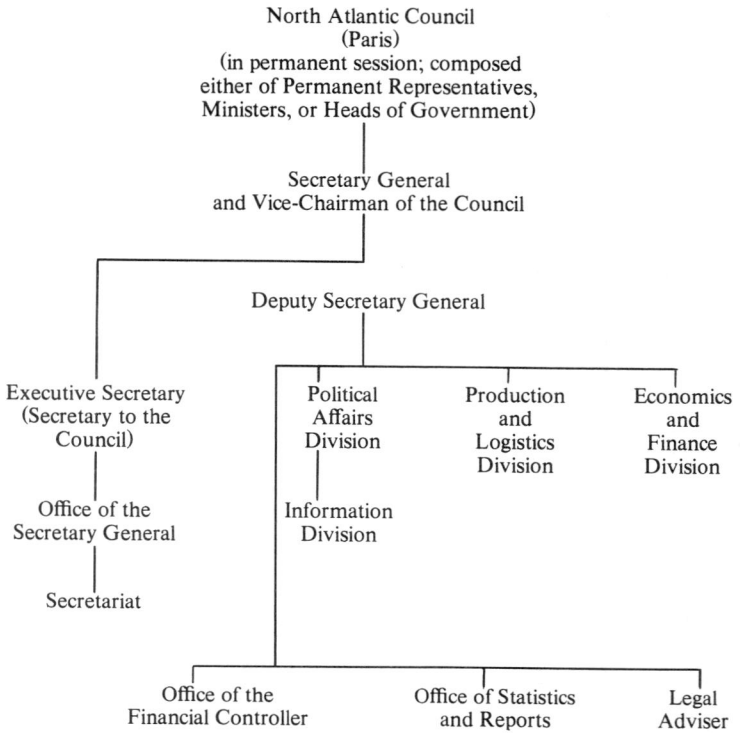

out altering in any way the purely defensive character of the North Atlantic Treaty Organization.' That agreement made possible the Council's decision during the same session to create an integrated force under the supreme command of an American officer.[113] 'All countries,' according to Brooke Claxton who was there, 'hoped and expected that it would be Eisenhower.'[114]

The idea took hold that it would be helpful if the North Atlantic Council were to express its preference for General Dwight David Eisenhower in advance of his appointment by the US President. Not only would this procedure give Eisenhower more authority in dealing with member countries – so Claxton reasoned – it could 'establish a precedent under which the practice might be established of sounding [the smaller members] out in advance.' Claxton was asked by the United States and United Kingdom representatives to move an appropriate resolution in the Council. 'Two or three nations had an inkling that I might be moving this,' Claxton recalled, 'and tried to beat me to it and to get what credit they thought there might be in it.'[115] When the Council met on 19 December, 'Acheson explained, a little coyly' – so the Permanent Representative reported to Ottawa – 'that if the Council wished to make a recommendation to the President, even suggesting the name of an officer if they so wished, the President would, he believed, act without delay. ... As Acheson had invited Mr Claxton ... to move the resolution, he did so in terms that were quickly agreed to...'[116] These were those terms.

The Council having agreed with the recommendation of the Defence Committee that a Supreme Allied Commander, Europe, should be appointed as soon as possible as an essential action in proceeding with the prompt establishment of an effective NATO Defence Force in Europe;

Recognizing that the ultimate success of such a force lies in its sound initiation and that, for this reason, the selection of the first Supreme Commander is a question of the utmost importance;

Reposing the greatest faith in General of the Army Dwight D. Eisenhower as a commander of incomparable prestige, proven ability and highest order of leadership;

Unanimously recommends to the President of the United States that he designate General of the Army Dwight D. Eisenhower as the first Supreme Allied Commander, Europe.[117]

'I am glad,' Claxton recorded of this event, 'to have been the instrument for an expression of view which was part of the chain which gave President Eisenhower the great success he achieved.' It would still take some time before Ike's success as NATO's Supreme Commander silenced its in-house jesters who compared the structure of their alliance to that of the Venus di Milo: 'all SHAPE and no arms.'

HOW MUCH MORE THAN 'MERELY MILITARY'?

Canada's commitment to making the North Atlantic Treaty something more than 'an old-fashioned military alliance' ought to have led her to lobby for ways of pursuing non-military objectives. But her government, so far from seeking to translate the aspirations of Article 2 into practical accomplishments, held back on implementing it. It was as if it had been Canada's objective throughout the negotiation of the Treaty to avoid obliging its signatories to work for political and economic co-operation – whereas exactly the opposite had been the case. Once the Treaty was signed and ratified, Canada's enthusiasm vanished, her motto became 'Solvitur ambulando.' What accounts for that?

In May 1949, the High Commissioner at London advised the Department of External Affairs that he would in all likelihood soon be asked by the British government what his own government proposed to do to implement Article 2. 'It is the feeling of the United Kingdom authorities,' Norman Robertson observed, 'that this article was included largely at Canada's request' – as, indeed, it had been. How was the High Commissioner to respond? 'I should be grateful,' Robertson concluded, 'for any guidance.'[118]

Little guidance was forthcoming. 'It is true that the Government attach importance to the provisions of Article 2,' A.D.P. Heeney cabled in reply, 'but Ministers have not as yet considered the possibility of establishing special machinery in that connection.'[119] (Ministers were becoming preoccupied with their campaigns for the General Election of 27 June.)

A telegram from the Ambassador at Washington anticipated what would become Canadian policy. 'I am glad to notice the cautious attitude which you have taken about the possible establishment of agencies to give effect to Article 2,' Hume Wrong cabled to A.D.P. Heeney on 3 June.

[F]rom a very early stage in the negotiation of the Treaty the Canadian representatives (both Mr Pearson and myself) took the line that while Canada attached great importance to the inclusion in the Treaty of a pledge of economic collaboration, it was not our purpose to urge the establishment of special North Atlantic economic agencies. Without such an assurance we should never have secured the agreement of the Secretary of State and the Senate Foreign Relations Committee to the inclusion of the last sentence of the Article.*

The objections taken during the negotiations to the inclusion of an economic pledge in the Treaty arose in part from the belief that a North Atlantic economic organization would cut across and complicate the work of other international agencies in the economic field, including the OEEC [Organization for European Economic Co-Operation], the ITO [International Trade Organization], the Economic Commission for Europe and other United Nations bodies.

To overcome these objections it was agreed that the pledges which now appear in Article 2 were general pledges designed to be fulfilled by the parties individually or bilaterally or multilaterally as occasion arose. You may recall that we pressed for an economic clause primarily because we believed that it would be useful in negotiating on economic questions with the United Kingdom and United States...

There was in any case to be new machinery on the economic side: a supply agency was to implement the commitment in Article 3 to provide mutual aid. 'I think that our best line would be to concentrate on this,' Wrong concluded, 'and to encourage it to take in a fairly wide field. This

---

* 'They [the Parties] will seek to eliminate conflict in their international economic policies and will encourage economic collaboration between any or all of them.'

would relate economic collaboration to the central purpose of the Treaty, the organization of collective defence.'[120]

This general scepticism within the policy community about the need for new machinery to implement Article 2 there was joined by its fear lest any new institutions might lead to the making of invidious comparisons among member countries' performances. It was at one stage proposed that an Economic Committee be created precisely for the purpose of evaluating respective contributions to the common cause. Canada's representative was at once instructed to oppose such an innovation. 'It would be most unfortunate if ... an "Economic Committee" were to be established to go into the relative "sacrifices" made or anticipated of the various signatories,' he was informed by Ottawa. 'In fact such a Committee's deliberations might very seriously affect the effectiveness of the Pact and would certainly make Canadian participation very difficult.'[121] More would be heard of the politics of pooling – much more.*

In its efforts at squelching or stalling proposals for new institutions for economic co-operation, the government was doubly handicapped. In the first place, the problem of implementing Article 2 was of its own making: had Canada not worked so assiduously to include an article on non-military co-operation in the North Atlantic Treaty, there would have been no Article 2 to require implementation. In the second place, the policy community did not see eye to eye on what, if anything, needed to be done. Among its senior officials, Escott Reid along considered implementing Article 2 to be urgent. Others were indifferent or hostile. 'Our Department of Finance remained sceptical of ideas advancing Article 2,' L.B. Pearson stated in his memoirs. 'Trade and Commerce and the Bank of Canada were, at best, doubtful supporters of the idea.' Their scepticism and doubt were the results of what Pearson admitted to be 'our failure to consult [them] ... adequately before we began our campaign to establish in the Treaty the basis for a larger Atlantic Union.'[122] Escott Reid confirmed this explanation: '[O]fficials and ministers became involved in the decision-making process who knew little or nothing of the policies which Canada had pursued in the negotiations or the reasons for the policies. This was one reason why, after the treaty was signed, the Canadian government was half-hearted over implementing those non-military provisions of the treaty for which it had fought so hard during the negotiations.'[123]

But even those senior officials of the Department of External Affairs who had known of the gestation of Article 2 were indifferent to its up-

---

* See below, Ch. 5, 300-18.

bringing. Sidney Pierce, a liaison official for his own Department with the Departments of Finance and Trade and Commerce, was far from wanting to convert them to his Minister's cause. 'I feel pretty strongly that we have enough objectives and for the moment enough machinery in the economic field. [Herbert] Evatt [foreign minister of Australia] used to score pretty heavily ... with the old one about too much harness and not enough horse,' Pierce wrote to the Under Secretary of State for External Affairs on 20 April 1950. 'I think we are somewhat better off in that we have both horse and harness; but what we need now is hay. In short, our European partners need money or markets in which to earn money; we should examine our actions largely in this light.'[124] 'The idea of the creation of a "political Commonwealth of the North Atlantic",' Hume Wrong wrote bluntly from his Washington Embassy on 15 October 1951, 'is in present circumstances so remote from attainment that to discuss it as an aim of current policy is unrealistic.'[125] Dana Wilgress was even more crushing. 'I have long been mystified as to what exactly was the reason why we sponsored Article 2 of the Treaty,' Wilgress wrote from his High Commission at London on 30 October 1951. 'I have never been able to take seriously the proposal for closer integration of the North Atlantic countries.'[126]

In spite of these expressions of disenchantment from senior officers of his own Department, its Minister took Article 2 and North Atlantic integration seriously. 'Without any illusions, I kept hammering away at the maximum possible application of Article 2 to further co-operation and unity within the Atlantic Alliance,' L.B. Pearson recalls in his memoirs. 'I remained on the side of the angels, however remote they were.'[127]

Foreign service officers believe that it is not enough to be on the side of the angels: one's feet must be on the ground. Out of respect for Pearson's seriousness more than from conviction, the policy community gave thought to how Article 2 might be used. A first step in this direction was to try to make the North Atlantic Working Group on economic and financial machinery receptive to the creation of such machinery. The Canadian representative on the Working Group was told on 15 September 1949 to obtain 'broader terms' which 'should at least not preclude the establishment of an Economic Committee for the purpose of considering the economic collaboration envisaged by Article 2.'[128] Other members of the Working Group bridled at this suggestion, and the Canadian representative decided to abandon the initiative. To this the Department of External Affairs was agreeable. However, Hume Wrong was instructed to inform the Working Group 'that the Minister will make a statement in the Council probably to the effect that the Canadian Government continues to attach importance to Article 2 of the Treaty and recording his understanding that the establishment of such machinery is not precluded by the Working Group's report.'[129] The statement was duly delivered by the Canadian foreign minister at the first session of the North Atlantic Council at Washington on 17 September 1949. The following day, Hume Wrong asked the Council to create a committee to study ways and means to implement Article 2. The US Secretary of State, Wrong reported, 'neatly returned the ball to me by asking me to propose at an early meeting of the Council the terms of an instruction to the Working Group.'[130] This adroit move, Pearson commented retrospectively, 'put it strictly up to us. It also postponed any further consideration of the matter until the next Council meeting, at the earliest; and this was no doubt what Acheson wished.'[131]

Pressed by L.B. Pearson to come up with something, the policy community remained perplexed – perhaps genuinely so – about what was to be done. 'I have puzzled my head about the duties which could appropriately be given to a North Atlantic economic agency,' Hume Wrong confessed, 'paying due regard to the activities of GATT [General Agreement of Tariffs and Trade], the [World] Bank and [International Monetary] Fund, OEEC [Organization for European Economic Co-operation], the Economic Council for Europe. ... I have not come up with any answer.'[132] But an answer was needed, if only because other governments now waited for Canada to follow through – the American government, possibly with faint malice, anticipated that Canada would be unable to follow through. It had become almost as important to head off what Wrong described as 'the suspicion that we are advocating the creation of some new international agency as an end in itself and not as a means to an end' as to devise the machinery and a rationale to justify it.[133] So an interdepartmental committee was struck and told to produce ideas.

There were consultations among officials from the Departments of External Affairs, Trade and Commerce, Finance, and from the Bank of Canada. Their verdict was unanimous: 'The time is not yet ripe.' Why not? For one thing, 'it is not yet clear what the real content of economic co-operation between the North Atlantic powers will be.' For another, 'the need for economic machinery under the North Atlantic Treaty will not become pressing until the European Recovery Programme is much nearer its close.' For yet another, 'the close economic co-operation of the North Atlantic Community would be neither desirable nor possible until there has been some resolution of the problems of the sterling area.' All this left the Canadian position in limbo. 'It will ... be necessary for our representatives in the Working Group to stall for quite some time,' the

Economic Division of the Department of External Affairs concluded frankly.[134] As Pearson later conceded: 'Our interdepartmental committee failed to produce a single concrete proposal for the implementation of Article 2...'[135]

Undeterred, Pearson drafted a pro-Article 2 speech for the meeting of the North Atlantic Council at London in May 1950. He subsequently described his remarks as 'a careful statement designed to allay fears that we were rushing NATO into economic activities for which it might not be suited, or which would overlap and conflict with the work of other international agencies.' It contained the following paragraph.

The most important way for us to give effect to Article 2 is for each of our countries always to act in accordance with it. If the spirit is there, co-operation and elimination of conflict will follow rapidly enough. However, it will probably help us all to practice what we preach if, at our Council meetings, we have some pretty frank talks about each other's behaviour. I have in mind a mixture between a confessional and a Quaker meeting. Finally, I think we should consider, very seriously and without haste, what sort of machinery, if any, we should set up to give further effect to Article 2.[136]

An American despatch from the scene summarized Pearson's appeal pithily: 'Citing Article 2 expressed hope that mutual obligations assumed thereunder can be clarified and that they can be correlated with broad question of economic cooperation in Western world.'[137]

'If the spirit is there...' L.B. Pearson would later write: 'The reality is that the spirit to implement the economic aspects of Article 2 was *never* there. ... [P]erhaps it simply took me too long to realize this...'[138] Until he did, meanwhile, further efforts would be made to get Article 2 off – or above – the ground.

The first of three attempts to breathe life into the still-born article of the North Atlantic Treaty arose from the Ministerial meetings of the Council in mid-September 1951, at which a committee was created to study how to promote practical co-operation among the member governments. The committee was made up of NATO's smaller countries – Canada, along with Belgium, Italy, The Netherlands, and Norway. 'For my pains I was appointed to preside over the Committee of Five,' L.B. Pearson recalled, 'and Canadian officials did most of the work.' This quintet had not much clout. 'We soon found out, as we had feared we would, that the attitude of our most powerful members made the prospects for any broad advance under Article 2 negligible. ... [T]here was not much point in making specific recommendations that would be rejected by the Big Three and, as a consequence, would merely emphasize the division within the Alliance.'[139] This the Committee of Five reported limply to the North Atlantic Council at the meetings in Lisbon in February 1952; the Ministers asked the Permanent Representatives on the Council to continue the quest.

The second attempt arose in February 1955. The Permanent Representative on the North Atlantic Council had sought to revive interest within the policy community in what almost all its participants had come to regard both as a lost cause and a dead issue. This initiative from Dana Wilgress – who five years earlier had professed scepticism about Article 2 – suggests that he had meanwhile been influenced by the NATO International Staff/Secretariat which, like any bureaucracy, sought to augment its authority and saw in the implementing of Article 2 one way of expanding its role. 'What we are now considering,' Wilgress reported from Paris on 23 February, 'is the possibility of providing for discussion on the broad politico-economic aspects of economic collaboration in the NATO Council – preferably at ministerial level.' The NATO Staff/Secretariat, Wilgress suggested, might undertake a special study of the subject, which could be reviewed by a special working group or by the Annual Review Committee, and the result incorporated within the general chapter of the Annual Review Report.* 'This method,' Wilgress observed, 'may present an opportunity for NATO to take official cognizance of the economic provisions of Article 2. Without setting up any special machinery to examine these questions, a review of the situation could be prepared for the information of Ministers when they were considering the Annual Review at the December meeting of the Council. This would afford the opportunity for any minister, who so desired, to raise a question pertaining to economic collaboration.'[140]

This modest proposal promptly evoked a hostile response within the Department of External Affairs. The Economic Division greeted it 'with a good deal of scepticism. ... It can perhaps be argued that from the political standpoint closer economic integration and more intimate economic consultation among NATO countries is required to revivify the alliance,' the head of that Division, A.E. Ritchie, countered. 'But Mr Wilgress' proposed method of accomplishing this (through a search for "conflicts" in the international economic policies of the various NATO countries) would seem open to a number of objections...'[141] Within the Defence Liaison Division there was equally strong opposition on three main grounds. First, if Canada put forward such a suggestion, she would be expected and obliged to give some sort of lead in discussions of it both in the Perma-

---

* See below, Ch. 5, 301-4.

nent Council and at ministerial meetings (where neither the Minister of Finance, Walter Harris, nor the Minister of Trade and Commerce, C.D. Howe, were 'prepared to interest themselves in such discussions or even to attend future ministerial meetings'). Second,

It is difficult to see how any survey of economic policies and problems prepared for such discussions could avoid dealing with the fundamental difference of approach between Canada and to a lesser extent the United States, on the one hand, and the European member countries on the other, with respect to the economic and commercial policy that should govern relations between Western Europe and North America. Further discussion of this matter in NATO would be likely to give rise to the same recrimination, ill-feeling and embarrassment that it has already done in OEEC and GATT, and to harden further the positions already adopted.

Third, it was doubtful, whatever was said during the discussions, that the European members would as a result alter 'their existing economic policy of protection.' To which A.E. Ritchie added: 'In fact discussion of the extremely controversial economic issues in NATO might tend to discolour consideration of political and strategic matters on which NATO is now making some progress.'[142] A final douche of cold water came from the Department of Finance. '[R]ecent experience has shown that even the most advanced and responsible of our NATO allies do not see eye-to-eye with each other in economic matters,' A.F.W. Plumptre, then Director of the International Economic Relations Division of that Department, pointed out to the Under Secretary of State for External Affairs. 'I have sometimes considered the possibility of using NATO as a forum in which to support direct representations in Washington concerning US policies. However I have become increasingly doubtful whether this would lead to any useful results...'[143]

This negative consensus, unaffected by any dissent from Escott Reid (who had taken up the High Commissionership at New Delhi and with whom his Ottawa colleagues had not consulted), produced a despatch to Paris on 24 March in which the Permanent Representative was informed that he should refrain from pushing his project further. When Pearson saw the despatch he was displeased. 'I think that our attitude is too negative...,' he told his Under Secretary, Jules Léger, 'and I am sorry that telegram ... was sent.'[144] A mollifying message duly went out from Pearson to Wilgress. 'I would not want you to think from my previous telegram that we have not got under continuous review the non-military aspects of the Treaty,' the Minister reassured the Permanent Representative. 'I hope to have a word with you about this when I am in Paris.'[145]

When in Paris for the NATO Ministerial Meetings in mid-June 1955, L.B. Pearson left with Dana Wilgress a number of papers setting out the objections of officials of his own Department and of the Departments of Finance and Trade and Commerce to a Canadian initiative to implement Article 2, and asked him to respond. Wilgress provided a spirited rejoinder.

If I may say so, I think the officials in Ottawa have misunderstood my motive in putting forward the proposal. This is not to be wondered at, because, as I see it, the tangible advantages to be gained from a discussion in NATO of the broad politico-economic aspects of economic collaboration are the political advantages; the less tangible and elusive ones are the economic advantages. The principal advantage would be to keep the second sentence of Article 2 alive as a positive instrument of international policy. Properly handled, this would help to engender gradually a sense of the North Atlantic Community which we are so desirous of fostering, as the sense of the European Community has been engendered among the members of OEEC by the discussions which have been taking place in that body. A subsidiary advantage would be that by keeping alive the second sentence of Article 2 as a positive instrument of international policy, useful resort might be taken of it on some later occasion.

Wilgress was unmoved by word that the Ministers of Finance and Trade and Commerce would be so unenthusiastic about leading a discussion on economic collaboration that they might skip the meetings. 'Without being in any way disrespectful towards either Mr Harris or Mr Howe,' he rejoined, 'my view is that you would be the most effective Minister to take the lead in such a discussion on account of your close identification with the idea of the North Atlantic Community. Without presuming to indicate the line you should take, I can see how you could make a very effective intervention by describing in general terms the realities behind the North Atlantic Community. ... In other words,' Wilgress continued, 'your leadership could be to place the consideration of the second sentence of Article 2 on the broad and high plane of politico-economic considerations, of which other countries could take advantage if they felt there was any specific area of conflict to which they wished to draw attention.' To the objection that such discussion would lead to 'recrimination, ill-feeling and embarrassment,' Wilgress observed that it would depend on how the discussion was conducted. 'It is unlikely that the simple insertion of an Article 2 catalyst could alter entrenched positions and it would of course be unwise to stretch the Atlantic Community to the breaking point. If this was not done, however, there would appear to be no logical reason why a broad discussion of economic problems in the context of Article 2 might not build up an attachment for the Community principle. This could only be done, however, if difficult issues were approached carefully and tact-fully. ... I have thought over my position,' Wilgress concluded his persua-sive reply, 'and have decided that what is essential in my proposal is that the second sentence of Article 2 should be made a subject for discussion at the December Ministerial Meeting of the Council...'[146]

These arguments hit home. 'From the strictly political point of view there is a good deal of merit in Mr Wilgress' suggestion,' Jules Léger concurred in a memorandum for his Minister on 11 July.

The principal argument in favour is that the military side of NATO is likely gradu-ally to become less important over the next few years, and it is imperative that, if NATO is to maintain its strength, we start building it on a sound political and economic base now.

...If we allow NATO to continue on a purely military base, and then have that base undermined, it will be difficult to retain the alliance in the political-military form which we think necessary for our security. If this is a correct assumption, then it follows that we should start now, while the military base is still solid, to reinforce the political side. We have made a good start this year with the successful political meetings of the Council. I think it would be logical to complement this with some progress in creating at least the impression of greater economic and cultural unity among the members of the North Atlantic community.[147]

Put to L.B. Pearson, all of this was preaching to the converted. Put, as Pearson did in identical letters of 26 September, to C.D. Howe and Walter Harris, it was preaching to agnostics. Developing the non-military aspects of NATO, Pearson emphasized at the outset, was 'of particular importance at the present time when the tactics of the Soviet Government are reduc-ing the sense of military threat and thereby tending to weaken the incen-tives for the continuation of NATO as a military alliance.' An item on the agenda of the forthcoming ministerial meeting to allow comment on cur-rent economic policies and international arrangements would, he be-lieved, help to avert that danger. 'The aim *would not* be to arrive at any agreed conclusions, to set up new economic machinery or to detract from the functions of existing organizations,' Pearson was careful to stress. 'It *would* be to invoke explicitly in the NATO Council the positive statement of international policy contained in Article 2 which requires member countries to "seek to eliminate conflict in their international economic policies and ... encourage economic collaboration between any or all of them".' Nor was it the intention to move towards common North Atlan-tic policies. 'What I have in mind ... is discussion by governments on their respective policies and not an attempt to reach a common or a "NATO approach".'[148]

L.B. Pearson was well aware of the intense scepticism with which his two colleagues would read this letter, which was in consequence inordinately long. But the hallmark of the agnostic is the capacity to be converted. Both the Minister of Finance and the Minister of Trade and Commerce gave their consent to Pearson's proposal, if a bit grudgingly and replete with reservations. 'While I am personally somewhat doubtful about the usefulness of general rather than particular debates in international bodies,' Walter Harris replied,

I am willing to accept your judgment concerning the desirability of discussing economic matters from time to time in the North Atlantic Council when it meets at the Ministerial level. Therefore ... I would not object.

Harris had doubts about timing. Noting that at a recent meeting of the Canada-United States Committee on Economic Affairs, the US Ministers had been unreceptive to proposals for economic collaboration, he wondered whether they would be any less so 'in Paris in December, with their President ill and with an election only a few months off. ... Further, if Canada put the item on the agenda, our representatives would be expected to take a leading part in the discussion, and I think we might find it very difficult at this juncture either to attack or to support the US representatives. In short,' the Minister of Finance concluded, 'I wonder whether the introduction of this topic at this particular time might not do more harm than good!'[149]

The Minister of Trade and Commerce was also qualified in his approval. While sharing Pearson's concern at the 'regrettable lack of new initiatives in the field of international economic relations,' and appreciating the 'distinct danger of international trade relations slipping backwards,' C.D. Howe believed that these disappointing trends arose from the domestic policies of the United States and, to a lesser degree, of the United Kingdom, which discussion within the NATO Council was unlikely to affect. 'When one examines the particular reasons which exist for present policies in these countries,' Howe observed, 'it is difficult to see in what way a debate in NATO might result in altering the policies of any of the major trading countries or in persuading them to produce new and constructive initiatives.' Like his colleague the Minister of Finance, Howe recalled the dismaying protectionism expressed by Americans in the Canada-United States Committee on Economic Affairs. 'If the United States were to participate in a debate in NATO by restating the views on trade policy which were stated there, the effect upon the various European countries might be quite unfortunate. ... You may consider these dangers of sufficient weight to defer the approach you are considering until a more auspicious time,' was how the Minister indicated his own preference for postponement, adding that 'I am quite happy, however, to leave the tactical decision in your hands as to whether you should take this new initiative at NATO.'[150]

On these green lights from his colleagues – accompanied by a cautionary show of orange – the Secretary of State for External Affairs decided to move. Before he could, however, Italy jumped out in front. Dana Wilgress does not appear to have been concerned that his proposed initiative had been pre-empted. 'I feel we should not be too unhappy about the Italians beating the gun through proposing that an item covering Article 2 should be included in the agenda for the December Ministerial Meeting,' Wilgress cabled from Paris on 21 November. 'Some of the doubts expressed by the Ministers of Finance and Trade and Commerce about the proposal ... arose out of the fears that Canadian initiative in proposing a discussion of Article 2 might be misunderstood. The Italian initiative relieves us of this possibility.'[151]

Article 2 was duly discussed within the North Atlantic Council meetings in mid-December 1955. The discussion appears to have been perfunctory. 'A resolution was passed reaffirming that closer co-operation between members of the Alliance, as envisaged in Article 2, was a very good thing,' is how L.B. Pearson almost sarcastically described the proceedings in his memoirs, 'and that the Permanent Council should examine once again how this could best be brought about. Naturally, I supported the resolution, though I was sceptical that anything would happen. ... I was right.'[152]

The third – and final – attempt to move Article 2 from rhetoric to reality occurred during the weeks leading up to the NATO Ministerial Council Meeting of May 1956. Once again, L.B. Pearson gave the lead. '[C]an it be agreed,' Pearson inquired of the Permanent Representative on 5 March, 'that the comparatively limited time of the next Ministerial Meeting will be devoted to a discussion of co-operation between NATO members in the non-military fields, i.e., consultation on political and economic problems common to members...?'[153] And once again it was the Department of Finance which expressed its apprehension. 'Any attempt to push NATO into an active, continuing programme on the economic front seems to me misguided and even dangerous,' A.F.W. Plumptre wrote to the Under Secretary of State for External Affairs on 27 March.

Neither the Secretariat nor the delegations are properly staffed or organized for this kind of activity. Other international organizations organized for the purpose have developed well-defined responsibilities in the field of economic co-operation, and NATO could not and should not attempt to duplicate their activities. Moreover, the economic interests of NATO members are not always the same, and there is a real danger that an attempt to make NATO into an active force on the economic front would merely emphasize the divergency of interests which exists, thereby weakening the common ties which have bound NATO members together. These ties seem hardly strong enough at the moment to run the risk of further strain...'[154]

When the North Atlantic Council met on 4 May 1956, L.B. Pearson was encouraged by what he took to be 'a renewed impetus to re-examine non-military co-operation; fresh and serious thinking seemed to have been given to the problem.' Pearson was by this time under no illusion that progress would be likely. 'I kept my fingers crossed. My caution was justified; when the US Secretary of State later spoke at the Council meeting ... he seemed less concerned about non-military co-operation than in ensuring that any strengthening in this area should not be at the expense of the collective military effort.'[155] All that emerged from the meeting was yet another study committee.

Once more the Secretary of State for External Affairs donned the mantle of North Atlantic seer, this time in the company of Halvard Lange of Norway and Gaetano Martino of Italy. This Committee of Three, Pearson recalled, 'was immediately, and inevitably, handicapped by being dubbed "The Three Wise Men." There were moments when I thought that it might more appropriately be called "The Three Stooges".'[156] The Committee of Three reported to the North Atlantic Council in December 1956. Most of its report dealt with the topic of political consultation, so spectacularly lacking during the convulsing crisis over Suez. The outcome of the intensive efforts of the Wise Men and their staffs over nine months of work was, in Pearson's view, 'neither startling nor likely to form a consensus for action.'[157] By 1956, he recorded, 'I was losing hope that NATO would evolve beyond an alliance for defence...'[158]

The failure of the Canadian government's campaign to put Article 2 to some use probably inspired – so L.B. Pearson later speculated – 'some ironic reflections in Washington and London.'[159]

There were reflections in London, but not ironic. Gladwyn Jebb (later Lord Gladwyn), has since described his objection to the idea of an Atlantic community as 'fundamental,' and his objection to Article 2, while not so deeply rooted, was likewise unequivocal: 'Of course there would, and there should, be institutions – even political institutions – to regulate the intimate relationship between Europe and America. The North Atlantic Council ... seemed to me admirably adapted to this purpose. But ... I was against giving it any economic or social jurisdiction, since that, if exercised, would appear to conflict with the successful working of bodies such as the OEEC and the GATT...' In spite of Gladwyn's opposition to Article 2, he did not fault Canada for supporting it: on the contrary, he praised her most enthusiastic supporter for his far-sighted view of the national interest.

Escott Reid was not only concerned on ideological grounds to introduce into the treaty some provision tending in the direction of Atlantic unity: he was anxious to do so in order to protect the special position of Canada. He saw very well that if Western Europe ever one day really "jelled" and the famous dumb-bell became a reality, it was not clear what the role of Canada would be, or how it would be expected to protect its special interests.[160]

Reflections of a different kind came from Washington – reflections not so much ironic as acerbic. 'Article 2 has continued to bedevil NATO,' Dean Acheson remarked in his memoirs. 'Lester Pearson has continually urged the Council to set up committees of "wise men" to find a use for it, which the "wise men" continually have failed to do.'[161] And again, elsewhere: 'The plain fact ... is that NATO is a military alliance. Its purpose was and is to deter and, if necessary, to meet the use of Russian military power or the fear of its use in Europe. This purpose is pretty old-fashioned. Perhaps to avoid this stigma, Canadian draftsmen had Article 2 inserted in the Treaty. That article calls for joint action by the signatories in economic and cultural fields as well as in the military; but despite studies by two groups of "wise men" guided by Canadians, no promising areas were discovered.'[162]

The most telling criticism from Washington of Canada's failure to implement Article 2 comes not from an opponent of the Article but from a supporter. 'We were fully in sympathy with the Canadian point of view that [a North Atlantic pact] ... should be much more [than a military alliance],' Theodore C. Achilles, Acheson's colleague and fellow negotiator, recalled in 1970. (The 'we' in this instance refers to himself and John D. Hickerson of the US State Department, not to himself and Acheson.)

We wanted a flexible Article 2 which would really lead towards close cooperation and coordination, not merely in the military field but in the political and economic fields...

...[A]t the Lisbon ministerial meeting in 1952, we had just done something to Canada ... probably some restrictions on the import of pulp and paper – and Mike Pearson ... asked us if Washington would object seriously if Canada brought an accusation against the United States under Article 2 of the Treaty for violating this commitment to coordinate and harmonize economic policy. I said, "That sounds like a good idea. Let's try it out on Washington and see what they say." We telephoned Washington that night and got back a reply, "Sure, let Canada go ahead and bring something on that. We don't mind; we think this will be a very interesting exercise." I told Mike that but Ottawa apparently decided against going ahead with it. It would have been ... a way to get a little life into Article 2. ... The Americans were willing to see how far it would go. ... But the Canadians lost their nerve...[163]

The most scathing reflections are those of a Canadian policy maker. Escott Reid viewed Article 2 as the ark of the covenant, the *raison d'être* of the North Atlantic Treaty, the 'chrysalis' out of which would emerge in time a North Atlantic community and a North Atlantic union. While in Ottawa and from abroad, Reid continued to bombard his Minister with proposals for using Article 2 to bring these into being. Ideas dropped as in Chinese water torture: the governments of North Atlantic countries might concert their policies within UN specialized agencies, acting as 'a ginger group ... in making the agencies more effective...'; they might agree to merge some of their national apparatus – their meteorological bureaux, their air transport boards, their atomic energy agencies – into common North Atlantic apparatus; they might agree to allow among themselves free movement of goods, capital, and people. Such proposals, as ingenious as they may have been impracticable, brought little or no response. There was no 'action this day,' or any other day. 'Canada was not so active in pressing for the implementation of Article 2,' Reid later observed with considerable understatement, 'as it had been in pressing for its inclusion in the treaty.'[164]

For this inaction, Escott Reid blames his Minister. L.B. Pearson might have (in his own phrase) 'hammered away at the maximum implementation of Article 2,' but Reid believes that he had not hammered accurately or hard enough, that he lacked sufficient acumen in economics or sufficient stamina in politics – possibly lacked both – to see the project to completion.

Part of the explanation of Canada's half-heartedness was that Pearson was never at his best in dealing with economic issues. He may, indeed, have failed to grasp the implications of the argument ... that the path of development from alliance to community was for the alliance to meet practical problems, such as defence production and defence finance, successfully, and with as much fairness as possible to all the member states of the alliance. Or perhaps he realized very clearly the domestic political difficulties in the way of this kind of development and he was not prepared to undertake the struggles with the Cabinet, the Liberal Party, Parliament and the electorate which would be required to overcome these difficulties.[165]

A stern judgement. Is it justifiable? The verdict is left for the statesman's biographers to deliver. 'Biography is about chaps': national security studies are (mostly) about gaps.

4

Mobilizing the Deterrent

'So he's not going to rescue us?'
'Not he!'
'Then who will? What about NATO?'
'We only know one thing for certain about NATO – it can't get a force into the field in less than six weeks.'

Nancy Mitford

RETURNING TO EUROPE

'In order more effectively to achieve the objectives of this Treaty' – so the North Atlantic Treaty's third article recites – 'the Parties, separately and jointly, by means of continuous and effective self-help and mutual aid, will maintain and develop their individual and collective capacity to resist armed attack.' During the first year as a North Atlantic ally, the government of Canada considered how to implement this commitment.

Of three ways of doing so – sending a force to Western Europe, building up its own armed forces, helping Western Europe to defend itself – no thought was given to the first. A contribution by Canada to an allied force-in-being, stationed during peacetime in Western European countries, was rejected out of hand. 'There is no use asking the US, Canada and Britain to maintain large land and air forces on the continent in time of peace':[1] such was the opinion of a senior Army officer in June 1949; it was also the opinion of his government. So strong was Canada's fear that her membership in the Alliance might bring pressure to station troops in Western Europe that Ottawa initially opposed locating the Pact's headquarters there, preferring Washington to Paris. The Canadian government was 'concerned', the Ambassador at Washington explained to officials of the US State Department on 3 August 1949, 'lest such an arrangement [as a Paris headquarters] would cause undue pressure on the United States and Canada for more extensive and exacting commitments as to the use of their troops on the continent of Europe.'[2]

That Canada's NATO membership required an immediate and sizeable increase in her armed forces, and hence in the amount of her defence budget, was disputed by almost all members of the policy community in 1949. Escott Reid was the exception. In a memorandum to L.B. Pearson written on 12 March 1948 as the first of scores to come, Reid argued that it 'would be dishonest for us to enter an Atlantic pact unless we are prepared to increase considerably our defence appropriations in order to have a striking force immediately available.' Pearson, Reid recorded, 'made no comment on this.' When during the summer of 1948 Reid told Pearson that he 'assumed that the creation of the alliance would be followed by an increase in the defence expenditures of Canada,' the Under Secretary of State for External Affairs demurred. 'Pearson replied that he saw no reason for this; under the alliance, national armed forces would become part of a balanced collective force; there would be joint planning; all this would increase the efficiency of the allied forces – that, and not an increase in defence expenditures, was all that would be required.'[3] This view was expressed in the report of the Department of National Defence for 1949-50. 'The North Atlantic Treaty is a pact of peace,' the report declared. 'Its final result will not be to increase the expenditures which every nation on our side must take. By pooling reserves, the effect of the pact should be to reduce the total expenditures which each of the 12 countries would have found necessary for their security had there been no pact.' The report prudently hedged a bit: 'That result is some distance off,' it conceded, 'and in the meantime, Canada will have to make such modifications of her plans as may be found necessary to meet the situation.'[4] The Department's guarded formulation left plenty of room for manoeuvre – either down or up.

Its Minister, as was to have been expected, wanted to manoeuvre up. To a meeting of the Cabinet Defence Committee on 23 November 1949 Brooke Claxton brought two sets of figures, each projecting national defence expenditure to 1954-5. One set was based on the assumptions that no new equipment would be procured and no new commitments entered into. The other set was what Claxton called his 'desired' programme. Its figures incorporated what the Minister of Finance had asked for – 'the best forecasts that can be made ... of our prospective requirements under the Treaty, whether for military services and facilities (e.g. reciprocal training arrangements), or the provision of equipment and supplies, either from stocks or production.'[5] The two sets of figures were as shown in the table overleaf.

One External Affairs officer pronounced the figures in the first two columns to be 'rather startling' – meaning, presumably, rather startlingly

	Existing Programme (projected)	Desired Programme (projected)	Actual Programme[*]
1949-50	$382.9 million	—	384.9
1950-1	507.8	633.2	782.5
1951-2	494.1	586.0	1415.5
1952-3	466.7	619.4	1971.2
1953-4	427.0	589.3	1853.7
1954-5	416.1	584.9	1684.7

[*] The expenditures for 1952-3 and the two years following include those for Defence Production. (Source: *Canada Year Book, 1952-53, Canada Year Book, 1956.*) The cost of national defence for 1954-5 was 37 per cent of the federal budget in that year of $4529.8 million.

high. (Had he known what figures would come to occupy the third column, he would have been more than startled.)

A third way of implementing Article 3 – besides contributing to a standing force or reinforcing the existing armed services – was to contribute to Western European forces. Pressure on Canada to make such a contribution was soon exerted. By June 1949 the United States administration had prepared a programme for military assistance to Western Europe soon to be scrutinized by the Congress. The US programme stood a better chance of passing if the administration could tell its critics that Canada was embarking on a similar programme. With this message Congressional leaders and State Department officials called upon the Ambassador at Washington. It would be extremely helpful to them, these visitors informed Hume Wrong, if they were able to say publicly that Canada would be a contributor of military aid to Western Europe.

There was no enthusiasm in Ottawa for these importunings. The Under Secretary of State for External Affairs, after consulting his Minister – 'the observations which follow are my own, but you can take it that they also reflect accurately Mr Pearson's views' – instructed Hume Wrong to tell his American callers that their visits were premature and inopportune. 'It is quite impossible to forecast at this time the nature and extent of Canada's contributions to her Atlantic allies,' A.D.P. Heeney informed Wrong on 15 July 1949.

Any pressures from the United States for a commitment at this stage, indeed any public reference to the part which Canada should play, might well have quite serious results, ... We sometimes think that officials there ignore the reactions which the American attitude in such matters is bound to have in this country; at the same time they continue to emphasize the importance of our example in their own political difficulties.

The most the Americans could be told was that the Canadian government 'fully recognizes the obligations which Canada has undertaken under the Atlantic Pact and Canada can be counted upon to play her just and proper part in the common effort to achieve the purposes for which it was signed '[6]

The Ambassador at Washington carried out these instructions on 19 July. 'Canada fully recognized its obligation under Article III of the Atlantic Pact' – so the US State Department records Hume Wrong as having told two of its officials on that date. '[H]owever, the Canadian Government did not propose to announce any parallel program of interim aid at this time. It did not feel in a position to make commitments of this nature, at least until the Atlantic Pact had been ratified, the machinery under it set up, some form of over-all military plan put in shape and an allocation of responsibilities arrived at under such a plan. It was not seen by the Canadians how military aid could be intelligently distributed until that stage in the process had been reached.' The Ambassador buttressed this argument with two additional considerations. One was that the United States programme was in part the outcome of commitments of military assistance to countries threatened by Soviet power – Greece, Turkey, Iran – which had been entered into prior to the creation of the Atlantic Pact: 'In other words, the US interim aid program would probably have had to be brought forward in consequence of these commitments without regard to the Pact. Canada had assumed no such commitments.' The other was that the US aid program could be sustained by weapons and supplies from existing stockpiles: 'Canada, on the other hand, had scarcely any stocks.' For these reasons, the Canadian government 'would not be in a position to agree to any testimony before the US Congress which would do other than refer to Canada's acknowledgment in general of its obligation under Article III, its past record and its general reputation among nations.' When US State Department officials suggested that Canada, while deficient in military equipment, might be able to provide 'raw materials and other non-finished products to the common endeavour,' the Ambassador, referring again to the fact that he was speaking from instructions at the Cabinet level, responded that he was unable to comment upon that suggestion. Hume Wrong concluded the interview by emphasizing that 'while Canada was not at present willing to make a direct contribution parallel to the MAP [Military Assistance Program], it should be recognized that Canada was not seeking any grants-in aid, as virtually all other [North Atlantic Treaty] countries were.'[7]

With this negative response from Canada, the United States administration had to put up, though not contentedly. However, the Canadian government soon came to see that its policy of refusing to send military aid to Western Europe while the United States was contributing to its defences on such a lavish scale was unwise. Four considerations led Ottawa to adopt a different stance.

The first, and most insistent reason, was the crying need of Western European countries for all the aid that could be sent to them. The region lay exposed to an onslaught from the Soviet Union, to all intents and purposes 'defenceless under the night.' The Minister of National Defence, after visiting Western Europe in December 1949, had reported that all the armed forces there were 'appallingly short of vital items of equipment (particularly aircraft, tanks, motor vehicles, and anti-aircraft weapons).' Wartime occupation had denuded them not only of weapons but of personnel and technique – 'experienced and war-proven officers of all ranks ... design teams ... industrial know-how.'[8] Western Europe required arms and supply as a matter of utmost urgency. That fact – so it seemed to the Department of External Affairs at least – 'is the most compelling argument in favour of making a positive contribution to the partnership on which the national security of Canada largely depends.'[9] The argument became all the more compelling in the light of the fact that – contrary to what Hume Wrong had argued to the US State Department officials at Washington – there were lots of weapons and military supplies in Canada (granted not the most modern types) left over from the Second World War. From that stockpile some of Western Europe's needs might readily be met. 'We had a great deal of equipment that was not required for such forces as we could envisage being raised by Canada before the equipment became totally obsolete,' Brooke Claxton wrote later. 'None of the European countries had much equipment at all apart from what the Americans or ourselves had left behind us when we came home. It would make sense if we gave away as much equipment as we could safely part with and later replace this with the most modern type, in most cases American type. ... On this basis we would have large stocks of surplus military equipment to give away to European countries.'[10]

A second reason why it came to be recognized in most quarters of the policy community that Canada ought to move swiftly to implement Article 3 was that her image might be damaged if she didn't. 'Considering the pioneering role which we played in the creation of the North Atlantic Treaty,' officials of the Department of External Affairs commented in a memorandum to their Minister, 'our partners, including the United States, may question our sincerity if we make no mutual aid contribution.'

Comparisons would be drawn between Canada's performance and those of other NATO members, and such comparisons would be invidious at Canada's expense. 'Under their Mutual Defence Assistance Act,' the officials pointed out,

the United States are giving $1 billion in 1950 and 1951 for military supplies for North Atlantic countries. ... The United Kingdom Government will probably be giving the equivalent of about $125 millions. ... This places their contribution to mutual aid roughly on a par with that of the United States in proportion to a national income (8:1). ... By the same yardstick Canada would during the next two years have to contribute about $75 millions ... to make a comparable mutual aid contribution. (Taking our 1950-51 defence budget of $425 millions, our contribution towards "self-help" – our own defence forces – is less than half that of the United States, and about half that of the United Kingdom, in proportion to national income; and we are currently making no contribution to the economic recovery of Europe nor to the military security of areas outside the North Atlantic.)

The officials admitted that some comparisons would be misleading. 'Ours is not the major role; we are the only country of the North Atlantic Pact that will be paying for all our supplies from the United States; no other North Atlantic country probably pays such a high proportion of US dollars for its military equipment, including components; we have a thinly spread population and a vast area to defend; and our political problem is complicated by a tradition of extremely small peacetime forces and correspondingly low defence budgets...'[11] Yet, even so, other countries, particularly the United States, might not – or choose not to – understand all this. 'We may anticipate ... considerable needling from our North Atlantic partners,' A.D.P. Heeney warned his Minister, adding: 'Indeed, we have already been subject to some pressure.'[12]

Reinforcing these two arguments – Western European need, Canadian image – was a third arising from expediency. Sooner or later, Canada would be obliged to offer something. If it were later rather than sooner, Canada would be pressed to provide what had not yet been made available by others. 'There is nothing to be gained by waiting until we have been asked,' Dana Wilgress, then High Commissioner at London, pointed out,

and much to be gained by announcing our position on our own initiative. .. A "wait and see" policy would probably result in our being pressed eventually to contribute in a form less satisfactory to us. If we delay, we shall almost certainly find ourselves later being called upon to make our contribution entirely in the form of those goods which the United States and the European countries themselves are unable or unwilling to make available to one another. By thus narrowing the range of our contribution (but probably not reducing its size), such a delaying policy could quite well have a much more disturbing effect on our economy and on the pattern of our munitions production than would have been the case if we had made our contribution earlier and had made it in the lines that were most convenient for us. It would clearly seem desirable, from the Canadian point of view, for us to begin contributing as soon as possible...[13]

The Ambassador at Washington also supported a mutual aid initiative, Hume Wrong agreeing with Wilgress that 'delaying ... might result in our being confronted with a list of items which none of the other signatories could or would wish to produce.' Wrong added from his vantage point at Washington a supplementary argument.

The Mutual Aid Programme will be coming up for consideration by the Congress early in the session and I would hope that, if we make our views known early enough to the Administration, we might be able to influence changes in the existing US laws governing military procurement in the direction of easing our own position. ... One of the most objectionable features under the present Mutual Defence Assistance legislation is the omission of any authorization for the United States to purchase in Canada equipment for their military forces. I think that if we show a willingness to make a direct contribution ourselves to the strengthening of the defences of Western Europe we would assist those in the Administration who recognize the importance of helping us...[14]

There was one more reason adduced within the policy community for Canada's making a contribution immediately to Western Europe's defence requirements. Mutual aid, judiciously selected, might help stimulate the Canadian economy and relieve unemployment.

Here was an argument previously neglected. In so far as Ottawa had weighed the economic consequencs of mutual aid, it had dismissed them as detrimental. The principal hold-out against an early Canadian contribution had been the deputy minister of Finance, W.C. Clark. The federal treasury was then being depleted of funds allocated to supplement the unemployment insurance programme: the dreaded post-war recession was believed by some to be about to descend upon the land. Clark, and his minister Douglas Abbott, accordingly looked askance at any additional spending in what A.D.P. Heeney acknowledged to be 'our very tight budgetary situation' that was not directly aimed at relieving unemployment and stimulating the economy.[15]

Officials making their case for a Canadian mutual aid contribution accordingly began to stress the economic advantages to Canada that could accrue from carefully selected contributions. Shipments of agricultural products and minerals to be stockpiled in Western Europe could alleviate anticipated surpluses while generating employment in farming and mining. 'It would, perhaps, be stretching the word "contribution" too far,' a Department of External Affairs memorandum acknowledged, 'to consider stockpiling our anticipated food surpluses such as apples, salmon and eggs, but there would surely be a good argument for stockpiling wheat, or other staple bulk foods that would have to be carried across the Atlantic, in the event of war, by the hazardous and wasteful process of convoying...'[16] As for such strategic items as aluminum, zinc, copper, 'and a few other base metals that we can produce in greater quantity than we can sell either at home or abroad,' it was considered that 'spending the public funds in order to supply raw material stockpiles for the defence industries of the European industrial countries would be a worthy contribution to meeting their needs which, at the same time, would help to support important parts of the Canadian economy.'[17]

Providing military equipment out of existing stores would do little or nothing to help the domestic economy in the short run, but the consequent necessity of re-equipping with later models would help the Canadian defence industry, particularly if such weaponry were supplied to Western European countries as well. 'Orders for military supplies for the Canadian Armed Forces alone will not be sufficient to maintain or develop in Canada even the essential nucleus of an armament industry that would be vital to us in time of war, unless we sell or give arms to other countries.' A case in point was that of the Canadair plant in Montreal, where F-86 production for the Royal Canadian Air Force would taper off by 1952 in the absence of overseas demand, and might then be forced to close. 'If we see our role in a future war as an immediately available arsenal for Europe, the nucleus of our defence industry must be built up...'[18]

All these arguments were duly transmitted to the government. By such a formidable array of advocacy ministers were bound to be impressed. But there were opposing arguments which ministers took even more seriously. A memorandum prepared within the Department of External Affairs recited the countervailing considerations as follows.

The Government would be extremely reluctant to add to the great pressures which have already been placed upon the budget in a year when our revenues will be substantially reduced by last year's taxation cuts and probably by a declining level of economic activity as well, while, at the same time, there are more demands than ever for domestic expenditure, e.g., for defence and to meet unemployment and welfare demands. The alternatives of increasing taxation within a year of the election, or budgeting for a deficit while we are near the top of the economic cycle, are equally distasteful...[19]

Escott Reid, chafing at Canada's reluctance to follow through after working so zealously at negotiating the Treaty, wrote in evident exasperation: 'We are "able" to pay for twice as large a programme. It is not a question of ability but of willingness.'[20] That willingness, like Western Europe's arms and soldiers, was in short supply.

During the year which had elapsed since the Canadian government signed the North Atlantic Treaty on 4 April 1949, its contribution under Article 3 was confined to an offer to train in Canada 250 officers from Western European armies and air forces. The cost of such training (apart from paying the trainees) would be borne by the Department of National Defence, and since the amount was not impressive the idea was floated within the policy community 'that, in order to obtain the greatest political credit abroad for our efforts, a generous estimate might be made of the cost of such training facilities...'[21] The offer was conveyed to the NATO Defence Committee by Brooke Claxton. 'Our officer training plan went over exceedingly well,' Claxton reported, 'very much better than I expected. It was received with real enthusiasm. Several of the people said it was the best thing that had happened yet, the first sign of genuine co-operation. The timing of this seems to have been just right...'[22] An official of the Department of External Affairs described the offer as 'a fine gesture'[23] – a compliment perhaps intended to be back-handed. It was, at any rate, the only offer of its kind – or indeed of any other.

In late March and early April 1950, NATO's committees met at The Hague to consider the results of military planning embodied in the Medium Term Defence Plan. This Plan set forth in detail what forces were considered to be essential for the effective defence of the North Atlantic area by 1 July 1954 – the date by which the planners considered the Soviet Union to be capable of launching 'a major atomic attack.' The Plan envisaged an available force of ninety army divisions, with air and naval forces to match. A Canadian diplomat on the scene reported with brutal candour that 'the military plan approved by the Defence Ministers is not one which they expect can ever be put into effect. ... Until the United States is committed to a military and economic aid programme for her North Atlantic partners until at least 1954, at an annual rate of about $3 billion or so, the security of the North Atlantic Community will continue to rest more on political bluff than on military and economic strength...'[24]

A year after the signing of the North Atlantic Treaty, NATO remained a paper tiger. On paper some twenty divisions existed (including troops in Canada, the United States, and the United Kingdom which might – or then again might not – be committed to the Western European battleground.)* Half of these were ill equipped. Brooke Claxton was later to

---

* The question of whether or not these troops should be committed in advance to the defence of Western Europe was discussed by General Charles Foulkes and other senior Canadian officers with Air Marshal Sir William Elliot, Chief Staff Officer to the United Kingdom Ministry of Defence, at the British Embassy in Paris on 28 Novem-

describe these forces as 'literally nothing' – an obviously inaccurate description but a fitting rhetorical flourish. 'Even the American, British and French occupation troops were really garrison forces, neither deployed, trained nor organized for effective defence.'[25] As Claxton reported at the time from The Hague: 'The three major problems are obvious deficiencies of immense proportions between requirements of adequate plan and available resources, secondly, uncertainty [about] future United States assistance on which everything really depends and, thirdly, lack of confidence regarding security which seriously interferes with real progress regarding standardization of equipment and resulting integration of industry and economic power.'[26] One of those present on the Canadian delegation summed up his impressions of Atlantic achievement thus far:

The military machinery now set in motion will enable the North Atlantic area to spend its defence dollar to better effect; but it is by no means certain that it will enable a community of more than twice the population and industrial resources of the Soviet Union to produce armed forces capable of defending itself effectively in the event of a Soviet attack by 1954. As one delegate put it privately: "The cost of living everywhere has gone up; the cost of freedom has gone up too."[27]

As of 25 June 1950, no member of the Alliance – Canada included – seemed prepared to pay its price.

The attack by North Korea on the Republic of Korea transformed the mood of NATO members, much as the Nazi assault on Western Europe ten years previously had shaken the surviving democracies out of their inertia and complacency. Apathy changed, almost overnight, to concern. 'Up to the present, the Western powers have fought a phoney cold war,'

ber 1949. The discussion made clear that previous assurances such as that given to British senior officers by General Foulkes in April 1949 that 'we would likely be putting a Corps plus two Armoured Brigades into a theatre of operations at M plus 12' were made for the purposes of raising Western European morale and had no real operational significance. 'I emphasized that in my view the short and the long term considerations were greatly divergent,' Foulkes recorded of this discussion.

From the short term view in winning the cold war it was perhaps advantageous for the UK, US and Canada to give immediate assurances of support in both divisions and squadrons of aircraft in the initial stages of a battle in Western Europe. By so doing we would raise the morale of the Western European nations and this would assist them in doing more for themselves. But from the long term and practical standpoint this was military nonsense. There were insufficient divisions and squadrons available to in any way satisfy the immediate requirements of the Regions in Europe. ... At the present time it looks like two divisions from the UK, and maximum of four divisions from the US and two from Canada. If these were detailed before the battle began it would seriously tie the hands of any Supreme Commander...

DEA files, 50030-B-40.

was Escott Reid's characteristically trenchant way of putting it. 'This phoney cold war has now turned into a war which is neither phoney nor altogether cold. The change in the international climate is as abrupt and as grave as that which occurred in the spring and summer of 1940.'[28] One of his colleagues observed: 'The present international atmosphere has certainly made everybody much more anxious to get something done fast in a practical way...'[29] Years later, Brooke Claxton recalled the impact of Korea on the Atlantic Alliance:

NATO owes the fact that it has built up its strength to the communist aggression in Korea. ... To meet the challenge of Korea required a build-up of our forces comparable to what was needed to meet our commitments in Europe. Almost more important is the change that it made in public opinion. Korea made our people realize what was involved in communist aggression and what was needed to stop it. Moreover it accustomed the people of Canada (and of other NATO countries) to the idea of having large numbers of men and large amounts of money tied up in our common effort to protect our freedom.

The momentum we gained in the Korea war carried through to the build-up of our collective strength in Europe. In Canada we did everything possible to bring it home to the people that Korea and NATO were just two aspects of the same operation; two places where we met the communist challenge in precisely the same way, namely by building up our strength.[30]

The impact of the Korean War was first felt by the armed forces. All of the three Services were deemed to need more men, more weapons, and therefore more money. At a meeting of the Chiefs of Staff Committee on 18 July 1950, each of the Service commanders outlined his proposals for rearmament.

The Royal Canadian Navy proposed to add two destroyers and a minesweeper to its fleet; to upgrade firepower and fire-control on the nine Tribal class destroyers; to store additional ammunition in new facilities on each coast; to improve the seaward defences for St John's and Halifax; to provide a dozen additional Sea Fury aircraft for the carriers *Magnificent* and *Bonaventure*; and 'to procure, refit or build sundry items in radar, communications, stores, properties, buildings and such.' Naval and civilian personnel should be recruited to run the enlarged establishment.

The Canadian Army proposed to bring units of the Brigade Group up to full strength and to increase the anti-aircraft element.

The Royal Canadian Air Force was the most ambitious. The Chief of the Air Staff recommended the immediate acquisition from the United States Air Force of 100 Mustang fighter aircraft; the acceleration of F-86 fighter production to seven aircraft a month, and of CF-100 fighter production to five a month; an increase in aircraft establishment of two squadrons of maritime patrol planes, of twelve aircraft each; acceleration of production facilities for (though not production of) fifty Orenda engines per month; construction of three new heavy radar sites; and increases in manpower.[31]

When these proposals became known to the Department of External Affairs, it seemed to at least one of its officers that they erred on the side of insufficiency. This was no time to be thinking small. 'I gather that National Defence are proposing rather modest increases in the Defence programme with a view to speeding up re-equipment of Canadian forces,' R.A. MacKay wrote to the Under Secretary.

I think it would be a great pity if Cabinet got the impression that this is all that needs to be done. You might like to have a word with the Minister, pointing this out to him and suggesting that he might like to bring into the discussion the very great need for building up our European allies. It seems to me that the Korean situation underlines the necessity for forces in being and on the ground prepared to offer effective assistance from the outset, rather than mobilization potential...[32]

L.B. Pearson must have put this argument to the Cabinet on 19 July, for a statement made public after its meeting revealed a new sense of urgency.

The Korean situation cannot be viewed in isolation. The attack on the Republic of Korea has increased the cohesion of resistance to aggressive Communism in other parts of the world. ... We are increasing immediately our defence effort and expenditure. We are also giving consideration to further measures of aid by this country to our North Atlantic partners.[33]

At this meeting, Cabinet minutes record, approval was given to 'a general increase in defence expenditure, as submitted by the Minister of National Defence, involving an additional cash commitment of between $40 and $50 million and an increase in personnel for the three armed forces of 5 to 6 thousand.'[34] The increased cash commitment amounted to roughly ten per cent of the 1950-1 defence budget of $425 million, while the increase in personnel amounted to roughly twelve per cent of an active defence force which at the time stood at 47,185. These increases were scarcely staggering. But they were only the beginning.

Until the outbreak of war in Korea, Canada had contributed no equipment to Western European defence forces under Article 3 of the North Atlantic Treaty. Some weapons transfers were studied but the weaponry involved – a few guns here, some ammunition there – was niggardly. It began to dawn on members of the policy community that the scale of the proposals (on which action had yet to be taken) was too modest. 'We can no longer expect to get very much credit or gratitude for a small contribution of second-hand and somewhat out-moded equipment,' an official of the Department of External Affairs commented in July 1950. 'I do not think that at present anything very substantial by way of a mutual aid contribution in the form of military equipment is contemplated.'[35] Advocates of something 'very substantial' spoke up. 'I feel strongly that now is the time for the Canadian Government to consider the possibility of taking an immediate decision on the question of contributing equipment on a divisional scale from existing stocks to the European countries in the North Atlantic Treaty,' the High Commissioner at London cabled to L.B. Pearson on 25 July. 'An announcement to this effect, coupled with a general statement of the increase in our own defence programme, would, in my opinion, not only help the United States Administration, but would be evidence to other North Atlantic countries of our determination to play our part.'[36]

An event which reinforced this argument was the announcement by the United States Administration towards the end of July 1950 that it would be asking Congress for an additional $10 billion appropriation for defence and for a substantial increase in the funds for mutual aid. From an overall defence outlay of less than $15 billion the Americans proposed to move to an expenditure of between $25 and 30 billion, a decision described by a senior official in Ottawa as 'one of the most important events in post-war history.'[37]

By this decision United States pressure on Atlantic allies to increase their defence expenditures in turn was greatly intensified. The pressure was soon felt in Ottawa. On 26 July, the US Ambassador left an *aide mémoire* with the Secretary of State for External Affairs. L.B. Pearson's immediate response was recorded by the US State Department two days later. 'Canadian FonMin reacted favorably to our approach but he cautioned [Ambassador Stanley] Woodward that some of his colleagues were still "lagging" re increased defense effort. FonMin stated however that popular demand for greater Canadian effort will probably influence cabinet to reconvene Parliament earlier than originally contemplated. In order to avoid further opposition and press criticism, he thought announcement re this question might soon be forthcoming. Woodward notes increasing awareness in official Canadian circles that Canada's effort has fallen short as compared with UK and other countries.'[38] A written reply to the US Ambassador's representations was forthcoming on 11 August. It recounted the steps taken by the Canadian government to upgrade the strength of the armed forces – 'the costs of these are being estimated, but I am unable at present to give you any satisfactory figures' – and reported that 'the Government has been urgently examining the problem of stepping up production of defence equipment both for Canadian needs and for supplying other North Atlantic countries.' The reply pointedly noted that Canada's capacity to furnish mutual aid would be greatly improved if the United States were to remove its own restrictions on defence purchasing in foreign countries, or at least in Canada.[39]

Further pressure on the government was exerted with the approach of a meeting of the NATO Council of Deputies, at which each representative would be expected to describe in specific terms what his government proposed to do to strengthen North Atlantic defence. The Cabinet accordingly authorized additional defence expenditures – what the Minister of Finance later described to the House of Commons as 'the huge total of $409,257,821' – for 'aircraft, ships, guns and the other paraphernalia of modern defence' and an additional $300,000,000 'for the purpose of producing extra defence equipment and supplies, either for our own armed forces or for those of allies under the North Atlantic Treaty.'[40] At the NATO Council of Deputies meeting on 24 August, the Canadian representative, according to the US record,

indicated Canada's principal role would be maintain strategic reserves, defend sea lanes, and supply military equipment. He said Canada anxious carry its responsibility and in respect military production urged NATO state specific requirements. He said Canadian Government will shortly ask Parliament remove financial impediment to Canadian transfers military equipment...[41]

Canada's first contribution to West European armed forces was of United Kingdom-type equipment for one infantry division, furnished in the expectation that it would be replaced by United States-type equipment. Payment for the equipment would be made from the $300,000,000 appropriation for which the government sought Parliament's approval on 6 September 1950. That appropriation, the Minister of Finance explained to the House of Commons, would

get under way the Canadian portion of that large increase in the production of defence supplies and equipment which the North Atlantic Council has found to be so urgently needed now. It will be used to produce those things which the government considers will be most immediately useful in the common cause after receiving information and advice from the appropriate bodies created under the treaty. These may be turned over to our own forces, either increasing their plans or holdings beyond the current scale, which is provided for under our own defence programme, or replacing equipment or stores which they may make available to our allies in Europe. On the other hand, if it appears these new arms can be most effectively used or held in the common cause by our allies in Europe, they will be dispatched to them without delay and without payment. ... We are sure that this amount, and probably more, will be needed from Canada during the next year and a half...[42]

The next day, the Ambassador at Washington discussed the stepped-up program with the US Secretary of State. 'Mr Acheson,' Hume Wrong reported, 'was inclined to query whether we could not do more.' Some people are never satisfied.

At this time it was first publicly suggested that Canada should send troops to Western Europe. The US Secretary of State had raised this possibility privately with Hume Wrong on 7 September: Wrong, expressing his personal opinion, told Dean Acheson that 'it would be unwise and unprofitable to suggest that Canadian ground forces should be so employed. The problems of maintaining a force of the size which might conceivably be furnished by Canada would be too great to make the operation worth while.'[43] On 9 September, the *Washington Post* ran an article urging Canada to send troops to Western Europe. 'While I have thought that this question would arise in a concrete form at some time,' Wrong cabled at once to Ottawa, 'I had not expected it to be posed so soon.'[44] A few days later a more sonorous call to arms was heard in the British House of Commons. 'There should certainly be 10 divisions from the United States, two or three from Canada, and six or eight from this island.' The speaker was the Leader of the Opposition, Winston Churchill.

Shades of Chanak!* In 1950, as in 1922, Churchill's words made banner headlines in Canadian newspapers, among them the *Montreal Gazette*'s 'Churchill Hits UK Defence Plan.' In the House of Commons on 13 September, the day after Churchill had spoken out at Westminister, the Prime Minister read out the *Gazette*'s headline and the subhead that ran beneath it: 'Asks Seventy-Division European Army, Two or Three Divisions from Canada Suggested.' Noting that Churchill occupied the same position in the British parliament as did George Drew in the Canadian, L.S. St Laurent commented sarcastically: 'In this country it may be surprising to some, but I am sure not to very many, that decisions about the formation and use of Canadian armed forces are to continue to be made by the government of Canada, and by the House of Commons responsible to the electors of Canada.' St Laurent used the occasion to reiterate that the government was 'not considering the raising of Canadian forces to despatch to Europe as a deterrent to aggression in Europe, and has not before it any such suggestion from any of the governments of the North Atlantic Treaty nations.' He continued:

Personally I do not expect that those governments will suggest that the armed effort of a nation of some fourteen million people for the purpose of deterring aggression in Europe should be twenty or thirty per cent of the armed effort of a

* See *In Defence of Canada*, I, 20-5.

nation of 14 million people. Nor do I feel they are apt to suggest that the best value to be obtained from Canada's contribution would be by sending men to Europe, and housing, clothing, feeding and providing for them there, rather than by using these men here to help in our production of arms and equipment for men available in Europe whose need of arms and equipment is greater than the European countries themselves can meet...

Our present view is ... that the most effective immediate contribution Canada can make to the joint strength in Europe of the North Atlantic nations is the provision of arms and equipment which will enable the young men of the nations of Western Europe to have effective means of providing security for their own homelands, and of building up their combined strength as a deterrent to aggression from any quarter...[45]

Churchill's intervention had been – in Canada, at least – unhelpful to his cause.

On the eve of the first meeting of the North Atlantic Council since the outbreak of the war in Korea, the Under Secretary of State for External Affairs submitted to his Minister 'a general appraisal, as we see it, of the utility and shortcomings of the North Atlantic Organization, not as it may be in 1954, but as it is in 1950.' The appraisal was stark.

Since the Korean crisis, the tempo of the defence efforts of all North Atlantic countries has been sharply increased. Defence budgets have, on the average, gone up by about 40% – representing a spread of from 114% (for the United States) to 3.8% (for Portugal). Yet, it remains true that a year and a half after the signature of the Treaty, the Western Union citadel of our European partners remains, in the opinion of their commanders-in-chief, indefensible...[46]

Such was the situation confronting the North Atlantic Council when it met at New York on 15 September 1950.

While the main preoccupation of the Council during its week of intense discussions was the question of German rearmament,* it was also deeply preoccupied with the related question of the defence of Western Europe – item 4 on its agenda. In leading off debate during the first meeting of the session, the US Secretary of State had declared that 'action this item was key to future NATO.' Dean Acheson – according to the US record of the proceedings –

solicited views on this most important question. Netherlands opened by stressing need for defense line as far east in Germany as possible and raised both question of more troops in Europe (US, UK and Canada) or possible German participation in European defense. UK emphasized need for west to use maximum strength to avoid occupation and the necessity for military planners to know what forces they

* See below, Ch. 6, 327-8.

might expect in planning defense. French favored increased US, UK and Canadian forces in Europe but expressed reservations re arming of Germany. US closed session by emphasizing that alternatives suggested by Netherlands were not alternatives and that both courses suggested by Netherlands would be necessary to build sufficient strength. In recessing ... Secretary stated his opinion in duty of all Council members to speak and with absolute frankness on this vital question...[47]

Acheson's shaft was aimed at, among others, the Canadian representative who had remained silent throughout this first meeting. When L.B. Pearson spoke at the second meeting that afternoon, it was to endorse the principle that German manpower be 'appropriately used in defense of the west'; he said nothing of using Canadian manpower.[48] A Canadian reference to that matter was not made until the fifth meeting on 18 September and – as the US record implied – it was more oblique than what the Americans and West Europeans would have liked to have heard.

On integrated force, [Pearson] welcomed ideas of US...

Explained unique position Canada as small overseas nation with local defense problems. Stated Canada forming new army for UN and NATO but made clear no commitment now how Canada would be associated with unified force. Asked for NATO guidance on disposition of equipment Canada prepared make available, through stocks and new production from $300 million program...[49]

Pearson's statement evidently made little impression on the US Secretary of State: in reporting to President Truman 'some impressions of my own about these various meetings,' Dean Acheson did not mention Canada.[50] Chinese entry into the fighting in Korea made the Canadian government all the more determined to give its NATO commitments top priority. 'The main front is Western Europe,' L.B. Pearson reminded the Canadian representative at the United Nations on 11 November 1950, 'and we must resist efforts of the Soviet Union to get us committed to a theatre of secondary importance.'[51] That was also the message brought by the Canadian representative to the North Atlantic Council meetings during December. 'It is a cardinal point of Soviet policy to involve Western nations in long-drawn-out hostilities in Asia, so that our capacity for defending the West may be weakened,' declared Brooke Claxton on 19 December (Claxton stood in at the meetings for Pearson, who was preoccupied at the time in the UN Korean Cease-Fire Commission).

The Canadian Government believe that Europe must take first place in the conception of the global strategy of the free nations. We believe that the area covered by the North Atlantic Treaty is the heart and centre of any effective resistance to Soviet aggression. ... The Canadian government believe that it is essential that we should all press forward at a much accelerated speed to attain the goal of security which we have set ourselves in the North Atlantic Treaty Organization...

Claxton concluded his statement to the Council by declaring that his government would, 'in view of the need for intensifying and accelerating the rearmament programme of NATO ... have to re-examine our present programme in the light of the new time-table required by the new circumstances.'[52] The Minister's statement was recorded in the minutes taken by the US delegation as follows.

The increase in Communist aggression had been a source of great concern to Canada. Canada had taken steps to increase her defense effort just after the Korean hostilities and would continue to press on with them. An important aspect of the Korean situation was that it showed the strategy of the USSR to be that of involving the western nations heavily in Asia. Canada was convinced that the defenses of Europe must be strengthened and that Europe was in essence the heart of the strength of the West. Europe must take first place in our global strategy, and the NATO area is the key to defense against the USSR. He spoke of the need to press on with the building of military strength and said that political and other progress must be carried along with the military plan. Canada was ready to carry its part in the effort. The acceleration of production was an essential part of the defense build-up and this involved many activities such as standardization and coordination in placing of defense orders. All of these things must be worked out with the greatest possible speed.[53]

China's intervention, and the quickening tempo of Western rearmament which had resulted from it, were the subjects of a review prepared for the Cabinet by the Secretary of State for External Affairs and the Minister of National Defence. The document, dated 28 December 1950 and signed by both Ministers, affirmed bluntly that the lesson to be drawn from these events was that 'the Soviet Government have shown that they are willing to run the risk of a third world war.' The calculations of NATO planning had been rendered obsolete. It was not during late 1953 and early 1954 that the 'period of greatest danger' would begin. 'Now, the only safe assumption is that the period of greatest danger has already begun.' The main front to be defended was in Europe. Consequently, L.B. Pearson and Brooke Claxton concluded, 'we will all require to press forward at a much accelerated rate.' (The text of this memorandum, 'The International Situation,' is printed below as Document 4.)

NATO's Standing Group had already determined what Canada's minimum contribution ought to be – a commitment of one-third of a division of troops to serve in Western Europe; twenty-eight anti-aircraft regiments totalling 20,000 men; and seven additional warships with sixteen crews to man them. The most burdensome demand was for airpower – eleven squadrons in Western Europe were required of Canada, nineteen in North America, a total of 678 aircraft.[54]

These requests were placed before the Cabinet by the Minister of National Defence on 13 December 1950. The Standing Group had requested member governments to respond to its proposals by 10 January 1951. The government of Canada did not meet this deadline. By mid-January the Chiefs of Staff were still far from agreement – so the Defence Liaison Division of the Department of External Affairs noted disapprovingly – 'even as to the assumptions on which the estimates should be prepared.' Agreement had been reached, however, on the amount of the annual defence budget up to and including 1954 – $1.5 billion – and on the overall strength of the armed forces by 1954 – 104,500. That last figure, to the jaundiced eye of an External Affairs official, appeared as 'an artificial compromise, based on political premises, not on military requirements. Under such restrictions of manpower ... we would not do anything towards bridging the gap between these force tabs and the minimum forces required by NATO for the common defence...'[55]

As the build-up proceeded, it became evident to some of those concerned with it that the long-term costs of mobilization would exceed by far any sum that had been forecast. The Minister of National Defence complained at the weight of the burden in his statement to the North Atlantic Council session at Rome during November 1951. 'Up to now' – so Brooke Claxton recalled his remarks on this occasion –

we had been doing our planning both as an organization and, in all probability, in each separate country as if we had a definite target that would be achieved on June 30, 1954. Governments and NATO itself had both been proceeding as if we were on a kind of "crash plan," as if building up our armed forces was a one-time operation. To some extent we had been going along as if, having once got a complete suit of ships, aircraft, tanks and other weapons, all we would have to do would be to maintain them in a proper state of readiness. But, I said, nothing could be further from the truth. In Canada we had just completed a survey of aircraft requirements for the next seven years. Far from indicating that we would achieve a peak of preparedness and then level off or even level down, our survey had shown that the cost of building up and maintaining our air force at its present pitch of strength and preparedness relative to other air forces would take an expenditure of something like $500 million a year or more than 25% of the projected defence budget – this was a minimum. Like Alice in Wonderland, "it takes all the running you can do to keep in the same place."

In other words, simply to stay where we were relatively would take larger and larger sums of money. Apart from physical construction, there was really no such thing as "capital goods" for defence. The "hardware" – ships, aircraft, tanks and weapons – was becoming obsolete after a length of useful life which was becoming shorter and shorter. Practically all major weapons were technically obsolete before the first production numbers were coming off the line. This was true in the sense that there was already somewhere on the drawing board work on equipment which would be so greatly superior that the next one back would cease to be competitive. "Soft goods" – clothing, barracks, stores and so on – had to be replaced. Training, training operations, personnel maintenance and other similar expenditures totalled close to two-thirds of the defence dollar. After anxious study I had reached the conclusion that to carry on our contribution to NATO at its present high level of efficiency and to do what was necessary in continental defence would take more money than we were spending today – not less...

...[F]ar from adding to our forces, we would be fortunate if we were able to maintain them at about their present levels. The implication of what I had said was that the TCC [Temporary Council Committee]* in recommending increases had been quite unrealistic, as in fact it was.[56]

'Field Marshal Montgomery, faced by the possibility of an assault on Western Europe by upwards of 170 Soviet divisions (80 of which might be deployed against Western Europe at any time), supported by tens of thousands of tanks and aircraft, has only 8 divisions for the immediate defence of the Rhine.'[57] Such was the bleak assessment of NATO's military situation placed before the government of Canada during the autumn of 1950. The government responded by reversing its policy. Men as well as equipment would be supplied to SHAPE. Five years after leaving Europe, Canadian forces would return.

On 5 October 1950, the Cabinet Defence Committee agreed that the Special Force then being recruited and trained for service in Korea should, in the event of its not being needed in the Far East if hostilities ceased there, be made available to NATO for whatever role SHAPE's planners might recommend. On 12 October, the Cabinet Defence Committee agreed to make this decision known at the forthcoming meetings of the NATO Defence Committee, together with an intimation that Canada was planning to send a fighter squadron of aircraft to the United Kingdom for operational training, to be followed possibly by two more squadrons. On 30 October, the Minister of National Defence told the NATO Defence Committee at Washington that 'if the United States were to take part in an integrated force in Europe, Canadians would too, subject to parliamentary approval as required by our law.'[58]

At the same session of the NATO Defence Committee, the Standing Group's Medium Term Defence plans were approved. These plans asked Canada to provide one-third of an infantry division and eleven squadrons of aircraft for service in Western Europe. The government considered that such forces were beyond Canada's capacity at that time. In December, the Minister of National Defence reported to the Cabinet Defence

* See below, Ch. 5, 291-300.

Committee that NATO's planners had come to consider the likelihood of war much greater than they had estimated six months earlier. Brooke Claxton also pointed out that the enormously expanded defence program then being undertaken by the United States would make Canada's not so strenuous exertions more difficult to justify. Everything possible should be done, Claxton told the Committee, to assign to NATO's Integrated Force a brigade group and to indicate that the fighter squadrons proceeding to the United Kingdom, with others to follow, might be made available to the Supreme Command. On 28 December 1950, the Cabinet Defence Committee decided to accept these recommendations, as did the Cabinet the following day.

That Canadian forces would be returning to Europe for service there in peacetime was first officially announced in the Speech from the Throne on 30 January 1951: 'You will be asked early in the Session,' Members of Parliament were told, 'to authorize Canadian participation in the integrated force as part of our programme for national defence and security.'[59] On 5 February the Minister of National Defence explained the reason for the decision. 'We feel that equipment without men is even less useful than men without equipment. ... Accordingly, we propose, if Parliament approves, to place in the integrated force elements of the Canadian Army.'[60] On 11 April, the Cabinet decided that the contingent to be sent to Europe should not be drawn from the Special Force but should be recruited in addition to it, and instructed the Department of National Defence 'to raise for the Army as many men as possible, through the reserves, in order to provide an additional brigade group or regimental team of about 6000 officers and men, together with officers and men required as reinforcements and for rotation in Korea and Europe, against the possibility of the government deciding at a future date to send an army formation to the Integrated Force.'[61] Finally, on 4 May, Claxton told the House of Commons that the Army would be enlisting more recruits so as to make available 6670 officers and men who would form the 27th Infantry Brigade Group that would be sent to serve in Western Europe.

The creation of the 27th Infantry Brigade Group gave rise to a number of issues – of timing, of status, of command, and of control.

In notifying the Standing Group on 5 February 1951 that Canada would provide a brigade for the integrated force, the government had not committed itself to any date for beginning the tour of duty before 1954. However, as the Chairman of the Chiefs of Staff Committee reminded his Minister in April 1951, 'it has been indicated that a Canadian contribution to the Integrated Force would be made about the same time as the American formations were sent to Europe, and in conversations with the

Americans it has always been contemplated that a formation of about a Brigade would be sent sometime in the latter part of 1951.' That understanding, General Foulkes admitted, was on the assumption that the Canadian army contribution to the United Nations forces in Korea wou d be that of a battalion only, whereas a brigade had been contributed. Furthermore, when the 25th Infantry Brigade went to Korea, Canadien authorities had warned the United States Chiefs of Staff that this troop movement could have an adverse effect on the planned contribution :o the Integrated Force. The Americans ought thus to be aware of the ie constraints. Even so,

there will still remain in the minds of General Eisenhower, the Western Europe in countries and to some extent the Canadian public that Canada had promisec a contribution to the Integrated Force this year. ... While there is no legal responsi-bility on Canada to fulfill this commitment, there is no doubt a moral obligation and one which we should attempt to fulfill...[62]

The moral obligation apart, it was obvious that the sooner the Canadians arrived, the better off NATO would be. Accordingly, the government agreed that the 27th Infantry Brigade Group should be sent to Western Europe as soon as possible. Troops began leaving Canada during October 1951. By the end of the year they had become fully operational. With some reduction in strength in 1969, Canadian forces have been in Western Europe ever since.

A second issue concerned their status on arrival. Were they, like British and American forces in Western Europe, to do double duty as occupation troops? The Minister of National Defence, who had been instrumental in getting the Canadian Army out of the chores of occupation duty in 194€,* most emphatically thought not. 'We are greatly concerned here,' Brooke Claxton cabled on 12 October 1951 to the Chief of the General Staff, General Simonds (who was then in Paris for consultations with the Standing Group and the Supreme Commander),

about the status in Western Germany our forces will have. If it is at all possible by any means we want to avoid necessity of their being regarded as occupying forces. Preliminary discussion here indicates possibility that Government might postpone whole movement until occupation ended rather than accept that status.

Accordingly I would be glad if you would be extremely careful to avoid any action or discussion which would tend to indicate that we might be willing to accept rôle as part of occupying forces. ... Matter is of greatest urgency, importance and complexity...[63]

---

* See *In Defence of Canada*, III, 187-92.

Claxton's agitation indicates a row within the Cabinet at the possibility that the 27th Infantry Brigade might become, or appear as, part of the British army of occupation; it is likely that St Laurent himself had initiated the threat to hold up its move to Western Europe. The issue subsided as quickly as it had arisen, and no further question was raised about the status of the Brigade.

What caused the question to have arisen in the first place was the government's decision to send the Brigade to Germany under British command rather than to France under American command, for it was only in the former country that allied forces doubled as occupation troops. The issue of where the Brigade ought to be stationed and under which command was heatedly debated within the Chiefs of Staff Committee during the summer of 1951. General Charles Foulkes, just appointed to the newly created position of Chairman of the Chiefs of Staff Committee, favoured placing the Brigade in France under United States command. Such a decision, Foulkes argued, followed ineluctably from the government's earlier decision to equip the Brigade with United States weaponry. He considered it doubtful that the Americans would supply troops outside of their command and lines of communication. But the Army Chief of Staff, General Guy Simonds – between whom and Foulkes little love was lost* – disagreed. (Simonds testified years later that he had opposed the creation of the Air Division – doubtless because he feared its high cost of up-keep would divert funds from his own service.)†

Simonds stated his case in a lengthy memorandum which Arnold Heeney (in a compliment to a military mind rarely paid by the civilian) described as 'a powerfully written document' deserving 'careful reading in full.'[64] First among some half-dozen arguments why the Brigade should be placed under British command in Germany rather than under American command in France was the need to provide 'a counter-balance to the disproportionate and preponderating influence of the United States.' That consideration, Simonds insisted, did not arise from any anti-American sentiment. It was merely facing facts. The United States, while swiftly rising to 'an unprecedented position of dominance in the modern world,' was still inexperienced in the art of what would later come to be called crisis management. 'Without some balancing restraint, it is just conceivable that in the grip of sudden emotion, the US might carry the democratic

---

*   See *In Defence of Canada*, III, 61-6.
†   'I did not agree with the course that the Air Force were taking in setting up the Air Division in Europe in the first place, but that was a decision of the government.' House of Commons Standing Committee on National Defence, *Minutes of Proceedings and Evidence*, no. 34, 16 March 1967, 2186.

world to the very débacle it is attempting to avoid in accepting the leadership of the US under the North Atlantic Treaty – namely, to a Third World War.' It could not be credibly contended that where Canada's small contingent of troops was stationed in Western Europe would play a decisive part in constraining the American giant; but one had to start somewhere. 'The best interests of Canada will be served by helping to promote a counter-balance to the power of the US rather than by augmenting that power. Many of the smaller NATO countries take their lead from Canada,' Simonds pointed out, 'and if our contribution goes towards augmenting the power of the US theirs will go also, and we may lead a movement which will wreck all possibility of eventually establishing a balance.'

The question of how best to preserve Canadian identity was also, in Simonds' view, an important consideration. 'British leaders have learned to respect and even to be indulgent towards the national wishes and peculiarities of armed forces of other countries serving with them.' The same could not be said of their American counterparts. 'We have had ample and recent experiernces of the tendency on the part of US military leaders to ignore Canadian national susceptibilities in matters concerning continental defence.' Given that Canadian forces were going to be more and more closely associated with United States forces in defence of their common continent, 'it seems desirable that outside of North America there should be a counter-balance to integration and absorption.'

Nor to be overlooked was the opportunity to improve the performance of allies. 'The prestige of the Canadian Army stands very high with both the Belgians and the Dutch. ... The presence of a Canadian brigade to set an example in vigorous military training might well spark the Belgian and Dutch military efforts into far greater and more realistic activity.' An additional factor was that relations between the German population and the troops of occupation were better in the British zone than in the American. And because of the smaller number of troops in the British command sector compared with that in the American command sector, the Canadian contribution if grouped in the former would be less likely to be dismissed as a token and more likely accepted as significant in a material sense.

Finally – and here Simonds wrote from the heart – the Army preferred working with the British to working with the Americans. 'Canadian officers and men have confidence in the professional capacity and skill of British commanders. ... If Canadian forces are grouped with British forces it represents merely the continuation of an association which has existed in two world wars and which has been profitable and deeply satisfying to both parties. To group with the US forces now means severing a past connection and establishing a new. Both in the UK and among the other Commonwealth countries, this will be interpreted as a drift from that association at a time when it is in greatest need of support...' Simonds concluded:

Taking all factors into consideration, it is recommended that the 27th Canadian Infantry Brigade Group be despatched to Europe in October 1951, that it be grouped under British command in Germany where it will be serving in co-opera- tion with British, Dutch and Belgian troops, and that the UK and US governments be informed of this decision forthwith.[65]

The issue was thrashed out at a meeting of the Chiefs of Staff Commit- tee on 14 August. General Foulkes stuck to his preference for grouping with the Americans in France on the grounds that a force equipped with United States weapons and maintained with United States rations and supply ought logically to operate under United States command. He did not agree with Simonds that the balance of power within NATO was of significance. 'The Canadian position within NATO must be judged on the merits of each case,' Foulkes argued,

and not on any idea of acting either for or against the US. The main reason for US domination in NATO was because it is the one country who could afford at this time to assist the others by reason of her internal strength and prosperity. It should therefore behoove the one country who does not need US help (Canada) to always strive in any way she can to merge and reconcile the differences of points of view that may arise from time to time within NATO. This could best be achieved not by aligning ourselves with any particular group of nations but con- sidering and deciding our course of action on each problem as it arose...

The Under Secretary of State for External Affairs told the meeting that his Department had found considerable merit, from the political stand- point, in the arguments advanced by General Simonds, and described his reflections on balancing power within NATO as 'impressive.' But it was the intervention by the Chief of the Air Staff that made way for a compro- mise. Air Marshal Wilfrid Curtis was able to demonstrate to the satisfac- tion of all that the Air Division should be grouped in France under United States command. 'The RCAF and the USAF were closely associated in the integrated air defence system of North America, and as a result had deve- loped common operational doctrine and used common equipment.' The Chief of the Naval Staff then suggested that 'the answer might be to group the army units under the UK command but the Air Force contribu- tion with the USAF.' Curtis quickly agreed. 'By having the Army operate with the British Army and the RCAF with the USAF, it would be clear that the Canadian forces were not aligned with any particular power.'[66]

And that is how – and why – it was done, not however before the Chiefs of Staff went through their arguments once more, on 22 August. A week later, reporting to Pearson that the Chiefs were still at loggerheads over where to send the Brigade, A.D.P. Heeney noted that they had agreed to send the Air Division to France under the command of General Lauris Norstadt, United States Air Force. 'It would be a rather happy solution,' he remarked, 'to have the Canadian Army grouped with UK forces.'[67] The government, after taking the precaution of having Brooke Claxton consult informally with the Supreme Commander, accepted this solution. On 18 September, the Minister of National Defence announced that with General Eisenhower's concurrence 'for military reasons,' the Brigade would be 'deployed in the Northern Army sector in association with the United Kingdom, Netherlands and Belgian forces...' Foulkes had lost: a rare experience for him.*

A fourth issue to arise from the decision to contribute an infantry brigade group to the North Atlantic Integrated Force concerned the conditions under which the Supreme Commander might exercise control over it, both preceding and during combat. Since the First World War, successive Canadian governments had experienced well-founded apprehension lest the armed forces be committed to some unwise or unduly perilous operation without their consent. In the NATO context, A.D.P. Heeney illustrated the problem as follows: 'Should the Canadian Government have the right (a) to be consulted on, and (b) to veto, a proposal by the

---

* The two principal antagonists in what General Foulkes described as 'a critical dispute' each recalled his version of it years later in testimony to a parliamentary committee. 'We easily reached agreement that our air division in Europe should be stationed in the US zone and supplied by the US supply system,' was how Foulkes remembered the affair.

But General Simonds insisted that the Army brigade group should be stationed with the British forces and get its supplies through them. All the rest of us in the Chiefs of Staff Committee believed that the Brigade should be near the RCAF contingents and that they should both be supplied through US channels. This would have been more reliable and certainly more economical, but General Simonds took his stand on tradition and sentiment, and his plan was adopted.

According to General Simonds, General Foulkes' version was 'not a correct statement. ... The decision as to the positioning of the Canadian brigade in Europe the Canadian government had decided to refer to General Eisenhower, and General Eisenhower made the decision.' (Canada, House of Commons Standing Committee on National Defence, *Minutes of Proceedings and Evidence*, no. 34, 16 March 1967, 2183.) Whether Foulkes' statement is incorrect or not, Simonds' certainly is incorrect: the decision was the Canadian government's, not Eisenhower's, and had been announced as such by Brooke Claxton in the House of Commons: 'The intention is that this brigade should be grouped with the British forces. ... This was decided upon after a review of all considerations and after taking the advice of the Supreme Commander.' (Canada, *H.C. Debates*, 1951, 2nd Session, I, 280.) Old soldiers fade away: they also forget.

Supreme Commander to move the Canadian Brigade from Western Germany to, say, Western Berlin?'[68]

Within the policy community, officials differed as to how this question should be answered. General Foulkes felt that there was no (or not much) need to worry. 'The allocation of Canadian troops to SHAPE [Supreme Headquarters, Allied Powers in Europe],' he pointed out,

is in a much different category than the allocation of troops under a foreign commander or a British commander as was done in the last war. In the present case, the Canadian Government has been able to voice an opinion on whom the Supreme Commander should be and [on] his terms of reference. Further, General Eisenhower himself has made it quite clear that he realizes that he is responsible for his actions to the 12 Governments under NATO. ... I feel that the Supreme Commander in charge of operations should have as free a hand as possible regarding the troops under his command. Further, with regard to General Eisenhower's experience in handling Allied troops, I certainly would have complete confidence in his knowledge of how far he can go in dealing with allied troops under his command...[69]

The representative to the North Atlantic Council agreed. 'The Canadian Government was given ample opportunity,' Dana Wilgress noted, 'to scrutinize and comment on the documents dealing with the creation of an integrated European defence force, the establishment of a Supreme Headquarters in Europe and the re-organization of the NATO military structure. ... So long as a Supreme Commander operates within his terms of reference and in an impartial manner to the various national forces under his command, it would seem to be undesirable to place him in the position of having to consult with the various governments on the precise manner in which their forces would be employed in carrying out approved military plans.' Such a position would prove untenable for him.

The Supreme Allied Commander Europe will have under his command military forces from some ten or eleven nations, speaking seven or eight different languages, with assorted types of military equipment, and he will be required to mould these into an effective integrated force with which to carry out the mission he has been assigned. The varied nature of problems such as language, type of equipment, locating in peacetime national forces as close as possible to their own territories, will make the Supreme Commander's task very difficult. Both in peace and in the event of hostilities, there will be a limited number of ways in which the Supreme Commander can group and regroup his forces without seriously reducing their overall effectiveness. ... Should each government demand to be consulted by the Supreme Commander before he regroups his forces within the area in which he is authorized to operate, I feel he will have great difficulty in carrying out the task which these governments have given to him...

Of the example raised by Heeney as to whether the Supreme Commander should be able to move Canadian troops into Berlin without consultation with their government, Wilgress remarked: 'I think it would be unwise for individual governments to prohibit the Supreme Commander from employing their forces there.' If all twelve governments refused to deploy their troops in a particular theatre or for a particular purpose, the Supreme Commander's task would become not merely very difficult but 'impossible.'[70]

These representations notwithstanding, the Canadian government was unable to provide the Supreme Commander with the kind of categorical assurance that would have been so welcome to him. Returning from a meeting at SHAPE at the end of 1951, Pearson told his officials that 'General Eisenhower is most anxious to know whether he has the authority to order the troops under his command into action without reference to national governments. He has in mind, for example, a situation where Danish troops might be attacked and he would wish to order the Canadian Brigade into action.' Pearson expressed the opinion that the Supreme Commander already had that authority, but that he was 'against an open discussion or statement on this point...' A departmental memorandum reviewing the problem described it as 'very difficult and complex.'[71]

No resolution of these difficulties and complexities seemed in sight until May 1952, when an unforeseen episode in the Far East strengthened the hand of those within the policy community who argued that the Supreme Commander should be required to consult with member governments concerning the disposition of their troops. This was the affair on Koje Island in South Korea.* Canadian troops serving under United Nations command had been ordered by the UN Commander, US General Mark Clark, to guard prisoners-of-war who had rioted to protest extreme maltreatment. The Canadian government was not consulted. News of the troop movement reached Ottawa only after the Canadians had arrived on Koje. The government felt with good reason that Canada was being used (to employ a venerable but applicable phrase) to pull others' chestnuts out of the fire. A strong protest was left with the US State Department on 20 June 1952, which Pearson read later that day to the House of Commons. 'It has ... been a long established policy of the Canadian government,' that statement declared in part,

that Canadian forces dispatched abroad for military operations should remain under Canadian command and control and that, except in the event of a military emergency which does not permit time for consultation, no part of these forces should be detached therefrom except after consultation and with the agreement of the Canadian government.

* The episode, and Canadian reaction to it, are carefully examined in Denis Stairs, *The Diplomacy of Constraint: Canada, the Korean War, and the United States* (Toronto 1974), 246-58.

The Canadian government therefore views with concern the dispatch of a company of the 25th Infantry Brigade to Koje island without prior consultation with the Canadian government. ... The Canadian government also wishes to be reassured that, if it is proposed in the future to detach any Canadian forces from Canadian command and control for military or other duties, this will be done only after consultation and with the consent of the Canadian government, except in the event of a military emergency which does not permit of time for such consultation.[72]

A few days later, Pearson asked his officials to 'consider what action should be taken to prevent similar unsatisfactory incidents in Europe.' J.W. Pickersgill, then Secretary to the Cabinet, 'was of the opinion that the Canadian Government should forthwith send some communication to SACEUR [Supreme Allied Commander, Europe] to ensure that the "principle of the separate entity" of the Canadian Brigade is respected.' The official in charge of the Defence Liaison division of the Department of External Affairs 'questioned the wisdom' of that advice, and in all likelihood it was not acted upon.[73] The Canadian government's continuing insistence that SHAPE observe the principle of consultation when sending Canadians into action – 'except in the event of a military emergency which does not permit of time for such consultation' – must have added, if only marginally, to the mounting worries and anxieties of NATO's military leaders.

If NATO lacked power on land, it was even weaker in the air. 'There are not enough aircraft to meet our collective needs,' the Canadian government was told by its advisers in September 1950. 'Assuming their maximum production capacity is utilized regardless of cost from now through 1954, our Western Union partners alone estimate that they will have a deficiency of 2000 aircraft in 1954.' The Secretary of State for External Affairs was about to attend a ministerial meeting of the North Atlantic Council in New York. 'Could you indicate at the Council meeting,' L.B. Pearson was asked by his advisers, 'that the Canadian Government is contemplating sending operational units of the RCAF to be stationed in Western Europe in peacetime as a contribution to the strengthening of North Atlantic forces in being in Western Europe?'[74]

That was asking for too much too soon. Pearson said nothing at the Council meeting about sending RCAF squadrons overseas in peacetime. Instead, he pointedly reminded his fellow ministers that '3000 miles of ocean ... did make it difficult for countries like Canada to reach decisions about committing forces overseas in peacetime.' Canada supported the concept of an integrated force, he told the Council, and 'would play its part within the limits of our conception of what was possible...'[75]

An important contribution to the government's attitude on sending forces, both land and air, to Western Europe during peacetime was made by J.W. Pickersgill, then (September 1950) head of the Prime Minister's office and a close adviser of Louis St Laurent.* Pickersgill had pondered the statement by St Laurent in the House of Commons on 13 September that 'The government of Canada at this time is not considering the raising of Canadian forces to despatch to Europe as a deterrent to aggression.' A 'deterrent to aggression' was precisely what Canada's forces should be, Pickersgill reflected, and he argued the case in a memorandum for the Prime Minister.

I have been trying ... to think out, as clearly as I could, how our position can best be presented in order to achieve the maximum public acceptance at home and the least avoidable friction with our allies, particularly the United States.

It seems to me that we have all the elements both of the right policy and the right presentation but that they need to be put together in a more coherent way than we have done yet. Norman Robertson made an observation to me yesterday which I feel provides the key. It goes roughly like this: We have appealed for support of the policy of strengthening the forces of the North Atlantic powers as a *deterrent to aggression*, but our defence plans are still based on the tacit assumption that our defence forces are being organized *to resist aggression after it has happened* ... [italics in original]

In relation to the North Atlantic, surely what we should do is to look at every dollar of defence expenditure primarily from the point of view of a deterrent, and only secondarily from the point of view of providing for resistance after aggression actually occurred.

So far as ground forces are concerned, what this obviously means is establishing as quickly as possible the greatest possible number of trained and equipped army formations in Western Europe, without regard to the nationality of their components except to the extent that the participation of ground forces of certain peripheral nations, particularly the United States, may be necessary in order to ensure a genuine will to fight on the part of the nations of continental Europe. This consideration certainly does not apply to Canada but it may be that to maintain reasonably good relations with the United States, and to satisfy a pretty wide section of the public at home, some kind of undertaking will be unavoidable..

Pickersgill agreed with St Laurent that for Canada to keep any considerable ground forces in Europe 'would be, in a military sense, expensive and wasteful of men and resources.' But this was not the case, or not as much the case, with an air force commitment. 'A trained Air Force is extremely mobile, the ratio of machines to men is very high, and we have, in Canada, both exceptional capacity for Air Force training and a

* See above, Ch. 1, 26n.

population more than usually adaptable to service in the air. If, as is probable,' Pickersgill concluded,

the combined pressure of public opinion at home and in the United States is going to make it necessary for us in 1951 to increase substantially our forces in being, as an effective component of an integrated force designed to deter aggression, it is hard to escape the conclusion that the intelligent course would be to concentrate on enlargement and acceleration as far as possible of the Air Force, and to revise our defence planning as rapidly as possible with a view to giving priority to deterrent planning rather than that to planning for actual combat once a war has started.[76]

The government was evidently impressed by this reasoning. On 28 December 1950, the Cabinet Defence Committee agreed to provide the integrated force with one squadron of aircraft, subject to parliamentary approval, and to promise SHAPE two squadrons more. At a Cabinet meeting on 1 February 1951, the Minister of National Defence outlined proposals to contribute to the integrated force a total of eleven squadrons by 1954 – three of day interceptor aircraft (F-86Es), making seventy-five aircraft in all; seven fighter bomber squadrons, making 112 aircraft; and one fighter reconaissance squadron, of sixteen aircraft.[77] This contribution was approved by the Cabinet. Brooke Claxton explained the decision in the House of Commons on 5 February. 'Air power is especially needed,' Claxton asserted. For that reason, 'Canada's most substantial contribution to the planned force in being will be our air force participation.' Canada would place at the disposal of the Supreme Commander a full air division – 'eleven squadrons at full fighting strength, equipped with F86E and Canuck aircraft.' (The 3-7-1 allocation approved on 1 February had given way to an all-fighter commitment.) 'You can see,' Claxton told members of Parliament, 'that the air force participation in the integrated force will require a very large portion of our total defence budget.'[78] Two-thirds of it, to be exact.

At a meeting of the Cabinet on 17 January 1952, it was decided to increase the contribution by 1954 from eleven squadrons to twelve, on the understanding that each squadron would initially be composed of sixteen F-86Es rather than twenty-five. 'We have the squadrons with the men and the aircraft to comply with the requirements for the Air Force,' Claxton assured the House of Commons on 3 April 1952, 'and expect to do so, subject only to the possibility that the necessary airfields may not be available.'[79] A year later he reported: 'We have today six squadrons of Sabre fighters abroad, the most formidable fighter aircraft in operation today. ... Three more squadrons are on their way over. We shall complete our full commitment of an air division of twelve squadrons to NATO by the date set and we shall do that in the belief – which I think is shared by all Canadians – that the best place to defend Canada and to prevent aggression is as far away from our shores as possible.'[80] And, on 14 April 1953:

We have sent abroad a wing of three squadrons of Sabre fighters which are now stationed at North Luffenham, England, and form an important ... part of the defences of the North Atlantic area in England. They were followed by a second wing in a remarkable operation called "Operation Leapfrog" when all the aircraft of the second wing were flown across by their own pilots to take up their station at Grostenquin, France. A third wing is on its way over and is arriving at Zwei-brucken in the French zone of Germany. When I visit it for the first time next week I expect to hand it over to the control of SHAPE and complete three-quarters of our air force commitment on the target date.

A fourth wing is now being formed in Canada with officers and men joining their squadrons and being equipped with Sabre fighters as they come off the lines and are tested. That wing will leave for overseas later this year to complete the forma-tion of our air division of twelve squadrons of Sabre fighters plus a divisional headquarters, plus a repair depot and the other supporting units, which will com-plete our air commitment to NATO right on the target date.[81]

Handing the Air Division 'over to the control of SHAPE' did not mean that SHAPE controlled the Air Division. The Canadian government claimed the right to be consulted before the Air Division was committed either to battle or to some new peacetime mission. On 13 March 1953, L.B. Pearson recalls in his memoirs,

a telegram was received by Brooke Claxton ... from our NATO air representative which indicated that General Norstadt, Deputy (Air) at SHAPE, might want to move Canadian F-86 squadrons from their bases in France to the frontiers of West Germany, or even into the air corridor to West Berlin, as protection against MIG attacks. There had been two such attacks, one against a US fighter plane on the Czech border and one against a British bomber in the north. Feeling was high, especially in the press, and it was felt that some protective measures should be taken. As the RCAF had the only F-86s in Europe, they would obviously be con-sidered for such a move. The situation, however, was not an easy one from our point of view, because we did not wish to become involved in any move arising out of occupation policy or, indeed, to become involved in any retaliatory inci-dents. Nevertheless, our forces in Europe were part of the NATO forces, and had to accept duties as such. Claxton was all for instructing Air Marshal Campbell, Air Officer Commanding, Canadian Air Division, Europe, to tell Norstadt that he had better find some other aircraft for these purposes.* I was anxious that we take no such negative attitude, but merely point out some of the considerations involved and wait to see if a formal request would be made. ... I had a talk with the PM and

---

* Claxton's reaction was the same as during the Berlin airlift of 1948-9, when he opposed RCAF participation therein; see above, Ch. 1, 45-6.

he agreed that we should proceed very cautiously in this matter and hope that public opinion would die down and no dramatic retaliatory protective action would be required.

In the event, Pearson recorded, 'Nothing further was heard of the possibility of moving RCAF jets to border areas.'[82] (The official history of the armed forces treats the issue of how the Air Division is controlled in a rather elliptical fashion: '...[O]perational control is vested in the Fourth Allied Tactical Air Force ... commanded by a US officer. ... However, the direction of the Canadian Air Division is almost entirely a Canadian affair, because Fourth ATAF is mainly concerned in promoting effective cooperation and ... assumes full operational command only in an emergency.'[83])

'BRIDGING THE GAP'

'NATO was bedeviled by a continuous conflict between estimated military requirements, on the one hand, and political and financial limitations, on the other,' Brooke Claxton recollected of that period of Alliance mobilization during which he was in charge of Canada's defence. 'This conflict tended to create a sour note. Instead of the countries being encouraged by the real progress that was being made, the NATO agencies, largely under American lead, tended to create a feeling of failure because of deficiencies in meeting requirements. We were always talking about "the Gap"...'[84]

Talk about 'the Gap' was never more garrulous than during the months immediately after the adoption by the NATO Ministerial Council meeting during February 1952 of what became known as 'the Lisbon levels.'

On the recommendation of NATO's Supreme Commander, forces available to SHAPE were to be spectacularly increased. By the end of 1952, SHAPE should have at its disposal not the dozen or so divisions then available but no fewer than fifty divisions of land forces, together with 4000 aircraft and 'strong naval forces.' By 1954, the Supreme Commander counselled, these forces ought to be augmented still further. Land forces should number ninety-six divisions, of which twenty-five were to be at battle-readiness on the central European front. These recommendations were accepted by the North Atlantic Council. 'The decisions which the Council took at Lisbon,' the Organization's first Secretary General observed, 'have made that session a landmark in the history of NATO.'[85] Just so – but a landmark in the field of futility.

Even at the time, the participants at Lisbon knew very well how utterly unreal were such stupendous force goals as those to which they had allowed themselves to become committed – though no one of them said as much in public. Later, they would admit it: 'The military force goals set and accepted at Lisbon,' L.B. Pearson wrote in retrospect, 'were quite unrealistic.'[86]

Who was to blame for that? Civilians, with justification, blamed the military. Brooke Claxton in later years was scathing in his criticism of the 'top military personnel, [who] with what I continued to regard as a grave lack of responsibility, continued to set military requirements at figures beyond any reasonable hope of realization. They said it was up to the military leaders to say what was militarily necessary and they put everything in.'[87] That foible was by no means confined to officers at SHAPE; leaders of the armed forces of member countries were equally to blame. 'The Chiefs of Air Staff of the United States, the United Kingdom and France got together in Paris [in the autumn of 1951] and drew up a plan for closing the air gap,' Claxton recalled.

This became known as the "Paris Plan" which included something like nine or ten thousand aircraft needed for the Alliance. Our Air Force, though not our government, had been represented in these discussions and I believe took an active part in them. They resulted in allotting to Canada an additional bomber wing, which would have brought our contribution to NATO to something close to one thousand aircraft, or more than the number to be contributed by either the United States or Britain. Nothing but the unbridled enthusiasm of our airmen could have produced such a result. I was exceedingly annoyed when I heard about it and made our Air Force go right back to the Paris group and say they had acted entirely without instruction and that we would not be adding any aircraft whatever. Later on we might consider substituting CF-100s for F-86s. While I found the action of our own Air Force annoying, this whole episode I am sure was an attempt by the Chiefs of Air Staff to do an end-run around the NATO Military Command so as to bring about pressure for a substantial increase in the over-all aircraft strength, even though this might be at the expense of what had been generally agreed as a proper contribution to our balanced international force. At the next meeting of the Military Committee at Rome [during November 1951], the "Paris Plan" was entirely eliminated...[88]

Claxton was not alone in blaming the brass for inflating force goals. 'The military ... were operating in a watertight compartment,' A.D.P. Heeney wrote in his memoirs, 'insulated from the Council and making plans which, by any realistic assessment, they were quite incapable of fulfilling.' The generals in turn blamed the civilians, holding 'the shortfall between Lisbon profession and Paris performance [to be] ... the fault of the Permanent Council. Field Marshal Montgomery ... did not hesitate to attribute such failures to the weakness of the permanent representatives in Paris.' A third set of villains were found within the Secretariat, whose zealous officials 'sought to take the initiative and develop an independent role to effect the goals. Because of the attitude of most national governments this effort proved quite unrealistic...'[89]

All this recrimination lay in the future. At the time, the obvious villain – in Canada at least – was neither the military nor the diplomats nor yet again the NATO bureaucrats. It was the government of Canada for allowing the 'Lisbon levels' to go forward without demur. Both as the spokesman for that government in foreign affairs and as the minister who had presided at the Lisbon meeting of the Council, L.B. Pearson faced a barrage of criticism in the House of Commons on his return to it in March 1952.

The Conservative Leader of the Opposition, George A. Drew, criticized the government for encouraging wishful thinking and false expectations. 'It is difficult to understand what would prompt those responsible for such a statement to announce that there would be fifty divisions in the European army by the end of this year,' Drew declared on 6 March. 'If we were to accept a statement of that kind we would be simply deluding ourselves. Most certainly it will not fool the Russians.'[90] The leader of the Co-operative Commonwealth Federation (CCF) Party, the country's democratic socialists, hit closer to the bone by averring that the government had betrayed its own ideals and undermined its much publicized commitment to making NATO more than a military alliance. 'I want to say to the Minister and to the House,' M.J. Coldwell declaimed, 'that you cannot build defence when there is economic disease in Europe or anywhere else. ... The policy outlined at Lisbon jeopardizes the peaceful and defensive objectives which brought the Organization into being...'[91]

Privately, Pearson agreed. But as spokesman for the government, he could hardly concede such criticism. Nor did he. Rounding on a portion of a statement released some days before by the National Council of the CCF affirming that 'NATO seems to have fallen completely under the control of the military to the exclusion of necessary social and economic considerations in the building of western collective security,' the Secretary of State for External Affairs denied the charge. 'NATO has not fallen completely under the control of the military,' Pearson insisted, adding: 'If it had fallen completely under the control of the military I doubt very much whether Canada would be very anxious to participate in its activities.' Quoting again from the CCF statement – 'a substantial proportion of the total sums involved should be diverted from crippling and excessive military preparedness to necessary economic re-building in Europe and elsewhere,' Pearson offered this rejoinder.

I ask myself the question: Will qualified support, conditional support of that kind, strengthen NATO at a time when the North Atlantic Treaty Organization is our strongest bulwark for peace, and when defence weakness is the greatest provoca- tion to aggression? If that aggression should occur, then what chance shall we have in NATO, in the United Nations or anywhere else to promote that economic and social progress about which we have all spoken so many times, and as to the importance of which we all sincerely agree? What chance will any of us have to promote that economic and social progress which remains an objective of NATO second only – but still second – to acquisition of that minimum strength necessary to prevent war?[92]

Of his performance in an unusually spirited debate Pearson would later remark: 'This was the best case I could make but it did not satisfy our critics; or, indeed, completely satisfy me.'[93]

On 3 April 1952, the Minister of National Defence presented to Parlia- ment a summary of Canada's mobilization efforts during the three years since the signing of the North Atlantic Treaty. Brooke Claxton quoted and agreed with the report issued on the preceding day by General Eisen- hower on the first anniversary of his appointment as Supreme Com- mander: 'There is no real security yet achieved in Europe; there is a beginning.' Claxton also quoted approvingly from Eisenhower's refer- ence to air power, which the Supreme Commander had described as 'the dominant factor in war today. It cannot win a war alone, but without it, no war can be won.' That was the reason, the Minister explained, 'why in the Canadian programme we put the greatest emphasis, and spend by far the greatest proportion of the defence dollar, on the air force.' Claxton de- scribed his defence estimates for 1952-3, amounting to $2001 millions, as a 'huge sum.' Canada's NATO program for 1952 would provide twenty- four ships, one-third of a division, and four squadrons of fighter aircraft (to be increased to twelve squadrons by 1954). He offered the following survey of what had been done in defence of Canada during the twenty months since the outbreak of the war in Korea.

The navy has commissioned nine ships and launched six others; it has twenty- seven more on order, with forty awaiting refitting. It is operating sixteen schools. In Korean waters alone it has sailed over 450,000 miles. Its ships have made cruises like that of the *Ontario* to Australia and New Zealand, and that of the *Magnificent*, the *Micmac* and *Huron* to the Mediterranean and North Atlantic. It has steadily built up its strength, largely at sea.

In the army, we have raised, equipped and trained the 25th and 27th brigades; provided for their reinforcement and rotation; maintained the mobile striking force and continued the training for airborne and Arctic warfare...

There has been an increase to twenty-four squadrons of the regular and auxiliary air force. One squadron has had a tour of duty in the United Kingdom and has

returned to Canada, and two more are in the United Kingdom. We have provided
the manning and training machinery, and the aircraft, for the build-up at a rate of
approximately one squadron every two months, equipped and manned with aircrew and ground crew, until the total of forty squadrons for N ATO and the defence
of Canada is reached. We have added nearly 500 aircraft, 1300 aircrew, and
10,500 ground crew to the strength...

Here by any standards other than a super-power's was a major effort; for
a middle power it was an effort not far short of herculean. Was it enough?
How much was enough? Here is a conundrum for every defence policy
aimed not so much at fighting a war as at deterring aggression: the Minister
of National Defence did not try to answer. There would be those who, using
hindsight, would say the government had done too much; or, possibly, too
little. 'We do not know which will be right, but,' Brooke Claxton added in
conclusion, 'we should never forget that the ability of anyone to exercise
any hindsight at all is made possible by the fact that we have had three years
of peace...bought by the price we have paid for the prevention of war.'[94]

'From the point of view of planning for our effective defence, together
with our allies, it of course would be more desirable not to make, each of
us in turn, these figures available to the only possible aggressor.'[95] So the
Minister of National Defence had observed when telling the House of
Commons of Canada's defence commitments to NATO for 1952. Strategic
studies were then in infancy, and Brooke Claxton may be pardoned for
failing to grasp that where the objective is to deter aggression, conceal-
ment of the power to deter works to the disadvantage of those possessed
of it. No matter. What members of the Atlantic Alliance were required to
conceal during 1952 – and for several years thereafter – was evidence not
of strength but weakness.

Those within the policy community privy to documents marked 'COS-
MIC' – the security classification by which NATO's inner secrets were
designated – might well feel perturbed at their tales of enfeeblement and
disarray. The Supreme Commander had not erred on the side of pessim-
ism in pronouncing that 'there is no real security yet achieved in Europe.'
Indeed there was not. 'It is a shock to read of the existence of limitations
on our air strength which would have "disastrous effects",' the Under
Secretary of State for External Affairs wrote to his Minister after perusing
SACEUR's 'Report to the Standing Group on the Status of Forces in his
Command.' Its litany of shortcomings was doleful. The report stated

that there is airfield storage for only seven days' fuel reserves; that the Northern
European Emergency Defence Plan could not be implemented (and this was

based on forces *in existence* in January 1952); that the Southern Command could not control the battle for lack of communications facilities; that officers, NCOs and specialists are, even in the units in existence, at one-half the acceptable minimum; that there are "acute shortages" in supporting troops; and that a lack of intelligence will reduce the warning of the outbreak of hostilities with critical effect on the employment of the forces available...

With all this, SACEUR reports that throughout the Command, morale is high, but if war were to break out within the next six or eight months, one has a picture of unsupported troops gallantly repelling a surprise attack with little chance of relief, their inadequate supplies dwindling unreplenished, as they fight isolated engagements while their commanders vainly attempt to control the battle in the face of inadequate signals communications and transport...

The implications for policy of this alarming assessment – alarming to its Canadian readers not least for their concern at the likely fate of the 27th Infantry Brigade in such a fracas – were pretty plain. 'A state has clearly been reached where the shortages must be made good as soon as possible,' Dana Wilgress commented, 'or else the efforts which have already been made to provide troops in being will be wasted. ... We suggest that the Canadian approach to SACEUR's paper should be positive and general, not restricted simply to assessing the extent to which Canada can remedy any default in our agreed commitment. We should investigate how, within the existing budget, Canada could minimize the grave difficulties SACEUR describes.'[96]

On 1 October 1952, on the eve of a visit by the Standing Group to confer with the Permanent Representatives on the North Atlantic Council, the Canadian Representative set down some impressions of NATO's problems and their consequences for Canadian policy. 'When you were in Paris,' A.D.P. Heeney reminded L.B. Pearson, 'you expressed concern about increased goals for 1953. You hoped the efforts of NATO next year might be devoted primarily to fulfilling effectively the programme for 1952. It appeared to you sounder to complete the present programme in terms of reserves and logistical support rather than to embark at once on a larger one.' In Heeney's estimation, this no longer represented (if it ever did represent) the views of the European members of NATO who were likely – not least in order to get even greater United States aid – to believe 'that the better course is to continue to develop forces on a broad scale...' It seemed to him to be probable that the Canadian government would to step up the tempo of the overall defence effort.[97]

Responding to these observations – 'of great interest and significance' – L.B. Pearson stated that he still thought that NATO would be 'well advised from publicizing higher figures for 1953,' adding 'I am not sure that our own Service people would agree with me on this point.' In any event, Pearson informed Heeney,

I feel strongly that we should not plan in any way for any new Canadian overseas formations beyond those for which we are already committed for the first few months of war. It is unrealistic to press us for further forces on the ground that the war will be decided in the first few weeks, because there would be no possibility of getting those forces into action during that time.

...There is no possibility of increasing our defence effort next year, either in Mutual Aid or any other way. The feeling here is that we are already doing our full share and there will, indeed, be a strong temptation to reduce that effort in 1953 by stretching our plans a bit...[98]

SHAPE's analysis of and recommendations for the Canadian defence programme during 1953 arrived at Ottawa in early February. Its main recommendations were: to maintain the 27th Infantry Brigade at its war-ready level of preparedness as 'an M-Day [for May Day] unit' (ie, one that would be expected to bear the first shock of battle); to provide by the end of 1954 an air depot in Western Europe; to contribute to the defence of those European airfields at which RCAF aircraft would be based; to help correct the existing imbalance of equipment and reserve stocks. These recommendations struck Pearson as 'pretty formidable.'[99] Even so, they paled by comparison with the recommendations of SACEUR and SACLANT which were made to Canada later in the year. SACEUR proposed that Canada should allocate a wing of all-weather fighters by the end of 1955 or, alternatively, offer such fighters to Western European air forces as part of Mutual Aid; and that Canada should increase her contribution of support units in Western Europe to back up her land and air forces there. SACLANT proposed that Canada should add to the number, improve the quality, and advance the dates of availability of escort vessels; and add to the number of maritime patrol aircraft, replacing these by modern types as soon as possible.[100]

The Canadian government rejected each and every one of these recommendations – in one case not without some argument. On 29 September 1953, the Chiefs of Staff Committee discussed

SACEUR's suggestion that Canada make all-weather jet fighters available. General Foulkes said that the Minister could not accept this. ... Air Marshal Slemon replied that from the military point of view, he was prepared to recommend that a wing of CF-100s be made available. In the discussion that followed, Air Marshal Slemon admitted that this would involve an additional expenditure of some $200 million and that there were manpower difficulties which might make such a proposition unattractive to the political authorities.

...Air Marshal Slemon made the point that functions of the Chiefs of Staff should be clarified. It was his duty, he thought, to make military recommendations in the light of military considerations and for the Minister to consider these. The Minister could then make his decision in the light of political considerations and these would be implemented by the Air Force. He did not think that the military should make military decisions in the light of political considerations. ... Both the Chief of the Naval Staff and the Chief of the General Staff strongly agreed with the Chief of the Air Staff on this subject.[101]

Whether or not the Chairman of the Chiefs of Staff Committee was doing his duty by saying so,* General Foulkes was correct in stating that his Minister would not accept SACEUR's proposal. 'There is no possibility whatever of our supplying CF-100s to Europe until we have equipped the squadrons needed for the defence of Canada,' Brooke Claxton wrote to L.B. Pearson on 16 October. 'I expect that this will be well under way and even possibly completed in the fiscal year 1954-55 when we can again look at the matter but I would certainly not do anything at this time to hold out any hope of our being able to furnish any considerable number of these very expensive aircraft and still see to our other defence requirements.'[102] Claxton would later refer to the SACEUR proposal as 'preposterous. It would have meant our having in Europe considerably more effective fighter strength than either Britain or the United States. The suggestion,' he wrote,

that this might be done by a country of fourteen million people was flattering but unacceptable. However, it did point to the appalling shortage of all-weather fighters in the NATO forces and to our wisdom or good luck in having the best aircraft for the purpose. With single-seater interceptors of the types available, our allied forces would only be able to fight effectively in fine weather. It happened that Canada's CF-100 was well in advance of all other aircraft of this type. As the doctrine seemed to be that there should be one all-weather squadron on each airfield with these eight squadrons of single-seater fights, our having twelve squadrons of all-weather fighters would mean that we would have at least nine squadrons attached to British and American bases. What we held out as a long term possibility was the replacement of one or more of our squadrons of Sabres with CF-100s...[103]

(In December 1954, the Cabinet agreed that CF-100s could be transferred from Canada to Europe, and in 1955 a squadron of these aircraft was flown across the North Atlantic for active service there.)

---

* General Foulkes' propensity to inject political considerations into military decisions caused General Simonds to charge that the Chairman's role had been 'to protect the government against the receipt of unpalatable advice.' See *In Defence of Canada*, III, 61-6, 115.

The government was next obliged to communicate to NATO its refusal to accept SHAPE's recommendations, and in such a way as to lose as little face as possible and cause the minimum of recrimination and backsliding. The explanation took place in two stages. The first was during the Annual Review examination,* held in Paris on 2 November. There the Canadian representative devoted the major portion of his statement to the air production programme. The Canadair plant at Montreal was producing F-86E interceptor day fighters at the rate of two completed aircraft per working day. A total of some 740 F-86Es had been delivered, including 370 during 1952-3 which had been offered as Mutual Aid and allocated by the Standing Group to the United Kingdom. 'I am glad to be able to state at this time,' the Canadian representative then added, 'that the Canadian Government has approved the inclusion of an additional quantity of 164 F-86E aircraft in our mutual aid programme.' This offer was intended to take some of the sting out of what next had to be revealed about the CF-100s. 'Production continues to make progress, but this is a vast industrial undertaking and to date only 63 aircraft have been completed since the production line was set up. ... It is impossible to predict the production schedule at this stage for more than a few months ahead but it would seem that we shall be more than busy for two years with completing our own urgent requirements for equipping of squadrons for the defence of North America.'[104] With that explanation NATO authorities had to be content. It seems that they were. 'Our examination took place yesterday,' the Permanent Representative to the North Atlantic Council reported to Ottawa on November 3. 'The general tone was most satisfactory. We were in the fortunate position of being rather more positive and constructive than many other delegations. We made a statement on the position of Canadian production and mutual aid ... and this was very well received. ... Even when resisting the proposal that Canada should send a AWX [all-weather interceptor] wing to Europe, we managed to emphasize the positive side of Canadian production and plans for North American defence...'[105]

The final stage of justifying the defence programme before NATO took place at the ministerial meeting of the Council during December. There the Minister of National Defence reiterated the theme of his statement to the meeting at Rome during November 1951.† According to the summary of his speech reported to Ottawa by the Permanent Representative,

Mr Claxton said that the cruising speed seemed likely to be about as expensive as the acceleration; this had been clearly illustrated by recent Canadian studies of the

* See below, Ch. 5, 301-18.
† See above, 208-9.

cost of maintaining and equipping the RCAF. Accordingly, there was now very little elasticity in national defence programmes and national defence budgets. While he did not imply that there was no room at all for change, the NATO agencies concerned should keep it in mind that the very success we have had in the build-up narrows the scope for acceleration.

He briefly reviewed the recommendations appearing in the Canadian country chapter. Having referred to the lack of elasticity in budgets, he pointed out that the recommendations relating to an all-weather fighter force would, if accepted, cost an additional $150 to $200 million per annum, four or five times as much as the Brigade in Germany...

In conclusion, after emphasizing the relative rigidity of present defence programmes, he noted that NATO forces had now learned to work together; this was a great deterrent to attack and a great contribution to peace...[106]

By 1954, the pace of NATO's build-up slowed. 'Acceleration,' in Brooke Claxton's phrase, had given way to 'cruising' – the costs of which, it had been discovered, were far higher than anticipated. Keeping member governments in line was still a major preoccupation of the Alliance, but the difficulties had altered. 'When NATO was engaged in a rapid build-up of forces,' a member of the Department of External Affairs' Defence Liaison Division (I) noted, 'the problem then was to reconcile the military requirements with the economic and political situation of member countries. Reconciliation in this sense is no longer seriously undertaken. With the momentum of the build-up decreasing in the face of an apparently less imminent threat, the problem is now to maintain, over a long period, the present high level of defence preparedness and to avoid a dangerous relaxation of effort.'[107] In the parlance of the Alliance, this objective became referred to as 'the long haul.' (NATO's members are hauling to this day.)*

If the haul were to be sustained for long, NATO's governments and publics would have to continue to believe that the Soviet Union posed a military threat to their security and freedom.

In October 1952, the Permanent Representative on the North Atlantic Council asked his foreign minister if the threat of Soviet aggression had diminished. 'I feel it has,' L.B. Pearson responded, 'but I would not sug-

---

* 'To emphasize the growing Canadian involvement [in NATO, Minister of National Defence Barney Danson] gave other defence ministers dark-blue neckties covered with golden leaping leopards, symbol of Canada's recent $200-million purchase of Leopard tanks from West Germany. ... General Laurie Farrington, director-general of Canadian defence information service, said that ... the public generally seems to be getting the idea that NATO still has a vital role to play...' *The Globe and Mail* (Toronto), 7 December 1977, 'NATO Praises Canada's Defence Program, Danson Says.'

gest at the moment that you should put this as a Canadian Government view in the Council.' Assessment of the threat, Pearson reflected, was not easily done.

One cannot ... be very dogmatic about this, for it is impossible to come to any firm conclusion without more information on the military capabilities and strength and strategy of both the potential enemy and the United States. When, for instance, it is said, as we so often say, that if the USSR wished to begin a war of aggression it would have done so a year or so before NATO began to grow in unity and strength, we assume that the Soviet Union, relative to ourselves, was stronger than it is now. As far as I am concerned, this is only an assumption, and I have never seen any authoritative statement which would justify it or invalidate it. The difficulty, of course, is two-fold: the lack of information about the USSR, and the reluctance of the Pentagon to share what information they have on the USSR and on their own plans with other governments and political agencies such as the NATO Council. There is also always the uneasy feeling that the military information we get is given us in support of a particular policy rather than as a basis for formulation of policy. ... My own feeling ... is that, in essence, the risk remains the same, but it is not now so likely to express itself in a calculated aggression in Western Europe...[108]

Such an assessment might be vouchsafed to senior members of the policy community, but the public was told a somewhat different story. Stalin's death in March 1953, the people of Canada were instructed by their government, had brought a change of leadership – even, as Brooke Claxton put it in the House of Commons on 20 May 1954, 'a change in attitude, in behaviour and perhaps in manners' – but not a change 'in fundamental objective. ... The North Atlantic treaty nations at their meeting in Paris,' Claxton told the House, 'affirmed their decision to continue to build up their strength on the assumption that there was no change in the fundamental Soviet objectives of imperialism and aggrandizement.'[109] A year later, Claxton's successor as Minister of National Defence offered a similar opinion. 'The present climate of international affairs appears to be moderating,' R.O. Campney stated in Parliament on 16 June 1955, 'but we cannot be sure that the better weather of recent months will endure. Our objective remains fixed before us – to make peace permanent. ... To do this, we must go on as far as we can see, year after year, investing a substantial part of our national production in defence.'[110] In November 1955, the Department of External Affairs examined the current military situation of the Atlantic Alliance. The condition of NATO was found to be 'disturbing.' What the Department's analysts found worrisome was not any change for the worse in the policies of the Soviet Union. On the contrary. 'It is not the political intentions of the Soviet Government which are causing most concern to the NATO civil and military staffs,' their memorandum noted. 'Provided that an adequate deterrent in land, sea and air forces is maintained, and provided that there is tangible evidence of determination in NATO to use such forces should the need arise, the NATO staffs believe that the Soviet leaders will wish to avoid war in the foreseeable future.' The source of their apprehension was the trend to complacency among Alliance governments and peoples. 'The balance of capabilities,' the Department analysts concluded, 'is tilting against the Atlantic Community as the milder tactics of the Soviet leaders, and the growing public feeling that no nation will deliberately run the terrible risks of all-out nuclear warfare, produce a relaxation of effort on the part of the NATO countries. Already this has gone so far that the military threat, in the estimation of the NATO commanders, is greater than ever before...'[111]

The perils of complacency were singled out for special attention in R.O. Campney's statement to the House of Commons accompanying his presentation of the estimates for the Department of National Defence on 20 June 1956. 'To maintain the deterrent power of the free nations will not be an easy task,' the Minister warned the Members,

essential though it is to our survival. Paradoxically, as the existence of the deterrent continues to protect the peace, the continuance of that peace itself may tend to soften up the very deterrent force on which it depends, for it tends to give credibility to smiling assurances and friendly, folksy visits, all propagating the view that the day of world brotherhood has dawned at last, and suggesting that we can now safely set aside our defence programmes, with their heavy costs, and concentrate on the much more pleasant task of raising our material standard of life.

To thus relax our defence effort might be an inviting policy for the free nations, but it would be a very dangerous policy...

That was why, Campney affirmed, 'Canada is building and maintaining a defence effort that is really out of all proportion to our status as a middle power.'[112]

DEPLOYING THE ATOM

Soon after the surrender of Japan, General Maurice Pope* was detailed to do a paper on the consequences of the atomic bomb – a project comparable in scope and daunting to doing a paper on the human condition. 'This I was naturally reluctant to attempt,' Pope recalled in his memoirs, 'for I

---

* See *In Defence of Canada* III, 50-1.

did not know, nor as I thought did anyone else at the time, what those consequences would be other than that they would be profound. ... I remember writing that, amid all the obscurities surrounding the subject, one thing was clear. ... [T]he United States could not be disposed to reveal the secrets of this tremendous discovery to even their closest allies.'[113]

So it turned out. Canada and the United Kingdom were denied access to the secrets of the American post-war atomic energy programme. Their crucial contributions to the success of the Manhattan Project were to count for nothing. The principle of tripartite collaboration between the three countries on all aspects of atomic energy, agreed upon at Quebec in 1943, was abruptly jettisoned in 1946. Irrational panic at the prospective loss of the new-found font of power, joined by somewhat less irrational fear of espionage, produced the US McMahon Act with its draconian penalties against offering with intent 'to secure an advantage to any foreign nation' any data about atomic weapons, the production of fissionable materials, and their use in generating energy.

For Britain, the consequences of this sudden and unexpected deprivation were drastic. The shock pushed its policy-makers down the path to an independent nuclear deterrent system the strategic justification of which is questionable,* and the drain of which upon an economy hard-pressed to provide butter along with all the guns is evident today.

For Canada, by contrast, the consequences were negligible. Seeing no strategic requirement for nuclear weapons of her own in any kind of role, her policy-makers could take the cut-off in their stride – and did. 'When, in December 1946, the British told the Canadians that they were going to return to the charge over collaboration with the United States Government, Mr [C.D.] Howe was not prepared to join in. It was true, he said, that Canada had received very little information from the United States and this delayed by some months the operation of her pile, but she was prepared to accept this position.'[114] The official historian of British atomic energy describes the Canadian attitude as 'relaxed and generous': Canada

---

*   A mounting body of evidence shows that strategic considerations played a small part in the taking of this decision to those of status and prestige. One story is especially revealing. There is discussion, probably in 1947, between the British Prime Minister and Foreign Secretary. Ernest Bevin speaks: 'PM, I don't care a damn about these arguments. No other Foreign Secretary should have to sit in front of the US Foreign Secretary and be talked to as I have been talked to by Byrnes. It shouldn't happen, and the only way to stop it is to have the plants in this country with the Union Jack on top.' Quoted in Michael Howard, 'The Quiet Architect of the Air Force,' *Sunday Times*, 19 March 1978, 39. 'Such are the true reasons why countries become nuclear powers,' Professor Howard comments, 'perhaps indeed why they go to war...'

was 'ready to help the British and Americans without bothering too much whether she got back as much as she gave.'[115]

Irritation occasionally marred this mood: Canada's policy-makers were generous, they could not be expected to be saints. One policy-maker in particular was made restive by the cut-off. General A.G.L. McNaughton* was at this time both Chairman of the Canadian Section of the Permanent Joint Board on Defence and Chairman of the Canadian Atomic Energy Control Board; on a trip in the former capacity, McNaughton told a US State Department officer of his concerns in the latter. 'He said that he was deeply concerned over the present legal situation in the United States which prevented American officials and scientists concerned in atomic energy matters in this country revealing information to him and his Canadian Board,' the official recorded on 26 February 1947.

He said that before the McMahon Act there had been free exchange in both directions and each side had obviously benefitted enormously. Now, however, it was a "one-way traffic" of information from Canada to the United States and he personally was very fed up. He added that this situation was not going to do Canadian-American relations any good and that he personally was indignant about it. He said that some of his fellow Board members in Canada, and other Canadian officers and scientists concerned, were advocating retaliation, but he had given them orders that they were to continue to give information without restriction to the Americans. He said that a number of Americans who had come to Canada to gain information had expressed themselves as "ashamed" to be in a position of asking without being able to give anything in return...

General McNaughton is of course a man of deep conviction but he spoke with extra feeling about this problem and he ended up by saying "I wish you would tell your State Department how strongly I feel about this"...[116]

Some months later, McNaughton expressed himself in this vein again, this time to his American colleague on the United Nations Atomic Energy Commission. 'Under the McMahon Act no classified information is permitted to go from the United States to Canada,' that official noted on 29 October 1947. 'He considers the McMahon Act very badly drawn in this respect, and while he has been able to sit on the lid effectively, the situation is now causing him deep anxiety. He feels he cannot go on quite in this way very much longer.'[117]

Nor was he required to. By the end of 1947 the three governments had worked out a new deal: the British agreed to release uranium ore to the United States in exchange for information in certain specified areas, which would also be forthcoming to Canada. This *modus vivendi*, as it was called, was to expire by the end of 1949 but broke down in 1948 when the US Atomic Energy Commission learned to its acute dismay that the Brit-

---

* See *In Defence of Canada* III, 16-19, 284-95.

ish were heading for bomb production. '[W]e have got to protect our information,' President Harry S. Truman told its chairman with characteristic bluntness, 'and we certainly must try to see that the British do not have information with which to build those atomic bombs in England because they might be captured.'[118]

Another North Atlantic tangle, the knottiest yet, was in the making. But the Canadian government, distressed to see it so, took little if no part in the unravelling. Canada's own atomic programme was unaffected by the dispute. C.D. Howe's declaration to the Combined Policy Committee on 20 September 1949 was couched (according to its minutes) in terms of unruffled serenity.

Mr Howe stated that Canada's position in the field of atomic energy was well known. Canada had no plans for military use of atomic energy. Her materials and facilities were employed for purposes of research only, and everything that Canada had accomplished in this field had been passed on to her associates. In addition, Canada was an important source of raw materials. ... With regard to the present modus vivendi, Canada had no complaint. It was felt that the information that had come to Canada had been put to good use. While more information could have been used to advantage, perhaps there was some benefit and gain from the fact which had made it necessary for Canadian scientists to work out many problems for themselves.[119]

While Canada might accept with equanimity her exclusion from much of the product of American research and development in the fields of science and technology, her leaders were more and more put on edge by her exclusion from the secrets of American strategy for nuclear war. Two events caused the Canadian 'need to know' to become both urgent and self-evident. One was the signing of a treaty. The other was the exploding of a bomb.*

The advent of the North Atlantic alliance and of Soviet nuclear capability transformed the situation of Canada and the expectations of her government.

Canada had now become the ally of a nuclear weapons state (and of another state intent upon equipping itself with nuclear weapons), whose stockpile of such weapons had been made possible by and would in future depend upon Canadian resources.† A major atomic exchange between the

---

* See *ibid.*, 317-18.
† Pitchblende and uranium ore. Much of the latter would come from a mine located in the constituency of Algoma East, represented from 1949 to 1968 by L.B. Pearson. By the early 1950s three-quarters of the ore needed to sustain US bomb production came from the Belgian Congo, but Canada was the only assured foreign supplier. Even so, her government never so much as considered a threat to cut off exports to the United States unless the American government undertook to consult with it on atomic strategy, such as the proposed use of nuclear weapons.

United States and the Soviet Union would in all likelihood contaminate her airspace and her lakes and turn her lands into a killing-ground. Her industry would become a prime supplier of military equipment for the armed forces of Western Europe. Her troops and airmen would serve in the West European integrated force – the 'shield,' for which the US Strategic Air Command would provide the 'Sword.'

If, then, it was 'absurd' – the adjective is used by the British official historian of these matters – 'that the one topic which could not be discussed together' between Britain and the United States 'was the most powerful weapon in the Allied armoury – atomic bombs and atomic strategy,'[120] it was – taking the aforementioned factors into account – horrendously absurd that it could not be discussed together between the United States and Canada – except under threat to any American discussant of heavy fines and years in jail.

American policy-makers by no means chafed under the constraints imposed upon them by the legislation known as the McMahon Act. They preferred to be hamstrung in that way. To share nuclear know-how with foreigners – even with friendly allied foreigners – might spill precious secrets to Soviet power. (It had happened not long ago, it would happen soon again.) And by soliciting the opinions of their allies on when (if ever) atomic bombs might be used, they would run the risk of degrading their ultimate weapon by allowing US strategy to be shaped by the inhibitions of irresolute governments.

That American concern on this latter score was neither irrational nor ill founded is shown by a disagreement which arose over the wording of a paragraph on the use of the bomb in the basic alliance planning document entitled 'Strategic Concept for the Defense of the North Atlantic Area.'* This document came under scrutiny at meetings of the Military Committee and the Defence Ministers at Paris on 29 November and 1 December 1949. Under the heading of 'Military Measures to Implement Defense Concept,' the drafters of the document – American, British, and French officials – had set out a number of so-called 'Basic Undertakings.' The first of these was to

Insure the ability to carry out strategic bombing including the prompt delivery of the atomic bomb. This is primarily a US responsibility assisted as practicable by other nations.

The Danish Chief of Staff told his colleagues on the Military Committee that this formulation was unacceptable. According to an American offi-

* See above, Ch. 3, 166.

cial, 'the Danes apparently advanced a number of reasons including the fact that if the Concept paper should leak, the USSR might, upon the outbreak of war, use this phrase as a pretext for dropping an A-bomb on Copenhagen.' The American representative, General Omar Bradley, succeeded in overcoming the objections of his Danish counterpart, and the paragraph survived to be considered by the meeting of the Defence Ministers the following day. When US Secretary of Defense Louis Johnson arrived at Paris for the meeting, he was told by the defence minister of Norway that 'a serious contretemps might arise in the Defense Ministers' meeting since the Danish Minister was under categoric Cabinet instructions from his Government not to agree to the reference to the atomic bomb.' This possible impasse was adroitly avoided by Johnson, who agreed to take the reference to the atomic bomb out of the wording of the Basic Undertaking, providing that the minutes of the meeting contained a statement to the effect that 'strategic bombing included the use of the atomic bomb.' To this the Danish defence minister was able to assent. The first of the Basic Undertakings in the Alliance's Strategic Concept was accordingly revised; it is to

Insure the ability to carry out strategic bombing promptly by all means possible with all types of weapons, without exception. This is primarily a US responsibility assisted as practicable by other nations.

The US State Department official on the scene was unhappy with this wording because, as he reported later in Washington, 'it might imply bacteriological and other forms of warfare.'[121]

The United States administration would have preferred to have been able to keep its tight-lipped silence on all matters pertaining to atomic energy and strategy. Certain developments, however, were making such silence more difficult to keep – especially with the government of Canada. There were five of these developments in all (listed here in no order of importance except for the fifth which, intrinsically the most important, had practically the least consequence):

First, the US administration was proposing that Canada should make her territory available for storing (and possibly for testing) nuclear weapons.

Second, the US administration was proposing that Canada should make her territory available for bases from which the Strategic Air Command could fly its missions of deterrence and retaliation.

Third, the Canadian government was contending that, because Canada was the ally of the United States most likely to be devastated in a nuclear exchange, it had the right to be consulted about the use of nuclear weapons in any theatre or cause.

Fourth, it would become, after December 1954, the policy of SHAPE to use nuclear weapons in Western Europe to repel a Soviet attack with conventional weapons.

Fifth, certain US officials were attempting to alter the American negotiating position on the international control of atomic energy, following the Soviet Union's detonation of a nuclear device.

By the summer of 1949, American policy-makers had begun to worry about the consequences of Britain's becoming a nuclear state. Their concern derived in part from the prospect of what in time would be called the problem of proliferation – the heightened uncertainty and danger produced by the addition of further sets of nuclear decision-makers to the international system and the family of man. Their concern also derived from the prospect that a stockpile in Britain of several score of nuclear weapons* might tempt the Soviet Union to try to seize it – as might British bomb production plants when built.

Out of these concerns emerged a proposal whereby the Americans would ask the British to stop all production in exchange for a number of bombs in the United States arsenal to be earmarked for United Kingdom use. Quite apart from its evident impracticality – stored in cave or canyon, whom could such bombs deter? – the proposal was considered by the US Secretary of Defense and the Chairman of the US Atomic Energy Commission to be (in the latter's words) 'so humiliating ... considering their place in the world and their contribution to this enterprise, that it would do more harm to make the offer than just to ride along...'[122] A modified proposal was devised to take its place. Plutonium produced in the United Kingdom plant would be shipped to the United States and there combined with U-235 to make atomic bombs which would remain on the American side until the British wished to retrieve them. The British Chiefs of Staff found this unacceptable on several grounds. They 'had examined yet again the arguments about the vulnerability of atomic weapons in the United Kingdom, and yet again had found them baseless; it would be senseless to store weapons outside Britain because they would be needed for use in a strategic air offensive at the very moment when the threat would be increasing. If all stocks were stored in the United States, the United States would in effect be in sole control and Britain would virtually

---

* In 1947, the British Chiefs of Staff had called for the production of 200 atomic bombs by 1957 – a figure termed 'quite arbitrary' by the official historian of the United Kingdom atomic energy programme. Margaret Gowing, *Independence and Deterrence: Britain and Atomic Energy, 1945-1952*, I, *Policy Making* (London 1974), 216. Arbitrary or not, this figure was probably unknown to American authorities in 1949.

be in the position of having to seek their agreement to use her own bombs.'[123] Yet another variation was then produced: build the bombs in Britain, store the bombs in Canada. Problems of accessibility would remain, but the problem of American control would not. Would Canada oblige by playing host to British bombs?

The storage issue came before the Combined Policy Committee – that Anglo-Canadian-American body formed in September 1943 to co-ordinate wartime atomic energy production and which had continued to meet, for long periods desultorily, during the post-war years – in September 1949 as part of an overall plan for nuclear co-operation among the three countries intended to operate to 1955. The fifth of the eight provisions of the plan was as follows:

(v) Complete co-ordination on the design, production, storage and delivery of atomic weapons, with combined testing of them. In view of the reduction of the United Kingdom production programme, the United States would provide Britain with enriched material and other components for making improved weapons. The weapons would be stored in the three countries "in accordance with common strategic concepts."[124]

Reporting on the plan to Ottawa, the Canadian representative expressed the hope that the government could see its way to approving it. 'We have just ended a meeting of the Canadian delegation,' Hume Wrong wrote on 27 September from Washington, 'and we are all agreed that the British draft contains nothing that we are unwilling to put forward to the Canadian Government, provided that the Canadian Government is prepared to accept at this stage a contingent responsibility for storage of United Kingdom nuclear weapons in Canada...' Wrong emphasized that the bombs would not actually arrive in Canada until towards the end of the proposed five-year period: it would take at least two years to produce any nuclear weapons from British plutonium, and the United Kingdom authorities would want to retain within their country those initially produced before shipping any out. 'We think that we should approve a submission to Governments on the lines under discussion,' Wrong continued, 'and I am ready to do so without further guidance from Ottawa unless the possibility of weapons storage in Canada is totally unacceptable. If it is unacceptable,' he cautioned, 'the arrangement under consideration might come to pieces since the Americans attach considerable importance to it both for military reasons and in influencing Congressional and public opinion.'[125]

The government was not enthusiastic about storing atomic bombs for Britain or any other country. Nevertheless, it decided on 29 September to allow Canada to become their custodian if need be. Its decision while remarkable is not surprising. The traditional mission of Canada's foreign policy had been to bring the United Kingdom and the United States back together in the wake of their falling out: Anglo-American relations had been badly strained as the result of the breakdown of post-war co-operation on atomic energy. The 'store-British-bombs-in-Canada' proposal was not an end in itself but part of an overall plan to restore the harmony of old. Canada would do much for that.

The effort within the Combined Policy Committee to produce what Hume Wrong from the scene described as 'a continuation of the full wartime partnership and ... a specialized contribution by the three countries to the defence of the North Atlantic area and the free world which they alone are in a position to make'[126] continued until the end of 1949 while the American and British teams attempted unavailingly to convert each to the other's proposals. At the crux of the negotiation was whether Britain was to receive all the benefits of American research and know-how in atomic energy matters while at the same time proceeding with its own bomb production assured of access to its stockpile by having at least part of it – the British Chiefs of Staff fixing on the figure of 'about 20' – located within the United Kingdom and the remainder located in Canada (in order to avoid the political and constitutional problems that could arise if the stockpile were located in the United States).

The Canadians were mainly onlookers at this debate. During an adjournment in October, the head of the British team, Sir Roger Makins, described them to his government as regarding 'themselves as full atomic partners with the United States and Britain but looked upon the present talks as raising primarily Anglo-American issues.'[127] Hume Wrong described his delegation's attitude on the Anglo-American differences over the British weapons program as one of 'interested neutrality.' The problem of storage in Canada, Wrong wrote to Ottawa as the talks progressed, was more complicated than it had appeared at first sight. 'The main reason given for storage in Canada rather than in the United States,' he reported, 'is the delay which might arise pending action by Congress in the event of a declaration of war, which might deprive the United Kingdom of the use of atomic bombs in the early stages of war. This, however, raises the question whether we would consent to allow the United Kingdom to withdraw bombs even though Canada were not at war.'[128] Then there were bombkeeping problems: who would guard the stockpile, defend the storage area, attend to and pay for the upkeep of the arsenal? Being custodian of a nuclear stockpile could be onerous – the more so when it belonged to someone else.

In the event, these questions did not require answering. On 2 February 1950, Klaus Fuchs, the British atomic scientist who had worked at Los

Alamos before joining the staff at Harwell, was arrested for spying for the Russians. All deals were off. The British went ahead on their own.

As work proceeded at Aldermaston – the first plutonium weapon left that production site on 5 June 1952 – a quest began for where to test. During the summer of 1950, Dr William Penney, Chief Superintendent of Armament Research and in charge of British atomic bomb production, visited Canada to investigate possible sites. The official historian of the British atomic energy program states that a feasibility study was prepared by Penney jointly with the Chairman of the Defence Research Board, Dr O.M. Solandt.* 'This was a feasibility study only,' Professor Margaret Gowing remarks, 'since there was no ministerial authority on either side for Anglo-Canadian collaboration in weapon testing.' In any case, nothing came of it: the British turned instead to the hospitable perimeter of Sir Robert Menzies' Australia. But the Penney-Solandt – or Penney – report, cogently summarized by Gowing, is none the less of interest.

Penney was seeking more than a site for the first test, and the joint report which he and his Canadian colleagues produced looked forward for some years. It defined three types of trials: (i) to test the functioning of a weapon; (ii) given a weapon of known power, to discover certain physical effects (for instance, the effect of an explosion in shallow water); and (iii) to prove the functioning and ballistics of an operational weapon. The first British trial would combine objectives (i) and (ii). If a tripartite agreement were reached on a common proving ground in Canada, the report continued, there might be one or two trials a year for several years; the site would have to be generously staffed and equipped with instruments. Assuming complete Anglo-Canadian integration but no tripartite agreement, the staff required for the first trial would be 200 scientists, 50 technicians and 100 industrial workers. Most of the scientists would be provided by Britain, with help from the Canadians in chemical analysis and radiological safety, and most of the industrial workers by Canada; Canada would undertake the construction work; costs would be shared on an agreed basis...

The report set out the requirements for a site: a detonation area; a temporary camp at least 10 miles away upwind; a base camp, with laboratories, workshops and signals office, at least 25 miles away upwind. It would have to be isolated, with no human habitation downwind in a wide sector; prevailing winds should blow contamination over the sea but clear of shipping. It should be large enough to accommodate the detonation of about a dozen weapons over several years; since

*   See *In Defence of Canada* III, 49. 'I cannot recall any collaboration with Bill Penney on a report,' Dr Solandt has kindly commented in reply to a request for clarification. 'I think that what Dr Gowing must have encountered is Bill Penney's own outline of the requirements for a trial site. I am reasonably certain that this was never submitted formally to the Canadian government. As I recall it the Canadian attitude toward the whole idea of participation in [a] nuclear weapon program was so negative that it was not pursued beyond the informal discussion stage.' Omond M. Solandt to the author, 8 February 1978.

each explosion would cause severe contamination over an area of about 500 yards radius which could not be used again, each detonation would have to be at least 3 miles from the previous trial. Of the seven Canadian sites investigated, one near Churchill, Manitoba, on the west coast of Hudson Bay, seemed ideal...[129]

An innocent abroad.

Some of Canada's vast territory – nearly half of NATO countries' total area – was either remote enough from human habitation to permit testing of nuclear weapons, or remote enough from the Soviet Union to store nuclear weapons – or close enough to the Soviet Union to provide bases from which to deliver nuclear weapons to targets in that country. For this last purpose, the United States was interested in acquiring base rights in Canada. Was Canada interested in ceding these?

The question was first asked during the autumn of 1949 at meetings of the Combined Policy Committee in Washington. The Canadian representative sought guidance from his government. 'Is Canada prepared to co-operate in the provision, equipment and defence of bases for the launching of atomic weapons?,' Hume Wrong inquired of Ottawa on 21 October.

An important aspect of the United States proposals is the consideration of methods for the improvement of deliverability of atomic weapons against probable targets in the event of war. This involves not only weapon development, improvement of bomb-carriers, and target intelligence, but also the provision of launching sites and the protection of such sites.*

Two considerations accounted for the earnest desire of the Pentagon for this agreement with the Canadian Government. First, there was a need for the utmost secrecy between the two governments arising out of the need for prior consultation and notification. There was also the need, however, for swift action to enable the US Strategic Air Command to undertake a strategic air offensive for the mutual defence of Canada and the United States if, as the Pentagon Paper says, "war is joined by the North Atlantic Treaty Organization nations." What the US Department of Defense is seeking ... is a "canopy" of an agreement reached at the highest political level which would enable the US Chiefs of Staff, acting under the authority of the Secretary of Defense, to take prompt action, through channels of maximum security, such as from General Vandenberg to Air Marshal Curtis, to notify the Canadian authorities involved of any particular action to be taken under the terms of the general agreement...[131]

Prompting so urgent and drastic a request was American fear, following the retreat of United States armies in Korea at the hands of the Chinese,

---

* By 'launching sites' Wrong probably meant bomber runways. However, the use of missiles as nuclear bomb carriers had been under study by the United States armed forces since 1948. See Edmond Beard, *Developing the ICBM: A Study in Bureaucratic Politics* (New York 1976), 44.

that there was greater danger than ever before of what a USAF officer in *Dr Strangelove* is pleased to call 'nuclear combat toe-to-toe with the Ruskies.'

The government of Canada was in effect being asked – even implored – to help assure the performance of the two-fold mission of the US Strategic Air Command – deterrence and retaliation – by agreeing to regard North America, for military purposes at least, as virtually a single state. And its agreement would have to be in secret. Here was a tall order, even for the most ardent continentalist; L.B. Pearson referred to its 'delicacy and difficulty.'[132] The Americans forwarded a draft of the proposed '"canopy"' agreement to Ottawa on 3 January 1951. This was discussed 'at the highest political level' in February. The Cabinet's reaction was unfavourable. A reply to the United States' request was prepared, but Pearson did not like it: '[O]ur initial comments should be tougher than in the original draft.' The ensuing revision was judged unsuitable for leaving with the US State Department in the form of an *aide-mémoire* – presumably because of its political sensitivity. 'These comments should be transmitted to the U.S. Government orally,' Pearson instructed Hume Wrong, 'and as coming from me.'[133]

Further discussion of the matter at a high, if not 'the highest,' political level took place at Ottawa on 2 April. The participants were Pearson, Brooke Claxton, Arnold Heeney (then Under Secretary of State for External Affairs), Norman Robertson (then Clerk of the Privy Council and Secretary to the Cabinet), General Charles Foulkes (Chairman of the Chiefs of Staff Committee), and Air Vice Marshal A.L. James (the RCAF officer in charge of North American air defence). After the meeting, Heeney reviewed the American proposal for the Ambassador at Washington and informed him of the reaction of the officials who had discussed it.

[The agreement] would constitute, in effect, advance consent to the use, subject to notification, of facilities in Canada by Strategic Air Command in preparing for carrying out operations in atomic warfare. ... In short, the canopy agreement as outlined would seem to leave the Canadian Government with little, if any ... control over the use for operational purposes by Strategic Air Command of facilities in Canada...

The desire of the United States authorities in view of responsibilities under NATO for strategic air operations, to have a free hand, subject to notification, for the Strategic Air Command to overfly Canada and to use Goose Bay and Harmon Field for operational purposes is fully appreciated. At the same time, if the Canadian Government agree to such an arrangement, it might well forego any opportunity it may have of influencing policy in the use of atomic weapons by reason of Canada's geographical location. In the event of an all-out war, it would perhaps be unrealistic for the Canadian Government to hope that it could really exercise an effective influence on such policy. But it would clearly seem unwise for it to "throw in its hand" in advance.

Such an argument, of course, can scarcely be put to the United States authorities. It might, however, be pointed out to them that although the United States has a responsibility under North Atlantic Treaty arrangements for strategic air operations, and although the Canadian Government would not wish in any way to hinder the United States in the fulfilment of those responsibilities, it is felt that it would be improper for Canada as a sovereign nation to permit unrestricted use in peacetime of facilities in Canadian territory for these operations, even on assurance of notification in advance of use.

These considerations, Hume Wrong was informed, applied particularly to storing fissionable components on Canadian territory, to the overflight by American aircraft carrying atomic bombs, and to nuclear strikes from bases in Canada. 'These are matters on which it is felt the Canadian Government should be consulted in each case at the highest political level. The channel for such matters should be civil rather than military.' This process of consultation through the civilian side of government – from the US State Department to the Ambassador at Washington to the Department of External Affairs and thence to Minister or Prime Minister – would present problems of command and control, but these, it was felt, were not insuperable. 'There should be no more delay in getting a decision from the Ministers if a request were to come through diplomatic channels than if it were to come through military channels.' If the American authorities considered these requirements acceptable and wanted to negotiate an agreement in which they would be embodied, then, Wrong was told by Heeney,

I suggest the agreement should be placed squarely upon agreed arrangements under the North Atlantic Treaty. A reference might be written into the introductory part of the United States Note to our common obligations under the Treaty, to the special responsibilities of the United States for strategic air operations, and to the agreement of Treaty nations through the Council Deputies that member nations should agree to give immediate and special attention to the granting to the United States of appropriate facilities for the fulfilment of its responsibilities...[134]

The Ambassador conveyed these views to the US State Department, whose officials responded by disclosing more candidly than usual some aspects of American strategy. The Pentagon's interest in the Newfoundland bases stemmed from the fact that in certain circumstances they were regarded as essential to preserve the vital national interest of the United States. These bases were no mere back-up air fields, third- or fourth-string substitutes on the American offensive team; they might be needed on the starting line-up. 'It was possible, in the event of an emergency,' Hume Wrong was informed, that nuclear components would not have been deployed to Strategic Air Command bases in the United Kingdom or to other strategic locations along the periphery of the probable targets. If such deployment had not taken place, the United States would wish to use Goose Bay as *the base from which initial strikes against the enemy would take place...* [author's italics]

Nor was that all. To return from targets in the Soviet Union to bases in Western Europe or the United Kingdom, the bombers would require mid-air refuelling. As much of their fuel was consumed by takeoff, the bombers could be refuelled soon afterwards. Facilities for basing tankers at Harmon Field were sought as well, for Goose Bay could serve no strategic purpose without them.[135]

The revelation that the United States authorities regarded the Newfoundland bases as conceivably indispensable for mounting strategic atomic retaliation against the Soviet Union put their request in a different light. How could Canada refuse? '[I]t may be very difficult indeed for the Canadian Government,' Brooke Claxton wrote in another connection, 'to reject any major defence proposal which the United States Government presents with conviction as essential to the defence of North America.'[136] So it now seemed to the Ambassador at Washington. 'Do you think it would be unreasonable for the Canadian Government,' Hume Wrong inquired of A.D.P. Heeney on 10 April, 'to give prior consent in advance to strikes with atomic weapons from Goose Bay or Harmon Field *in the event of a clearly established Soviet air attack on North American territory* [Wrong's italics] subject to as much prior notification as might be possible in the circumstances? It seems to me,' he continued, 'that we could not reasonably refuse our agreement to the use in such conditions of Canadian facilities and air space, and that we would in fact be anxious to see a counter-offensive undertaken with the minimum of delay. Furthermore, we might find in such an event that wire communication between Washington and Ottawa was severed and that it would take some time to discover alternative means of communication...'[137]

On 4 May – four months after the Pentagon's overture – the government had settled on its position. The Ambassador was to tell the US Secretary of State that Canada expected to be consulted, as distinct from being notified, through diplomatic channels at the highest political level, about possible atomic strikes from bases in Canada, the storage of nuclear weapons on Canadian territory, and the overflight by aircraft carrying nuclear weapons of Canadian territory. The government was willing, however, to waive these requirements 'in the event of a major outright Soviet attack against continental North America,' in which case 'we would not object to immediate retaliation by the US Strategic Air Command with all available means and from all available bases. ... In these circumstances, we would not insist on prior consultation, but would, of course, wish to have as much prior notification as possible...'[138]

A further overture to Canada by US defence authorities was made during the autumn of 1956. Their object was to secure the assent of the government to the establishment in Canada of bases from which United States aircraft could carry out aerial refuelling of bombers of the Strategic Air Command based in the United States. The Ambassador at Washington was invited to the Command's headquarters at Omaha, Nebraska, for briefings. A.D.P. Heeney's host on this occasion was 'the legendary General Curtis Lemay ... I was greeted,' Heeney recalled,

by a guard of honour, ruffles, national anthems and the works. Lemay met me at the ramp. ... I was sure that one of the reasons for the warmth of my welcome was that the United States at that period wanted permission to establish tanker bases in Canada which would provide a ten-fold increase in the range of their B-47s and a four hour saving on operations. The briefings were slanted that way and there was little question of the value they set upon a northern facility.

Already, lavish hospitality and awesome display of technological prowess had come to mark the efforts of the Omaha Command to convince visitors, usually from the US Congress, that, as its motto put it, 'Peace is Our Profession' and that, accordingly, no sacrifice for SAC could be too great. Its Canadian visitor on this occasion appears to have been favourably impressed.

As always a closer association with the nuclear striking arm of the United States posed political problems for Canada. Once more we were encountering the issue of effective participation in the ultimate decision to use these weapons. I thought perhaps this current request for tanker facilities might give us an opportunity to clarify and re-emphasize our right to hear and be heard and the political necessity for our doing so. The practical implications and the working out of this proposition were difficult. I myself saw no way to avoid co-operation in this matter if we were to participate in the joint defence of the continent. Subsequently the facilities were permitted.[139]

In the event, the United States did not avail itself of this 'northern facility:' replacement of B-47 bombers by longer-range B-52s made preferable other arrangements.

Consultation on the use of atomic bombs had two aspects. First, there was the question of Canadian control over the launching of nuclear strikes by United States bombers stationed in Canada. Second, there was the question of consultation on American use of the bomb from bases other than those in Canada.* In respect of the latter, ought a right to such consultation exist? Did it in fact exist? Would it be observed in practice?

This second issue assumed sudden importance on 30 November 1950 when, in a few sentences at the weekly presidential news conference, the President of the United States allowed himself to be understood as stating that nuclear weapons could well be used in the Korean War. A reporter, striving for accuracy – perhaps wishing to give President Truman the opportunity to retract or qualify – asked him further:

Q. ...Did I understand you correctly to say that the use of the atom bomb is under active consideration?

A. It always has been, Smitty. It is one of our weapons...

The exchange, brief as it was and swiftly followed by US official 'clarification' intended to allay alarm, brought the Prime Minister of Britain flying posthaste to Washington, caused what an historian describes as 'the lowest point in the graph of Anglo-American relations since Pearl Harbor,' and created consternation within the policy community at Ottawa. '[T]his incident,' L.B. Pearson wrote in his memoirs, 'really made us shudder. ... [O]ne more atomic bomb dropped by the United States anywhere in Asia would have had disastrous political consequences. I felt very strongly that whatever might be the military result of dropping an atomic bomb, whatever its tactical value, it would be a political disaster which would haunt the Western world for a long time.'[140]

What was to be done? 'Since President Truman's statements on November 30 about the possibility of using the atomic bomb in Korea,' Pearson cabled to Hume Wrong in Washington on 4 December, 'I have been considering our position. ... I think we should waste no time in informing the US government of some of the considerations which weigh most heavily with us ... on this most delicately and vitally important problem – the use, or the threat of use, of the atomic bomb.'[141]

These considerations were formulated in a memorandum entitled 'Korea and the Atomic Bomb,' in the writing of which Pearson himself took a major part and which bears his signature. (It is printed below, as Document 3.) The memorandum reiterates the thesis of Pearson's paper 'On Atomic Warfare' of 8 November 1945, wherein he had written: 'The atomic bomb is not merely a new weapon in a long succession of weapons, since man first began to fight with clubs, but something revolution-

---

* The wording of these two sentences is identical with those in the official history of the British post-war atomic energy program, substituting 'Canadian' and 'Canada' for 'British' and 'Britain.' Gowing, *Independence and Deterrence*, I, 310.

ary and unprecedented; a new departure in destruction and annihilative in effect.'* To use such a weapon against Chinese cities might confer some military advantage, but would put at risk 'the cohesion and unity of purpose of the Atlantic Community,' to say nothing of 'the links that remain between the Western world and the people of the East.' Because of the contributions made by Canada to the nuclear arsenal of the United States, 'the Canadian Government would be inevitably involved, and in a specially close sense, in the consequences of the use of the atomic bomb. ... [B]efore a decision of such immense and awful consequence, for all of us, is taken,' the memorandum concluded, 'there should be consultation among the governments principally concerned.'[142]

The Secretary of State for External Affairs gave much thought to how this message might most effectively be placed before the American authorities. He did not want them to feel that they were being made the recipients of 'an unnecessary homily.' While there was something to be said for delivering the message orally, 'in a matter of this moment,' Pearson told Hume Wrong, 'I think there should be some written record.' He would leave to Wrong's judgement the manner of its presentation. He noted that 'the memorandum has been deliberately prepared without reference to President Truman's statement so that it could be taken as an independent appreciation, for the use of the Canadian Government, a copy of which we are giving to the US Government for their information as an indication of our thinking on the subject of the greatest common interests to both Governments...'[143] The Ambassador did not wholeheartedly approve of the analysis. 'Several passages ... seem to me to convey the impression that the Canadian Government believes that a unilateral decision to authorize the bomb in Korea is likely to be taken and probably soon,' Wrong cabled to Pearson on 4 December. 'I am sure that this is not the case. ... I am certain,' he added, 'that little consideration has been given to the use of atomic weapons in Korea or Manchuria. It is doubtful whether the military results that could be achieved would be sufficiently great to warrant their use on military grounds alone...'† Despite Wrong's reservation, the text of the memorandum was handed on 6 December to

---

* 'Pearson's memorandum on atomic energy control deserves a place among the great diplomatic state papers...' *In Defence of Canada*, III, 279. It is reprinted in full in J.A. Munro and A.I. Inglis, 'The Atomic Conference 1945 and the Pearson Memoirs,' *International Journal*, XXIX, 1, Winter 1973-4, 94-9.

† Hume Wrong to SSEA 4 December 1950 (telegram), DEA files, 50069-A-40. Wrong's surmise that there was really little probability that the US President would authorize the bomb to be used in Korea is borne out in subsequently published records of policy discussion within the Truman administration; see *Foreign Relations of the United States, 1950*, VII, *Korea* (Washington, DC 1976), 1041ff.

Gordon Arneson – the most senior official of the US State Department to deal exclusively with atomic energy matters, who for that reason was selected to receive Canada's representations.

'Korea and the Atomic Bomb' had asserted the right of Canada, as a contributor to the development of the weapon, to be consulted before its use. On 13 April 1951, the Ambassador at Washington informed the Department of External Affairs that the United States government had offered Canada with respect to consultation 'the same arrangement as had been offered to the United Kingdom.'[144] Did that mean that the United States had assented, for the first time, to the right to which Canada had been trying to lay claim?

Prime Minister Attlee had based his belief that the US President would seek British consent to the use of atomic weapons on a verbal assurance from Truman.* That belief imputed to the President more than he had said, or meant to say. L.B. Pearson was quick to sense that disagreement loomed. 'There is a very real risk, I think,' Pearson wrote to his Under Secretary on 20 March 1951,

of a misunderstanding between the United States, on the one hand, and the United Kingdom authorities and ourselves, on the other, as to the nature of the commitment already given by President Truman to Mr Attlee – and extended to us – regarding the use of atomic bombs by the United States. There is no doubt that the United States is satisfied that there is no commitment in regard to prior consent from any other government before atomic bombs are used. ... The misunderstanding that may arise will be over the relationship of "consultation" to "consent." In our case that misunderstanding may be more difficult to avoid because of the agreed occupation by the United States of Canadian bases from which an attack could be mounted. How can we agree to this without the reservation that we too must be at war! But if we are not going to permit the United States to fly atomic bombs from Canadian bases without prior agreement (except in the case of an immediate retaliation against an atomic or air assault), then, to us, prior

---

* President Truman's version of what passed between himself and Prime Minister Attlee on the use of atomic weapons was recorded as follows by Philip C. Jessup of the US State Department.

> The President said he had just talked with the Prime Minister and that they had discussed the atomic bomb and its use. The President reminded Mr Attlee that the Governments of the United Kingdom and the United States had always been partners in this matter and that he would not consider the use of the bomb without consulting with the United Kingdom. The Prime Minister asked whether this agreement should be put in writing, and the President replied no that it would not be put in writing, that if a man's word wasn't any good it wasn't made better by writing it down. The Prime Minister expressed his thanks.

> *ibid.*, 1462. Only a single copy was made of Jessup's transcription, for retention in the office of the Secretary of State.

consultation does, in certain circumstances, really imply consent. I agree ... that it is going to be difficult to impose specific conditions on the United States in regard to this matter...[145]

Discussion over the use of the bomb continued between British and American representatives in Washington, with the Canadians playing their usual role in these issues of grand atomic strategy as interested but quiet spectators. The negotiation got nowhere – 'almost as fruitless,' in the estimation of the official historian of the British atomic energy programme, 'as the long negotiations to integrate atomic energy production.'[146] There being nothing to negotiate, talk shifted from problems of consultation and consent – the Americans would under no circumstances submit a decision to use atomic weapons for the consent of any ally, and would use their own discretion about consulting any ally – to problems of formulating conditions in which atomic weapons might or might not be used. This, too, proved pointless. 'Considering that the value of the atomic bomb as a deterrent rests partly on the uncertainties in any potential aggressor's mind as to how, when or whether it could be used,' Hume Wrong remarked to Ottawa, 'any definition of the occasions for its employment would remove some of the deterrent value.'[147]

Nevertheless, L.B. Pearson remained convinced that the atomic bomb, being a weapon unlike any other, was not to be used as an instrument of any single national policy. So awesome a weapon was in a moral sense in the custody of mankind even if in a physical sense in the custody of – so far – two governments. Pearson took this idea for the theme of a nation-wide radio broadcast on 5 December 1950. To his fellow-Canadians, and any Americans tuned in, he granted that the atomic bomb, from a strictly legal point of view, 'is merely another weapon, and can be used like any other weapon.' But the legal view, as nearly always, provided a too limited perspective.

The political instinct of people throughout the world ... has insisted – and I think rightly – that the atomic bomb is different from other weapons. Not only is its destructive power far greater than that of any other weapon, but it was created as a result of the deepest penetration that man has yet made into the fundamental secrets of Nature, and if used widely enough might destroy all life on this planet. Whether or not to use a weapon of that kind should surely not be decided by the application of the same criteria applicable to other weapons, or by unilateral decision, no matter what the technical and legal position may be. At a time of military reverses, when soldiers are trapped and encircled and are dying desperately, there will naturally be a strong temptation to sanction the use of the atomic bomb. Anyone considering such authorization, however, must remember that the fate of the whole world may depend on the decision. The atomic bomb is universally regarded as the ultimate weapon. It should be treated as such.[148]

These heart-felt reflections were rudely jolted on 12 January 1954, when the US Secretary of State delivered what soon became known as 'the massive retaliation' speech at the Council on Foreign Relations in New York.

On the assumption that a foreign minister will attempt to practice in public life what he may have preached in private life, the address by John Foster Dulles ought not to have taken his colleagues in government by surprise. An article written by Dulles had appeared in *Life* magazine for 19 May 1952, with the deliberately provocative title of 'A Policy of Boldness.' Its contents were even more provocative. To counter the Communist 'strategy of encirclement and strangulation' the United States needed – so Dulles there affirmed – 'to hit with shattering effectiveness the sources of power and lines of communication of the Sovietized world.' The speech of 12 January 1954 delivered its threat of nuclear retaliation, 'almost verbatim, in the vivid language of his 1952 article in *Life*' as 'a terse, choppy lawyer's brief.'[149] The gist of Dulles' statement was as follows.

Since the end of the Second World War, United States policies had been reactive, 'in the main emergency action, imposed on us by our enemies.' The Eisenhower administration proposed to seize the initiative from those enemies 'by placing more reliance on deterrent power, and less dependence on local defensive power.' What Dulles called 'massive retaliatory power' – the phrase that gave the speech its name – would be given pride of place in the United States' repertoire of policy initiatives. No longer would the United States need to be prepared to fight on any scale in any theatre – 'in the Arctic and in the tropics; in Asia, the Near East and in Europe; by sea, by land and by air; with old weapons and with new weapons.' Basic presidential decisions had changed this outmoded defence posture and replaced it by a new doctrine: 'to depend primarily upon a great capacity to retaliate, instantly, by means and at places of our choosing.'[150]

These remarks created what used to be called 'a fluttering of dovecoats in the chanceries.' No chancery could have been more shocked by them than was the East Block at Ottawa. Dulles' speech had been delivered without notice to the government of Canada which, of all United States' allies in NATO, would be most affected by the new doctrine (soon to be dubbed 'the New Look'). Canada had deserved to be forewarned. There had been no forewarning. 'There was no prior consultation or agreement with Canada,' L.B. Pearson informed the Prime Minister on 3 February, 'before these important policy statements were made, and we have not yet had an opportunity to discuss their implications with the United

States.'[151] Taking counsel with senior officials of his Department, Pearson formulated his first reactions in a memorandum for Louis St Laurent. (The text of this memorandum, dated 2 February 1954, is printed below as Document 5.) 'There is little doubt that far-reaching changes have been made in Washington in respect of defence policy and strategy,' Pearson told St Laurent. 'Mr Dulles' speech on January 12 in New York greatly strengthens this view. It is too early to come to any conclusion as to the exact nature of these decisions, but it is safe to say that their consequences will be of the greatest importance, not only for the United States but for other countries as well, including Canada.' In the portion of the memorandum dealing with the new doctrine of massive retaliation, Pearson wrote as follows.

This new concept of defence by the threat of swift and effective retaliation is meant to give United States military strength more flexibility. But it also makes flexibility in diplomacy even more necessary. In a sense, it will keep the potential aggressor guessing. But it may also keep the allies of the United States guessing.

Furthermore, it is important to know what Mr Dulles means by "our" in this context; especially when the "means" would appear to be largely atomic. Certainly this new strategy makes full consultation – being asked rather than told – more important than ever. The Korean situation in 1950 illustrates this. If the United States had chosen at that time not to work through the United Nations – after they had made up their own minds – but to retaliate instantly by overwhelming air action, or if later they had made the same decision to retaliate against Peking, would they have had time to consult us? Or would we have been involved automatically in action which, at least in the case of Peking, might have led to general war? It is clear that the new strategy is going to make diplomacy, both in its inter-allied aspects and in relations with the communists, more important than before.

It is also clear that the weapon of overwhelming retaliation, or the threat of it, is one which can only be exercised when the issue is clear-cut and decisive. There will, however, be many blurred and unclear situations constituting aggressive action when it could not be used. Indeed, it can be argued, as a practical proposition, that local aggressions cannot be answered by atomic bombs on Moscow. If so, the threat of massive retaliation "by means and at places of our choosing" may become a somewhat hollow one. The new strategy may result, therefore, in greater rigidity, rather than greater flexibility, of policy. If it becomes a question of the atomic bomb and all-out war, or nothing, it may be, too often, nothing.[152]

A paper prepared for the Chiefs of Staff Committee offered, on 10 February, a few tentative conclusions. The 'New Look' should not be taken to mean that the United States was contemplating preventive war, a prospect that was pronounced 'inconceivable.' It was evident, however, 'that the US have relaxed the former restriction on the use of "A" weapons and are now planning their use in any type of military action. Therefore, because of our close association with the US in the military field we may find ourselves involved in an atomic war without much consultation.' Accordingly, the paper recommended a number of cautionary measures: the improvement of intelligence at every level about United States strategic thinking and plans, training for Canadian forces 'under conditions and in areas where atomic explosions have occurred,' a greater emphasis on civil defence and survival training, and the reconsideration of Canada's position on the storing of atomic weapons on Canadian territory and their transport through Canadian air space.[153]

The first opportunity for Canadian officials to discuss the meaning of the 'New Look' with United States officials occurred early in March – by which time the US Secretary of State and other Administration spokesmen had been compelled by public furore in their own country to tone down considerably the bristling belligerency of the Dulles formulation.* The Chairman of the Chiefs of Staff Committee confronted his opposite number in Washington at the Pentagon to seek clarification of the Dulles doctrine, in the framing of which Admiral Arthur Radford, the Eisenhower administration's appointee as chairman of the Joint Chiefs of Staff, had been influential.[†] General Charles Foulkes' cross-examination of Radford was justifiably relentless. 'I ... raised several points in regard to

---

* 'Public reaction was ... an uproar of confusion, consternation and disbelief. ... [T]he press and public read it either as the serious intent of the US government to transform every border incident into a nuclear showdown, or else as a glaringly transparent bluff that would ... serve to weaken the credibility of American policy everywhere. The tactical advocate had loosed a verbal rocket at the Kremlin, but the side effects spread psychological devastation in a hundred other capitals. All the logical weaknesses of the doctrine, all the awkward questions, which his presentation had consciously or unconsciously pushed under the rug, were now embarrassingly thrown up to the administration in a thousand protests. A hasty and endless attempt was made to answer them, which led Walter Lippmann to the comment that "official explanations of the new look have become so voluminous that it is almost a career in itself to keep up with them".' Townsend Hoopes, *The Devil and John Foster Dulles* (Boston, Toronto 1973), 199-200.

† At a key meeting of the US National Security Council on 13 October 1953, Radford 'undertook to argue that the desired economies might well be feasible if the basis for military planning were more sharply defined – that is, if, instead of having to develop forces for a wide range of contingencies ... the Joint Chiefs of Staff were allowed to make plans on the assumption that nuclear weapons would be used whenever it was technologically advantageous to do so. ... [T]hese remarks of Radford's were soon to become the heart of the "New Look" doctrine...' Radford's appointment as Chairman of the Joint Chiefs had been highly political, designed to satisfy Republican complaints of the Administration's over-emphasis on Europe. '[T]he dashing, articulate naval commander (whose maxim as a carrier admiral in the war against Japan had been "kill the bastards scientifically") advocated a "strong" and "positive" policy toward China, and was known to favor primary reliance on air and sea power.' *ibid.*, 195-6, 194.

the "new look" which I was not too clear about,' Foulkes reported of his interview.

The first point was "prompt retaliation at places of our choosing," etc. Admiral Radford explained that this was an effort to regain the initiative and not continue to be drawn into local aggressions on the ground of enemy choosing. It was designed mainly as a warning to the Communists that the US will not hesitate to risk a major war to prevent future aggression. The theory is based on the assumption that the Communists will not risk a major war unless they are prepared to wage an all-out war and it is in accordance with their preconceived plans. Admiral Radford continued by saying that the statement was meant mainly as a warning to the Soviets. He admitted that there were many practical difficulties in working out such a policy. I asked the question "What about your allies in such circumstances?" He replied that of course they would have to be consulted and I replied that this appears to nullify the word "prompt" in the policy statement. I pursued the point by referring to the circumstances in case of hostilities again in Korea. Admiral Radford replied that he did not think hostilities would be reopened but if I wanted to discuss this situation as a case in point he would go along. I suggested that if shooting started again in Korea, especially at night, who would know or who would admit who reopened the war. He agreed that this would create a difficult problem and he replied that this was a case where the A bomb could not be used immediately, but he emphasized that if the Korean war reopened that the US could not accept the Yalu sanctuary and would insist on using all nuclear weapons at their disposal to bring the war to a speedy conclusion. However, he reiterated that A bombs would only be used against military targets and not against Chinese cities. He said that much more had been read into the statement of "places of our choosing" than was intended, and that it did not imply bombing Peking and Moscow. Admiral Radford continued that he was convinced that the Chinese had only entered the Korea conflict after they had ascertained sufficient information from the UN and other sources such as India, that if they entered the Korean war there was little likelihood that the UN forces would extend the war to the mainland of China. Therefore, they were prepared to take a calculated risk fully expecting to be able to drive the UN forces into the sea with little risk of A bomb retaliation on the mainland of China. I then asked about the use of the A bomb in the event of further Chinese aid to Indo-China, [and] here again he said it would be hard to prove further Chinese aid and there were no suitable targets on which to use A weapons.

'By this time,' General Foulkes' report concludes, 'I was convinced that the statement about "prompt retaliatory action at places of our own choosing" was mainly for propaganda purposes and would not be applied without consultation with allies.'[154] From the standpoint of the Canadian government, this conclusion was overly optimistic. Within a week of meeting with Foulkes, Admiral Radford was advocating (together with Vice-President Richard M. Nixon) a series of United States air strikes on North Vietnamese positions surrounding the beleaguered French garrison at Dien Bien Phu – not necessarily with nuclear weapons, but with nuclear weapons if necessary. This plan was vetoed not by the United States' allies (which, with the exception of France, were not consulted), but by Radford's commander-in-chief.

Meanwhile in Ottawa, officials were wondering whether the time had come to abandon 'quiet diplomacy' for some form of public remonstration. The Defence Liaison division of the Department of External Affairs opposed speaking out. 'We have prepared notes for the Minister on United States defence policy, as requested,' the division reported to the Acting Under Secretary on 2 March. 'At the same time, however, I think we should express our misgivings about the advisability of making such remarks in a public statement in the United States at this time.' Notes for the proposed speech by the Secretary of State for External Affairs made it seem that L.B. Pearson would be commenting on the new US strategy, 'and particularly Mr Dulles' exposition of it;' they would be 'bound to be taken by the Administration and the public of being critical of certain aspects of United States policy (which they are).' The memorandum concluded:

Such questions as are posed in these notes can and should be raised with the United States authorities through official channels. There will undoubtedly be opportunity to discuss them. ... I think, however, that it might be taken amiss if the Minister ... enters into public discussion on the subject. It might be regarded as an appeal to the American people over the heads of the Administration or as outside interference in the lively debate which Mr Dulles' statement has set off. Such false impression might jeopardize the chances of our getting sympathetic hearing in private talks with the Administration.'[155]

Only two months earlier, L.B. Pearson had pleaded before an audience made up of public relations professionals for a greater reliance on diplomacy for the solution of international problems. 'By diplomacy I mean something more than monologues at international gatherings, or public press conferences, or calculated leaks to frighten potential adversaries or "put the heat on" reluctant friends, or even political quiz programmes before the microphone or camera. There should be more room for and greater reliance on quiet and confidential negotiation...'[156] It is a measure of the depth of Pearson's concern about the Dulles doctrine that he now chose to over-rule advice from his own officials which was so much in keeping with his chosen diplomatic method. He decided to speak out, using for the purpose the most powerful amplifier in the world – the microphone at the National Press Club, Washington, DC.

Pearson's speech, entitled 'A Look at the New Look,' was delivered on 15 March. It contained the following passage.

Mr Dulles, in a speech on January 12, which may turn out to be one of the most important of our times, announced, as a basic principle for defence planning, a

Washington decision, and I quote from his speech, "...to depend primarily upon a great capacity to retaliate, instantly, by means, and at places, of our choosing."

The key words in this sentence, as I see it, are "instantly," "means," and "our."

This statement has aroused intense interest in this country. That interest is hardly less among your friends in other countries; especially, I suspect, among those whose territories are only a few hundred miles from those great communist armies who could also act as an instrument of retaliation.

From our point of view, it is important that the "our" in this statement should mean those who have agreed, particularly in NATO, to work together and by collective action, to prevent war or, if that should fail, to win it. Indeed, an earlier part of Mr Dulles' statement gives that wise interpretation, when he said: "The way to deter aggression is for the *free community* to be willing and able to respond vigorously at places and with means of *its* own choosing."

But what effect will that have on the other words "instantly" and "means"? Collective action means collective consultation, but that must be reconciled with the necessity for swift and effective decision. This reconciliation is not always easy, even within a single government. It is less easy between governments.

I want to emphasize that I am not criticizing this new defence concept which may turn out to be the best deterrent against aggression. It does, however, I think make diplomacy not less but even more important; especially when we contemplate the "means" – including atomic – that may have to be used, the occasions when this should be done, and the effect – explosive possibly in more respects than one – it may have.

Diplomacy includes two things: first the effort, patient and persistent, to settle differences with those whom we rightly fear, though at times, with a fear that seems to freeze us into diplomatic immobility or fire us at other times into something almost like panic. Secondly, there is the other kind of diplomacy, now also more important than ever: the search for agreement between friends on policies and tactics and timing, so that "our choosing" will mean an agreed collective decision, without prejudicing speedy and effective action in an emergency. Indeed, such agreement, after consultation and discussion, is, to put it bluntly, necessary, if this policy of preventing aggression by the threat of immediate and overwhelming retaliation is to work collectively.

The stakes are now higher than ever, and the necessity for co-operation and consultation greater than ever. It is essential that we work together in any new defence planning and policy – as we have already been working together in NATO – if the great coalition which we have formed for peace is not to be replaced by an entrenched continentalism which, I can assure you, makes no great appeal to your northern neighbour as the best way to prevent war or defeat aggression, and which is not likely to provide a solid basis for good United States–Canadian relations.[157]

L.B. Pearson's 'Look at the New Look' – as forthright an address speech as any delivered before an American audience by a Canadian spokesman – had its intended effect. Widely and favourably reported, it produced what the Washington correspondent of a Canadian newspaper described as 'the most notable spate of reaction, both official and otherwise, accorded to observations by a foreign statesman in at least the last year.'[158] Looking back at it, Pearson commented:

I said quite a lot in that speech. ... [A]lmost before my speech was over, Foster Dulles ... had me on the phone to see if I'd have dinner with him that night. ... We had a very good talk and I succeeded, I think, in convincing him that night that we weren't trying merely to be mischievous or difficult but that he must put himself more often in the shoes of other people and see how certain things looked to them. For a Canadian, massive retaliation, when the decision would be made in effect by the United States because they were the only people who had the massive arms, was frightening. I think I removed some of his misapprehensions...[159]

On the day following this conversation, the US Secretary of State delivered himself of yet another 'clarification' by declaring that the Administration would consult with its allies before launching nuclear attacks – but adding the crucial qualification 'in most cases.'*

Those officials within the Department of External Affairs who had advised their Minister to forego a speech on this subject presumably had mixed feelings of chagrin and relief on learning of its success. Asked for guidance by the Canadian Broadcasting Corporation on how to prepare comment on the speech for shortwave transmission to its audiences around the world, officers of the Department displayed reluctance to provide it: '[T]here is only a certain way the Department can or should go,' an internal memorandum commented, 'in trying to interpret what the Minister himself had in mind...' Subject to that *caveat*, the Department of External Affairs offered these observations.

The main aim of Mr Pearson's speech was probably not to criticize United States policies as such but to draw attention to the fact that collective action must stem from collective consultation, and that a policy for the common defence of the NATO countries can hardly receive their whole-hearted support unless they are consulted in its formation.

---

*   *The Globe and Mail* (Toronto), 17 March 1954. A year earlier, the US Secretary of State had revealed his attitude towards Canada in testimony before the US House of Representatives Committee on Appropriations, in testimony which he mistakenly believed to be off-the-record (and which he caused to be stricken from the record when he discovered his mistake): '"He takes a few slams at Canada – their inferiority complex, their ambivalent attitude to the US – but points out that it's a very important piece of real estate and should be humoured along".' Quoted in Leonard Mosley, *Dulles: A Biography of Eleanor, Allen and John Foster Dulles and Their Family Network* (New York 1978), 329.

In this sense, therefore, Mr Pearson *was* being critical, critical of the inadequate amount of consultation that had preceded Mr Dulles' speech on instant retaliation in New York on January 12. ... [T]he emphasis should be placed not on this critical note but on Mr Pearson's desire to ensure that further efforts are, in future, made to overcome the admittedly serious difficulties in the way of carrying out effective consultation on this vital question.[160]

On 25 March, L.B. Pearson spoke at length of his 'look at the "New Look"' in the course of his survey of international affairs in the House of Commons. 'So far as I am concerned,' Pearson told the House, 'I do not criticize the view that this kind of strategy is a valuable deterrent against aggression, and a shield for defence. ... What I thought was important, however, was to clarify some of the ambiguities of this new strategy, and to make it as clear as possible to us all where we stood as friends and allies in relation to it.' He noted that within the past few weeks 'some very important and reassuring clarifications have been made in Washington of what seemed to some of us to be obscurities. I believe that has been a good result. I know that personally I feel better after having heard some of these statements. ... We now have a fairly clear and reassuring idea of what this new strategy and this new planning for defence is.'[161]

A Canadian historian, writing of this episode, concludes that 'two months after Mr Dulles's speech, Canadian qualms in regard to Mr Dulles's policy had presumably been removed.'[162] That was a large presumption, seemingly unfounded. A.D.P. Heeney, ambassador at Washington at the time, offers a different judgement: 'Early in 1954 Dulles made his "massive retaliation" speech indicating that the United States would retaliate with considerable force and even use atomic bombs anywhere in the world. From that time on Ottawa was almost continuously anxious about the course of United States foreign policy...'[163]

L.B. Pearson's remarks on 'massive retaliation' during 1954 did not challenge the doctrine as such. The strategy, he stressed, would be valid and effective, provided that Canada and other NATO allies were consulted if feasible, and that they concurred in what the United States proposed to do. Only later would he express reservations about the strategy itself. These reservations were stated in the first of a series of lectures which Pearson gave at Princeton University in the early summer of 1955. He proposed, he told his audience, 'to re-examine some loose thinking, and loose talk, that has occurred about this doctrine and about the theory of the deterrent. The capacity for massive retaliation,' Pearson continued,

and the unambiguous and declared resolve in certain circumstances to use that capacity is, it seems to me, a necessary deterrent against the possibility that a potential aggressor might yield to the temptation of launching an all-out attack in the hope of quick and final victory. But any idea that such capacity for massive retaliation should or would be used by our side in retaliation against a local attack or conflict, or as a defence against an attack which may not be massive, is something else. The acceptance of such a theory could mean that the very future of the world would hang on the decision whether to reply to a threat against a big battleship or a small island by an H-bomb attack on a continent.

There is something very frightening about the idea of playing "all or nothing" with any kind of weapon. In an era where two sides possess thermonuclear weapons, the application of the theory of the maximum deterrent for other than the maximum attack might be fatal to both sides.[164]

To replace the doctrine of massive retaliation, Pearson proposed what was being termed 'graduated deterrence,' a concept then much discussed by strategists (particularly in the United Kingdom, where thermonuclear attack was tantamount to national destruction). The new doctrine arose from the realization that the striking power of the US Strategic Air Command was not likely to serve as a deterrent against conventional military assault. Conscience and common sense would not tolerate the certain death of scores of millions of innocents (half or more of whom would be on the retaliating side) as a reprisal against a non-nuclear foray. There came dimly into view what an as yet obscure American analyst (Henry Kissinger) identified as 'one of the most serious and at the same time novel' paradoxes of nuclear strategy: 'The deterrent effect on its diplomacy of a power's own deterrent arsenal.'[165] Massive retaliation, so far from deterring conventional attacks, seemed likely to encourage them. To overcome the paralysis induced by the very awesomeness of the destructive power of which both sides were possessors, the West needed to devise a new strategy – a strategy which fitted punishment to crime and deployed the proper proportions of force. It was not the first time that the new doctrine had been enunciated, but Pearson enunciated it more clearly than some.

[E]xcept in the event of a reciprocal spasm of mutual annihilation, the free world's force should be used only for limited political objectives, of which the chief will be to deter aggression; or if it breaks out, to localize it, defeat it, and prepare the way for a peace settlement.

This is something different from the doctrine of massive retaliation.[166]

The doctrine of graduated deterrence gained still more adherents as new types of nuclear weapons came to be deployed in so-called tactical or battlefield roles.

During the first years of the atomic era, nuclear weapons were widely believed to possess a single strategic property: the ability to deter the

Soviet Union from all-out war upon the West. But as early as 1948, the US Army had been studying how to use atomic weapons to help turn the t de of battle once war had broken out.[167]

Because of the American taboo against sharing nuclear strategy with other governments, no Canadian official or officer knew of this development. They were kept in ignorance until late in 1949 when the Chief of the General Staff, lunching at the Pentagon, was told by his host that ' he American Chiefs of Staff had under active consideration the use of he atomic bomb in a tactical role to prevent the crossing of the Rhine.'[168]

General Foulkes, receiving this information, must have thought it highly secret. But any satisfaction at being made a confidant would have evaporated the following week on reading in the *Saturday Evening Post* for 15 October an article (necessarily declassified weeks or months earlier) by General Omar Bradley, Chairman of the Joint Chiefs of Staff, which cis-cussed in specific terms why nuclear weapons should be deployed on he battlefield. The article, 'This Way Lies Peace,' first told the melancholy tale of 'the Gap' and then proposed a way of closing it.

Give the defensive forces' superiority in fire-power, in mobility and in the air – an advantage well within the industrial ability of the Western world – and the entire picture changes. The defenders will then be able to turn back invaders far superior in number. And here atomic weapons may well enter the tactical equation.

The atomic bomb has been thought of as exclusively a strategic, offensive wea-pon. It is deadly over several square miles, and thus terribly effective aga nst industrial centers. But it is not militarily economical to use such a weapon aga nst troops dispersed over large stretches of country. It could not stop invading armies well spread out, advancing against negligible opposition.

But suppose the defenders can stop the initial rush and set up a strongly held defensive line. The only way to crack such a line is to concentrate heavy forces for a break-through. These concentrations would provide a target for the skilful use of atomic weapons on the tactical defensive. Note that this strengthens the defen-sive power of an army.

Thus the A-bomb, in its tactical aspect, may well contribute towards a stable equi-librium of forces since it tends to strengthen a defensive army...[169]

Drawing these paragraphs to the attention of the policy community at Ottawa, Hume Wrong commented that they referred – 'so far as I know for the first time publicly – to the possible tactical use of atomic weapons in defence.'[170]

The Minister of National Defence remained unimpressed by this argu-ment. 'At this time,' Brooke Claxton recalled – he is writing of May 1950 – 'very little weight seemed to be attached to the atomic bomb as a means of stopping [the Russians]. Probably this was the right concept because our side did not have enough ground forces to produce concentrations of the Russian troops which would make good targets for atomic weapons. ... I remember feeling that it was unlikely that any country, still less all the countries, would be able to produce the ground and air force necessary to slow up a Russian advance seriously without atomic weapons. But I did find that it would be possible to build up the strength to hold on long enough to bring atomic weapons into full play.'[171]

By 1952, military authorities in the United Kingdom were also becoming keen on the battlefield use of nuclear weapons in Western Europe. On 12 September, L.B. Pearson and A.D.P. Heeney paid a visit to the British Ministry of Defence (then in charge of a former governor general of Canada). 'There was a good deal of talk about the importance of the "A" weapon in NATO strategy and tactics,' Heeney recorded, 'and I thought that both Lord Alexander and General [Sir Ian] Jacob were pretty optimistic about the effectiveness of this type of warfare in the early stages of the battle for Europe.'[172] Heeney continued to monitor this British enthusiasm, doubtless enhanced by the successful detonation on Monte Bello Island on 30 September. '[T]he UK Chiefs of Staff have developed views of their own,' he reported to Ottawa the following day. 'They may argue either that the requirements for conventional forces have diminished, or ... the United Kingdom may suggest that, given the current political conditions, it may be worthwhile taking some risk now in the rate of build-up so as to develop newer and more effective weapons which may be more economical and in the long run more decisive...'[173] To this, L.B. Pearson responded:

[W]e are in a dilemma. We have to rely exclusively on what the Americans tell us about [the] ... effectiveness [of nuclear weapons] now and later, and there is no way of checking this opinion. This leaves us with an uneasy and restless feeling that we are planning in the dark. It will, in the long run, be impossible for a military coalition to work effectively if, for instance, a major on General [Matthew] Ridgeway's staff knows more about certain essential factors on which strategy and tactics must be based than the Commander-in-Chief of the Land Forces, Field Marshal Montgomery. ... I agree that we would be well advised now to take some risk in the rate of build-up against the likelihood of those weapons becoming effective in a shorter time than has been suggested.[174]

The appeal of nuclear weapons to NATO's military planners at this early stage is understandable. 'Military planners generated a requirement for shield forces to hold the line in Europe,' an American authority has since written, 'and these requirements were not met. At the same time, the American stockpile of fissionable material was estimated to exceed that of the Soviets by a good deal. In the short run, we could obviously draw upon our superior supply of fissionable material to substitute for NATO's deficiency in troops.'[175]

But that substitution – as even slight reflection showed – was not without grave drawbacks. It was true that when the NATO forces were built up in Western Europe, the Supreme Commander would be able to force the attacker to mass and concentrate its armies, so providing worthwhile targets for atomic counter-attack. But during the same period, the Soviet Union's own nuclear stockpile would mount, and NATO military planners could no longer assume that the Soviet Union would be so short of fissionable material that it would not retaliate in kind. '"Taking war back to the battlefield" is a fine slogan,' an American critic observed, 'but if it is used to rationalize unlimited theatre deployment of atomic weapons, it becomes a mockery to allies over whose territory they are being employed.' Moreover, the battlefield use of nuclear weapons by both sides, so far from solving NATO's problem of a chronic troop deficiency, would intensify it: 'Force requirements go up as estimated casualties soar in number, offsetting the substitution of atomic weapons for troops.'[176]

Early proponents of the use of atomic weapons on the battlefield had assumed that the same type of bomb held in readiness for demolishing Soviet cities would be deployed against Soviet divisions.* But by 1953 new kinds of weapons were appearing in US ordnance, referred to as 'tactical' less for their role than for their characteristics. These were spectacularly miniaturized. There existed, for example, an artillery shell which after being fired from a four-inch cannon exploded in fission with a force equivalent to about 3000 tons of TNT (compared with the 20,000 tons of the first atomic bomb or the roughly 14,000,000 tons of the first hydrogen bomb). Such weapons, later dubbed 'mini-nukes', were hailed for providing the opportunity to 'bring war back to the battlefield' with a vengeance. Whereas the hydrogen bomb was at best a deterrent against all-out attack,[†] at worst the tocsin of apocalypse, the tactical atomic wea-

---

* 'Hiroshima-type' bombs were used in the series of troop manoeuvres in Nevada which began on 1 November 1951 for the purpose of developing a US atomic fighting force. In consequence, many of the thousands of army personnel exposed to intense radiation at short range developed illness in later years; some died young. Patrick Huyghe and David Konigsberg, 'Grim Legacy of Nuclear Testing,' *The New York Times Magazine*, 22 April 1979.

† The best-known proponent of the optimistic view of the advent of hydrogen bomb era was Sir Winston Churchill who, in his last major address in Parliament as prime minister, mused that mankind had 'reached a stage where safety might well be the child of terror and life the twin of annihilation.' Churchill had rehearsed this theme in discussion at a Commonwealth Prime Ministers' meeting on 2 February 1955, as L.B. Pearson noted in his diary.

  He really let himself go on the H-bomb – the shattering implications of which, on our society, he has fully grasped. His sweeping imagination and range of mind has

pon could be fired upon enemy formations with relative impunity. So the United States Administration stated with all the emphasis at its command, President Eisenhower himself declaring that 'in any combat where these things can be used on strictly military targets and for strictly military purposes, I see no reason why they should not be used just exactly as you would use a bullet or anything else.'[177] The US Secretary of State put it more precisely: '[I]f the United States became engaged in a major military activity anywhere in the world ... [tactical atomic weapons] would come into use because ... they are more and more becoming conventional and replacing what used to be called conventional weapons.'[178] As such, they quickly entered NATO's arsenal. 'Under the twin pressures of economy and recognition of what were believed to be the strategic implications of inevitable technological change, the Eisenhower administration seemed to allow for the battlefield employment of nuclear weapons in all circumstances short of what came to be called "brushfire wars". ... Dutifully, the NATO Council followed suit in December 1954.'[179]

L.B. Pearson referred to that NATO decision in his Princeton University lectures some six months later.

At the ministerial meeting of the NATO Council held in Paris in December 1954 we took a decision of which one feature, which seemed to me particularly significant, was that it made possible the development of plans for the tactical use of atomic weapons for the defence of the NATO area to supplement the already existing plans for defensive strategic use. At the same time a form of strategy was agreed on, which in the event of aggression against Western Europe should enable SHAPE to defend more effectively the territory of the European NATO members by the provision of a shield which would have a good chance of holding the attack. A feature of great significance in this new strategy, which is based on new strength –

that is, the additional firepower supplied by tactical atomic weapons –

is that it should ultimately make it possible for NATO to rely less exclusively on the nuclear capacity to retaliate against the centres of Russian life and to rely more on NATO's ability to hold and throw back the invading armies.[280]

sensed that this discovery has made all the old concepts of strategy and defence as out of date as the spear or the Macedonian phalanx. He is horrified and comforted at the same time; by the immensity of the bomb, and by its value as a deterrent. He finds solace in the fact that the Moscow men are cold-blooded realists who know what power means and don't wish to be destroyed. So he thinks the bomb may be the destruction of war, not of humanity.

Quoted in *Mike* II, 80. The Minister of National Defence agreed with this view. 'I think that there can be no doubt,' Brooke Claxton declared on 20 May 1954, 'that the possession of this power of mass destruction is a powerful deterrent to war. There can be no doubt of that fact.' Canada, *H.C. Debates*, 1954, v, 4904

To regard tactical nuclear weapons as serving the cause of a humanitarian ideal – the sparing of life and suffering – was characteristic of L.B. Pearson's sunny optimism.* But such a view could not withstand serious analysis; nor did it.

The decision taken in December 1954 to deploy tactical nuclear weapons in the defence of Western Europe – in so far as it was thoroughly thought through – rested on three assumptions. First, that the attackers to be repulsed by atomic firepower would not themselves be equipped to return it in full measure. Second, even if the attackers had tactical nuclear weapons and used them, the battle atomically contended on both sides would not wreak unacceptable havoc within the battlefield countries. Third, that a battle fought with tactical atomic weapons by one side or by both could be contained to such, and not 'escalate' – the term would soon be common in the jargon – into all-out or world-wide war.

A moment's cogitation would reveal each of these assumptions to be implausible. The Soviet Union had proven itself proficient in the production of strategic nuclear weapons: why would it not be capable eventually of producing tactical nuclear weapons or prudent enough to wait until these had entered service before mounting an attack against defenders known to be similarly equipped? A limited atomic war fought up and down the peninsula of Western Europe would create unimaginable disaster, not only among the rival armies but on the populations that the NATO forces had been created to defend. During the summer of 1955, when Chancellor Adenauer was trying to get his Volunteers' Bill through the Bundestag, an ill-timed publicity placed before the people of West Germany the results of Operation 'Carte Blanche,' a NATO war games exercise in Western Europe in which for the first time tactical atomic weapons had hypothetically been used to destroy a presumed invader. '335 bombs had been "dropped" in the crowded space between Hamburg and Munich,' the West German press reported, 'and ... according to unofficial calculations – 1,700,000 Germans had been "killed" and 3,500,000 "wounded," not counting possible casualties from radiation.'[181] NATO's new strategy seemed to result mainly in the extermination of West Germans. Finally, there was no assurance – quite the reverse – that such a conflict, conducted initially with low-yield weapons, would not bring high-yield weapons into play. Even L.B. Pearson, relieved that NATO's new tactical weapons might down-grade the priority of Soviet cities on SHAPE's list of targets, expressed apprehension lest limited atomic war were to run amok. 'A war which begins on an island,' Pearson warned his audience at

* See James Eayrs, 'Sunny Side Up,' *Weekend Magazine*, 17 December 1977.

Princeton, 'may soon spread to a world. The use by one side of tactical A-weapons may, under the dread and ruthless momentum of fear, hate and destruction, lead to strategic H-bombs against a metropolis.'[182]

The case against relying on tactical nuclear weapons to destroy or drive back Soviet divisions could hardly be overstated. Such weapons – and their delivery systems – as an authority has since written of them, 'were vulnerable to pre-emption on the ground, they offered no obvious advantage to the defending side, they transgressed the one unquestionable qualitative firebreak or breakpoint in weaponry, they promised to accelerate the escalation of what might otherwise remain a local war, and they would certainly devastate the allies that they were supposed to be defending.'[183] All too true. Nevertheless, there they were, deployed eventually to the extent of perhaps as many as 10,000 warheads – excluding the Warsaw Pact's.

For Canada, deployment of tactical nuclear weapons in Western Europe created two major problems. One of these – the problem of access – lies beyond the period with which this study is concerned.* The other was the problem of use. In what circumstances, on whose orders, might these weapons be used in battle?

On 19 December 1954, L.B. Pearson discussed this question with John Foster Dulles at the US Embassy in Paris, where both foreign ministers were attending the NATO Council meetings at which it was decided to rely on tactical nuclear weapons for the defence of Western Europe. 'Mr Dulles was worried,' Pearson recorded at the time,

about the possibility of subsequent discussion in the Council as to how the governments would exercise their right of decision in regard to the use of atomic weapons if an emergency developed. He felt, and I agreed with him, that any such discussion would likely not be helpful and might be dangerous. It simply was not possible to work out in advance an agreement between fifteen nations on a subject of this kind which would cover every situation. ... He admitted that there might be some understanding reached with the powers principally concerned, notably the United Kingdom, France and Canada,† as to the procedure which should be followed for making quick and necessary decisions if an emergency developed. He thought, however, that any such arrangements should be kept very secret and that NATO Council discussions of these matters, let alone public discussion, should be discouraged. I told him that I was inclined to agree with him...[184]

---

* On 13 January 1963, L.B. Pearson, then leader of the Opposition, announced his conversion to a policy of acquisition of tactical nuclear weapons for the Canadian armed forces under conditions of United States custody and control – a decision implemented after Pearson became Prime Minister later that year, and which reportedly caused him 'much personal anguish.'

† Also, presumably, on attaining NATO membership, West Germany.

So much for the dictum, once uttered in public by Pearson, that 'No genuinely democratic state can or should countenance commitments secretly entered into; or adopt policies or make engagements without the people knowing about them and Parliament passing on them.'[185]

The foregoing sections make amply plain that the incentives to overcome the US Administration's inhibitions against sharing nuclear secrets with its Canadian ally arose from desire to deploy the atom rather than to control it. By 1949, when the two countries became military allies committed to each other's defence and to the defence of Britain and Western Europe, negotiation on atomic energy control had all but petered out. The United Nations Atomic Energy Commission continued to meet in New York; General A.G.L. McNaughton was Canada's representative as he had been from the beginning.* But no progress was forthcoming, no progress was expected.

'Heard about Vermont from C.D. [Howe],' C.J. Mackenzie noted tersely on 20 September 1949. When the unpalatable news of the first atomic detonation by the Soviet Union (for which 'Vermont' had been the code name) had been digested in Washington, a move developed there to rethink United States negotiating positions on the international control of atomic energy. The leader of this effort was George F. Kennan, then finishing his term as the first director of the US State Department's Policy Planning Staff. Kennan set about trying to convert his colleagues to his belief that the Baruch Plan, which had rigidified into what were known as the 'majority proposals' before the UN Atomic Energy Commission, should be replaced by one which stood some chance of acceptance – as the Baruch Plan did not – by the Soviet Union.

Kennan embodied his views on this issue in a memorandum of 20 January 1950, 'International Control of Atomic Energy,' which its author later described as being 'in its implications one of the most important, if not the most important, of all the documents I ever wrote in government.'† In the memorandum, Kennan had addressed himself in part to the steps the United States government might take 'if we *had* reviewed our military concepts, if we *had* come to the conclusion that we would no

---

* See *In Defence of Canada* III, 282-95.
† The memorandum is summarized in George F. Kennan, *Memoirs: 1925-1950* (Boston, Toronto 1967), 472-3. Kennan's summary is from memory: 'I do not even have any notes on the document,' he wrote, and added: 'I regret that government policy precludes its publication at this time.' The memorandum was published (minus its fourth part of seventeen pages) nine years later: see *Foreign Relations of the United States, 1950*, I, *National Security Affairs: Foreign Economic Policy* (Washington, DC 1976), 22-44.

longer rely on mass destruction weapons in our planning for a future war, and if we *had* resolved to work ourselves out of our present dependence on those weapons as rapidly as possible.' The first thing to be done in these eventualities, Kennan had written, 'would be to discuss this new state of mind with our allies in the Atlantic Pact group...'[186]

As a trial run for such discussion, Kennan had ventured to share his ideas with the Canadian diplomat who sat as General McNaughton's deputy on the UN Atomic Energy Commission, Arnold C. Smith. Their conversation took place over lunch on 8 November 1949. Kennan was careful to emphasize to his Canadian friend that he was speaking for himself and not for the US Government.

According to Arnold Smith's report of Kennan's remarks to him, the American diplomat told Smith that he thought the time had come to inform the Russians that the United States was now willing to call off the atomic arms race. An American proposal, Kennan suggested, might be formulated on the basis of three new policies which each side would undertake to implement. First, both would abandon large-scale atomic production and renounce attempts to use atomic energy as a source of power. Second, both would accept permanent inspection of raw material sources and declared facilities, to ensure that if any production was in progress it was only small in scale. Third, both would agree to sequester their existing stockpile of nuclear weapons with some international authority, possibly the United Nations, as its custodian.

These were radical proposals: not for the first time nor for the last was the US State Department's 'in-house intellectual' swimming against a strong tide. Reporting the conversation to the Under Secretary of State for External Affairs, Smith sought to strike a balance between the fact that the views expressed emanated from an individual whose maverick tendencies were already notorious and the fact that, as he put it, 'at least several others in the State Department are working with him in trying to evolve a policy along these lines.' But the policy – as Kennan himself knew and admitted* – was virtually a *volte-face*. 'Kennan's suggestions,' Smith pointed out to A.D.P. Heeney,

would involve giving up the main military deterrent to aggression which the United States now holds. ... Kennan did make clear that he does not attach very

---

* 'It may be adduced, with regard to the above discussion,' Kennan had written at the conclusion of his paper,

> that it charts out a course replete with a whole series of difficulties and obstacles and that there is little likelihood ... that we would ever successfully make our way to the end of it. ... This is a respectable argument...

Ibid., 43.

great importance to military deterrents; he said "Everyone seems to think the Russians want to jump Western Europe. I'm certain they do not: not at the present stage. They have a long-term programme for the world. The present stage is consolidation and economic development; this will take years." Kennan, in many conversations with me over the past few years, has stressed this, and made it clear that he considers the cold war much more important than any danger of a shooting war. It will be recalled that for some time he opposed, as unnecessary, the idea of having a North Atlantic Pact.* ... On the other hand he has been a firm advocate of the political and strategic possibilities of rolling back the Soviet grip by economic and political measures.

Arnold Smith concluded his report of Kennan's proposals by passing on to Ottawa the opinion of their author that negotiations along their lines 'might be desirable within the next six to twelve months...'[187]

Within Canada's policy community – the only one outside the United States where Kennan's comments circulated – these ideas drew sharp reaction – almost all of it unfavourable.

The response of the Under Secretary of State for External Affairs (to whom Arnold Smith had first reported his conversation with Kennan) was one of gratification that an American official, however removed from the mainstream of policy, had deigned to discuss such arcane mysteries with a Canadian counterpart. 'It looks rather as if ... the United States might be preparing to retire suddenly from our joint defence of the majority plan,' A.D.P. Heeney observed, 'after encouraging the rest of us to fight to the last man, and I am glad to see that this time they are taking us into their confidence at an early stage in the preparation of what may be their new position.' On the substance of Kennan's proposals, Heeney made no comment. 'Although we may have our doubts as to how a new position should be formulated,' the Under Secretary observed noncommitally, 'I think it is ... desirable that the whole subject should be re-examined and that we should give very thorough consideration to any and all proposals for a compromise solution of any kind that would guarantee us an acceptable degree of national security in the Western democracies. We must surely recognize that no plan can ever give us complete security,' Heeney added, 'but a compromise might give us relatively more than we shall otherwise have in a few years.'[188]

Other members of the policy community, however, did not accord to George Kennan's proposals even this qualified measure of approval. Three responses to them may be described as hostile.

The Defence Liaison Division of the Department of External Affairs, closer than any other to the Department of National Defence, was un-

---

* See above, Ch. 2, 79-82.

likely to be sympathetic to proposals for radical change in arms control; nor was it. Kennan's proposals, James George wrote of them, bristled with difficulties. It was unrealistic to expect the Russians to forego the benefits of developing nuclear power for industrial, as distinct from military, purposes. 'To give up power development would be a much greater sacrifice for the Soviet Union, and to a lesser extent for the United Kingdom, than for the United States and Canada...' The degree of inspection which the proposals envisaged would not offer reasonable assurance that the Soviet Union was not embarked clandestinely on more than small-scale production. The suggestion to sequester existing stockpiles of nuclear weapons under international control was one of those solutions to problems such that, were the conditions for their implementation to exist, the solutions would be unnecessary.

I do not see how the Russians could agree to any kind of international inspection or control within their territories unless the United States were not only to declare that it would not use atomic weapons but was prepared to place them under United Nations escrow at a point where they could not readily be seized. Of course, there are all kinds of difficulties that immediately come to mind. Neither the United States nor the Soviet Union could be sure that the other had in fact turned over its entire stockpile to the United Nations guards...

Finally, James George did not share Kennan's sense of urgency about the need for winding down the atomic arms race, which he described as 'being exaggerated in the press. Although both sides are making a very considerable effort, particularly in order to stockpile nuclear fuels, the total expenditure for defence on both sides is not, relatively, out of keeping with their respective national income, considering the vulnerability of modern states to attack across intercontinental distances.'[189]

Another member of the Department of External Affairs to weigh in against Kennan's proposals was George Ignatieff, at that time alternate representative to the UN Atomic Energy Commission. Ignatieff shared the doubt of his colleague within the Defence Liaison Division that the Soviet Union would to forego the advantages of the peaceful application of nuclear power. Nor did he believe that the prospects for peace would be enhanced by the elimination of nuclear weapons from the arsenals of both sides, even if that were possible.

The best way to avoid the use of the atomic bomb by Russia is to prevent a general war from starting. Although it must be assumed that the Soviet Government, consistent with the Marxist theory, believes that a final collision with the Western world is inevitable, it is unlikely to attack unless it believes that its chances of victory are very good. Therefore, any action which the Western powers may take to diminish the chances of Soviet victory also diminish the chances of war. Although the strengthening of the Western world through collective action in the political and economic field is quite as important as in the military, among the important military factors, the strategic use of the atomic weapon is an essential element at the present time.[190]

The most severe critic was the President of the National Research Council, then the policy community's leading authority on atomic energy matters. C.J. Mackenzie considered Kennan's proposals wholly unrealistic – not only unacceptable to the Soviet Union but also unacceptable to the United States. 'I think Mr Kennan would have very great difficulty,' Mackenzie wrote, 'in persuading the atomic energy and military authorities in the United States to give up the large-scale production of fissile material. ... This, of course, means in fact a rather complete stoppage of all atomic energy research and development and, apart from the strictly military aspects, I doubt if anyone would agree to stop dead in its tracks a great technological development. Personally,' Mackenzie added, 'I do not think anyone is wise enough nor sufficiently far-seeing to properly appraise the possible benefits to mankind against the obvious disagreeableness of atomic bombs.' Mackenzie shared James George's view that to place atomic bombs in escrow would be impossible. 'I cannot see where the stocks could be sequestered without being in reality under the control of one of the major powers. Certainly the United States would not permit their stock to be stored in Europe, in Russia, or in any place vulnerable to seizure by the Russians and I am quite sure that if the suggestion is to store them in America the Russians would not feel that in any emergency any conceivable United Nations force could be capable of preventing the Americans from taking over.' Mackenzie expressed strong scepticism about the capacity of international law to constrain governments in the use of nuclear or indeed of any types of weapons.

From the personal standpoint the suggestion of an international convention to outlaw atomic weapons always leaves me cold as I do not believe that in a final war for survival between East and West any conventions that would interfere with the effectiveness of military victory would be respected. The Germans did not observe the convention about gas warfare in 1915 and neither Great Britain nor Germany would, I believe, have done so in the past war had there been an overwhelming advantage to be obtained from the use of gas. While all the countries without atomic bombs might be very pleased to outlaw atomic bombs, I cannot see the United States military authorities accepting any such limitation at the present time. The suggestion ... for the renunciation of the use of atomic weapons for the purpose of aggression is again to me meaningless as in modern wars no nation is ever an aggressor in its own eyes and thus would not be bound by any such agreement. If we are to have conventions at all why not go the whole limit and outlaw war itself?...[191]

Presumably, all these criticisms of Kennan's proposals were being made within the American own policy community as well as the Canadian. On 11 January 1950, the Ambassador at Washington reported that 'it appears that Mr Kennan's ideas have not won support in the Administration.'[192] Indeed they had not. On 31 January the President of the United States released the following statement:

It is part of my responsibility as Commander in Chief of the Armed Forces to see to it that our country is able to defend itself against any possible aggressor. Accordingly, I have directed the Atomic Energy Commission to continue its work on all forms of atomic weapons, including the so-called hydrogen or super-bomb...[193]

When George Kennan heard this announcement, he wrote in his memoirs, 'I knew that my labor had been, once again, in vain.'[194]

L.B. Pearson was not as resolutely sceptical as his advisers about the prospects of reaching some useful agreement between the United States and the Soviet Union on the international control of atomic energy. On 3 April 1950, Pearson, joined by Hume Wrong and R.G. Riddell, Permanent Representative to the United Nations, conferred in Washington on the subject with three senior officials of the US State Department. According to the latter's record of the meeting,

Pearson spoke of the question of the advantages of a general prohibition on the use of atomic bombs as against the importance of the bomb as a deterrent. He felt that with the development of Russian atomic power we should have a new look at this proposition. He said that their people in re-evaluating the evidence wondered whether it was true the Russians really had the atomic bomb. Mr [Dean] Rusk pointed out that it would be quite inadvisable to proceed on the assumption that they did not.[195]

Pearson also spoke at some length of the need to pursue negotiations with the Soviet Union for the favourable propaganda that a seemingly zealous commitment to arms control would generate for the West. 'The general Canadian attitude seemed to be that it would be desirable to keep on talking even though there were no great expectation of concrete results in the form of agreement,' the U.S. State Department noted. 'Pearson seemed to feel that from a public relations point of view we should frequently propose or initiate conversations and let the Russians have the onus of turning them down.' It was for this reason that he felt it wise to resume talks with the Russians on atomic energy. 'He said that there had never really been an exploration of the points which Vishinksy raised last fall.* He was not sanguine that the Russians had anything in mind, but he seemed to be reflecting Canadian Parliamentary and popular opinion in suggesting the desirability that we should not only take a fresh look at our own proposals ... but that we should also find ways to continue talks with the Russians. ... It was my opinion' – so Philip Jessup of the US Department of State summed up the visitors' view – 'that the Canadians would like to resume more formal conversations with the Russians, again largely from the point of view of public relations.'[196]

The Secretary of State for External Affairs again stressed the importance of at least keeping up the appearance of an interest in negotiating with the Soviet Union on the control of atomic energy, during a discussion in London some six weeks later at which the British Prime Minister and Foreign Secretary, the American Secretary of State, and some senior Foreign Office officials were present. According to the report of this meeting prepared by Dean Acheson, L.B. Pearson

raised the question of proceeding informally with the talks among the sponsoring powers in the United Nations on atomic energy. He suggested this, he said, not with any idea that any substantive progress would be made, but because the so-called Vishinsky proposals of last fall were being used by Communist propaganda to make it appear that the Russians were willing to move toward international control, and that the Western powers were blocking it...[197]

In the academic literature on techniques of negotiation, the approach which Pearson here commended is termed 'bargaining for side-effects,' where the desired side-effect is to create a good impression; in more general parlance it is known as bargaining in bad faith.

The problems which have been discussed above received at the time little attention from the public. Lack of popular concern with them was due in part to the secrecy in which officials then felt it desirable to discuss and devise atomic strategic and atomic weapons. But it was also due to the public mood. Canadians were not only not permitted to know; Canadians did not want to know.

Thinking about the unthinkable is hard enough at the worst of times: the years 1949 to 1955 were, for most Canadians, the best of times. Their attention focused not on the prospects for apocalypse but on the prospects

---

* Andrei Vishinsky, the Soviet foreign minister, had introduced a resolution at the Fourth Session of the UN General Assembly in September 1949 which proposed the unconditional abolition of nuclear weapons and appropriate international control; the simplicity and boldness of this proposal had attracted world attention. Pearson described Vishinsky in his memoirs as 'the most gifted, energetic, articulate, and unscrupulous of the communist polemicists at the UN.' *Mike* II, 122.

for prosperity. These, so a Royal Commission on Canada's Economic Prospects duly found, were excellent; it presented its findings on the assumption 'that a global war will be avoided. Such an assumption,' its authors affirmed – their affirmation reflecting faithfully popular complacency – 'would seem to be obligatory for anyone with faith in the human species. In any case,' they added in extenuation of their stance, 'it seemed to us pointless to consider what Canada's economic prospects would be in a world laid waste by radioactive dust.'[198] Caught up in a wave of good fortune, bewitched by forecasts of a future more glittering still, the citizens of Canada in the middle of the century which Sir Wilfrid Laurier had predicted would belong to them had no desire to dwell on the idea that it could end with there being no one for it to belong to – save cockroaches and the hardy slimes.

5

Sharing the Burden

Give all thou canst; high Heaven rejects the lore
Of nicely calculated less or more.

William Wordsworth

HOW FAIR IS 'FAIR'?

As North Atlantic Treaty countries first began to mobilize, they faced a set of crucial questions. What were to be the rules by which the collective burden of rearmament was to be shared among them? How to define the criteria by which the costs of security should be borne among its benefi-ciaries? How to tell whether each of the dozen governments concerned was really pulling its weight? How to spot slackers and free riders? How to goad, scold, or shame these into doing their proper bit? Justice and com-mon sense required that the 'price of freedom' be fairly paid. Fair was only fair. But how to know how fair was 'fair'?

These questions assumed special importance for Canada. Alone of other North Atlantic Treaty members, Canada did not receive aid from the United States. Hence every NATO government but Canada's acquired a vested interest in raising projected force requirements to the highest possible levels. 'All the Atlantic countries except Canada,' the Minister of National Defence explained in Cabinet on 13 December 1950, 'were ex-pecting to get financial aid from the United States. For such countries, disregarding financial limitations was not unrealistic. There was, more-over, an incentive to put figures at a high level in order to get as much aid as possible.' This practice was made more pernicious by the United States government which, so far from looking askance at it, gave it every en-couragement so as 'to raise the sights of Congress when questions of assistance were under consideration.'[1] Brooke Claxton had himself 'heard

Americans urge representatives of European countries to agree to put in figures that were quite unrealistic in order to show Congress what a big contribution the European countries were making.'[2] Nor was that all. Canada, with the United States, was unlike other NATO members in Europe in that her contributions made for their defence 'would not be immediately available for direct national defence as well.'

For these reasons, Brooke Claxton told his Cabinet colleagues, 'Canada had special difficulties. An effort had been made to explain to other representatives individually the peculiar position of Canada, but,' he added, 'it was not entirely clear that it was understood or accepted.'[3]

If the government's frank exposition of 'the peculiar position of Canada' had failed to gain the understanding of other NATO delegations, its spokesmen were unlikely to satisfy those Canadians (mostly supporters of the Conservative Party) who felt that a greater defence effort was required by a necessarily more guarded argument. Herein lay their dilemma. To explain to the public in candour could be detrimental to the Alliance. To offer no explanation would be detrimental to the government. The only way out of the dilemma was to try to put Canada's contribution in the most favourable light. Thus the Minister of National Defence pointed out in a radio broadcast on 24 April 1950 that the government's proposed defence estimates for the coming year amounted to '$31.50 for each man, woman and child in Canada, nearly 18 per cent of the national budget and nearly 3 per cent of the national income' – in the hope that these figures would be more impressive than a defence budget of $425 million. 'At current rates of exchange,' Brooke Claxton told his audience, 'Canada is spending more on defence per capita than the other nations in the British Commonwealth except the United Kingdom, and more than the other nations in the North Atlantic Treaty Organization except the UK and the US.'[4] But this argument did not still criticism, either at home or abroad.

Foreign criticism wounded most. Within the Department of External Affairs, glum concern was expressed at the publication of articles in the *New York Times* and the London *Economist* comparing the defence expenditures of NATO countries in proportion to their national incomes – a method of comparison invidious to Canada. What could be done about it? One official thought not much. It would be unwise, he considered, for the government to 'make a great play of the fact that we are spending on defence 3.2% of our national income, instead of 2% as quoted in the press articles, as even 3.2% leaves us about eighth or ninth among the North Atlantic countries.' However, information officers abroad might be told to point out prudently to editors and journalists that 'comparisons based on data that are not prepared in a comparable manner are very misleading; that 'we make a much better showing on the basis of per capita defence expenditures'; and that 'our defence expenditures are 50% greater this year than last and 17 times greater than our normal pre-war defence budgets.'[5] But to publicize the proper explanation for the lag in Canada's performance – that other NATO members (except for the United States) did not pay for all they got – was thought to be unstatesmanlike.

On 26 June 1950 – the day after the outbreak of war in Korea – the Minister of National Defence again attempted to silence criticism that Canada was not doing all it should be doing in defence of the Western alliance. Brooke Claxton posed the question squarely: 'Is the amount of $425 million that we are spending on defence enough to enable us to see that we carry our fair share of the load under the North Atlantic treaty?' The Minister's unsurprising answer was that 'It is the belief of this government that it is enough,' and he went on to state the reasons for its belief. Repeating the comparisons he had made in his earlier broadcast – comparisons based on expenditure *per capita* – Claxton continued:

On other bases of comparison, it is more than a good many other of the countries concerned are spending, either as a proportion of national product or as a percentage of national budget, although some of the countries of Europe are spending more. But when we include with the $425 million some of the other items that might properly be allocated to defence under the accounting systems in force ... in ... other countries – such as, for example, married quarters built for defence by Central Mortgage and Housing Corporation; some part of the cost of civil aviation and navigational aids; some part of the cost of the RCMP ... the figure can be built up to something over $500 million...[6]

Half a century earlier, Sir Wilfrid Laurier and his colleagues, asked by British ministers what Canada was doing to help defend the Empire, had responded by citing recent improvements on the Canadian Pacific Railway: Brooke Claxton's argument was much the same – and just as unconvincing. For by such semantics of accountancy every dollar spent by government could be presented as outlay upon the national defence.

The Minister continued to try to allay criticism that Canada was not pulling her weight in NATO. 'The defence appropriation this year will be $1600 million,' Brooke Claxton told a meeting of the National Liberal Federation on 26 February 1951. 'This will be more proportionately, either on a per capita basis, or as a percentage of national income, or as a percentage of the national budget, than any other country in the North Atlantic Treaty Organization except the United States. From the financial point of view, on any basis of comparison, we shall be doing more than The Netherlands, Italy, Belgium, Denmark, Norway, Portugal, France and the United Kingdom; and our defence bill this year is ten times what it is in Australia.' By any fair comparison, Claxton insisted, Canada was pulling her weight. But he made plain his feeling that all comparison was odious and fair comparison impossible. 'These comparisons that appear in the newspapers are dreadfully misleading. We do not like making comparisons because you cannot make a fair one. But if people go on making comparisons that misrepresent the position in Canada, I will make then so as to represent Canada's position in the most favourable light.' And again: 'I must say that I deprecate such comparisons if for no other reason than that it is almost impossible to make them on a fair basis; and almost certainly such comparisons will result in pressure and recrimination as between nations which should be working closely together.'[7]

'The peculiar position of Canada' had a geopolitical dimension. The country lay squarely across the northern approaches that would be used by bombers of the Soviet Union in an attack upon the United States. No other NATO member could claim that unenviable distinction. This aspect of the peculiar position of Canada also affected how Canada's share of NATO's burden ought fairly to be assessed.

If a government is guided by *realpolitik* alone, Canada's could have relied upon the United States to bear by itself the entire burden of defending their common continent, secure in the knowledge that the Americans, in their own self-interest, could hardly do otherwise.* But human feelings intruded upon so ruthless a calculation – not least those of pride and self-respect. It was clear at the outset that Canada would share to some degree the costs of defending North America. It was also clear that this commitment was bound to affect the degree to which she would share the costs of defending Western Europe.

In the beginning, the connection between the two commitments was considered by some Canadian officials to be a topic unsuitable for discussion – at least with West Europeans, for it might unsettle their morale. One Canadian alerted to their alarm was the Chief of the General Staff. General Charles Foulkes reported to his Minister in May 1948 that on a recent visit to Western Europe he had been repeatedly questioned by his counterparts 'regarding Canadian preparations and expenditures in the Canadian North. ... It was with some difficulty,' Foulkes admitted to Brooke Claxton,

---

* 'Sometimes a nation may have a geo-political position (e.g., behind an alliance member serving as a buffer state) such that it would be usually difficult, if not impossible, to deny it the benefits of alliance protection.' Mancur J. Olson, Jr and Richard Zeckhauser, 'An Economic Theory of Alliances,' *Review of Economics and Statistics*, XLVIII, 1966, 273.

that I was able to convince various Defence leaders that no extensive expenditures are being made solely for the protection of North America. There is every indication that large expenditures in the Canadian Arctic would be misunderstood by the Benelux countries, who still suspect that the United States and Canada may be more concerned with their own territorial defence than with really fighting the war where it may occur. ... It is my opinion that ... no expenditures or preparation should be made in the Canadian Arctic which cannot also be used for the offensive in the early stages of any war.

I also feel that there should be no publicity about developments in the Arctic, as this would lead to a confirmation of the views held in Europe that Canada and the United States still share an isolationist view...[8]

The Canadian government had since 1946 successfully resisted United States pressure – on occasion, very strong pressure – to join with the US Air Force in implementing its plans for defending North America – plans which included basing US fighter-interceptors as far north in Canada as feasible.* During the early 1950's American pressure was revived – this time to secure Canadian agreement to, and help in, construction of the Distant Early Warning system designed to give the bombers of the Strategic Air Command sufficient time to mount its mission of retaliation – and so enabling it to perform its function of deterrence. On 30 March 1953, the Chairman of the Chiefs of Staff Committee informed the inter-departmental committee created to consider how much and what kind of Mutual Aid equipment should be offered to NATO that 'Canada is receiving a series of demands for the defence of the North American continent, and within the last month Canada has been advised of US plans to develop an early warning radar chain in the Far North.' The United States authorities were making 'extraordinary efforts,' General Foulkes reported, to install test stations by the end of the year and, the tests proving successful, planned to proceed with 'a project that may run to three or four hundred millions of dollars for installations, most of which will be in Canadian territory. This poses a very difficult problem for Canada,' Foulkes observed. 'There is a feeling here that this is only the beginning of a large number of requests for operational facilities which may run into untold millions.' But one conclusion was already clear: 'Until the Service Chiefs ... know or have some intimation of the size and nature of these requests, it will be inadvisable for Canada to undertake any additional military obligations.'[9]

By the end of 1953, Canada and the United States had begun work on the radar warning systems – the Mid-Canada line across the 55th parallel,

* See *In Defence of Canada* III, 336-44.

which Canadian scientists made possible and Canadian tax-payers would finance; the 'seawing' extensions of that line, which the United States would provide and pay for; and the enormously costly Distant Early Warning line across the High Arctic at the 70th parallel, for which the United States would also pay. By then, too, the impact of this activity was beginning to impinge upon Canadian defence spending.

Not only had it become impossible to conceal these preparations for continental defence from the two North American countries' West European allies, it was no longer from Canada's standpoint advisable to do so. The trick was to convince the West European governments that the defence of North America was as much in their interest as the defence of Western Europe was in the interest of Canada and the United States. Most of a statement made by the Permanent Representative to a meeting of the NATO Secretariat on 24 September 1953 had such conviction as its purpose. He had thought it well, L.D. Wilgress explained to Ottawa, 'to call attention to the emerging problems and requirements of North American defence. We felt that the Europeans were likely to overlook these requirements. Moreover,' Wilgress added, 'it is the requirements of North American defence which supply one of the basic reasons why Canada cannot accept SACEUR's main recommendation, i.e., that Canada should supply all-weather fighters to Europe either as a Canadian wing or as mutual aid.'[10] The CF-100s were needed in North America. They would best serve NATO there. 'You will, I am sure, appreciate that when Canada decided on her programme two years ago,' the Permanent Representative told members of the Secretariat, 'a choice had to be made.'

This choice lay between European defence and North American defence.* There were those who felt that the Government's primary responsibility lay in building up North American defence. There were even those who whispered that, with Russia so far ahead of us, Europe was indefensible. Nevertheless, the Canadian

---

* The Minister of National Defence, examining this statement after it was made, emphatically disagreed with it. 'No such choice was made,' Brooke Claxton pointed out to L.B. Pearson on 16 October,

> and it would be most unfortunate if the impression went out that such a choice had even been considered. As you know, the defence of Canada here has always been stated as one of the objectives of our defence programme. Long before NATO came into existence we had started to create the kinds of forces and equipment best suited to defend Canada. ... For the Air Force ... we obviously required a long-range all-weather fighter to back up radar defences. To bring these into existence has taken a considerable time but we have been pressing ahead with them just as fast as we could. It is only now that the construction of the necessary radar stations and communications services and the production of the CF-100 are beginning to make a positive contribution to continental defence.

DEA files, 50107-C-40.

Government decided to direct virtually the whole of the Canadian buildup of forces and production towards European defence, including, of course, the defence of the sea-lanes between Europe and North America.

Now, however, Canada's share of the agreed programme for European defence is nearing completion. It is, therefore, natural and inevitable that the Canadian Government should devote increasing attention to doing what has been left to a large extent undone during the past two years. This explains why, in 1953, unlike 1952, we have included in our replies to the Annual Review Questionnaire,* data relating to our forces designed for North American defence. Had we not done so, our NATO partners would not have before them the full picture of our defence buildup...

Our programme for North American defence ... consists of two main parts. In the first place, we must provide a small and highly mobile striking force in Canada. In the second place, we must develop North American air defence and this includes both the provision of certain air forces, composed primarily of all weather fighters, and also the installation and manning of Canada's share of a comprehensive radar screen. Both parts of this programme are essential and of increasing urgency as the long-range striking power of our potential enemies increases. The Canadian public would not understand if its government chose at this stage to neglect either part of the programme. Indeed, in the recent election campaign, many voices were raised in criticism of the Government which was alleged to be defending Europe while leaving Canada's defences virtually bare.

There is a further point that I would like to make regarding North American defence. This programme must naturally be undertaken in the closest collaboration with the United States, whose plans, naturally and properly, are far more extensive and expensive than our own. In the course of this collaboration, the Canadian Government has agreed to the installation of US equipment in Canada and the stationing of US personnel there. The Canadian public certainly would not understand if their Government continued to place forces and equipment at the disposal of SACEUR and SACLANT while allowing US personnel and equipment to occupy an undue share of the radar screen in Canada. It is essential that we should contribute our fair share along with the United States to North American defence...

Wilgress concluded his statement to the NATO Secretariat by affirming his government's continuing commitment to the defence of Western Europe 'which we regard as the main bulwark of the North Atlantic Community.'[11]

Even as a first attempt to tell Canada's NATO allies why they should regard her expenditure for the defence of North America as a contribution to their own defence, this argument is barely passable. While alluding to the unpalatable political consequences at home of continuing to put commitments to the defence of Western Europe ahead of commitments

---

*   See below, 301-18.

to the defence of North America, Dana Wilgress failed to demonstrate that the two commitments were strategically interconnected. Perhaps he with those who helped him with the statement felt that it would be labouring the obvious to make the point emphatically; or perhaps they did not see the point themselves.

That the relationship of North American to Western European defences had not been thoroughly thought through could be inferred from L.B. Pearson's statement at the NATO Ministerial Council meeting in December 1953. 'Mr. Pearson turned the discussion of atomic weapons towards their possible use by the Soviets against North America,' the Permanent Representative reported to Ottawa. 'Continental defences were now being developed by Canada and the United States and these defences should be recognized as a part of the general NATO defences because Europe could not fight very long with the industrial power of North America knocked out.'[12] That was indubitably true, but the sort of truth which holds that there is no life if everything is dead: Canadian strategists, it seems, were still at primary school. Not until 1955 were they to hit the nail on the head in a statement provided to the Permanent Representative for delivery to the North Atlantic Council on 9 March. 'The development by the Soviet Union of the hydrogen bomb together with their improved capacity to deliver it,' Dana Wilgress at last declared,

has made indispensable to the strength of the North Atlantic Community the provision of additional early warning systems on the North American continent, not only for the protection of a firm base for the support of operations in the defence of Europe, but also to defend the retaliatory capacity of North America itself. Canada, together with the United States, has undertaken the construction of two additional early warning systems across Canada. Canada's share involves substantial capital outlays over the next few years, together with continuing costs which at the moment are of an unpredictable order of magnitude...

Bearing in mind the foregoing considerations, the appropriation for Mutual Aid for the fiscal year 1955-56 which the Canadian Government will propose to Parliament amounts to $175 million...[13]

(Three years earlier, it had appropriated $324 million.) An even clearer statement was contained in the memorandum which accompanied the Canadian reply to the Annual Review Questionnaire for 1955: 'The defence of the retaliatory capacity of the United States Strategic Air Force, which is a matter of primary importance to all NATO countries, will require Canada to undertake much more extensive measures for early warning and interception in North America, involving a larger proportion of our defence facilities than heretofore for this purpose.'[14]

The highest mark for correctly setting out the relationship between the defence of North America and the defence of Western Europe is earned by L.B. Pearson. Pearson's exposition occurred not at any NATO meeting but in *tête-à-tête* with the US Secretary of State during December 1954. Pearson had taken advantage of the discussion to explain to John Foster Dulles what he described in his diary as

> some new problems that had arisen for Canada in respect of the NATO collective defence effort; problems which arose, as we had pointed out in a statement to the Council, over the increasing importance attached to northern defence, particularly through the setting up of early warning systems. We were anxious to emphasize that this was an important part of NATO defence, because without such effective early warning arrangements the retaliatory power of the United States might be destroyed and, in present circumstances, this would be as fatal for Europe as for America. Canada was anxious to play a full part in these northern defence developments, especially in respect of those which were on Canadian territory. This might result eventually in reducing somewhat our air defence contribution in Europe and the transfer of some of our squadrons back to Canada to back up the early warning systems...[15]

To establish once and for all that what Canada was contributing to North American defence was part and parcel of the defence of the Treaty area in general and of Western Europe in particular, L.B. Pearson took up with enthusiasm the idea of deploying Western European armed forces in the defence of the Canadian Arctic. 'I believed that the North American sector should be considered an integral part of the North Atlantic defence structure,' Pearson would write later. 'It seemed to me, for example, that Norwegian contingents should operate in our Arctic just as Canadian forces occasionally took part in exercises in Norway. Canada's contribution to Arctic defence, therefore, should be accepted on the same basis as her contribution to overseas defence.' But it could not be done. 'The Americans would have none of this concept which, they thought, would interfere with their own control. Our own service people also, I suspect, preferred bilateral dealings and arrangements with Washington. Canadians had become accustomed to serving overseas in Europe; the idea that even token European contingents might share the responsibility of our continental defence was a novelty unworthy of serious consideration.'[16] A good idea, but one whose time would never come.

THE BURDEN OF SHARING

Even before war in Korea caused North Atlantic Treaty countries to mobilize in earnest, they had come to the conclusion – stated in the communiqué put out at the end of the fourth session of the North Atlantic Council in May 1950 – that 'the problem of adequate military forces and necessary financial costs' should 'be examined as one and not as separate problems.' If it was a truism that they should be so examined, it was also of the utmost importance – and fraught with difficulties both practical and theoretical.*

In October 1950 the Council Deputies authorized the creation of an Economic and Financial Group. The Group's members were to be recruited from NATO countries' delegations to the Organization for European Economic Co-operation (to which all of them belonged). 'This new working group,' NATO spokesmen announced to the press,

> will enquire how statistical information provided to the OEEC by NATO countries may be adapted so as to serve the purposes of NATO. This working group will recommend what additional information should be furnished by NATO countries in order to assess the impact of their defence efforts on their economies, and also their respective abilities to carry the burden of expanded defence requirements...[17]

Here was the origin of that process of collective scrutiny of the defence programmes of individual NATO members that would come to be called 'performance assessment' and to be institutionalized as the 'Annual Review.'

To this project Ottawa was hostile from its inception and remained so, its initial doubt that an annual review was necessary becoming reinforced by concern lest decision-making shift in the process to Paris. The first of many memoranda on sharing the burden – the government came to regard it as the burden of sharing – emanated within the department made most agitated by the concept – the Department of Finance. 'Our views on the whole question of attempting to arrive at an equitable distribution of economic burdens in carrying out the medium term defence plan,' wrote an officer of that Department, John Deutsch, on 31 October 1950, are

> that decisions in this field are basically political and must in the final analysis be taken by participating governments. It is accordingly essential, in any plans for preparatory and statistical work, that the essentially expert nature of this work, as distinct from policy formulation, be clearly retained. ... A strictly objective approach to this project must be made if results of any value are to be obtained.

---

* This section discusses the practical difficulties only; the theoretical difficulties have given rise to a considerable literature. See Edward S. Mason, 'The Equitable Sharing of Military and Economic Aid Burdens,' *Proceedings of the Academy of Political Science,* XXVII, May 1963, 256-64; John A. Pincus, *Sharing the Costs of Military Alliance and International Economic Aid* (RAND Corporation paper RM-3249-ISA, Santa Monica 1962); and Mancur Olson, Jr and Richard Zeckhauser, 'An Economic Theory of Alliances,' *Review of Economics and Statistics,* XLVIII, 1966, 266-79.

No attempt should be made for instance by the group itself to solve any problems of a policy nature...[18]

The Department of External Affairs, also, was sceptical about the value of the exercise; its scepticism grew after its officials perused two papers on burden-sharing prepared within the British and American governments.

The British paper – suspected in Ottawa of being largely the work of the Labour Government's Chancellor of the Exchequer, Hugh Gaitskell – was dismissed almost derisively. 'It puts forward principles which may be summed up in such texts as (a) from each according to his ability, to each according to his need; or (b) bear ye one another's burden; or (c) share the wealth.' These were defensible imperatives, the Department's commentator observed in furnishing guidance for the Council Deputy to help him formulate desirable tasks for the new Economic and Financial Working Group, and are regarded by 'millions of people ... as the highest and noblest ideals.' But

we are not aware that any NATO government has a mandate from its electorate to put them into full force either on a national or – far more difficult – on an international basis. This is certainly true of the Canadian government.

Each NATO government can go along the path of burden-sharing at a certain pace, depending on its present mandate and its willingness to seek a further mandate in the future. An attempt to force the pace of the slower governments is likely to make them stall. Further, an attempt to get agreement on ultimately international philosophies, between governments whose domestic philosophies differ widely, will surely produce little but disharmony and disunity. We would urge that the United Kingdom should not divert our eye to the distant scene; one step at a time along the path of burden-sharing will be enough. Let us keep our feet on the ground.

The American paper envisaged an intensive investigation of the 'sources and use of each country's economic resources.' Ottawa disliked this approach on every count. Such an investigation would not only be a 'staggering' task, it would expose previously hidden processes of policy formation to the eyes of other governments, and expose who knew what else. It would be idle to pretend that the kind of study proposed in the American paper could be 'value-free;' it was bound to be value-freighted. 'The study would entail the consideration of the relative priorities to be assigned to various items in national budgets, the structure of taxation and the objectives of national policy. It is unrealistic to think that fundamental political matters of this kind can be evaluated or decided by dispassionate statistical processes...[19]

In the general scepticism that greeted these proposals for burden-sharing, some officials were more sceptical than others. 'Finance is pretty rigid on the issue,' commented a member of the Department of External Affairs. In that rigidity, the officers at Finance partook of the attitude of their Minister. Douglas Abbott made decisions – so one of his colleagues has commented – 'without always seeming to reflect with becoming gravity on the pros and cons,'* and on this issue Abbott came down quick and hard on the cons. 'Mr Abbott says he will not go one step beyond the instructions sent to Mr Wilgress,' an official reported to the Under Secretary of State for External Affairs.

He is quite ready for us to participate in economic exercises up to the limit laid down in those instructions but beyond that limit he will not go. He does not wish Canadian representatives either to supply economic data about Canada or to participate in the preparation of general material going beyond this limit.

...Mr Abbott feels very strongly on these points. He emphasized that he regarded the decisions to be made as largely political. The extended economic analysis is "nonsense." If Canada participated in it we would be misleading other countries into believing that we were going to base our decisions on it. Hence "We won't participate in any way"...

Informed that the Department of External Affairs held somewhat different views, Abbott retorted that 'he would be glad to discuss the matter with our Minister, or, in his absence, with the Prime Minister.'[20]

There was more to this disagreement than ordinary departmental feuding or the occupational bias – one of wary frugality – in whomsoever might hold the Finance portfolio. Chickens were coming home to roost: the government was now experiencing the consequences of the failure of senior officials of the Department of External Affairs to keep key cabinet ministers sufficiently informed during 1948 and early 1949 of the negotiation of the North Atlantic Treaty.† Its Article 2 – 'the Canadian Article' – while not pledging the signatories to share the burden of defence could be invoked in support of burden sharing (and on at least one occasion was invoked for such a purpose).** For that reason the main opponent of 'the Canadian Article' turned out to be a Canadian minister – not Dean Acheson, US Secretary of State, but Douglas Abbott, Minister of Finance.

---

*   J.W. Pickersgill, *My Years with Louis St Laurent: A Political Memoir* (Toronto 1975), 216. See *In Defence of Canada* III, 18-19.
† See above, Ch. 3, 177.
** In 1955, when Italy placed on the agenda of the North Atlantic Council an item for the consideration of ways and means of implementing Article 2. 'They wish, no doubt, to emphasize the burden-sharing aspects,' the Permanent Representative commented disparagingly, 'and in this manner make Article 2 an additional instrument for burden-sharing...' L.D. Wilgress to Department of External Affairs, 21 November 1955 (telegram), DEA files, 50105-E-40.

Abbott's refusal to participate in an exercise strongly favoured by both the British and American governments – and probably by Western European members – created some stir within the Department of External Affairs. 'Canadian views ... happen to diverge from those that are uppermost in other countries,' one External Affairs official noted anxiously. 'Indeed, we find ourselves in a position of splendid isolation.' That, for Canada, was never a comfortable position. 'What other countries will really believe that we are taking our stand purely on the merits of an academic issue? Surely all of them will really believe that we are simply trying to shirk our responsibilities.' A restrictive participation in the statistical exercise, which was the most that Abbott appeared ready to countenance, 'would be impossibly embarrassing for the Canadian participants. They would be contributing Canada's data in the form of half bricks, not whole bricks, and even though the half bricks could be used in the structure they would be a continual and aggravating reminder of Canada's peculiar position. ... We must not put our representatives abroad in such a position.'[21]

The pros and cons of Canadian participation were set out in a paper prepared within the Department of External Affairs for the Economic Defence Panel (the inter-departmental group created to recommend policy on economic aspects of defence). Partial involvement in the proposed study was rejected outright. It should be all or nothing at all. There was a respectable case for staying out. Pressure for an extensive investigation, the paper noted pointedly, came from United States officials, who had special reasons for applying it.

They wish to have massive economic paraphernalia in order to support MDAA [US Mutual Defense Assistance Act] appropriations in Congress. In short, they wish to get, for MDAA purposes, the same sort of comprehensive material that they have collected in the past in Paris through OEEC for ECA [US Economic Cooperation Administration] appropriations. The purpose of the material is, at least supposedly, two-fold: first, to secure as large a pie as possible and, second, to serve as a guide in slicing it...

There was no reason for Canada's involving herself in any of this, good reason for her not to.

In the past Canada has been scrupulously careful to avoid being a beneficiary under lend-lease, ECA or MDAA. Canada has taken all sorts of special precautions to avoid dependence on USA and to avoid getting into the same boat as the UK and European countries. Similarly, when Canada has given aid to overseas countries it has been done independently in a pattern of our own, and not merely as a minor adjunct of US aid. If we go in for the fully-fledged US exercise in burden-sharing we are exposing ourselves to two dangers: We may be pushed around by the US as if we were receiving US aid and, at the same time, we may be expected by other countries to put in our Canadian two cents' worth just as a slight premium on top of the American dollar.

These were persuasive arguments. But the case for Canadian participation was perhaps a shade stronger. 'Some very undesirable results might flow from our decision to stand apart,' the authors of the paper commented.

We would appear to flout the principles of "pooling resources" or "sharing the burden" on which France and the United Kingdom have laid such stress and to which we can, at least in a limited degree, subscribe. Moreover, if the Atlantic Pact is going to work at all, it will only work if individual countries are willing to accept majority decisions. Thus we are in danger of doing serious damage to the whole fabric of North Atlantic unity, a fabric which Canada has done so much to build and strengthen. And finally, and most invidiously, our motives would never be understood; we would always be suspected of willingness to play the game only as long as it did not cost too much, or of unwillingness to allow our partners even to look at the rich resources that we might be devoting to the common cause. Thus we would lose the respect and confidence of other countries and, in a measure, lose our place of influence and prestige among them.[22]

These arguments were considered by the Economic Defence Panel on 14 November 1950. A.D.P. Heeney made the case for full Canadian participation. 'I received fairly general support,' he reported afterwards to L.B. Pearson, 'particularly from Foulkes [Chairman, Chiefs of Staff Committee], and Drury [Deputy Minister of National Defence], and I think Robertson [Clerk of the Privy Council and Secretary to the Cabinet]. Mackenzie [President, National Research Council] was non-committal although worried about the embarrassment ... involved in abstaining. ... I am very disturbed indeed,' Heeney told his Minister,

by the proposal that we should in any way dissociate ourselves from any burden-sharing exercise, even though we may doubt its usefulness and fear possible embarrassments. Indeed, I can well understand the strong desire of both the United States and the European members to go ahead with some sort of study, though I am prepared to agree with Dr Clark [Deputy Minister of Finance] that this particular basis for a study seems ill-conceived. Having stated our case at various levels in NATO, however, I cannot see that the possible political advantages of staying out are in any way comparable to the certain disadvantages of doing so. We find it difficult to fathom what fears are preoccupying the Department of Finance and exactly what they think might embarrass the Canadian Government. ... Personally, I am confident that we can prove to the satisfaction of our partners that we are pulling our weight. Our post-Korean level of defence expenditures, including our mutual aid programme, will bear comparison on any statistical basis with the efforts of other North Atlantic countries. Our calculations show that on the basis of percentages of national income, only those Atlantic countries having overseas dependencies are spending more on national and collective defence than we are.

Heeney added the suggestion that Pearson should put these points to the Prime Minister, noting that Abbott might have already tried to gain St Laurent's ear. The matter would have to be settled at the next meeting of the Cabinet.[23] Pearson responded that he was 'quite confident' of the outcome. Justifiably: on 22 November, the Cabinet approved Canadian participation in the burden-sharing study.

The message to the Council Deputy conveying this news, which must have been welcome, stressed that 'it should be kept in mind at all times that neither the Council of Deputies nor any participating government is necessarily bound by the results of the Paris study.' It instructed Dana Wilgress to say as much when announcing Canada's agreement to participate, and to repeat that *caveat* should need arise. He was further told not to expend too much energy: 'It is doubted whether the study will turn out to be very useful and therefore Canadian representatives participating in it should protect the Canadian position rather than taking any general initiative.[24] The Secretary of State for External Affairs felt it necessary to send to Wilgress a further message of explanation and advice. 'I feel sure,' L.B. Pearson cabled on 23 November 1950,

that you have explained fully ... the basis of our opposition. It is not that we have anything to hide, nor, indeed, that we are apologetic for what we have done or propose to do.

Information received during the last day or two from Washington indicates that the Americans themselves are becoming uneasy about these studies, which are apparently being referred to in some Washington circles as "Operation Mousetrap." The "Mousetrap," however, is strictly US manufacture, and it is surprising that they had not realized earlier that they might be the first victims. The fact that it is a share-the-burden operation for them, and a share-the-wealth operation for others, should have given them cause to worry.

However, this is all water over the dam and we must now do our best to make sure that the difficulties and dangers which we have always anticipated are reduced to a minimum. It is the feeling of the Government, which I share, that while we should participate honestly in the work, we should, nevertheless, not allow ourselves to become involved in needless investigations and useless research work which would take up the time of Canadian officials here, in England, and in France, who are already over-burdened...[25]

The Economic and Financial Working Group, with Canadian representatives participating, drew up a series of 'extensive and detailed' questionnaires dealing with such subjects as 'relative national and individual incomes, existing tax burdens, industrial capacity, and raw material resources.'[26] The questionnaires were sent to member governments, the responses of which were to form the basis of a report. Awaiting that report, the Council Deputy admitted to Ottawa that 'we have had to reply to a great extent in guesswork as to the nature, importance and end-use of [it]. ... Specifically, we do not know what influence the report can, or will, have, in any NATO burden-sharing discussions; nor do we know what use will be made of it in aid allocations.' Wilgress noted that the United States and the United Kingdom were intending to devote 'a great deal of personnel, time and effort to the report and are anticipating that each national submission will be carefully probed. ... The report would seem to have a very direct relevance to Article 2 of the Treaty,' Wilgress added, 'since it is likely to stand as the first and perhaps, for some time to come, as the most serious and comprehensive attempt at collecting data on the economic consequences of rearmament and the distribution of the burden.'[27]

By the time all twelve governments had responded to the questionnaires prepared by the Economic and Financial Working Group, the latter body had been disbanded and replaced by a new permanent NATO committee, the Financial and Economic Board, which held its meetings at Paris so as to be close to the expertise within the OEEC. The Canadian government's first reaction was to oppose the creation of this machinery – again, out of its concern lest an elaborate and permanent North Atlantic burden-sharing bureaucracy come to impinge upon its own decision-making. The Council Deputy was dismayed to be told to oppose formation of this Board. Not only would Dana Wilgress be a minority of one in opposition, but it seemed to him that Ottawa's instructions were inconsistent with its earlier policy. 'Having regard ... to our initial sponsorship of Article 2 of the Treaty,' Wilgress wrote to A.D.P. Heeney, '...you will understand how difficult it is for me to fathom the reasons for the instructions which have come to me from Ottawa. ... I am hoping that ... we will not be required to take a position which will have no support from the other members of NATO.'[28] Heeney, on second thought, agreed. 'I must say this letter does a good deal to dispel my concern re FEB,' he wrote. 'Provided it takes the place of all other agencies of NATO & provided its relations with the Deputies are correct ... provided in fact that the new regime represents a genuine simplification of machinery & saving of effort, and that the Council (& their Deputies) are in control I wd. accept the proposal.'[29]

The first task of the Financial and Economic Board was to assess the replies to the questionnaires and produce realistic recommendations. By September 1951 its interim report was ready. The contents have been described by NATO's first Secretary General.

This report cosidered the question of how to achieve the ''equitable'' sharing of
the defence burden between member countries. ... It stressed that no simple and
generally acceptable formula could be devised: the complex factors which determined each country's capacity to undertake defence could not be reduced to
mathematical terms.

On the vital question of assessing the desired increase in the total NATO defence
effort, the FEB pointed out that it was impossible to arrive at final conclusions in
the absence of close military guidance. ... Still more important was the fact that the
existing defence programmes of many countries were already causing considerable economic strain. The FEB urged that any final decision about the size of the
defence burdens should await a careful appraisal of the economic risks involved in
undertaking increases against the military risks of *not* doing so. That was a task
which the Board was neither empowered nor competent to perform.

For these conclusions – or non-conclusions – Lord Ismay awarded the
Board high marks – for effort only. Noting that the interim report had
been prepared within only a few months of its creation, Ismay wrote: 'It is
a tribute to them that they were able so quickly to bring these issues to a
head.'[30] The historian of the NATO International Staff/Secretariat is blun-
ter: 'Even this Board, with its international staff, and its high-ranking
membership coming directly under the Council Deputies, was unable to
master the problem.'[31]

That problem was the enormous discrepancy, which the work of the
Financial and Economic Board had helped to uncover, between what
member governments stated that they were able and therefore prepared
to offer for the defence of Western Europe, and what the Supreme Commander and his advisers insisted was the necessary minimum. The latter
greatly exceeded the former. Here was 'the Gap.'

A chance for governments to try to close the gap came at the next
meeting of the North Atlantic Council, in September 1951 at Ottawa.
Here the task of reconciling the fulfillment of 'a militarily acceptable
NATO plan for the defence of Western Europe and the realistic political-
economic capabilities of the member countries' was entrusted to a specially created committee – the Temporary Council Committee (TCC),
consisting of a minister (or ambassador) from each member country:
hence the 'Twelve Apostles.' An inner group – Averell Harriman of the
United States, Sir Edwin Plowden of the United Kingdom, and Jean
Monnet of France – became its Executive Bureau: hence the 'Three Wise
Men.'

The TCC took over from the defunct Financial and Economic Board its
device of interrogation by questionnaire, to which they added the device
of cross-examination. When submitting a questionnaire,

the TCC wanted to know about the numbers and reserve groups countries were proposing to raise, the state of their training, the types of equipment available for future defence production and the plans for using it. Questions were asked about the cost of defence programmes, their impact on all sectors of the economy, the measures which were being taken to meet this impact, and additional measures which could be taken by the countries, acting together, to strengthen their economies.[32]

The material contained in the responses of member governments was scrutinized by the staff of the Executive Bureau, and 'assembled ... into a form useful for further individual and comparative study.' Then came cross-examination.

Each country had its reply appraised by a committee of experts and by the Bureau. When a particular country's programme was considered, the representative of that country on the TCC sat with the Executive Bureau. The Bureau could add other members when it felt that they were needed, which was especially the case when the programmes of the United States, the United Kingdom, and France were under consideration. When this process had been completed, the full TCC met in order to make a final examination of the work of the Executive Bureau. This examination was characterized by a frankness which was unusual in such delicate matters, invading as they did the innermost recesses of a nation's national existence...[33]

Or, as Lord Ismay remarks, 'that sovereign governments submitted to this searching cross-examination by an international staff, parted with some of their most jealously guarded secrets and debated in common measures affecting matters of high policy, was a signal victory for the NATO spirit.'[34]

Canada's representative on the TCC was her Minister of Finance, Douglas Abbott, whose hostility towards NATO bureaucrats who intruded – so he considered – needlessly and unjustifiably into the business of the government must have made that duty irksome. 'It was hoped that it would be an instructive experience for the Department of Finance,' an official of the Department of External Affairs commented slyly, 'to be exposed directly to pressure from an international body to supply information and statistics urgently.'[35]

Within a month of its creation the Executive Bureau, or 'Three Wise Men,' had set about its business. Its first demands upon the member governments were for each to offer its estimate of the cost to it of the national force contribution suggested by the Standing Group, and to outline the economic problems involved in present and proposed defence programmes. 'You will have received ... the text of the "questionnaire to permit a realistic analysis of our military position" as well as a request for "country analysis of politico-economic capabilities in relation to defence requirements'',' the representative at OEEC cabled to the Department of External Affairs on 17 October 1951. 'I now understand that trio of wise men deputies ... are now ready with eight – repeat eight – pro forma tables to be used in country submissions on military questionnaire, replies being required by October 29.'[36] That did not leave Ottawa much time. The government told it representatives that filling out the economic section of the questionnaire could not be done before the week of 5 November. From London, the Council Deputy urged Ottawa to do better. Dana Wilgress reported to the Department of External Affairs that he was 'seriously concerned' by the news that the Canadian reply would be late. 'A long delay ... may interfere seriously with the whole programme, and it would create an unfavourable impression if our replies were submitted a week after all other replies.'[37] This appeal had no effect on the government's time-table. 'Material must go before Cabinet Defence Committee,' Wilgress was reminded. 'Apart from this difficulty we are much concerned with the desirability of turning in a thorough and responsible contribution.'[38]

The Cabinet Defence Committee met on 8 November. The meeting was unusually prtracted. Its members had before them an attempt by a committee of senior officials 'to ascertain as quickly as possible a reasonable figure for the fulfilment of the 1952-53 portion of Canada's contribution to the NATO Medium Term Defence plan.' The officials had arrived at a figure of $2455 million. The Minister of Finance observed that this figure was too high. '$2455 million, added to expected expenditures of roughly $200 million on defence production, atomic energy, civil defence and other projects in the general field of defence, represented about 13% of the anticipated gross national product in that year and more, he felt, than the country would be prepared to pay or the economy could stand.' Abbott added, however, that he would 'not object to the Executive Bureau being informed that the present estimates of expenditures in the next three years were initial approximations of costs that had still to undergo further screening.' The Cabinet Defence Committee agreed that the Minister of Finance should tell the Executive Bureau that 'at present the government did not expect cash disbursements in excess of $2.4 billion, including some $200 million for ... other projects in the general field of defence, to be authorized for defence purposes in 1952-53.'[39] Abbott's intervention had lopped $250 million off the estimated total.

The Canadian reply then went forward to the Executive Bureau. The reply was late, but so were others. Canada's examination was set for 16 November. It was a long day for Douglas Abbott and his aides.

The morning session brought them before the Executive Bureau's Screening and Costing Staff, whose chairman, General Joseph T. McCarney, US Army (flanked by representatives from Britain, France, and Belgium), conducted an interrogation into the military aspects of the defence programme. All went routinely until General McCarney offered his opinion that 'if Canada had national service, she could increase the size, or improve the readiness of, her forces.' Abbott then acquainted McCarney with the Golden Rule of Canadian politics: 'Thou shalt not conscript for military service in peacetime.' McCarney's suggestion, a Canadian present recorded cryptically, 'was not pursued further.' McCarney also observed that when the Korean War ended, Canada would be in a position to provide an entire division of infantry troops for service in Western Europe, thereby trebling their number; he was told that 'this would entail ... an undesirable and unwise use of Canadian manpower,' and that 'such a contribution by Canada would be quite out of proportion to the United States commitment.'[40]

The afternoon was given over to the economic aspects of the defence programme. The first part of the interrogation, during which Canada's economic situation was scrutinized was 'largely mechanical and routine,' but what followed – a smaller informal meeting with the Three Wise men – was unprecedented. 'Monnet, supported to some extent by Harriman, expressed the opinion that the present Canadian defence effort did not constitute a burden as heavy as those being undertaken by most of the other NATO countries.' They suggested that Canada increase her contribution of mutual aid, preferably in the form of wheat, aluminum, and copper to be stockpiled in Western Europe. Abbott robustly deflected these demands. 'He did not think that the Canadian Government or Parliament could be persuaded, in the present circumstances, to commit more than the maximum of $2.4 billion projected for 1952-53, and that he would not recommend an increase,' the representative to the OEEC who was present at the meeting reported to Ottawa. Abbott stated further that

the heavy outlay on expansion of vital raw materials in Canada was in many respects as important as the direct defence effort and imposed an additional substantial impact on the economy which was not included in the direct defence expenditures. Consequently, they could not attach a great deal of weight to simple comparisons of GNP. ... Mr Abbott said that the Canadian public still had a clear recollection of the over-commitment in assistance to European countries which Canada took upon itself during 1946 and 1947 and the results therefrom in objectionable restrictions and taxation. He said it was the policy of the Canadian Government to avoid, as far as possible, the recurrence of such a situation...[41]

Douglas Abbott's presentation, an External Affairs official, A.F.W. Plumptre, commented after reading the report of the proceedings at Paris on 16 November, 'could not have been entirely convincing to his audience.'[42] But its unreceptivity, Plumptre noted elsewhere, could not fairly be attributed to any deficiency of style or preparation on Abbott's part. 'It would probably be impossible to give a reply, from the Canadian point of view, that would seem completely convincing and satisfying to the UK and Continental members of NATO,' he wrote to the Under Secretary of State for External Affairs on 22 November.

All of them are floundering in a sea of economic troubles, evidenced by inflation, budgetary difficulties, and import restrictions. None of them is likely to be entirely sympathetic to a statement that Canada, in seeking to assist NATO, is trying to keep clear of the same troubles. On the other hand, just because most of the NATO countries are already in serious difficulties, economic and political, it does not necessarily follow that NATO would be strengthened if Canada got itself into similar difficulties. Indeed, one could argue the opposite: unless and until these other NATO countries get their own houses in better shape, any aid Canada can give them will be of negligible assistance and Canada will do well to keep its own house in good order in the meantime. Unfortunately, it is difficult if not impossible to make this argument without giving offence to our less fortunate or less competent fellow members of the Pact, and the effect of our policy, insofar as it has an influence on the Alliance, is likely to be divisive rather than cohesive. This would seem to be a serious matter which should be kept in mind.[43]

After more questioning by the TCC of the Minister of Finance and other Canadian officials, the object of the entire exercise – the TCC's report – was prepared and distributed among member governments by mid-November 1951. Only three of them – the American, British, and Portuguese – were judged by the TCC to have been making a contribution to NATO which fairly matched their capabilities. The rest were judged capable of doing more.

NATO's first assessment of performance held Canada's in disfavour. Rejecting the arguments put by her representatives to the Executive Bureau and the Temporary Council Committee on 16 November and 4 December 1951, the TCC recommended that the Canadian government contribute during 1952-53 an additional $250 millions in mutual aid in the form of raw materials and commodities. How did the Canadian government react to such a judgement?

The Department of External Affairs Committee on NATO Affairs considered the TCC report on 15 December. The report's recommendations on the military side were deemed to be reasonable. 'The suggestion regarding economic aid, however' – so the Committee's minutes record – 'could not be accepted as Canada could not undertake the type of assistance recommended – that of giving primary products, the sale of which constitutes our chief trade. All that Canada would be prepared to do would be, in the years subsequent to 1952-53, to make available as mutual aid military assistance....'[44]

The reaction of the Minister of Finance to the TCC's assessment of Canadian performance was to feel incensed at it. Exactly what Douglas Abbott had feared at the outset seemed to be taking place: an international bureaucracy either indifferent towards or ignorant of Canadian realities was attempting to shape Canada's economic policies. Abbott became more determined than ever to hold fast to a $2.4 billion expenditure on defence. An official of the Department of External Affairs described his position as 'very arbitrary.'[45] Officials of his own Department, scrounging for any additional military equipment which could be used as mutual aid, had found some $50 millions' worth of ammunition and between $20 and $30 millions' worth of artillery. These stores Abbott was prepared to transfer only if other outlays on defence were reduced by an equivalent amount. The Department of External Affairs considered this gesture inadequate. 'There has been no serious attempt to find out what additional defence production could be made available to NATO countries,' A.D.P. Heeney commented to L.B. Pearson, and he termed Abbott's insistence on sticking to the $2.4 billion limit as 'a quite inexplicable addiction.' Part of the problem was caused by the fact that the funds for mutual aid came out of the money voted for the Department of National Defence. That meant, as Heeney pointed out, that National Defence had 'little positive interest in the programme, apart from some convenience in releasing equipment. Indeed,' Heeney added, 'if there is a ceiling on total defence expenditures, the interest of the Department of National Defence lies in reducing mutual aid to the minimum.' For this reason, he considered, it would be desirable to transfer the mutual aid vote to the Department of Defence Production – providing that its Minister, C.D. Howe, could be counted on to take 'a positive and constructive interest in the Canadian mutual aid programme.'[46]

Early in 1952, the Under Secretary of State for External Affairs took stock of the situation on the eve of the 'important decisions' which would have to be made 'regarding Canadian mutual aid for North Atlantic countries.' There was something to be said for the $2.4 billion ceiling, after all. The sum, A.D.P. Heeney pointed out,

represents a really heavy burden for Canada and a 50% increase over the amount programmed for the current year (about $1.6 billions). The figure of $2.4 billions also stands up reasonably well when realistic comparisons are made between the proportions of gross national product likely to be spent in Canada and the proportions likely to be spent in other North Atlantic countries. Finally there are valid reasons why Canada should not embark on a permanent NATO programme of giving away basic raw materials.

On the other hand, we have never been too impressed by suggestions, which have come from the Department of Finance, that the Canadian economy was in a highly precarious condition and in danger of being overturned by an extra hundred million dollars or so...

Two hundred million dollars represents only 1% of the gross national product. Considering all these things and considering the burdens being carried by other NATO countries and the difficulties confronting them, it seems essential that, in response to the TCC recommendation, we should make a respectable increase to our planned mutual aid programme for the coming year.

A 'respectable increase,' Heeney considered, would mean an additional mutual aid transfer in the amount of about $150 million, over and above the $228 million already in the programme, making some $375 million overall. 'Canadians are doing reasonably well,' Heeney observed, 'if they provide one twentieth of the amount put up by the Americans' for foreign aid. The Americans were expected to put up roughly $8 billion in 1952-3 for aid around the world. Canada, with $375 million allocated to Western Europe and $25 million to South and South-East Asia under the Colombo Plan, would be giving roughly that one-twentieth – 'a very respectable role.' But Heeney thought the TCC recommendation of an extra $250 million to be 'unduly high.' An extra $150 million was quite enough.[47] L.B. Pearson concurred. 'In giving out this figure we are not, in fact, committing ourselves to that exact amount,' Pearson noted. 'We are merely saying that out of the total appropriations for next year, we will hope to increase our mutual aid by this amount.' Doing so might be good for Canada domestically as well as internationally: it might 'even help to relieve pockets of unemployment in certain areas.'[48]

But the struggle within the government over the size of the defence budget, and therefore that of the Mutual Aid appropriation, was far from over. Abbott's $2.4 billion turned out not to be sacrosanct after all. The Department of Finance proposed to cut the budget – first to $2.2 billion, then to $2.0 billion. By this last reduction, the Department of External Affairs was appalled. An official reported to its Under Secretary that he had been 'disturbed' to discover from talking with officials in Finance 'that our specific proposal for an additional $150 million ... had not "sunk in"' at all...'[49] Notice was served on the Council Deputy in London that all was not well in Ottawa. 'I know you will appreciate that planning at this end is exceptionally difficult,' A.D.P. Heeney cabled to Dana Wilgress on 25 January, 'because this Department has not been able to accept the present position of the Department of Finance that the Canadian defence programme for 1952-53 should be reduced to $2.0 billon including only $223 millions for mutual aid.'[50] Wilgress found this news 'disturbing.' It would make it more difficult to explain to the TCC why Canada would not accept its recommendation to provide mutual aid in the form of raw materials and commodities.[51]

At this juncture, the Department of External Affairs played its highest, and only, card: an appeal through its Minister to the Prime Minister for him to see things its way. L.B. Pearson stood as high in Louis S. St Laurent's estimation as did any other member of his government. Their working relations were always close: 'With their offices just a few doors apart on the second floor of the East Block, St Laurent and Pearson met frequently, going over the voluminous dispatches received from other parts of the world, and working out the Canadian policy together,' writes St Laurent's biographer. 'While the Prime Minister allowed Pearson an unusual amount of freedom of action, the Secretary of State for External Affairs never abused that confidence, keeping his superior closely informed of all developments, discussing his ideas with him, and obtaining his approval for any significant initiatives.'[52] Pearson now sought that approval for his own, and his Department's, conviction that Canada should raise its Mutual Aid contribution, and that, to make this possible, the estimates of the Department of National Defence should be kept at a figure of $2.4 billion rather than be cut, as the Department of Finance was recommending, to $2.0 billion. Pearson made his case in a letter to the Prime Minister of some 3000 words in length. The heart of his argument is contained in the extracts that follow.

The development of NATO has now reached an important point, as it moves from its planning stage into its operational stage. It is, I think, not too much to say that the future of the alliance will be determined by the decisions we have to make shortly, national and collective decisions. Apart from the TCC report itself, the move for European re-armament, including the organization of the European Defence Community, seems to be gathering momentum and our security depends in part on its maintenance. Thus the question naturally arises: Are NATO plans going to be put into operation? Are individual countries willing, not to be ordered, because we don't want that, but at least to be guided by NATO recommendations; or are they going to go their own way independently, each in the light of the local situation as interpreted by it? Each NATO country is thus eying all the others: good examples and bad examples will count, I suppose, for more this year than they may ever likely count again.

In this situation, I believe that the position taken by Canada is of real significance, both at home and abroad. The outstanding part which this Government has played in the origin and development of NATO is widely recognized. Canada's attitude is a matter of importance. Further, if we are not reasonably co-operative, there may be widespread misconceptions of our motives. A simplified version may run that Canada is a rich and stable country and that if the Canadian Government feels unable to respond, in some measure, at least, to the Executive Bureau recommendations, other countries in Europe, with more unstable economies, should not be invited to make further sacrifices, or even continue those which they feel they are now making. Our natural irritation with this unfair over-simplification of Canada's position should not, I think, blind us to the importance of any action we take or do not take at this time.

Accordingly we run risks of unfortunate results if we completely reject the economic recommendations of the Executive Bureau. There is, first of all, the risk that, encouraged by our example, our less fortunate European allies may be encouraged to follow. ... In the second place, our complete rejection of the Bureau's economic recommendations would increase the difficulties faced by the United States administration in carrying forward its defence programme in the face of Congressional obstacles. This would have less concern for us if our own security did not depend heavily on the preparedness of the United States. Finally, our action would also, I believe, have some effect on relations between Canada and the United States. It is impossible to ignore, though it is easy to exaggerate, the concern expressed by US representatives in Washington and Ottawa regarding the Canadian comment recently submitted to the TCC.* I do not wish to over-emphasize these aspects of the problem or to suggest that they are determining factors. But they can hardly be overlooked, especially by anyone particularly concerned, as I am, with foreign relations.

For all these reasons I believe we should think seriously before completely rejecting the economic proposals of the Executive Bureau. I am acutely aware of the shortcomings of the TCC procedure, and I have always been very sceptical of the value of any statistical exercise in burden-sharing. Nevertheless, I do not think we should reject out of hand the recommendations of such men as Mr Harriman, Mr Monnet and Sir Edwin Plowden and their competent staff. Nor should we forget that we had something to do at Ottawa with the setting up of the TCC and the Executive Bureau.

...I wonder whether the Department of Finance may not be over-emphasizing our financial dangers.

It is my belief, and certainly it is the belief of most commentators both at home and abroad, that the Canadian economy is in a strong and healthy condition. This country has seldom experienced so vigorous and so prosperous a period. Our weakest point is, of course, our heavy dependence on the import of US capital, and there is always a risk that, by undertaking greater defence burdens, we may disturb confidence at home or abroad. However, confidence seems to be pretty firm and pretty well founded at present and I find it difficult to believe that it will suffer if our defence programme goes somewhat beyond $2.0 billions. Only two months ago Cabinet Defence Committee agreed that Mr Abbott might put forward $2.4 billions as a maximum figure for defence, and since that time there are evidences

---

* See above, 294-5.

of growing strength rather than weakness. We have removed all restrictions on foreign exchange transactions. We have had a further increase in our reserves of gold and US dollars. We have found it possible to relax some of our consumer credit restrictions. As an index of the confidence felt in the future of this country, the Canadian dollar has moved up to parity with the US dollar. In the face of these well-known circumstances it will surely be difficult to persuade our allies – frankly it is difficult to persuade me – that we are *unable* to carry out any of the economic recommendations of the Executive Bureau.

Pearson accordingly recommended to the Prime Minister that Canada provide NATO members in Western Europe with an additional $150 million's worth of Mutual Aid in the form of military equipment, and concluded: 'If a total mutual aid programme of, say, $375 millions is approved, if we carry out the full spirit of our undertaking to the TCC regarding our defence programme, if we include in the grand total the defence estimates of the Department of Defence Production (about $100 millions) and of some other Departments and agencies (about $60 millions), and if we take into account recent indications that the NATO infrastructure programme will be substantially greater than has seemed likely up to the present, then I believe we shall come out with a programme that is not too far below our originally agreed figure of $2.4 billions as qualified by Mr Abbott. We shall be going a considerable way to meet the economic recommendations of the Executive Bureau.'[53]

This powerful plea had part, but only part, of its desired effect. The Cabinet did not accept all the cuts proposed by the Department of Finance. Neither did it accept all the increases proposed by the Department of External Affairs. The government compromised on an intermediate sum. The Mutual Aid appropriation for 1952-3 could be (and was) raised by about $100 million (from $223 million to $324 million), rather than to the $375 million proposed by Pearson. That, with other programmes, put the 1952-3 defence estimates at $2.106 billion.* Had the Three Wise Men not brought their weight to bear, these would have been at least $106 million less.

THE POLITICS OF POOLING

Canadian officials had helped to bring about the scrutiny by the Temporary Council Committee of member governments' contributions to the

---

*   Actual expenditure, as distinct from estimates, amounted to $1.971 billion: '[A]s is all too obvious, the Canadian budget estimates are not accurate within a range of a couple of hundred million dollars.' Under Secretary of State for External Affairs, memorandum for the Minister, 'Canadian Aid for NATO and UK,' 8 January 1952, DEA files, 50030-AL-40.

common defence. But they had neither expected nor hoped that their co-operation would lead to the review's becoming an annual event. They regarded the exercise as emergency treatment for transitory ailments. 'I do not think we should endorse or give undue praise to the TCC procedure,' L.B. Pearson commented after reading its first report. 'The procedure, as such, may have been necessary for this particular situation, but would, I think, have very unhappy results if it became normal. ... This kind of international inquisitorial operation into national defence policies,' Pearson added, 'will run into every kind of trouble unless it is done very carefully.'[54]

The decision to conduct the review on a yearly basis was taken by the North Atlantic Council at Lisbon in February 1952, on the recommendation from the Temporary Council Committee that 'something akin to the TCC exercise be made a regular feature of NATO's work, so as to ensure a continuous appraisal of defence programmes in the light of economic and political developments.'[55] The job of running the review was entrusted to the new International Staff/Secretariat, recently moved from London to Paris. In the words of the historian of that institution, 'the Council thus deposited on the International Staff/Secretariat a problem which had vexed the Alliance almost from its beginning, and which had reached such proportions that it had been lifted out of the regular context of Alliance activity and organization and incorporated into a "crash" operation' – that is, the TCC exercise of 1951 – 'of the first magnitude.'[56] The review process, thus institutionalized, was time-tabled.

January-March	– drafting of the Questionnaire in the light of previous experience and agreeing on a modified procedure for the Review;
March-July	– issue of planning guidance by Supreme Commanders, visits to each capital by special military teams, and completion of the Questionnaire by member governments;
July-October	– analysis and discussion of national programmes and drafting of final report;
November	– consideration of report by governments, followed by Council meeting at Ministerial level for adoption of force goals.[57]

A NATO fiscal year was set – 1 January to 31 December. But the eight member governments whose own fiscal years did not coincide with the calendar would not alter theirs to match NATO's: members of the Alliance could no more harmonize their budgetary processes than they could standardize their weapons systems.

The first of the regular Annual Reviews proved to be the most trying of the lot – partly because of lack of experience on the part of all concerned, partly because 'the Gap' that loomed as the result of the decisions on force goals adopted at Lisbon in February 1952 was greater than it had been before or would be again.*

By May 1952, the policy community at Ottawa was already preparing the defence estimates for 1953-4. At issue, as usual, was how much of the defence appropriation should be allocated to Mutual Aid for that year. The new Under Secretary of State for External Affairs (who had then just traded jobs with A.D.P. Heeney who had been transferred from the East Block to the Palais de Chaillot) was from his experience on the Council Deputies a committed advocate of a substantial Canadian contribution.' I feel strongly ... that an amount of $350 millon should be included for mutual aid in the defence programme being planned for 1953-54,' Dana Wilgress told Escott Reid on 12 May. 'Any amount less than this sum would be sure to make us subject to attack during the course of the forthcoming annual review of NATO defence build-up.'[58]

By June, Dana Wilgress had learned that the Department of National Defence was planning to spend $2.4 billion during 1953-4, including $143 million for Mutual Aid. 'There will be very strong pressure,' Wilgress predicted to L.B. Pearson, 'to reduce the total ... probably down to something like $2 billions.' Such a reduction would be painful: 'I understand that there is a natural lump or bulge in the National Defence programme for 1953-4. The general plans of recruitment and equipment ... involve extra heavy expenditures in that year.' Vigilance would be required, if the Mutual Aid appropriation were not to shrink in the process; Wilgress wanted it enlarged, not shrunk.

I am greatly impressed by the importance of Canada taking a really constructive position in the forthcoming Annual Review of NATO. For the current year we have agreed to put up $324 millions [for Mutual Aid]; it is most desirable that we should go a bit beyond this for the coming year...

Even if we cannot go beyond this year's figure for Mutual Aid of $324 millions I think we should fight very hard to equal it in the coming year; it would be very desirable to press forward but it would be most undesirable to slip backward...

And, if slipping backward proved unavoidable, it would be more undesirable still to slip too far: '[I]f it is impossible to maintain this figure in the face of the pressures that are developing, I would hope you would be able to hold the line at $250,000,000. ... While any reduction below this year's figure will be embarrassing in our NATO relationships I think we could probably "live with" a figure of $250,000,000; I think it would be very difficult indeed to live with any lower figure.'[59] Wilgress's readiness even to contem-

---

* See above, Ch. 4, 222-5.

plate a Mutual Aid appropriation $100 million less than that which, before taking up his new duties as Under Secretary of State for External Affairs, he had himself proposed was produced by intense pressure on the government to cut expenditure – pressure more palpable in Ottawa than overseas.

Meanwhile, at Paris, the process of preparing the Annual Review questionnaire had begun. This time the government was determined to avoid the detailed statistical inquiry conducted the year before by the Temporary Council Committee. A first look at the Secretariat's draft questionnaire was not encouraging. 'The feeling was that it followed the TCC pattern too closely,' the Department of External Affairs reported to the Permanent Representative to the North Atlantic Council. 'The same kind of exhaustive statistical investigation of countries' capabilities that gave rise to so much difficulty in the TCC exercises seems to be contemplated. ... The proposed procedure would give undesirable emphasis to the economic position of the various countries which is only one, and in many cases not the decisive, factor in determining the defence burden which can be supported.' What then did the government want? 'In our view the questionnaire should be designed to bring out the main *facts* about each country's economic position, and should avoid unnecessary statistical requests and argumentation about political factors and limitations on national defence efforts. The questionnaire should be ... as simple as possible.'[60] A.D.P. Heeney, attempting to put the case for simplicity to the Secretary General and officials of the Secretariat, reported that 'the going was tough.'[61]

The going was made much tougher when the US administration decided to support the elaborate and intrusive type of questionnaire which the Canadians wanted to head off. 'We are strongly opposed to the military tables proposed by the US,' the government informed the Permanent Representative on 5 June 1952, 'and to the view expressed by the US representative that the Annual Review should become a screening operation designed to put pressure on NATO countries.'[62] The Secretary of State for External Affairs informed the Ambassador at Washington that 'a fundamental difference of approach has appeared between the United States and most of the other delegations. ... The US representative on the questionnaire working group, apparently under firm instructions, has been pressing strongly for tables embodying a detailed costing exercise. ... I am concerned,' L.B. Pearson told Hume Wrong, 'lest in this way the intent and scope of the Annual Review questionnaire might be prejudged without out the Council having had an opportunity of considering the question of principle involved. I am therefore asking Heeney in Paris to raise this question in the Council as a matter of urgency...'[63]

The Permanent Representative went through the motions of protest within the Council but, as A.D.P. Heeney had reported beforehand, the conclusion was foregone: it would prove impossible for Canada to work major changes in a procedure favoured by the NATO Secretariat, the United States and, most recently, the United Kingdom. Of his first, and failed, assignment on the North Atlantic Council, Heeney could only tell Ottawa that his delegation had done its best.

We made energetic efforts, at different levels, to have the issue settled from the start. ... This continual battle conducted at numerous interminable meetings has frayed everyone's temper. ... The small countries took the line that they could not quite understand the purpose of the exercise but, if the United States wanted the tables filled in, they were prepared to do so. The shadow of mutual aid had obviously been cast over the whole proceedings...

The net result has been that we have been largely unsuccessful in preventing the adoption of a considerable number of complicated and forbidding tables for which we can see no use and with respect to which the United States could give no really plausible explanation of the use to which they would be put. We have managed to eliminate some complete tables and a fair amount of detail within the tables themselves but we have been merely nibbling at the edges and the large, hard core remains...

To sum up, we have fought the battle against statistics on all sectors of the Paris front. ... But for all practical purposes the jig is up and the big battalions of our determined friends have but to occupy the field...[64]

That 'large, hard core' which constituted the questionnaire for the 1952 NATO Annual Review turned out to be 200 pages long. The tome arrived in Ottawa at the end of June; it was meant to be returned, duly filled in, at the end of July. The Secretariat had estimated that the length of the average completed questionnaire would be 'at least 300 pages. ... In other words, the International Staff/Secretariat would receive approximately 4000 pages to be reproduced and distributed, totalling over 1,000,000 reproduced pages.' These demands upon its facilities, the historian of the International Staff/Secretariat has commented, 'was a formidable challenge ... especially as the need for these papers was immediate.'[65]

The questionnaire – in two parts, five sections and 200 pages – was a formidable challenge to the patience of officials in Ottawa who had sought to forestall its distribution. There it lay, massively, in their in-baskets. While it could not be ignored, need each and every query be painstakingly filled in?

Some officials, while disliking the task, felt that it had to be performed in full. Others favoured filling in the forms only to the end of the government's fiscal year – that is, to 31 March 1953 – leaving the rest for completion later on. On 15 July the Cabinet decided in favour of submitting an incomplete return; NATO authorities, the Cabinet agreed, were to be given an explanation, in the form of a preface to Canada's return, why all their questions could not be answered.

Drafting that explanatory preface – the Department of External Affairs considered it to be 'an important political document' – proved to be troublesome; several officials and at least two ministers tried their hand at it. The Deputy Minister of National Defence was first in the field with 'three short paragraphs ... I have endeavoured,' C.M. Drury explained to the senior officials among whom these were circulated, 'in so far as possible to avoid any negative statements.'[66] The first paragraph announced the intention of the Canadian Government 'to make available on the dates shown, the forces described in Part I of this paper,' and it added pointedly: 'In making available such forces, the Canadian Government will not be seeking external financial assistance.' The second promised that the data omitted after 31 March 1953 would be forwarded 'as soon as they can be ascertained.' The third paragraph noted, even more pointedly: 'The present programme would appear to be as extensive as the Canadian public will support, and it is unlikely that additions to it will be possible.'[67] A later draft by L.B. Pearson, based on Drury's, reversed the order of the second and third paragraphs, deleting from what had become the second the reference to the unlikelihood of additions being made. In yet another draft, to which several officials contributed, the statement had grown to seven paragraphs, including these:

This year the situation is also affected by the possibility of a General Election in 1953 in which the next budget would be an issue before the Canadian people. Therefore, the Government would have to be closer to the next fiscal year before it could say what the country would be asked to support.

This position is not to be interpreted as indicating in any way a disposition to reduce the Canadian force commitments. The Canadian Government will take the necessary action to carry out its declared physical programme and to finance it without outside assistance, but, as the Council has recognized, political, as well as economic and military factors, must be taken into account in determining a defence programme, and it is essential, in the Canadian view, that the Canadian plans for NATO expenditures be such that they will have a reasonable chance of being approved by the Canadian people. The present estimate of political capabilities indicates that the financial programme cannot exceed that for the current year and may have to be reduced. Thus, the possibility of achieving economy without reducing the physical programme may have to be studied.[69]

Each of these draft paragraphs drew withering criticism from the Permanent Representative (who would be the first to experience the hostile reaction which he was sure they would provoke). It was inappropriate,

A.D.P. Heeney felt, to bring up the subject of the impending general election; the second paragraph seemed to him 'repetitious and ... too defensive in tone. We will have difficulty no doubt in maintaining our position,' Heeney predicted from Paris, 'but we have no need to be too apologetic in the circumstances.'[69]

The battle of the drafts continued for more than two months. By early September, two versions of the explanatory preface remained in contention – one the work mainly of C.M. Drury and Brooke Claxton of the Department of National Defence, the other the work of officials of the Department of External Affairs. The Minister at External Affairs pronounced the draft produced wthin National Defence to be 'unsatisfactory as it stands' but salvagable with certain changes. 'Frankly I think our own draft is much better than the National Defence draft, even as amended,' L.B. Pearson wrote testily on 8 September, 'but if they will accept these amendments, we might agree to the rest of their text. If this is not agreeable to them, then I suggest we have no preface at all.'[70]

The delay in producing the preface held up the return of the questionnaire. At a Chiefs of Staff Committee meeting on 17 September, it was said that the delay was all to the good: other member governments were 'holding back,' and if the Canadian return was first or early in the field, it would, 'to our disadvantage,' receive 'the undivided attention of the examining staff.' Dana Wilgress, to whom this argument was relayed, asked the Permanent Representative 'whether there would be any advantages to Canada in delaying the tabling of our reply or whether it is, as I should imagine, to the greater interest of ourselves and all the members of NATO that the returns be submitted as soon as possible in order to assist the Secretariat and perhaps help to generate some much needed enthusiasm, which is so sadly lacking in the Annual Review exercise this year.'[71] A.D.P. Heeney replied: 'We are already in an embarrassing position and we hope that there will be no deliberate delay of our returns or part of our returns. We would therefore request that the Canadian returns should be made available at the earliest possible date, even if the data is sent forward piecemeal.'[72]

The text of the explanatory preface finally agreed to was as follows.

The Government of Canada is not yet in a position to give any firm figure for the expenditures which it expects to make in the fiscal year 1953-54.

On the other hand there is no disposition to reduce the Canadian force commitments.

In general it may be said that while the Canadian Government will take the necessary action to complete and finance its declared physical programme, it appears unlikely that the Canadian financial appropriation for defence will exceed that for the current year.

Detailed information regarding future fiscal years will be forwarded as soon as possible.[73]

Canada's return, late and incomplete, was followed by Canada's interrogation. The process began in mid-October with the submission to her delegation of some ninety questions, arising from the return, prepared within the NATO Secretariat in conjunction with other national representatives. (These 'supplementaries' were both intrusive and extensive: one list of questions submitted by a fellow delegation was 125 pages long. 'The countries were frankly curious as to how their allies were conducting their military programmes.')[74] Members of the delegation then worked with members of the NATO Working Group which was to conduct the examination to divide the ninety-odd questions into three parts. 'Most of the questions were relegated to Parts Two and Three, indicating either that they had been answered satisfactorily informally or that they could probably be dealt with informally at the technical level. All the rest – Part One – seemed to involve policy considerations of some sort.'[75] The questions in Part I were put to Canada's delegation in the examination held on 23 October in the Council Chamber of the Palais de Chaillot, attended by about sixty or seventy members of the NATO Secretariat and national delegations.

Before the questioning began, the meeting was addressed by the Permanent Representative, who offered a statement which had been designed, as A.D.P. Heeney told those present, 'to assist with Working Group in understanding the position of the Canadian Government, particularly with respect to the omission of certain figures requested in the Questionnaire.' The adoption of this tactic, Heeney later explained to Ottawa, had been decided upon as being 'not only ... in our own interest but also in the general interest of the Annual Review procedure.' After reading out the four 'key sentences' of the explanatory preface to the return (on which so much effort had been expended at Ottawa), the Permanent Representative discussed 'quite frankly ... the reasons why it was not possible for us to provide certain of the data called for by the Questionnaire.' Heeney informed the meeting that the basic difficulty had been 'one of timing in relation to our fiscal year and our established constitutional practice.' Anticipating the obvious rejoinder – that with the same fiscal year and constitutional practice, Canada had nonetheless managed to provide a complete return in the TCC exercise of 1951 – Heeney offered the following explanation.

[L]ast year, for the purposes of what was regarded as an abnormal, emergency operation, the Canadian Government did in fact depart widely in this respect from our normal practices. We did communicate to the TCC some highly tentative figures regarding possible expenditures for the fiscal year to come, and, indeed, for following fiscal years. One result is that certain of these figures, particularly those involving the longer forecasts, are turning out to be very wide of the mark and, therefore, quite misleading. Furthermore, the Government ran into criticism on the ground that important matters which should, at the least, have first been discussed in the House of Commons were being discussed – and commitments in fact being made – with other governments. The traditions of budget secrecy and parliamentary control of the purse are very deep seated in our country.

Heeney then adduced two additional reasons why the government had felt unable to follow its own example of the year before – the uncertainties that other members of the Alliance were experiencing in deciding what their own defence programmes would be in 1953; and the impending general election: 1953 was 'likely to be [a year] ... of special political activity in our own country.' The Permanent Representative concluded by pledging 'to do our best to give such information within the limitations which we have stated.[76]

Reaction to this statement was mixed: there was appreciation of its frankness, regret at its necessity. For Canada had been the only North Atlantic Treaty member to submit an incomplete return. 'The attitude of the Working Group,' Heeney reported to Ottawa, 'was one of regretful, and provisional, acceptance of the Canadian position.'[77]

The meeting turned next to what questions remained after the winnowing. Of three military questions outstanding, one was fundamental: To what extent could Canada increase her planned force contribution in 1953, 1954, and 1955 in military forces or military aid? 'As [the question] involves major policy issues, which can be resolved only at the highest governmental level,' Heeney explained in his report, 'we had no alternative but to accept the Working Group's decision that it should be carried forward into the subsequent stages of the Annual Review.'

The surviving questions on defence expenditure had been for the most part answered by Heeney's opening statement. A question on production was deflected by stating that an answer 'would be tantamount to giving a forecast on ... expenditure. ... We were not able to give that type of information...' Not enough was yet known about the next slice of 'infrastructure' to be able to estimate Canada's likely contribution to its cost.

These replies disposed of all but the economic questions which, Heeney reported,

had been arranged to lead up to the final one. After exploring whether our national production was not expanding satisfactorily and perhaps more rapidly than we had forecast, after looking into the extent to which our actual defence outlays seemed to be rather less than the amounts we had been willing to entertain as possible a year ago, after noting that our balance of payments had proved more satisfactory than we had expected at the time of the TCC exercise – after reviewing these and other features of our situation, the final "$64-question" as the Chairman remarked) was, in brief, whether Canada could not do more, physically or financially?

To that question – more like $164 million than $64 – Heeney could only reply that 'any material changes in the Canadian defence programme were matters of government policy, and the 1953-54 programme was presently under active consideration.'

At the end of the day, the Chairman (an American official, David Luxe Hopkins, business executive and philanthropist who in June 1952 had become NATO's first Assistant Secretary General), summing up, remarked that the examination of Canada's return had identified six major issues which should be resolved either 'in considering further the Canadian submission' or 'during the reconciliation process.' These issues, the Permanent Representative reported, were as follows.

(a) the possibility of Canada increasing her military forces or mutual aid at the disposal of the alliance;
(b) the difficulties in conducting the Annual Review arising out of the inability of Canada to provide financial data after March 31, 1953;
(c) the fact that Canadian production is likely to be higher than anticipated when our submission was drawn up;
(d) the increased emphasis placed by Canada this year on the political side of the discussion of politico-economic capabilities;
(e) the problems Canada may face in converting production from defence requirements, if and when the defence build-up tapers off;
(f) the importance Canada places upon resource development and its close connection with the defence effort.

And so the first round was over. There had been some awkward moments for the examinee, but no humiliation. 'We were given a fair first run,' the Permanent Representative told Ottawa afterwards, 'sympathetic and critical in the proper sense of both words.'[78] Later, reflecting on the experience, Heeney considered the outcome to have been 'reasonably satisfactory. We should not by any means infer, however, that we will have no difficulty in the rounds which remain – and there will be many. We have gone back to our corner without any change in our reputation if anything, we may have slightly improved the betting odds.'[79]

The final stages of the first Annual Review were the preparation of the report, its consideration by member governments, and its presentation to the NATO Council in December. The approach of this climacteric unsettled the participants. 'Tension over the annual review and national contributions increased,' Arnold Heeney recalls in his memoirs.

The French were insisting, to the point of virtual ultimatum, on the strict application of a rigid burden-sharing formula. ... Meantime, the French government itself was introducing a defence budget openly conditional upon a level of US aid which the United States did not, and certainly would not, accept. The soldiers still pressed for their military goals with no apparent appreciation of the political and economic difficulties, and SACEUR's report continued to include what I characterized as "cardboard targets" for the next year. The United Kingdom delayed replying to the secretariat's questionnaire, the EDC Treaty remained unratified by France, and finally, the United States elections had taken place and the US delegation had concluded that the reconciliation between what NATO should have and what it could have would have to wait until the following spring.[80]

It was, in short, business as usual for the Atlantic Alliance.

In Ottawa, the first Annual Review report was awaited more or less with resignation. 'We believe that the Annual Review should present a survey of what has been achieved and a statement of *accepted* objectives,' the Department of External Affairs informed the Permanent Representative at Paris. 'It may not of course be practicable in the early stages of the review to avoid some suggestions or hints of suggestions unpalatable to Canada. No useful purpose would be served, however, by including in the *final* report a statement to the effect that thirteen countries think Country X should do so and so if Country X, after being subjected to considerable pressure in the negotiation stage, cannot see its way clear to accept the proposed commitment.'[81]

By mid-November, it was becoming evident that the NATO Secretariat – deluged by documents, dogged by inexperience, hampered by member governments' policy disagreements – would not be able to produce the final report in time for presentation to the December meeting of Council Ministers. Should that meeting be postponed until the report was ready? 'The arguments for postponement are strong if the Annual Review is not completed or nearly completed,' L.B. Pearson conceded. 'On the other hand, I am worried about the implications of the position that we cannot hold a NATO Council meeting unless military planning considerations make it possible. That certainly underlines with a vengeance the military character of our association. ... I am becoming increasingly worried,' Pearson admitted, 'by the impression we are creating in the North Atlantic Council that Ministerial meetings are now admittedly held only or at least primarily for military planning purposes.'[82]

The Ministerial meeting was in the event convened on the assumption that the final report would be available but in the knowledge that in all probability it would not. 'We now have reason to hope that the Ministe¬s' discussions in December of the Annual Review and the future NA¬O defence programme will be confined to general issues,' A.D.P. Heen₃y wrote to his Minister on 24 November, 'and not focussed upon impossible statistical gaps between what we have and what the soldiers think ¬e should have.'[83]

Meanwhile, the NATO Secretariat and the national delegations had be₃n driving themselves. 'The pressure to complete the first Review was so great that the Annual Review Committee had to meet late into the night,' the historian of the NATO Staff/Secretariat has stated,[84] and his observation is confirmed by those who did. 'All of us are tied up in interminable meetings,' the Permanent Representative reported on 6 December, 'morning, afternoon and night.'[85] His delegation was not so much ccncerned with meeting the deadline as with rendering the section dealing with Canada's performance as innocuous as possible. In that effort, A.D.P. Heeney considered, they were obtaining good results. 'We have been successful in having most of your changes incorporated into t₃e section on Canada. There is now doubt whether in fact any coun¬ry studies will be included. The general sections of the review are being substantially amended and we are not worried about the final outcome as we were when we saw the first drafts.'[86]

The Secretariat had been forced to lower its sights: it was no longer trying to finish the final report but rather to produce an interim report ¬or the Ministers to mull over on 20 December. A special North Atlantic Council meeting was convened on 9 December to consider the Sec¬etariat's draft of this document. The delegation took an active part in the proceedings. 'The objects of our endeavours related partly to substar ce and partly to form,' A.D.P. Heeney informed Ottawa. 'Our primary ccncern was that the Report as a whole should lay a satisfactory basis ¬or Ministerial consideration and for the work of the months immediately beyond. ... In addition, we proposed, and other delegations readily agreed, that an attempt should be made to relieve the almost unmitigated gloom of the original Secretariat drafts; they bristled with slippages, deficienc.es and other forms of failure.'[87]

The December meeting of Council Ministers, in Heeney's recollection, 'went off much better than we had anticipated,' if only because 'our expectations in Paris had not been high.'[88] The Secretariat then resum₃d work on the completion of the final report, and member governme₃ts girded themselves for 'reconciliation' – in NATO's parlance, that proc₃ss whereby what the Alliance's military commanders say they must have is blended, meshed, or melded with what member governments, whose programmes and capabilities have been subjected to scrutiny and criticism for most of the year, are when all is said and done prepared to give.

By early 1953, the Department of External Affairs had concluded that any reconciliation reported to the next Ministerial meeting of the Council scheduled for April would be scanty. 'Most national programmes for 1953 will have become firm by then,' the Secretary of State for External Affairs pointed out to the Permanent Representative on 16 January,

and modifications in them would have to be restricted to minor reallocations of expenditure within presently planned defence budgets. These budgets will presumably take some account of the suggestions already made in the Country Panels, of the general guidance given by Ministers in December, and perhaps also of such further suggestions as may be made in the next couple of months, particularly with respect to standards of readiness. Because of the timing of this Annual Review, the Council will inevitably be faced with virtual *faits accompli* as regards the size of national programmes.

Canada's own defence budget will have been tabled, and from our point of view, therefore, it would be most undesirable that proposals involving high policy for 1953 should be put forward at all...

In these circumstances, we envisage that the process of "reconciliation" at the next Ministerial meeting will not amount to much more than adjusting the Lisbon force goals for 1953 to the economic and political capabilities of member countries as revealed by their planned defence programmes...[89]

A week later, the Under Secretary of State for External Affairs observed that 'the TCC-type "reconciliation" appears to have been discarded.'[90] A.D.P. Heeney quickly sought to disabuse Dana Wilgress of this wishful thought. Heeney reminded the Under Secretary that while 'we expressed the opinion that burden-sharing, with all that it implies regarding recommendations and reconciliation, is on the wane,' 'we warned that final judgment should be reserved. At yesterday's meeting,' he reported,

some revival of burden sharing was pressed by Norway ... and supported by UK ... and others. They admitted the deficiencies attached to any particular set of statistics. On the other hand they did not think that the present position was satisfactory in which each NATO partner simply claims that it is doing the maximum that it thinks it can under all the circumstances...

He thought that 'the most important single element' in the Annual Review then being concluded, as in annual reviews to come, would be their assessments of the NATO supreme commander's recommended national force contributions. 'There are obvious advantages in basing annual reviews on proposals of the supreme commanders. On the other hand, there is a danger that these proposals may get substantially out of line with political and economic capabilities...[91]

Member governments were required by the time-table for the reconciliation process to meet with the International Secretariat during March of each year for yet another examination of their proposed commitments to the common defence. Canada's turn fell on 16 March 1953. At this meeting, unlike the confrontation on 23 October 1952, representatives from other national delegations were absent – a feature which to the Permanent Representative appeared to be advantageous all round: 'A frank talk with the International Staff alone is more effective than an attempt to cover the same sort of ground, much of it very delicate, in a meeting at which other countries are present.'

Presiding at this meeting was NATO's first Deputy Secretary General, Henry van Vredenburch, who before his arrival at Paris in 1952 had been a senior member of the foreign ministry of The Netherlands. At the end of the meeting, van Vredenburch appealed to Canada to give more than she had offered. 'Although an international civil servant' – so A.D.P. Heeney's record shows him to have said – 'he sometimes remembered that he was a Dutchman and that his country owed a great deal to Canada. It was personally embarrassing to him even to suggest that Canada should do more in any direction. However, he felt bound to convey to us the sincere feelings of himself and his colleagues and hoped we would take their suggestions in the spirit in which these were made. He very much hoped that Canada, not so restricted by economic difficulties as many other countries, might be able to show a measure of further leadership in meeting urgent needs of NATO commanders for forces and equipment.'[92]

What could Heeney say in reply? Only, as he reported to Ottawa,

that, whatever Canada did, real leadership of NATO inevitably rested elsewhere. We recognized that the observations that had been made concerning possible increases in Canada's contribution had arisen from a desire to strengthen NATO. We would certainly report them to Ottawa. However, we would like to remind them that, while many other countries had felt forced to stretch out or water down their Lisbon goals, the Canadian Government had been, with the exception of minor slippages, fulfilling its undertakings and was proposing to continue to do so. This was a position in which we took some pride...[93]

By the end of March 1953, the so-called 'country chapter' portion of what would be the Annual Review's final report – that is, the NATO Secretariat's analysis of and recommendations for the defence programme of each member government – had reached Ottawa at last. The country chapter contained several recommendations. One recommendation was that Canada should double her appropriation for Mutual Aid over the next two years.

Ottawa was dismayed by this proposal, which would have required the government to raise the existing Mutual Aid appropriation of $324 mil-

lion to something like $490 million in 1953 – half-way to the recom-
mended total of $750 million for 1954. That was a tall order. Already the
existing appropriation was expected to be greater by as much as $75 mil-
lion than the sum which would actually be spent – a surplus caused by
delays in defence production. Officials in the Department of Finance welcomed the discrepancy, for the government was short of cash and (as an
official of the Department of External Affairs put it) 'Finance would
apparently be considerably embarrassed if it became necessary to find the
cash with which to finance purchases to fill out the $324 million.'[94] Where
would it find the cash to finance purchases to fill out $490 million?

Nor was that all. Officials were upset by the Secretariat's tactics, for
they had often warned it of the dangers involved in making recommendations that governments could not be expected to accept. From Paris, the
Permanent Representative expressed his misgiving at the turn of events.
'We foresee the greatest difficulties and confusions arising in respect to
the country chapters,' A.D.P. Heeney cabled to Ottawa on 25 March.
'The Secretariat will certainly resist attempts to emasculate their recommendations. ... On the other hand, if, as we are led to believe, the Secretariat has made sweeping recommendations for many countries, it will be
absolutely impossible to get agreed versions hammered out in full committee.' A year's work had ended in a mess. Speculating as to what could
have caused such an egregious error of judgement, Heeney was inclined
to attribute it to the possibility 'that the Secretariat suffers slightly from an
inferiority complex. ... In order to justify their existence, they feel impelled to go forward with a programme of recommendations without fully
realizing that these are not likely to gain acceptance or realizing the consequences of the resulting situation...'

All that was now water over the dam. What was to be done? Heeney
could think of only one way out. Every member government would have
to 'put in and have included as part of the report an addendum to
[its] ... country chapter. This addendum would cover, from the country's
own viewpoint, those points remaining in the country chapter with which
the country itself cannot agree. To put the matter in another way, there
would be a report on each country by the Secretariat together with comments on that report by the individual countries.' To put the matter yet
another way, each member government should be given the opportunity
to file a minority report on its country chapter in the NATO Secretariat's
final report on the 1953 Annual Review. To that remedy, Heeney remarked, 'we are most unwillingly forced.'[95] And no wonder unwillingly:
the remedy would require further time and effort, it would add even more
material to what was already a document of inordinate length (the report

placed before the Ministerial meeting of the NATO Council in April 1953 'contained some 360 pages of typescript'),[96] most grievously, it would expose for all to see and deride the futile result to which the Annual Review had led. But there was no alternative.

Accordingly, the delegation at Paris picked out those parts of the country chapter on Canada with which it could not agree. In doing so, it was deliberately uncritical of the Secretariat for, as A.D.P. Heeney explained to Ottawa, 'while we think the Secretariat has done some unwise things, it is very much against our long-term interests to bring them into ridicule or disrepute.' So the delegation paid tribute to 'the industry, the impartiality and the courage with which the Secretariat has approached its difficult task.' It then set forth the reasons why the Canadian government could not accept its recomendations, particularly the recommendation that the amount of Mutual Aid be doubled in value over the next two years.

First, while Canada is passing through a period of exceptional prosperity it is partly based on quite unusual and temporary factors: these include phenomenal harvests, favourable terms of trade, and a heavy inflow of United States capital for direct investment; experience indicates that it is not prudent to make commitments based on such a singularly favourable set of circumstances. Second, while the Canadian standard of living may seem 'very high' when viewed from Europe, it remains substantially lower than the only foreign standard with which the vast majority of Canadians are familiar. Third, Canada has neither the world wide interests and responsibilities of the United States, the United Kingdom and France, nor has it, in NATO and other international organizations, the same voice and authority; hence the Canadian Government could not accept any implications emerging from close comparisons between the overall defence efforts of Canada and such countries.

The delegation then attempted to put the Canadian Mutual Aid programme 'in proper perspective.' The programme, it pointed out, already was a heavy one, amounting to fifteen per cent of the defence budget. Aid programmes overall, including contributions to NATO, the Colombo Plan, and the United Nations, amounted to eight per cent of the budget. 'It would seem to the Delegation that, unless there were some substantial changes in general circumstances, such proportions as these would probably represent the maximum practicable.' The paper concluded by noting that the Canadian government had accepted SACEUR's recommendation of force goals, and had under consideration its recommendations to help defend airfields and to establish an air depot in Western Europe. Only the recommendations of SACLANT did not appear 'feasible at this time from the viewpoint of the Canadian naval authorities.'[97]

In the event, the Secretary of State for External Affairs decided not to send the document containing these observations to the Secretariat for publication in the report. Perhaps L.B. Pearson disliked the device (suggested by Heeney to circumvent, in the interests of saving time, the necessity of discussion of the text in Cabinet) whereby the document was to have been submitted in the name of the delegation rather than of the government. Perhaps Pearson did not like its tone, or perhaps he felt that 'Never complain, never explain' was the better course. Perhaps something of all three.

Instead of submitting as part of the final report rebuttals to the country chapters, those member governments which would not accept the Secretariat's recommendations agreed to treat Part III of the report (in which the country chapters were contained) as 'solely Secretariat documents which did not commit delegations.' A note to this effect was included in the report. Further, the Ministerial Council meeting in April 1953 did not 'approve' the report, it merely 'considered' it. These nuances escaped the authors of the Summary Record, for this affirms that the Council had 'approved' the report. 'It was generally understood, however,' an official of the Department of External Affairs pointed out to his Minister at the end of the year, 'that the governments were *not* committed by the views of recommendations contained in the country chapters.'[98]

And so the first Annual Review came to its anticlimactic close. Was it all worth while? The Permanent Representative thought, on balance, it had been. 'The Annual Review, 1952, has been carried on under difficult conditions,' A.D.P. Heeney wrote to Ottawa in an appraisal of the exercise, citing the 'disturbances caused by the recent move of the NATO Civil Headquarters to Paris, the inexperience of the new international staff, the long delays in the replies of many countries to NATO questionnaires, and the inability for different reasons of the United States, the United Kingdom and France to give clear leadership.' Nevertheless, Heeney considered that there had been some 'very important achievements.' New force goals would be established for 1953 and 1954, and important improvements in the quality of NATO forces were under way. Further, 'the international staff has played an important (and hitherto little appreciated) role ... by persuading the military authorities to drop many suggestions of an impractical character, thus reducing the gap between military proposals and national political-economic capabilities.'[99]

Practice did not make the Annual Review perfect but, over the years, practice made it less imperfect. 'The first Annual Review was by far the most difficult,' the historian of the International Secretariat which conducted it has written. 'After the International Staff/Secretariat, the military planners, and the delegations had become acquainted with their tasks and with each other, after procedures had been worked out, and after the mass of information had been sifted and analyzed, subsequent Reviews became increasingly more routine. The questionnaires were progressively reduced in length and complexity.'[100]

Even so, there were those in Ottawa who felt the questionnaire could be pared further – could even be dispensed with. R.O. Campney, who replaced Brooke Claxton as Minister of National Defence on 1 July 1954, asked an official of the Department of External Affairs 'why it was necessary to go on year after year putting in so much effort on the Annual Review. He said that he could not see that the exercise was of much value to Canada and he wondered whether it was really of great value to NATO.' Campney's question evidently took the official aback, for he reported that he 'did not even try to explain the difficulties which would be created if Canada were to reduce its co-operation with NATO as a whole in the matter of the Annual Review.'[101]

The Annual Review's most sceptical critic was the Chairman of the Chiefs of Staff Committee. As early as June 1953, General Charles Foulkes had questioned its value. 'What do we do,' Foulkes asked rhetorically at an interdepartmental meeting, 'when the Annual Review becomes merely a series of ditto marks?' He added that it 'was becoming a statistical exercise for the information of the US although they had the facilities for obtaining the information elsewhere.'[102] By 1955 – two Annual Reviews later – Foulkes' patience had run out. He wrote to the Under Secretary of State for External Affairs to express his 'doubts as to the real value of the Annual Review process, at least as far as Canada is concerned. We are meeting our force goals,' the General went on acerbically, 'and this Annual Review exercise has not added one extra Canadian serviceman to the NATO forces. It would appear, therefore, that our only purpose in taking part in the review is to sastisfy the International Staff who wish to impel some of the nations who are falling behind in the attainment of their force goals.'[103] By 1956, Foulkes, frustrated in his effort to secure the abandonment of the exercise, proposed that it be drastically simplified. 'Over the course of the last four Annual Reviews,' he wrote to the Under Secretary of State for External Affairs,

the Canadian force goals have not changed materially nor is there likely to be any substantial changes in them for the 1956 Review. Every year, therefore, it has been necessary to produce essentially the same information for the Annual Review. This has involved a tremendous amount of detailed work on the part of a great many people not only at this Headquarters, but also in other Government Departments and in Paris. This situation applies, I am sure, not only to Canada, but also to many of the other NATO countries who are in a comparable position.

I consider, therefore, that the time has come when strong representations should be made to the Annual Review Committee that the purpose of the Annual Review could be satisfied by the submission of amendments, where required, to the reply to the last Annual Review Questionnaire. I suggest that rather than issue an annual questionnaire which would require a complete reply, the Annual Review Committee should simply request nations to bring their last reply up to date.[104]

The Secretary of State for External Affairs thought this to be a reasonable compromise, and the Permanent Representative was told to 'make a definite proposal along these lines and report the reaction...'[105] Dana Wilgress (back at the North Atlantic Council for a second stint) reported that the British delegation had already floated a similar proposal, which had met with 'a very cold reception by all concerned.'[106] Bureaucracies find it easier to start something than to stop it, and NATO's bureaucracy was no exception to this rule. Too many people for too many reasons had acquired a vested interest in the Annual Review for it to be abandoned.

Among the ministries of government, the Department of External Affairs remained alone in continuing to be convinced that the Annual Review was worth the trouble and inconvenience that it caused from one year to the next. '[I]t was as important to the coalition,' L.B. Pearson later stated in his memoirs, 'as it was occasionally irritating to governments. This annual survey,' Pearson added, 'with its praise and blame and its recommendations, had, of course, no binding effect on member governments. These remained masters of their own policies and appropriations, but the surveys were bound to influence their planning for, and participation in, the common defence.'[107]

6

Expanding the Membership

Germany ... is the greatest prospective asset in the possible struggle.

Ambassador at Bonn

Turkey is the only thing that really matters...

Ambassador at Ankara

GERMANS (1)

'[I]n view of Canada's participation in the war, it would not be sufficient merely to present views to the Deputies of the Council of Foreign Ministers and then withdraw. Canada should rather play a more active role, and if possible make an effective contribution to the settlement.'[1] Such had been the consensus of a group of officials at Ottawa on 24 December 1946 which met to determine how best to obtain a seat for their country at the table where the future of Germany would be decided.

But it was not to be. Canada's immediate post-war policy for Germany had been to quit it as soon as possible; her last troops had left by the fall of 1946. Having declined post-war occupation duty, the government had failed to secure a position for Canada on the Allied High Commission and Control Council. (During Germany's brief period of transition from conquered people to sovereign state, Canada's interests were looked after by a Military Mission to the Control Council.) The method by which Canada's views on a peace treaty with Germany were to be presented to the Great Powers was rejected by the government as being, in the words of the Secretary of State for External Affairs, 'a procedure ... entirely inadequate ... for associating Canada with the peace settlement.'[2] A sense of having been badly dealt with in this way may have been partly responsible for Canada's decision to refuse to serve in the airlift of supplies to Berlin under blockade.* Finally, Canada played no part in the shaping of

* See above, Ch. 1, 38-51.

the policy by which West Germany was permitted to draw up a constitution and become the Federal Republic on 23 May 1949. In the light of Canada's bloody conflict with and over Germany during two world wars, this role of onlooker after the second of those wars struck many Canadians as both incongruous and unworthy.

Canada's role as a mere spectator of the attempts at settling the future of Germany ceased abruptly with the coming into force of the North Atlantic Treaty. The Treaty's Article 6 committed Canada to consider as an armed attack upon herself an armed attack 'on the occupation forces of any Party in Europe.' By an agreed interpretation (not made public at the time), British and American forces in the Free Territory of Trieste were understood to be occupation forces. The British, American, and French forces in Germany were obviously occupation forces. Canada was bound to come in aid of them if needed.

Canada's first official statement on the Federal Republic and its future was made in the House of Commons by the Secretary of State for External Affairs on 16 November 1949. Granting that judgement of Germany's 'fitness to enter European society' should be passed primarily by that country's 'European neighbours who have suffered so much in the past from German aggression,' L.B. Pearson expressed the opinion 'that before this judgment can be given Germany must have a democratic and responsible government composed of representatives of the German people qualified to speak for them in the Council of Europe.' For that reason, Pearson declared, his government 'welcomes the establishment of a democratic Federal Republic of Germany whose mandate we hope will soon run over a united Germany. The participation of such a democratic republic in the European community,' he concluded, 'I think is fundamental to the rehabilitation of that community.'[3] Of the rearmament of Germany it was too soon to speak – or even whisper.

At least in public. General Maurice Pope, head of the Military Mission in Berlin, had heard 'word' of the rearmament of Germany as early as March 1949, 'after which,' he records, 'I had heard no more.' A year later, Pope's senior official and right-hand man in the Mission heard more gossip on the policy which, as yet, dared not speak its name.

In mid-March Pete Molson told me that, at a dinner party the previous evening in the British sector, he had gathered that rearmament was now considered to be essential, even though this might not yet be the view held in London. Molson had expressed mild surprise whereupon he had been told that he was probably unaware of the military and strategic considerations. Nor was I, for while I was clear enough in my mind that this development was inevitable, and while I was convinced that all that had been done, and would be done in the future, to fulfil the provisions of the Atlantic Treaty were sound and would make for peace, I felt that in this case it would be wise to make haste slowly.[4]

The policy community at Ottawa was divided whether to rearm Germany. The military planners favoured German rearmament. A document of the Joint Planning Committee dated 24 April 1950 concluded with the recommendation that 'immediate pressure be exerted by the United States, United Kingdom and Canada to impress more forcibly on the other countries of NATO that if Western Europe is to be defended effectively, Western Germany must be accepted as a military partner.' A Department of External Affairs minute on that recommendation rejected it succinctly: 'Nonsense.'[5]

A more considered opinion is to be found in a memorandum prepared within the Department of External Affairs for the guidance of its minister on the eve of the North Atlantic Council session during May 1950. The Department did not expect that German rearmament would be discussed by the Council at its formal sessions: 'It is still too explosive a subject for anyone to raise in such mixed company. It may, however, be discussed behind the scenes in United States-United Kingdom talks.'

The Department of External Affairs' paper addressed itself to two aspects of the German problem: how to associate West Germany with the rest of Western Europe; and whether or not West Germany should be permitted to rearm. The former had already created all kinds of difficulty. Logic and reason led to a policy of including West Germany in any Western European organization. Fear and emotion led to a policy of keeping West Germany down, if not out. More than any North Atlantic Treaty country, France was torn between the two. The French had sought to bring the United Kingdom into the Council of Europe as a counterweight to West Germany, but the British had refused to join. The French had then proposed the creation of a new international organization to include the OEEC countries, West Germany, the United States, and Canada. 'The idea of yet another international organization will certainly not prove attractive to the United States,' the Department's memorandum commented, 'or perhaps to ourselves.' The Department had hoped 'that by keeping machinery flexible enough we might bring Germany and other OEEC countries under the umbrella of the Atlantic Treaty on the political and economic side without associating them with its military aspects.' This approach was not promising. 'In Europe the North Atlantic Treaty is, of course, regarded primarily as a military alliance. Countries like Sweden and Switzerland would be very shy of being associated with it in any way. To associate Germany with it would bring instant protest from France and other European signatories who would feel that this was the first step towards accepting Germany as a military partner.' The 'German problem' was being handled badly. 'Grudging gestures, displays of strength followed by hurried and embarrassed concessions to the Germans are creating that very impression of uncertainty and weakness which has always fed the German appetite for domination.' As the Department saw it, 'the present conglomeration of committees and of alphabetic labels should not obscure ... the necessity for a major political and diplomatic manoeuvre which will bring Germany into a grouping of which the United States and ourselves are members. That is the underlying and perhaps crucial question.' Canada might even give a lead, being 'less directly engaged with squabbles with the Germans over minor points in occupation policy.' 'When the question of associating Germany with a wider grouping ... comes up,' Canada's role should be 'to secure that the objective is clearly delimited, that the consequences of accepting Germany as a partner are accepted without fear or fuss, and that any German attempts to exploit differences between us are met with unity and firmness.' The Department's commentators conceded that 'all this is easier said than done.'

It would be more easily done by aiding West German economic recovery and the revival of democratic institutions while firmly opposing West German rearmament in any form. 'Unfortunately,' the Department's memorandum observed, 'it is becoming more and more difficult to do this. The temptation to utilize German manpower and German industry in the defence of Western Europe may in the end prove irresistible and there are some who urge that we should begin this process now.' The Department was not among the advocates of an early activation of the German war machine. There were two main reasons why. 'In the first place, the association of Germany as a military partner in the North Atlantic Treaty would probably at this stage or even in any foreseeable future break the Treaty wide open. ... The French would simply refuse to accept Germany's membership and the same is probably true of Belgium and The Netherlands.' In the second place, West German rearmament would provoke the Russians. 'It is difficult to imagine that the Soviet Government could sit by and watch the recreation of the German armaments industry and the German army which so nearly overwhelmed the Soviet Union only a few years ago with the knowledge that this formidable military machine was backed by United States power. The very knowledge that such a development was planned might precipitate a decision by the Soviet Government to take over Western Europe at any cost before the threat had materialized.' There was a third reason for delay: 'The German

Chancellor, Dr Adenauer, has publicly declared that Germany has no wish to be rearmed, a view with which the German Socialist Opposition Party have associated themselves.' The Department's paper wound its way to its conclusion.

As there is still insufficient equipment to rearm our Western European allies and while the fear of Soviet aggression has still not precipitated any desire for German rearmament among Western European countries, it would be premature to embark on so dangerous a course. The more so as no one can predict what course both a rearmed and politically resurgent Germany might pursue. Instead of being the bulwark of Western resistance to Soviet aggression, Germany might prefer to play the role which she played in 1939 and we might be faced with a new version of the Ribbentrop-Molotov Pact. We must remember that once Germany is rearmed and politically independent we shall have no further real control over her actions. Thus we reach the conclusion that while German political and economic restoration and close association with the North Atlantic bloc is desirable and should be pursued, the risks of German rearmament at this stage outweigh the advantages.'[6]

The government of Canada agreed – at least until 25 June 1950.

The first parliamentary exchange of opinion about German rearmament before the Korean War took place in the House of Commons on 8 June 1950. It did not elicit much information. The questioner, Douglas Harkness (a future Minister of National Defence), spoke bluntly.

I think it is ... extremely unlikely that, without the armed manpower of western Germany, any of the western European nations with the exception of the peninsulas – Italy, possibly, and more likely Spain, and of course Great Britain because of her island position – could be held successfully. But apart from those countries it would seem to me most unlikely that the North Atlantic pact countries ... could be saved from occupation unless that large pool of manpower in western Germany is utilized.

I should like to know whether this aspect of the matter has been considered in formulating our defence policy, and what the conclusions have been with respect thereto. I know that this whole question is a very thorny one, concerning which most governments in western Europe do not wish to commit themselves, because there is still a large body of opinion mortally afraid of a rearmed Germany. However, in my view this is one of the most important questions to be faced – indeed, perhaps the vital one – if this new strategy is to be carried into effect.

If our government has any opinion in the matter, then we should be told about it in the House of Commons. If our military leaders have anything like the view I have enunciated, we should be told. If they do take that view, then we as a country should be prepared to press for its adoption. Someone has to take the lead in these matters, and, well removed from Europe, without any undue internal difficulty, we could quite readily take that lead, whereas, in a country like France the internal difficulty would be much greater...[7]

It is a fair guess that Harkness had been primed by the military which (as noted above) was pressing for action along the lines of his question. But the Minister of National Defence would not be drawn by it. 'It would not be proper for me to express any views ... at this time with regard to the question raised by the hon. member,' was Brooke Claxton's guarded reply. 'I do not think that would help the situation, which is one that has to be worked out over quite a long term in conjunction with our allies. ... I am not in a position to make any further comment...'[8]

'German rearmament was the product of the war in Korea.'[9] A scholar citing this dictum pronounces it to be 'only slight exaggeration,' but in truth it is no exaggeration at all. The attack on South Korea by a North Korean army lavishly supplied for that purpose with heavy weapons by the Soviet Union upset, to the extent that it did not confirm, all of NATO's operating assumptions. 'The Korean War made a new set of operational premises valid even if they had not been proven correct. Among these were: the Soviet Union would expand militarily if not checked by visible countervailing power; local imbalances which favoured Russia or a satellite would lead to further "Koreas"; and the most inviting local imbalance was in Central Europe.'[10]

There was more to it than even that. Was not the most probable venue, the most plausible scenario, for 'future Koreas,' to be found in the two Germanies? 'The analogy between Korea and Germany – both divided, each with a government aligned with one of the sides in the cold war, with the Communist part militarily superior and supplied with Soviet weapons – was superficially persuasive and deceptively neat.'[11] Superficial or not, deceptive or not, the analogy was accepted where it mattered – in Washington, by the President of the United States. If history was not to be permitted to repeat itself, the step to take was obvious. 'Without Germany, the defense of Europe was a rearguard action on the shores of the Atlantic Ocean,' Harry S. Truman recorded in his memoirs. 'With Germany, there could be a defense in depth, powerful enough to offer effective resistance to aggression from the East. The logic behind this situation is very plain. Any map will show it, and a little arithmetic will prove what the addition of German manpower means to the strength of the joint defence of Europe.'[12] Canada's head of mission to the government at Bonn had likewise been doing his sums. 'When you size up the situation over here,' T.C. Davis wrote in his first dispatch from his new post,

and eliminate France as the major protective power on the continent, what have you left? Italy, is, I suppose, better with you than against you; but Italy has never been able to resist anything very much for very long. Holland and Belgium, are, after all, little States, both with small populations, comparatively speaking. They may fight better next time, but they have never helped anybody very much to date. The Scandinavian countries won't help much in a European struggle with Communism. All in all, there isn't such a great deal over here with which to wage war.

Germany, and even West Germany, is the greatest prospective asset in the possible struggle. Her people are virile, intelligent, hard-working and vigorous...

The time has come when I think that we should be actively starting to think in terms of the possibilities of war. This is no time for wishful thinking...[13]

On 31 August 1950, L.B. Pearson, in the course of a speech said to have 'stunned both politicians and the press' by its cogency and power,[14] dealt squarely with the impact of the Korean war upon the German problem. Gone now was the restraint which, less than three months earlier, had caused the Minister of National Defence to decline even so much as to mention German rearmament. 'The first characteristic of Soviet communist imperialism which I should like to stress today,' Pearson told the House of Commons, 'is that its operations – we know now as never before – are on a world-wide scale. ... The masters of the Kremlin survey every part of the world in their calculations. Today there is fighting in Korea. ... Tomorrow there may be ... a civil war fomented in Germany.' He accepted without qualification the analogy between 'Korea' and the perils inherent in the division of Germany.

The conditions of those two countries, superficially so contrasting, offer some striking parallels at the present time. Both are cut in two by an artificial line of division; in both countries the Soviet-dominated section has powerfully equipped armed forces; while the other section is comparatively unarmed and open to attack. It is, I think, becoming increasingly obvious that the disparity between the military forces of eastern and western Germany must be redressed. It is no longer a question of whether or not Germany is to be rearmed, because the communist part of Germany has already been rearmed, and by Soviet Russia which controls it. If western Germany therefore is to be defended – and certainly that defence is important to the defence of western Europe – it must be given arms with which to assist in its own defence, or alternatively, other western countries must assume even heavier responsibilities...

Here was the first ministerial mention in Parliament of the hitherto forbidden topic of German rearmament. The Secretary of State for External Affairs, far from mentioning it matter-of-factly, stressed from its outset the perils of such a policy.

There are of course risks entailed in rearming western Germany. By grim experience we know that Germans with arms in their hands can be dangerous; but that risk already exists in eastern Germany, and I think it will be minimized in western Germany if that part of Germany, and eventually all of free democratic Germany, could be increasingly and effectively integrated economically, militarily and ultimately politically with the other countries of western Europe. That way, I think, lies the road to safety. But that process of course will raise problems in its turn. And yet I cannot help but feel that that policy alone provides safeguards against the dangers involved in allowing western Germany to rearm, apart from western Europe, or even the more dangerous position of allowing her to remain defenceless against a Russia armed and controlled eastern Europe.[15]

War, General Wolfe once wrote, is an option of difficulties. So – as Pearson's listeners might have reflected on this occasion – is peace.

On 9 September 1950, the Under Secretary of State for External Affairs informed his Minister that the question of German rearmament would be before the North Atlantic Council during its session a week hence. 'In this context,' A.D.P. Heeney advised L.B. Pearson, 'the term "rearmament" cannot be interpreted in the narrow sense. It does not refer merely to the strengthening of German police forces and the expansion of German industrial capacity. It includes also the recreation of German armed forces and German rearmament production.' There were thus three aspects to consider: police, industry, and rearmament in the widest sense. Of these three, policy on police presented the least difficulty: 'On the need for strengthening the Western German police forces there is now general agreement between the Western Powers.' On industry: 'The initiative in the matter of removing some of the restrictions imposed on German industry by the Prohibited and Limited Industries Agreement has already been taken by the United States authorities.' On rearmament in the widest sense: 'To embark on the rearmament of Western Germany would be to reverse the policy of demilitarization which France, the United Kingdom and the United States have pursued with considerable success since 1945. If the inadequacy of Western European defences makes rearmament necessary, it is not surprising that the prospect should be regarded with special concern by France which has suffered so much from German aggression in the past, and that French thinking on the subject should tend to lag behind that of its two partners. Even so the gulf between the Anglo-Saxon and the French points of view is now perhaps less great than might be expected...'[16] Events would shortly show this assessment to be too optimistic.

On 14 September 1950, a few hours before the great debate on German rearmament would take place within the North Atlantic Council, the US Secretary of State conferred with the foreign ministers of Norway, The Netherlands, and Canada to tell them what had transpired at an earlier meeting of the foreign ministers of the United Kingdom, France, and the

United States. There had been no agreement on German rearmament, Dean Acheson disclosed:

He outlined in some detail the position of the US on the question of integrated forces, combined staff, German participation, etc. He expressed the hope that he would get support from the other Ministers present and urged that a complete and thorough discussion take place in the Council. He said that he hoped no one would "pull any punches."

For Canada, the US minutes of this meeting record, 'Mr Pearson said that his Government was prepared to support Mr Acheson's stand.'[17]

The debate in the North Atlantic Council on 15 September was described by L.B. Pearson as having been conducted in 'the frankest possible way. ... I spoke towards the end of the discussion,' Pearson reported,

along the general lines of my statement in the House of Commons on August 31. I emphasized the importance and difficulty of the subject, and that the representative of a country like Canada must approach it with special diffidence, as we were geographically and psychologically further removed from Germany than other members. We were in a sense the only Western hemisphere country represented at the Council because the strength and power and influence of the United States extended far beyond this hemisphere. I said that we must all admit with the French and other European countries that while in the past the overseas democracies had been given time to rearm after war had broken out, in the future they might not have the time, or indeed the right to gather their strength behind the ramparts of sacrifices made by others. I agreed that France had the right to ask that her maximum effort to defend herself should be supplemented by the collective effort of us all, so that the next time she would not require to be liberated. At the same time, we across the ocean had the right to ask that everything possible should be done in Europe to give us the assurance that the effort to defend freedom in Europe would be successful. That brought up the question automatically of German rearmament.

If we agreed, as we all did, that the menace of Russian Communist aggression was great and immediate, then we had to ask the question how could we secure enough forces to meet it in Europe as far to the East as possible, that is in Germany. One answer was to do this without Germans – at least Germans on our side – because there would certainly be Germans against us. I felt that this was not possible militarily or desirable politically. The other answer was to include German units, though not a German army, in the Western European forces, which would also include forces from the USA. Of course, there were risks in this course. Everybody admitted such risks, but we felt that this was the best choice of risks to take, especially as rearmament had already taken place in that part of Germany under communist control. I argued that this course did not mean that the Germans should be armed before their allies, nor did it mean that the rest of us would slacken our defence effort. I then asked that we accept at this Council meeting the principle of using in some way German manpower for the defence of freedom in Europe, so that defence might be successful and be conducted as far away as possible from the borders of those countries which have suffered so much from

German aggression in the past, and might suffer even more in the future from Russian Communist aggression if we did not take effective action in time...[18]

L.B. Pearson's plea for a decision then and there in favour of German rearmament – if only a decision in principle – failed to persuade the opponents of that policy. 'France, Belgium, the Netherlands, Denmark and Norway ... had vivid memories of Nazi aggression and occupation and feared a recrudescence of German militarism,' Pearson recalled in his memoirs. 'They were not going to be rushed into a solution of the problem by Washington'[19] – much less by Ottawa. 'The French are out of step,' Pearson reported on 17 September 1950. 'They cannot agree to accept immediately in principle the participation of German units in an integrated force, and they cannot accept Western Germany producing any complete items of military equipment...' He observed that the debate, while emotional, had been conducted without bitterness. 'We all realize that the complete lack of diplomatic preparation for this major decision has presented the French and others at this Council with a most awkward political problem and, with the best will in the world, a solution must take a little time.'[20] By that he did not mean five years.

During the three months which elapsed between rejection and acceptance of the principle that West Germany must somehow be rearmed, members of the policy community pondered the dilemma, according it the intense and careful analysis which the issues by their gravity deserved.

The Ambassador at Washington provided one of the longest and most thoughtful of the many dispatches he would compose at that busy post – a worthy example of what a colleague described as his mind's 'rational quality and its pragmaticism.'[21] Hume Wrong began by noting that the North Atlantic Council had decided against the recreation of a German national army and that 'the question to be considered will be, not whether a German armed force should be formed as an independent national unit, but whether it would be desirable to have German participation in an integrated force for the defence of Western Europe.'

Wrong then took up the issue of that desirability.

German rearmament can be justified at this time only for the reasons which have dictated the rearmament of the democratic nations, namely, the threat of Soviet aggression in the various forms which have been experienced in the past few years. German association with the rearmament efforts of the North Atlantic countries would, therefore, be for the purpose of deterring Soviet aggression or ensuring its defeat should aggression occur. Any other justification would be unthinkable, especially in view of Germany's own record of aggression and the dangers that oppressive forces will again be brought into play in Germany once any degree of rearmament is permitted in that country.

A Soviet attack upon Western Germany should be anticipated in any of three forms. The first, that of internal subversion, had been the concern of the three Western occupying powers in deciding to allow West Germany to establish mobile police formations for the maintenance of internal security. The second was armed aggression on the Korean model, in which the Soviet Union would use East German troops as its proxy for an attack. The third was outright attack by the Soviet Union itself, using its own armed forces. Of these two latter possibilities, Wrong considered the threat of attack by proxy to be the more probable, 'since the use of Soviet forces would involve a general war and a resulting retaliation with atomic weapons.' Nevertheless, the threat of a direct Soviet attack was one for which deterrence was required, and effective deterrence could not for much longer be conferred by atomic weapons alone.

If it is agreed that heretofore a Soviet attack on Western Europe has been held in check by the prospect of retaliation with atomic weapons by the United States, the development of atomic weapons by the Soviet Union may be expected to create a comparable deterrent to the use of atomic weapons by the democratic powers. To restore the balance, it is now argued that the ground forces of the North Atlantic Treaty countries must be built up to a point at which an integrated force can readily be put into the field which can cope with the mobilized divisions of the Soviet Union. If this formidable increase in strength is indeed now required to deter Soviet aggression, the question of utilizing German manpower becomes all the more urgent, and it is difficult to conceive from what source the necessary divisions will be forthcoming for the defence of Western Europe without an adequate contribution of manpower from Germany...

Wrong, like L.B. Pearson, saw the dangers of rearming West Germany. He identified a two-fold hazard – 'the revival of a German military caste, and a German military spirit, and secondly, the revival of German military potential...' Both of these perils could be preempted only by integrating Western Germany 'economically, militarily and politically with the other countries of Western Europe, in such a way that any decisions involving the defence of Western Germany are subordinated to the requirements and plans of the democratic world, and not to the nationalist aspirations and policies of the German Government.' Wrong agreed with the decision to prohibit West Germany from producing weapons (so-called 'military end items'), but noted that some arrangement would have to be contrived in order to forestall its benefitting economically by being able to export materials for the Alliance's arms build-up while receiving free of charge the equipment necessary for its own defence. The best form of overall control, Wrong considered, would derive from West Germany's admission, 'before too long,' to the North Atlantic Treaty Organization.

It is well to recognize this at the beginning. That the democracies which twice in thirty years have exerted themselves to the point of exhaustion to defeat German aggression should now assist in re-creating German forces is distasteful enough; and it will take a good deal of education of public opinion for the people of the North Atlantic countries to accept the idea of admitting Germany as an equal party in the North Atlantic Alliance. The masters of the Kremlin have shown themselves to be industrious pedagogues in this respect; but such an outcome must rest on more solid ground than fear of the Soviet Union – i.e., on confidence that the German people have earned the right to be trusted.

Wrong concluded his dispatch by observing that public opinion in the United States had, since the outbreak of war in Korea, 'taken a sharp turn in favour of rearmament of Western Germany. Whereas the weight of sentiment was against it as recently as May of this year,' he pointed out, 'the results of the Gallup Poll published on August 16th indicate that 71% of the people of the United States favour assisting the Western Germans to build up an army at least equal in size to the military forces of the Eastern zone.' Such a shift of key by the *vox populi* of the United States, Wrong commented, 'indicates how quickly public opinion in this country can change in the face of an imminent danger.'[22]

Another member of the policy community to offer reflections on German rearmament was the former head of the mission at Bonn. General Maurice Pope (who in mid-June had been transferred to Brussels as Ambassador) counselled that the people to whose wishes most heed should be paid was the West German public itself, to which 'too much attention cannot be given. ... I am inclined to wonder,' Pope continued,

if the German authorities at Bonn really entertain as great a fear of the possibility of a western march of the Soviet armies as is apparently entertained in other quarters. If they do not, and I think they do not, then I am inclined to believe that Herr Adenauer and his principal advisers are content, for the time being, to press the Western Occupying Powers materially to increase their forces of "occupation" so as the better to be able to discharge the responsibilities which they assumed on the cessation of hostilities.

From another aspect I think it should always clearly be borne in mind that the Germans have as much pride in themselves and their great country as any other people on earth. In any event, they have every justification for being so. Consequently, any idea that the Germans can be summoned to contribute their quota of defence forces, almost in the form of mercenaries, is, I suggest, very likely to lead to disillusionment. That they would do so without exacting complete equality with the Atlantic Treaty countries is, I think, doubtful.

For myself, I think that the rearmament of Germany pretty well on terms of equality is an inevitable consequence of the Western Occupying Powers' decision some two and a half years ago to set up the Federal Republic. From this course there can be no turning back. The question of timing, however, is of great importance as it is in all political questions. To my mind ... the time may not yet be opportune. Many obstacles, e.g. French reluctance, and the price which Herr Adenauer would wish to exact, would have to be overcome...[23]

From Paris, Ambassador Georges Vanier gave his opinion that 'French reluctance' might not be so formidable an obstacle as other NATO capitals, including Ottawa, supposed. 'We have as you know expressed the view that French public opinion could be brought without too much difficulty to accept a measure of German rearmament if the Government were to give up its obduracy and were to take a reasonably bold line.'[24] Events would show that the word 'if' in that succinct comment bore much freight. Even at the time, officials in Ottawa remained sceptical. 'The failure of the North Atlantic Council ... to reach agreement on the German question was largely the result of French adamance,' the Department of External Affairs responded to Vanier's dispatch. 'We find it difficult to reconcile the government's inflexible attitude with optimistic estimate of the progress of French public opinion conveyed in your despatches. This matter requires careful re-examination as it is of especial concern to us at the present time. It is, therefore, of considerable importance to us to have a clearer analysis of the situation as you see it as soon as possible.'[25] (1950 was a year of heavy weather for the Vanier embassy: it was concurrently under rebuke by Ottawa for what officials there considered its unduly optimistic and overly superficial analysis of the French cause in Indochina.)

The head of the mission at Bonn also experienced the East Block's reprimand for his reporting on the German scene. T.C. Davis – an experienced if opinionated observer* – had offered Ottawa, on 5 September 1950, a blunt and bleak appraisal: 'The only final alternative to a Russian-dominated Europe is a Europe to a considerable extent dominated by Germany.' This position, as officials of the Department of External Affairs promptly told the head of mission, was 'at variance with the policy that the Canadian Government has followed with respect to Germany since the end of the war.' Davis ought not to have ventured such a view without 'the closest possible analysis' with which to support it. The Under

---

* 'Little...escaped Davis' notice. That he was given in succession several difficult assignments (he was Canada's first ambassador to West Germany) suggests that his work was prized by his superiors in Ottawa.' Norman Ward, 'A Prince Albertan in Peiping: The Letters of T.C. Davis,' *International Journal*, XXX, 1, Winter, 1974-5, 33.

Secretary of State for External Affairs had his officials prepare such an analysis, which was sent to the head of the mission at Bonn for his guidance.

On this as on other subjects Canadian policy should not be static in such a changing world; nor should it be at the mercy of every new idea or theory which might find favour with one power or another. You are familiar enough with our efforts in bringing about and strengthening the United Nations organization and the North Atlantic Treaty to realize that our whole policy aims at achieving international security through international co-operation and not on the domination of one continent or region by one power or another. It would not be in the spirit of the United Nations Charter or the North Atlantic Treaty to have a Europe dominated either by Soviet Russia or Germany.

Secondly, our European North Atlantic partners, particularly those which have suffered German occupation, would be reluctant to accept a measure of German remilitarization which might eventually lead to German domination over Europe. The fears of our Western European partners are an integral part of European thinking and have to be taken into consideration even if at times they seem to have a paralyzing effect. To ignore those fears would be to force upon our allies a policy which would not command the support of their governments or their people. We can try to quicken the pace if it is considered too slow, but this should be done in an atmosphere of co-operation and not of coercion.

Thirdly, the experience of the last fifty years has proven that the "virility of the German people," as you describe it, could very well enable that country, if given the opportunity, again to dominate Europe to a considerable degree, eventually to try and dominate it fully. Hitler accomplished this in less than a decade. The threat of a new form of world imperialism should not make us forget so rapidly the lessons of the last two wars...

...Our policy and that of other peace-loving nations would be extremely shortsighted if it led to the restoration of Germany to a place of military pre-eminence in Europe. Germany should be given an opportunity to play a constructive role in Europe without thoughts or means of domination; the plans which are now being made to integrate Germany into the Western community should, in my estimation, be based on that premise. We are apt, at the present time, to consider all problems purely in terms of their military and strategic implications; it appears to me that our role is to try to prevent mistakes which might serve to place the military in charge once more. Even if the worst comes to the worst and this had to be done, we should persevere in our efforts to build up a world free from the German as well as the Russian menace.

Our gravest and most immediate threat is from Communist imperialism and it might be that the Germans can help us to face it; but the assistance which they might give should not be such as to encourage aggressive designs on their part.

It is our policy that Germany should be reunited; it is a fact that once Germany is reunited she will have become numerically and economically the greatest power in Europe apart from the USSR. It seems to me that it is up to us to find a solution whereby, notwithstanding her "greatness," Germany will remain a willing partner and not become a harsh leader. This is a most intricate problem and will tax to their limit the wisdom and understanding of statesmen of the Western world. It seems to me that ... the formula of slowly integrating Germany in the North Atlantic Treaty Organization is a good one. In a camp where the United States would be ever present, Germany would surely find it difficult to dominate.[26]

T.C. Davis' reply to this reprimand was swift and apologetic. 'I am most grateful that you have written me as you have done,' Davis began, perhaps unconvincingly. 'I have read and re-read your letter and thoroughly agree with the statement of policy which it contains. Germany must be integrated into a Western bloc but in such a way that we will not ultimately find ourselves facing a possible German menace as well as a Russian one.' That much conceded, Davis sought next to clarify and justify the view which had caused offence. He admitted it had been infelicitously expressed.

Perhaps my use of the word "dominate" was not the happiest choice. ... The word is open to the construction, and perhaps the natural one, of a powerful force running roughshod over others. It is perhaps the one which comes naturally to mind in the light of German history over the last one hundred years. I did not have quite that idea in mind when I used the word.

Let me try and explain just what I had in mind. Here in the heart of Europe lies Germany, a nation of nearly eighty million people. Here she is and here they are and here they both remain.

...Under the old set-up Germany could be and was sort of a third power. In the face of Russia she can no longer be such. The continent is now definitely divided into two camps, viz., Russia and her satellites and the Western and free portion of Europe. Germany must ally herself with one or the other. Russian policy forces a nation to be either with her or against her. There is no middle course.

If Germany allies herself with Russia, then Russia definitely controls the whole of Europe. If she allies herself with the West, then there is a balance of power which tips towards the West. It is, therefore, essential that Germany be allied with the West.

The Germans know they are in a bargaining position and being Germans they propose to make the most of it. They will use their position to the utmost to secure a complete return of freedom and national sovereignty and the relinquishment of further claims for reparations, etc.

I am sure that Western Germany will move in with the West. She can in the final analysis do nothing else. When Germany becomes united, it is another question...

...It is essential that there be a joint defence to protect Western Europe. It is inevitable that Western Germany will be represented therein. A separate German Army would be fatal. This joint set-up must be in being before control of Germany is completely released. If sooner released, there would be great danger of her rearmament and thus an increase of her bargaining power. In any event, the inclusion of Germany must be done slowly. ... A powerful joint defence force excluding Germany should be in being before steps are taken to include Germany in it. Finally, Germany should come in freely of her own volition and it must be clear that the bulk of public opinion is behind her doing so. Care should be taken to see to it that she is not brought in as a result of bargaining which would be fatal.

If she can be brought in this manner into this joint force, then I am not alarmed about her military domination of Western Europe nor would I greatly fear her throwing her weight around too much...

...In conclusion, my idea was to express my opinion of the importance of Germany in the North Atlantic set-up and to bring a realization of the fact that restored in power and might as she is bound to be, she will be a powerful influence. I might hesitate to use the word "dominate" but she will be a dominating influence. How will that do?...[27]

A more tersely expressed statement of the views of Ottawa's man in Bonn was despatched on 2 November: 'To recapitulate,' T.C. Davis then wrote. 'I think that a unified force without Germany and with a Supreme Commander should be evolved at once and when it shows real signs of strength that Germany should then be invited to join such an organization in being.'[28]

Further reflections on German rearmament within the policy community at this time are contained in a letter from Jules Léger (then in charge of the Department of External Affairs' European Division and, as such, the drafter of the reprimanding dispatch sent over the signature of the Under Secretary to the head of mission at Bonn) to a fellow official. 'It appears to me that the problem of German rearmament is being seriously mishandled,' Léger wrote on 20 October.

I think that the bluntness of the American approach to that problem has done great harm.

I am wondering if we should not start from the premise that the French, for all practical purposes, are at present no better equipped than the Germans to face a possible Soviet aggression. If the Russians decided to invade Western Europe they would not encounter much more resistance in France than they would in Western Germany. At this stage it is not so much a question of morale as it is one of armament. Within this context it is easy to see why the French are so adamant in accepting discussions of German rearmament simultaneously with discussions of their own rearmament, since they realize that under such conditions they would be the losers in the very near future. The theory of immediate and simultaneous rearmament for France and Germany cannot therefore be accepted by the French without very serious misgivings.

Another very important current, however, cuts across this in France and makes me believe that a solution could be found. At this juncture in their history the

French are willing to give up certain attributes of their national sovereignty in exchange for security on their Eastern frontiers. The best illustration of this is the Schuman Plan [for the integration of the French and West German coal and steel industries]. To me this is an indication that the French are taking a longer term view of the problem of intra-European relations than the Americans are. War or no war the French realize that they will have to continue to live next to the Germans and that any increase in the military strength of the latter could eventually lead to another occupation of their country, while the Americans seem to envisage German participation in a common pool of defence as an immediate requirement without thinking of its future implications. All told the United States and France are, therefore, looking at different problems in different perspectives. The United States are thinking in terms of strategical necessities for the immediate future, while the French are thinking in terms of their permanent quarrel with their next door neighbour. This is a pretty tragic situation: on the one hand you have the United States willing to help both militarily and economically at a rate unheard of in their history and, on the other hand, you have the French who are willing to give up part of their national sovereignty to settle once and for all the problem of their relations with the Germans. And still with all this goodwill on both sides no satisfactory solution seems to be forthcoming. This is so much more tragic because the decisions which are taken now might well lead to the establishment of equilibrium on the European continent for years and years to come, an equilibrium which could lead us to another disaster.

If the French continue to be so stubborn about it, the United States might very well turn to the Germans and rearm them notwithstanding objections. The Germans are probably waiting for this opportunity since they have been placed in such a good bargaining position. The French would be left to stew in their own juice. If war comes the French won't fight and once the war is over the Germans will dominate the continent, since I take it, for the sake of argument, Soviet Russia would have been eliminated. One could argue that the United States are in Europe to stay in perpetuity, but no one will ever convince me of that. If there is no war it means that Russian pressure will decrease, that the Germans will have been rearmed, that the United States will leave Europe, and that the European continent will be dominated again by the Germans.

In terms of immediate strategical requirements, German manpower appears to be essential; if a longer term view is taken, German rearmament is a real danger. Is a *quid pro quo* not possible? Could a discussion of German rearmament instead of being placed in the North Atlantic Treaty context not only remain in a more European context but be discussed jointly with French plans for European integration? It seems to me that one cannot go wrong if one subscribes to any solution which would eliminate one of the more important causes of war apart from Communism, i.e. Franco-German rivalry. Each month that goes by makes a solution on those lines more difficult.

If the rearmament of Western Germany were placed in its European context there is another point that confuses the issue and which would have to be cleared, i.e., the "*splendide isolement*" of the United Kingdom as far as European integration is concerned. This weakens the Western will to resist since the average Frenchman and Italian just does not understand. Could a way not be found for other members of the Commonwealth to press the United Kingdom into being more co-operative in their dealings with their immediate European neighbours? The fiction of Commonwealth ties as against Commonwealth co-operation plays an enormous role in this sort of thinking. To my mind ... a closer integration of the United Kingdom into European affairs would strengthen the morale of continental countries.

It looks as if I were trying to disassociate Western German rearmament with the North Atlantic Treaty; this is not so. I am only trying to bring the North Atlantic Treaty back to its original conception. This is where Canada would have a pretty important role to play. We seem to have lost quite a lot of our proselytism about Article 2 of the Treaty which is rapidly becoming unrecognizable. It has military lines and nothing else now. It appears to me that the democracies, within the North Atlantic Treaty, if they were willing to work together, could offer guns and butter at the same time. The difficulty here is that since the North American housewife has butter anyway, emphasis on this continent has to be placed on guns. This is a very North American way to look on the North Atlantic Treaty, however. The European way might well be that emphasis on butter could lead to a better handling of guns.

One last word: when the problem of German rearmament is discussed, there are those optimists who believe that, under certain guarantees, it can be made fool-proof. I cannot agree with this: if the Germans are permitted three divisions for next year, they will have ten divisions in five years. If this deterrent force prevents Communist Russia from attacking us, the only way other European countries can be safe from an eventual German domination of the continent is by a perpetual occupation of Europe by United States troops. Such a situation is unthinkable; it just won't happen. The Americans are not built that way nor are we and once we think that the situation has become more stable we will all go back home and the Europeans will be left to the Germans once more. It is, therefore, very urgent that the French position of integrating Germany and France and other European countries in a unit where real power in certain spheres will be given to a higher authority should materialize...[29]

These reflections – far-ranging, imaginative, partly prophetic – were duly placed before the Secretary of State for External Affairs. L.B. Pearson considered them 'an excellent statement of the situation in terms of long-range political realities as distinct from the immediate pressure for German rearmament.' So favourably impressed was Pearson by Léger's letter that he sent a copy to the Ambassador at Washington with the suggestion that 'you might, if you agree, take an opportunity to [give] it to Dean Acheson as it may serve to counter-balance in some measure the current irritation with the French by putting the case rather better than M. Monnet seems to have been able to. After all,' Pearson added, 'this is not only or even principally a problem of French security, but one of the balance of forces in Europe which, in the long run, may affect us all.'[30] Hume Wrong replied that Léger's letter had not reached him until after the last meeting of NATO Defence Ministers held in Washington at the end of October, and that 'in the light of what went on at those meetings, it would be unwise for me to adopt your suggestion of passing on to Dean Acheson the opinions of Léger.' Wrong's response makes clear that he thought it just as well that 'the opinions of Léger' arrived too late, for he disagreed with them. 'Léger omits what is to me a most important factor,' Wrong wrote to Pearson on 2 November.

The Germans are not going to remain unarmed for much longer, no matter what Adenauer and the Socialists may say. The time within which the rearmament of Germany can be conducted by agreement between the Western Powers is thus limited. We must always remember what happened after the first war: the methods whereby von Seeckt retained the professional core of the army and used it to give training to very large numbers of Germans, and the defiance which Hitler later displayed to all restrictions. Legal rearmament under such safeguards as can be agreed with the German authorities is infinitely preferable to illegal rearmament, and there is still some chance that we can get it.

Another factor is that unless the Germans soon begin to play some effective part in their own defence, it will, I think, become politically impossible for the United States to maintain substantial forces in Western Europe. It is possible that Canadian opinion would be moved so far in the same direction that we could not send the Special Force to Europe...

I agree with Léger that the question of German rearmament should not be divorced from the problems of closer European integration, and I have much sympathy for the apprehensions over the long term which are held by the French about the revival of German military power. To the continental European, however, and especially to the Danes, Dutch, Belgians, Germans and the French themselves, the immediate need is the adoption of measures to make the line of the Elbe rather than the line of the Rhine the basic defensive position against the Russians. This requires, *inter alia*, the presence in Europe of the US Divisions which President Truman has indicated can be supplied, and I gravely doubt that they will be forthcoming unless we start now to use German manpower in some way or other to assist in the defence of Western Germany...

... [T]he idea stuck in my crop at the rest of us assisting the Germans to re-establish German armed forces other than police formations. We must, however, weigh danger against danger, and I am now satisfied that, unless we are all grossly exaggerating the danger from the Soviet Union, we must begin to make use of German manpower while at the same time encouraging as far as possible in other respects the integration of Western Germany both with Western Europe and the whole group of Atlantic nations...

If Pearson wanted to put some views on German rearmament before the US Secretary of State, Wrong stated, they should come from him as foreign minister of Canada and should carry as well the support of the Minister of National Defence. 'I should think it is essential that Brooke Claxton be consulted first. ... We are now,' Wrong added grimly, 'in the midst of a great crisis in the development of the North Atlantic Treaty. If it is not solved quickly, the Treaty may become meaningless. Failure to find a solution will tend to drive the United States towards withdrawal from Europe and concentration on North American defence.'[31]

Out of this discussion – in which, it will be observed, no participant opposed German rearmament outright and only one (General Pope) considered that the time was not yet propitious for such a move – did any policy emerge?

Not much – necessarily. The members of the Alliance were in deadlock. The United States insisted on rearming Germany then and there. The French had just as insistently refused. The debate was to be resumed at the meetings of the North Atlantic Defence Committee to be held in Washington late in October 1950. As guidance for the members of the military establishment who would be participating in the talks, the Department of External Affairs had prepared a memorandum on 'some tentative views as to the political setting...'

There were three of these. The first foreshadowed Hume Wrong's subsequent warning that no safeguards would be foolproof. '[S]afeguards, however carefully framed, may not endure much longer than the establishment of a fully independent West German government. From this reasonable expectation it follows that, in the final analysis, only the integration of Western Germany in the Western community can ultimately protect the other nations of Western Europe from a resurgence of German militarism.' The second proposition was that the United States should maintain a military presence in Western Europe for the foreseeable future, and that the French and other allied governments there could be persuaded that American troops would not be prematurely withdrawn. Third: 'Our final proposition is that we should not be led by the logic of the purely military argument into pressing the French too hard for an immediate agreement on a programme that has immense political difficulties for them, and, in any case, cannot be implemented immediately.'[32]

Such were the outlines of the policy which Canada's delegation hoped would emerge from the meeting of NATO's Defence Committee at Washington at the end of October 1950. That meeting took place immediately after the French National Assembly had approved in principle the plan placed before it by Premier René Pleven, eventually to bear his name, for creating a European Army under the direction of European political institutions in which formations of German troops would be organized as the smallest units possible (which the French believed should be at the level of combat regiments). The Pleven Plan, one authority has commented, 'must be considered a masterpiece, if for no other reason than because it sounded so attractive on so many counts – it would bring military strength, Franco-German reconciliation, European unification...' It would also bring maximum delay in giving arms to Germans. 'By presenting the European army plan in such fashion that it could be undertaken only after the many details of the Schuman Plan had been agreed to, and only after the supranational European political edifice had been erected, the French Government sought to assure itself that considerable time would pass before a German in uniform could appear – and if he did, he would not be in a German but a European uniform.'[33]

Canadian authorities, while favourably impressed by the Pleven Plan's technical virtuosity, doubted whether it would prove to be politically feasible. 'I felt, I think our whole delegation agreed,' Brooke Claxton was to write in retrospect, 'that not only would the terms of this [Plan] prove unacceptable to Germany but that the project would not even be accepted by France. Certainly not in any workable form. No doubt it had been put forward and pushed through in all sincerity by M. René Pleven but its effect was to hamstring progress on this both at our meeting and in Europe.'[34]

That appraisal was written with benefit of hindsight. At the time, Brooke Claxton was more cautious, although he made no attempt to hide Canada's concern about the practical difficulties which the Pleven Plan presented. 'Our ties of blood with France and our actions in their defence and liberation in two world wars' – so Claxton declared (according to Hume Wrong's report) to the Defence Committee

made it clear that we fully appreciated the sincerity of their point of view. The French proposals were indeed revolutionary; but so were those of the United States which had never before contemplated sending troops to Europe in peacetime...

As regards the political difficulties of the French plan, we would do everything possible to be of assistance but did not feel it proper to discuss the issue in detail. As regards the military difficulties, however, we did feel it would delay matters. It would mean creating a European Army in which Germans would be second-class soldiers which would not encourage them to co-operate as they must to make the endeavour worthwhile. Also, there might be difficulties in working out a satisfactory relationship between the European Army and Canadian and United States forces serving separately under the Supreme Commander. These difficulties might tend to make the force less effective than that which we know the Communists have today.

While we have made astonishing progress, we cannot believe ... that our choice was between the French plan and doing nothing. We must get on with the rest of the job without delay...[35]

Claxton's own recollection of his statement to the Defence Committee confirms his insistence on 'the necessity for getting on with the job. I said,' he recalled in his memoirs, 'that while the proposal for re-armament of Germany might appear to be premature and put forward with insufficient preparation (a colossal understatement), we must think in terms of time. Looking back we could now see that there were times when it might have been possible for the Second World War to have been averted if at the time the pre-Hitler offers of co-operation by Germany had been taken at some value, if not their full face value, and if the United States had been willing to guarantee the peace of Europe. Now we had a moment, a breathing spell in history, when Germany was willing to co-operate and the United States was willing to guarantee the peace of Europe. This combination of circumstances might not last forever. What if the attitude of either Germany of the United States changed? And the spirit being shown at our meeting' – Claxton described it as 'the worst scene I remember in NATO' – 'was just the kind of thing which, if known to the public, might well lead either the Germans or Americans, or both, to change...'[36]

Two other officials present at the meeting conveyed their impressions of it to Ottawa. 'Once again a top North Atlantic body has been faced with major new proposals which, with the best will in the world, could not possibly be dealt with in one session from a standing start,' A.D.P. Heeney observed. 'At New York [in September] the Council was faced with the American proposals. Here' – at Washington – 'we have been confronted with the still more far-reaching French plan which the French themselves asked should not be discussed, as it could have been, in the preparatory group which met for several days before the Defence Ministers arrived. General Marshall and Mr Acheson decided very sensibly to leave most of the running to the Europeans who were being asked under the French plan to deferate [sic: procrastinate]. With the exception of Luxembourg, none of the European representatives showed any inclination to do so – at least they did not want to hold up present defence plans during the elaborate process of negotiating a European union. On this point, therefore, the French were virtually isolated and their "take it or leave it" attitude did their cause no good. In the discussion on procedure, however,' Heeney's account continued,

the French almost succeeded in isolating the United States and the United Kingdom, who kept insisting that the military aspects of the problem could and should be separated from the political. The rest of us did not disagree that the Military Committee should assist in the examination of this problem, but we could not see much point in it coming back to the Defence Committee alone as, at the ministerial level, the decisions are bound to be primarily political.

The United States have chosen to risk the let-down in public opinion to which Mr Claxton drew attention in order to make the French face up to the consequences of their present policy. General Bradley told the French and ourselves privately that he could not possibly testify to Congress in favour of sending the United States troops to Europe and building up an integrated force unless that force could be made a going concern; and in his opinion that required German participation in a form which they could accept with at least some measure of enthusiasm. As [the United Kingdom defence minister Emmanuel] Shinwell pointed out, all the non-continental Governments would be in the same position of finding it almost impossible to send troops to the defence of Germany while the Germans simply sat back and watched. The question of course remains as to what the Germans themselves would accept. Certainly the longer we wrangle the better will be their bargaining position.

The alternative United States policy, which was privately advocated by some United Kingdom military representatives, would have been to announce that, in spite of the French, the United Kingdom and the United States were going to arm the Germans in their zones. In our opinion, this would have been fatal; for, if the defence of the West is impossible without Germany, it is equally impossible without France. The United States have chosen to wield their second biggest stick. There is to be no Supreme Commander and no integrated force until the French give some earnest of their willingness to compromise. If and when they do, the United States will probably go a short distance towards meeting them – for example, on the size of German units. But, the present United States attitude to the French has been considerably hardened by the attitude of the French in blocking further progress by attaching conditions that cannot possibly be accepted at least within the time which may be given the West for building up its defence. As one of them said, they have been "Moched"! Although [the French defence minister Jules] Moch presented his case with great clarity, the ill-concealed satisfaction of his stone-wall performance has thoroughly annoyed the Americans.

'It would appear,' Heeney concluded, 'that the lesson we have still to learn is that, in the final analysis, no member of the North Atlantic Community, neither France nor the United States, can really afford to call another's bluff. In our present danger we are too inter-dependent; and for that reason a great effort will have to be made in the meetings of the Deputies and the Military Committee that are to follow in the next two weeks or so before the Defence Ministers resume their meeting.'[37]

To A.D.P. Heeney's impressions, Hume Wrong added his. 'If you had listened to the speeches round the table at the Defence Committee,' the Ambassador at Washington told his Minister, 'you would, I think, agree that it would only be irritating to Acheson to present criticisms of the position adopted not only by the United States, but far more emphatically by the United Kingdom with strong support from the Norwegians, Danes, Belgians, Dutch, Italians, Portuguese, and Canadians. Moch, who is an accomplished performer, stuck to his inflexible instructions. Shinwell tactlessly goaded him by taking the first opportunity of asking, contrary to the judgment of his own advisers, a series of leading questions which Moch was impelled to answer categorically. ... The hope is,' Wrong concluded, 'that some middle ground can be discovered between the Pleven Plan and the measures which the United States and apparently most of the other governments consider to be essential. Moch, however, gave no reason at the meetings (or at his press conference yesterday) for hope that this common ground existed. Unless it is discovered we are unlikely to have any Supreme Commander, any agreed medium term plan and any integrated force.'[38]

Back in Ottawa, the Under Secretary of State for External Affairs pondered how the government might assist the principal antagonists to find a way out of the deadlock. 'I think we should begin now to put some ideas on paper,' A.D.P. Heeney wrote on 2 November in a memorandum to his colleagues, 'working within the general policy of the Government to leave the prime initiative on this subject to those countries more directly concerned with German participation than we are. In our judgment,' Heeney continued,

the extremely grave situation we are now faced with can only be resolved if the French government are prepared to modify their proposals. This almost certainly means modification in substance. If the French can be brought to this course, the United States would, we think, be prepared to compromise on the details of their proposals. The problem is, therefore, how best to move the French.

In the first place, we think that both the French and the United States Governments may have an inflated idea of their respective bargaining positions. The Americans feel that the piper will, in the final analysis, be able to call the tune. The French believe that Western European defence is hopeless without their participation and that the United States will have to come around and produce their reinforcement of Western Europe if the most co-operative French government possible in present circumstances is to remain in power and France is to produce the twenty divisions she has promised by 1953. Before there can be successful negotiations, both sides will have to realize their interdependence. On the one hand, therefore, it seems to me we should be urging on the French the political, psychological and military risks of delay, and on the other hand, trying to impress the United States with the dangers of any attempt to steamroll the French, which would only get their backs up and strengthen French "neutralism."

On points of detail, we must be careful that the military Committee do not introduce political assumptions, for example, as to the size of units that would be politically acceptable to the United States. ... For this reason, I think our military paper should address itself to the problem of the smallest German units that would make sense from a military point of view in the near future...[39]

Brooke Claxton took advantage of Jules Moch's visit to Ottawa follow-ing the meeting of NATO's Defence Committee at Washington to try to persuade the French defence minister that his government's proposed level of integration of German troops on the basis of the regimental unit was unrealistic. 'In my talks with Moch,' Claxton recalled in his memoirs, 'I went for the natural compromise of the brigade or brigade group. I pointed out that this was likely to become the smallest complete fighting forma-tion. A regiment' – so the former regimental sergeant-major affirmed from his experience – 'could not fight alone'. Moch, too, had fought n the Great War. 'He must really admit, as an experienced soldier ... that it was ridiculous to speak about having a German regiment alongside a French or other NATO regiment in a formation smaller than a brigade group. On the other hand, a brigade group was an effective fighting formation as we had shown and learned in Korea.' At this point in the conversation, which took place over dinner, Claxton sketched a plan on the menu. 'The dessert was held up for a few minutes...He led me to believe that in the end I had convinced him.'

Convincing Moch, as Brooke Claxton knew, would be more than half the battle: the Americans and British would then fall into line. But what about the Germans? 'Almost certainly they would insist on having com-plete German divisions and I could not blame them very much,' Claxton wrote six years later. 'However, I thought that on this Adenauer would be reasonable and it would be possible to point out to him that the force we had in Korea, and would be sending to Germany, was ... a brigade group, a small division. As the tendency undoubtedly would be to have divisions smaller and smaller, what they agreed at the outset to call a division or brigade did not matter very much. The end of this debate was a long way off and we were to have many more go's at it. ... Meanwhile,' Claxton's account concluded, 'I kept talking to each trying to bridge the gap be-tween their very different views on the part that Germany would play in the defence of Western Europe. It was like trying to keep two balls in the air...'[40]

If October 1950 was a month of havering on the issue of German rearma-ment, November was a month of negotiating. 'The meetings were long and difficult, with the representatives' capacity to reach compromise tested to the utmost.'[41]

In Washington, Hume Wrong turned his formidable analytical talent to the issues yet to be resolved on 'this explosive subject.' All of these, Wrong noted at the beginning of his analysis of them, 'have both political and military content, but they can perhaps be divided between those primarily military and those primarily political in nature, the former being mainly of concern to the Military Committee and the latter to the Deputies. I start from the assumption,' Wrong continued,

that the political superstructure of the Pleven plan, although it may be attractive in the perspective of several decades, is so impracticable in the context of the next five years that it must be discarded. A European Army financed by a common budget and directed by a European Minister of Defence might come about as a consequence of a strong federal movement in Europe but could hardly be its beginning. Furthermore, the feat of political architecture involved is fantastic, since the European Defence Ministry would be responsible simultaneously to a European Assembly, a European Council of National Ministers, and in part also to SHAPE when established. No one except the French has defended this proposal as a means of meeting the issues with which we are now confronted. Although it cannot be accepted because of its political implications, it is desirable clearly to establish in the Military Committee that it is also impracticable on military grounds.

Primarily military questions:

(a) If the Pleven proposal were to be put into effect, could the European army become an efficient fighting force? I think there is no doubt of the answer which the military advisors of nearly all NAT Governments (and a good many French soldiers) would give.

(b) How long an interval must lapse before, under any scheme, German formations can be recruited, equipped and trained? Some definite idea on this is needed for many reasons, such as the progressive build-up under the medium-term plan, the possibilities of diluting the United States proposal for German divisions so as to make it more acceptable to the French during the next three or four years, and the prospects of equipping the new divisions of other NAT countries.

(c) What is the smallest German unit which could effectively be employed in an integrated force? This may turn out to be a crucial question during the next stage of this negotiation. The French have gagged at the idea of German divisions, but in spite of Moch's assertions, they might swallow German brigades. The military advisers should study whether any common ground.... between the French and the United States plans could be found through time – phasing the creation of German forces over a period of years from battalions and lines of communication troops through brigades to divisions. It is another question whether the Germans would agree to play ball without knowing where they were going – i.e., without public recognition from the first that German divisions would be set up.

(d) Is the defence of the West beyond the line of the Rhine (or even at that line) possible by 1953 or 1954, without the substantial employment of German manpower?...

(e) Does the United States plan adequate army and general staff?

Primarily Political Questions:

(a) If no German forces are raised by agreement, how much time are the NAT countries likely to have before covert German rearmament begins? The choice is probably between overt rearmament under agreement, and there-fore subject to control and integration with NATO, and covert rearmament following the pattern of the period between the wars.

(b) Will the United States in particular, but also other North Atlantic countries, continue to contribute substantial forces for the defence of Western Germany unless Germans participate in their own defence? This is a point not yet seized on strongly by public opinion, but it is clearly one which is likely to arise in an acute form before long if nothing is done...

(c) Would West German forces ever fight against East Germans?...

(d) How solid is the political backing in France of the Pleven Plan or, in other words, to what degree did M. Moch's intransigence in the Defence Committee represent French public opinion? The Pleven Plan is only a rough sketch, and we must assume that it is not the only method that the French can accept...

(e) What are the consequences of a continuing stalemate on this subject for the North Atlantic countries? At the moment they look grimmer than they would probably turn out to be. If, however, the French attitude is based on a greater fear of a revived Germany than of Russia, the French will continue to be unco-operative. It seems that the French people still have to be convinced by their leaders of the imminence and extent of the danger from Russia.

(f) If the issue brings about the break-up of the French Government, is it likely that another French government could reach an agreement with the other NAT countries?...

'If the great experiment now evolving in the North Atlantic Community is to succeed,' Wrong concluded, 'it is essential that the defensive line in Western Europe be pushed as far east as the Elbe. This forward strategy, contemplated in the medium-term plan, cannot have sufficient armed forces behind it for three or four years at least. If 1951 and 1952 should be accepted as the most critical years and if efficient German forces cannot be trained and equipped by that time, the problem of German rearmament is not of immediate importance...'[42]

At this juncture of events, the government played one of its few cards. The Ambassador at Paris was instructed to exploit his 'excellent personal relations' with the French foreign minister, Robert Schuman, by appealing to him personally 'to use his wise influence to facilitate a solution...I am much disturbed over these developments,' the Secretary of State for External Affairs declared to General Georges Vanier of the French re-

fusal to compromise over the Pleven Plan and their continued insistence
that European political integration should precede any measure of West
German rearmament, 'which, as you will readily appreciate, put in jeopardy the whole concept of the NATO integrated forces in Europe and
threaten to arrest the forward movement of NATO plans for the defence of
Europe.' L.B. Pearson gave Vanier detailed instructions on how he should
conduct the interview with Schuman.

(a) You should express my own concern which I am sure he will share at the
    divergence of views revealed in the Defence Ministers' discussions, and you
    might add that we in Canada, although not directly involved in this divergence
    of views, are prompted by long-standing ties of blood and friendship with
    France to appeal to Mr Schuman...

(b) You should explain to Mr Schuman that we share French apprehensions re-
    garding the potential dangers involved in any measure of German rearma-
    ment. Like the French we approach this problem in a spirit of great caution
    and with the desire to obtain the maximum safeguards against the resurgence
    of German militarism. Moreover we also sympathize with the broad lines of
    French policy which aim at the creation of a political and economic framework
    on a Western European scale with which Germany should be closely asso-
    ciated. You might remind Mr Schuman in this connection that I have already
    publicly expressed my sympathy with the aims of the Schuman Plan.

(c) While I think we all share the same long term aims the problem seems to us to
    be primarily one of timing. It is our belief that on the military level a compro-
    mise could and should be worked out at once. Military planning could there-
    upon go forward as rapidly as possible. We would hope that simultaneously
    with the advance of military planning other steps could be taken in the direc-
    tion of building up the political and economic framework of Western Europe
    and that co-operation in military planning would itself be a stage in political
    development. We agree with the French that the military and political ele-
    ments in the situation are closely inter-related. We fear however that if no
    progress can be made on the military side until agreement is reached on prob-
    lems of European integration, this delay may present difficulties and
    dangers...

Vanier was told as well to remind the French foreign minister of the fluc-
tuating attitudes of the American electorate and the US Congress. 'We in
Canada are naturally particularly close to the mood of public opinion in
the United States and we feel that there is a very real danger that if there
is delay in implementing these policies opinion may swing in the opposite
direction and that the strong undercurrent of resistance to such essentially
unpopular decisions as the extension of the term of military service and
the stationing of United States forces in Europe will come to the surface.
Indeed the same forces in public opinion manifest themselves in Canada.'
The Ambassador was also to point out to Schuman the danger that a

prolonged delay during which Western governments opposed to and in favour of rearming Germans continued to wrangle would 'encourage the tendency of the Germans to play off one side against the other and thus to strengthen their bargaining position. This would be a very unhealthy development leading straight in the direction which the French, like ourselves, are so anxious to avoid.' Pearson's message concluded by relating to Vanier three of the impressions made on the Canadian delegation during the Defence Committee's deliberations at Washington a few days earlier. 'First, that the French thought that in any case United States forces would be stationed in Europe in peacetime and that they therefore were in a position to stand on their own plan without risk. Second, that M. Moch was satisfied with the deadlock at the Defence Ministers' meeting as it delayed the whole problem of German rearmament. (This, we are sure, is a very shortsighted view.) Third, that M. Moch's personal opposition to any measure of German rearmament made compromise more difficult.' Vanier was asked (not for the first time) to provide Ottawa with his own assessment of the French domestic political situation. 'Do you think that Mr Pleven and Mr Schuman fully share Mr Moch's uncompromising attitude?'[43]

The Ambassador was received by the foreign minister of France on 8 November. It was by Vanier's account a most cordial encounter. 'As your message was quite a long one,' the Ambassador reported, 'I made a French translation which I read to M. Schuman "in toto." At the end after listening intently, M. Schuman said, "Will you please thank your Minister for his message which I look upon as a mark of personal friendship." He then added at once much to my pleasure and may I add a little to my surprise: "Je *te* souscris entièrement à tout ce que M. Pearson dit d'un bout à l'autre." In other words he shared all your views without the smallest reservation.' Schuman told Vanier that Moch's conduct at Washington had made him feel '"consterné" – which as you know,' Vanier commented to Pearson, 'is a very strong word, best translated by "dismayed"...' Schuman told Vanier that Moch 'did not reflect the opinion of the French Government.' Schuman, Vanier reported further, thought it would be most unwise to interfere with the advancement of NATO military planning. 'He went so far as to say that he would not even be stopped by the question of the size of the units or formations. ... M. Schuman said that the French and Germans were in complete accord, that he and Adenauer saw eye to eye...'[44]

The intelligence supplied by the Ambassador at Paris that the French cabinet was divided on the issue of German rearmament caused the policy community at Ottawa to refrain, for the time being, from taking any initiative of its own. 'Until this French domestic division has sorted itself out,' A.D.P. Heeney commented to Brooke Claxton, 'I should be inclined to advise great caution in putting forward in Washington any proposals for a compromise based on our conversations with M. Moch. We do not wish to get into the position of being "plus royaliste que le roi," "le roi" being in this case M. Schuman and, according to M. Schuman, M. Pleven also.'[45] 'We are reluctant,' representatives at Washington and overseas were informed, 'to put forward anything that might be labelled a Canadian compromise plan.'

Meanwhile, discussions were continuing on the safeguards intended to prevent any West German forces being used for any purpose other than that of the defence of Western Europe. By the end of November 1950, there had been some progress. 'Important concessions have been made on both sides,' A.D.P. Heeney reported to his Minister. 'On the size of basic units, the Americans have come down from divisions to brigade groups, while the French have gone up from battalions to brigade groups.' That much, at least, seemed settled. But no political alternative to the European army concept had as yet been proposed. 'For this reason,' Heeney explained, 'we are joining with the Americans in gently indicating to the continental European members that we think that they should at least agree to sit down now to work out an acceptable scheme for a European Army within the framework of NATO. ... Mr Wilgress has been instructed not to take the initiative, in accordance with Cabinet decision that Canadian representatives on North Atlantic bodies should leave the problem of German participation largely to those more immediately concerned.'[46] The US record of how Dana Wilgress complied with that instruction at the Council Deputies' meeting on 28 November is as follows.

Canadian deputy supported US proposal ... basing support on urgency immediate progress formation NATO integrated force with safeguarded German participation. US proposal offered best chance progress this direction and left latitude for European countries try work out long-range program pursuant French proposal which acceptable course if accomplished within reasonable time after which if no agreement participants should consider alternatives. Believed that in transitional period occupying powers would learn more of German attitudes and become better able judge feasibility of alternative military arrangements. European countries had primary political concern and his government chiefly concerned quick build-up adequate NATO defense. However, emphasized crucial importance in American opinion which in event undue delay defense preparations might begin to question whole possibility building effective West European defense. Though appreciative French reasons for different view and believing interested European countries should have opportunity work out methods attaining French objective, Canada agreed with US that it was imperative to begin now with steps toward German military participation. Hoped views European countries would be sufficiently flexible permit their considering long-range alternatives to French proposals should Paris conference fail practical results. He believed there had been too much talk on two conceptions as conflicting. Whichever conception was adopted, military effectiveness should be guiding criterion. Creation integrated force would advance concept Atlantic union...[47]

The United States Council Deputy considered Wilgress's statement for Canada to have been 'helpful and effective.'[48]

The communiqué released by the North Atlantic Council at the conclusion of its session at Brussels on 18 and 19 December 1950 reported that its members had 'reached unanimous agreement regarding the part which Germany might assume in the common defense. The German participation would strengthen the defense of Europe without altering in any way the purely defensive character of the North Atlantic Treaty Organization.' This discreet formulation, as one analyst later noted, hid more than it revealed. 'The "unanimous agreement on the part which Germany might assume" ... was not further explained. The communiqué did *not* spell out the German role in European defense, or even mention German rearmament. The word "participate" hardly went beyond the language of the September NATO Council's communiqué which mentioned a German "contribution." The reason for this vagueness is not obscure. There had been no agreement at all on the German rearmament issue...'[49]

NATO's non-decision duly taken, Canadians along with other North Atlantic peoples waited for the day when a European army would appear at last upon parade. Few foresaw that when the time arrived for Germans in uniform to march once more they would do so as a *Wehrmacht.* No one foresaw that France would be responsible for the *Wehrmacht's* reappearance.

GREEKS AND TURKS

Waiting for Germans to join the Integrated Force, where else could NATO turn for help in repulsing that all-out attack which, if it ever came, would bring – so its planners calculated – the armed forces of the Soviet Union to the Channel ports within three weeks, to the Pyrenees within three months?

Greece and Turkey, first post-war recipients of American military aid, disposed between them of some half a million men under arms, capable, it was thought, of holding down a significant part of the Red Army on the Soviet Union's southern flank. Both countries were ready, Turkey even eager, to commit their forces for this purpose – in exchange for NATO membership. Was it a good deal for NATO to admit them?

On 25 August 1950, Turkey's ambassador at Ottawa called on the Department of External Affairs to sound out the government on its attitude towards his country's prospective membership of the Atlantic Alliance. Its response must have been tepid: soon afterwards, the Secretary of State for External Affairs informed the ambassador at Washington that 'I am instructing our missions in North Atlantic countries to avoid discussing this matter, if possible, or, if pressed, to make it clear that Canada is not taking any firm position and will not take any unless and until the attitude of the powers more directly concerned is known.'[50]

An opportunity to test NATO member governments' opinions was provided by the meeting on 20 September of the North Atlantic Council, which considered the admission of Turkey and Greece (and possibly of Spain whose candidacy was being pressed by Portugal), for which Ankara was actively in search. The consensus of the Council was that admission of new members at that time 'would unduly complicate the work of the Organization and would extend commitments beyond those acceptable to certain present members.' The Council decided that Greece and Turkey might be associated with appropriate NATO planning bodies for Mediterranean defence. That, for the moment, was as far as NATO would go.[51]

For Turkey and (to a lesser extent) for Greece, that did not go far enough. And by the spring of 1951 it did not go far enough for the United States. The US administration, impressed by Turkey's troop commitment to the UN command in Korea (the Turks were fighting there with great ferocity) and placing an even higher premium on the value of additional manpower as the result of Chinese intervention in the Korean war, had by then decided to support the admission of Greece and Turkey to full membership of the Alliance. Messages to other NATO governments seeking their approval and support of this new American policy were flowing forth from Washington.

Ottawa's preliminary reactions, as circulated privately within the policy community, were evasive. 'We are rather hesitant to comment on the views expressed to you by the State Department about the method of improving the security of the Eastern Mediterranean,' the Secretary of State for External Affairs attempted to explain to the Ambassador at Washington,

because we feel that, apart from the possibility of the inclusion of Greece and Turkey in NATO, the area is one in which Canadian interests are remote except in a general sense and we would not wish to give the impression that we are suggesting to the great powers methods whereby the security of the area under consideration could be increased by further commitments on their part while, at the same time, Canada would be unwilling to accept further commitments itself...

We do not wish to convey the impression that, were it so decided after careful consideration in Washington, we would be unwilling to consider the applications of Greece and Turkey...[52]

The policy community's reticence arose in part from a feeling that the two applicants, Turkey in particular, simply did not belong in an alliance composed (mostly) of free and democratic countries. Turkey had last figured in the headlines of a Canadian newspaper – during the Chanak crisis in September 1922 – as 'the beast of Asia'; and while its reputation for bestiality had diminished over the years, the regime of President Ismet Inönü was not notable for that 'faith in human rights and fundamental freedoms, in the worth and dignity of man and in the principles of parliamentary democracy, personal freedom and political liberty'[53] which was regarded by Escott Reid, L.B. Pearson, and L.S. St Laurent himself as a basic qualification for membership. Turkey could not accurately be described as part of that 'Western Christendom' which, in Canadian rhetoric at least, the Atlantic Alliance had been created to defend. Turkey's membership would make that much more difficult the use of the alliance (as Escott Reid would later put it) 'as a chrysalis for the North Atlantic community.'[54] Finally, Turkey's membership would extend the Treaty area a further thousand miles eastward to the town of Ani on the 312 mile-long Turkish frontier with the Soviet Union – an extension which, arguably, could cause other NATO members to lose more on the commitment roundabout than they stood to gain on the manpower swing.

Over all these unfavourable factors there loomed an additional and crucial consideration: the probable reaction of the Soviet Union. Would the admission of Greece and Turkey to NATO provoke the Kremlin into a new phase of adventuristic militarism? 'I think consideration should be given to the provocative aspect NATO would assume were it extended to Greece and Turkey,' the Under Secretary of State for External Affairs cabled to the High Commissioner at London on 30 May 1951. 'It may be that the military planners in Washington have already come to the conclusion that a Soviet attack on Greece and/or Turkey would immediately lead to a world war. If that is one of the premises on which they base their case for the admission of Greece and Turkey, it becomes even more important that the provocative aspect of the admission towards the USSR be studied...'[55] From Canada's standpoint, the enterprise seemed dubious in almost every way.

And not only from Canada's. L.B. Pearson discovered, during a quick visit to Europe during the summer of 1951, that the Dutch, the Norwegians, and the Danes were almost as sceptical about the value of bringing

Greece and Turkey in and apprehensive about the consequences. 'Stikker certainly shares the doubts of some of the rest of us in regard to the wisdom of this,' Pearson noted after talking with the foreign minister of The Netherlands on 2 July. 'He thought that it might fatally weaken the idea of the North Atlantic Pact as the basis for social, political and economic development. I concurred in this...' Norway's Halvard Lange was also opposed to the admission of Turkey, as was the Danish foreign minister, Ole Kraft. The foreign minister of Sweden 'expressed his anxiety that the accession of Turkey and Greece would serve to confirm Russian fears that the alliance was an encircling and provocative one. I agreed with him,' Pearson commented, 'that in a sense this changed the whole concept of the North Atlantic Pact, but I still hoped that some of the less happy results of the proposed accessions could be avoided...'*

In opposing the admission of Greece and Turkey to NATO, the Canadian government was not alone: the Norwegian, Netherlands, and Danish governments were judged to be 'firmly opposed,' the French government somewhat less than 'firmly.' The Canadian official best placed to know – the representative on the NATO Council of Deputies, Dana Wilgress – feared that further efforts to press forward with the United States proposal were 'likely to arouse lasting resentment among the existing members and render a unanimous decision on this issue impossible to achieve.' For this reason, Wilgress recommended that Canada float the idea of a Mediterranean or Middle East Pact as a means of accomplishing American objectives. Pearson, however, shied away from the idea of giving a lead along these lines, even though some such proposal 'would suit our own requirements in this instance.' The government wanted 'to avoid at all costs the impression that anything in the nature of a "Canadian plan"' existed.[56]

The consequence of Canada's continuing evasion of the issue was that the government, by the end of July 1951, was the only NATO member (Iceland apart) not to have offered its opinion on what it felt should be done. One senior official, at least, felt that the dodging had to stop. 'I cannot help feel that on a matter of such major importance to NATO,' Dana Wilgress cabled from London, 'we must ourselves look at the whole question in the light of the arguments which have been presented for the two main solutions of full membership and a Mediterranean Pact. ... In view of the fact that at the Council meetings we shall be required to take a

---

* Pearson's record of this conversation with Östen Undén is the only one not included in his memoirs: the omission is curious, for of the four discussions that with the foreign minister of Sweden is the most revealing. See *Mike II*, 71-2, for the talks with Stikker, Lange and Kraft; and for that with Undén, DEA files, 50030-A-1-40.

stand on the alternative solutions, I think there is every reason to formulate our ideas as rapidly as possible...'[57]

Spurred on by this advice, the Department of External Affairs faced the issue squarely for the first time – a year after it had arisen. The argument in favour of admitting Greece and Turkey had meanwhile been strengthened by the decision of the United Kingdom government to support it. 'It is obviously going to be extremely difficult,' the Under Secretary of State for External Affairs admitted to the High Commissioner at London, 'for the opponents of admission to make their viewpoint prevail.' A.D.P. Heeney went on to report the results of the Department's assessment of the problem. Officials had considered four 'fundamental questions.' First, they had asked themselves whether the admission of Greece and Turkey would extend Canada's commitments. They had concluded that it would not: 'Canada and NATO as a whole would be involved almost certainly in the event of an attack on Turkey and probably in the event of an attack on Greece, whether these countries were members of NATO or of a Mediterranean Pact, or, in all probability, if they had no treaty obligations at all with the Western powers beyond those which exist at present.' Second, they had considered whether their admission to NATO would unduly provoke the Soviet Union. They had concluded that while it might, the move would be no more provocative than the alternative project of creating a new Mediterranean Pact. Third, they had sought to determine whether their admission would hamper the development of NATO in the direction of an Atlantic community. On this their judgement was as follows:

No doubt the inclusion of two countries so far removed geographically and in some respects politically and culturally from the North Atlantic Community may complicate such a development. On the other hand, if powerful forces, political and economic, once really begin to move in the direction of the creation of a North Atlantic Community, this process will hardly be arrested by the mere fact that certain countries which are unable or unwilling to participate in this development are co-signatories of the North Atlantic Treaty.

Finally, the question had been posed as to whether insisting on some alternative solution, such as a Mediterranean Pact, might be the cause of a 'dangerous delay in making arrangements for the security of this exposed flank of the North Atlantic area.' There was general agreement that a delay would ensue, and that it was desirable to avoid it.

Such lines of reasoning appeared to lead inescapably to admitting Greece and Turkey to NATO. However, the Department of External Affairs was not yet ready to recommend such a policy. Weighing against it was the precedent that would be set by their admission. 'We may certainly anticipate a request from the German Republic...,' and 'we may well be subject to "arm twisting" for the inclusion of Spain...' Admission of Greece and Turkey would, moreover, change the character of the Alliance. 'The question arises as to whether NATO is to become a conglomerate association of anti-communist nations or whether it is to retain its original character and purpose.' For these reasons, A.D.P. Heeney informed the Council Deputy, the Department of External Affairs continued to prefer a solution which would not bring Greece and Turkey into the Alliance as full members. On the other hand, the Department was not prepared to recommend to the government that Canada should make a determined effort to try to keep them out. 'While we are anxious to go along with our friends The Netherlands, Norwegians and Belgians whose doubts about the admission of Greece and Turkey we share, we must not get ourselves into a false position by allowing them to believe that we could maintain a position of last-ditch resistance...'[58]

At this juncture the policy community began to receive advice from the Ambassador at Ankara.

Major General Victor Odlum* possessed to a degree fairly described as quirkish the susceptibility of diplomats to the country where they represent their own – a susceptibility long recognized by themselves to be an occupational malady of their profession dubbed 'localitis.' Odlum did not so much contract localitis as to purposively infect himself. As a technique for diplomatic reporting, he deliberately set out to see events and personalities as he imagined his hosts, people and government alike, envisaged them. Odlum had adopted this method when minister to China on his arrival at Chungking in 1943. 'My decision is that I must commence to see everything from a pro-Chinese angle,' Odlum explained candidly to his Prime Minister. 'I will always seek the favourable, the Chinese, interpretation. If I do not do this, I will never win the confidence of those who really matter.'[59] He retained this method of reporting on taking up his posting at Ankara in 1947. By 1951, near the end of his term of duty and of his diplomatic career, and after four years of service in Turkey (an unusually long posting by most foreign office standards), Odlum had become thoroughly suffused with the Turkish way of looking at the world. His perspective was identical to that of the Inönü government, and he argued its case for admission to NATO with as much fervour as if he had been Turkey's ambassador to Canada rather than Canada's to Turkey. His

---

* See *In Defence of Canada* III, 49-50; also Kim Richard Nossal, 'Chungking Prism: Cognitive Process and Intelligence Failure,' *International Journal*, XXXII, 3, Summer 1977, 559-76.

dispatches and letters – Odlum tended to go over the heads of Department of External Affairs officials to reach his Minister direct – took up the Turkish cause with zeal.

In my telegram dated August 18, 1951, I referred to the political situation in Turkey as one likely to be fraught with grave danger should Turkey's application for membership in NATO fail to receive favourable action. For some time I have been conscious that Turkey's early enthusiasm for NATO has slowly turned, delay having followed delay, as Turkey views the record, to a wide-spread resentment against the Western democracies which have stood in the way of Turkey's realization of her ambitions...

During the last few months, I have had to listen to many Turks talking ... about the wound to Turkish pride inflicted by those who opposed acceptance of her application for NATO membership. In every case, I have had to be almost silent for I have had little guidance from the Department concerning long-term Canadian policy...

At this distance, it would seem that the NATO powers may have to make a choice between sticking to their original broad programme – including its long-range political objectives – and thereby taking a chance of losing the active support of what is today the strongest army in Europe, the Turkish army. ... It is convenient and politically wise to talk of Turkey *and* Greece; but Turkey is the only thing that really matters when strength for battle is considered. I am in sympathy with the long-range purpose which gave birth to and shaped NATO in its early days; but I am convinced that, even to attain the original goal, it is first necessary to win a third world war, should one happen to come. To win the war, I believe the all-out support of the Turkish Army is necessary...[60]

And, in a letter to Pearson: 'From the start I preached North West Africa, Spain and Turkey. As a soldier, I cannot underrate them...'*

These interventions from the Ambassador at Ankara were timely – the meeting of the North Atlantic Council in Ottawa where the decision would be made was only three weeks off – but they could hardly have been decisive in determining Canada's policy. At most they reinforced

* Victor Odlum to L.B. Pearson, 3 September 1951, DEA files, 50030-v-3-40. Odlum's military background encouraged in him the belief that he possessed a special aptitude, deriving from professional experience, for assessing the strength of armed forces. His assessments of the comparative strengths of the military dispositions of the Kuomintang and the Communists in China from 1943 to 1946 were, however, extraordinarily inaccurate: see Nossal, 'Chungking Prism,' 574-5. Odlum's previous miscalculation, notorious within the Department of External Affairs, probably caused its senior officials to discount his assessment of the Turkish Army as 'the strongest ... in Europe.' In Turkey as before in China, Odlum was at least aware of his own bias: 'My sympathies are so strongly with Turkey,' he confessed to L.B. Pearson, 'that I might easily go beyond the limits which you would place if you were directing me as to what I should say...' Ambassador at Ankara to Secretary of State for External Affairs, 20 August 1951, DEA files, 50030-v-3-40.

what the Canadian government came to support willy-nilly after both the United States' and the United Kingdom's had agreed that Greece and Turkey should come in. The Cabinet had already decided on 8 August that the Secretary of State for External Affairs should 'support the admission of the two countries to NATO when the matter comes up at the North Atlantic Council meeting.'[61]

On 18 September 1951, L.B. Pearson delivered his statement to the Council, then meeting in Ottawa. Pearson admitted that 'the Canadian government has adopted a fairly cautious attitude towards this issue,' a caution dictated by 'concern for the future of NATO lest by setting a precedent for extending membership in this way its original purpose and character be lost and the whole organization be converted into a purely military alliance of anti-communist states.' For that reason, the Canadian government had preferred the solution of creating a new Mediterranean pact in which Greece and Turkey would belong to that of admitting them to the existing North Atlantic Pact. But 'in view of the stand taken in Turkey and Greece, insistence on this alternative course might have provoked trouble in those countries, the net result of which would have been, to say the least, disadvantageous for us all.' That was why, Pearson concluded, 'the Canadian government has come to the conclusion that despite the obvious merits of a Mediterranean Pact, admission of Greece and Turkey to full membership in NATO is the only practical solution at this time.'[62]

A Protocol of Accession brought Greece and Turkey into the North Atlantic Treaty Organization as full members on 22 October 1951. Pearson lived to regret it. It 'made nonsense of the North Atlantic character of our association,' he wrote in his memoirs, 'diminished our credibility as the foundation for an Atlantic community, and gave greater validity to the criticism that we were purely and simply a military alliance.'[63]

GERMANS (2)

'I feel the world is fortunate that Dr Adenauer is the head of the government here,' the head of the mission at Bonn wrote in August 1951. 'He is a practical man and he is sound, sane and decent.'[64] The West German Chancellor was also determined, wily, and astute. '[H]is main concern in foreign policy,' an authority has written since, 'was to tie the Federal Republic irrevocably into the West European community and the Western military alliance – naturally, on terms which would maximize her status and meet her specific interests.'[65] Adenauer's *Westpolitik* was not beyond – indeed, it relied upon – taking advantage of the long delay in reconciling Franco-American differences over West German rearmament and skilfully parlaying what one commentator described as 'a contribut on of non-existent German troops to a non-existent European Army' into a seriers of implacable demands.

In February 1952, a spate of new terms for German participation in the European Defence Community was approved by the Bundestag. These included membership of NATO; settlement of the Saar problem; release of war criminals; an equal voice for Bonn in seeking German reunification; removal of all restrictions on German industry; equal financial treatment in the sharing of defence costs; and an end to the occupation. In short, West Germany was prepared to contribute to the defence of Western Europe only as a fully sovereign state, with all vestiges of war guilt expunged from its record. For the Canadian diplomat whose service in post-Second World War Germany had been as envoy not to a national government but to a committee of conquerors, it was too much. 'As I see the tide going steadily against us to the point that a spirit of Rappallism [sic] is not only growing in the German heart and mind but also being given expression,' General Maurice Pope wrote to L.B. Pearson from his Brussels embassy, 'I am convinced that the only course now open to stop the rot would be to tell the Germans publicly, and in no uncertain fash-ion, that we have decided to give the question of German re-armament an indefinite hoist. And I am equally convinced,' Pope added, 'that the chances of getting Washington to agree to such a bold course of action are precisely nil.'[66]

The invocation by the Ambassador at Brussels of the analogy of the agreement at Rappallo in 1922 between the two pariah polities of Europe – Germany and the Soviet Union – was perhaps more prescient than he knew. A month later – on 10 March 1952 – the Soviet government, n a note to the three Western powers, called for a reunified, neutral Germany which would be permitted to have its own national military forces. This brazen overture set off reverberations around the North Atlantic capitals.

At Ottawa, L.B. Pearson referred obliquely to the Soviet move. 'Very difficult, complicated and indeed explosive,' was Pearson's comment in the House of Commons on the scene that now presented itself to NATO statesmen.

There are two extreme trends which might develop dangerously in Germany at the present time. On the one hand there is the revival of militarism, nazi militar-ism; and there is the other extreme, the rejection of all defence responsibilities by the Germans and the creation of a power vacuum in the centre of Europe. We know what happens when a vacuum of that kind is created. We have a pretty good idea who would try to move into that vacuum in present circumstances. Nevertheless, the fact remains that Germany, as I see it, is bound to become stronger and is bound to become united ultimately. Surely it is better that this should be done in association with the Atlantic powers than in isolation, or on a purely nationalistic basis, or in association with the communist east which would have no scruples about a Germany armed to the teeth, with Nazi leaders back in harness, provided that that were done by a communist government under Moscow orders.[67]

The leader of the Co-operative Commonwealth Federation (CCF) party, an opposition group of democratic socialists, viewed the Soviet intervention in a different perspective. 'It is now reported, and authoritatively reported, that Russia is proposing, as part of a German unification plan, the remilitarization of Germany, setting up a German army, and granting the right to manufacture instruments of war and indeed the remilitarization to the extent that former German officers, even if they were former Nazi officers, shall have the right to regain positions in the new German army,' M.J. Coldwell told Members of Parliament on 21 March. 'If that is the case, then it seems to me that the talk about the rearmament of Germany that we have been indulging in on our side has enabled the Russians to do something that is rather clever, and to outbid us for the support of the German people.'[68] It is more than likely that it seemed that way to Pearson, too, although he did not see fit to say so in the House. To his Prime Minister he confided on 2 May: 'My own view has been that it is unwise for the West to oppose the strong German drive for unity which is not likely to lose its force...'[69]

The grand negotiation over the rearming of Germany reached its climax and its anticlimax in May 1952 and September 1954, respectively.

In May 1952, 'only twenty months after the American demand for the raising of German troops, treaties intended to meet the desires of France and Germany, which amounted to preconditions to the rearmament of the Federal Republic, were ready to be signed.' On 27 May they were signed. 'The May treaties amounted to a vast number of accords which together comprised a web of agreements emerging from discussions among the EDC Six; the EDC states and Britain; the Six and NATO; and the occupying powers and the Federal Republic. They included the contractual agreements between Germany and the Big Three; the EDC treaty and related protocols; reciprocal guarantees between NATO and EDC; the guarantee treaty between Britain and EDC; and the joint declaration of the United States, the United Kingdom and France, with the one condition for entry into force of all the others the ratification of EDC.'[70]

Never in diplomatic history had so many documents been signed to so little purpose. On 29 August 1954, the National Assembly of France defeated the government's motion to ratify French membership of the European Defence Community. By that defection, the structure of Western European unity so carefully built over the past twenty months was demolished.

What could be built – quickly – in its place? The Secretary of State for External Affairs lost no time in putting forth, in public, a proposal for a substitute. Within twenty-four hours of the historic vote, L.B. Pearson had declared that NATO's members would as a result of it have to deal with Germany in 'an Atlantic context.' Pearson developed this proposal on 7 September in a speech devoted entirely to 'The Position of Germany in International Defence.' The defeat of the European Defence Community, he told his audience at the Canadian National Exhibition in Toronto, should be regarded 'not as putting an end either to the healing and hopeful process of European integration, or to the association of Germany with the Atlantic collective defence system, but as necessitating an urgent search for an alternative method by which these essential objectives can be achieved with a minimum of delay.' He ticked off the options: to keep Germany neutralized and disarmed; to do nothing and see what happened; to give West Germany full sovereignty and 'hope for the best'; to gather up the shattered pieces of the European Defence Community and try to reassemble these in a form which France could live in. All were found wanting: the neutralization and disarmament of Germany as both impractical and dangerous; doing nothing as 'futile and negative'; restoring German sovereignty as destructive of both European and Atlantic unity; rebuilding a European Defence Community as too difficult and time-consuming. 'There is left, then,' Pearson concluded,

the association with NATO of a Germany, with her sovereignty restored and the occupation ended, brought about in such a way that will remove the anxieties of Germany's neighbours, and which will strengthen the whole Atlantic system of collective defence and, therefore, strengthen the peace...[71]

A conference of foreign ministers from the six countries which would have formed the since defunct Community, together with those of the United States, the United Kingdom, and Canada, opened at London on 28 September. Its purpose was retrospectively described by L.B. Pearson as that of finding 'a new solution to the problem of German accession to the North Atlantic Treaty.' Pearson flew from the UN General Assembly session – 'the situation,' he wrote in his memoirs, 'seemed to require an exercise of that instant diplomacy made possible by air travel' – in time to engage in informal discussion with the principals, of whom the most consequential was the leader of the French delegation, Pierre Mendès-France. 'His views on the Conference depressed us more and more as the evening went on,' Pearson recalled. 'He talked about conditions which must be acceptable to the French Parliament before Germany could even be considered for membership in NATO: settlement of the Saar, control of arms production, etc. Eden began to get more and more impatient and finally told him very frankly that insistence on these views would mean the failure of the Conference; the withdrawal of the United States from the Atlantic Alliance; a policy of peripheral strategy in Washington; Germany would be the favourite friend. ... I tried to back Eden up in this,' Pearson remembered, 'especially in insisting on the disastrous effect of the failure of the Conference on United States policy.'[72] Of his own part, he wrote as follows:

I soon found that the other Alliance Foreign Ministers were worried about the possible failure of the conference, and impatient with the attitude and manners of Mendès-France. I was urged, since as a Canadian I was not directly involved, to be an "honest broker" in the search for agreement. I could only counsel patience and the avoidance of doing or saying anything that would isolate Mendès-France. At the conference my interventions were designed to prevent the impasse which seemed to be developing by putting forward various suggestions for a discussion, even for rejection. We needed time. As it happened, the conference, though once or twice seeming to be on the verge of disaster, eventually managed to work out the broad lines of an agreement associating West Germany with NATO on the only basis (I expressed strongly my own views to the conference on this) which she could accept – equality and non-discrimination.[73]

As with the defunct European Defence Community agreements, so with the emerging Protocol of Accession of the Federal Republic to NATO: Adenauer insisted upon and was formally accorded 'equality and non-discrimination' while tacitly accepting a number of practical inequalities. Four major limitations were imposed. First, West Germany's forces were to be subject to a ceiling – 500,000 troops organized into not more than twelve divisions and backed by no more than 1350 fighter aircraft. Second, all West Germany's armed forces were to be placed under NATO command. Third, West Germany was not to manufacture atomic, biological, or chemical weapons, long-range aircraft, guided missiles, or any but small warships. Finally, West Germany specifically pledged 'never to have recourse to force to achieve the reunification of Germany or the modification of the present boundaries of the German Federal Republic.' Of these safeguards, L.B. Pearson later remarked: 'It would be difficult to devise a more impressive set...'[74] But they could be ignored, or violated, or – as was indeed the case – altered.

Resumed at Paris to permit the remaining North Atlantic Treaty countries to approve of these arrangements, the Conference closed on what L.B. Pearson reported to his Prime Minister on 25 October to have been 'a very high and happy note. ... It has really been a very great achievement...'[75] The Protocol admitting West Germany to the North Atlantic Treaty Organization became effective on 5 May 1955 – ten years to the day after a Canadian general had accepted the surrender of German armies in The Netherlands and north-west Germany. On 16 June, the Minister of National Defence welcomed the new member to the club. 'I should like to say,' R.O. Campney told the House of Commons, 'that Canadians, in general, welcome the German people as our full and equal partners in NATO.'[76]

Campney's 'in general' gave fleeting recognition to the fact that there were Canadians, in and out of Parliament, of every province and region of their country, from every walk of life, who did not extend that welcome. Rearming Germans may have been regarded by their government as tangential to its main concerns; but not many Canadians then over the age of twenty-five were indifferent to that policy, and some Canadians passionately opposed it. Speeches in Parliament were accordingly delivered at an unusually high level of seriousness and intensity.

The debate was conducted over a period of four days following the moving of a resolution in the House of Commons by the Secretary of State for External Affairs on 20 January 1955: 'That it is expedient that the Houses of Parliament do approve the Protocol to the North Atlantic Treaty on the accession of the Federal Republic of Germany, signed by Canada at Paris on October 23, 1954, and that this House do approve the same.'

L.B. Pearson opened the debate in a lengthy speech which drew plaudits from Opposition members for its lucidity and eloquence. Pearson began by noting that the Protocol for which the government sought Parliament's approval would make West Germany a member not merely of the North Atlantic alliance but also of the North Atlantic community. 'The Soviet government and its satellite governments are seeking to prevent this development by an unparalleled campaign of intimidation, of cajolery and distortion, by the exertion of every kind of pressure through the lure of promises and the threat of punishment. In our own country,' Pearson pointed out, 'the communists are doing all they can, of course, to further this campaign, by a propaganda barrage focusing on the statement that a vote for this Protocol is merely a vote for German rearmament. ...

Their campaign unquestionably strikes some response in the hearts of many honest and sincere Canadian patriots, who have good reason to remember and fear the dread of German arms.' Rearmament, Pearson pointed out, was but one of three significant features of the Paris agreements. 'It is I think reasonable to expect that in the long run the most fundamental and durable of these features will be, first, the restoration of German freedom and sovereignty ... second, acceptance of the voluntary adherence of these people to the western coalition. ... The third feature of course is the provision that is being made for the Federal German Republic, in the exercise of the first right of sovereignty, to bear a fair share of the common burden of defence of the North Atlantic Treaty Organization...' That right, Pearson contended, was not being demanded in any spirit of militarism. 'The fact is that in Germany, as elsewhere, there is revulsion against war and militarism from which Germans as well as the rest of us have suffered so much and so recently. ... Where rearmament is supported in Germany today ... it is generally regarded at best, as indeed it is here, as a tragic necessity.'

Turning next to the series of safeguards which West Germany would be required to accept, the Secretary of State for External Affairs conceded that at some later date they might be disregarded or abandoned. 'I frankly admit ... that we have every right to be concerned with German good faith in this series of agreements. Many Canadians, including many of us in this House, and even more of our allies who are taking this decision with us and with all its consequences, bear on their bodies and in their minds scars from the German war machine. We remember how Hitler, with shocking and unscrupulous design, and with Soviet connivance and assistance, started World War II in 1939. We do not forget how the Nazis conducted that war with savage brutality, and how the German people supported it. While we do not forget that and cannot forget it, it is my considered view that support of these agreements with the safeguards I have described is both wise and farsighted, and of all the courses that are open to us this is the best course to follow in our effort to shape a better future.' History had demonstrated after the First World War how dangerous it was to make Germans feel like outcasts. 'Quite apart from the pressing fact of the Soviet threat to western Europe it would, I submit, be wrong and foolish to deal with Germany now as a rejected, unequal people in international society. If we do so they will soon conclude that their choice lies only between isolation and a brooding introspection, or seeking domination and aggressive strength on their own. Surely the sensible course, even if the threat of communist aggression were removed, would still be to bring the Germans into the West European community, and into the North Atlantic Organization where they would be only one of 15 members, including the United States, and which they could not hope to dominate...'

Towards the end of his address, Pearson considered what he described as 'the most impressive' of the arguments against the policy he advocated – that it would be dangerously provocative to the Soviet Union and so increase rather than diminish the danger of war. He urged the House not to take Soviet threats at their face value. Soviet threats, like Soviet promises, were tactics 'to weaken our resolve and confuse our purposes.' He admitted – and in so doing became one of the first among Western statesmen to make such an admission in public – 'the constant danger of conflict from a misunderstanding on both sides of each other's motives. In the west we remain with good reason alarmed by the threatening and aggressive policies of the USSR in recent years. In turn I think it is not inconceivable, given the atmosphere of totalitarian isolation and ignorance in Moscow, that the Soviet people, and even certain Soviet leaders, may at times consider – sincerely consider – that they are threatened by the west. One of the great tasks in the next few years in diplomacy is to try somehow to bridge this gap in misunderstanding...'[77] (It may be that in saying this, Pearson had in mind his forthcoming trip to the Soviet Union in October where, as the first NATO foreign minister to be invited on a state visit to Moscow, he would have the opportunity to attempt to remove whatever misperceptions of reality he encountered in the Kremlin.)*

The spokesman for the Conservative Party on foreign affairs, John G. Diefenbaker, congratulated the Secretary of State for External Affairs for 'a speech powerful in delivery and cogent in its lucidity. He drew a dark picture,' Diefenbaker declared. 'He produced a calm in this House that I have never before witnessed.' The Conservative spokesman regretted that the information in Pearson's speech had not been previously divulged. 'If the speech which my hon. friend has made today and the details which he has given had been given to the Canadian people earlier, much of the

---

* 'One of the advantages...,' L.B. Pearson reported to Ottawa of his visit, 'was the opportunity to dispel misapprehensions and remove misunderstanding and distortion.' During a free-wheeling two-hour talk with Nikita Khrushchev, Pearson got 'the chance to say that I might be willing to agree that the Soviet Union was justified in its fear of Germany if NATO were not a purely defensive organization. I was about to explain why NATO should not be so regarded when Khrushchev broke in with the remark, "You should let us into NATO – we have been knocking at the door two years." I replied that if the world situation were such as to permit entry of the USSR into NATO it would also presumably permit proper functioning of the United Nations in the security field...' (Quoted in *Mike* II, 206). A perfect rejoinder. J.G. Diefenbaker had described the Soviet bid for NATO membership as 'analogous to Satan joining the anti-hell society.' (Canada, *H.C. Debates*, 1955, I, 375.)

feeling that has been aroused would have been allayed, diminished or eliminated.' He noted that it was 'the first time in the history of Canada that the House of Commons has been in a position where an adverse vote would not only defeat the motion before us but would render nugatory and ineffective the favourable decisions by parliaments in Britain, West Germany, France and the other members of this union.' With the substance of the Minister's speech, Diefenbaker had no major disagreement.[78]

While the Conservative Party's support for the resolution was predictable, that of the other opposition party, the CCF, was not. The first sentence of its leader's speech may have come as a surprise. 'I rise,' M.J. Coldwell declared, 'to support the motion.' Coldwell had chosen to break, after 'long and anxious thought,' with several of his followers. 'The overriding consideration which has governed my own decision,' he told the House,

is that the failure of Russia to co-operate in the United Nations with a view to setting up the Military Staff Committee, and to participate in the security measures provided for and envisioned in the United Nations Charter, made the organization of the regional defensive alliance known as NATO necessary and inevitable...

Now the time has come when a proposal is before us for recognition of the ... sovereignty of Germany. As the Minister said this afternoon, sovereignty surely involves the right of a nation to defend itself against aggression. How shall that be done?

The alternatives as I see them are to drift along until Germany rearms of her own volition and without supervision or control, or to see her rearmed with the support of one or more friendly powers, perhaps the United States, or to recognize her right to limited rearmament under safeguards and supervision outlined in the treaties. To my mind the limited and supervised rearmament within NATO is the alternative I must support.[79]

But others within the CCF parliamentary caucus, reflecting the views of a considerable body of CCF supporters within the country, could not support a rearmed Germany, even within NATO.* The first to speak for them in the debate was Stanley Knowles, the Member for Winnipeg North Centre who represented survivors of the Holocaust and relatives of those who perished. Knowles explained his opposition to the motion on three grounds.

---

*   This split within the CCF reflected an earlier and continuing rift within the party over the desirability of Canada's becoming a member of the Atlantic Alliance. 'There was some division in the party,' T.C. Douglas recalled. 'M.J. [Coldwell] and a majority of the caucus and party supported Canada going into NATO. Others wanted us to stay out...' Quoted in Doris French Shackleton, *Tommy Douglas* (Toronto 1975), 222.

First of all, I shall register my opposition from a deep personal conviction. It is my judgment that the rearming of Western Germany at this time is a step we should not now be taking. My second reason for rising to express this opposition is that I am satisfied, as other members are – indeed as other members have said – that there are thousands of good, solid, patriotic Canadians – never mind the others – from one end of the country to the other who are concerned about this step...

I also take this position because ... it is the position of the movement to which 24 in this House have the honour to belong. ... At our national convention in August 1954 a decision was taken against the rearming of Germany at this time...

...We in this group regret that in our attempt ... to bring our best judgment to bear on the question, we have not come out with the same conclusion. Regret that fact though we may, I think I can say for my leader as well as for myself that we are proud of the fact that, so far as our party is concerned, we feel that it is our right and our duty to express our personal convictions on this issue and to vote on the motion in the way that each of us feels is best for the future of this country and best for the future of mankind...[80]

If the Member for Algoma East delivered what was by all accounts the most powerful speech of the debate, the Member for the Toronto constituency of Spadina delivered the most poignant. 'I believe this House knows my background, upbringing and family tradition,' one of its two Jewish representatives declared.

Seared and burned in my memory are names that will forever live in infamy. I have had thousands of representations and many delegations which have made a very deep impression on me. There is scarcely a house in my riding that has not suffered. I am a man torn. I have done much soul-searching. My heart, instinct, intuition and emotions say no. My head, logic and realism say yes. ... With great reluctance and a heavy heart I shall do what needs to be done at this time, without joy and with the Everest of misgivings.[81]

David A. Croll and 212 other Members voted in favour of the motion; twelve (all CCF) voted against.

Canada's Parliament had become the fourth North Atlantic legislature to approve the Protocol of Accession of the Federal Republic. By so doing, Canada was – as L.B. Pearson put it some months later – 'only a few years after the ... Morgenthau plan for reducing Germany to the level of an agrarian economy ... welcoming a rearmed Germany into our coalition.'[82] Such were the strains of growing up allied.

End of vol. IV

DOCUMENTS

CHRONOLOGY OF EVENTS

NOTE ON THE SOURCES

REFERENCES

INDEX

DOCUMENT 1

EXTRACTS FROM A MEMORANDUM BY L.B. PEARSON
FOR THE PRIME MINISTER, 1 JUNE 1948 (KING PAPERS)

...One argument which is particularly strong from the Canadian point of view is that it would be far more difficult for Canada to collaborate in planning defence against Soviet aggression on the basis of a unilateral United States assurance than it would be if both countries were parties to an Atlantic Treaty. Furthermore, under such a treaty the joint planning of the defence of North America would fall into place as part of a larger whole and the difficulties arising in Canada from the fear of invasion of Canadian sovereignty by the United States would be diminished. If the present state of affairs is maintained or even if there is merely a Presidential or Congressional declaration, the advocates in Canada of a policy of aloofness would be able to strengthen their position. An Atlantic treaty would go a long way towards lessening the political difficulties of defence planning in Canada by bringing the United Kingdom, the United States and Canada into partnership.

A further advantage to Canada of an Atlantic Treaty is that it would help to ensure that Canada was not pushed out ahead of the United States in the event of war. In the last two wars Canada has gone to war more than two years before the United States. A treaty commitment by the United States instead of a congressional resolution would lessen the danger that this might happen again.

Another disadvantage to Canada of a mere Congressional resolution is that, unless it were followed quickly by the calling of a conference to frame an Atlantic treaty, the Canadian Government might be placed in a somewhat difficult position. There might be demands in Canada that the Government take some action similar to that taken by the United States Congress or even going beyond it, but it might be difficult to decide what action the Canadian Government could wisely and usefully take to supplement the public statements already made by the Prime Minister and by Mr St Laurent.

The military planning which would follow the conclusion of a treaty would tend to modify the present rather unrealistic concentration of United States and Canadian planners on the passive defence of North America from outside attack. If the North Atlantic is bridged by a defence alliance, the problems of North American defence would be seen as a small part of a larger plan, the purpose of which would be to defeat the enemy by offensive operations.

There are a number of North Atlantic countries which, like Canada, would find it politically easier to grant defence facilities to a North Atlantic union than to the United States...

Moreover, a multilateral security agreement reflects the realities of the situation much more faithfully than a unilateral guarantee by the United States. The United States and Canada need the assistance of the Western European democracies just as they need ours. A Russian conquest of Western Europe would mean for us war, and war on most unfavourable terms. A unilateral guarantee smells of charity (in the worst sense of the word); the Western European democracies are not beggars asking for charity, but they are potential allies whose assistance we need in order to be able to defend ourselves. They are Canada's first line of defence. This is a point which will have to be made clear to the people of the United States and Canada. The difficulties of doing this would be great in any case but they will be increased if the United States gives a multilateral guarantee instead of entering into a multilateral security agreement.

Most important of all, a unilateral guarantee would be nothing more than a pledge of military assistance. If the peoples of Western Europe are to throw their full weight in the scales against Russia, they need a good deal more than this from North America, especially since, if there is a war within the next year or so, the Western European countries run an almost certain danger of being occupied for many years by Soviet armies. Russia's allies in Western Europe are not so much now the Communists as the forces of apathy, despair, doubt and fear. It is therefore very important that the peoples of the Western democracies should make a bold move to raise in the hearts and minds and spirits of all those in the world who love freedom that confidence and faith which will restore their vigour. Just as the last war was a "struggle for the control of men's minds and men's souls," so is the present cold war. What is now needed is a treaty which is not merely a treaty of military guarantee but something along the lines of the Brussels Treaty; it should contain provisions for closer political, economic and cultural co-operation; it should set up new international institutions; it should set forth the principles of Western society which we are trying not only to defend but to make the basis of an eventually united world. By concluding such a treaty, the Atlantic Community could become "a model of what we hope the whole world will some day become."

Pearson

DOCUMENT 2

'COMMENTARY ON THE WASHINGTON PAPER OF SEPTEMBER 9, 1948,'
6 DECEMBER 1948 (DEPARTMENT OF EXTERNAL AFFAIRS FILES, 283(s);
ALSO IN US STATE DEPARTMENT FILES, PA/HO RESEARCH FILES, LOT 57-D271)

Introduction

1 At the beginning of October on instructions from the Cabinet, the Governments of Belgium, France, Luxembourg, The Netherlands, the United Kingdom and the United States were informed that the Canadian Government had considered the proposals set forth in the Washington paper of September 9, 1948, for a "North Atlantic Security Pact" and was ready to enter into a treaty with these countries, and such other countries as might be agreed, on the general lines of the annex to that paper.

Reasons for Canada Entering into the Treaty

2a The march of events has shown that the Soviet Union is seeking world domination by aggression, direct or indirect. Nation after nation has succumbed to these tactics. The only world war which might occur in the foreseeable future would be a war for domination by Soviet communism. Such a war would in time involve all the Western powers who would either have to fight or fall. No matter how much Canada might desire to do so, this country could not avoid being involved in such a war.

b The only way to prevent the further spread of communism through nation after nation is for the free nations to stand together now. That is the lesson of two world wars. The only way to avoid conflict or conquest is to prevent both by standing together.

c In these circumstances, the only way to prevent war is to make it clear that the Soviet Union could not win. In order to convince the Soviet Union of this it must be confronted with an overwhelming preponderance of force organized for peace. This force must be organized in such a way as to ensure that it is so used as to guarantee that the free nations will not be defeated one by one, thus jeopardizing the security of Canada.

d The organization of such a preponderance of force under a North Atlantic Security Pact is the one and only solid base for the defence of Canada.

e It could establish a constitutional basis for the collective organization of defensive power in peace and for the devolution of power in war from the members of the alliance to its organs and agents. This would contrast favourably with the concentration of power in the hands of the Big Two or the Big Three during the last war.

f It could contain within itself possibilities of growth and of adaptation to changing conditions.

g The North Atlantic countries already constitute, in fact, a group of nations sharing similar democratic ideals and cultural traditions. The creation of a "collective security system" among them may well provide a basis on which it may be possible to build, in the course of this generation, a closer unity of the North Atlantic world.

Primary Objective of the Forthcoming Negotiations

3 The objective of the forthcoming negotiations should be:

a to establish, within the framework of the United Nations Charter, a treaty for collective self-defence among the countries bordering on the North Atlantic, based on continuous and effective self-help and mutual aid, and

b to strengthen the national security of each contracting state by the establishment under the treaty of joint agencies, which would in peacetime be agencies of recommendation and which could in wartime become agencies of military decision.

The Treaty and the United Nations

4 It is important that the organization established by the treaty should be kept strictly within the framework of the United Nations.

Organs to be Established under the Treaty

5 It will be necessary for the treaty to contain a provision setting up a council (presumably of foreign ministers) empowered to establish such organs as from time to time seem necessary. These might be similar to those now set up by Western Union.

6 Should signature of the treaty not take place for some time, or should it seem likely that some months may elapse between the signature of the treaty and its coming into force, it might be necessary to make provision at the time of signature for setting up an interim council empowered to establish interim organs.

Canadian Control

7 The association of the Canadian Government with the proposed treaty must be based upon due constitutional processes. This means not only that the treaty must be approved by the Canadian Parliament but also that the ultimate control by the Canadian Government of any measures recommended by the council which may entail military or economic contributions by Canada must be preserved.

Non-Military Provisions

8 In order to emphasize the positive and moral content of the treaty, it should include provisions for consultation, co-operation and common action in the eco-

nomic field, and also a provision under which the contracting states would accept without qualification the compulsory jurisdiction of the International Court on any legal dispute which may arise among them. Moreover, the preamble should set forth, in much the same language as the preamble to the Brussels Treaty, the belief of the signatories in the values and virtues of their common civilization, and their common determination to work for the promotion of their mutual welfare and the preservation of peace, which is the aim of the treaty. The language of the treaty should be simple and clear and "officialese" and pedantic terms should be avoided.

Original Members of the Organization

9 It is desirable that the original signatories should include, if possible, the Scandinavian countries, Iceland, and Ireland, as well as the participants in the Washington discussions. If one of them should refuse to join, it will be necessary for those willing to join to give careful consideration to whether the Organization can extend guarantees to any country which does not reciprocate, although the strategic importance of bases in one of the countries might justify special arrangements with the Organization once it had been set up and the country concerned.

10 It would be difficult to support an invitation to Italy to become a member of a North Atlantic Organization since Italy not only does not fall within the North Atlantic region, but she could contribute little to the common pool of resources. In view, however, of Italy's strategic importance, the Organization once it has been set up might make special arrangements with Italy, under which Italy would receive a promise of defence by the North Atlantic Organization and, in return, agree to grant defence facilities to the Organization.

The Undertaking

11 It would seem wise to limit the undertaking to give mutual assistance under the treaty to attacks on members or on states with which the Organization has made defence arrangements, but the undertaking should not apply to non-self-governing territories outside the North Atlantic region, unless such territories are specifically included. The undertaking should be as close as possible to that in the Brussels Treaty, which reads as follows:

> If any of the High Contracting Parties should be the object of an armed attack in Europe, the other High Contracting Parties will, in accordance with the provisions of Article 51 of the Charter of the United Nations, afford the party so attacked all the military and other aid and assistance in their power.

Duration

12 The treaty might remain in force for, say, twenty or twenty-five years.

DOCUMENT 3

MEMORANDUM BY L.B. PEARSON, 'KOREA AND THE ATOMIC BOMB,' 3 DECEMBER 1950
(DEPARTMENT OF EXTERNAL AFFAIRS FILES, 50069-C-40; ALSO IN HOWE PAPERS)

1 The military authorities may argue that the atomic bomb is just another weapon. But, in the minds of ordinary people everywhere in the world, it is far more than that and has acquired an immensely greater intrinsic significance. The anxiety with which the possibility of the use of the bomb, by either side, is regarded has been strikingly and increasingly evident of late among our friends in Europe and in Asia. This is the main reason for the appeal, even in free countries, of the cynical Communist "peace" campaign.

2 The psychological and political consequences of the employment of the bomb, or the threat of its employment, in the present critical situation would be incalculably great. The risk of retaliation, to which our allies in Europe feel themselves to be exposed, would affect materially their will to resist, and the imminent prospect of atomic war over Korea, when our defences elsewhere are still weak, cannot fail to stimulate the tendencies toward "neutralism" which the development of strength and unity on our side is beginning to overcome.

3 The strategic use of the bomb against Chinese cities might conceivably change the course of military events in Asia now, but at the risk of destroying the cohesion and unity of purpose of the Atlantic community. Certainly its use, for a second time, against an Asian people would dangerously weaken the links that remain between the Western world and the people of the East.

4 The atomic bomb is the most powerful deterrent element in the arsenal of the free world. To what extent this is because of actual military potential, to what extent to psychological factors, it is impossible for us, and probably for anyone, to know. In any event it is universally regarded as the ultimate weapon. It should be treated as such. The effectiveness of the bomb as a tactical weapon cannot be fully appreciated. The very uncertainty of its capabilities in the tactical role must add materially to its deterrent value. Once it has been used tactically, however, much of its force as a deterrent may disappear, unless its use for this purpose has proven overwhelmingly successful.

5 The Canadian people would hold their Government responsible for making the Canadian views known to the United States before the atomic bomb were to be used. This is especially true in present circumstances because of the United Nations character of the operation in Korea.

6 Furthermore, in atomic matters, the Canadian Government has, from the beginning, been a partner in the tri-partite co-operation which stemmed from the Quebec Agreement between President Roosevelt and Mr Churchill in 1943. Mr Mackenzie King was associated with the Joint Declaration of November, 1945, by the heads of the three Governments directly concerned. Through its membership

in the Combined Policy Committee, the Canadian Government has continued to assist in the development of our joint resources of raw materials and of scientfic knowledge. Canada has made a direct contribution to building up the atomic stockpile. Although the *modus vivendi* of the Combined Policy Committee concluded in January 1948 does not include, as did the Quebec Agreement, the clause providing for prior consultation, the Canadian Government would be inevitably involved, and in a specially close sense, in the consequences of the use of the atomic bomb.

7 The mass intervention of the Chinese Communists in Korea may lead to the third world war. In the present critical military situation, those who have their own men engaged (and this applies, of course, particularly to the United States), are obviously entitled to have full consideration given to the use of every available means of supporting the ground forces fighting under the United Nations Command. This is natural and inevitable. But, before a decision of such immense and awful consequence, for all of us, is taken, there should be consultation among the governments principally concerned.

DOCUMENT 4

MEMORANDUM BY L.B. PEARSON AND BROOKE CLAXTON FOR THE CABINET,
'THE INTERNATIONAL SITUATION,' 28 DECEMBER 1950 (DEPARTMENT OF
EXTERNAL AFFAIRS FILES, 50069-D-40)

1 In North Atlantic planning the period of greatest danger was, until a few months ago, assumed to begin in late 1953 or 1954. Now, the only safe assumption is that the period of greatest danger has already begun.

2 By their support of the Chinese intervention in Korea, the Soviet Government have shown that they are willing to run the risk of a third world war. In such a war the Soviet Union would have, initially, and probably over the next two years, a preponderance of land and air forces in the conventional methods of warfare. Also they would probably have a small stockpile of nuclear weapons.

3 In addition, the events of the last few weeks have sharply revealed the danger that, even if a third world war can be avoided for the time being, the forces of Soviet imperialism throughout the world may be able to seize so many additional areas in Asia and Europe that the position of North America will eventually become very serious indeed.

4 Although we have differed with the United States on a number of issues of Far Eastern policy, there is agreement between the Canadian and United States Governments that:
a   peace is now in jeopardy;
b   the expansion of Soviet imperialism must be opposed;
c   the principle of collective resistance to aggression must be maintained; and
d   the main front which must be defended is Western Europe.
Our disagreements arise only in deciding how our agreement on these basic points should be translated into immediate policy and action, taking into account the present military strength of the Soviet Union and their friends and satellites and the present military weakness of the free world.

5 This relative weakness is most dangerous in Western Europe. This is where the initial Soviet attack would probably be made in the event of a general war. Europe is open to Soviet attack whenever the USSR is prepared to run the risk of atomic bombardment of its cities and industries. It is estimated that under present conditions the Red Army could occupy Western Europe to the Pyrenees within three months.

6 The present military weakness of Western Europe is one of the basic reasons why we have contended that all possible steps should be taken to avoid becoming embroiled in a war with Communist China. In such a war a decision would be almost impossible to secure. Even the atomic bomb would probably not be

decisive since suitable targets are few, life is cheap and manpower virtually inex-
haustible. Meanwhile, every day such a war lasted would be wasting inadequate
Western resources of trained manpower and military equipment.

7 Assuming that a major war with China can be avoided, it must, nevertheless,
be recognized that the defeat which the United Nations have suffered in Korea
makes more likely Communist attacks on other parts of Asia, the Middle East and
Eastern Europe. A full-scale attack on Indo-China, in particular, must be regarded
as an early possibility. And, if Indo-China is lost, the whole of South-East Asia,
including Burma, Malaya and Indonesia with their important natural resources,
might well fall under Communist control. The position of India and Pakistan, in
these events, would become precarious. This, incidentally, is an aspect of the
situation which emphasizes the political importance of outside financial assistance
for the economic development of these countries to strengthen their will and
capacity to assist in the struggle against Communist imperialism.

8 Persia and the Middle East are also vulnerable. The governments of these
countries and the rivalries between them are such that there is little ground for
hoping that, with the exception of Turkey, they would offer much effective opposition to armed aggression. Another potential ally of substantial strength which is
immediately threatened is Yugoslavia whose power to resist has been seriously
weakened by present economic difficulties.

9 In short, recent Communist successes disclose the stark possibility that, either
in the course of a general war or as a result of piece-meal attrition, the whole of
Asia and Europe, apart from the United Kingdom, Spain and Portugal, might fall
rapidly under Soviet domination. The position of North America would then be
worse than in 1940. If the Soviet Union were in control of all the productive
resources of Europe and Asia, it would have at its disposal steel and oil production
comparable to that of North America. Its supplies of raw materials and skilled
manpower would be greater and more varied.

10 Because of their lack of forces in being the North Atlantic Treaty countries are
obliged to go as far as they can to gain time. That is one of the purposes of the
present negotiations for a cease-fire in Korea. It must not be lost sight of, however, that action by Communist China or by the Soviet Union may at any time
precipitate a general war.

11 The employment by the Western countries of their present great economic
superiority and resources of skilled manpower in such a way that the prospect of
eventual victory over them is slender remains the greatest deterrent to war. This
has been their purpose especially since the North Atlantic Treaty came into
effect. But the danger has increased more rapidly than our combined efforts to
meet it.

12 The new defence programmes which the North Atlantic Treaty countries
undertook in August of this year have not yet brought about any substantial and
immediately effective net increase in their military strength. A substantial part of
the defensive strength which has been added has been diverted to Korea.

13 Last week the North Atlantic Council appointed a Supreme Commander for Western Europe and agreed upon a scheme for the establishment of an "integrated force." The representatives of the NATO countries pledged themselves to step up their defence programmes. They also agreed upon proposals for the participation of Western Germany in the joint defence.

14 The gravity of the situation has been recognized in all the North Atlantic Treaty nations, but none more than in the United States.

On December 16, President Truman adopted the unprecedented course of declaring a national emergency in peacetime. In this he said: "Recent events in Korea and elsewhere constitute a grave threat to the peace of the world. ... World conquest by Communist imperialism is the goal of the forces of aggression that have been loosed upon the world. ... The increasing menace of the forces of Communist aggression requires that the national defence of the United States be strengthened as speedily as possible."

Since the attack on Korea on June 25, the United States has sharply increased its defence appropriations and preparations. Both directly and through NATO the United States has urged the other free nations to adopt similar action. The action taken in other countries has naturally been referred to in Congress and comparisons have been made both there and in the various agencies of NATO between the defence expenditures of various countries.

15 The defence of the West depends on continued and increased participation and assistance by the United States and this will be more likely to be forthcoming if Congress and the American people believe that their effort is being matched by a comparable effort in other countries.

Further, increased fear of Russia will combine with any trend towards isolation on this continent to focus more attention on home defence against direct attack. Only if the home front is felt to be secure will public opinion support the employment of forces in Europe on the scale necessary to deter aggression.

16 The USSR may be tempted to wage war in the near future in order to prevent the free world attaining the position where it could check Soviet imperialism by the threat of effective force. Also the action taken by NATO at Brussels with respect to Western Germany involves some immediate risk of Russian reaction.

17 It seems essential that, in common with other countries of the North Atlantic, we should re-examine our defence programme in the light of these sombre developments. We will all require to press forward at a much accelerated speed if we are to attain the goal of security which is set by the North Atlantic Treaty.

18 The position of the Canadian Government, in the new emergency, was referred to in instructions sent to the Canadian representative at the Brussels meeting and then made the subject of a statement by him. Copies of that statement have been circulated to Ministers.

DOCUMENT 5

MEMORANDUM BY L.B. PEARSON FOR THE PRIME MINISTER,
'UNITED STATES DEFENCE POLICY,' 2 FEBRUARY 1954
(DEPARTMENT OF EXTERNAL AFFAIRS FILES, 50115-P-40)

There is little doubt that far-reaching decisions have been made in Washington in respect of defence policy and strategy. Mr Dulles' speech on January 12 in New York greatly strengthens this view. It is too early to come to any conclusion as to the exact nature of these decisions, but it is safe to say that their consequences will be of the greatest importance, not only for the United States but for other countries as well, including Canada.

The implementation of any decisions taken will, of course, be gradual and every effort will be made to act in a way to cause the least possible anxiety among friends and allies. As Mr Dulles put it in New York:

> It was imperative that change should be accompanied by understanding of our true purposes; sudden and spectacular change had to be avoided. Otherwise there might have been a panic among our friends and miscalculated aggression by our enemies.

There are a good many straws which show the way the defence wind is now blowing in Washington.

One is the fact – clearly demonstrated at the last NATO Council meeting – that NATO countries are no longer subject to American pressure to increase defence expenditures. Indeed, Mr Dulles now talks about "readjustments in the NATO collective security effort," and he probably means readjustment downwards, at least in terms of cost for both the United States and its NATO allies.

NATO defence forces in Europe are now to be stabilized at about fifty divisions, plus whatever Germany can produce. There is no longer any Pentagon talk, at least in public, about ninety-five or one hundred divisions as being essential to the peace in Europe. On the other hand, there is much talk of the "new look" and the "long haul," and economic stability as the foundation for defence effort. All these concepts, the validity of which is unquestioned, are now put forward by Mr Dulles, specifically at Paris in December and in his New York speech, as a new American discovery and a new NATO policy. The fact is, of course, that they had previously been advocated at NATO meetings by British and other delegates, and opposed by the Americans.

The United States delegates in those earlier days strongly deprecated talk of more defence for less cost by relying on quality and "new weapons." But all this has now changed. No attempt is now apparently to be made to build up NATO forces in Europe to a point which the American military, at least, considered necessary a year or so ago if Western Europe was to be successfully defended against liberation.

It is true that the Lisbon force goals were recognized generally as being unrealisti-
cally high long before the December NATO meeting. Mr Dulles now confirms the
validity of this position. It involves a calculated risk but one perhaps not much
greater than was always involved in NATO planning.

This is said, not in criticism of the NATO defence concept of the "long haul," but
merely to support the view that there is now a new approach in Washington to the
problems of United States defence policy. Our Embassy in Washington has given
its view that no radical change in defence policy (in so far as it means United
States commitments within the structure of collective security) is under consideration. I hope they are right, but I feel myself that this conclusion may be too
optimistic. Even, however, if there is no fundamental change, the new approach
and the new principles of strategy have important implications for not only the
United States itself, but for its friends.

These shifts in United States defence policy may be due to a genuine belief in the
efficacy of new methods and weapons and of defence by retaliation; also, in part,
to a feeling that the crisis has eased. But they may also be due to a new American
policy of "disengagement," inspired by budgetary as well as by strategic considerations. This, at least, is a possibility that cannot be dismissed.

The present position of the European Defence Community may have a bearing
on this new American approach. Indeed, it may be that frustration and disappointment over the delay in bringing the EDC into effect is one reason for the shift in
policy that is taking place. Alternatively, focussing attention on this delay may be a
rationalization of, or even an excuse for, this shift. The Americans may now
argue that as Europe will not unite to defend itself, they are relieved of certain
responsibilities for that defence which can, in any event, now be left predomi-
nantly to the Germans! This being the case, United States strategy should now
become peripheral, holding a sea and air line running roughly from Norway to the
United Kingdom through Spain and the Mediterranean to Greece and Turkey – and Pakistan? From this line, in case of war, victory by atomic retaliation
can be assured.

More and more stress is being placed on this new doctrine of the prevention of
war or, if it comes, the achievement of victory, by developing, to use the words of
Mr Dulles, "massive retaliatory power." As the Secretary of State put it in New
York:

> The basic decision was to depend primarily upon a great capacity to retaliate,
> instantly, by means and at places of our choosing.

This new concept of defence by the threat of swift and effective retaliation is
meant to give United States military strength more flexibility. But it also makes
flexibility in diplomacy even more necessary. In a sense, it will keep the potential
aggressor guessing. But it may also keep the allies of the United States guessing.

Furthermore, it is important to know what Mr Dulles means by "our" in this
context; especially when the "means" would appear to be largely atomic. Certainly this new strategy makes full consultation – being asked rather than told –
more important than ever. The Korean situation in 1950 illustrates this. If the

United States had chosen at that time not to work through the United Nations – after they had made up their own minds – but to retaliate instantly by overwhelming air action; or if later they had made the same decision to retaliate against Peking, would they have had time to consult us? Or would we have been involved automatically in action which, at least in the case of Peking, might have led to general war?

It is clear that the new strategy is going to make diplomacy, both in its inter-allied aspect and in relations with the communists, more important than before.

It is also clear that the weapon of overwhelming retaliation, or the threat of it, is one which can only be exercised when the issue is clear-cut and decisive. There will, however, be many blurred and unclear situations constituting aggressive action when it could not be used. Indeed, it can be argued, as a practical proposition, that local aggressions cannot be answered by atomic bombs on Moscow. If so, the threat of massive retaliation "by means and at places of our choosing" may become a somewhat hollow one. The new strategy may result, therefore, in greater rigidity, rather than greater flexibility, of policy. If it becomes a question of the atomic bomb and all-out war, or nothing, it may be, too often, nothing.

How is this policy of "massive retaliation" to be carried into action? By building up a strategic reserve, featuring atomic weapons and "highly mobile air and amphibious units"?

It is true that there is a large stockpile of atomic bombs and that other atomic weapons are increasing in volume and effectiveness. Indeed this must have made easier the decision to adopt the new strategy. On the other hand, there is to be a reduction of $4 billions in defence expenditure, and 10% in manpower. It is stated that this can be brought about without any weakening of defence strength, or withdrawing from any commitments undertaken in Europe. That remains to be seen.

The announced withdrawal of two divisions from Korea will also, presumably, assist in forming the strategic reserve.

Furthermore, this strategy, of course, may permit a "thinning out" of American forces in Europe (this has begun but has not yet affected combat strength) and "bringing the boys home," which will be popular in the United States.

Naturally, every effort will be made by the United States to remove fears that commitments for collective defence are going to be weakened, or that there will be extensive or immediate withdrawals from European soil. Indeed, adherence to NATO policies will be re-affirmed. President Eisenhower did, in fact, give such a re-affirmation in his State of the Union speech. There is no reason to believe that this was not genuine, nor is there any evidence that the United States Administration has lost interest and is withdrawing its support from NATO.

But the implications of the new doctrine do, I believe, make this result possible; and may easily bring about "Operation Disengagement."

If these changes in American strategy are to be made without abandoning or even weakening the North Atlantic collective security arrangements, this will require skill and care in Washington. It will also require an appreciation by Congress of the collective issues involved and the feelings and fears of allies.

If this appreciation is not shown, the new policy may be carried out in such a way that the whole NATO system will be weakened and even disappear. It may be taken for granted that the communists, for whom NATO remains the chief enemy, will interpret and exploit new American defence and strategic developments so as to facilitate this disappearance. They will undoubtedly try to show that the Americans are abandoning NATO and leaving the Europeans to their fate, while themselves taking refuge in atomic bombs and continental defence.

Mr Dulles himself has given some ammunition for this attack when he admitted in New York that one consequence of the new strategy would be less emphasis on "local defensive power." While he added that such local defensive power would always be important, he felt that it alone would never be enough to contain the mighty land array or the communist world.

This is certainly true and has always been accepted by NATO political and military planners. But bringing it out into the open, in the context of the new American strategy, is going to create uneasiness among Europeans and increase fears that the United States may consider that Europe, if not expendable, will have to be defended by its own forces, assisted by overseas weapons, rather than by overseas men. Europeans, in short, will fight in the old-fashioned, bloody, man-to-man way, while victory will come from the skies by atomic retaliation. If such victory comes only after occupation and destruction and liberation, it will have little appeal for Europeans. To this the Americans may well reply that European countries are now strong enough themselves, with some British and American help – but not too much – to hold the Russians off; especially if they will only unite!

Commenting on these European fears, aroused by the new United States strategy, Mr Wilgress writes from Paris:

> The French and a number of European countries will not accept an arrangement whereby they will be expected to contribute largely manpower while the United States will concentrate on a small highly mobile reserve force supplemented by intricate scientific weapons of mass destruction. They will wish to be supplied themselves with these weapons, they will also try to effect such economies as may be compatible with the agreed requirements of effective defence and they will press to have a voice in the shaping of the strategy which will determine the use of such weapons.

While it is too soon to be dogmatic about what the final effect will be of decisions taken in Washington, we shall have to watch their development carefully, especially as they concern our own commitment abroad, and our own defence policies.

Canadian defence policy has been firmly, and rightly, founded on NATO, and we should do everything we can to keep this foundation strong. On the other hand, it is not going to be easy, politically, to maintain at full and unimpaired strength our forces overseas, if our neighbours begin to reduce their commitments through "new decisions" and new strategic concepts.

It may be that the American Administration will not be the only ones who will, before long, have to make an "agonizing reappraisal" of foreign policy.

CHRONOLOGY OF EVENTS, 1947-55

WORLD	CANADA	PERSONNEL

1947

January

| | | 1 Marshall US Secretary of State |

11 UK decides to produce atomic bomb

March
10 Council of Foreign Ministers in Moscow
12 US aid to Greece and Turkey

April

Reid Assistant Under Secretary for External Affairs

June
 5 Marshall offers aid to Europe (Marshall Plan)
29 USSR rejects Marshall Plan aid

July
   Kennan's 'X' article

September

18 St Laurent speech at UN

23 Cominform

30 Canada on UN Security Council

November
25 Council of Foreign Ministers in London

December
15 Council of Foreign Ministers adjourns *sine die*

WORLD	CANADA	PERSONNEL

1948

January

| | | 19 Howe Minister of Trade and Commerce |

February
25 *Coup d'état* in Prague

March
  US European Recovery Program
10 Masaryk dead

11 Attlee telegram

17 Brussels Treaty

22 'Security Conversations' in Washington

April
18 Italian election

June
11 Vandenberg Resolution
22 Berlin blockade

July

1 St Laurent Minister of Justice

6 'Exploratory Talks' in Washington

August

7 St Laurent Liberal leader

September

Reid Acting Under Secretary of State for External Affairs
10 Pearson Secretary of State for External Affairs

November
  US presidential election

Truman US President
15 St Laurent Prime Minister

WORLD	CANADA	PERSONNEL

December

'Exploratory Talks'
resume

1949

January

20 Acheson US Secretary
of State

March
4 Norway joins
'Exploratory Talks'

15 Heeney Under Secre-
tary of State for Exter-
nal Affairs; Reid Deputy
Under Secretary of State
for External Affairs;
Robertson Clerk of the
Privy Council and Secre-
tary to the Cabinet;
Wilgress High Commis-
sioner at London

April
4 North Atlantic Treaty
signed

29 North Atlantic Treaty
ratified

May
12 Berlin blockade lifted
23 Basic Law for West
German State

June

27 Liberal Government
re-elected

August
29 USSR atomic bomb

September
21 People's Republic
of China
Federal Republic
of Germany
23 US-UK announcement of
USSR atomic bomb

WORLD	CANADA	PERSONNEL

October
10 German Democratic
   Republic

1950

January
31 Truman orders
   hydrogen bomb

February
14 Sino-Soviet Friendship
   Treaty

May

| | | Wilgress Council Deputy |

June
25 War in Korea

July
   US defence budget
   doubled

August

| | 7 Announcement of decision to send land forces to Korea | |

September
   North Atlantic Council
   debates German
   rearmament

November
   Chinese troops
   in Korea

December
 4 Attlee flies to
   Washington

| | | 14 Eisenhower Supreme Commander, Allied Forces in Europe |

WORLD	CANADA	PERSONNEL
1951		
January	31 Announcement of decision to send land and air forces to Europe	
February		1 Foulkes Chairman Chiefs of Staff Committee; Simonds Chief of the General Staff
March		Morrison UK Foreign Secretary
April		1 Howe Minister of Defence Production
2 Supreme Headquarters, Allied Powers in Europe, activated		
October UK general election		Churchill UK Prime Minister; Eden UK Foreign Secretary
	20 Advance party of 27th Infantry Brigade leaves for Integrated Force in Europe	
22 Greece and Turkey enter NATO		
November	First RCAF F-86 squadron crosses Atlantic for Air Division in Europe	
1952		
February North Atlantic Council in Lisbon		

WORLD	CANADA	PERSONNEL
April		
		Heeney Permanent Representative on North Atlantic Council Ismay NATO Secretary-General
May 27 European Defence Community agreements signed		
June		
		1 Robertson High Commissioner at London; Wilgress Under Secretary of State for External Affairs 2 Pickersgill Clerk of the Privy Council and Secretary to the Cabinet
October 3 UK atomic bomb		
November 1 US thermonuclear explosion ('Mike' test)		Reid High Commissioner at New Delhi; Ritchie Deputy Under Secretary of State for External Affairs
4 US presidential election		Eisenhower president-elect
1953		
January		
		20 Dulles US Secretary of State
February		
		12 Campney Associate Minister of National Defence

WORLD	CANADA	PERSONNEL

March
5 Stalin dies

15 Malenkov chairman
USSR Council of
Ministers

June

12 Bryce Clerk of the Privy
Council and Secretary
to the Cabinet

July
27 Armistice in Korea

Heeney Ambassador at
Washington

August

10 Liberal Government
re-elected

12 USSR thermonuclear
explosion ('Joe 4')

Wilgress Permanent
Representative on
North Atlantic Council

September

13 Khrushchev First Sec-
retary of Communist
Party of USSR
Wrong Under Secretary
of State for External
Affairs

1954

January
12 Dulles' 'massive
retaliation' speech

April
Fall of Dienbienphu
26 Geneva Conference on
Korea and Indochina

July

1 Campney Minister of
National Defence;
Harris Minister of
Finance

WORLD	CANADA	PERSONNEL
	28 Membership on Indochina Truce Supervisory Commissions	
August		
		Léger Under Secretary of State for External Affairs
30 French National Assembly rejects European Defence Community		
September 9 South East Asia Collective Defence Treaty signed		
October 23 Paris agreements on West Germany signed		
1955		
January		
	26 NATO Protocol on accession of West Germany ratified	
February 8 Malenkov resigns		Bulganin USSR Premier
May 5 Federal Republic of Germany enters NATO as sovereign state 15 Austrian State Treaty		
July 18 Geneva Conference of Big Four Heads of Government		
October	5 Pearson in USSR	

NOTE ON THE SOURCES

The published sources on which this book mainly relies may be ascertained by the frequency with which these are cited in the references; they include debates of the House of Commons; reports of the Departments of External Affairs and National Defence; statements and speeches; memoirs by L.B. Pearson, A.D.P. Heeney, and J.W. Pickersgill; and a reconstruction of the negotiation of the North Atlantic Treaty by Escott Reid. An important, if incongruous, source are the documents published by the US State Department in its series *Foreign Relations of the United States*; this collection contains much material pertaining to Canada, including classified Canadian state papers.

The unpublished documents on which this book is based are in the collections listed below: each collection is described by the name by which it is referred to in the references, which is followed by that of its custodian.

Ministers and Public Servants

King Papers (Public Archives of Canada)
Howe Papers (Public Archives of Canada)
Claxton Papers, including unpublished memoirs (Public Archives of Canada)
Foulkes Papers (Literary Executors of General Charles Foulkes)

Institutions

Department of External Affairs files (Historical Division, Department of External Affairs)

REFERENCES

CHAPTER ONE: CREATING THE COALITION

1 Associate Under Secretary of State for External Affairs [hereafter AUSSEA], memorandum, 'Impressions of the First General Assembly of the United Nations,' 27 February 1946, in *Documents on Canadian External Relations*, 12, *1946* (Ottawa 1977),
674-5, 680 [hereafter cited as *Documents* 12]

2 Quoted in J.W. Pickersgill and D.F. Forster (eds.), *The Mackenzie King Record*, III,
1945-1946 (Toronto 1970), 183-4 [hereafter cited as *Record* III]

3 Quoted in *Mike: The Memoirs of the Right Honourable Lester B. Pearson*, II, *1948-1957*
(Toronto 1973), 39 [hereafter cited as *Mike* II]; also in *Documents* 12, 2045

4 Hume Wrong, memorandum, 'The Possibility of War with the Soviet Union,' 28
June 1946, King Papers

5 Ambassador at Moscow to Secretary of State for External Affairs [hereafter SSEA],
21 March 1946, *Documents* 12, 2050

6 United Kingdom Foreign Office Paper, 'Russia from the Political Angle,' 16 September 1946, quoted in Don Page and Don Munton, 'Canadian Images of the Cold War
1946-7,' *International Journal*, XXXII, 3, Summer 1977, 582n

7 C.S.A. Ritchie, 'Political Appreciation of the Objectives of Soviet Foreign Policy,'
30 November 1946, in *Documents* 12, 1703-7

8 Quoted in Page and Munton, *op. cit.*, 589-91

9 Quoted in Escott Reid, *Time of Fear and Hope: The Making of the North Atlantic
Treaty, 1947-1949* (Toronto 1977), 29

10 'The Constitution of the United Nations,' Free World Research Bureau, April 1945,
11

11 Quoted in J.W. Pickersgill (ed.), *The Mackenzie King Record*, I, *1939-1944* (Toronto
1960), 532

12 Quoted in Thomas T. Hammond, 'Atomic Diplomacy Revisited,' *Orbis*, XIX, Winter
1976, 1427

13 Quoted in *Mike* II, 38-9; also in *Documents* XII, 2046

14 H.H. Wrong to L.B. Pearson, 23 March 1946, *Documents* 12, 2052

15 Pearson to Mackenzie King, 16 January 1947, King Papers

16 Ambassador at Moscow to SSEA, 21 March 1946, *Documents* 12, 2051

17 Escott Reid to Norman Robertson, 29 October 1947, Department of External Affairs
[hereafter DEA] files, 211-J-s

18 L.B. Pearson, 'International Co-operation,' speech at the Directors' International Day
Luncheon, Canadian National Exhibition, Toronto, 2 September 1947, DEA Information Division, *Statements and Speeches*, no. 47/13 (Ottawa, mimeographed)

19 Hume Wrong, 'Canada, the United Nations and the United States,' speech at Tarrytown, NY, 16 September 1947, DEA Information Division, *Statements and Speeches*,
no. 47/14 (Ottawa, mimeographed)

20 Mackenzie King to Sir Alfred Zimmern, 17 October 1947, DEA files, *op. cit.*

21 Willson Woodside, 'Unity of War-Winning Coalition Tested in Trieste and Poland,'
Saturday Night, 26 May 1945, 13

22 Woodside, 'First Peace Session a Failure, Speeds Drift towards Blocs,' *Saturday
Night*, 6 October 1945, 13

23 Quoted in *Mike* II, 40

24 *Globe and Mail* (Toronto), 17 June 1947

25 Canada, *H.C. Debates*, 1947, VI, 5077-8

26 *Mike* II, 40

27 Escott Reid to Hume Wrong, 20 October 1947, DEA files, *op. cit.*
28 Reid, 'Canada's Role in the United Nations,' speech at the Canadian Institute on Public Affairs, Lake Couchiching, Ontario, 13 August 1947, DEA Information Division, *Statement and Speeches*, no. 47/12 (Ottawa, mimeographed)
29 Reid, *Time of Fear and Hope*, 31
30 *Ibid.*
31 Reid, 'The Birth of the North Atlantic Alliance,' *International Journal*, XXII, 3, Summer 1967, 426-7
32 Quoted in Page and Munton, *op. cit.*, 594
33 Quoted in *ibid.*, 592, 593
34 *Ibid.*, 596-7
35 Escott Reid, *Time of Fear and Hope*, 32
36 *Mike* II, 41
37 Quoted in Reid, *Time of Fear and Hope*, 33
38 Quoted in *Mike* II, 41
39 Reid, *Time of Fear and Hope*, 32-3
40 *Mike* II, 41
41 Escott Reid to Hume Wrong, 20 October 1947, DEA files, *op. cit.*
42 *Mike* II, 41
43 Dale C. Thomson, *Louis St Laurent: Canadian* (Toronto 1967), 219
44 Louis S. St Laurent, 'Some Observations on the United Nations General Assembly, 1947,' speech to the Canadian Chamber of Commerce, Quebec City, 7 October 1947, DEA Information Division, *Statements and Speeches*, no. 47/16 (Ottawa, mimeographed)
45 Thomson, *op. cit.*, 219-20
46 Escott Reid to Hume Wrong, 5 November 1947, DEA files, *op. cit.*
47 Reid, *Time of Fear and Hope*, 35
48 Reid to Hume Wrong, 5 November 1947, DEA files, *op. cit.*
49 G.R. Riddell to L.B. Pearson, 5 December 1947, *ibid.*
50 Escott Reid, 'The Birth of the North Atlantic Alliance,' 427
51 Quoted in J.W. Pickersgill and D.F. Forster (eds.), *The Mackenzie King Record*, IV, *1947-1948* (Toronto 1970), 108 [hereafter cited as *Record* IV]
52 Quoted in *ibid.*, 111
53 Quoted in *ibid.*, 116
54 Quoted in *ibid.*, 119
55 Quoted in *ibid.*, 133
56 Quoted in Reid, *Time of Fear and Hope*, 36
57 *Foreign Relations of the United States, 1947*, II, *Council of Foreign Ministers; Germany and Austria* (Washington, DC 1972), 815-16
58 *The Memoirs of Lord Gladwyn* (London 1972), 209
59 Theodore H. White, *Fire in the Ashes: Europe in Mid-Century* (New York 1953), 287-8
60 Mackenzie King to Sir Shuldham Redfern, 8 August 1947, King Papers
61 Quoted in *Record* IV, 427
62 *Mike* II, 132
63 *Mike* II, 40-1
64 Oral History Project on Canada's Role in the Formation of NATO, York University, interview by T.A. Hockin and G. Wright with L.B. Pearson, Ottawa, 7 May 1970
65 J.W. Pickersgill, *My Years with Louis St Laurent: A Political Memoir* (Toronto 1975), 45
66 Escott Reid, *Time of Fear and Hope*, 68
67 Reid, 'The Birth of the North Atlantic Alliance,' 428
68 Quoted in *Record* IV, 154-5
69 Escott Reid, 'The Birth of the North Atlantic Alliance,' 428
70 L.B. Pearson to L.S. St Laurent, 17 January 1948, DEA files, 277(s)

71 Escott Reid, 'The Birth of the North Atlantic Alliance,' 428
72 Reid, 'Memorandum for Mr Soward,' 20 June 1951, DEA files, 50030-40
73 Jebb, *op. cit.*, 210-11
74 Hume Wrong to L.B. Pearson, 7 February 1948, DEA files, 277(s)
75 Quoted in *Record* IV, 164
76 Thomson, *op. cit.*, 229-30
77 L.B. Pearson to D.C. Abbott, 3 May 1948, DEA files, *op. cit.*
78 Dana Wilgress to Pearson, 25 May 1948, King Papers
79 Quoted in *Record* IV, 167
80 'Personal Message for Mr Mackenzie King from Mr Attlee, dated 10th March, 1948,' King Papers
81 Quoted in *Record* IV, 166
82 Thomson, *op. cit.*, 229
83 Quoted in *Record* IV, 166
84 Mackenzie King to C.R. Attlee, 11 March 1948 (telegram), King Papers
85 Quoted in *Record* IV, 166
86 Quoted in *ibid.*, 167
87 Quoted in *ibid.*
88 Quoted in *ibid.*
89 Quoted in *ibid.*, 168
90 Quoted in *ibid.*, 169
91 Quoted in *ibid.*, 170
92 Quoted in *ibid.*
93 Quoted in *ibid.*, 171-2
94 Thomson, *op. cit.*, 229
95 Quoted in *Record* IV, 173
96 Quoted in *ibid.*, 174
97 Canada, *H.C. Debates*, 1948, III, 2303
98 *Ibid.*, 2306
99 *Ibid.*, 2312
100 Quoted in *Record* IV, 174
101 'Mr. King's Pledge', *Winnipeg Free Press*, 29 March 1948
102 Quoted in *Record* IV, 175-6
103 Quoted in *ibid.*, 175
104 Quoted in *ibid.*, 177
105 Quoted in Reid, *Time of Fear and Hope*, 23
106 Gaddis Smith, 'Visions and Revisions of the Cold War: The Berlin Blockade through the Filter of History,' *New York Times Magazine*, 29 April 1973
107 Quoted in *Record* IV, 108
108 Quoted in *ibid.*, 109
109 Quoted in *ibid.*, 114
110 Quoted in *ibid.*, 133
111 Quoted in *ibid.*, 275-6
112 Quoted in *ibid.*, 189
113 Quoted in *ibid.*
114 N.A. Robertson to SSEA, 28 June 1948 (telegram), DEA files, 11840-40
115 L.B. Pearson to L.S. St Laurent, 'Situation in Berlin,' 29 June 1948, *ibid.*
116 Quoted in *Record* IV, 189-90
117 L.B. Pearson to N.A. Robertson, 30 June 1948 (telegram), DEA files, *op. cit.*
118 Quoted in *Record* IV, 190-1
119 Quoted in *ibid.*, 192
120 Quoted in *ibid.*, 193
121 Quoted in *ibid.*
122 L.B. Pearson, memorandum for SSEA, 30 June 1948, DEA files, *op. cit.*

123 Brooke Claxton to L.S. St Laurent, 30 June 1948, *ibid.*
124 Escott Reid, memorandum for L.B. Pearson, 13 July 1948, *ibid.*
125 Canada, *H.C. Debates*, 1948, VI, 6212
126 Quoted in *Record* IV, 193
127 James Eayrs, *In Defence of Canada*, II, *Appeasement and Rearmament* (Toronto 1965), 95
128 L.B. Pearson, memorandum for SSEA, 3 August 1948, DEA files, *op. cit.*
129 L.B. Pearson to N.A. Robertson, 1 July 1948 (telegram), DEA files, *op. cit.*
130 Pearson, memorandum for SSEA, 3 August 1948, *ibid.*
131 *Ibid.*
132 Pearson to SSEA, 3 September 1948, *ibid.*
133 Brooke Claxton to Pearson, 22 September 1948; extract from Cabinet minutes, 25 September 1948, *ibid.*
134 General Maurice Pope to L.B. Pearson, 8 September 1948, *ibid.*
135 Hume Wrong to Escott Reid, 1 November 1948, *ibid.*
136 N.A. Robertson to Acting Prime Minister [Brooke Claxton], 12 October 1948 (telegram), *ibid.*
137 Robertson to Escott Reid, 26 October 1948 (telegram), *ibid.*
138 Hume Wrong to Reid, 1 November 1948, *ibid.*
139 Reid to SSEA, 13 October 1948, *ibid.*
140 L.B. Pearson to Reid, 29 November 1948 (telegram), *ibid.*
141 Reid, memorandum for SSEA, 20 December 1948, *ibid.*
142 Canada, *H.C. Debates*, 1949, I, 906
143 T.B. Millar, *Australia's Defence* (London and New York 1965), 26-7
144 Canada, *H.C. Debates*, 1948, VI, 5551
145 Quoted in Donald Creighton, *Harold Adams Innis: Portrait of a Scholar* (Toronto 1957), 132-4
146 Quoted in *ibid.*, 133
147 Frank H. Underhill, 'The Lights Go Out in Czechoslovakia,' *Canadian Forum*, XXVIII, 327, April 1948, 5-6
148 Quoted in Donald Liesemer, 'The Nature of Canada's Crusade for NATO' (unpublished MA dissertation, Bishop's University 1973), 122
149 Quoted in *ibid.*, 128
150 Alex I. Inglis, 'The Institute and the Department,' *International Journal*, XXXIII, I, Winter 1977-8, 98
151 Leslie Morris, *Peace is in Your Hands* (Toronto, April 1949), 5, 24, 26
152 *Ibid.*, 28
153 Quoted in Walter D. Young, *The Anatomy of a Party: The National CCF, 1932-61* (Toronto 1969), 280
154 Quoted in Liesemer, *op. cit.*, 130
155 *Ibid.*, 139
156 Quoted in *ibid.*, 139
157 Young, *op. cit.*, 280
158 *Ibid.*, 281
159 Quoted in Liesemer, *op. cit.*, 140
160 Quoted in J.L. Granatstein and J.M. Hitsman, *Broken Promises: A History of Conscription in Canada* (Toronto 1977), 32
161 Quoted in Thomson, *op. cit.*, 230
162 Escott Reid to J.W. Pickersgill, 6 December 1948, DEA files, 283(s)
163 Quoted in DEA Information Division Reference Papers, No. 33, 'Statements made by the Canadian Government on the Proposed North Atlantic Treaty, 20 January 1948-25 October 1948,' 29 October 1948 (Ottawa, mimeographed)
164 Quoted in *ibid.*
165 *Ibid.*

166 Liesemer, *op. cit.*, 150
167 Escott Reid, 'Memories of Louis St Laurent, 1946-9,' in Norman Penlington (ed.), *On Canada: Essays in Honour of Frank H. Underhill* (Toronto 1971), 80-1
168 Canada, *H.C. Debates*, 1948, IV, 3449
169 *Winnipeg Free Press*, 1 May 1948
170 'At Last a Foreign Policy,' *Globe and Mail* (Toronto), 1 May 1948
171 Thomson, *op. cit.*, 231
172 *Globe and Mail* (Toronto), 14 May 1948
173 Escott Reid, 'Memories of Louis St Laurent,' *op. cit.*, 80
174 Canada, *H.C. Debates*, 1948, VI, 5551
175 DEA Information Division, *Statements and Speeches*, No. 48/35 (Ottawa 1948, mimeographed)
176 League of Nations, *Records of the Fifth Assembly* (1924), 221
177 Walter Millis (ed.), *The Forrestal Diaries* (New York 1951), 423
178 *Foreign Relations of the United States, 1948*, IX, *The Western Hemisphere* (Washington, DC 1972), 406 [hereafter cited as *FRUS, 1948*]
179 *Ibid.*, 406
180 Quoted in *Record* IV, 260
181 Quoted in *ibid.*, 263
182 Quoted in *ibid.*, 267
183 Quoted in *ibid.*, 267
184 Quoted in *ibid.*, 263-4
185 Quoted in *ibid.*, 264
186 *FRUS, 1948*, 410-11
187 L.B. Pearson, memorandum for the Prime Minister, 1 June 1948, King Papers
188 Quoted in *Record* IV, 269-70
189 Canada, *H.C. Debates*, 1955, I, 366
190 John Holmes to L.B. Pearson, 9 April 1948, King Papers
191 L.B. Pearson to Gen. Georges Vanier, 13 August 1948, quoted in Escott Reid, 'Canadian Conception of the Nature and Purpose of the North Atlantic Treaty,' 14 April 1950, DEA files, 50030-40
192 N.A. Robertson to SSEA, 21 April 1948, DEA files, 277(s)

CHAPTER TWO: DRAFTING THE TREATY

1 H.H. Wrong to L.B. Pearson, 13 March 1948 (telegram), DEA files, 283(s)
2 Pearson, memorandum for the Prime Minister, 'Proposed Pact of Mutual Assistance,' 14 March 1948, King Papers
3 Escott Reid to Pearson, 18 March 1948, DEA files, *op. cit.*
4 Escott Reid, *Time of Fear and Hope: The Making of the North Atlantic Treaty* (Toronto 1977), 71
5 Claxton memoirs, 1219
6 Reid, *op. cit.*, 71
7 *Ibid.*, 72
8 *Mike: The Memoirs of the Rt Hon. Lester B. Pearson*, II, *1948-1957* (Toronto 1973), 48 [hereafter cited as *Mike* II]
9 *The Memoirs of Lord Gladwyn* (London 1972), 216
10 *Ibid.*, 216
11 Robert Cecil, 'Legends Spies Tell: A Reappraisal of the Absconding Diplomats,' *Encounter*, L, 4, April 1978, 11
12 Reid, *op. cit.*, 81
13 Quoted in *Foreign Relations of the United States, 1948*, III, *Western Europe* (Washington, DC 1974), 59-61 [hereafter cited as *FRUS, 1948*]
14 L.B. Pearson to Escott Reid, 23 March 1948 (telegram), DEA files, *op. cit.*

15 Reid to Pearson, 23 March 1948 (telegram, not sent), *ibid.*
16 Pearson, memorandum for the Prime Minister, 27 March 1948, King Papers
17 *FRUS, 1948*, 65
18 Hume Wrong, memorandum, 'Reference Today's Discussion,' 23 March 1948, DEA files, *op. cit.*
19 *FRUS, 1948*, 66-7
20 L.B. Pearson, memorandum for the Prime Minister, 27 March 1948, King Papers
21 *Mike* II, 46
22 Quoted in J.W. Pickersgill and D.F. Forster (eds.), *The Mackenzie King Record*, IV, *1947-1948* (Toronto 1970), 181
23 L.B. Pearson to Hume Wrong, 29 March 1948, DEA files, *op. cit.*
24 Wrong to Pearson, 7 April 1948, *ibid.*
25 *FRUS, 1948*, 69
26 *Ibid.*, 70-1
27 *Ibid.*, 74
28 *FRUS, 1948*, 72
29 Privately communicated
30 Escott Reid, 'The Birth of the North Atlantic Alliance,' 439
31 George F. Kennan, *Memoirs*, I, *1925-1950* (Boston, Toronto 1967), 407-9
32 L.B. Pearson to Hume Wrong, 18 May 1948 (telegram), DEA files, *op. cit.*
33 Wrong to Pearson, 19 May 1948, *ibid.*
34 *FRUS, 1948*, 128
35 Quoted in Escott Reid, *Time of Fear and Hope*, 110
36 Reid, 'Canada and the Creation of the North Atlantic Alliance, 1948-1949,' in Michael G. Fry (ed.), *Freedom and Change: Essays in Honour of Lester B. Pearson* (Toronto 1975), 115-16
37 Quoted in *ibid.*, 116
38 Quoted in Reid, *Time of Fear and Hope*, 111
39 L.B. Pearson to Hume Wrong, 18 May 1948 (telegram), DEA files, *op. cit.*
40 *FRUS, 1948*, 136
41 Quoted in Reid, *Time of Fear and Hope*, 91
42 Reid, 'Canada and the Creation of the North Atlantic Alliance, 1948-1949,' 129-30
43 Reid to N.A. Robertson, 22 March 1948, DEA files, *op. cit.*
44 Reid, memorandum for L.B. Pearson, 18 March 1948, *ibid.*
45 Hume Wrong to Reid, 17 June 1948, *ibid.*
46 Reid, memorandum for L.B. Pearson, 26 June 1948, *ibid.*
47 Reid, memorandum, 'Proposed North Atlantic Defence Treaty,' 30 June 1948, *ibid.*
48 *FRUS, 1948*, 151
49 Reid, *Time of Fear and Hope*, 75
50 Quoted in *Mike* II, 50
51 *Ibid.*
52 *FRUS, 1948*, 175-6
53 *Ibid.*, 182
54 Reid, *Time of Fear and Hope*, 55
55 *Mike* II, 50
56 L.S. St Laurent to Hume Wrong, 27 July 1948, DEA files, *op. cit.*
57 L.B. Pearson to Pierre Dupuy, 27 July 1948, *ibid.*
58 *FRUS, 1948*, 216-7
59 *Ibid.*, 218
60 *Mike* II, 50
61 L.B. Pearson to Gen. Georges Vanier, 13 August 1948, quoted in Escott Reid, 'Canadian Conception of the Nature and Purpose of the North Atlantic Treaty, 14 April 1950, DEA files, 50030-40
62 *FRUS, 1948*, 238
63 *Ibid.*, 245

64   *Ibid.*, 249-50
65   Hume Wrong to L.B. Pearson, 11 September 1948, DEA files, 283(s)
66   Escott Reid, 'Canadian Conception of the Nature and Purpose of the North Atlantic Treaty,' 14 April 1950, DEA files, 50030-40
67   Quoted in *ibid.*
68   Reid, 'Comments of the Canadian Government on the Paper dated September 9, 1948, resulting from the Washington Exploratory Talks on Security,' 6 November 1948, Claxton Papers
69   N.A. Robertson to Reid, 9 November 1948 (telegram), *ibid.*
70   H.H. Wrong to Reid, 12 November 1948 (telegram), DEA files, 283(s)
71   Reid, memorandum for the Prime Minister, 'Proposed Statement of Views by the Canadian Government on the North Atlantic Treaty,' 15 November 1948, *ibid.*
72   H.H. Wrong to Reid, 19 November 1948 (telegram), *ibid.*
73   Reid to L.B. Pearson, 20 November 1948 (telegram), *ibid.*
74   A.D.P. Heeney, 'Memorandum for Mr Reid,' 20 November 1948, *ibid.*
75   L.B. Pearson to Escott Reid, 21 November 1948 (telegram), *ibid.*
76   Pearson to Reid, 22 November 1948 (telegram), *ibid.*
77   Reid to Hume Wrong, 20 November 1948 (draft telegram, not sent), *ibid.*
78   Wrong to Reid, 24 November 1948 (telegram), *ibid.*
79   Reid to L.B. Pearson, 7 December 1948 (telegram), *ibid.*
80   Brooke Claxton, 'North Atlantic Treaty: Draft of Proposed Memorandum for Guidance of the Canadian Representative in the Second Series of Informal and Non-Commital Discussions in Washington,' 1 December 1948, Claxton Papers
81   Hume Wrong to Escott Reid, 11 December 1948 (telegram), DEA files, *op. cit.*
82   Reid, 'Memorandum to SSEA,' 17 December 1948, *ibid.*
83   Reid, *Time of Fear and Hope*, 230, 277 (note to 230)
84   Reid, 'Canada and the Creation of the North Atlantic Alliance, 1948-1949,' in Fry (ed.), 131n
85   Reid, *Time of Fear and Hope*, 228
86   *Ibid.*, 219-20
87   *FRUS, 1948*, 316-17
88   *Ibid.*, 335
89   *Ibid.*, 70
90   Hume Wrong to L.B. Pearson, 7 April 1948, DEA files, *op. cit.*
91   Escott Reid, *Time of Fear and Hope*, 147
92   Quoted in *Foreign Relations of the United States, 1949*, IV, *Western Europe* (Washington, DC 1975), 74 [hereafter cited as *FRUS, 1949*]
93   *Ibid.*, 80
94   Hume Wrong to SSEA, 9 February 1949 (telegram), DEA files, *op. cit.*
95   Escott Reid, *Time of Fear and Hope*, 150
96   *Ibid.*, 150
97   *Ibid.*, 151
98   Quoted in *ibid.*, 151-2
99   *FRUS, 1949*, 109
100 Ambassador at Washington to DEA, 15 February 1949 (telegram), quoted in Escott Reid, *Time of Fear and Hope*, 152
101 Ambassador at Washington to DEA, 16 February 1949 (telegram), quoted in *ibid.*, 152
102 L.B. Pearson to Hume Wrong, 17 February 1949 (telegram), DEA files, *op. cit.*
103 Minutes of Ambassadors' Meetings, North Atlantic Treaty, Washington, DC, 6 July 1948-15 March 1949, 13th meeting, 25 February 1949, *ibid.*
104 Escott Reid, *Time of Fear and Hope*, 156
105 *Mike* II, 58

106   Oral History Project on Canada's Role in the Formation of NATO, York University, interview by T.A. Hockin and G. Wright with L.B. Pearson, Ottawa, 7 May 1970
107   *The New York Times*, 19 March 1949
108   Canada, *H.C. Debates*, 1949, III, 2098
109   *Mike* II, 55
110   Quoted in Escott Reid, *Time of Fear and Hope*, 199-200
111   DEA, 'Commentary on the Washington Paper of September 9, 1948,' 6 December 1948, DEA files, *op. cit.*
112   *FRUS, 1948*, 327, 330
113   Hume Wrong to L.B. Pearson, 4 January 1949, DEA files, *op. cit.*
114   Wrong to SSEA, 15 January 1949 (telegram), *ibid.*
115   L.B. Pearson to Wrong, 17 January 1949 (telegram), *ibid.*
116   Escott Reid, *Time of Fear and Hope*, 206
117   Minutes of Ambassadors' Meetings, North Atlantic Treaty, Washington, DC, 6 July 1948-15 March 1949, 13th meeting, 25 February 1949, DEA files, *op. cit.*
118   Escott Reid, *Time of Fear and Hope*, 213
119   *FRUS, 1948*, 327
120   Dale C. Thomson, *Louis St Laurent: Canadian* (Toronto 1967), 250
121   Hume Wrong, 'Memorandum for Mr Reid,' 8 January 1948, DEA files, *op. cit.*
122   Quoted in Reid, *Time of Fear and Hope*, 215-16
123   *Ibid.*, 216
124   *FRUS, 1949*, 32
125   Hume Wrong to SSEA, 15 January 1949 (telegram), DEA files, *op. cit.*
126   *FRUS, 1949*, 33
127   Hume Wrong to SSEA, 15 January 1949 (telegram), DEA files, *op. cit.*
128   Quoted in *Mike* II, 55
129   *FRUS, 1948*, 334-5
130   Escott Reid, *Time of Fear and Hope*, 168
131   *Ibid.*, 171
132   Oral History Project ... interview by T.A. Hockin and G. Wright with John D. Hickerson, Washington, 27 October 1969
133   Dean Acheson, *Present at the Creation: My Years in the State Department* (New York, Toronto 1969), 365-6
134   Escott Reid, *Time of Fear and Hope*, 171
135   Quoted in *ibid.*, 171
136   Hume Wrong to L.B. Pearson, 7 February 1949 (telegram), DEA files, *op. cit.*
137   Minutes of Ambassadors' Meetings, North Atlantic Treaty, Washington, DC, 6 July 1948-15 March 1949, 12th meeting, 8 February 1949, *ibid.*
138   *Ibid.*
139   Hume Wrong to SSEA, 9 February 1949 (telegram), DEA files, *op. cit.*
140   L.B. Pearson to Wrong, 9 February 1949 (telegram), *ibid.*
141   Escott Reid, *Time of Fear and Hope*, 179
142   *Ibid.*
143   *Ibid.*, 178-9
144   Hume Wrong to SSEA, 14 February 1949 (telegram), DEA files, *op. cit.*
145   *Mike* II, 57
146   Thomson, *op. cit.*, 258
147   Hume Wrong to SSEA, 19 February 1949, DEA files, *op. cit.*
148   Escott Reid, *Time of Fear and Hope*, 179
149   Quoted in *ibid.*, 175
150   Quoted in *ibid.*
151   Quoted in *ibid.*
152   Hume Wrong to SSEA, 23 February 1949 (telegram), DEA files, *op. cit.*

153　Escott Reid, *Time of Fear and Hope*, 175-6
154　Oral History Project..., *op. cit.*
155　Quoted in Escott Reid, *Time of Fear and Hope*, 176
156　Minutes of Ambassadors' Meetings..., 13th Meeting, 25 February 1949, DEA files, *op. cit.*
157　Hume Wrong to SSEA, 25 February 1949 (telegram), *ibid.*
158　SSEA to Wrong, 27 February 1949 (telegram), *ibid.*
159　*FRUS, 1949*, 160
160　Oral History Project..., *op. cit.*

CHAPTER THREE: ORGANIZING THE ALLIANCE

1　*Foreign Relations of the United States*, 1949, IV, *Western Europe* (Washington, DC 1975), 172 [hereafter cited as *FRUS, 1949*]
2　*Mike: The Memoirs of the Rt Hon. Lester B. Pearson*, II, *1948-1957* (Toronto 1973), 59 [hereafter cited as *Mike* II]
3　Oral History Project on Canada's Role in the Formation of NATO, York University, interview by T.A. Hockin and G. Wright with John D. Hickerson, Washington, DC, 27 October 1969
4　Dean Acheson, *Present at the Creation: My Years in the State Department* (New York, Toronto 1969), 374
5　*Mike* II, 60
6　Quoted in Escott Reid, *Time of Fear and Hope: The Making of the North Atlantic Treaty, 1947-1949* (Toronto 1977), 221
7　Elliott R. Goodman, *The Fate of the Atlantic Community* (New York 1975), 538
8　Quoted in Reid, *Time of Fear and Hope*, 222
9　Robert S. Jordan, *The NATO International Staff/Secretariat, 1952-1957: A Study in International Administration* (London 1967), 19
10　Ambassador at Washington to SSEA, 6 August 1949 (telegram), DEA files, 50030-40
11　A.D.P. Heeney, 'Memorandum for SSEA,' 23 March 1949, *ibid.*
12　General Charles Foulkes to Brooke Claxton, 21 February 1955, Foulkes Papers
13　*Ibid.*
14　Escott Reid to Hume Wrong, 14 January 1949 (telegram), DEA files, *op. cit.*
15　Wrong to Reid, 17 January 1949, *ibid.*
16　Lt-Gen. Charles Foulkes to Maj.-Gen. A.M. Gruenther, 7 March 1949, Foulkes Papers
17　Col. R.L. Raymont to Foulkes, 25 March 1949 (telegram), *ibid.*
18　Foulkes, 'Memorandum for the Minister,' 16 March 1949, *ibid.*
19　Foulkes to Maj.-Gen. A.M. Gruenther, 7 March 1949, *ibid.*
20　Foulkes, 'Memorandum for the Minister,' 16 March 1949, *ibid.*
21　Col. R.L. Raymont to Foulkes, 25 March 1949 (telegram), *ibid.*
22　A.D.P. Heeney, 'Memorandum for Mr Reid and Mr Crean,' 25 March 1949, DEA files, *op. cit.*
23　USSEA, memorandum for SSEA, 'Re Defence Organization under North Atlantic Treaty,' 1 April 1949, *ibid.*
24　A.D.P. Heeney, 'Chiefs of Staff Committee: Defence Organization under North Atlantic Treaty,' 18 May 1949, *ibid.*; Lt-Gen. Charles Foulkes to Col. R.L. Raymont, 18 May 1949 (telegram), Foulkes Papers
25　DEA memorandum, 'North Atlantic Treaty – Military Organization,' 11 May 1949, DEA files, *op. cit.*
26　A.D.P. Heeney to H.H. Wrong, 24 August 1949 (telegram), *ibid.*
27　SSEA to Ambassador at Washington, 25 August 1949 (telegram), *ibid.*
28　H.H. Wrong to A.D.P. Heeney, 1 September 1949 (telegram), *ibid.*
29　Heeney to G. Ignatieff, 2 September 1949 (telegram), *ibid.*

30 L.B. Pearson to Heeney, 3 September 1949, *ibid.*
31 DEA, 'Memorandum for the Minister,' 5 September 1949, *ibid.*
32 DEA, 'Memorandum for Mr Claxton,' 7 September 1949, *ibid.*
33 *Ottawa Citizen*, 3 September 1949, 'Canada May be Excluded from Groups'
34 L.B. Pearson, 'Memorandum for Mr Heeney,' 3 September 1949, DEA files, *op. cit.*
35 Brooke Claxton to T.W.L. MacDermot, 3 October 1951, Claxton Papers
36 Oral History Project on Canada's Role in the Formation of NATO, York University. interview by T.A. Hockin and G. Wright with L.B. Pearson, Ottawa, 7 May 1970
37 Claxton memoirs, 1242
38 *Ibid.*
39 *Ibid.*, 1261-6
40 *Ibid.*, 1267
41 *Ibid.*, 1241-2
42 Chiefs of Staff Committee memorandum, 'Concept of North Atlantic Defence Organization,' 30 June 1949, DEA files, *op. cit.*
43 Chiefs of Staff Committee memorandum, 'A Concept of North Atlantic Defence Organization' (no date), *ibid.*
44 A.D.P. Heeney to H.H. Wrong, 2 August 1949 (telegram), *ibid.*
45 General Charles Foulkes, 'Notes on Discussion with Generals Bradley and Gruenther on the Military Organization of the Atlantic Pact,' 15 August 1949, Foulkes Papers
46 Charles Ritchie, 'Memorandum for the USSEA' [Under Secretary of State for External Affairs, hereafter USSEA], 18 July 1950, DEA files, *op. cit.*
47 SSEA to High Commissioner at London, 22 July 1950 (telegram), *ibid.*
48 SSEA to Permanent Representative on North Atlantic Council, 3 October 1952 (telegram), DEA files, 50107-40
49 Permanent Representative on North Atlantic Council to SSEA, 13 January 1953, DEA files, 50115-P-40
50 Minute by L.B. Pearson on USSEA, 'Memorandum for the Minister – NATO and Global Planning,' 24 January 1953, *ibid.*
51 Brooke Claxton to L.D. Wilgress, 15 July 1952, DEA files, 50030-L-5-40
52 J.W. Pickersgill to C.M. Drury, 24 July 1952, *ibid.*
53 Ambassador at Paris to SSEA, 26 July 1952, *ibid.*
54 Quoted in *The Pentagon Papers: The Defense Department History of United States Decisionmaking on Vietnam* (Senator Gravel edition), I (Boston 1971), 10
55 DEA, Defence Liaison Division I, memorandum for Acting USSEA, 28 July 1952, DEA files, *op. cit.*
56 Minute by L.S. St Laurent on memorandum by USSEA for L.B. Pearson (no date , *ibid.*
57 R.G. Robertson, 'Memorandum for Mr Pearson,' 18 August 1952, *ibid.*
58 Ambassador at Washington to SSEA, 6 August 1949 (telegram), DEA files, 50030-40
59 A.D.P. Heeney to H.H. Wrong, 24 August 1949 (telegram), *ibid.*
60 Quoted in Jordan, *op. cit.*, 20
61 R.A. MacKay, 'Memorandum for Mr Reid,' 13 September 1949, DEA files, 50030-A-40
62 Hume Wrong to A.F.W. Plumptre, 2 May 1950, *ibid.*
63 Escott Reid to L.B. Pearson, 31 March 1950, *ibid.*
64 A.D.P. Heeney, 'Memorandum for the Minister – Notes for Cabinet on Agenda for North Atlantic Council,' 19 May 1950, *ibid.*
65 SSEA to Ambassador at Washington, 21 April 1950 (telegram), *ibid.*
66 L.B. Pearson to A.D.P. Heeney, 18 May 1950, *ibid.*
67 Pearson, 'Report of Meetings of North Atlantic Council and Council Deputies held in New York, September 15-20, 1950,' *ibid.*
68 DEA memorandum, 'North Atlantic Council Meeting,' 13 December 1950, *ibid.*

69   Quoted in Reid, *Time of Fear and Hope*, 242
70   L.B. Pearson, minute on DEA 'Memorandum to the Minister,' 14 October 1953, DEA files, 50102-E-40
71   C.L. Sulzberger, *A Long Row of Candles: Memoirs and Diaries, 1934-1954* (New York and Toronto 1969), 940
72   Lester B. Pearson, *Democracy in World Politics* (Toronto 1955), 52
73   Quoted in *Mike* II, 92
74   Canada, *H.C. Debates*, 1955, VI, 6673
75   Ambassador at Washington to SSEA, 21 November 1955 (telegram), DEA files, 50102-M-40
76   SSEA to Permanent Representative on North Atlantic Council, 23 November 1955 (telegram), *ibid.*
77   SSEA to Permanent Representative on North Atlantic Council, 12 December 1955 (telegram), *ibid.*
78   Delegation, North Atlantic Council, to DEA, 17 December 1955 (telegram), *ibid.*
79   SSEA to Permanent Representative on North Atlantic Council, 14 March 1956 (telegram), DEA files, 50102-N-40
80   SSEA to Permanent Representative on North Atlantic Council, 17 March 1956 (telegram), *ibid.*
81   Quoted in L.D. Wilgress to SSEA, 20 March 1956 (telegram), *ibid.*; Lord Ismay to L.B. Pearson, 2 May 1956, DEA files, 50105-F-40
82   L.D. Wilgress to SSEA, 3 April 1956 (telegram), DEA files, 50102-N-40
83   USSEA, memorandum for the Minister, 'General Review of NATO Ministerial Meeting, May 4-6, 1956,' 23 April 1956, *ibid.*
84   SSEA, 'Appreciation of NATO Ministerial Meeting, May 4-6, 1956,' 11 May 1956, *ibid.*
85   L.B. Pearson, Memorandum for the Prime Minister, 'North Atlantic Council Meeting, Paris, December 11-14, 1956,' 18 December 1956, DEA files, 50102-P-40
86   L.B. Pearson to DEA, 5 May 1957 (telegram), DEA files, 50102-R-40
87   L.B. Pearson, *Diplomacy in the Nuclear Age* (Toronto 1958), 30-1, 26, 31
88   SSEA to Ambassador at Washington, 2 May 1950 (telegram), DEA files, 50030-A-40
89   L.B. Pearson to L.S. St Laurent, 9 May 1950 (telegram), *ibid.*
90   Quoted in *Mike* II, 70
91   Arnold Heeney, *The Things that are Caesar's: Memoirs of a Canadian Public Servant* (Toronto, 1972), 106-7
92   *Ibid.*, 108
93   Quoted in *ibid.*, 108
94   Claxton memoirs, 1238
95   Lord Ismay, *NATO: The First Five Years, 1949-1954* (Paris 1956), 27
96   *FRUS, 1949*, 357
97   Brooke Claxton, 'Defence Meetings, November 26 to December 14, 1949,' Claxton Papers
98   Claxton memoirs, 1252-3
99   Claxton to Hume Wrong, 4 April 1950, Claxton Papers
100   Claxton memoirs, 1252-3
101   L.B. Pearson to L.S. St Laurent, 9 May 1950 (telegram), DEA files, *op. cit.*
102   *Foreign Relations of the United States, 1950*, III, *Western Europe* (Washington, DC 1977), 328 [hereafter cited as *FRUS, 1950*]
103   *Ibid.*, 462-4
104   *Ibid.*, 524-5
105   *Ibid.*, 573
106   Jordan, *op. cit.*, 27-8
107   DEA, Minutes of Meeting of Departmental Committee on NATO Affairs, 15 December 1951, DEA files, 50030-AJ-40
108   Ismay, *op. cit.*, 55
109   Jordan, *op. cit.*, 39

110   Claxton memoirs, 1314-15
111   Quoted in *Mike* II, 126
112   *Mike* II, 77
113   Ismay, *op. cit.*, 34-5
114   Claxton memoirs, 1275
115   *Ibid.*, 1275-6
116   A.D.P. Heeney to SSEA, 19 December 1950 (telegram), DEA files, 50030-AB-40
117   Ambassador at Brussels to SSEA, 19 December 1950 (telegram), *ibid.*
118   High Commissioner at London to SSEA, 25 May 1949 (telegram), DEA files, 50030-40
119   SSEA to High Commissioner at London, 27 May 1949 (telegram), *ibid.*
120   Ambassador at Washington to SSEA, 3 June 1949 (telegram), *ibid.*
121   A.D.P. Heeney, 'Memorandum for the Minister,' 31 August 1949, *ibid.*
122   *Mike* II, 61
123   Escott Reid, *Time of Fear and Hope*, 86
124   Sidney Pierce to A.D.P. Heeney, 20 April 1950 (telegram), DEA files, 50105-50
125   Quoted in *Mike* II, 62
126   Quoted in *ibid.*, 62
127   *Ibid.*
128   A.D.P. Heeney to H.H. Wrong, 15 September 1949 (telegram), DEA files, 50030-40
129   Heeney to Wrong, 16 September 1949 (telegram), *ibid.*
130   Wrong to SSEA, 18 September 1949 (telegram), DEA files, 50105-40
131   *Mike* II, 63
132   Hume Wrong to SSEA, 18 November 1949 (telegram), DEA files, *op. cit.*
133   *Ibid.*
134   DEA, Economic Division, 'Memorandum for Mr Heeney,' 17 December 1949, DEA files, *op. cit.*
135   *Mike* II, 64
136   Quoted in *ibid.*, 64
137   *FRUS, 1950,* III, 105
138   *Mike* II, 66-7
139   *Ibid.*, 76
140   Permanent Representative on North Atlantic Council to SSEA, 23 February 1955 (telegram), DEA files, 50105-E-40
141   DEA Economic Division to DEA Defence Liaison Division I, 2 March 1955, *ibid.*
142   DEA Defence Liaison Division I to USSEA, 4 March 1955, *ibid.*
143   A.F.W. Plumptre to USSEA, 23 March 1955, *ibid.*
144   SSEA, memorandum for USSEA, 27 April 1955, *ibid.*
145   SSEA to Permanent Representative on North Atlantic Council, 28 April 1955 (telegram), *ibid.*
146   L.D. Wilgress to L.B. Pearson, 22 June 1955, *ibid.*
147   Jules Léger, memorandum for the Minister, 'Article (2) of NATO,' 11 July 1955, *ibid.*
148   L.B. Pearson to Walter Harris and C.D. Howe (separate and identical letters), 26 September 1955, *ibid.*
149   Harris to Pearson, 17 October 1955, *ibid.*
150   C.D. Howe to Pearson, 19 October 1955, *ibid.*
151   L.D. Wilgress to DEA, 21 November 1955 (telegram), *ibid.*
152   *Mike* II, 91
153   SSEA to Permanent Representative on North Atlantic Council, 5 March 1956 (telegram), DEA files, 50102-N-40
154   A.F.W. Plumptre to USSEA, 27 March 1956, *ibid.*
155   *Mike* II, 92
156   *Ibid.*, 93

157 *Ibid.*, 97
158 *Ibid.*, 92
159 *Ibid.*, 64
160 Lord Gladwyn, review of Escott Reid's *Time of Fear and Hope*, *International Journal*, XXXIII, 1, Winter 1977-8, 254-5
161 Acheson, *op. cit.*, 366
162 Acheson, 'Canada: "Stern Daughter of the Voice of God'',' in Livingston Merchant (ed.), *Neighbours Taken for Granted: Canada and the United States* (New York, Toronto 1966), 141-2
163 Oral History Project..., interview by T.A. Hockin and G. Wright with Theodore C. Achilles, Washington, DC, 27 October 1969
164 Escott Reid, *Time of Fear and Hope*, 246
165 *Ibid.*

CHAPTER FOUR: MOBILIZING THE DETERRENT

1 Brigadier F. Clark to General Charles Foulkes, 21 June 1949, Foulkes Papers.
2 *Foreign Relations of the United States, 1949*, IV, *Western Europe* (Washington, DC 1975), 317 [hereafter cited as *FRUS, 1949* IV]
3 Escott Reid, *Time of Fear and Hope: The Making of the North Atlantic Treaty, 1947-1949* (Toronto 1977), 234
4 Department of National Defence, *Canada's Defence Programme, 1949-1950* (Ottawa 1949), 8
5 D.C. Abbott to Brooke Claxton, 16 November 1949, DEA files, 50030-T-40
6 A.D.P. Heeney to H.H. Wrong, 15 July 1949 (telegram), DEA files, 50030-L-40
7 *FRUS, 1949* IV, 311-13
8 Brooke Claxton, 'Defence Meetings, November 26 to December 14, 1949,' Claxton Papers
9 DEA Defence Liaison Division I, memorandum, 'North Atlantic Treaty: Canadian Mutual Aid,' 20 February 1950, DEA files, 50030-40
10 Claxton memoirs, 1245
11 DEA Defence Liaison Division I, memorandum, *op. cit.*
12 A.D.P. Heeney, 'Memorandum for the Minister: North Atlantic,' 20 February 1950, DEA files, *op. cit.*
13 L.D. Wilgress to Heeney, 12 December 1949, *ibid.*
14 H.H. Wrong to Heeney, 30 December 1949, *ibid.*
15 Heeney, 'Memorandum for the Minister: North Atlantic,' *op. cit.*
16 DEA memorandum, 'Canadian Contribution under Article 3 of the North Atlantic Treaty,' 18 January 1950, *ibid.*
17 DEA Defence Liaison Division I, memorandum, *op. cit.*
18 *Ibid.*
19 *Ibid.*
20 Escott Reid, minute on James George, 'Memorandum for Mr Ritchie, North Atlantic Defence and Finance Meetings,' 5 April 1950, DEA files 50030-B-40
21 DEA memorandum, *op. cit.*
22 Brooke Claxton to Hume Wrong, 4 April 1950, *ibid.*
23 James George, 'Memorandum for Mr Ritchie, North Atlantic Defence and Finance Meetings,' 5 April 1950, *ibid.*
24 *Ibid.*
25 Claxton memoirs, 1257
26 Claxton to L.B. Pearson, 29 March 1950 (telegram), DEA files, 50030-40
27 James George, 'Memorandum for Mr Ritchie,' *op. cit.*
28 Escott Reid, 'Appreciation of the Present International Situation,' 31 July 1950, DEA files, 50030-L-40

29 R.A. MacKay to E.W.T. Gill, 12 July 1950, *ibid.*
30 Claxton memoirs, 1258
31 Minutes of Chiefs of Staff Committee, 18 July 1950, DEA files, *op. cit.*
32 R.A. MacKay, 'Memorandum for the USSEA,' 19 July 1950, *ibid.*
33 Department of External Affairs, *Statements and Speeches*, no. 50/28, quoted in Dents Stairs, *The Diplomacy of Constraint: Canada, the Korean War and the United States* (Toronto 1974), 79
34 Minutes of Cabinet, 19 July 1950, DEA files, 50069-As6-40
35 R.A. MacKay to E.W.T. Gill, 12 July 1950, DEA files, 50030-L-40
36 L.D. Wilgress to SSEA, 25 July 1950 (telegram), *ibid.*
37 Escott Reid, 'Appreciation of the Present International Situation,' 31 July 1950, *ibid.*
38 *Foreign Relations of the United States, 1950*, III, *Western Europe* (Washington, DC 1977), 151 [hereafter cited as *FRUS, 1950* III]
39 L.B. Pearson to the Hon. Stanley Woodward, 11 August 1950, DEA files, *op. cit.*
40 Canada, *H.C. Debates*, 1950 (2nd Session), 269-70
41 *FRUS, 1950* III, 245
42 Canada, *H.C. Debates, op. cit.*, 270
43 Ambassador at Washington to SSEA, 8 September 1950 (telegram), DEA files, *op. ci.*
44 Ambassador at Washington to SSEA, 9 September 1950 (telegram), *ibid.*
45 Canada, *H.C. Debates, op. cit.*, 680-1
46 DEA, memorandum for the Minister, 'North Atlantic Council Meeting, New York. September 15-16, 1950,' DEA files, 50030-A-40
47 *FRUS, 1950* III, 309
48 *Ibid.*, 310
49 *Ibid.*, 328
50 *Ibid.*, 335-7
51 SSEA to R.G. Riddell, 11 November 1950 (telegram), DEA files, 50069-A-40
52 Statement by Brooke Claxton to the North Atlantic Council, 19 December 1950, DEA files, 50030-AB-40
53 *FRUS, 1950* III, 600
54 Minutes of Cabinet, 13 December 1950, DEA files, 50030-A-40
55 DEA Defence Liaison Division I, memorandum for USSEA, 17 January 1951, *ibid.*
56 Claxton memoirs, 1291-3
57 USSEA, memorandum for the Minister, 'North Atlantic Council Meeting, New York, September 15-16, 1950,' DEA files, *op. cit.*
58 Ambassador at Washington to SSEA, 30 October 1950 (telegram), DEA files, 50030-B-40
59 Canada, *H.C. Debates*, 1951 (1st session), I, 1
60 *Ibid.*, 94
61 Quoted in DEA Defence Liaison Division memorandum, 'Further Information on Canadian Force Contributions to NATO,' 5 November 1954, DEA files, 50107-D-40
62 Chairman, Chiefs of Staff Committee, memorandum for the Minister, 'Contributon to Integrated Force' (no date: probably April 1951), Claxton Papers
63 Brooke Claxton to General G.G. Simonds, 12 October 1951 (telegram), *ibid.*
64 A.D.P. Heeney, memorandum for the Minister, 31 July 1951, DEA files, 50030-x-40
65 General G.G. Simonds, memorandum for the Minister, 16 July 1951, *ibid.*
66 Minutes of 503rd meeting of the Chiefs of Staff Committee, 14 August 1951, *ibid.*
67 A.D.P. Heeney, memorandum for the Minister, 29 August 1951, *ibid.*
68 Heeney to H.H. Wrong, 6 March 1951 (telegram), DEA files, 50030-AB-40
69 Chairman, Chiefs of Staff Committee, to USSEA, 28 February 1951, *ibid.*
70 Dana Wilgress to A.D.P. Heeney, 11 March 1951, *ibid.*
71 DEA Defence Liaison Division memorandum, 'SHAPE's Authority to Order Troops into Action,' 20 December 1951, *ibid.*
72 Quoted in Stairs, *ibid.*, 253

73 DEA Defence Liaison Division I memorandum, 'Redeployment of Canadian Forces by SACEUR,' 25 June 1952, DEA files, *op. cit.*

74 USSEA, memorandum for the Minister, 'North Atlantic Council Meeting, New York, September 15-16, 1950,' DEA files, 50030-A-40

75 L.B. Pearson to USSEA, 17 September 1950 (telegram), *ibid.*

76 J.W. Pickersgill, memorandum for the Prime Minister, 'Re Canada's Position in North Atlantic Treaty Organization,' 22 September 1950, DEA files, 50030-I-40

77 DEA Defence Liaison Division I memorandum, 'Further Information on Canadian Force Contributions to NATO,' 5 November 1954, DEA files, 50107-D-40

78 Canada, *H.C. Debates*, 1951 (1st session), I, 95

79 *Op. cit.*, 1952, I, 105

80 *Op. cit.*, 1952-3, III, 3339

81 *Ibid.*, 3806

82 *Mike: The Memoirs of the Rt. Hon. Lester B. Pearson*, II, *1948-1957* (Toronto 1973), 81-2 [hereafter cited as *Mike* II]

83 Lt-Col. D.J. Goodspeed (ed.), *The Armed Forces of Canada, 1867-1967: A Century of Achievement* (Ottawa 1967), 223

84 Claxton memoirs, 1255

85 Lord Ismay, *NATO: The First Five Years, 1949-1954* (Paris 1956), 47

86 *Mike* II, 78

87 Claxton memoirs, 1253

88 *Ibid.*, 1290

89 Arnold Heeney, *The Things that are Caesar's: The Memoirs of a Canadian Public Servant* (Toronto 1972), 107-8

90 Canada, *H.C. Debates*, 1962, I, 157

91 *Ibid.*, 367

92 *Ibid.*, 390

93 *Mike* II, 81

94 Canada, *H.C. Debates*, 1952, I, 1083-8

95 *Ibid.*, 1085

96 USSEA, memorandum for the Minister, 'SACEUR's Report to the Standing Group on the Status of Forces in his Command,' 25 August 1952, DEA files, 50030-AB-40

97 Permanent Representative on North Atlantic Council to SSEA, 1 October 1952 (telegram), DEA files, 50107-40

98 SSEA to Permanent Representative on North Atlantic Council, 3 October 1952 (telegram), *ibid.*

99 L.D. Wilgress, memorandum for the Minister, 6 February 1953, *ibid.*

100 DEA Defence Liaison Division I, memorandum, 14 September 1953, DEA files, 50107-C-40

101 DEA, memorandum for Defence Liaison Division I, 30 September 1953, *ibid.*

102 Brooke Claxton to L.B. Pearson, 16 October 1953, *ibid.*

103 Claxton memoirs, 1288-9

104 'Statement by the Canadian delegation regarding Canadian Production and Mutual Aid during the Examination of Canada in the NATO Annual Review Committee,' 2 November 1953, DEA files, *op. cit.*

105 Permanent Representative on North Atlantic Council to SSEA, 3 November 1953 (telegram), *ibid.*

106 Permanent Representative on North Atlantic Council to SSEA, 17 December 1953 (telegram), DEA files, 50102-E-40

107 R.A. Macdonnell, memorandum for the Minister, 19 January 1954, DEA files, 50107-C-40

108 SSEA to Permanent Representative on North Atlantic Council, 3 October 1954 (telegram), DEA files, 50107-40

109 Canada, *H.C. Debates*, 1953-4, V, 4903

110 *Op. cit.*, 1954-5, V, 4867

111   DEA memorandum, 'Current Military Situation of the Atlantic Alliance,'
      10 November 1955, DEA files, 50107-E-40
112   Canada, *H.C. Debates*, 1955-6, V, 5209
113   Lt-Gen. Maurice A. Pope, *Soldiers and Politicians* (Toronto 1962), 276
114   Margaret Gowing, *Independence and Deterrence: Britain and Atomic Energy 1945-1952*,
      I, *Policy Making* (London 1974), 136
115   *Ibid.*, 328
116   *Foreign Relations of the United States, 1947*, I, *General: The United Nations* (Washing-
      ton, DC 1973), 797-8
117   *Ibid.*, 848
118   *The Journals of David E. Lillienthal*, II, *The Atomic Energy Years, 1945-1950*
      (New York, Evanston, and London 1964), 175-6
119   *Foreign Relations of the United States, 1949*, I, *National Security Affairs, Foreign
      Economic Policy* (Washington, DC 1976), 533 [hereafter cited as *FRUS, 1949*, I]
120   Gowing, *op. cit.*, 274
121   *FRUS, 1949* IV, 355, 357
122   Quoted in Gowing, *op. cit.*, 278
123   *Ibid.*, 286
124   Quoted in *ibid.*, 287
125   Hume Wrong to N.A. Robertson, 27 September 1949, Claxton Papers
126   Wrong to Robertson, 30 September 1949, *ibid.*
127   Gowing, *op. cit.*, 289
128   Hume Wrong to N.A. Robertson, 21 October 1949, Claxton Papers
129   Gowing, II, *Policy Execution*, 477-8
130   Hume Wrong to N.A. Robertson, 21 October 1949, Claxton Papers
131   Ambassador at Washington to SSEA, 3 January 1951 (telegram), DEA files,
      50069-C-40
132   L.B. Pearson, memorandum, 'US Strategic Air Command Projects,' 20 March 1951,
      ibid.
133   SSEA to Ambassador at Washington, 4 April 1951 (telegram), *ibid.*
134   USSEA to Ambassador at Washington, 2 April 1951 (telegram), *ibid.*
135   Ambassador at Washington to USSEA, 10 April 1951 (telegram), *ibid.*
136   Brooke Claxton, memorandum, 3 October 1953, Claxton Papers
137   Ambassador at Washington to USSEA, 10 April 1951 (telegram), DEA files, *op. cit.*
138   USSEA to Ambassador at Washington, 4 May 1951, *ibid.*
139   Heeney, *op. cit.*, 142
140   *Mike* II, 165
141   SSEA to Ambassador at Washington, 4 December 1950 (telegram), DEA files,
      op. cit.
142   L.B. Pearson, memorandum, 'Korea and the Atomic Bomb,' *ibid.*
143   SSEA to Ambassador at Washington, 4 December 1950 (telegram), *ibid.*
144   Ambassador at Washington to USSEA, 13 April 1951, *ibid.*
145   L.B. Pearson, memorandum, 'US Strategic Air Command Projects,' 20 March 1951,
      ibid.
146   Gowing, *op. cit.*, 315
147   Ambassador at Washington to USSEA, 10 April 1951 (telegram), DEA files, *op. cit.*
148   L.B. Pearson, 'Canadian Policy in the Present International Crisis,' DEA Information
      Division, *Statements and Speeches*, No. 50/51 (Ottawa, mimeographed)
149   Townsend Hoopes, *The Devil and John Foster Dulles* (Boston and Toronto 1973)
      197-8
150   Quoted in *ibid.*, 198
151   L.B. Pearson, memorandum for the Prime Minister, 3 February 1954, DEA files
      50115-P-40
152   L.B. Pearson, memorandum for the Prime Minister, 'United States Defence Policy,'
      2 February 1954, DEA files, *op. cit.*

153 CSC Paper 1883-1, 'A Study of Recent Changes and Trends in United States Defence Policy and the Implication It Might Have on Canadian Defence Policy,' 10 February 1954, DEA files, *op. cit.*
154 'Notes by General Foulkes on Conversations held in Washington on March 4 and 5, 1954,' DEA files, *op. cit.*
155 DEA Defence Liaison Division (I) to Acting USSEA, 2 March 1954, DEA files, *op. cit.*
156 L.B. Pearson, speech to the Public Relations Society, Montreal, 'International Public Relations,' 4 January 1954, in Lester B. Pearson, *Words and Occasions* (Toronto 1970), 124
157 L.B. Pearson, 'A Look at the "New Look",' DEA Information Division, *Statements and Speeches*, No. 54/16 (Ottawa, mimeographed)
158 *Montreal Star*, 18 March 1954
159 Oral History Project on Canada's Role in the Formation of NATO, York University, interview by T.A. Hockin and G. Wright with L.B. Pearson, Ottawa, 7 May 1970
160 DEA, Defence Liaison Division I, memorandum, 25 March 1954, DEA files, *op. cit.*
161 Canada, *H.C. Debates*, 1953-4, IV, 3329-31
162 Donald C. Masters, *Canada in World Affairs, 1953 to 1955* (Toronto 1958), 31
163 Heeney, *op. cit.*, 115
164 Lester B. Pearson, *Democracy in World Politics* (Toronto 1955), 23-4
165 Henry A. Kissinger, *Nuclear Weapons and Foreign Policy* (New York 1957), 74
166 Pearson, *op. cit.*, 33-4
167 Colin S. Gray, 'Mini-Nukes and Strategy,' *International Journal*, XXIX, 2, Spring 1974, 231
168 Lt-General Charles Foulkes, memorandum, 'Discussions with Major-General A.M. Gruenther,' 7 October 1949, Foulkes Papers
169 General Omar Bradley, 'This Way Lies Peace,' *Saturday Evening Post*, 15 October 1949
170 Hume Wrong to Brooke Claxton, 18 October 1949, DEA files, 50030-40
171 Claxton memoirs, 1256-7
172 A.D.P. Heeney, memorandum, 12 September 1952, DEA files, 50107-40
173 Permanent Representative on NAC to SSEA, 1 October 1952 (telegram), *ibid.*
174 SSEA to Permanent Representative on NAC, 3 October 1952 (telegram), *ibid.*
175 Malcolm W. Hoag, 'The Place of Limited War in NATO Strategy,' in Klaus Knorr (ed.), *NATO and American Security* (Princeton, NJ 1958), 116
176 *Ibid.*, 117-18
177 *New York Times*, 17 March 1955
178 *Ibid.*, 16 March 1955
179 Gray, *op. cit.*, 231
180 Pearson, *Democracy in World Politics*, 34
181 Quoted in Gordon A. Craig, 'NATO and the New German Army,' in William W. Kaufmann (ed.), *Military Policy and National Security* (Princeton, NJ 1956), 226
182 Pearson, *Democracy in World Politics*, 18-19
183 Gray, *op. cit.*, 232-3
184 Quoted in *Mike* II, 83
185 Pearson, *Words and Occasions*, 125
186 *Foreign Relations of the United States*, 1950, I, *National Security Affairs: Foreign Economy Policy* (Washington, DC 1976), 36 [hereafter cited as *FRUS, 1950,* I]
187 A.C. Smith, 'Memorandum for Mr Pearson,' 8 November 1949, Howe Papers
188 A.D.P. Heeney to Smith, 22 November 1949, *ibid.*
189 J. George, 'Memorandum for Mr Heeney,' 18 November 1949, *ibid.*
190 George Ignatieff, 'Proposals for a Short-Term Armistice with the Soviet Union,' no date, *ibid.*
191 C.J. Mackenzie to A.D.P. Heeney, 15 December 1949, *ibid.*
192 H.H. Wrong to Heeney, 11 January 1950, *ibid.*

193 Quoted in *FRUS, 1950*, I, 513n
194 George F. Kennan, *Memoirs 1925-1950* (Boston and Toronto 1967), 475
195 *FRUS, 1950*, I, 61
196 *Ibid.*, 60-1
197 *Ibid.*, 561
198 Royal Commission on Canada's Economic Prospects, *Final Report* (Ottawa 1957), 5

CHAPTER FIVE: SHARING THE BURDEN

1 Minutes of Cabinet, 13 December 1950, DEA files, 50030-A-40
2 Claxton memoirs (no page number)
3 Minutes of Cabinet, DEA files, *op. cit.*
4 DEA files, 50030-T-40
5 DEA Defence Liaison I memorandum, 19 May 1950, *ibid.*
6 Canada, *H.C. Debates*, 1950, V, 4127
7 Brooke Claxton, 'Address before Advisory Council Meeting, National Liberal Federation,' Ottawa, 26 February 1951 (typescript), Claxton Papers; Canada, *H.C. Debates*, 1950 (2nd session), I, 299
8 Lt-General Charles Foulkes, memorandum for Brooke Claxton, 18 May 1948, Claxton Papers
9 Air Commodore H.H.C. Rutledge to Secretary, Economic Sub-Panel, 30 March 1953, DEA files, 50107-40
10 Permanent Representative on North Atlantic Council to SSEA, 28 September 1953, DEA files, 50107-C-40
11 Statement by L.D. Wilgress at the Informal Meeting with NATO Secretariat, 24 September 1953, *ibid.*
12 Permanent Representative on North Atlantic Council to SSEA, 21 December 1953, DEA files, 50102-E-40
13 L.D. Wilgress, Statement at NATO Council Meeting, 9 March 1955, DEA files, 50030-L-40
14 'Memorandum to Accompany the Canadian Reply to ARQ(55),' 28 June 1955, DEA files, 50107-E-40
15 Quoted in *Mike: The Memoirs of the Rt. Hon. Lester B. Pearson*, II, *1948-1957* (Toronto 1973), 83-4 [hereafter cited as *Mike* II]
16 *Ibid.*, 84
17 Quoted in Robert S. Jordan, *The NATO International Staff/Secretariat 1952-1957: A Study in International Administration* (London, New York, Toronto 1967), 199-200
18 John J. Deutsch to A.F.W. Plumptre, 31 October 1950, DEA files, 50096-40
19 SSEA to High Commissioner at London, 4 November 1950 (telegram), *ibid.*
20 A.F.W. Plumptre, 'Memorandum to the USSEA,' 10 November 1950, *ibid.*
21 *Ibid.*
22 SSEA to High Commissioner at London, 11 November 1950 (telegram), *ibid.*
23 A.D.P. Heeney to L.B. Pearson, 15 November 1950 (telegram), *ibid.*
24 SSEA to High Commissioner at London, 23 November 1950 (telegram), *ibid.*
25 L.B. Pearson to L.D. Wilgress, 23 November 1950 (telegram), *ibid.*
26 Jordan, *op. cit.*, 201
27 High Commissioner at London to SSEA, 23 February 1951 (telegram), DEA files, *op. cit.*
28 L.D. Wilgress to A.D.P. Heeney, 4 April 1951, *ibid.*
29 Heeney, minute on A.F.W. Plumptre, 'Memorandum to USSEA,' 10 April 1951, *ibid.*
30 Lord Ismay, *NATO: The First Five Years, 1949-1954* (Paris 1956), 43-4
31 Jordan, *op. cit.*, 201
32 Ismay, *op. cit.*, 44-5
33 Jordan, *op. cit.*, 204-5
34 Ismay, *op. cit.*, 45

35 Minutes of Meeting of Departmental Committee on NATO Affairs, 3 November 1951, DEA files, 50030-AJ-40
36 Representative at OEEC to SSEA, 17 October 1951 (telegram), DEA files, 50030-AL-40
37 High Commissioner at London to SSEA, 30 October 1951 (telegram), *ibid.*
38 SSEA to Representative at OEEC, 30 October 1951 (telegram), *ibid.*
39 Minutes of Cabinet Defence Committee, 8 November 1951, *ibid.*
40 Representative at OEEC to SSEA, 19 November 1951 (telegram), *ibid.*
41 *Ibid.*
42 A.F.W. Plumptre, memorandum for the USSEA, 3 December 1951, *ibid.*
43 Plumptre, memorandum for the USSEA, 'Review of Canadian Programme by Executive Bureau of TCC,' 22 November 1951, *ibid.*
44 Minutes of Meeting of Departmental Committee on NATO Affairs, 15 December 1951, DEA files, 50030-AJ-40
45 A.D.P. Heeney, memorandum for the Minister, 20 December 1951, DEA files, 50030-AL-40
46 *Ibid.*
47 USSEA, memorandum for the Minister, 'Canadian Aid for NATO and UK,' 8 January 1952, *ibid.*
48 L.B. Pearson, 'Observations on Draft Commentary on TCC Report,' 11 January 1952, *ibid.*
49 A.F.W. Plumptre, memorandum for the USSEA, 14 January 1952, *ibid.*
50 USSEA to High Commissioner at London, 25 January 1952 (telegram), *ibid.*
51 High Commissioner at London to USSEA, 28 January 1952 (telegram), *ibid.*
52 Dale C. Thomson, *Louis St Laurent: Canadian* (Toronto 1967), 301
53 L.B. Pearson to L.S. St Laurent, 31 January 1952, DEA files, *op. cit.*
54 Pearson, 'Observations on Draft Commentary on TCC Report,' 11 January 1952, *ibid.*
55 Ismay, *op. cit.*, 46
56 Jordan, *op. cit.*, 211-12
57 Ismay, *op. cit.*, 92
58 L.D. Wilgress to Escott Reid, 12 May 1952 (telegram), DEA files, 50030-L-40
59 L.D. Wilgress, 'Memorandum for the Minister,' 13 June 1952, *ibid.*
60 SSEA to Permanent Representative on North Atlantic Council, 7 May 1952 (telegram), DEA files, 50107-40
61 Permanent Representative on North Atlantic Council to SSEA, 17 May 1952, *ibid.*
62 SSEA to Canadian Delegation, North Atlantic Council, 5 June 1952, *ibid.*
63 SSEA to Ambassador at Washington, 12 June 1952 (telegram), *ibid.*
64 Permanent Representative on North Atlantic Council to SSEA, 13 June 1952 (telegram), *ibid.*
65 Jordan, *op. cit.*, 218-19
66 C.N. Drury to J.W. Pickersgill, R.B. Bryce, and R.M.B. Brophy, 22 July 1952, DEA files, *op. cit.*
67 *Ibid.*
68 Escott Reid, memorandum for C.S.A. Ritchie, 23 July 1952, *ibid.*
69 Permanent Representative on North Atlantic Council to SSEA, 29 July 1952 (telegram), *ibid.*
70 L.B. Pearson, memorandum for USSEA, 8 September 1952, *ibid.*
71 USSEA to Permanent Representative on North Atlantic Council, 19 September 1952 (telegram), *ibid.*
72 Permanent Representative on North Atlantic Council to SSEA, 21 September 1952 (telegram), *ibid.*
73 'Statement by the Permanent Representative of Canada to the NATO Working Group for the Examination of the Canadian Reply, Annual Review, 1952,' 23 October 1952, *ibid.*
74 Jordan, *op. cit.*, 220

75 Permanent Representative on North Atlantic Council to SSEA, 27 October 1952, DEA files, *op. cit.*
76 'Statement...,' 23 October 1952, *ibid.*
77 Permanent Representative on North Atlantic Council to SSEA, 27 October 1952, *ibid.*
78 Permanent Representative on North Atlantic Council to SSEA, 23 October 1952 (telegram), *ibid.*
79 Permanent Representative on North Atlantic Council to SSEA, 27 October 1952, *ibid.*
80 Heeney, *op. cit.,* 109
81 SSEA to Permanent Representative on North Atlantic Council, 1 November 1952 (telegram), DEA files, *op. cit.*
82 L.B. Pearson to L.D. Wilgress, 12 November 1952 (telegram), *ibid.*
83 Quoted in Heeney, *op. cit.,* 109n
84 Jordan, *op. cit.,* 224
85 Permanent Representative on North Atlantic Council to SSEA, 6 December 1952 (telegram), DEA files, *op. cit.*
86 *Ibid.*
87 Delegation at North Atlantic Council and OEEC to USSEA, 10 December 1952, *ibid.*
88 Heeney, *op. cit.,* 110
89 SSEA to Permanent Representative on North Atlantic Council, 16 January 1953 (telegram), *ibid.*
90 USSEA to Permanent Representative on North Atlantic Council, 21 January 1953 (telegram), *ibid.*
91 Permanent Representative on North Atlantic Council to SSEA, 6 February 1953 (telegram), *ibid.*
92 Permanent Representative on North Atlantic Council to SSEA, 16 March 1953 (telegram), *ibid.*
93 *Ibid.*
94 DEA memorandum for USSEA, 15 January 1953, DEA files, 50030-L-40
95 Permanent Representative on North Atlantic Council to SSEA, 25 March 1953 (telegram), DEA files, 50107-40
96 Ismay, *op. cit.,* 96
97 Permanent Representative on North Atlantic Council to SSEA, 30 March 1953 (telegram), DEA files, *op. cit.*
98 DEA Defence Liaison (I) memorandum for the Minister, 30 November 1953, DEA files, 50107-C-40
99 Permanent Representative on North Atlantic Council to SSEA, 16 April 1953 (telegram), DEA files, 50107-40
100 Jordan, *op. cit.,* 223
101 M.H. Wershoff, memorandum for Defence Liaison (I), 30 November 1954, DEA files, 50107-D-40
102 K.W. MacLellan to Wershoff, 24 June 1953, DEA files, 50107-C-40
103 Chairman, Chiefs of Staff Committee, to USSEA, 8 February 1955, DEA files, 50107-E-40
104 Chairman, Chiefs of Staff Committee, to USSEA, 2 February 1956, DEA files, 50107-F-40
105 SSEA to Delegation at North Atlantic Council, 6 February 1956 (telegram), *ibid.*
106 Delegation at North Atlantic Council to SSEA, 13 February 1956 (telegram), *ibid.*
107 *Mike* II, 65-6

CHAPTER SIX: EXPANDING THE MEMBERSHIP

1 Minutes of a Meeting, DEA, 24 December 1946, *Documents* XII, 192
2 Canada, *H.C. Debates,* 1947, I, 6
3 *Ibid.,* 1949 (2nd Session), II, 1839-40

4   *Soldiers and Politicians: The Memoirs of Lt-Gen. Maurice A. Pope* (Toronto 1962), 377
5   Joint Planning Committee Report, 'The Problem of Western Germany,' 24 April 1950, DEA files, 50154-40
6   USSEA, memorandum for the Minister, 'Discussion of Germany at the North Atlantic Council,' 4 May 1950, DEA files, 10934-40
7   Canada, *H.C. Debates*, 1950, IV, 3357
8   *Ibid.*, 3381
9   Peter Calvocoressi, *Survey of International Affairs, 1949-1950* (London 1953), 168
10 Robert McGeehan, *The German Rearmament Question: American Diplomacy and European Defense After World War II* (Urbana, Chicago, London 1972), 26
11 *Ibid.*, 23
12 Harry S Truman, *Memoirs*, II, *Years of Trial and Hope* (Garden City, NJ 1956), 253
13 Head of Mission at Bonn to SSEA, 10 July 1950, DEA files, *op. cit.*
14 Denis Stairs, *The Diplomacy of Constraint: Canada, the Korean War, and the United States* (Toronto 1974), 106
15 Canada, *H.C. Debates*, 1950 (2nd Session), 90, 95
16 A.D.P. Heeney, memorandum for the Minister, 9 September 1950, DEA files, 50154-40
17 *Foreign Relations of the United States, 1950*, III, *Western Europe* (Washington, DC 1977), 303-4 [hereafter cited as *FRUS, 1950*, III]
18 L.B. Pearson, 'Report on Meetings of North Atlantic Council and Council Deputies held in New York, September 15-20, 1950,' DEA files, 50030-A-40
19 *Mike: The Memoirs of the Rt. Hon. Lester B. Pearson*, II, *1948-1957* (Toronto 1973), 85 [cited hereafter as *Mike* II]
20 L.B. Pearson, 'Report on Meetings...,' *op. cit.*
21 'H. Hume Wrong,' External Affairs (Ottawa), VI, 3, March 1954, 76
22 Hume Wrong to SSEA, 26 September 1950, DEA files, 50154-40
23 Lt-Gen. Maurice Pope to SSEA, 2 October 1950, *ibid.*
24 Ambassador at Paris to USSEA, 13 October 1950, *ibid.*
25 SSEA to Ambassador at Paris, 18 October 1950, *ibid.*
26 USSEA to T.C. Davis, 5 October 1950, *ibid.*
27 Davis to A.D.P. Heeney, 18 October 1950, *ibid.*
28 Davis to SSEA, 2 November 1950, *ibid.*
29 Jules Léger to Charles Ritchie, 20 October 1950, *ibid.*
30 L.B. Pearson to Hume Wrong, 28 October 1950, *ibid.*
31 Wrong to Pearson, 2 November 1950, *ibid.*
32 DEA, memorandum for Chiefs of Staff Committee, 20 October 1950, *ibid.*
33 McGeehan, *op. cit.*, 63-4
34 Claxton memoirs, 1268
35 Ambassador at Washington to SSEA, 30 October 1950 (telegram), DEA files, 50030-B-40
36 Claxton memoirs, 1270
37 A.D.P. Heeney to SSEA, 1 November 1950 (telegram), DEA files, *op. cit.*
38 Hume Wrong to L.B. Pearson, 2 November 1950, DEA files, 50154-40
39 A.D.P. Heeney to DEA, 2 November 1950 (telegram), DEA files, 50030-A-40
40 Claxton memoirs, 1272-4
41 McGeehan, *op. cit.*, 83
42 Hume Wrong to SSEA, 4 November 1950 (telegram), DEA files, 50154-40
43 L.B. Pearson to Ambassador at Paris, 6 November 1950 (telegram), *ibid.*
44 Ambassador at Paris to SSEA, 8 November 1950 (telegram), *ibid.*
45 A.D.P. Heeney to Brooke Claxton, 9 November 1950, *ibid.*
46 Heeney, memorandum for the Minister, 28 November 1950, DEA files, 50030-A-40
47 *FRUS, 1950*, III, 490-1
48 *Ibid.*, 494
49 McGeehan, *op. cit.*, 88

50 SSEA to Ambassador at Washington, 1 September 1950 (telegram), DEA files,
    50030-V-3-40c
51 DEA Defence Liaison Division I, memorandum, 'North Atlantic Council Meeting in
    New York, 20 September 1950,' DEA files, 50030-H-40
52 SSEA to Ambassador at Washington, 20 April 1951, DEA files, 50030-V-3-40
53 Escott Reid, memorandum, 14 March 1948, quoted in Reid, *Time of Fear and Hope:
    The Making of the North Atlantic Treaty, 1947-1949* (Toronto 1977), 136
54 *Ibid.*, 211
55 A.D.P. Heeney to High Commissioner at London, 31 May 1951 (telegram), DEA
    files, 50030-3-V-40
56 SSEA to ambassador at Washington, 10 July 1951 (telegram), *ibid.*
57 High Commissioner at London to SSEA, 17 July 1951 (telegram), *ibid.*
58 USSEA to High Commissioner at London, 24 July 1951 (telegram), *ibid.*
59 'Victor Odlum to Mackenzie King, 31 May 1943, quoted in Kim Richard Nossal,
    'Chungking Prism: Cognitive Process and Intelligence Failure,' *International Journal*,
    XXXII, 3, Summer 1977, 561
60 Ambassador at Ankara to SSEA, 20 August 1951, DEA files, 50030-V-3-40
61 SSEA to High Commissioner at London, 21 August 1951 (telegram), *ibid.*
62 L.B. Pearson, 'Statement at the Sixth Meeting of the North Atlantic Council,'
    18 September 1951, DEA files, 50030-A-1-40
63 *Mike* II, 85
64 Ambassador at Bonn to SSEA, 22 August 1951, DEA files, 10934-40
65 Roger Morgan, 'The Grandfather-Figure of Bonn,' *Times Literary Supplement*,
    30 December 1977
66 Ambassador at Brussels to SSEA, 12 February 1952, DEA files, 50154-40
67 Canada, *H.C. Debates*, 1952, I, 670
68 *Ibid.*, 681
69 L.B. Pearson, memorandum for the Prime Minister, 2 May 1952, DEA files, 50234-40
70 McGeehan, *op. cit.*, 204, 208
71 DEA, Information Division, *Statements and Speeches*, No. 54/39 (Ottawa, mimeo-
    graphed)
72 Quoted in *Mike* II, 89
73 *Ibid.*, 89-90
74 Canada, *H.C. Debates*, 1955, I, 369
75 L.B. Pearson to L.S. St Laurent, 25 October 1954 (telegram), DEA files, 50030-V-4-40
76 Canada, *H.C. Debates*, 1955, V, 4061
77 *Op. cit.*, I, 361-73
78 *Ibid.*, 373-9
79 *Ibid.*, 381-2
80 *Ibid.*, 393, 397
81 *Ibid.*, 460-1
82 Lester B. Pearson, *Democracy in World Politics* (Toronto 1955), 31

INDEX

*(Officers and titled persons are listed under the highest rank
and title attained during 1947-55)*